LEARNING
QUICKBOOKS® PRO 2009
A Practical Approach

Terri E. Brunsdon, CPA, CITP, JD

Prentice Hall

Boston   Columbus   Indianapolis   New York   San Francisco   Upper Saddle River
Amsterdam   Cape Town   Dubai   London   Madrid   Milan   Munich   Paris   Montreal   Toronto
Delhi   Mexico City   Sao Paulo   Sydney   Hong Kong   Seoul   Singapore   Taipei   Tokyo

VP/Publisher: Natalie E. Anderson
AVP/Executive Editor, Print: Jodi McPherson
Director, Product Development: Pamela Hersperger
Editorial Project Manager: Melissa Gill
Editorial Assistant: Christina Rumbaugh
Director of Marketing: Patrice Lumumba Jones
Senior Marketing Manager: Liz Averbeck
Marketing Assistant: Justin Jacob
Senior Managing Editor: Cynthia Zonneveld
Production Project Manager: Rhonda Aversa

Senior Operations Supervisor: Natacha Moore
Senior Art Director: Jonathan Boylan
Cover Designer: Jonathan Boylan
Manager, Rights and Permissions: Charles Morris
Cover Art: © Kimball Stock
Editorial Media Project Manager: Allison Longley
Production Media Project Manager: John Cassar
Printer/Binder: Webcrafters Inc.
Cover Printer: Lehigh-Phoenix Color/Hagerstown

10 9 8 7 6 5 4 3 2

Prentice Hall
is an imprint of

ISBN-10:   0-13-612320-1
ISBN-13: 978-0-13-612320-0

TABLE OF CONTENTS

PREFACE ix

CHAPTER 1   GET READY FOR QUICKBOOKS PRO 2009 1

    Learning Objectives 1
    Introduction to Accounting Software..1
    Application Software 3
    Launching QuickBooks and Loading Sample Data..4
    Opening and Closing Companies 12
    The QuickBooks Desktop 13
    Customize the Icon Bar 19
    QuickBooks Centers 22
    Customize Company Names 28
    QuickBooks Keyboard Shortcuts 29
    QuickBooks Help 31
    Backing Up Company Data Files 38
    Restoring Company Data Files..44
    Moving Data Between School and Home 48
    Exiting QuickBooks..48
    Summary 48
    End-of-Chapter Questions 49
    Practice Set 50

CHAPTER 2   QUICKBOOKS BASICS 51

    Learning Objectives 51
    Chart of Accounts..52
    Print the Chart of Accounts 53
    General Ledger Framework 55
    General Ledger Accounts 56
    QuickBooks Preference Options...61
    QuickBooks Drilldown Features 66
    Finding Transactions in QuickBooks 73
    The Reports Menu and Report Center..77
    Exporting and Emailing Reports 89
    Accounting Periods 100
    Summary 102
    End-of-Chapter Questions 103

CHAPTER 3   GENERAL JOURNAL TRANSACTIONS AND REPORTS.....................................105

    Learning Objectives 105
    Manual Accounting Procedures..105
    Basic Journal Entries 107
    Behind the Keys of a Posted Journal Entry 114
    Correcting a Posted Journal Entry 117
    Compound Journal Entries 119
    Adjusting Journal Entries 122
    Print the Trial Balance 123
    Print Financial Statements...125
    Close an Accounting Period 128
    QuickBooks Data Integration...130

Summary *131*
End-of-Chapter Questions *132*
Practice Set *134*

CHAPTER 4   CUSTOMER ACTIVITIES FOR A SERVICE BASED BUSINESS **136**

Learning Objectives *136*
Manual Accounting Procedures *137*
Customer Center *141*
Entering Sales Invoices *147*
Behind the Keys of a Posted Sales Invoice *154*
Correcting Sales Invoices *158*
QuickBooks Email Features *159*
Customer and Job Accounts *160*
Understanding Service and Non-Inventory Part Items *176*
Invoicing Customer Jobs *184*
Job Reporting *190*
Customer Payments *197*
Behind the Keys of a Posted Customer Payment *201*
Customer Payments with a Discount and Sales Receipts *203*
Correcting Customer Payments *209*
Customer Credits *210*
Customer Reporting and Reconciling Activities *213*
Write Off a Customer Invoice *214*
Customer Statements *216*
Summary *218*
End-of-Chapter Questions *219*
Practice Set *221*

CHAPTER 5   VENDOR ACTIVITIES FOR A SERVICE BASED BUSINESS **225**

Learning Objectives *225*
Manual Accounting Procedures *226*
Vendor Center *231*
Purchase Orders *236*
Correcting a Purchase Order *240*
Vendor Bills and Receipts For Purchase Orders *243*
Behind the Keys of a Posted Vendor Receipt and Bill *248*
Correcting a Vendor Receipt or Bill *255*
Vendor Bills for Vendor Receipts *256*
Vendor Accounts *259*
Vendor Bills for Expenses *263*
Memorized Vendor Bills *266*
Vendor Payments *270*
Behind the Keys of a Posted Vendor Payment *276*
Write Checks Without a Vendor Bill *278*
Voiding Vendor Payments *284*
Paying Sales Tax *287*
Vendor Credits *291*
Vendor Reporting and Reconciling Activities *294*
Summary *297*
End-of-Chapter Questions *298*
Practice Set *300*

CHAPTER 6   PAYROLL ACTIVITIES FOR A SERVICE BASED BUSINESS 303

Learning Objectives 303
Manual Accounting Procedures..303
Understanding Payroll Items 311
Employee Center 323
Managing Employees..325
Employee Time..339
Employee Time Reports 344
Paying Employees 346
Behind the Keys of a Posted Paycheck..366
Correcting Employee Paychecks..369
Allocating Salaried Employee Time to Jobs 374
Paying Employer and Employee Payroll Taxes 376
Quarterly and Year-End Payroll Reporting..385
Summary 399
End-of-Chapter Questions 400
Practice Set 402

CHAPTER 7   CLOSE THE ACCOUNTING PERIOD FOR A SERVICE BASED BUSINESS 414

Learning Objectives 414
Analyze Transactions 414
Adjusting Entries 422
Reconcile Bank Accounts 427
Financial Reports 438
Closing the Accounting Period 452
Summary 453
End-of-Chapter Questions 454
Practice Set 455

PROJECT 1   COMPREHENSIVE EXAM FOR A SERVICE BASED BUSINESS..459

CHAPTER 8   CUSTOMER ACTIVITIES FOR A MERCHANDISING BUSINESS..471

Learning Objectives 471
Manual Accounting Procedures..472
Customer Center 478
Entering Sales Invoices..484
Behind the Keys of a Posted Sales Invoice 491
Correcting Sales Invoices 496
QuickBooks Email Features 497
Customer Accounts 499
Understanding Inventory Items 510
Inventory Pricing and Price Levels 515
Inventory Reporting 522
Physical Inventory 525
Storefront Sale of Merchandise 528
Invoices for Out-of-Stock Merchandise 530
Customer Payments..531
Behind the Keys of a Posted Customer Payment..535
Customer Payments with a Discount..536
Correcting Customer Payments..541
Customer Credits 542
Customer Reporting and Reconciling Activities 544
Write Off a Customer Invoice 546
Customer Statements 548

Summary *551*
End-of-Chapter Questions *552*
Practice Set *554*

CHAPTER 9   VENDOR ACTIVITIES FOR A MERCHANDISING BUSINESS **558**

Learning Objectives *558*
Manual Accounting Procedures.. *558*
Vendor Center *563*
Purchase Orders... *568*
Correcting a Purchase Order *571*
Vendor Receipts and Bills for Purchase Orders *573*
Behind the Keys of a Posted Vendor Receipt and Bill *581*
Correcting a Vendor Receipt or Bill *584*
Vendor Bills for Vendor Receipts *585*
Vendor Accounts *587*
Vendor Bills for Expenses *592*
Memorized Vendor Bills *595*
Vendor Payments... *600*
Behind the Keys of a Posted Vendor Payment... *606*
Write Checks Without a Vendor Bill.. *607*
Voiding Vendor Payments *613*
Paying Sales Tax... *616*
Vendor Credits *620*
Vendor Reporting and Reconciling Activities *623*
Purchasing and Inventory Activity Reporting *627*
Summary *631*
End-of-Chapter Questions *632*
Practice Set *634*

CHAPTER 10   PAYROLL ACTIVITIES FOR A MERCHANDISING BUSINESS....................................**638**

Learning Objectives *638*
Manual Accounting Procedures.. *638*
Understanding Payroll Items *647*
Employee Center *661*
Managing Employees... *663*
Paying Employees *676*
Behind the Keys of a Posted Paycheck.. *699*
Correcting Employee Paychecks... *702*
Paying Employer and Employee Payroll Taxes *707*
Quarterly and Year-End Payroll Reporting.. *719*
Summary *733*
End-of-Chapter Questions *734*
Practice Set *736*

CHAPTER 11   CLOSE THE ACCOUNTING PERIOD FOR A MERCHANDISING BUSINESS...............................**746**

Learning Objectives *746*
Analyze Transactions *746*
Adjusting Entries *756*
Reconcile Bank Accounts *760*
Financial Reports *772*
Closing the Accounting Period *786*
Summary *788*
End-of-Chapter Questions *789*
Practice Set *791*

PROJECT 2 **COMPREHENSIVE EXAM FOR A MERCHANDISING BUSINESS** **796**

CHAPTER 12 **CREATE A NEW COMPANY** **811**

 Learning Objectives *811*
 New Company Data File Wizard *811*
 Chart of Accounts Setup *818*
 Company Preferences Setup *827*
 Customer Setup *832*
 Vendor Setup *835*
 Inventory Setup *838*
 Payroll and Employee Setup *845*
 Customizing Form Templates.. *863*
 Summary *870*
 Practice Set *871*

APPENDIX A **INSTALLING QUICKBOOKS PRO 2009**... **881**

APPENDIX B **CORRECTING TRANSACTIONS** **892**

APPENDIX C **BACKING UP AND RESTORING DATA FILES** **895**

APPENDIX D **IRS CIRCULAR E TAX TABLES** **912**

APPENDIX E **SOLUTIONS FOR YOU TRY EXERCISES** **917**

 Chapter 1 .... *917*
 Chapter 2 .... *917*
 Chapter 3 .... *918*
 Chapter 4 .... *921*
 Chapter 5 .... *931*
 Chapter 6 .... *942*
 Chapter 7 .... *946*
 Chapter 8 .... *950*
 Chapter 9 .... *957*
 Chapter 10 .... *970*
 Chapter 11 .... *972*

INDEX **976**

PREFACE

A Special Note to Students and Instructors from Terri Brunsdon
How This Textbook Teaches QuickBooks Pro 2009

Learning QuickBooks Pro 2009 is a comprehensive approach to teaching accounting concepts in a software environment. The text includes sample company data files designed to simulate real-world businesses so that students gain "hands-on" experience with initiating transactions, performing accounting activities, producing financial statements, and analyzing company performance.

This text uses a "WHoW" approach to teaching software by explaining *why* a task is performed, illustrating *how* to perform the task, and then explaining *what* the task affected. Chapters begin with an introduction to **Manual Accounting Procedures ("MAPS")** before illustrating transaction posting in the software. *MAPS* topics expose students to journals, ledgers, and audit trail concepts necessary to understanding why and how transaction posting impacts financial information. *MAPS* topics also provide insight for illustrations in *Behind the Keys* topics where students trace the audit trail for posted transactions. With *MAPS* and *Behind the Keys*, students learn to conceptualize accounting transactions and to correct posting errors.

The text provides step-by-step illustrations that guide students through posting transactions and performing other accounting activities. On occasion, students will be asked to complete a *You Try* exercise following a guided illustration to reinforce skills previously covered. Solutions for these exercises are located in Appendix E.

How Chapters Are Organized

- **Chapter 1** begins by explaining the role of accounting software and then illustrates activities such as opening, closing, and backing up company data files, working with QuickBooks help files and shortcut keys, and navigating the QuickBooks interface.

- **Chapter 2** illustrates customizing QuickBooks preference options, reviewing the chart of accounts, printing, customizing, and exporting reports, emailing documents, and locating information using find, drilldown, and hyperlink features.

- In **Chapter 3** students post basic and compound journal entries and then print financial statements. This chapter is intended to make students comfortable with posting basic transactions, printing reports, and locating information before tackling more complicated tasks involving sales, purchasing, and payroll transactions. After this chapter, the text branches into two distinct tracks that present accounting activities for a service based business and then a merchandising business.

- **Chapters 4 through 7** use a cycle-based approach to illustrate accounting activities for a service based business using job costing. This track begins by processing sales activities and then proceeds to separate chapters illustrating purchasing and payroll activities. The track concludes by reviewing postings, recording adjusting entries, printing financial statements, and closing the accounting period. After completing this series of chapters, students have worked with job costing and have completed an entire accounting cycle for a serviced based business. The text then presents a comprehensive project covering activities for a different service based business that can be assigned to test student skills.

- In **Chapters 8 through 11** the cycle-based approach is repeated for a merchandising business. After completing this track, students have worked with inventory and have completed an entire accounting cycle for a merchandising company. The text then presents a comprehensive project covering activities for a different merchandising business that can be assigned to test student skills.

- **Chapter 12** provides an opportunity for students to create a merchandising business from scratch and then record a month of transactions for the new business.

- **Appendix A** includes detailed instructions for installing QuickBooks Pro 2009. **Appendix B** includes comprehensive instructions for correcting posting errors. **Appendix C** provides data file backup and restore procedures that make data portable between school and home. **Appendix D** contains IRS Circular E tax tables used in the text for computing employee paychecks. **Appendix E** contains solutions to the You Try exercises that appear throughout the text.

Note: The author recommends that students complete Chapters 1 through 3 before embarking on either the service based business or merchandising business tracks. In addition, students should complete the Practice Set at the end of Chapter 1 where students load sample data files, customize data files with their initials, and backup the files for use in later chapters.

Where Student Data Files Are Found and How They Are Named and Used in the Text

Sample data files used with the text can be found at www.pearsonhighered.com/brunsdon and are named and used in the text as follows:

Data File Name	When to Use
Practice TEK Business	While reading Chapters 3
Graded TEK Business	End of chapter exercises in Chapter 3
Practice Astor Landscaping	While reading Chapters 4 through 7
Graded Astor Landscaping	End of chapter exercises in Chapters 4 through 7
Practice Baxter Garden Supply	While reading Chapters 1 and 2 and 8 through 11
Graded Baxter Garden Supply	End of chapter exercises in Chapters 8 through 11
Eragon Electrical Contracting Project	Service based company for Project 1
Olsen Office Furniture Project	Merchandising company for Project 2

Note: There is NO data file for Chapter 12 because students create the data file while reading the chapter.

Features That Help Readers Really Learn the Software AND Accounting

The following icons are placed in the margin of topics and exercises to signal:

 Step-by-step instructions for performing a task with illustrated solutions.

 You Try exercises with solutions in Appendix E.

 Manual Accounting Procedures (*MAPS*) illustrations.

 Behind the Keys procedures for tracing posted entries.

 Indicates a new feature in QuickBooks Pro 2009. The major change for 2009 is the new Company Snapshot window that summarizes accounting data. This feature is not discussed in the text.

 Web-based video tutorial is available to illustrate the topic.

LEARNING RESOURCES FOR STUDENTS

Companion Website located at www.pearsonhighered.com/brunsdon
- The book's website contains updates for the text and a link to student resources.

Student Data Files
- Sample company data files used with the text can be found at www.pearsonhighered.com/brunsdon under the link to student resources.

TEACHING RESOURCES FOR INSTRUCTORS

Instructor Resources
Instructors will find resources for the text located under the Instructor Resources link on the www.pearsonhighered.com/brunsdon website. These resources include an Instructors Manual with teaching tips and solutions, a sample syllabus, PowerPoint slides, and company data files with solutions by chapter.

Web-Based Tutorials and Test Bank
Check with your Prentice Hall representative for information on web-based tutorials designed for the text. These tutorials illustrate and explain tasks performed in the software and are perfect for use in the classroom or for implementing an on-line course. Your representative can also provide information on gaining access to the test bank developed for the text.

Online Instructors Resource Center located at www.pearsonhighered.com/brunsdon/
- The Instructor website contains links to instructor resource materials. Contact your local sales representative for access to this password-protected area.

Course Management Solutions
- WebCT Course Management
- Blackboard Course Management

Author Web site located at www.terribrunsdon.com
This companion site contains information on text updates and other news.

Product Development

The author would like to thank Bill Brunsdon, Jr. for accuracy checking practice sets and Susan Snow Davis, CPA of Green River Community College for accuracy checking the text.

About the Author

Terri Brunsdon is a Certified Public Accountant with undergraduate degrees in accounting and computer programming. She also has a Juris Doctorate in Law and a Masters in Tax. Terri has over twenty years of accounting experience and specializes in recommending and implementing accounting software solutions. In addition, Terri has six years of higher education experience in teaching accounting information systems and computer software applications. Terri is a member of the American Institute of Certified Public Accountants (AICPA) and is an AICPA Certified Information Technology Professional (CITP). She is also a member of the American Accounting Association, American Bar Association, Ohio Bar Association, and Ohio Society Certified Public Accountants.

More Computerized Accounting Software Texts by Terri Brunsdon

If you like the teaching and learning approach of this book, don't forget to review these other Prentice Hall textbooks by Terri Brunsdon

- *Learning Peachtree Complete Accounting*
- *Learning Microsoft Office Accounting Professional*
- *Introduction to Microsoft Dynamics 10.0: Focus on Internal Controls*

Dedicated to my husband and best friend, Bill Brunsdon

CHAPTER 1   GET READY FOR QUICKBOOKS PRO 2009

LEARNING OBJECTIVES

This chapter introduces QuickBooks Pro 2009 (QBP) by covering the following:

1. An introduction to accounting software and application software
2. Launching QBP and loading company data files
3. Opening and closing companies in QBP
4. Navigating the desktop
5. Customizing the icon bar
6. Using QuickBooks centers
7. Customizing company names
8. Using keyboard shortcuts
9. Using QuickBooks Help
10. Backing up company data files
11. Restoring sample data files
12. Moving data between school and home
13. Exiting the software

INTRODUCTION TO ACCOUNTING SOFTWARE

Accounting software simplifies capturing and posting accounting transactions. Although basic accounting procedures remain the same, accounting software eliminates tedious processes such as typing documents, manually posting and calculating transactions, and documenting the audit trail. The table that follows illustrates these differences.

Manual Accounting System	Computerized Accounting System
1. Business transaction occurs and is manually entered onto a source document.	1. Business transaction occurs and is entered into the accounting software.
2. Source document manually recorded in the subsidiary journal and posted to the subsidiary ledger and general ledger while documenting the audit trail.	2. Accounting software records transaction in the subsidiary journal and posts to subsidiary ledger and general ledger along with the audit trail.
3. Manually prepare trial balance.	3. Print computerized trial balance.
4. Record adjusting entries in the general journal and post entries to the general ledger.	4. Record adjusting entries in the general journal and software posts to the general ledger.
5. Manually prepare adjusted trial balance.	5. Reprint trial balance with adjusting entries.
6. Manually calculate and post closing entries.	6. Computer posts closing entries.
7. Manually prepare financial statements.	7. Print computerized financial statements.

Computerized accounting minimizes posting errors, thus protecting the validity of data. After correctly capturing an entry, the software coordinates posting, reporting, and the audit trail. In addition, the accountant can easily monitor transactions and analyze financial performance.

Naturally you need computer hardware and operating software to use computerized accounting software. Computer hardware encompasses the physical components such as keyboard, screen, hard drive, CD-ROM, mouse, memory, and printers. Operating software is the system software that translates user instructions to hardware components and application software. Microsoft's Windows XP, Windows 2000, and Vista as well as Linux and UNIX are examples of operating software.

APPLICATION SOFTWARE

Application software serves specific needs of the user and is installed over operating software. There are a wide variety of application software packages on the market and the following table outlines a few of the more familiar packages alongside their purposes.

Application	Purpose
Microsoft Word	Word processing
Microsoft Excel	Financial analysis
Microsoft Access	Database
Microsoft Explorer	Internet browser
Microsoft Outlook	Email and contact manager
QuickBooks Pro	Accounting software

Application software must match the computer operating system software. Therefore, you will often find multiple versions of the same software for installation with particular operating software.

Accounting Software

Accounting software is application software that automates manual accounting procedures. This software is normally organized by activities with each activity representing a specific functional area of accounting such as customer activities or vendor activities. QBP segregates accounting activities into company (general journal entries), customer (sales, accounts receivable, and cash receipts), vendor (purchases, accounts payable, and cash disbursements), employee (payroll), and banking (deposits and checks) activities. A visual depiction of these activities is illustrated in Chapter 3 under the topic that discusses data integration.

LAUNCHING QUICKBOOKS AND LOADING COMPANY DATA FILES

To cover concepts presented in this text, you will work with the sample company databases designed by the author and located on the **Website** for the textbook, located at *www.pearsonhighered.com/brunsdon*. The following table lists the data files and describes when a data file is used in the text. The table explains that companies containing **Graded** in the data file name are duplicates of companies containing **Practice** in the data file name. This design lets you practice tasks while reading a chapter, and then complete graded tasks at the end of the chapter without having to learn a new accounting structure for a different company.

Company Files	Description
Practice TEK Business	Service based consulting business used while reading Chapter 3.
Graded TEK Business	Duplicate of Practice TEK Business used while completing the Practice Set at the end of Chapter 3.
Practice Astor Landscaping	Service based landscaping business used while reading Chapters 4 through 7.
Graded Astor Landscaping	Duplicate of Practice Astor Landscaping used while completing Practice Sets at the end of Chapters 4 through 7.
Practice Baxter Garden Supply	Home and garden merchandiser used while reading Chapters 1 and 2 and 8 through 11.
Graded Baxter Garden Supply	Duplicate of Practice Baxter Garden Supply used while completing Practice Sets at the end of Chapters 8 through 11.

**Note: There are two additional data files, namely Eragon Electrical Contracting Project and Olsen Office Furniture Project. These data files are used in the comprehensive projects and can be downloaded before beginning Project 1 and Project 2.*

STEPS TO LOADING SAMPLE COMPANY DATA FILES

1. Begin by downloading the student data files from the textbook website. Open your browser and type in *http://www.pearsonhighered.com/brunsdon/*.

2. Click the **Student Resources** link for the Learning QuickBooks 2009 textbook to open a new browser window with links to the data files listed in the previous table. Click the link for **Practice TEK Business** and choose **Save**.

   If you are using the Vista operating system then the dialog box in Figure 1:1 opens. Double click to open the **Public** folder and then open the **Public Documents** folder. Next open the **Intuit** folder and then open the **QuickBooks** folder. Finally, open the **Company Files** folder and click **Save**. The file is now on your computer.

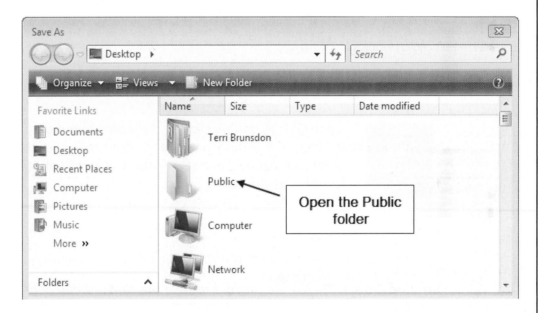

Figure 1:1

If you are not using Vista then click the dropdown list on the **Save in** box, select the **Shared Documents** folder, and then open the **Intuit** folder as illustrated in Figure 1:2.

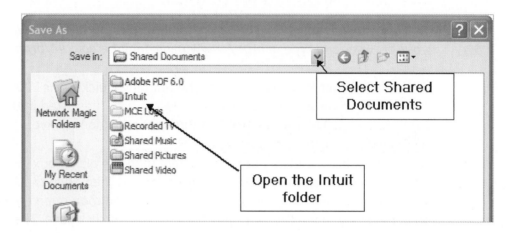

Figure 1:2

Return to your browser window and repeat this step until all files have been saved to your computer.

3. You will now open these files in QuickBooks.

 Open QBP by double clicking the icon on your desktop illustrated in Figure 1:3. If this icon is not present then click the Start button, point to Programs, and then point to QuickBooks to select QuickBooks Pro 2009.

Figure 1:3

(Note: If QuickBooks Pro 2009 is not installed on your computer, Appendix A will guide you through installation.)

4. The first time you open QuickBooks the screen illustrated in Figure 1:4 opens. The Live Community pane on the right is used to access online content. Click **X** to close this pane and in the window that opens, unmark the option to **Open Live community when starting QuickBooks**, mark the option to **Don't display this message again**, and click **OK**.

Finally, click **OK** to proceed to the next step.

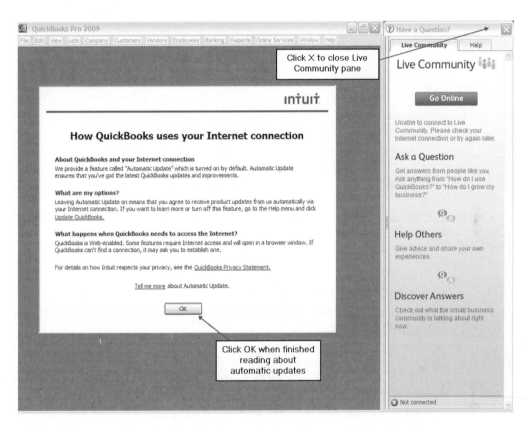

Figure 1:4

5. Click **Open an existing company file** as illustrated in Figure 1:5.

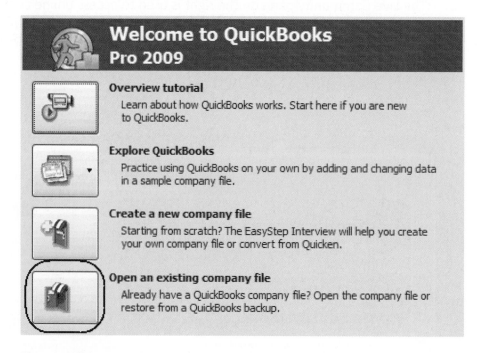

Figure 1:5

If the screen in Figure 1:5 fails to open, select *File>>Close Company* on the main menu and click **Open or Restore an existing Company** as illustrated in Figure 1:6.

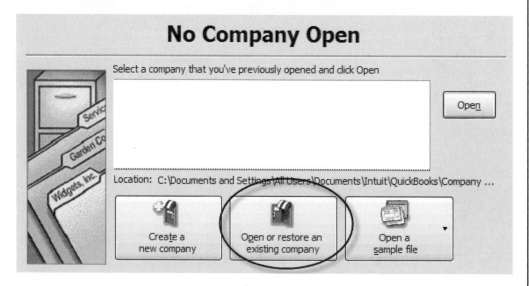

Figure 1:6

6. Select **Open a company file** and click **Next**. (See Figure 1:7.)

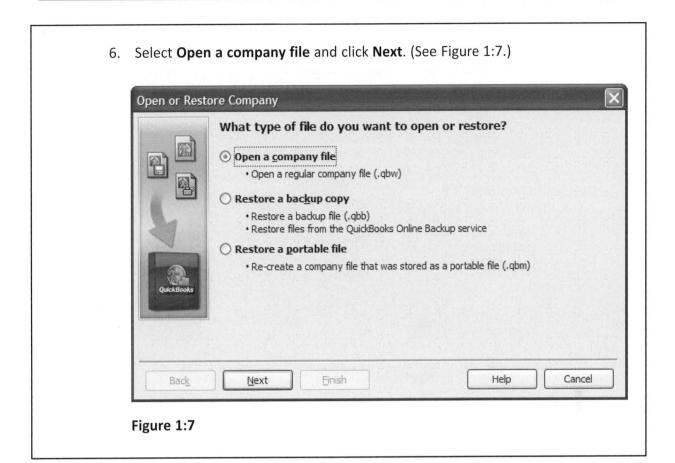

Figure 1:7

7. If you are using Vista then the window in Figure 1:8 opens for you to browse to where the data files are stored. Double click to open the **Public** folder and then open the **Public Documents** folder. Next, open the **Intuit** folder and then the **QuickBooks** folder. Finally, open the **Company Files** folder.

Figure 1:8

If you are not using Vista then use the dropdown list on the Look in box to select Shared Documents and then click the Intuit folders illustrated in Figure 1:9. Finally, click the Company folder.

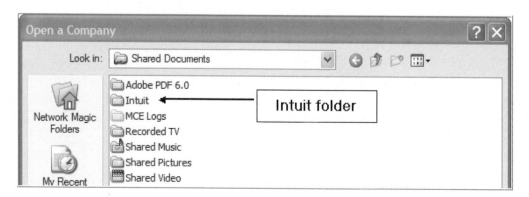

Figure 1:9

8. Highlight **Practice TEK Business** and click **Open**.

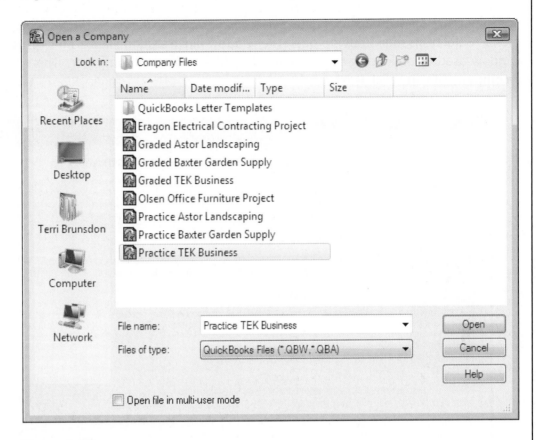

Figure 1:10

If you just installed QuickBooks you will be prompted to register the software. Verify that you are connected to the Internet and then click Begin Registration. Follow the onscreen prompts to complete registration. If you do not have an Internet connection, QuickBooks provides a toll free number to complete registration. If registering online, select "Use QuickBooks software, but without a paid subscription" and "No Thanks" when asked to use credit card processing.

If you are prompted to finish setting up an Intuit Account then click X to close the window.

9. *Select **File>>Open or Restore Company** on the main menu and repeat Steps 6 through 8 to load the five remaining Practice and Graded sample companies. (Note: Do not load Eragon Electrical Contracting Project or Olsen Office Furniture Project until assigned Project 1 and Project 2.)*

OPENING AND CLOSING COMPANIES

To change the open company in QBP select *File>>Open or Restore Company* on the main menu. Select this menu now to open the window illustrated in Figure 1:11. This is the same window used when loading the company data files onto your computer. This time click **Open a company file** and click **Next**.

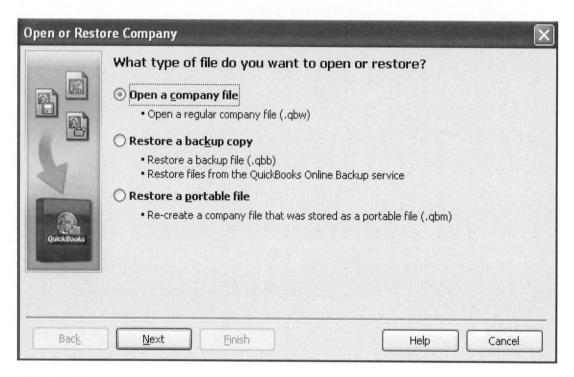

Figure 1:11

The Open Company window appears (not illustrated), listing company data files stored on your hard drive. Highlight **Practice Baxter Garden Supply** and click **Open** to open it. *(Note: Double clicking a company name will also open the company.)*

Note: You may receive the message illustrated in Figure 1:12 when opening a company. Clicking Yes will update your software and then update the data file; however, you must be connected to the Internet to make this selection. You can always click No and mark the option to turn off future messages without affecting tasks performed in the text.

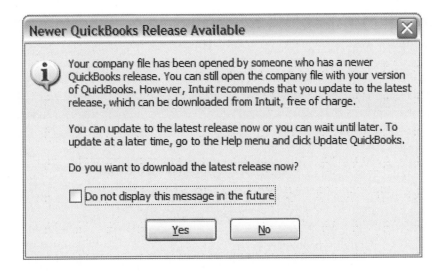

Figure 1:12

THE QUICKBOOKS DESKTOP

Baxter's desktop appears in Figure 1:13 with the **Home** page active. When the Home page is not displayed, you activate it by clicking the **Home** icon.

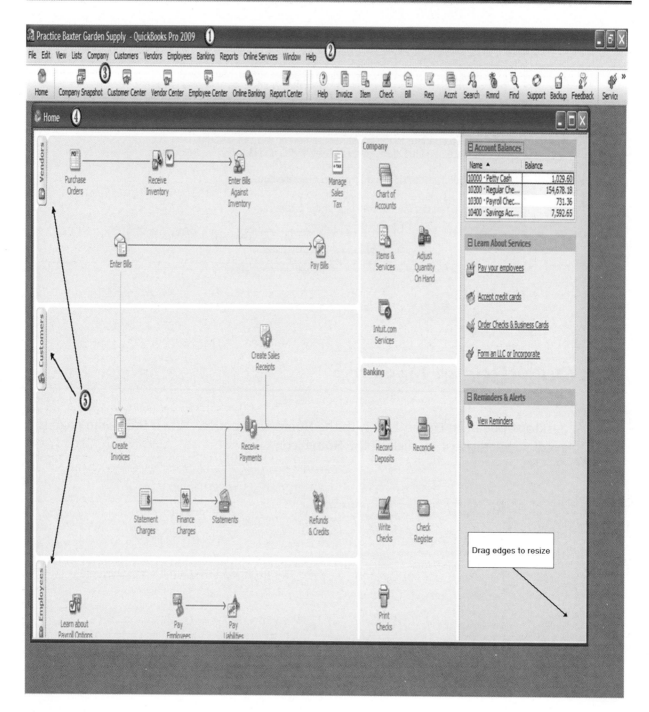

Figure 1:13

Figure 1:13 has been labeled so you can identify elements of the desktop and the table that follows explains these elements.

QUICKBOOKS DESKTOP ELEMENTS		
Section	Name	Description
1	Title Bar	Displays the name of the open company.
2	Main Menu	Menus for executing QBP commands.
3	Icon Bar	Quick access to frequently used tasks. Adding and deleting icons from this bar is explained later in the chapter.
4	Home Page	Icon access to vendor, customer, employee, company, and banking tasks with the workflow of tasks illustrated. Customizing the Home page is explained later in the chapter.
5	Center Icons	Icons for opening the Vendors, Customers, and Employees centers.

Before using the software it helps to become familiar with the location of menu commands, so the next table explains menus by categories.

MENU COMMANDS	
Main Menu	Description
File	Basic operations such as opening and closing companies, data backup, and recovery operations, printing, and printer setup.
Edit	Data manipulation features such as cut, copy, paste, delete, and undo. Submenus activate based on the task being performed. A calculator is also found here.
Lists	Commands for opening and managing master record lists such as customers, vendors, sales taxes, inventory, and chart of accounts.
View	Commands for viewing the Icon Bar and activating task windows.

MENU COMMANDS	
Main Menu	**Description**
Company	Company-related tasks such as entering company identifying information, closing the accounting period, establishing budgets, and setting reminders and alerts.
Customers	Customer-related tasks such as invoicing, receiving payments, and printing customer statements.
Vendors	Vendor-related tasks such as entering billings, remitting payment, and managing inventory activities.
Employees	Employee-related tasks such as creating paychecks, entering time cards, and paying payroll liabilities.
Banking	Banking-related activities such as making deposits, writing checks, and reconciling bank statements.
Reports	Menus for printing a variety of reports that analyze company performance.
Windows	Commands for activating an open task window when performing multiple tasks.
Help	QBP help files, license agreement, and software version.

We will now provide more information on using the Home page. (See Figure 1:14.)

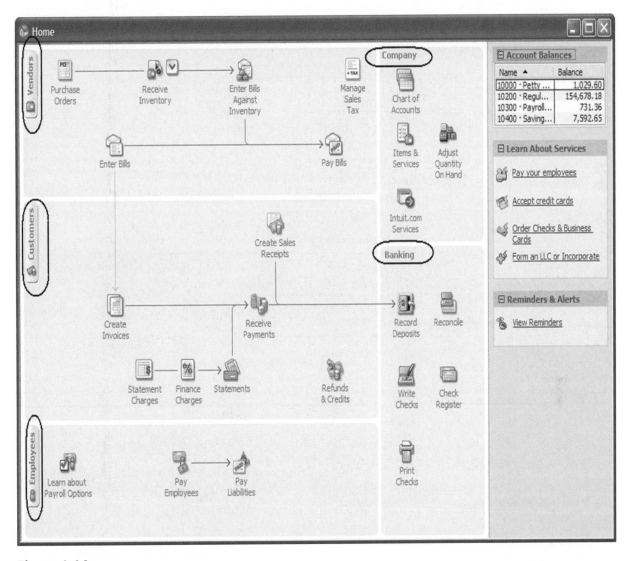

Figure 1:14

This page is divided into five distinct sections, namely Vendors, Customers, Employees, Company, and Banking. Each section contains icons for accessing specific tasks performed in that activity.

Arrows depict the normal workflow of tasks. Focus on the Vendors section. You can commence a vendor transaction by entering a purchase order. After entering the order, you continue processing it by recording a vendor receipt or a bill. Only after recording the bill can you then pay the vendor. The second line of icons shows that you can also commence a vendor transaction by entering a bill without entering a purchase order. Once again, the vendor is paid after recording the bill.

Arrows also depict the task workflow between activities. Notice that vendor bills will interface with customer invoices. In Chapter 4 we illustrate the interrelationship between customer invoices and vendor bills when you invoice a customer for vendor charges.

Finally, cash account balances appear to the right and company preference settings determine the task icons displayed on the page. Click **Edit** on the main menu and select **Preferences** to open the window illustrated next. Click **Desktop View** on the right and select the **Company Preferences** tab to view preferences for the desktop. (See Figure 1:15.)

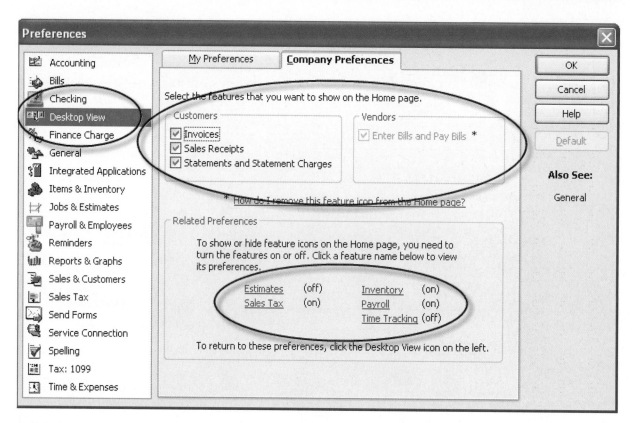

Figure 1:15

This window determines the icons appearing on the Home page. Baxter has chosen to turn on all icons except Estimates and Time Tracking. The display of icons is changed by clicking an option to turn the feature on or off. Click **OK** to close the window.

Home page icons avoid searching through menus to open frequently performed tasks. However, as illustrated above, you can only activate icons for the tasks listed in the Preference Window. Therefore, QBP provides another way of creating shortcuts to frequently used tasks. Shortcuts can be added by customizing the Icon Bar and this is the subject of our next topic.

CUSTOMIZE THE ICON BAR

Click **View>>Customize Icon Bar** on the main menu and the window in Figure 1:16 opens.

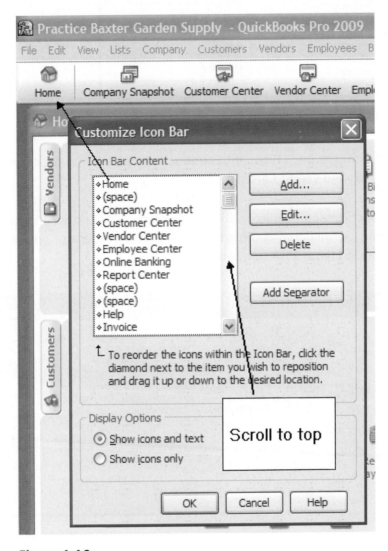

Figure 1:16

Scroll to the top of the list and notice that Home appears first. Icon Bar Content displays the names of icons appearing on the Icon Bar and the ordering of the icons on the bar.

Let us change the ordering of the Check and Bill icons. Scroll down the list to locate the Bill icon. Using the mouse, click the diamond in front of **Bill** and drag it until a hash line appears before Check. (See Figure 1:17.) Release the mouse and the ordering changes.

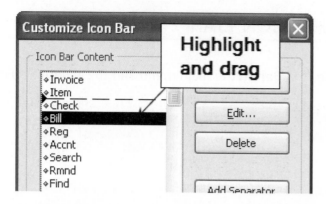

Figure 1:17

You will next remove icons from the bar. Highlight **Feedback** on the list and click **Delete**. Also delete **Accnt**, **Services**, **Payroll**, and **Credit Cards**.

Finally, you will add a new section and new icons for this section. Scroll down and highlight **(space)**. Click **Add Separator**. Scroll down and highlight the **(space)** separator you just added and click **Add** for the window in Figure 1:18 to open.

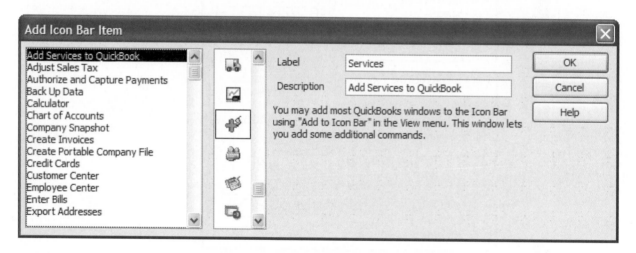

Figure 1:18

Now add the **Accnt** icon to this new section by highlighting **Chart of Accounts** on the list to the left. Notice that the icon to the right jumped to the picture for this item. The **Label** name will be Accnt. (See Figure 1:19.) Click **OK**. Click **OK** again to close the Customize Icon Bar window.

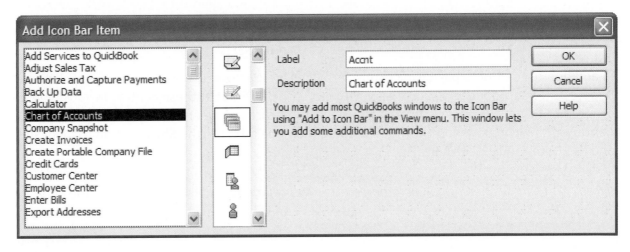

Figure 1:19

There is a different method for adding report shortcuts to the Icon Bar. Select *Reports>>Memorized Reports>>Accountant>>Profit & Loss* on the main menu. This action opened Baxter's income statement (not illustrated).

Now add the income statement to the Icon Bar. Click *View>>Add "Profit & Loss" to Icon Bar* on the main menu to open the window illustrated in Figure 1:20.

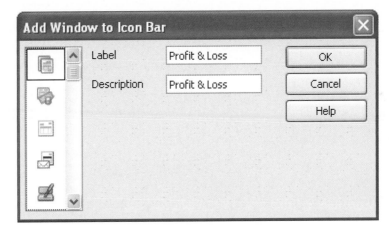

Figure 1:20

Change the **Label** to "P&L," click **OK**, and the report is added to the Icon Bar. Click **X** on the report to close it. Your Icon Bar will now resemble the bar in Figure 1:21.

Figure 1:21

QUICKBOOKS CENTERS

In addition to the Home page, QuickBooks provides the Customer, Vendor, Employee, and Report centers for managing activities. You will learn more about these centers in subsequent chapters. For now, learn to activate and use basic features on a center. Click **Customer Center** on the Icon Bar and select the **Customers & Jobs** tab. Set the **Show** option to Invoices and the **Date** to All. (See Figure 1.22.)

(Note: You can also open the Customer Center by clicking [🏠 Customers] *on the Home page.)*

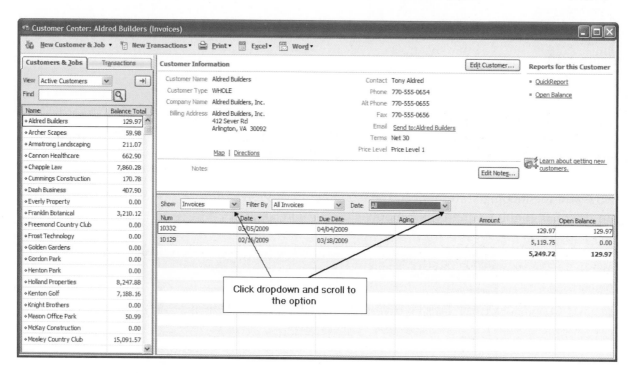

Figure 1:22

This center has a **Customers & Jobs** and a **Transactions** tab.

The **Customers & Jobs** tab lists customer accounts with balances to the left. Aldred Builders is the company currently highlighted on the left so Aldred's account information and transactions appear on the right.

Transactions listed at the bottom are viewed by setting the **Show**, **Filter By**, and **Date** options. These options are currently set to **Invoices** that are **Open Invoices** in **This Fiscal Year**. To change an option, click this [▾] dropdown list on an option to make a different selection.

Change the **Show** option to **All Transactions** and the **Date** to **All** so that the bottom section now displays the transactions illustrated in Figure 1:23.

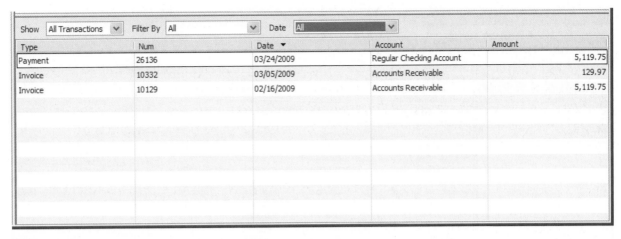

Figure 1:23

IMPORTANT: This window and report windows use your computer system date to determine the fiscal period. Thus, if your computer date falls in 2008 This Fiscal Year will display transactions recorded in 2009, but if your computer date falls after 2009, you will have to change the Date option to Last Fiscal Year or All.

Next look at information displayed on the **Transactions** tab. Click the tab and select **Invoices** on the left so that the center displays sales invoices for all customers.

Use the dropdown list to change the **Filter By** option to **All Invoices** and the **Date** to **All.** (See Figure 1:24.)

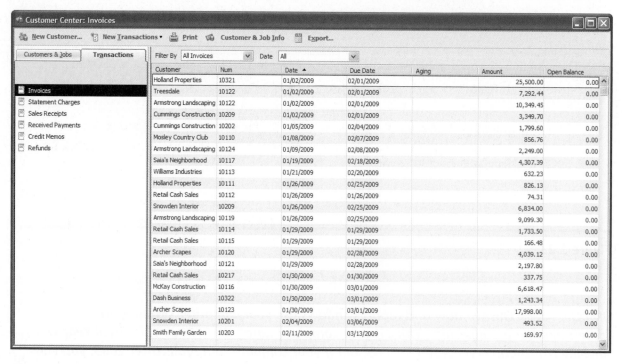

Figure 1:24

You now see all invoices posted in 2009. Remember that if your computer system date falls after 2009 you need to set the Date option to Next Fiscal Year or All.

This illustration shows that the Transactions tab displays transactions by type and the Customers & Jobs tab displays transactions by customer.

Click **X** to close the Customer Center and perform the exercise that follows.

PRACTICE NAVIGATING QUICKBOOKS

1. Click the **Vendors** button on the Home page to open the Vendor Center. *(Note: You can also click Vendor Center on the Icon Bar.)* This center operates similar to the Customer center.

    The **Vendors** tab lists vendors and account balances to the left and highlighted vendor information to the right. The **Transactions** tab displays all vendor transactions by type.

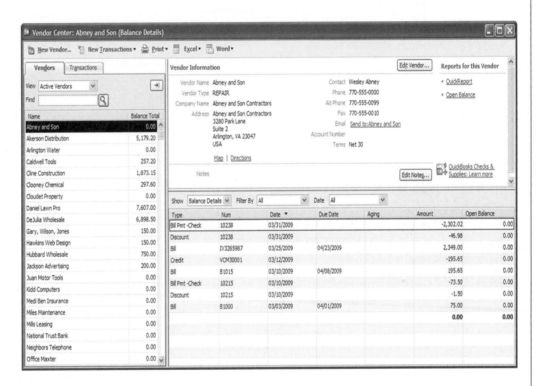

Figure 1:25

2. Click **Employee Center** on the Icon Bar. You can resize a center by using the mouse. Place your cursor at the edge of the center until it changes to ←||→. Use the left mouse button and drag to resize. You can also resize sections on the center by dragging the separator bar.

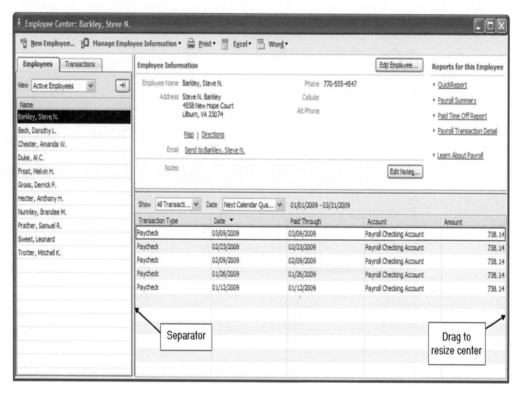

Figure 1:26

3. Now open the chart of accounts. Click **Lists>>Chart of Accounts** on the main menu or use the **Accnt** icon you added to the Icon Bar in the previous topic.

4. You now have three windows open. Click **Window** on the main menu. The list of open windows appears at the bottom and the active window is checked (Figure 1:27). Click **Employee Center** and the center moves to the front of all open windows, meaning it is now the active window.

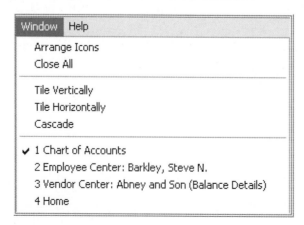

Figure 1:27

5. Click the Minimize button on the Employee Center.

Figure 1:28

The center drops to the bottom of the screen and appears as illustrated in Figure 1:29. *(Note: It may be hidden behind the Home page if you are viewing the Home page in full screen.)*

Figure 1:29

The Restore button will reopen the window to its original size. The Maximize button will reopen the window to full screen.

6. Click *View>Open Window List* on the main menu and the list illustrated in Figure 1:30 appears to the left.

Figure 1:30

Keeping this list open will let you navigate between tasks. A task is activated by clicking it on the list. Clicking **X** will close the Open Windows list.

7. Click to activate the Vendor Center and then click **X** to close it. Do the same for the Employee Center and Chart of Accounts. You now know how to multitask in QBP.

CUSTOMIZE COMPANY NAMES

Before performing tasks, you need to customize each company's name to identify QBP reports and other output as yours. With Practice Baxter Garden Supply as the open company, click **Company>>Company Information** on the main menu. Refer to Figure 1:31 and add your initials to the **Company Name** and **Legal Name**.

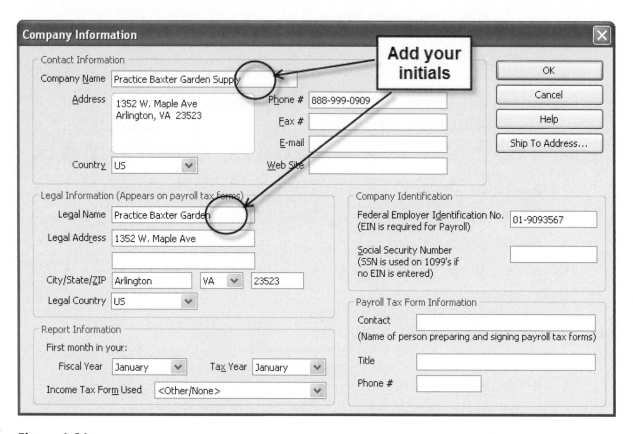

Figure 1:31

Before saving the changes, notice that the window shows Baxter's **Fiscal Year** and **Tax Year**. Both years begin in January, meaning that the company is on a calendar year accounting cycle. Click **OK** to save your changes. *(Note: Cancel will close the window without saving changes.)*

In the Practice Set at the end of the chapter you customize company names for remaining sample data files. Be sure to complete it.

QUICKBOOKS KEYBOARD SHORTCUTS

Keyboard shortcuts are a method of executing software commands without selecting a command from the menu. You may already be familiar with keyboard shortcuts by using other software applications. QBP sometimes lists the keyboard shortcut alongside the menu command. For instance, click *Edit* on the main menu and notice that **Ctrl+C** is the shortcut key for the **Copy** command. To use this shortcut, highlight the text to be copied, press and hold the Ctrl key on your keyboard, and then press the letter "C".

The following table lists frequently used keyboard shortcuts.

Editing Commands	Keyboard Action	Activity Commands	Keyboard Action
Cut highlighted text	Ctrl + X	Open help for the active window	F1
Copy highlighted text	Ctrl + C	Find transaction	Ctrl + F
Paste copied text	Ctrl + V	Create new transaction	Ctrl + N
Undo editing	Ctrl + Z	Open transaction journal	Ctrl + Y
Delete character to right of cursor	Del	Memorize transaction	Ctrl + M
Delete character to left of cursor	Backspace	Open chart of accounts list	Ctrl + A
Delete entire line	Ctrl + Del	Open dropdown list for an item	Ctrl + L
Delete entire transaction	Ctrl + D	Show list	Ctrl + S
Insert a new line	Ctrl + Ins	Open Quick Report for a transaction or to list items	Ctrl + Q
Move to next field	Tab	Print	Ctrl + P
Move to previous field	Shift + Tab		
Move to beginning of field	Home		
Move to end of field	End		
Move up or down a line	Up arrow or down arrow		

Date Shortcuts	Keyboard Action
Today	T
Date calendar	Alt + down arrow
Next day	+
Previous day	−

QUICKBOOKS HELP

 *QB 2009 added a Live Community tab to the Help window so you can easily search for help online.*

Help on using QBP is only one click away. The shortcut key **F1** will open the help window on the right. Use your mouse to resize this window as illustrated in Figure 1:32. You can also select ***Help>>QuickBooks Help*** on the main menu to open this window.

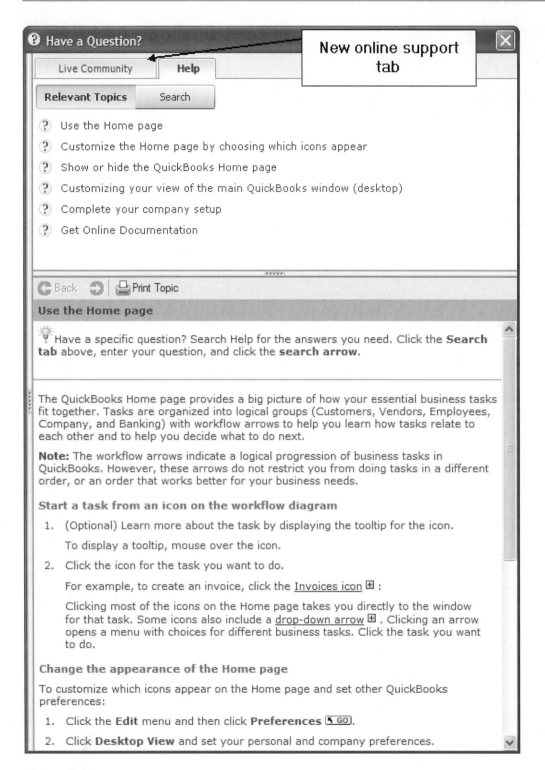

Figure 1:32

The **Relevant Topics** tab provides general help by topic and will open to show topics related to the window that was active when opening Help. In this instance the Home page was active when opening Help so the topics listed relate to topics on the Home page.

Close QuickBooks Help by clicking **X**. Click **Invoice** on the Icon Bar. *(Note: You can also click the Create Invoices icon on the Home page or select Customers>>Create Invoices on the main menu.)* Reopen the Help window and find that **Relevant Topics** now relate to invoices (Figure 1:33).

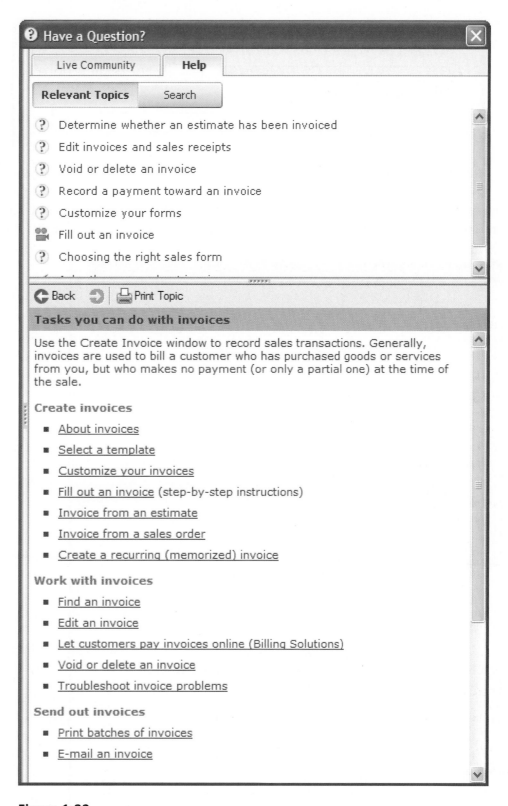

Figure 1:33

Next, click the **Search** tab to search for specific terms in a help topic (Figure 1:34).

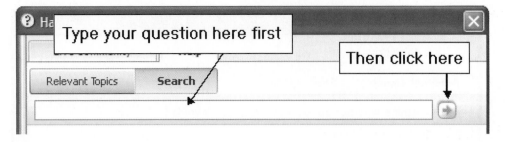

Figure 1:34

Type "saving sales invoices" in the search box and click the arrow to the right of the box or hit enter. Topics now focus on the question of saving sales invoices. (See Figure 1:35.)

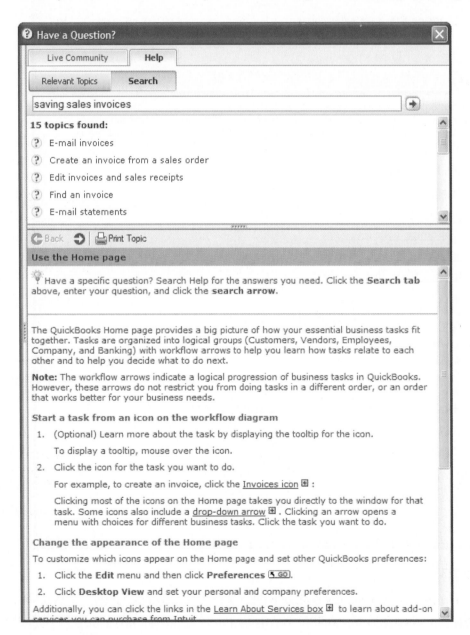

Figure 1:35

Click **Edit invoices and sales receipts** under topics and information for that topic displays at the bottom (Figure 1:36).

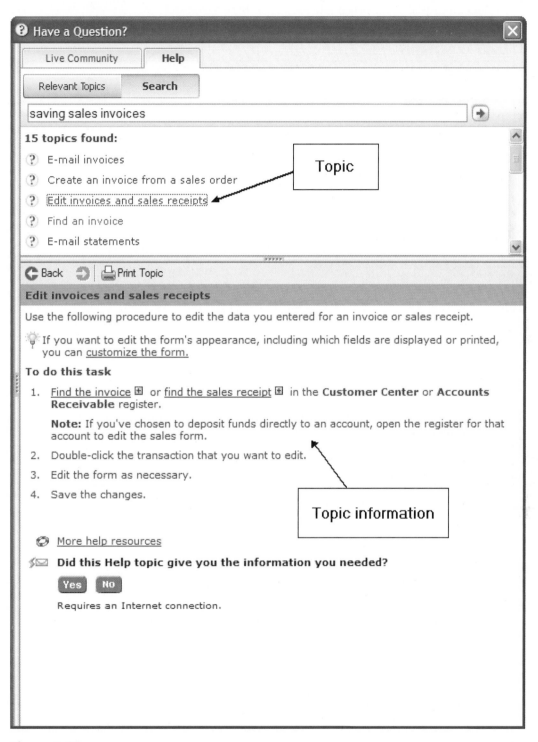

Figure 1:36

This topic was placed in the search results because QBP found the words "save," "sales," and "invoice" in the topic. You see that the search tab helps narrow down topics to specific tasks.

Underlined terms in the topic, such as "Find the invoice," have a plus symbol to indicate that clicking the term will display additional information. (See Figure 1:37.)

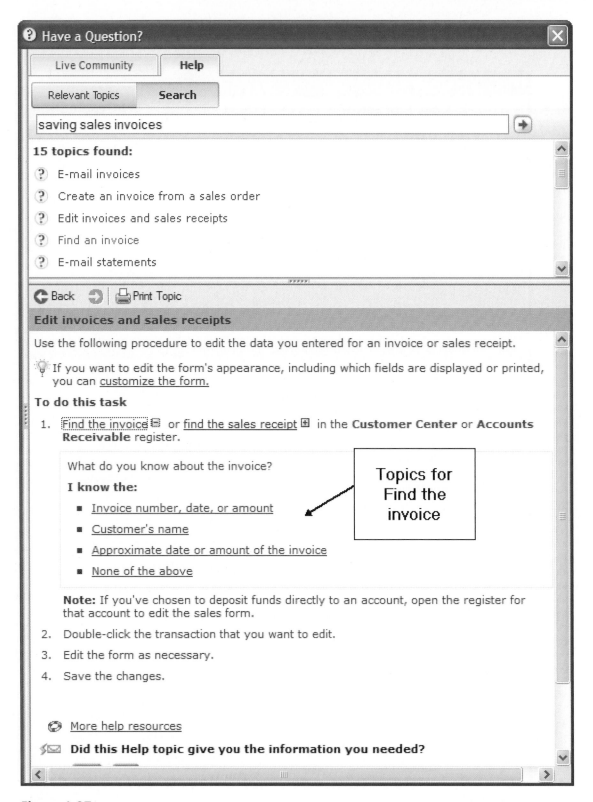

Figure 1:37

Click the **Invoice number, date or amount** link and you are shown topics about this subject. (See Figure 1:38.)

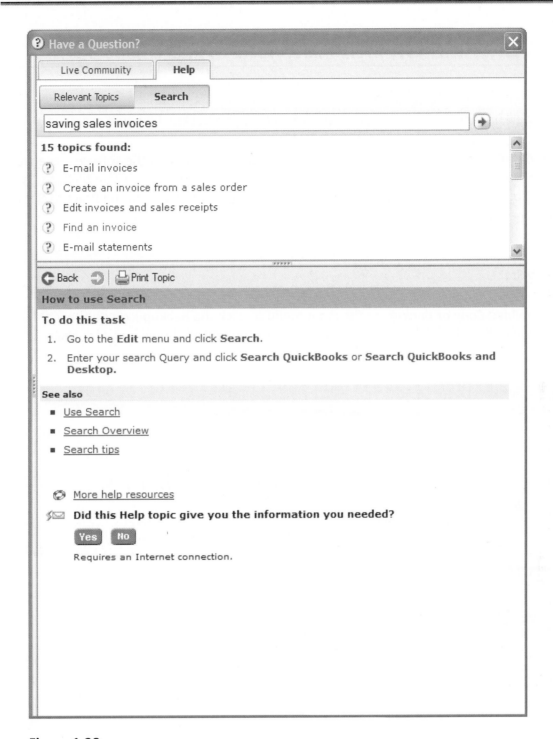

Figure 1:38

Click the Back icon 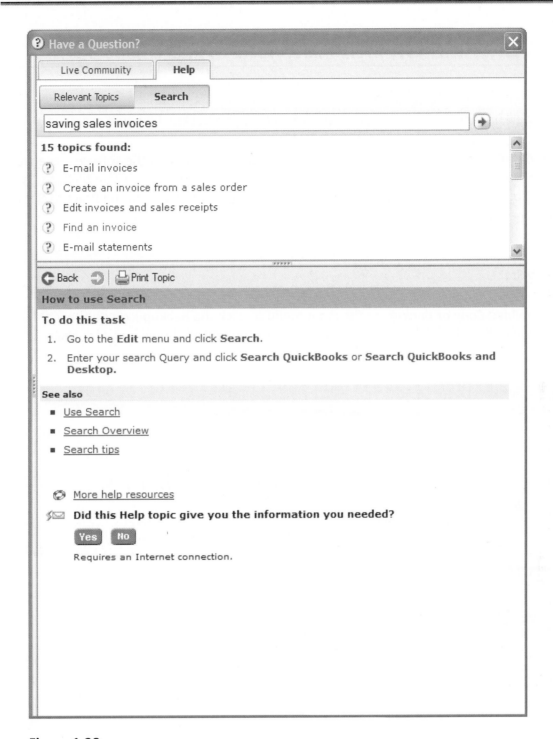 to return to the previous topic or click the Print Topic icon Print Topic to print the topic.

QPB provides icons at the bottom of help topics so you can submit comments that improve help topics. You can also use the Live Community tab to seek online help. An Internet connection is required for both features.

Click **X** on the help window and click **X** on the invoice window.

BACKING UP COMPANY DATA FILES

Data files should be backed up each time you finish working on a company. At a minimum, perform a backup whenever the text tells you to and use the backup filename provided.

The backup utility performs a backup of the company currently open in the software. Because this is now Practice Baxter Garden Supply, the steps that follow create a backup file for this company. You will create a backup file for remaining sample companies in the Practice Set at the end of the chapter.

❖ *Backup Step 1*

Select *File>>Save Copy or Backup* on the main menu or click the **Backup** icon on the Icon Bar to open the window illustrated in Figure 1:39. Choose the option shown and click **Next**.

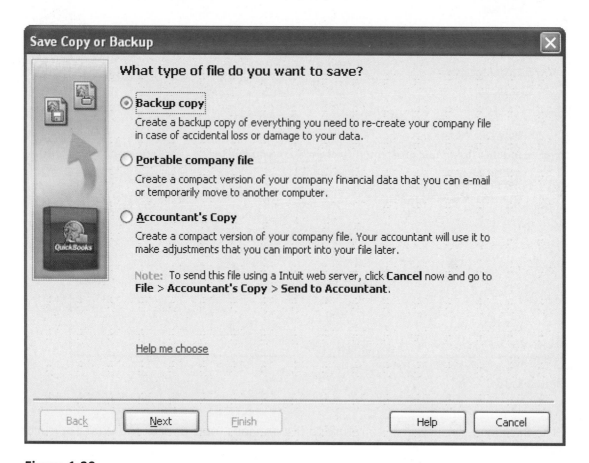

Figure 1:39

❖ **_Backup Step 2_**

On the screen illustrated in Figure 1:40 select **Local backup**.

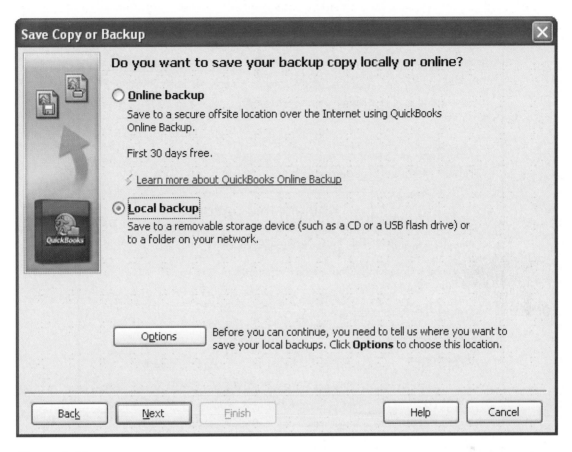

Figure 1:40

❖ **Backup Step 3**

Click **Options** to set options for creating the backup (Figure 1:41).

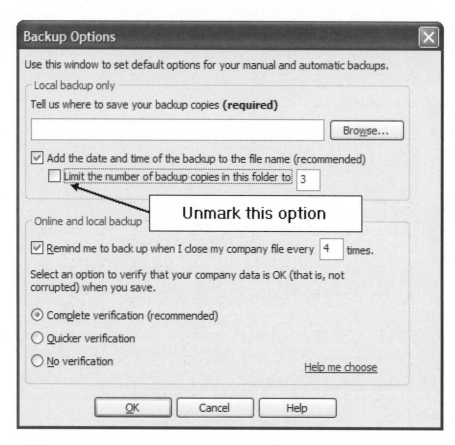

Figure 1:41

Click **Browse** to choose a path for storing the backup file. To make it easy to locate the file in the future, highlight **My Documents** and click **OK**. (See Figure 1:42.)

Note: You can also select the drive labeled CD-RW Drive. You can also select a USB drive, which is normally labeled "E." However, when storing backups to these devices you may need to use the instructions in Appendix C and create a portable backup to reduce the backup file size.

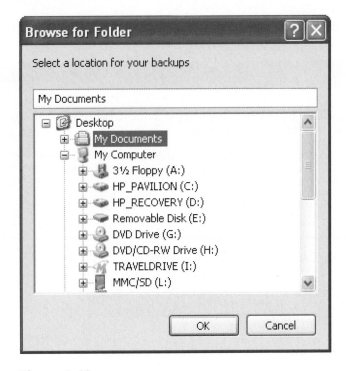

Figure 1:42

The window in Figure 1:43 now opens, showing the exact location for storing the backup file.

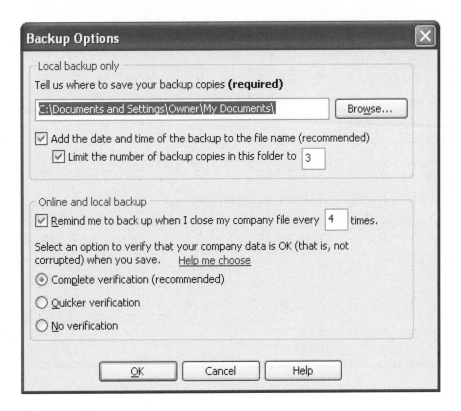

Figure 1:43

Click **OK** and you are prompted to change the location (Figure 1:44). Click **Use this Location.**

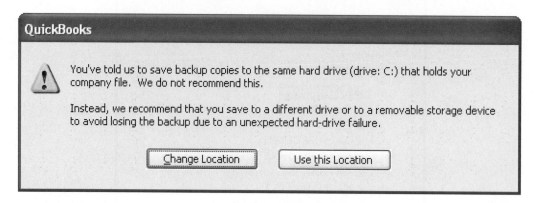

Figure 1:44

❖ *Backup Step 4*

Click **Next**, select **Save it now** (Figure 1:45), and click **Next**.

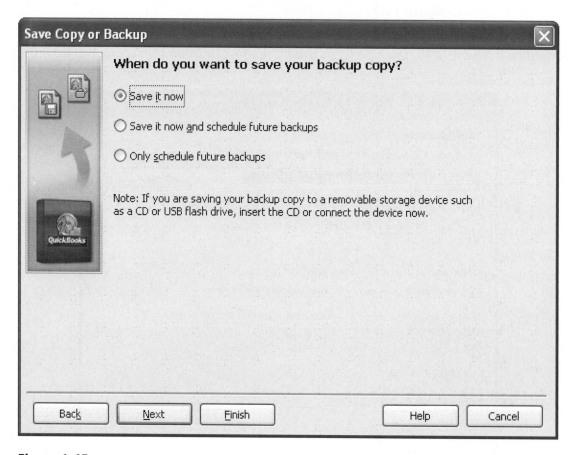

Figure 1:45

❖ **Backup Step 5**

We suggest replacing the date portion of the backup file name with the chapter name you are currently working on. Therefore, in the window illustrated in Figure 1:46 change the **File name** to *Practice Baxter Garden Supply Chpt 1* and click **Save**. *(Note: The software adds the QBB extension.)*

Figure 1:46

The company file closes and the backup begins. When Figure 1:47 appears the backup is complete. Click **OK** and the company file reopens.

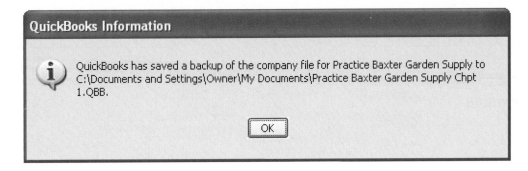

Figure 1:47

RESTORING COMPANY DATA FILES

This topic covers situations where you need to restore a company backup file, for instance, when you want to restart a chapter or move data files between school and home. *(Note: If restoring a portable backup, refer to the instructions in Appendix C.)*

Note: You cannot restore previous work unless you have created a backup file; however, you can always return to using the original data file that was downloaded from the textbook Website.

Note: Restoring a backup file overwrites all existing data. Therefore, you should backup existing data using a unique filename before restoring a backup file.

❖ *Restore Step 1*

Open the company to be restored by selecting *File>>Open or Restore Company* on the main menu. *(Note: You can actually open any company file.)* Choose the option illustrated in Figure 1:48 and click **Next**.

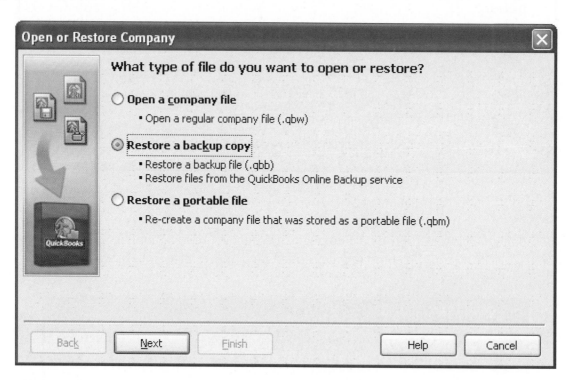

Figure 1:48

❖ *Restore Step 2*

Select **Local backup** and click **Next** (Figure 1:49).

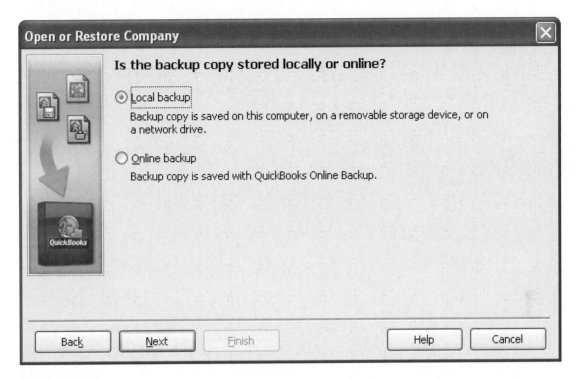

Figure 1:49

❖ *Restore Step 3*

Highlight the backup file name and click **Open** (Figure 1:50).

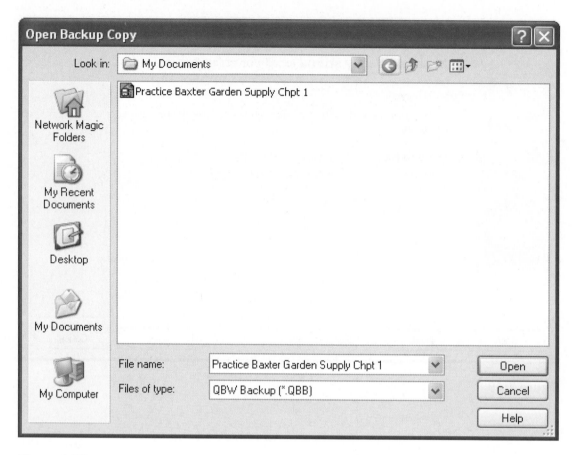

Figure 1:50

❖ *__Restore Step 4__*

On the window illustrated in Figure 1:51 click **Next.**

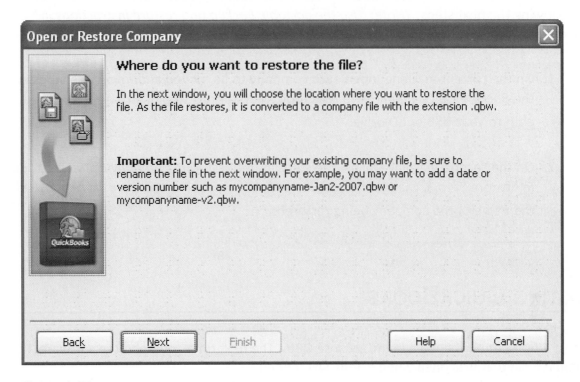

Figure 1:51

In the window that opens (not illustrated) highlight **Practice Baxter Garden Supply** and click **Save**. When QBP warns that the file already exists, click **Yes** to replace it.

The company closes and opens a confirmation screen to delete existing data by restoring data from the backup file (Figure 1:52). Type "YES" in all caps and click **OK.**

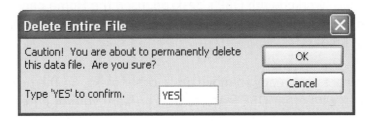

Figure 1:52

Click **OK** when QBP prompts and the company reopens.

MOVING DATA BETWEEN SCHOOL AND HOME

Using backup and restore procedures, you can move data files between home and school by following the next steps. *(Note: Use the portable backup and restore instructions in Appendix C if you need to reduce backup file sizes.)*

1. On the current machine, open each company to be moved and follow the steps in the *Backing Up Company Data Files* topic. For Backup Step 3, change the backup path to your USB or CD drive.

2. On the second machine, follow the steps in the *Restoring Company Data Files* topic. In Restore Step 3, change the data file path to your USB or CD drive. In Step 4, select the name of the company being restored.

EXITING QUICKBOOKS

Select **File>>Exit** on the main menu to close QBP. The next time you open the software, the company file that was open when exiting will reopen.

SUMMARY

In this chapter, you downloaded company data files from the textbook's Website to your computer and opened these companies in the software. You learned to customize company names with your initials, worked with QBP's desktop, used the Home page and centers, and customized the Icon Bar. You also worked with QBP's help files and learned to back up and restore company data files.

Congratulations! You are now ready to move on to other tasks. In the next chapter, your focus shifts to working with other QBP features that prepare you for entering transactions.

END-OF-CHAPTER QUESTIONS

TRUE/FALSE

_____   1. You can restore a company using a restore file.

_____   2. Icons on the Icon Bar are shortcuts to frequently used tasks and reports.

_____   3. QBP Help can be accessed by pressing F1.

_____   4. You must close a company before exiting QBP.

_____   5. You need only use the restore utility to relocate company files to a new computer.

MULTIPLE CHOICE

_____   1. You can identify the open company in QBP by looking at the ____.
   a. Main Menu
   b. Title Bar
   c. Icon Bar
   d. Window Bar

_____   2. Which of the following is considered operating software?
   a. Microsoft Office Professional
   b. LINUX
   c. Microsoft Windows XP
   d. Both b and c

_____   3. Which main menu command will open a view of the chart of accounts?
   a. File
   b. Lists
   c. Customers
   d. Vendors

_____   4. The Create Invoices icon appears on the _____ section of the Home page.
   a. Customers
   b. Banking
   c. Company
   d. Vendors

_____ 5. Which keyboard shortcut can be used to enter a new transaction?
     a. Ctrl + D
     b. Ctrl + S
     c. Ctrl + N
     d. Ctrl + L

PRACTICE SET

1. Open each sample company listed below. After opening, add your initials to the company name. Remember that the company name is changed by selecting *Company>>Company Information* on the main menu

   After adding your initials, back up each company using the file names indicated below.

Sample Company	Backup File Name
Graded Baxter Garden Supply	Graded Baxter Garden Supply Chpt 1
Practice Astor Landscaping	Practice Astor Landscaping Chpt 1
Graded Astor Landscaping	Graded Astor Landscaping Chpt 1
Practice TEK Business	Practice TEK Business Chpt 1
Graded TEK Business	Graded TEK Business Chpt 1

CHAPTER 2   QUICKBOOKS BASICS

LEARNING OBJECTIVES

This chapter works with the **Practice Baxter Garden Supply** data file used in Chapter 1. *If this company is not loaded on your computer then restore the Practice Baxter Garden Supply Chpt 1.QBB backup file created while reading Chapter 1.*

In this chapter you will review the QBP settings and options affecting transaction posting and learn to use features that help you locate posted transactions. The chapter covers the following:

1. Viewing and printing the chart of accounts
2. Understanding a company's general ledger framework and general ledger accounts, including creating accounts
3. Setting QBP preference options that control software behavior
4. Using report drilldown and find features to locate transactions
5. Using the reports menu and center
6. Printing, customizing, emailing and exporting reports
7. Setting accounting periods

You are probably ready to jump in and begin recording transactions, but accounting is more than posting entries. Accountants determine the "where and when" of transaction posting, for example, where to post a rent bill (i.e., prepaid asset or expense account) and when to recognize revenue (i.e., upon taking an order or shipping the goods). Understanding the where and when of transaction posting lets the accountant know what human intervention is required to ensure that financial statements are correct.

To understand the where and when of accounting software, you must understand QBP's behavior behind the keys. Therefore, this chapter looks at settings and options that control transaction posting and reporting. Before looking at these settings and options, you need to become familiar with the basic foundation for all accounting entries, namely the chart of accounts. This is the subject of our next topic. First, launch QBP and open **Practice Baxter Garden Supply**.

CHART OF ACCOUNTS

Open the chart of accounts by clicking the **Accnt** icon on the Icon Bar or by selecting *Lists>>Chart of Accounts* on the main menu. The list displayed in Figure 2:1 shows Baxter's general ledger account numbers and names along with current account balances and account types. *(Note: Amounts with minus signs are credit balances.)* Use the scroll bar to view accounts toward the bottom.

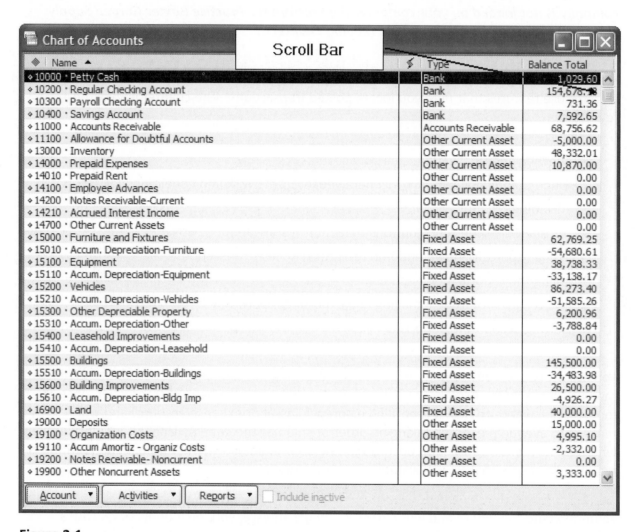

Figure 2:1

These accounts will be used for posting Baxter's accounting transactions and the balances will appear on financial statements and other reports. After reading the topics that follow, you will be familiar with Baxter's chart of accounts and ready to record transactions.

PRINT THE CHART OF ACCOUNTS

You begin familiarizing yourself with Baxter's COA by printing it. Click the **Reports** button at the bottom of the Chart of Accounts list and select **Account Listing**. *(Note: You can also print this report by selecting **Reports>>List>>Account Listing** on the main menu.)*

The scroll bar to the right of the report will let you view accounts toward the bottom (Figure 2:2). You can resize report columns by selecting the column separator and dragging it.

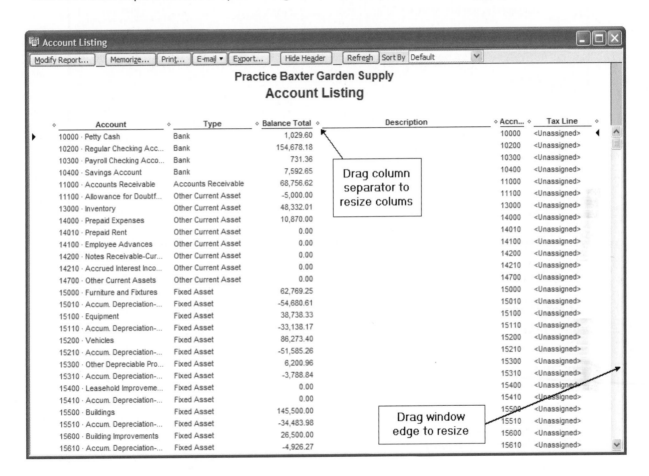

Figure 2:2

Click the **Print** button and the printer dialog window opens (Figure 2:3).

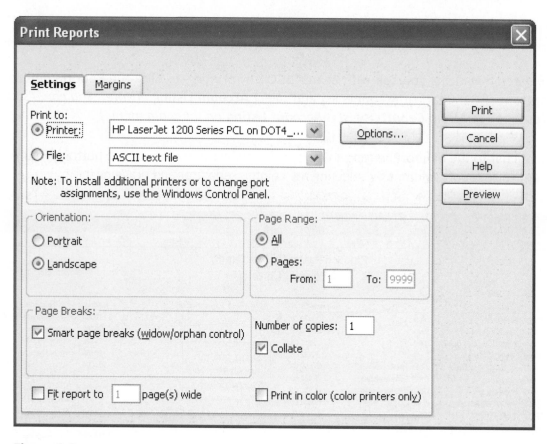

Figure 2:3

Use the dropdown list on the **Printer** field when you need to select a different printer. *(Note: Your printer name will vary from the printer name illustrated.)*

Click **Print** and a hardcopy is sent to the printer. Retain this report as a reference for posting transactions in subsequent chapters.

Click **X** to close the report. *(Note: If you resized report columns, QBP prompts to memorize the report before closing. Click **No**.)*

PRINTING THE CHART OF ACCOUNTS FOR OTHER SAMPLE COMPANIES

When you have the time, print the COA report for Practice Astor Landscaping and Practice TEK Business. You do not need to print the COAs for graded companies because these data files are replicas of practice companies. Keep these reports as a reference for posting transactions in subsequent chapters.

(Note: Solutions for this exercise are not provided in Appendix E.)

GENERAL LEDGER FRAMEWORK

Return to the Chart of Accounts List. The COA is comprised of individual general ledger accounts identified by account numbers and descriptions. Baxter has numbered its general ledger accounts using five numeric digits.

The first digit identifies when the account is an asset, liability, equity, revenue, cost of goods sold, operating expense, other income, or other expense account based on the following table.

First Digit	Type of Account
1	Asset
2	Liability
3	Equity
4	Revenue
5	Cost of Goods Sold
6/7	Operating Expense
8	Other Income
9	Other Expense

The second account digit used on asset and liability accounts indicates when the asset account is current or noncurrent or when the liability account is current or long-term. Current asset and current liability accounts will have 0 through 4 as the second digit whereas noncurrent asset and long-term liability accounts will have 5 through 9 as the second digit.

Review the COA report to gain a better understanding on Baxter's account numbering
framework.   Knowing the general ledger account framework will help you identify and select
accounts when posting transactions. In the real world, many companies use a similar general
ledger framework for numbering general ledger accounts.

GENERAL LEDGER ACCOUNTS

After reviewing Baxter's general ledger account framework, it is a good time to discuss creating
and managing general ledger accounts. On the **Chart of Accounts** list, highlight "10000 Petty
Cash" and click the **Account** button at the bottom to select **Edit Account**. This action opens the
window illustrated in Figure 2:4.

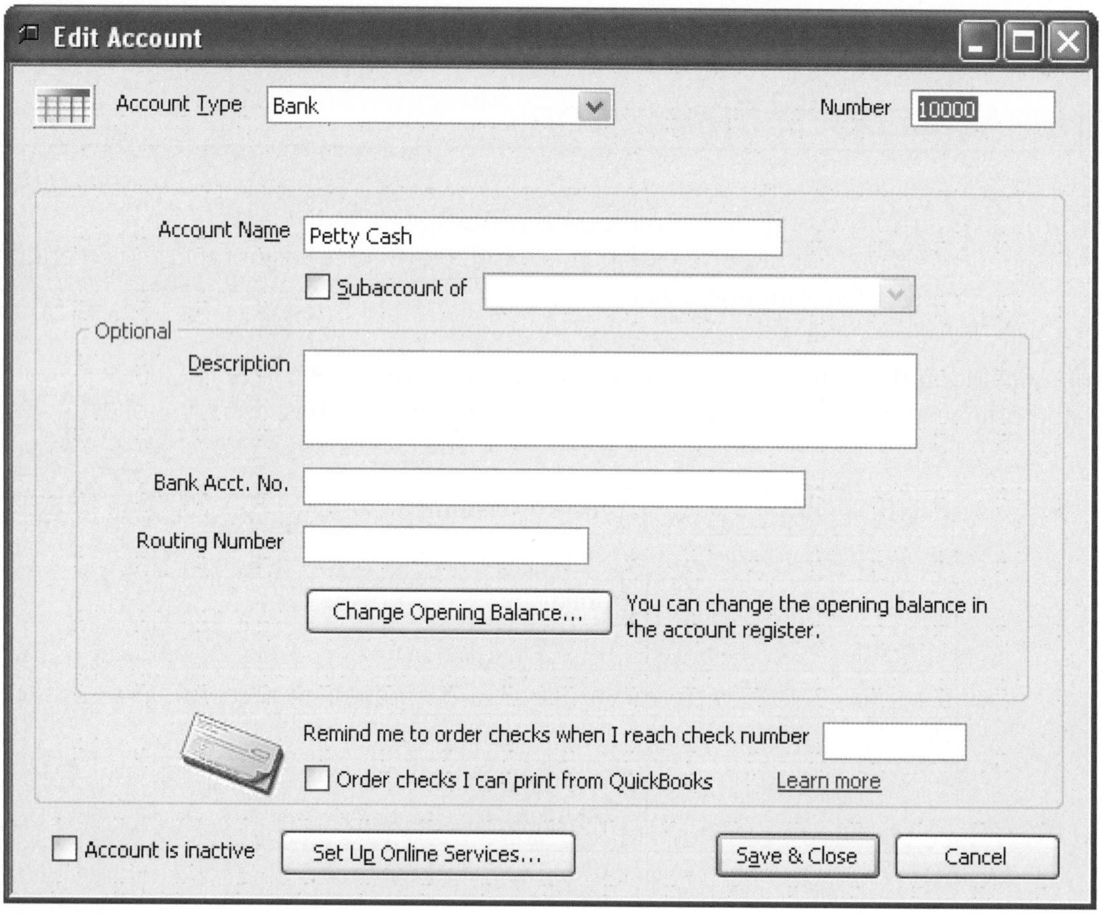

Figure 2:4

The following table explains the fields and buttons on an account.

Fields	Description
Account Type	Determines the account's normal balance (i.e., debit or credit) and the account's placement on financial reports. Selecting the dropdown list ⌄ lets you view available account types and these types are explained in the next table. Note: You may have to scroll up the list to see additional types.
Number	Unique number used to implement the general ledger account framework.
Account Name	Unique name to describe the account. The name should be concise and properly spelled and capitalized because it appears on financial reports.
Subaccount of	Option for linking an account to a related account. Linked accounts appear indented on the Chart of Accounts List and will be grouped on financial reports. Baxter's sales accounts are examples of linked accounts.
Description	Optional text field to provide an additional description. This information does not appear on financial reports but will appear on the COA report.
Bank Acct. No. or Note	Bank and credit card account types contain a Bank Acct. No. field for storing the bank account number. All other accounts replace this field with the Note field.
Change Opening Balance	Opens an account's register, which can be used to enter beginning balances. Beginning balances are entered when transferring accounting data from another accounting system.
Account is inactive	Toggles the account from active to inactive. QBP will deny transaction posting to inactive accounts.

Click **X** to close the Petty Cash account. In the exercise that follows, you will create a new general ledger account. Before performing that task, go through an accounting refresher.

The next table lists QBP account types alongside the accounting categories covered in your accounting courses. The table also lists an account category's normal balance. *(Note: The table is organized in QBP's order for types on the dropdown list.)* You can see that asset, cost of sales, and expense accounts have normal balances of debit whereas liability, equity, and revenue accounts have normal balances of credit. The normal balance is important because it determines if a debit or credit increases the account balance; for instance, accounts with a normal debit balance are increased by posting a debit.

QBP Account Type	Accounting Category	Normal Balance
Bank	Asset	Debit *(Note: This type interfaces with the account reconciliation window.)*
Accounts Receivable	Asset	Debit
Other Current Assets	Asset	Debit
Fixed Asset	Asset	Debit
Other Asset	Asset	Debit
Accounts Payable	Liability	Credit
Credit Card	Liability	Credit *(Note: This type interfaces with the account reconciliation window.)*
Other Current Liability	Liability	Credit
Long-Term Liability	Liability	Credit
Equity	Equity	Credit
Income	Revenue	Credit
Cost of Goods Sold	Cost of Sales	Debit
Expense	Expense	Debit
Other Income	Income	Credit
Other Expense	Expense	Debit

STEPS FOR ADDING A NEW GENERAL LEDGER ACCOUNT

1. From the Chart of Accounts list click **Account** and select **New**.

2. You will be creating a new expense account for equipment rentals so click **Expense** as shown in Figure 2:5 and then click **Continue**.

Figure 2:5

Note: When the account type does not appear as a listed option, use the dropdown list on Other Account Types to choose a type.

3. This account will appear right after rent expense for the office so enter "71120" as the **Number**.

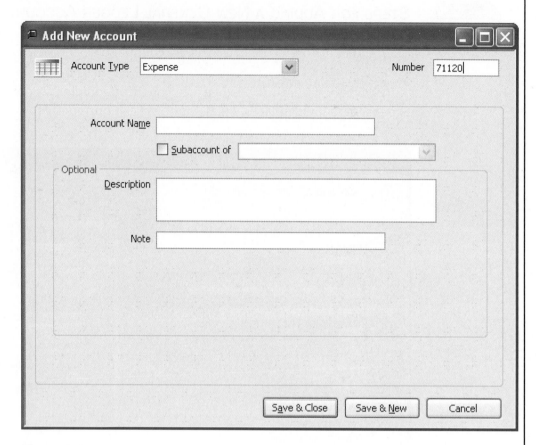

Figure 2:6

Note: If you made the wrong Account Type selection, use the dropdown list to change it.

4. Tab to **Account Name** and enter "Rent - Equipment".

5. Click the option box for **Subaccount** of and use the dropdown list to select account "71000 – Rent Expense". When finished, the new account appears as shown in Figure 2:7.

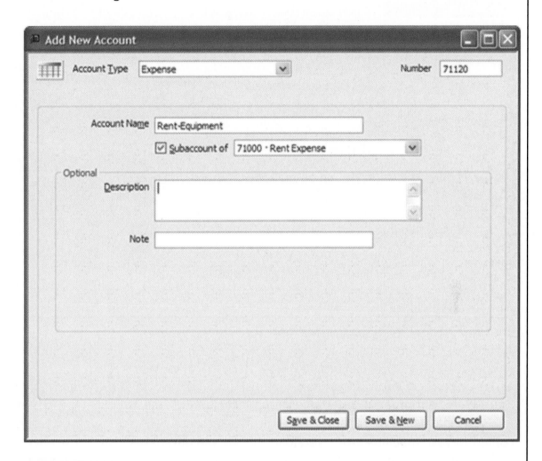

Figure 2:7

6. Click **Save & Close**. QBP returns to the Chart of Accounts. Scroll down to view the new account and then click **X** to close the Chart of Accounts.

 # QuickBooks Preference Options

In this topic you manage options that control transaction processing. Click **Edit>>Preferences** on the main menu, click the **Checking** preferences category to the left, and then select the **Company Preferences** tab. (See Figure 2:8.)

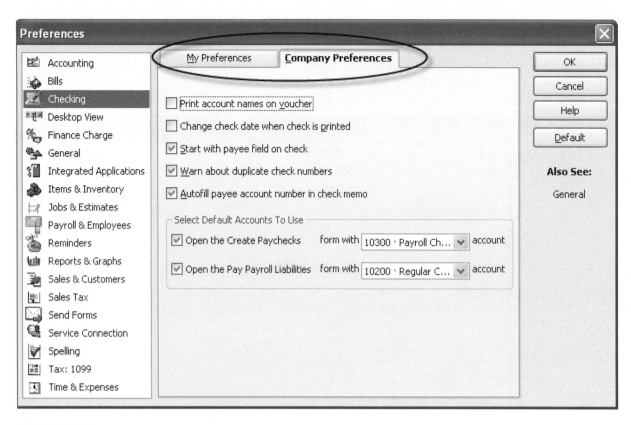

Figure 2:8

The Preferences window contains two tabs, namely Company Preferences and My Preferences. **Company Preferences** affect all users whereas **My Preferences** are customized for individual users. Company Preferences are stored with the company data file and will be copied to your machine when you load the sample databases. My Preferences are not stored with the data file, thus must be customized after opening a data file and are saved only on the current machine.

Company Preferences

You will look at only a few of the company preferences to learn why certain activities behave in a particular fashion. *Do not change any of these settings.*

Checking preferences (Figure 2:8) show that paychecks will post to 10300 Payroll Checking Account and payroll liability checks will post to 10200 Regular Checking.

Click **Accounting** and the Company Preferences tab shows that Baxter has activated general ledger account numbers.

Click **Bills** to see that vendor purchase discounts are automatically taken and the discount amount will post to 59500 Purchase Discounts.

My Preferences

Now focus on settings that control software behavior on your machine. ***You should set these options for each sample company.*** Furthermore, if you move data to a new machine, you may need to set these options again.

Go to the My Preferences tab for each preference discussed next. When you make changes, click a different category and QBP will prompt to save your changes. Click **Yes** to save the changes.

❖ **Checking Preferences**

Click **My Preferences** and select the regular checking account for each option illustrated in Figure 2:9. *(Note: The regular checking number may vary for each sample company.)* These options make sure that the correct checking account number defaults during transaction entry.

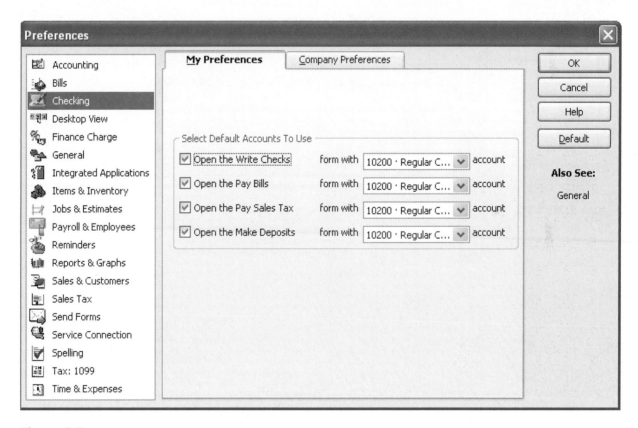

Figure 2:9

❖ **General Preferences**

Click **General** and choose the options shown in Figure 2:10. *(Note: Click **Save** when prompted to store your previous changes.)*

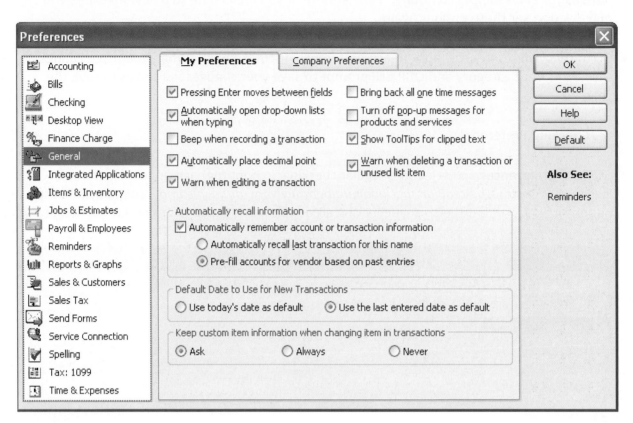

Figure 2:10

❖ **Reports & Graphs Preferences**

Click **Reports & Graphs** and verify that your options are the same as illustrated in Figure 2:11.

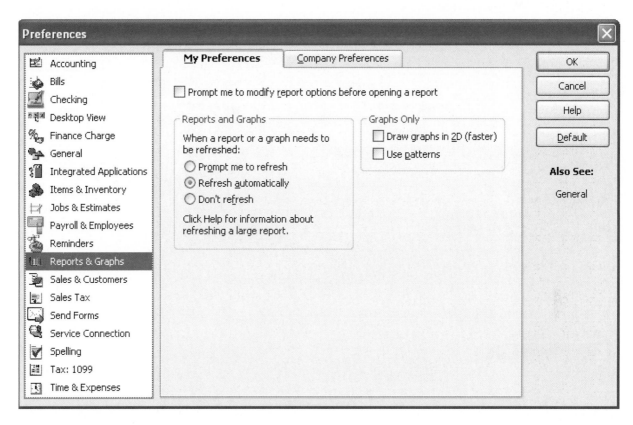

Figure 2:11

❖ **Sales & Customers Preferences**

Click **Sales & Customers** and verify that the option of **Ask what to do** is selected.

❖ **Send Forms Preferences**

Click **Send Forms** and uncheck the "**Auto-check the To be e-mailed**" checkbox.

❖ **Spelling Preferences**

Click **Spelling** if you want to customize spell check options (Figure 2:12).

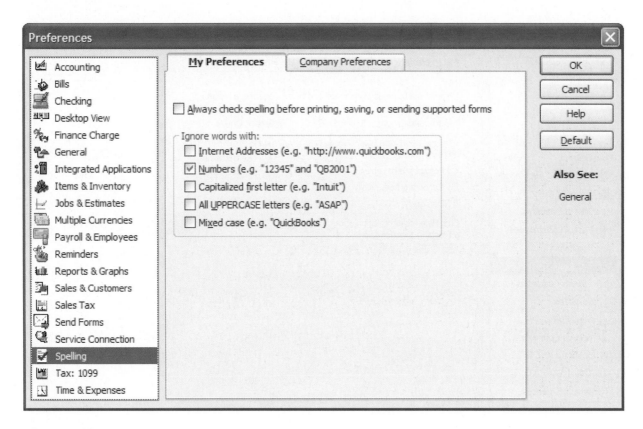

Figure 2:12

Click **OK** when finished. *Remember you will need to set these options for each sample company.*

QuickBooks Drilldown Features

Accounting software drilldown features offer a significant advantage over manual systems. Instead of sorting though general journal sheets, account ledgers, and other paperwork, you need only locate a transaction on a report or account and click to reopen the details. Let's begin by learning to use drilldown features on a report.

Open the Chart of Accounts list by clicking **Accnt** on the Icon Bar or by using the keyboard shortcut of **Ctrl + A**. At the bottom of the list, click *Reports>>Reports on All Accounts>>Other>>Trial Balance* (Figure 2:13).

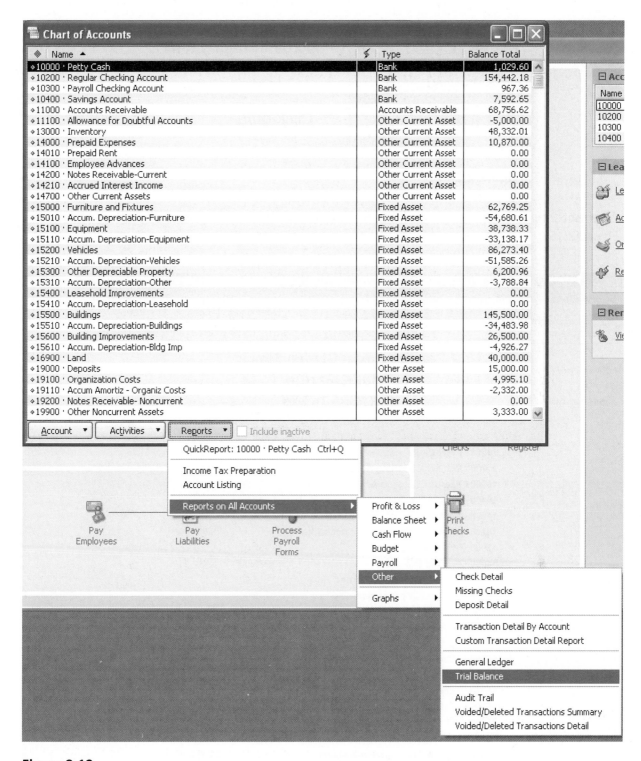

Figure 2:13

Set the report's date range to **From 3/01/2009** and **To 3/31/2009**. The first date can be entered by typing "3/01/2009" in the field or by clicking 🔳 to open the calendar feature. When using the calendar feature, dates are selected by scrolling through months to click a date. (See Figure 2:14.)

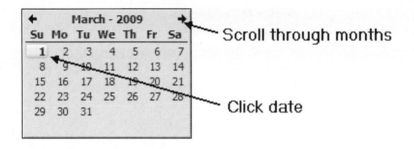

Figure 2:14

After entering the date range, click the **Refresh** button and the report redisplays as shown in Figure 2:15.

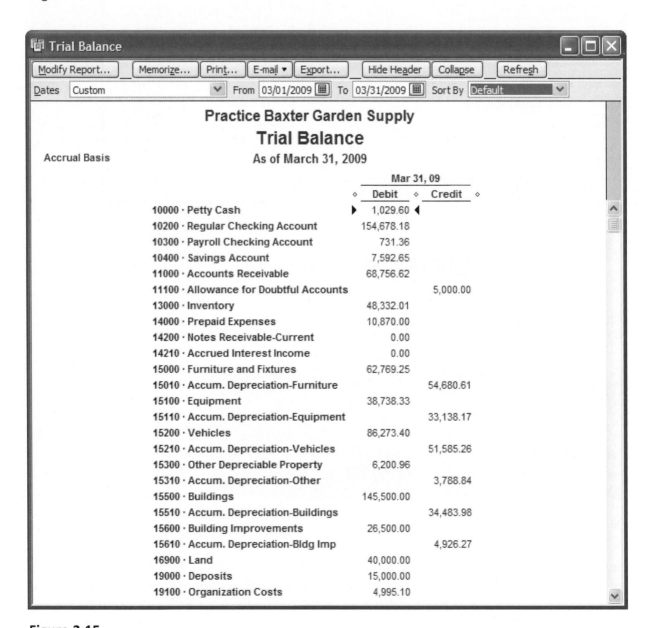

Figure 2:15

We are looking for a March sales invoice to Holland Properties. Hold your mouse over the balance on **Accounts Receivable** until the mouse changes to ⬚. *(Note: When you see this symbol, the report contains a drilldown feature.)* Double click and the Transactions by Account report opens (Figure 2:16).

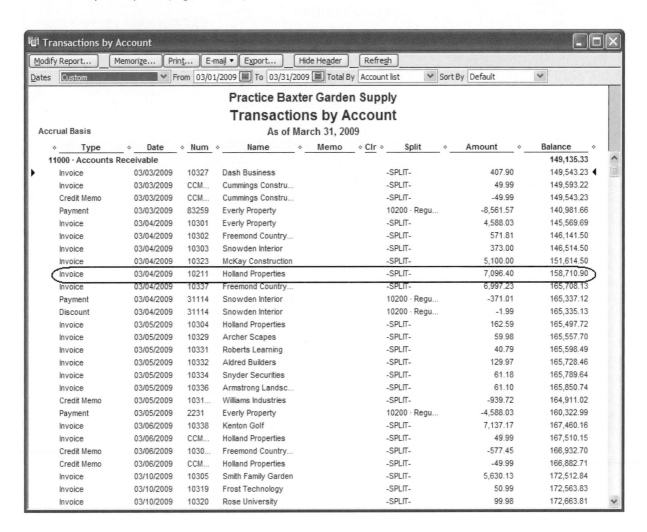

Figure 2:16

You should see **Invoice 10211** to Holland Properties. Hold your mouse over this invoice and again double click to open original invoice (Figure 2:17).

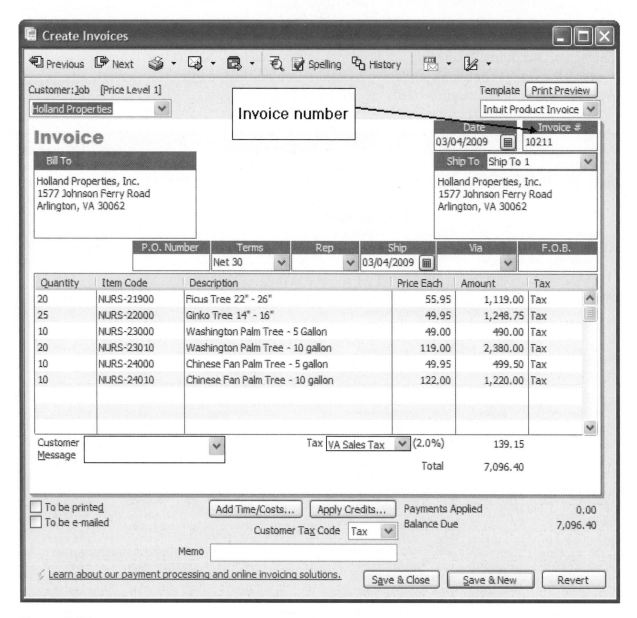

Figure 2:17

You have just used report drilldown features to locate an original transaction. Not all reports offer this feature. Drilldowns are only available when you see the magnifying glass.

So what information did you gain by drilling down to the invoice? First, you know that the transaction debited accounts receivable for $7,096.40 because this was the account balance you originally used to drill down to the invoice. You also know the inventory items sold, the sales tax charged, and the invoice total.

However, you cannot tell the general ledger sales account that was credited when posting the transaction. When selling inventory, the general ledger account used to post sales revenue defaults from the inventory item being sold, but the account is not listed on the invoice. *(Note: You will learn about setting default inventory item sales accounts in Chapters 4 and 8.)* Therefore, the next report shows you how to locate all accounts used when posting this invoice.

Click **Reports>>Transaction Journal** on the main menu and the report in Figure 2:18 opens. You can now view all general ledger accounts affected by this transaction.

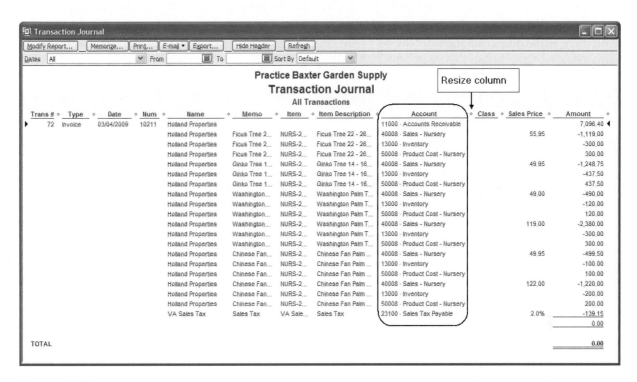

Figure 2:18

Click **X** to close the Transaction Journal report, the Create Invoices window, and the Transactions by Account report.

Click **X** to close the Trial Balance report and QBP prompts to save changes to the date range (Figure 2:19). Click the option illustrated to turn off future messages and click **No**.

Figure 2:19

Click **X** to close the Chart of Accounts.

There is another way to locate the Holland invoice. Assume that you know the customer and invoice number so click **Customer Center** on the Icon Bar, select the **Customers & Jobs** tab, and click **Holland Properties** on the left. On the right, change the **Show** option to "Invoices" and **Date** to "All." (See Figure 2:20.)

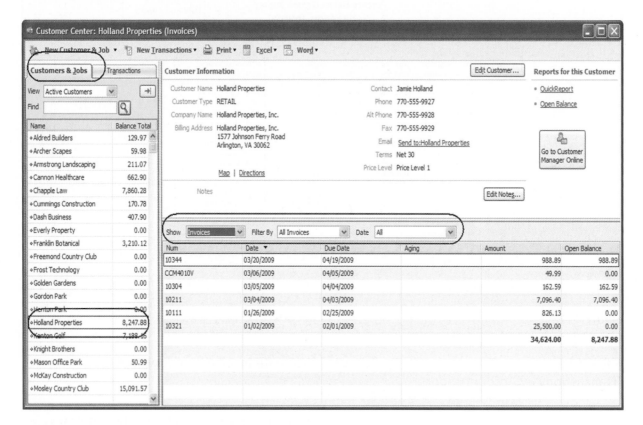

Figure 2:20

Highlight invoice number **10211** and double click. You are returned to the invoice transaction illustrated previously. Click **X** to close the invoice and **X** to close the Customer Center.

It is important to know where to locate a posted transaction. Reports are also useful when you spot a transaction and want more information on it. QBP's centers are also useful when you know the account name or transaction type; however, an account may contain too many transactions to efficiently find a specific transaction.   This is where QBP's Find feature can assist in locating a transaction and is the subject of our next topic.

FINDING TRANSACTIONS IN QUICKBOOKS

In this topic you use QBP's Find feature to locate Invoice 10211 issued to Holland Properties on March 4, 2009. Select **Edit>>Find** on the main menu or use the keyboard shortcut of **Ctrl + F** and select the **Simple** tab to view the window illustrated in Figure 2:21.

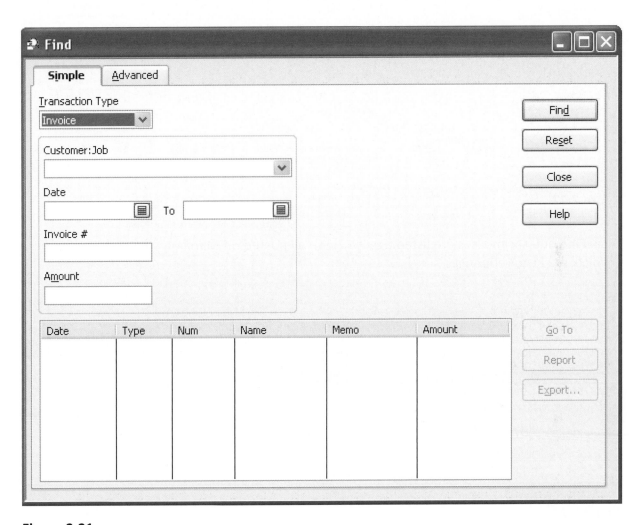

Figure 2:21

The Find window contains two tabs, one for performing a **Simple** search and the other for performing an **Advanced** search. We will use the simple approach first to locate Holland's invoice.

Click the **Transaction Type** dropdown list, select "Invoice," and then enter "3/04/2009" to "3/04/2009" in the **Date** fields. (See Figure 2:22.)

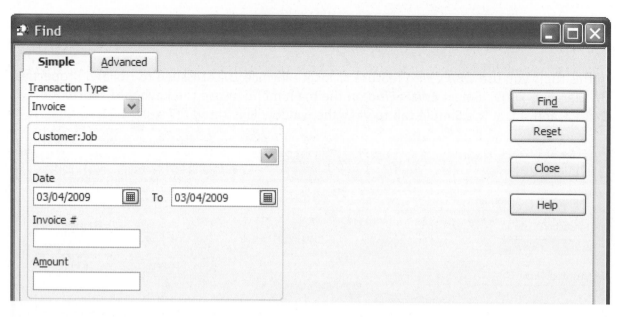

Figure 2:22

Click **Find** and six invoices are listed (Figure 2:23), all posted on March 4. You can double click Invoice 10211 to reopen it.

Date	Type	Num	Name	Memo	Amount	
03/04/2009	INV	10301	Everly Property		4,588.03	
03/04/2009	INV	10302	Freemond Cou...		571.81	
03/04/2009	INV	10303	Snowden Inter...		373.00	
03/04/2009	INV	10323	McKay Constr...		5,100.00	
03/04/2009	INV	10211	Holland Proper...		7,096.40	
03/04/2009	INV	10337	Freemond Cou...		6,997.23	

Go To
Report
Export...

Number of matches: 6

Figure 2:23

Now select the **Advanced** tab so we can illustrate using this method to locate inventory items sold to Holland. Filter choices on this tab appear on the left and current filters appear on the right (Figure 2:24). Click **Transaction Type** under **Choose Filter** and, using the dropdown list, select **Invoice** to add it to the filters listed under **Current Choices**.

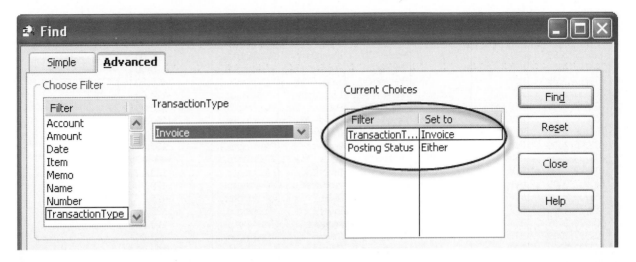

Figure 2:24

Return to the **Choose Filter** column, highlight **Item**, and then select "NURS-23000" using the dropdown list. Current Choices now show that you are filtering for a specific item on an invoice (Figure 2:25).

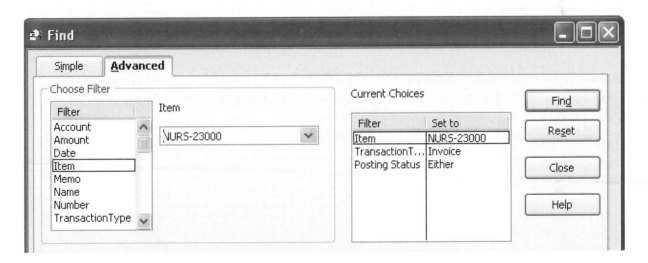

Figure 2:25

Click **Find** and every invoice selling this item appears at the bottom (Figure 2:26).

Date	Type	Num	Name	Account	Memo	Amount
03/17/2009	INV		Mosley Co...	Sales - Nur...	Washingto...	-490.00
03/17/2009	INV		Mosley Co...	Inventory	Washingto...	-120.00
03/17/2009	INV		Mosley Co...	Product Co...	Washingto...	120.00
03/17/2009	INV		Franklin Bo...	Sales - Nur...	Washingto...	-490.00
03/17/2009	INV		Franklin Bo...	Inventory	Washingto...	-120.00
03/17/2009	INV		Franklin Bo...	Product Co...	Washingto...	120.00
03/06/2009	INV		Kenton Golf	Sales - Nur...	Washingto...	-490.00
03/06/2009	INV		Kenton Golf	Inventory	Washingto...	-120.00
03/06/2009	INV		Kenton Golf	Product Co...	Washingto...	120.00
03/04/2009	INV		Holland Pro...	Sales - Nur...	Washingto...	-490.00
03/04/2009	INV		Holland Pro...	Inventory	Washingto...	-120.00
03/04/2009	INV		Holland Pro...	Product Co...	Washingto...	120.00
03/04/2009	INV		Freemond ...	Sales - Nur...	Washingto...	-490.00
03/04/2009	INV		Freemond ...	Inventory	Washingto...	-120.00
03/04/2009	INV		Freemond ...	Product Co...	Washingto...	120.00
02/27/2009	INV		Armstrong ...	Sales - Nur...	Washingto...	-490.00
02/27/2009	INV		Armstrong ...	Inventory	Washingto...	-120.00
02/27/2009	INV		Armstrong ...	Product Co...	Washingto...	120.00
02/27/2009	INV		Saia's Neig...	Sales - Nur...	Washingto...	-490.00
02/27/2009	INV		Saia's Neig...	Inventory	Washingto...	-120.00
02/27/2009	INV		Saia's Neig...	Product Co...	Washingto...	120.00
02/23/2009	INV		Archer Sca...	Sales - Nur...	Washingto...	-490.00
02/23/2009	INV		Archer Sca...	Inventory	Washingto...	-120.00
02/23/2009	INV		Archer Sca...	Product Co...	Washingto...	120.00

Go To   Report   Export...   Number of matches: 24

Figure 2:26

Now add the filter choice of **Name** and in the dropdown list select "Holland Properties." Click **Find** again and the list narrows to the invoices issued to Holland. (Not illustrated.)

You now know how to locate transactions in the Find window. Close the **Find** window.

THE REPORTS MENU AND REPORT CENTER

In this topic you learn to work with reports. Click **Reports** on the main menu to view the menu commands illustrated in Figure 2:27. This ▸ indicator on a menu means submenus are present.

Reports are categorized by activities; therefore, you can generally locate a report by identifying the type of reporting activity. For instance, financial statements are submenus under the Company & Financial menu whereas aged receivables reports are found under the Customers & Receivables menu.

Reports that you customize will be located under the Memorized Reports menu.

Click **Report Center** on the menu and the Report Center illustrated in Figure 2:28 opens. Notice that categories on the left of the center correspond to Reports menus.

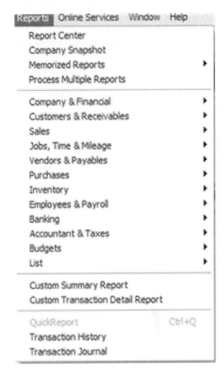

Figure 2:27

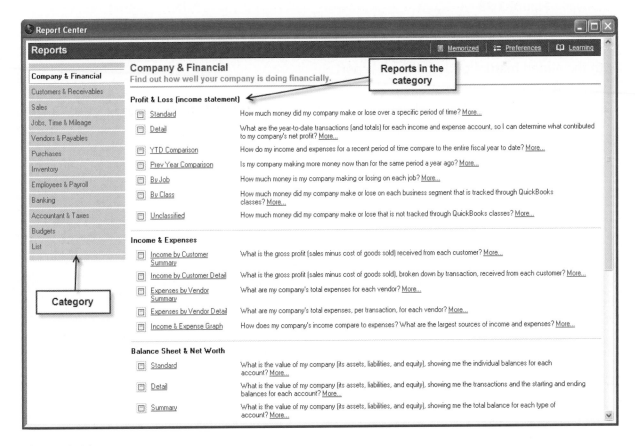

Figure 2:28

Highlight the Company & Financial reporting category on the Report Center and review the list of reports displayed to the right (not illustrated). This list of reports will correspond to submenus under the Company & Financial menu (Figure 2:29).

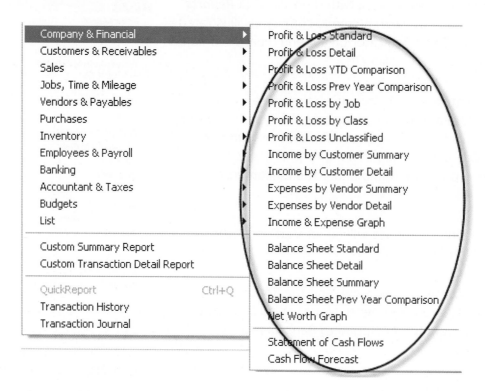

Figure 2:29

This shows you that the Report Center is merely an interactive replica of the Reports menu with the added feature of describing a report.

Click the **Accountant & Taxes** category and focus on the **Account Activity** section (Figure 2:30).

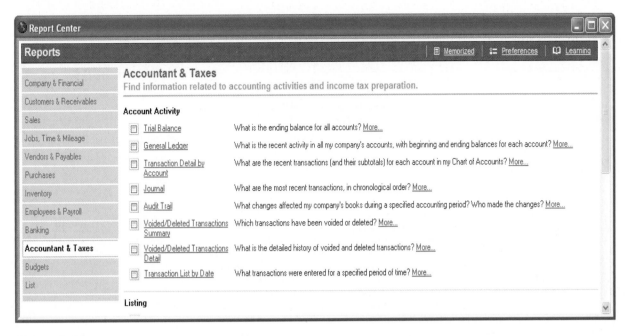

Figure 2:30

The Audit Trail and Voided/Deleted Transactions Summary and Detail reports are control reports that document user activity in the software. In subsequent chapters you will trace the audit trail on posted transactions and print reports that document this trail. We want to clarify that the Audit Trail report above does not document posted transactions. Instead, this report documents the users posting transactions.

Click **General Ledger** to open the report that documents the audit trail of a posted transaction. Enter the date range of **From 3/01/2009** and **To 3/31/2009** and refresh the report (Figure 2:31).

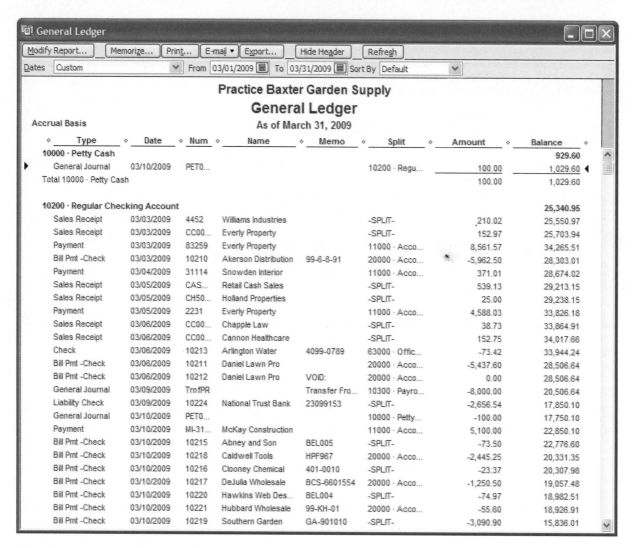

Figure 2:31

This report lists March transactions posted to all general ledger accounts. Whenever you see "-SPLIT-" in the Split column then the transaction posted to multiple accounts. For instance, the payment to Everly Property on 3/3/2009 affected accounts 10200 Regular Checking Account (i.e., the account you are looking at) and 11000 Accounts Receivable (i.e., the account listed in the Split column) whereas the Sales Receipt on 3/3/2009 to Everly Property affected account 10200 Regular Checking Account and more than one other account.

The following exercise steps through customizing this report and these steps will work for customizing any QBP report.

STEPS TO CUSTOMIZING THE GENERAL LEDGER REPORT

1. Click **Modify Report** to open the window in Figure 2:32.

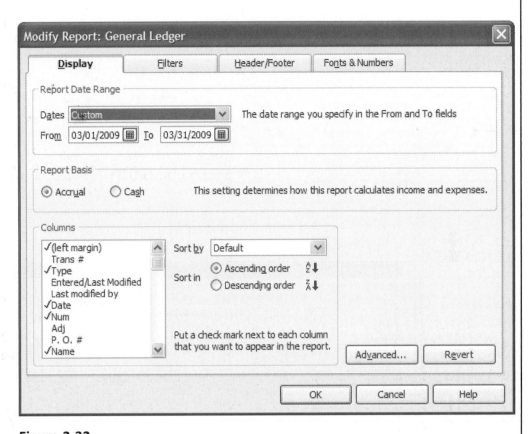

Figure 2:32

The Display tab sets the reporting period, data columns, and sort order for the report. There is an option for changing the Report Basis to Cash for companies that do not use the accrual method of accounting.

2. Scroll down the **Columns** section and locate the **Debit**, **Credit**, and **Amount** columns. Click Debit and Credit to activate these columns and click Amount to turn off the column (Figure 2:33).

Figure 2:33

3. Click **OK** and the report refreshes to display the column changes. Remember that you can resize columns by dragging the column separator.

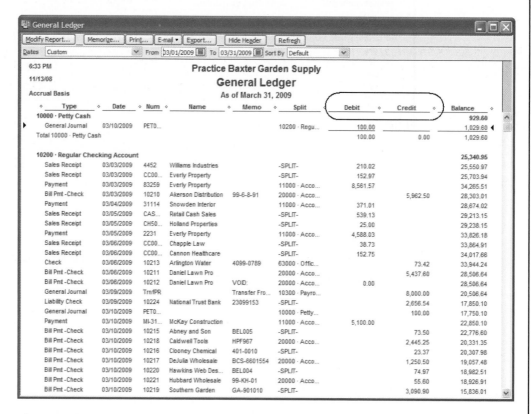

Figure 2:34

4. Now filter the report to display selected accounts. Click **Modify Report** again and then select the **Filters tab**.

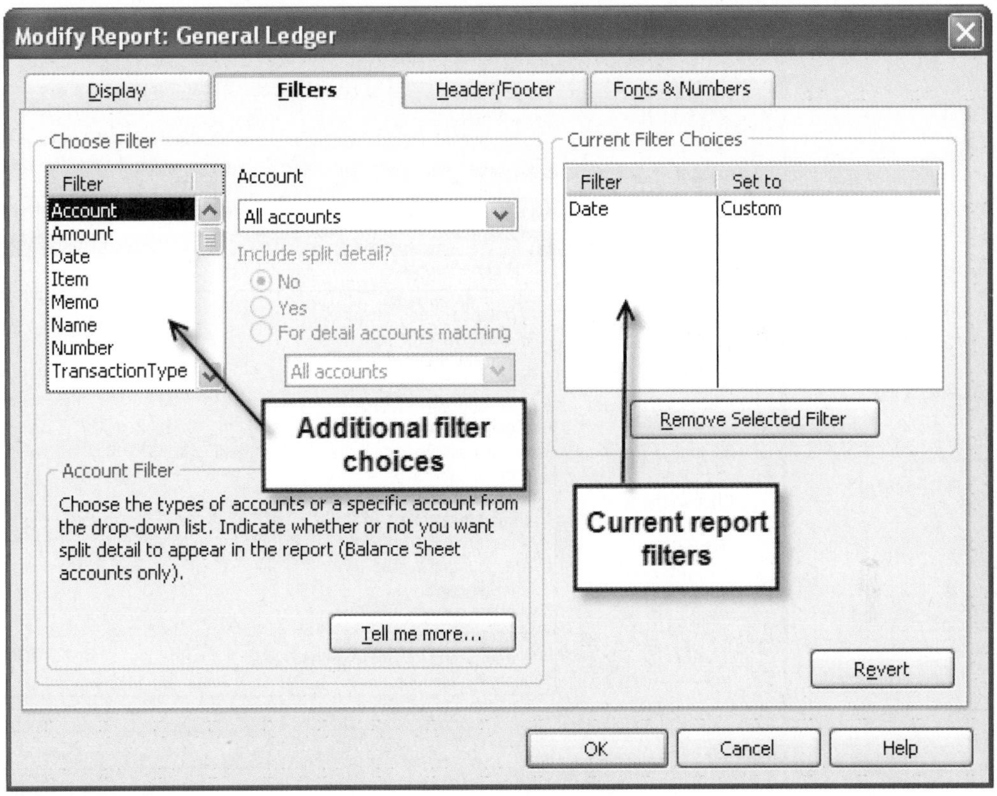

Figure 2:35

5. Highlight **Account** under **Choose Filter** and the filter box to the right will display "All accounts." Click the dropdown list to view filtering options (Figure 2:36).

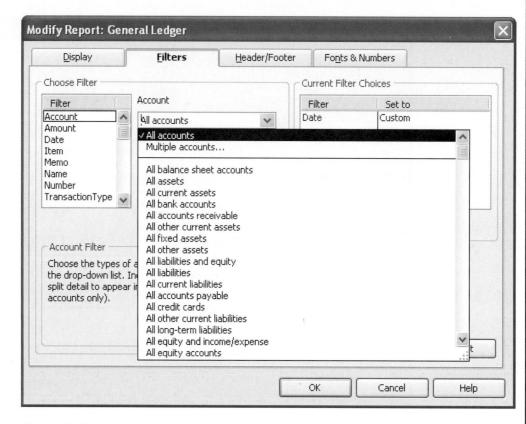

Figure 2:36

6. You are going to filter the general ledger report so that general ledger accounts 40001 to 40002 are the only accounts to display.

In the filter box select **Multiple Accounts** and the window in Figure 2:37 opens.

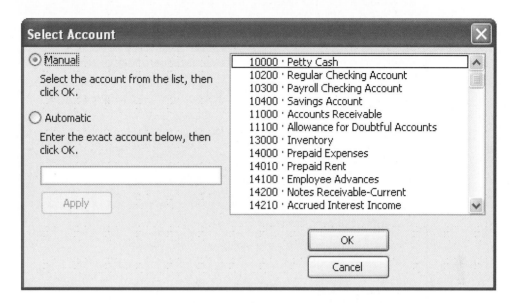

Figure 2:37

Scroll down and click **40001 Sales – Aviary** and **40002 Sales – Books** (Figure 2:38). Click **OK** after making these selections.

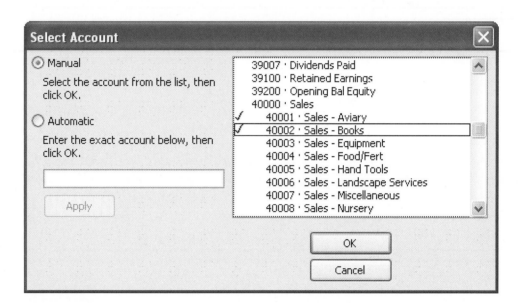

Figure 2:38

Current Filter Choices now displays Account as an additional filter. Click **OK**.

7. Although the report still lists all accounts, the accounts do not display transactions. Scroll down to find that only the two filtered accounts display transactions (Figure 2:39).

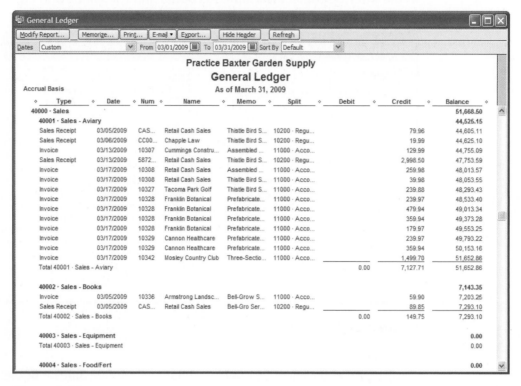

Figure 2:39

8. Click **Modify Report** again and select the **Header/Footer** tab. Header options print at the top of report pages, whereas footer options print at the bottom. The Alignment option is used to left justify, right justify, or center report information on the page.

Change the **Report Title** to "Customized General Ledger".

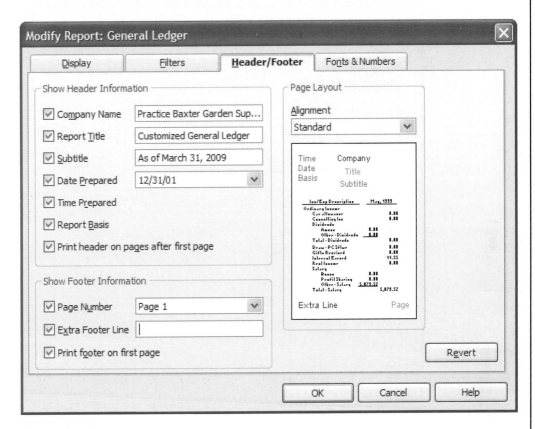

Figure 2:40

9. Click the **Fonts & Numbers** tab. These options change report fonts for data fields listed to the left. You can also change the appearance of negative numbers (i.e., options of Normally, In Parentheses, or With a Trailing Minus and In Bright Red).

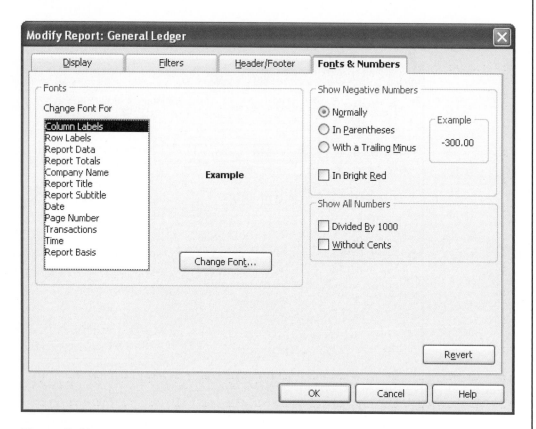

Figure 2:41

10. Click the **Filters** tab and highlight **Account** under Current Filter Choices. Click **Remove Selected Filter**.

11. Click **OK** and the report redisplays, listing transactions for all accounts. Click **Print** and the Print window opens to choose a printer. Click **Print** again and the report is sent to the printer.

12. You will now save the customized report. Click **Memorize** and, in the window that opens (Figure 2:42), enter the report name of Customized General Ledger and mark the option to save the report in the memorized report group named Accountant. Click **OK** and close the report.

Figure 2:42

13. Click *Reports>>Memorized Reports>>Accountant>>Customized General Ledger* on the main menu and your customized report reopens. Thus, the Memorize Report window in the previous step created a new submenu item beneath the Accountant menu.

14. Now place this report on the Icon Bar so you can easily access it in the future. Click *View>>Add "Customized General Ledger" to Icon Bar* on the main menu.

    Change the **Label** to "Custom G/L" and click **OK**. Close the report and the Report Center.

EXPORTING AND EMAILING REPORTS

Your professor may want you to export reports to Excel and then email the workbook. Click **P&L** on the Icon Bar to reopen Baxter's Income Statement. *(Note: This icon was added in Chapter 1. If you did not add it then select **Reports>>Memorized Reports>>Accountant>>Profit & Loss** on the main menu.)*

Click **Export** to open the window illustrated Figure 2:43.

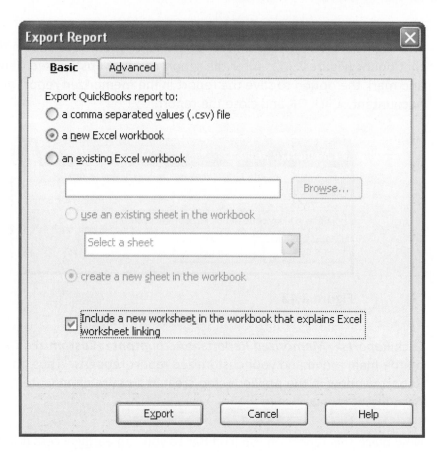

Figure 2:43

The **Basic** tab selects the type of export file to create. When you do not have Microsoft Excel software on your machine, you must export the report to **a comma separated values (.csv) file**. This file type can then be imported into Excel.

This topic focuses on using the Excel export features. The export options related to Excel are exporting **a new Excel workbook** or to **an existing Excel workbook**. *(Note: To export to an existing workbook the workbook must already be open in Excel.)*

Select the options illustrated in Figure 2:43 and click **Export**. A new Excel workbook is created, containing two worksheets (Figure 2:44). *(Note: The workbook is illustrated in Excel 2007. Your workbook will look different if you are using an earlier version of Excel. We will provide Excel commands for 2007 and earlier versions.)*

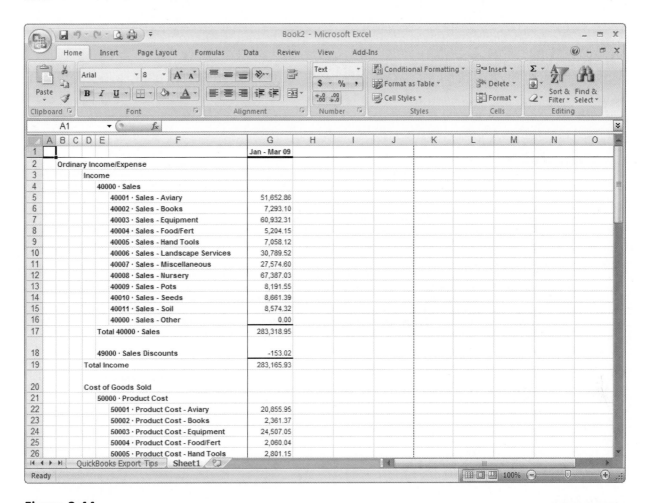

Figure 2:44

The worksheet named Sheet1 contains the exported data. Click to select this worksheet and scroll to the bottom. *(Hint: Use **CTRL + End** to jump to the end of the report.)*

Click the worksheet named **QuickBooks Export Tips** (Figure 2:45).

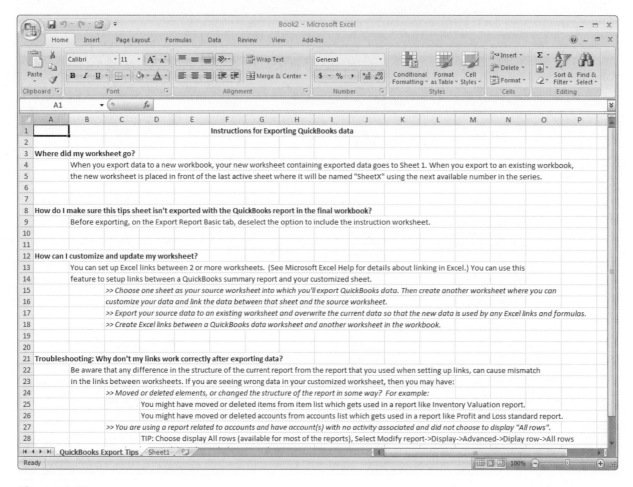

Figure 2:45

You can turn off exporting these instructions by turning off this option on the Basic tab of the export window.

☑ Include a new worksheet in the workbook that explains Excel worksheet linking

Click **X** to close the Excel workbook and click **No** to exit without saving.

Click **Export** again on the P/L report and this time select the **Advanced** tab.

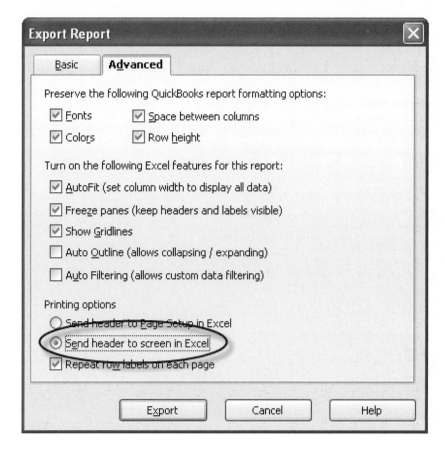

Figure 2:46

This tab contains export options for three areas:

Formatting options: Export the report preserving the fonts, colors, column spaces, and row heights set by QuickBooks.

Excel features: Activate the listed Excel features such as AutoFit and freeze panes.

Printing options: Place column headers in Excel's Page Setup or send headers to the first row of the Excel spreadsheet.

Set the **Advanced** options shown in Figure 2:46 and click the **Basic** tab and turn off exporting the instruction sheet. Click **Export**.

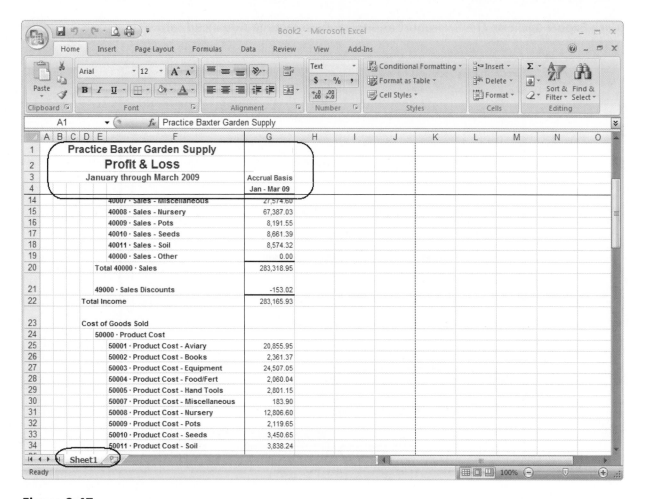

Figure 2:47

This time the workbook contains one worksheet with company information appearing in the top rows of the worksheet.

Save the new Excel workbook. Click this Office Icon 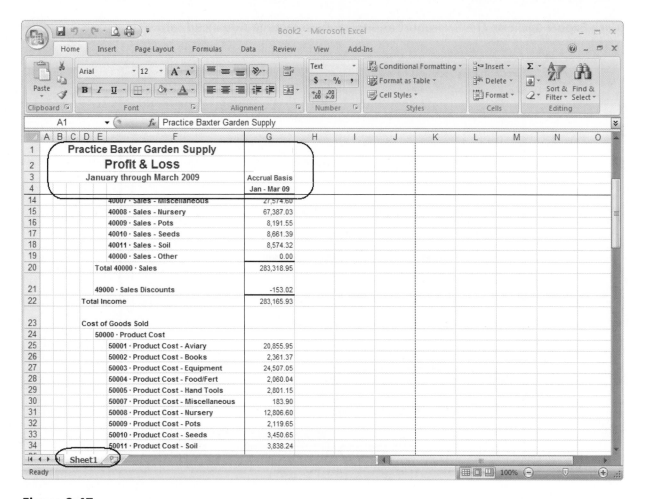 and select **Save As>>Excel Workbook** (Figure 2:48). (*Note: You can save it as an Excel 97-2003 Workbook when needed. For earlier version of Excel select File>>Save As on the main menu.*)

Figure 2:48

Using the Save in dropdown list, select **My Documents** as the folder and type "Baxter Income Statement" as the file name (Figure 2:49). *(Note: These instructions remain the same for earlier versions of Excel.)* Click **Save**.

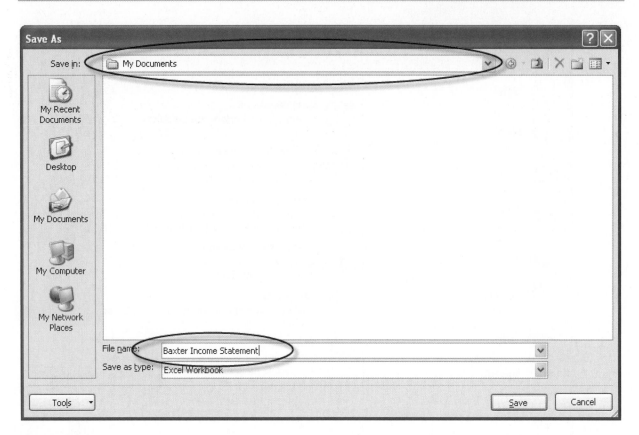

Figure 2:49

Now practice emailing the workbook. First, connect to the Internet and open your email software.

In Excel, click [icon] **>> Send>>E-mail** as shown in Figure 2:50. *(Note: For earlier versions of Excel click File>>Send To and select Mail Recipient (as Attachment).)*

Figure 2:50

When the email message opens (Figure 2:51), enter your email address and click **Send**. Check your email later to verify delivery.

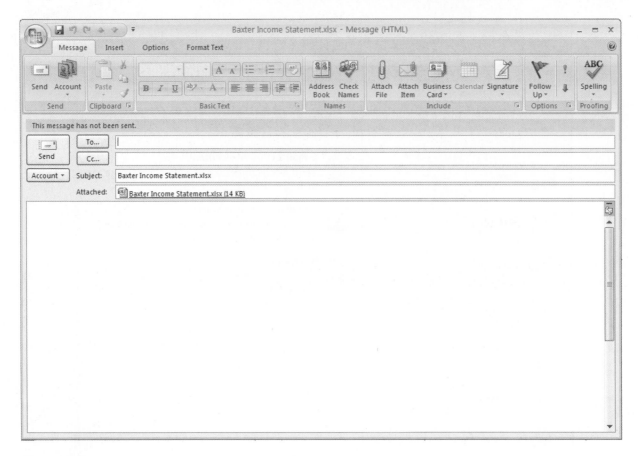

Figure 2:51

Close Excel and return to the P&L report in QBP.

Your professor may also want you to email reports in PDF format. Click **Email** and select **Send report as PDF**. *(Note: Notice that you could have emailed the Excel workbook without exporting it first.)*

When the following Email Security message opens, mark the option of "Do not display this message in the future" and click **OK**.

Figure 2:52

The email message now opens (Figure 2:53) with an attached PDF version of the report. Enter your email address and click **Send**. Check your email later to verify delivery. *Note: QuickBooks now utilizes Outlook for its e-mail service. If you receive a message informing you of this, click Close.*

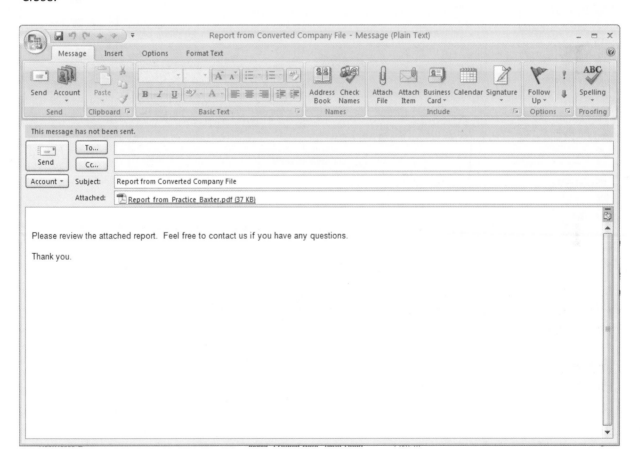

Figure 2:53

Close the report.

ACCOUNTING PERIODS

One final topic and you have covered QBP basics. Although the software will let you override this statement, you should only post transactions to the current accounting period. To locate Baxter's current period, click *Company>>Set Closing Date* on the main menu and open the Company Preferences tab illustrated in Figure 2:54.

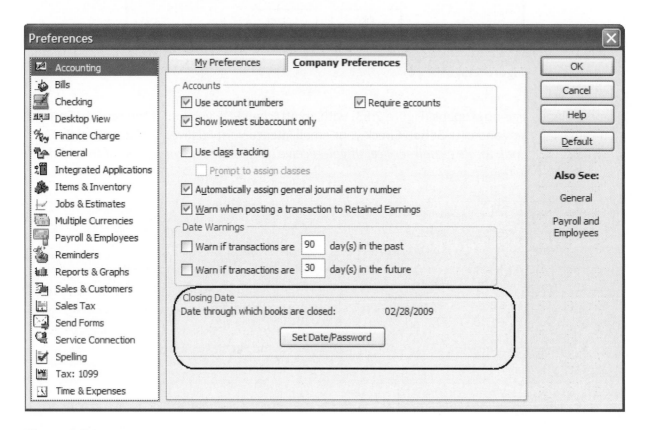

Figure 2:54

Baxter's books are closed as of 2/28/2009, meaning that the open accounting period is March 2009.

Click **Set Date/Password**. An accounting period is closed by entering a different date in the **Closing Date** field. (See Figure 2:55.)

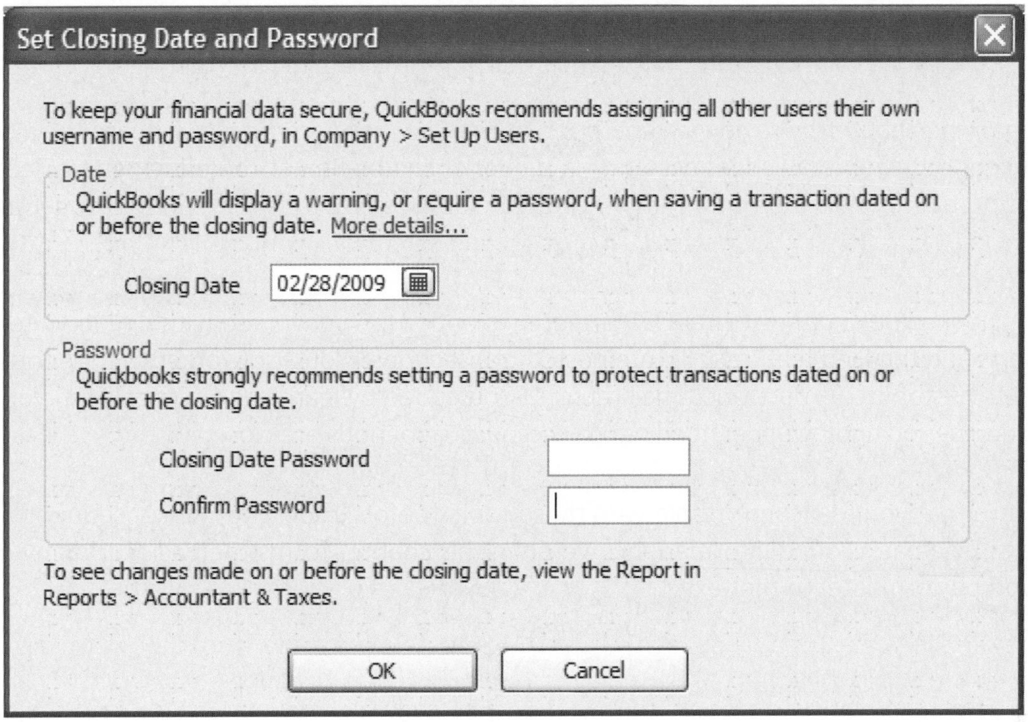

Set Closing Date and Password

To keep your financial data secure, QuickBooks recommends assigning all other users their own username and password, in Company > Set Up Users.

Date
QuickBooks will display a warning, or require a password, when saving a transaction dated on or before the closing date. More details...

Closing Date   02/28/2009

Password
Quickbooks strongly recommends setting a password to protect transactions dated on or before the closing date.

Closing Date Password

Confirm Password

To see changes made on or before the closing date, view the Report in Reports > Accountant & Taxes.

OK   Cancel

Figure 2:55

In the real world, you would also set a closing date password to prevent users from posting to a closed period without first entering an authorization password. Because this window does not contain a password, QBP will merely warn when attempting to post an entry to a closed period. You can permit the posting to occur by clicking Yes on the warning window. Click **Cancel** to exit this window.

You should always close an accounting period after finalizing transactions and issuing financial reports. Closing the period protects the integrity of reported data by preventing erroneous postings to a reported period.

One last thought. Although you can prevent posting to prior months (closed periods), you cannot prevent posting to future months. Therefore, be very careful to enter correct dates on transactions.

You have now completed this chapter so *make a backup of Practice Baxter Garden Supply to a file named "Practice Baxter Garden Supply Chpt 2". In Chapter 8, you will build on the work completed in this chapter.*

SUMMARY

You began the chapter by reviewing and printing the Chart of Accounts. You were then introduced to the general ledger account framework used by Baxter to define general ledger account numbers. With this information, you were able to create a new general ledger account.

You then looked *Behind the Keys* at QBP preference options. You worked with drilldown features on reports and the Find feature to locate posted transactions. You also worked with reports and learned to customize, export, and email reports. You ended by learning to recognize the open accounting period and by understanding why accounting periods are closed.

Make sure that you feel comfortable with these topics before moving on to subsequent chapters. The background information covered in this chapter forms the basis for many of the tasks you perform later in the text.

END-OF-CHAPTER QUESTIONS

TRUE/FALSE

_____ 1. For Baxter, liability accounts begin with "3."

_____ 2. The account type "Other Current Liability" would be assigned to an accounts payable account.

_____ 3. QBP will not let you post a transaction to a closed month.

_____ 4. QBP preference options control whether or not a decimal point will be required when entering a financial amount.

_____ 5. Exporting QBP reports to Excel requires owning the Excel software.

_____ 6. You can customize reports shown on the Report Center.

_____ 7. You can add new general ledger accounts using a button located at the top of the COA list.

_____ 8. For Baxter, the second digit on a general ledger account number identifies whether the account is an asset, liability, equity, revenue, or expense account.

_____ 9. The general ledger and trial balance reports contain the same information.

MULTIPLE CHOICE

_____ 1. For Baxter Garden, _____ is an account number used for sales revenue.
   a. 10200
   b. 11000
   c. 40000
   d. 49000

_____ 2. The income statement can be printed using the _____.
   a. Reports menu
   b. Report Center
   c. Lists menu
   d. Both a and b

_____ 3. Referring to Baxter Garden's COA, which account number would be appropriate for
an account named Consulting Expense?
   a. 85600
   b. 62610
   c. 50100
   d. 40100

_____ 4. Baxter uses which account to record accounts payable liabilities?
   a. 11000
   b. 20000
   c. 50000
   d. 27000

_____ 5. Report filters are set by using the _____ button.
   a. Print
   b. Memorize
   c. Modify Report
   d. None of the above

CHAPTER 3 GENERAL JOURNAL TRANSACTIONS AND REPORTS

LEARNING OBJECTIVES

This chapter introduces QBP general journal entries and works with the **Practice TEK Business** data file customized with your initials at the end of Chapter 1. *If this company is not loaded on your computer, then restore the Practice TEK Business Chpt1.QBB backup file created in the Practice Set at the end of Chapter 1.*

In this chapter you will:

1. Learn manual accounting procedures (MAPS) for recording general journal entries before posting entries in QBP
2. Post basic general journal entries
3. Look *Behind the Keys* at posted transactions by reviewing the Journal and General Ledger reports
4. Learn to correct posted journal entries
5. Post compound journal entries and adjusting entries
6. Print the trial balance and financial statements
7. Close an accounting period
8. Review QBP data integration

Launch QBP and open **Practice TEK Business**.

 ## MANUAL ACCOUNTING PROCEDURES

TEK is a startup company that began business on January 1, 2009. It provides technology consulting services and, on January 2, 2009, made its first cash sale for services rendered.

Before attempting to record this transaction, refresh your memory on using the T-Account method for balancing accounting entries. This method applied to TEK's cash sale is illustrated next.

Regular Checking Account			**Consulting Income**	
Dr.	Cr.		Dr.	Cr.
$1,000				$1,000

Accountants with years of experience still rely on this method to visualize entries before recording a complicated transaction. You should also rely on this method when encountering new and complicated exercises in the text.

You will now become acquainted with the manual accounting procedures (*MAPS*) used to record a cash sale through general journal entries. With *MAPS*, the accountant would record the journal entry on the general journal illustrated in Figure 3:1.

Audit Trail

TEK Business
General Journal   Page 2

Date	Account Post Ref	Description	Debit	Credit
01/02/09	10100	Regular Checking Account	1,000.00	
	40000	Consulting Income		1,000.00
To record cash sale				

Figure 3:1

The entry lists the transaction date, general ledger account numbers and descriptions, and the debit and credit amount. The entry balances and account numbers form part of the audit trail documenting the transaction. Finally, the transaction was recorded on the second page of the general journal and this page number becomes part of the audit trail in the next illustration.

After recording this entry in the general journal, the accountant next posts it to the general ledger accounts listed on the entry. These postings are illustrated in Figure 3:2.

General Ledger					
Regular Checking Account				**Account No. 10100**	
Date	Description	Post Ref	Debit	Credit	Balance
01/01/09	Beginning Balance				-
01/02/09		GJ 2		1,000.00	1,000.00

Audit Trail

General Ledger					
Consulting Income				**Account No. 40000**	
Date	Description	Post Ref	Debit	Credit	Balance
01/01/09	Beginning Balance				-
01/02/09		GJ 2	1,000.00		1,000.00

Figure 3:2

While posting entries to the general ledger, an audit trail is entered to cross-reference originating entries in the general journal. GJ 2 means that the entry originated on General Journal page 2. The audit trail becomes the path for tracing entries between the general journal and the general ledger.

BASIC JOURNAL ENTRIES

In this topic you post TEK's cash sale journal entry in QBP. Begin by clicking the **Home** icon to open the Home page. The zero account balances on the right reveal that the data file currently contains no financial transactions (Figure 3:3).

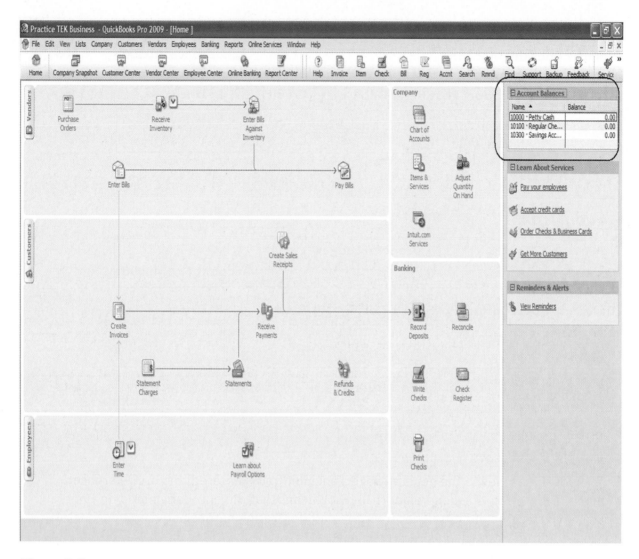

Figure 3:3

Before beginning the next exercise that posts the journal entry illustrated in the *MAPS* topic, read the following data entry tips.

	DATA ENTRY TIPS
Edit	Main menu commands for inserting or deleting transaction lines.
◀ Previous	Move to a previously posted transaction. Saves a transaction when clicked after entering a new transaction.
▶ Next	Move to the next transaction. Saves a transaction when clicked after entering a new transaction
🖨 ▾	Print the transaction in the window.
History	Open reports that view the history of transactions related to the current transaction. This button does not work on journal entries because other transactions are not linked to a journal entry.
Save & Close	Save the current transaction and exit the transaction window.
Save & New	Save the current transaction and remain in the transaction window to enter another transaction.
Clear	Appears only on the window of a new transaction and clears all data entered on the transaction.
Revert	Appears only on the window of a posted transaction and clears changes made to the transaction.

Steps to Recording A Journal Entry.

1. Click *Company>>Make General Journal Entries* on the main menu. If the window in Figure 3:4 opens then mark the option that turns off future messages and click **OK**.

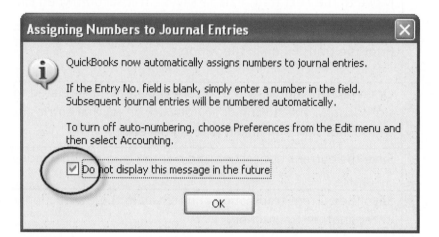

Figure 3:4

2.   Change the transaction **Date** to 1/2/2009 as shown in Figure 3:5.

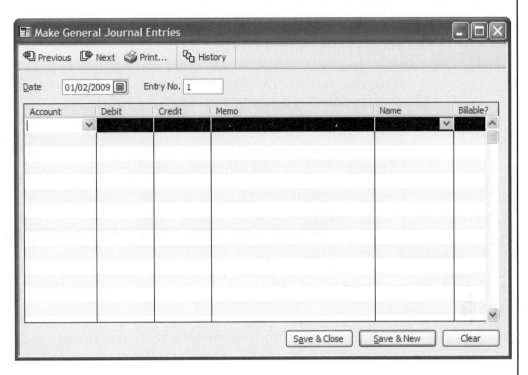

Figure 3:5

3.   Press **Tab** and the cursor stops at **Entry No**. The message in Figure 3:4 explained that QBP will automatically assign entry numbers and sequentially increments the number.

4. Press **Tab** and the cursor moves to the first line of the entry, stopping at **Account**.

    This is where you enter the general ledger account number of "10100 Regular Checking Account".

    Place your cursor on the field separator until it looks like a plus sign and drag to widen the Account field (Figure 3:6).

Figure 3:6

    There are two methods for entering account numbers. You will use the first method here and the second in a step that follows.

    With your cursor in the field, type "r" and QBP stops at the first account beginning with this letter (Figure 3:7), which happens to be the account you want.

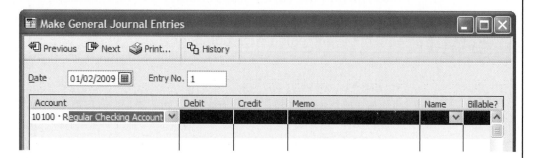

Figure 3:7

5. Tab to **Debit** and type in "1000.00" because this is the cash amount of the sale.

    *Note: Recall in Chapter 2 that you turned on the Preference option for QBP to automatically enter the decimal point. Therefore, you could also type "100000" to enter this amount. You must turn this option on in each company file. To verify that the option is active, select **Edit>>Preferences** on the main menu, select the **General** category and the **My Preferences** tab. The **Automatically place decimal point** option should be selected. Click OK to close.*

6. Tab to **Memo** and enter the short description of "Cash sale." The Memo field is optional and used when you want to describe the transaction.

7. Now widen the General Journal window size. Place your cursor to the edge of the window until a double arrow appears and then drag to resize (Figure 3:8). You have now increased the size of all columns.

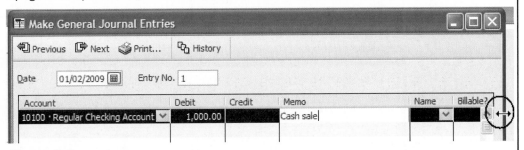

Figure 3:8

The **Name** field is used when a transaction affects a customer, vendor, or inventory account. Rarely should you use general journal entries to post these types of transactions; instead, you will learn to record these transactions using the accounting activities discussed in subsequent chapters.

The **Billable** field is used when the transaction amount will be billed to a customer. You will learn to record billable transactions in Chapters 4, 5, and 6.

8. **Tab** to the second row to enter the second **Account**. You will be selecting "40000 Consulting Income" by using the second method for selecting account numbers.

Type "4" and QBP opens the account lookup list, stopping at the first account beginning with this number (Figure 3:9). Since the correct account is already selected, press **Tab**. (*Note: You can select a different account by using your mouse or by pressing the down arrow on your keyboard to advance the account list.*)

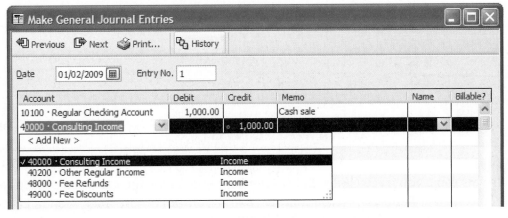

Figure 3:9

9. QBP has entered 1,000.00 in the **Credit** field because this is the amount needed to balance the entry. You can override the entry when needed and will do so in a different exercise. This is the correct credit amount so **Tab** to **Memo** and type "Cash sale".

10. The completed journal entry appears in Figure 3:10 and the entry balances. Unlike a manual system, QBP will not let you post an out-of-balance entry.

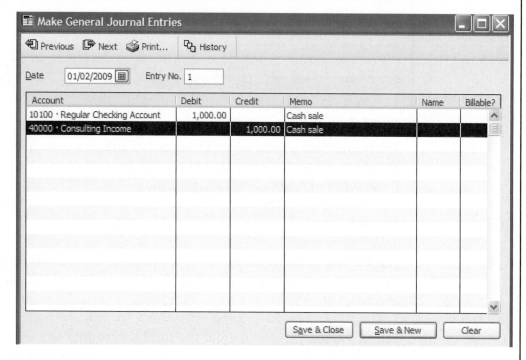

Figure 3:10

11. Click **Save and Close** at the bottom of the window and the entry posts.

On the Home page, review the Account Balances and notice that the balance for account 10100 Regular Checking has been updated to $1,000.00.

BEHIND THE KEYS OF A POSTED JOURNAL ENTRY

In this topic you trace QBP's *Behind the Keys* entries for the cash sale posted in the previous topic. Select **Reports>>Accountant & Taxes>>Journal** on the main menu. Enter the date range of **From 1/2/2009** and **To 1/2/2009** and refresh the report. (See Figure 3:11.)

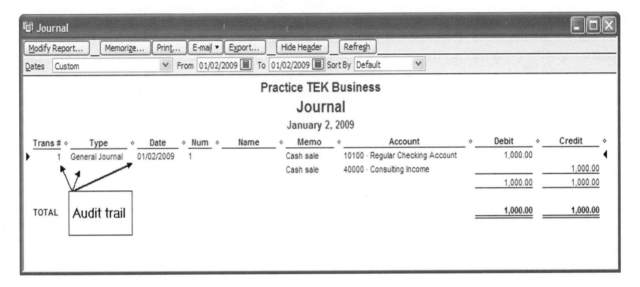

Figure 3:11

This is QBP's version of the *MAPS* General Journal.   The audit trail appears in the Trans #, Type, and Num columns.

Double click the entry to open the Regular Checking Account register (Figure 3:12). Registers are available for all balance sheet accounts except the Retained Earnings account.

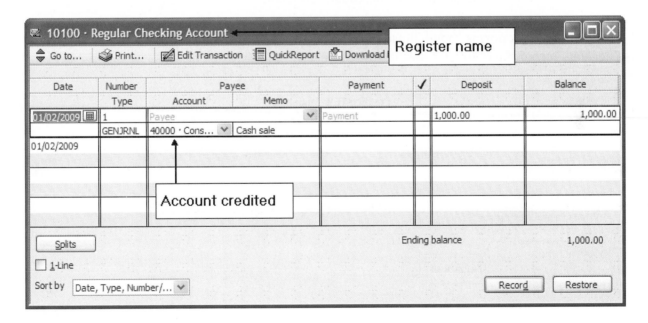

Figure 3:12

Figure 3:12 looks similar to your checkbook register. Notice that the sales amount appears as a deposit, meaning that the checking account was increased (debited) $1,000.00. The credit posted to 40000 Consulting Income and QBP entered GENJRNL and "1" as the audit trail code.

Although you can record entries using the register, this method can be confusing and will not be used in the text. Click **X** to close the register and **X** to close the Journal report.

You will now look for the postings on the general ledger. Select **_Reports>>Accountant & Taxes>>General Ledger_** on the main menu. In Chapter 2 you customized this report for Practice Baxter Garden Supply and added it to the Icon Bar.

Follow the next steps to customize TEK's General Ledger report and add it to the icon bar because you will use this report often.

        ○ Enter the date range of **1/1/2009** to **1/31/2009**.
        ○ Click **Modify Report.** Add the **Debit** and **Credit** columns and remove the **Amount** column. Click **OK**.
        ○ Resize the **Split** column so that the entire account number and name will display.
        ○ Click **Memorize** and name the report "Custom General Ledger" and save in the **Accountant** memorized report group.
        ○ Click **_View>>Add "Custom General Ledger" to Icon Bar_** on the main menu and enter "Custom G/L" as the **Label**. Click **OK**.

The customized report is shown in Figure 3:13, displaying entries recorded to 10100 Regular Checking Account and 40000 Consulting Income.

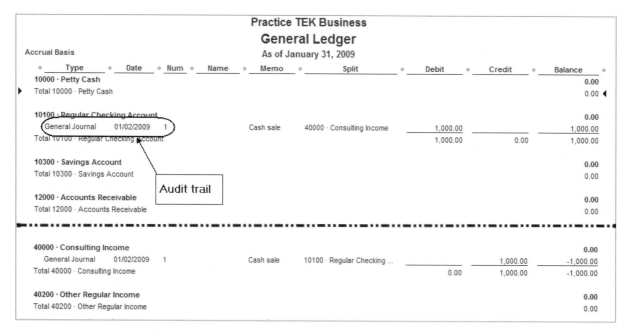

Figure 3:13

The audit trail code of **General Journal** is displayed in the Type column and the journal entry number in the **Num** column. You can also see where the **Memo** description appears.

Close this report and move to the next topic that explains correcting a posted journal entry.

CORRECTING A POSTED JOURNAL ENTRY

It is easy to correct a posted journal entry in QBP. First, locate the posted journal entry. Type **Ctrl + F** to open the Find window and change the **Transaction Type** to "Journal." Next, type "1" in **Entry. No.**, and click **Find**.

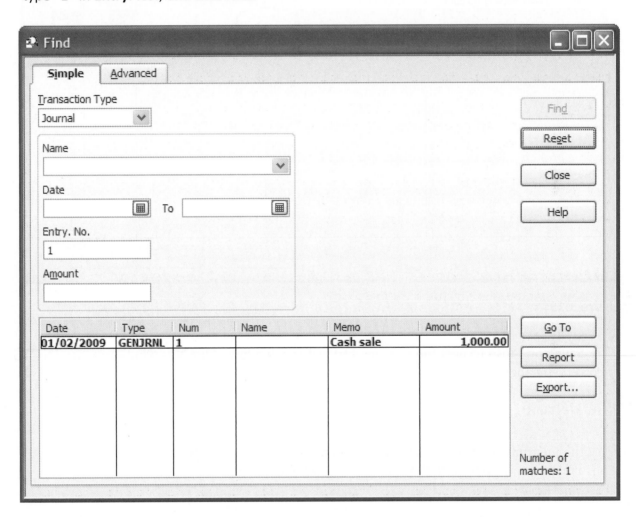

Figure 3:14

Double click the transaction displayed at the bottom to reopen the entry.

Now change the transaction. Place your cursor in the memo field for "4000 Consulting Income" and change the description to "Cash fees" (Figure 3:15).

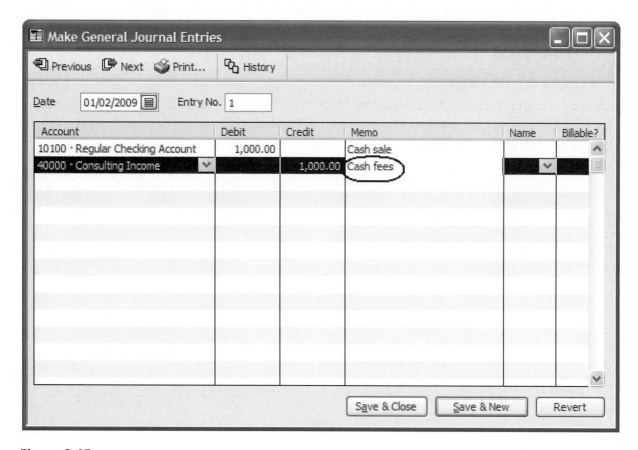

Figure 3:15

Click **Save and Close** to post the changes and exit the window. Click **Yes** when prompted to record the changes.

Close the **Find** window.

Click the **Custom G/L** icon button and reopen the report. Scroll down to account "40000 Consulting Income" and note the change in the Memo column.

Close the report and complete the next exercise.

You Try

RECORD TEK'S JANUARY TRANSACTIONS

Record the following January entries using the general journal. Enter a memo description on each transaction. For checks, include the check number in the description. All entries will affect the Regular Checking Account.

2009
<u>Jan.</u>

2	Owner deposit of cash to regular checking, $5,000.
5	Check No. 171 for office supplies expense, $250.
7	Check No. 172 for two months rent, $500. (Hint: use prepaid expense account.)
9	Cash received for fees earned, $1,375.
15	Check No. 173 for owner cash withdrawal from checking, $700.
20	Cash received for fees earned, $625.
23	Check No. 174 for telephone bill, $195.
26	Check No. 175 for January salaries, $975.

Print the January Journal report.

COMPOUND JOURNAL ENTRIES

Thus far you have recorded simple journal entries using two accounts. Often accountants record compound journal entries affecting multiple accounts.

On January 30, 2009, TEK's owner made another investment in the company. She invested $7,000 in cash, a car valued at $10,000, and computer equipment valued at $12,000. Follow the next steps to record the transaction.

STEPS TO RECORD A COMPOUND JOURNAL ENTRY

1. Open a new journal entry.

2. Enter the date of "1/30/2009".

3. Tab to **Account** on the first line and select "10100 Regular Checking Account". Tab to **Debit** and enter "7000.00". Tab to **Memo** and enter "Owner cash contribution".

4. Tab to **Account** on the second line and select "15200 Vehicle". Tab to **Debit** and enter "10000.00". Tab to **Memo** and enter "Owner car contribution". *(Note: You will override QBP's entry in the Credit field.)*

5. Tab to **Account** on the third line and select "15000 Office Equipment". Tab to **Debit** and enter "12000.00". Tab to **Memo** and enter "Owner computer contribution".

6. Tab to **Account** on the fourth line and select "39006 Owner's Contribution". QBP has entered "29,000.00" to the Credit field. *(Note: If you do not have this amount as a credit then check your previous entries.)*

7. Tab to **Memo** and enter "Owner contribution cash, car, computer". The completed entry appears in Figure 3:16.

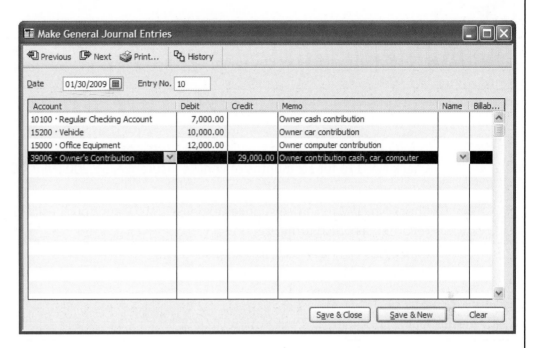

Figure 3:16

8. Click **Save and New**. *(Note: If you receive a message about fixed asset features, mark the option to turn off this message in the future and click OK.)*

Now complete the next exercise.

RECORD ADDITIONAL JOURNAL ENTRIES

Record the following journal entries and remember to enter a description for each transaction.

2009
<u>Jan.</u>

27	Check No. 176 for six months of vehicle insurance, $1,200 *(Hint: Use prepaid expense account.)*
28	Check No. 177 for office supplies expense, $210, and four desks, $3,250 recorded as office furniture.
29	Check No. 178 for electricity expense, $375.
30	Cash received for fees earned, $2,376.

Print the Journal report for 1/27/2009 to 1/30/2009.

ADJUSTING JOURNAL ENTRIES

Adjusting entries are journal entries that adjust account balances and record such transactions as expensing prepaid rent or recording depreciation expense.

After reviewing TEK's General Ledger report for January, the accountant asks you to post the following adjusting entries.

RECORD JANUARY ADJUSTING ENTRIES

Open the Journal Entry window and record the following adjusting entries for January 31, 2009.

a. Expense one month of the prepaid rent, $250.

b. Post January depreciation expense of $235.00 posted as follows.

>   Office equipment, $120;
>
>   Office furniture, $30;
>
>   Vehicles, $85.

Print the Journal report for January 31, 2009.

PRINT THE TRIAL BALANCE

The Trial Balance report differs from the General Ledger report because it lists accounts and balances without transaction detail. In addition, the report totals columns by debits and credits to make sure that general ledger accounts "balance." In a manual system, proving that the trial balance "balanced" was critical because it formed the basis for preparing financial statements.

In a computerized system, entries automatically balance. You have already seen that QBP will not post an out-of-balance entry. Therefore, accountants now use the trial balance to review account balances and to reconcile balances to external documents such as bank statements and asset reports.

Complete the following steps to print TEK's January Trial Balance report.

STEPS TO PRINT THE TRIAL BALANCE

1. Select **Reports>>Accountant & Taxes>>Trial Balance** from the main menu. Enter the dates of From: 1/31/2009 and To 1/31/2009. The refreshed report is shown in Figure 3:17.

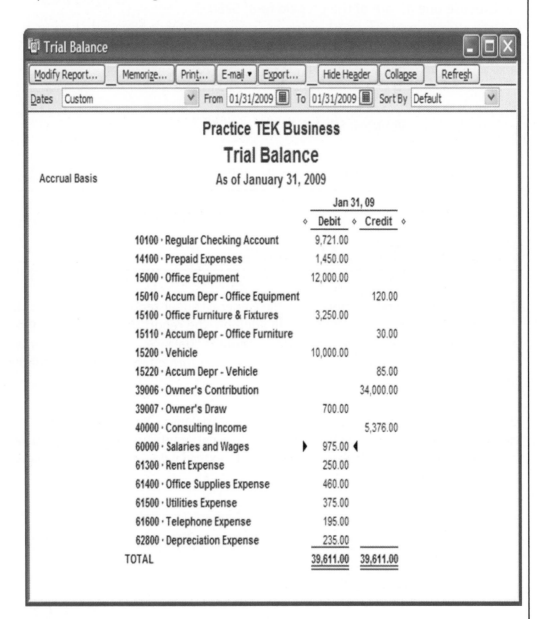

Figure 3:17

> 2. Click **Print**, choose a printer, and then click **Print** again to send the report to the printer. Click **X** to close the report and, when prompted, select the option to turn off future reminders on saving modified reports. Click **OK**.

PRINT FINANCIAL STATEMENTS

Financial statements include the Income Statement (sometimes called the Profit and Loss Statement) and Balance Sheet as well as the Statement of Retained Earnings and Cash Flow Statement. In a manual system, the Income Statement is prepared first because net income or loss from this statement is needed to create the Statement of Retained Earnings and Balance Sheet.

With a computerized system, financial statements may be printed in any order because the computer internally calculates net income or loss. Perform the next steps and print TEK's January Income Statement and Balance Sheet.

STEPS TO PRINT FINANCIAL STATEMENTS

1. Select **Reports>>Company & Financial>>Profit & Loss Standard** on the main menu. Enter the date range of From 1/1/2009 and To 1/31/2009.

2. Click **Refresh** and the report in Figure 3:18 displays. Click **Print** to send the report to a printer. Recall from Chapter 2 that you can also email and export reports. Close this statement.

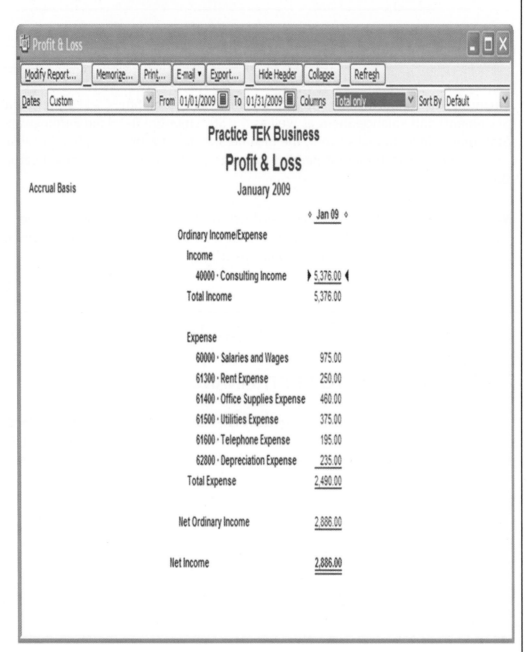

Figure 3:18

3. Select **Reports>>Company & Financials>>Balance Sheet Standard** on the main menu. Enter 1/31/2009 as the date. The refreshed report displays as shown. Click **X** to close the report.

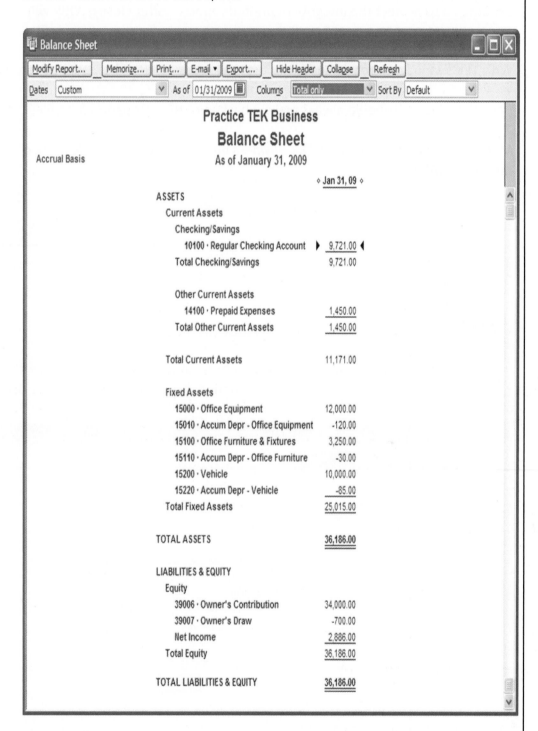

Figure 3:19

CLOSE AN ACCOUNTING PERIOD

As stated in Chapter 2, you should always close the accounting period after issuing financial statements to protect the integrity of printed reports. After closing, QBP will warn when you attempting to post to a closed period.

With TEK's January reports issued, you are now ready to close the January accounting period.

Before closing, you should always make a backup of the company's data file.

Make a backup of the Practice TEK Business data file to a backup file named "Practice TEK Business Chpt 3".

You will now close the January accounting period.

STEPS TO CLOSE AN ACCOUNTING PERIOD

1. Click ***Company>>Set Closing Date*** on the main menu and the Company Preferences tab under Accounting preferences opens (Figure 3:20).

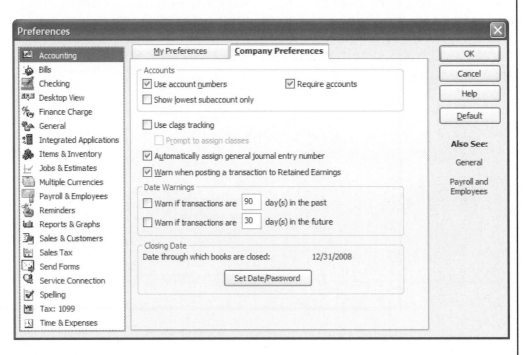

Figure 3:20

2. Click the **Set Date/Password** button and type "1/31/2009" in the **Closing Date** field.

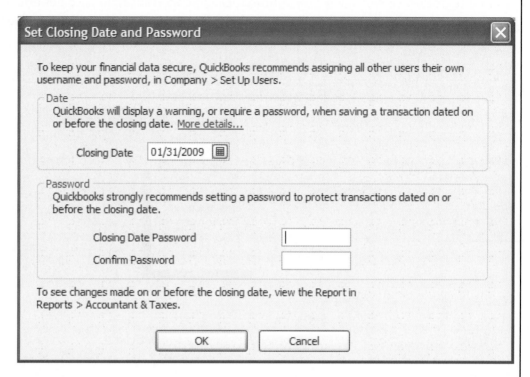

Figure 3:21

3. Click **OK**. A prompt appears to remind you to set a password. Mark the option to turn off future reminders and click **No**.

QUICKBOOKS DATA INTEGRATION

Data integration explains why QBP automatically posts transactions to general ledger accounts and customer, vendor, employee, and banking accounts. The next diagram visually depicts data integration.

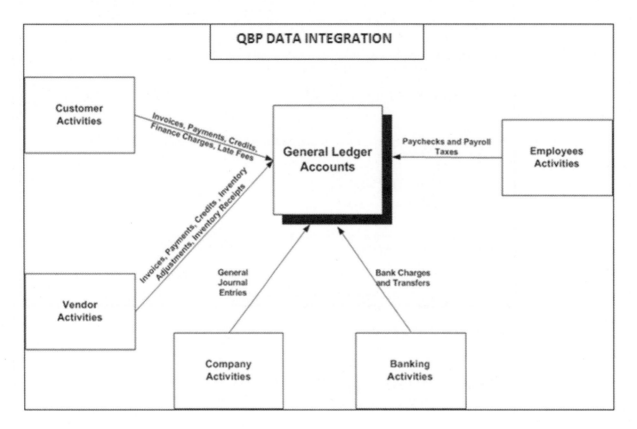

Figure 3:22

This diagram shows you that transactions posted in one activity flow through to the general ledger. Data integration saves time and reduces errors because you only enter data once instead of entering data in a subsidiary journal and then posting it to the general ledger. It also means that QBP automatically records the audit trail.

Subsequent chapters will focus on processing transactions for each activity depicted above. As in this chapter, you will begin by learning *MAPS* and then step through QBP transaction processing. Chapters 4 through 7 will cover customer, vendor, employee, and company/ banking activities for a service based business. Chapters 8 through 11 will focus on the same activities for a merchandising business.

SUMMARY

You began the chapter by looking at T-Accounts and *MAPS* for recording general journal entries. You then posted a general journal entry in QBP and went *Behind the Keys* of the posted transaction to trace the audit trail. You also posted compound journal entries and adjusting entries. You learned to correct entries and print the Trial Balance, Income Statement, and Balance Sheet. You finished by backing up TEK's data file and closing the January accounting period. Finally, you looked at the QBP integration that explains why computerized accounting saves times and reduces errors.

After completing the end-of-chapter materials, you can branch off and explore either the service based business or merchandising business tracks.

END-OF-CHAPTER QUESTIONS

TRUE/FALSE

_____ 1. You should always back up a company's data file before closing an accounting period.

_____ 2. You view posted journal entries by selecting *Company>>Journal* on the main menu.

_____ 3. QBP will let you drilldown on the Trial Balance report to view transactions in an account.

_____ 4. You can create a journal entry from the Chart of Accounts.

_____ 5. The Save button on a journal entry posts the transaction.

_____ 6. QBP will let you delete a posted journal entry.

_____ 7. The Print icon on the Trial Balance report opens a window for selecting a printer to receive output.

_____ 8. Journal entries are automatically posted to general ledger accounts when saved.

_____ 9. QBP will let you reopen a posted journal entry to correct it.

_____ 10. The General Ledger report displays General Journal and the entry number as the audit trail of a posted journal entry.

MULTIPLE CHOICE

_____ 1. Which report will list the details of transactions by account?
    a. Journal
    b. Balance Sheet
    c. General Ledger
    d. Trial Balance

_____ 2. You can print a General Ledger report using _____.
    a. *Reports>>Accountants & Taxes>>General Ledger* on the main menu
    b. the Reports command on the Chart of Accounts
    c. both a and b
    d. none of the above

_____ 3. QBP will let you change a report by _____.
      a. clicking the Modify Report icon
      b. entering custom dates on the face of the report
      c. changing the sort order on the face of the report
      d. all of the above

_____ 4. Adjusting journal entries are used to record _____.
      a. depreciation expense
      b. expired prepaid expense
      c. both a and b
      d. none of the above

_____ 5. Which report shows a company's financial position?
      a. Balance Sheet
      b. Chart of Accounts
      c. Profit and Loss
      d. General Ledger Trial Balance

_____ 6. Which of the following will not let you enter a range of reporting dates?
      a. General Ledger Trial Balance
      b. Profit and Loss
      c. Balance Sheet
      d. Both a and b

_____ 7. Which report is also known as the Income Statement?
      a. Balance Sheet
      b. Chart of Accounts
      c. Profit and Loss
      d. Trial Balance

PRACTICE SET

Before beginning this Practice Set, open the **Graded TEK Business** data file customized with your initials at the end of Chapter 1. *If this company is not loaded on your computer then restore it using the Graded TEK Business Chpt 1.QBB backup file created in the Practice Set at the end of Chapter 1.*

1. Enter TEK's January accounting entries listed below. Remember to enter a description on all transactions. All entries affect the regular checking account.

   2009

Jan 1	Owner initial investment of $24,000:

   > Cash $3,000
   > Office equipment $12,000
   > Office furniture $4,000
   > Vehicles $5,000

Jan 2	Check No. 178 for office supplies expense, $380.
Jan 5	Check No. 179 for six months of prepaid rent, $2,400.
Jan 7	Check No. 180 for advertising expense, $980.
	Check No. 181 to vehicle expenses, $1,700.
Jan 9	Cash received for fees earned, $7,625.
Jan 15	Check No. 182 for office salaries, $1,200
Jan 16	Cash received for fees earned, $3,300.
Jan 19	Check No. 183 for donation to local charity, $300.
	Check No. 184 to owner, $1,300.
Jan 28	Check No. 185 for electricity expense, $350.
	Check No. 186 for office salaries, $1,200.

2. Record the following adjusting entries as of January 31.
   a. Expense one month of prepaid rent.
   b. January depreciation expense of $355 posted as follows:
      Office equipment, $170
      Office furniture, $65
      Vehicles, $120

3. Print the following January reports.
   a. Journal
   b. Trial Balance
   c. Profit and Loss
   d. Balance Sheet

4. ***Back up the Graded TEK Business data file to a backup file named "Graded TEK Business Chpt 3". Close January's accounting period.***

CHAPTER 4   CUSTOMER ACTIVITIES FOR A SERVICE BASED BUSINESS

LEARNING OBJECTIVES

This chapter works with the **Practice Astor Landscaping** data file customized with your initials at the end of Chapter 1. *If this company is not loaded on your computer then restore it using the Practice Astor Landscaping Chpt 1.QBB backup file created in the Practice Set at the end of Chapter 1.*

The chapter focuses on using QBP to process customer activities for a service based business and covers the following:

1. The manual accounting procedures (*MAPS*) used to record customer transactions
2. Using the Customer Center to perform customer tasks
3. Recording a basic sales invoice
4. Going *Behind the Keys* of a posted sales invoice and learning to correct posting errors
5. Emailing a sales invoice
6. Managing customers and jobs
7. Understanding service and non-inventory part items
8. Invoicing job costs and printing job reports
9. Recording basic customer payments
10. Going *Behind the Keys* to view posted payments
11. Recording customer payments carrying a discount and sales receipts
12. Correcting errors after posting customer payments
13. Recording customer credits
14. Reporting on and reconciling customer activities
15. Writing off customer invoices
16. Preparing customer statements

Launch QBP and open **Practice Astor Landscaping**.

The following provides background information on Astor's business operations. The company supplies landscaping and lawn maintenance services to residential and commercial customers. Customers are not invoiced until services are provided. Astor uses QBP inventory features to track job material purchases and service pricing. Service labor costs are incurred by paying Astor employees or subcontractors and the accountant uses job costing to analyze job performance. The company's current accounting period is March 2009.

MANUAL ACCOUNTING PROCEDURES

Before processing sales transactions in QBP, become familiar with a manual accounting system. This topic walks through manual accounting procedures (*MAPS*) for processing customer sales transactions. We begin at the point where a customer initiates a transaction.

On March 24, 2009, John Chester contacts Astor salesperson, Jan Folse, requesting seasonal lawn maintenance. John has used the company in the past. Jan quoted John a price of $80.00 plus tax and the service is scheduled for March 27, 2009.

In a manual system, Jan writes up a service ticket, which an employee performing the service takes to the job. These tickets are not entered into the accounting records because the sale is not recognized until after performing the services. Recall that accrual accounting does not recognize revenue until earned and Astor does not earn revenue until the service is provided.

On March 27, Jeff Henderson picks up the service ticket and heads to John's home. After completing the service, Jeff has John sign the service ticket to acknowledge completion and returns the signed ticket to Jan. Jan then forwards the ticket to the accountant, Judy White, who prepares the following invoice.

Astor Landscaping
1505 Pavilion Place, Suite C
Arlington, VA 30093

Date: 3/27/2009

Customer:

Mr. John Chester
2404 Pleasant Hill
Danville, VA 30096

INVOICE   **No. 1020**

Seasonal Lawn Maintenance		
March 27, 2009	$	80.00
Sales Tax		4.00
Total	$	84.00
Please remit balance within 30 days		

Figure 4:1

Judy next records the invoice, along with other invoices for that day, in the Sales Journal. Her entries to the Sales Journal for March 27 appear next.

Astor Landscaping						
Date: 3/27/2009			Sales Journal			Page 15
Customer	Post Ref	Description	Accounts Receivable (Debit)	Maint. Services (Credit)	Hardscape Sales (Credit)	Sales Tax Payable (Credit)
John Chester	CHES001	Seasonal Maint. INV 1020	84.00	80.00		4.00
DBH Enterprises	DBHE001	Landscaping / Maint. INV 1021	3,383.15	290.00	2,916.78	176.37
Yango Software	YANG001	Seasonal Maint. INV 1022	290.13		275.00	15.13
Totals:			$ 3,757.28	$ 370.00	$ 3,191.78	$ 195.50
Acct Ref:			(11000)	(45000)	(42000)	(22000)
Audit Trail						

Figure 4:2

You see that Judy entered John's invoice as a debit to accounts receivable and as credits to maintenance services and sales tax payable. At the end of the day, Judy totals Sales Journal columns and cross-foots totals to verify that entries balance (i.e., debits equal credits). She then posts each invoice to the customer's account and posts column totals to the general ledger accounts noted at the bottom.

Figure 4:3 shows Judy's entry to John's customer account. *(Note: Entries for other customer accounts are not illustrated.)*

John Chester 2404 Pleasant Hill Danville, VA 30096		**Audit Trail**			Acct No:	CHES001
Date	Description	Post Ref	Debit	Credit	Balance	
03/01/09	Beginning Balance				0.00	
03/27/09	Seasonal Maint. INV 1020	SJ 15	84.00		84.00	

Figure 4:3

Judy's entries to general ledger accounts are illustrated next. *(Note: The entry to the sales tax payable account is not shown.)*

General Ledger

Accounts Receivable — Account No. 11000

Date	Description	Post Ref	Debit	Credit	Balance
03/26/09	Balance Forward				96,273.96
03/27/09		SJ 15	3,757.28		100,031.24

Audit Trail

General Ledger

Maintenance Services — Account No. 45000

Date	Description	Post Ref	Debit	Credit	Balance
03/26/09	Balance Forward				22,240.00
03/27/09		SJ 15		370.00	22,610.00

Audit Trail

General Ledger

Hardscape Sales — Account No. 42000

Date	Description	Post Ref	Debit	Credit	Balance
03/26/09	Balance Forward				55,290.00
03/27/09		SJ 15		3,191.78	58,481.78

Figure 4:4

As Judy posts, she is also entering posting references that form the audit trail. An audit trail documents entries from the Sales Journal to general ledger accounts, from the Sales Journal to customer accounts, and vice versa. You can imagine the posting errors that can occur in a manual system. Judy could record an entry backwards (e.g., enter a debit as a credit), record an out-of-balance entry, omit an entry, or forget to enter the audit trail.

On the same day that Judy posts invoices she also posts customer payments for outstanding invoices. These entries are recorded in a separate journal called the Cash Receipts Journal. Entries to the Cash Receipts Journal are illustrated next.

Astor Landscaping						
Date: 3/27/2009			Cash Receipts Journal			Page 3
Customer	Check No.	Post Ref	Invoice No.	Regular Checking (Debit)	Accounts Receivable (Credit)	Sales Discounts (Debit)
O'Hara Homes	993	OHAR001	993	1,000.00	1,000.00	
Sycamore Homes	9832	SYCA001	1012	20,291.72	20,681.95	390.23
Totals:				$ 21,291.72	$ 21,681.95	$ 390.23
Acct Ref:				(10200)	(11000)	(49000)

Audit Trail

Figure 4:5

As with postings on the Sales Journal, Judy posts each check to the customer's account and column totals to the general ledger accounts. This time she will use the posting reference of CRJ (Cash Receipts Journal) along with the page number. *(Note: These postings are not illustrated.)*

With QBP most of the posting errors are eliminated. You will see in subsequent topics that sales invoices and customer payments are posted when saving. In addition, QBP automatically posts entries recorded to the Sales and Cash Receipts Journals to customer accounts and general ledger accounts. QBP also enters the audit trail and will not post out of balance entries.

We will now focus our attention to processing customer transactions in QBP.

CUSTOMER CENTER

The **Customer Center** focuses on processing customer activities. Click the **Customers** button on the **Home** page to open the center and select the options indicated in Figure 4:6. We will now discuss this center's purpose.

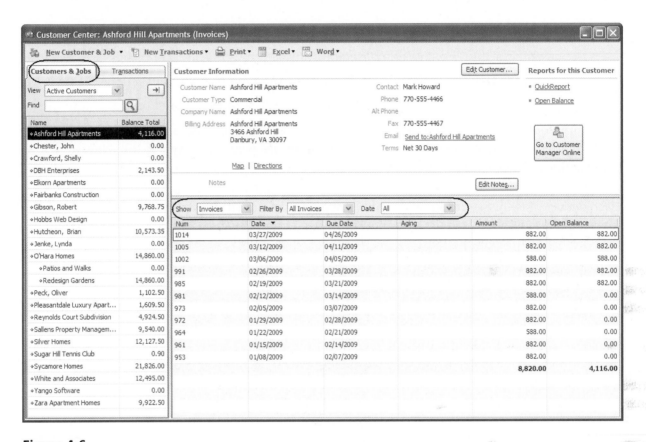

Figure 4:6

The **Customers & Jobs** tab lists transactions by customer account. Astor's customer accounts and balances appear to the left. The **View** option will toggle accounts for viewing All Customers, Active Customers, or Customers with Open Balances. You are currently viewing Active Customers.

This ⬜ button hides the Customer Information pane shown to the right. After hiding, this ⬜ button appears on the far right for redisplaying the pane.

The **Customer Information** pane displays transactions for the account highlighted to the left. This account is currently Ashford Hill Apartments.

The **Edit Customer** button opens the account for editing customer information and the **Edit Notes** button lets you enter account notes. There are also hyperlinks for creating **Reports for this Customer**.

Ashford's transactions are listed at the bottom of its account information. The filter options of **Show**, **Filter By**, and **Date** determine the transactions displayed. Click ⌄ to select a new option from the dropdown list. You are currently viewing **Invoices** that are **All Invoices** recorded on **All** dates. *(Remember that the fiscal year is based on your computer date.)*

Filter options work as follows:

- ❖ Show: Select the transaction type to list
- ❖ Filter By: Criteria based on transaction type
- ❖ Date: List all transactions for the type or only transactions recorded as of a specific date or range of dates

Now turn your attention to the task buttons for activities that can be performed while displaying the Customers & Jobs tab. These activities are **New Customer & Job**, **New Transactions**, **Print**, **Excel**, and **Word**.

Each activity has this ▾ dropdown symbol, meaning the activity contains multiple tasks. The next table discusses task choices by activity. Most actions perform the task on the customer account highlighted on the left.

Customers & Jobs Activities	Task	Description
New Customer & Job	New Customer	Create a new customer account.
	Add Job	Create a new job for the highlighted customer.
New Transactions	Invoices	Create a sales invoice for the highlighted customer.
	Sales Receipts	Record a sales transaction for the highlighted customer. Used when the customer is paying in full at time of sale. Do not use this activity when the customer is making a sales deposit. Instead, use Invoices.
	Statement Charges	Open the highlighted customer's register and enter charges that will print on a statement. This is an alternate method for billing customers that bypasses creating an invoice. It can also be used to record finance charges. The text will not illustrate this method.
	Receive Payments	Record payment receipt from the highlighted customer.
	Credit Memos/Refunds	Issue a credit to the highlighted customer or refund a customer overpayment.

Customers & Jobs Activities	Task	Description
Print	Customer & Job List	Print a customer list with balances. The report cannot be customized so you should consider using the Reports menu to print this information.
	Customer & Job Information	Print account information and notes for the highlighted customer. The report cannot be customized so you should consider using the Reports menu to print this information.
	Customer & Job Transaction List	Print the highlighted customer's transactions for the current fiscal year. The report cannot be customized so you should consider using the Reports menu to print this information.
Excel	Export Customer List	Create an Excel workbook or comma separated values (.csv) file containing account information for all customers along with account balances.
	Export Transactions	Create an Excel workbook or comma separated values (.csv) file containing current fiscal year transactions for the highlighted customer.
	Import from Excel	Import customer information and/or transactions from an Excel workbook or comma separated values (.csv) file.
Word	Customer communications	Create form letters for customers.

Next turn your attention to the **Transactions** tab, which lists transactions by type instead of transactions by customer. Click to activate the tab and select the options indicated in the next illustration.

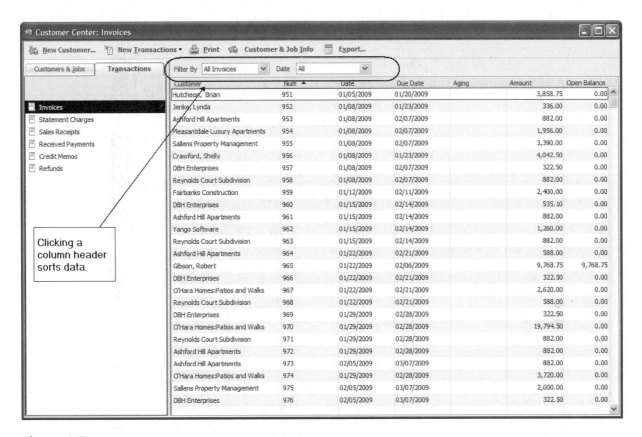

Figure 4:7

Transaction types are chosen on the left. **Invoices** is the type currently highlighted and the information displayed on the right lists **All Invoices** for **All** dates. Once again, the transactions displayed depend on the filtering options. You can change the sort order by clicking a column header.

Activities that can be performed on this tab are different from those that can be performed on the other tab. First, not all activities have additional tasks so clicking an activity immediately opens the task. The next table discusses activities for the **Transactions** tab.

Transactions Activities	Description
New Customer	Create a new customer account. Additional jobs must be added by using the first tab.
New Transactions	Contains the same tasks found on the Customers & Jobs tab but this time the user selects the customer.
Print	Print transactions listed to the right.
Customer & Job Info	Edit customer and job information for the transaction highlighted on the right.
Export	Create an Excel workbook or comma separated values (.csv) file containing transactions listed on the right.

As illustrated, you can perform a variety of customer activities from the Customer Center. You can initiate transactions, locate posted transactions, manage accounts, and create new accounts. Close the Customer Center.

In contrast, the customer section of the Home page (Figure 4:8) only initiates transactions but offers quicker access to such tasks. In addition, you can always use the **Customers** menu to perform customer activities.

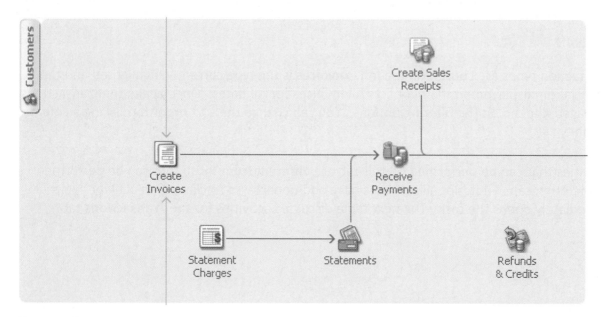

Figure 4:8

Now that you are familiar with locating customer activities let's begin recording customer transactions.

ENTERING SALES INVOICES

You will now return to John Chester's transaction illustrated in the *MAPS* topic to record his invoice in QBP. Read the following data entry tips before completing the exercise that follows.

Data Entry Tips

Tip 1:   The **Customer:Job** field links the transaction to a customer's account. The **Item** field links inventory items to the transaction. Customer accounts and items are also called master records. You will recognize a master record field because it contains lookups for selecting a record.

Tip 2:   You can either click the dropdown list on the **Customer:Job** or **Item** field to select a record or begin typing the name of the customer account or item to make a selection.

Tip 3:   If you select the wrong customer or item then return to the field and change the selection. Click **Edit** on the main menu when you want to add or delete invoice line items.

Tip 4:   QBP will create new master records "on the fly," meaning a new customer or item can be created while entering a transaction. Example: A new customer can be added by typing a customer name in the **Customer:Job** field and pressing tab. QBP will then prompt with the following:

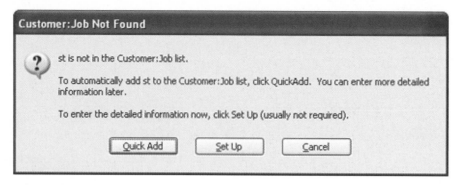

Figure 4:9

Clicking **Set Up** opens the New Customer window for entering all information on the new account. Clicking **Cancel** returns you to the **Customer:Job** field for selecting an existing customer. Clicking **Quick Add** creates the new account without opening the New Customer window. You will not want to use this option because it does not allow you to enter an address or other information for the new account.

Tip 5:   Figure 4:10 illustrates toolbar icons on the invoice window and a description of relevant icons follows the illustration.

Figure 4:10

Previous and **Next** scroll through posted invoices. QBP will prompt to save a new or modified transaction before moving to another transaction.

Print sends the current invoice to a printer. The dropdown list for this icon contains an option for previewing an invoice before printing it and an option for printing multiple invoices.

Send emails an invoice. The dropdown list for this icon contains options for emailing multiple invoices.

STEPS FOR ENTERING A SALES INVOICE

1. On the **Home** page, click **Create Invoices** to open the invoice transaction window.

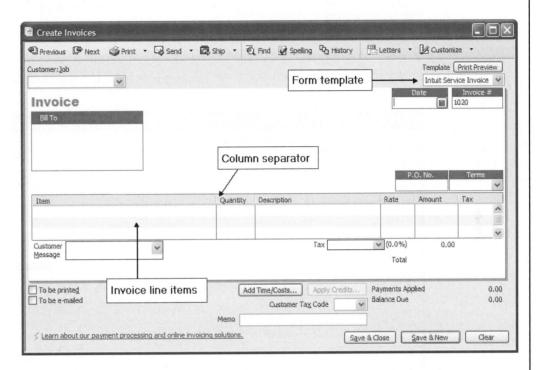

Figure 4:11

Make sure that the form template displays [Intuit Service Invoice ▼]. You can select the template from the dropdown list. The service invoice template determines the columns on line items and other fields displayed on the form.

To resize the window, drag the edges using the mouse. To resize line item columns, drag the column separators.

2. Place your cursor in **Customer:Job** and look up to select "Chester, John". The **Bill To** and **Terms** transfer from the customer account.

3. Place your cursor in **Date.** Type "3/27/2009" because this is the day that the services were performed. *(Note: You can also select the date using the field's calendar feature.)*

    *(Note: The first time you open a transaction window, QBP will set the transaction date to your computer date. **BE CAREFUL** and remember to always check transaction dates before saving.)*

4. Tab to **Invoice #** and enter "1020".

5. Place your cursor in **Item** on the first line item. Look up and select "SEAS MNTNCE – RESIDENTIAL" and QBP will display the item's description in the field.

   (Note: The lookup on Item signals that it links to a master record.)

6. Tab to **Quantity** and enter "2".

7. Press Tab and the completed invoice appears in Figure 4:12. Verify that the option of "To be printed" is marked.

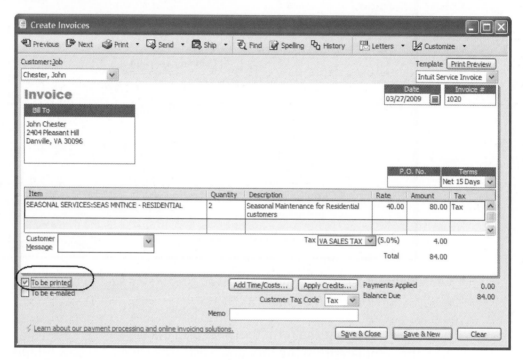

Figure 4:12

Before saving the invoice, review remaining fields in the window. You will normally not need to change data in these fields.

❖ **Description** and **Rate** defaulted from the item selected.

❖ **Amount** equals the **Quantity** times the **Rate**.

❖ The **Tax** field on a line item shows whether sales tax is normally charged on the item. You can mix taxable line items with nontaxable line items.

❖ Tax on the form (i.e., **VA Sales Tax**) sets the sales tax rate applied to taxable line items. The rate code defaults from the customer account.

❖ **Customer Tax Code** shows when sales to a particular customer are taxable. If the customer is not taxable then the invoice will not compute sales tax even when line items are taxable.

❖ *To be printed* flags an invoice for printing. *To be e-mailed* flags it for email delivery.

❖ The **Apply Credits** button is used when applying outstanding customer credit memos and overpayments to an invoice.

❖ Text in the **Customer Message** field will appear on the printed invoice whereas text in the **Memo** field stores internal notes.

8. Click [Print Preview] to view the invoice before sending it to the printer (Figure 4:13).

    (Note: If prompted about shipping labels, select the option that turns off future messages and click OK.)

    Scroll to the bottom of the invoice to view the total. You can click on the invoice to enlarge it.

    Click **Close** to return to the invoice transaction.

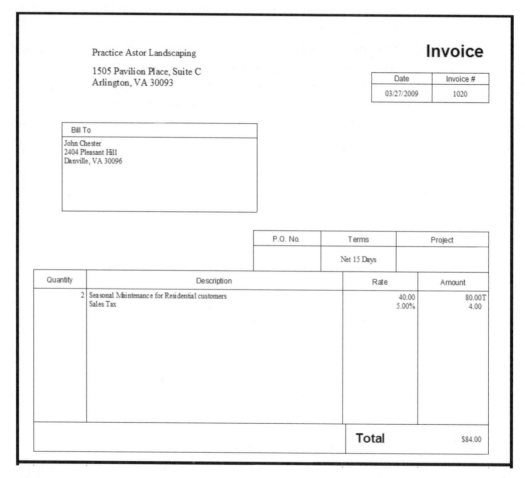

Figure 4:13

9. Click **Print** and QBP automatically saves the transaction before opening a window for selecting a printer (Figure 4:14). Use the dropdown list on **Printer name** if you need to select a different printer.

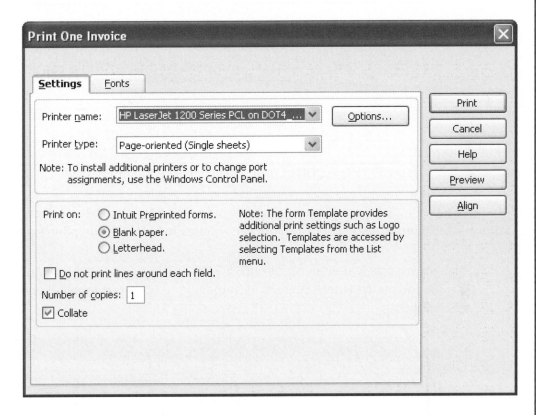

Figure 4:14

10. Click **Print** to send the invoice to the printer.

11. Click **Save & Close**. *(Note: Save & New will post a transaction and remain in the window for entering the next transaction.)*

In this exercise you entered a single invoice and then printed it. Normally you will enter several invoices before printing. To print multiple invoices, click the dropdown list on the Print icon and select Print Batch. QBP will then print every invoice with this option ☑ To be printed selected.

You do not have to recheck the *To be printed* option to reprint a posted invoice. Just reopen the invoice and click Print.

BEHIND THE KEYS OF A POSTED SALES INVOICE

In this topic you trace QBP's audit trail by locating the entries made when posting John's invoice in the previous topic. Remember that the audit trail in the manual system referenced the Sales Journal and the page number. Let's see how that compares with QBP's audit trail.

TRACE THE AUDIT TRAIL OF A POSTED SALES INVOICE

1. First, open the Sales Journal by selecting **Reports>>Memorized Reports>>Accounting Journals>>Sales Journal** on the main menu.

2. Enter the date range of **From** 3/27/2009 **To** 3/27/2009. Click **Modify Report** and on the **Filters** tab set the **Name** filter to **Chester, John**. Click **OK** to refresh the report.

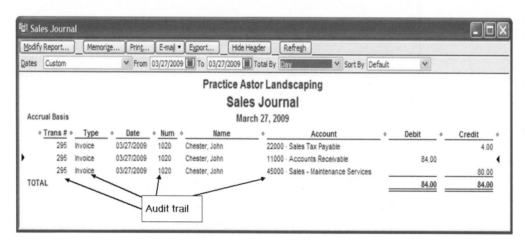

Figure 4:15

Recall that John's invoice entries on the manual Sales Journal debited 11000 Accounts Receivable for $84.00, credited 45000 Maintenance Services for $80.00, and credited 22000 Sales Taxes Payable for $4.00. This is exactly what QBP shows as the entries.

Note the audit trail codes under **Type** and **Trans #** because we will again refer to these codes. *(Note: Your Trans # may differ because numbers are assigned based on activity in the software.)* Close this report without saving changes.

(Hint: You can reopen the original invoice by double clicking any of the entries shown on the report.)

3.   Recall in the *MAPS* topic that after posting an invoice to the Sales Journal the invoice was then posted to the customer's account. You will now locate QBP's entries to John's customer account.

Click **Reports>>Customers & Receivables>>Transaction List by Customer** on the main menu.

Enter the date range of **From** 3/27/2009 and **To** 3/27/2009.

4.   Click **Modify Report**. Select **Trans #** under **Columns** to display this audit trail code (Figure 4:16). Scroll down and click **Split** to uncheck this column. Click **OK** and the report displays. (See Figure 4:17.)

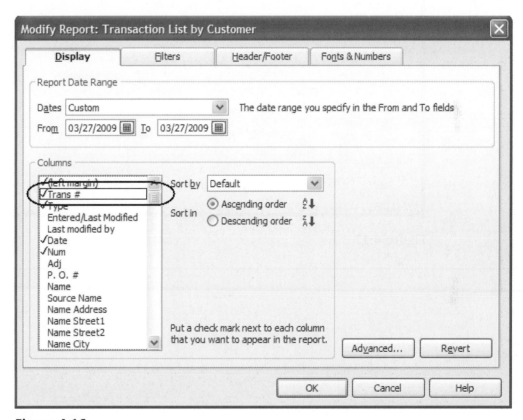

Figure 4:16

5. Notice that the **Trans #** and **Type** on John's account match the **Trans #** and **Type** on the Sales Journal. Close this report without saving changes.

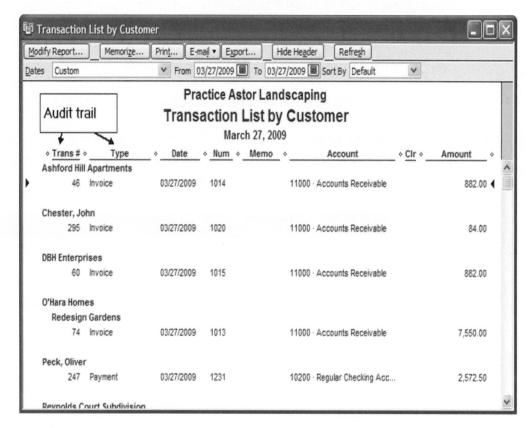

Figure 4:17

6. All that remains is tracing entries on the general ledger. Select **Reports>>Memorized Reports>>Accounting Journals>>General Ledger Detail Report** on the main menu. Enter the date range of **From** 3/27/2009 and **To** 3/27/2009 and click **Refresh** so the report redisplays as illustrated in Figure 4:18.

Practice Astor Landscaping
General Ledger Detail Report

Accrual Basis   March 27, 2009

Trans #	Type	Date	Num	Name	Memo	Debit	Credit
11000 · Accounts Receivable							
46	Invoice	03/27/2009	1014	Ashford Hill Apartments		882.00	
60	Invoice	03/27/2009	1015	DBH Enterprises		882.00	
74	Invoice	03/27/2009	1013	O'Hara Homes:Redesign Garde...		7,550.00	
90	Invoice	03/27/2009	1016	Reynolds Court Subdivision		808.50	
247	Payment	03/27/2009	1231	Peck, Oliver			2,572.50
248	Payment	03/27/2009	3251	Sugar Hill Tennis Club			1,598.50
253	Payment	03/27/2009	2613	Sycamore Homes			11,025.00
295	Invoice	03/27/2009	1020	Chester, John		84.00	
Total 11000 · Accounts Receivable						10,206.50	15,196.00
22000 · Sales Tax Payable							
46	Invoice	03/27/2009	1014	VA Sales Tax Department	Sales Tax		42.00
60	Invoice	03/27/2009	1015	VA Sales Tax Department	Sales Tax		42.00
74	Invoice	03/27/2009	1013	VA Sales Tax Department	Sales Tax	0.00	
90	Invoice	03/27/2009	1016	VA Sales Tax Department	Sales Tax		38.50
295	Invoice	03/27/2009	1020	VA Sales Tax Department	Sales Tax		4.00
Total 22000 · Sales Tax Payable						0.00	126.50
45000 · Sales - Maintenance Services							
46	Invoice	03/27/2009	1014	Ashford Hill Apartments	Weekly Main...		840.00
60	Invoice	03/27/2009	1015	DBH Enterprises	Weekly Main...		840.00
90	Invoice	03/27/2009	1016	Reynolds Court Subdivision	Weekly Main...		770.00
295	Invoice	03/27/2009	1020	Chester, John	Seasonal Ma...		80.00
Total 45000 · Sales - Maintenance Services						0.00	2,530.00
Total 40000 · Sales						0.00	10,080.00

Audit trail

Figure 4:18

Once again you see that the **Trans #** and **Type** on John's entries match the Sales Journal audit trail. Close this report without saving changes.

You have now followed QBP's audit trail and can see the advantages to using a computerized accounting system. You were able to capture a sales invoice and QBP posted entries to the Sales Journal, customer account, and general ledger when saving it. In addition, the accountant is better equipped to answer customer inquiries, provide customer support, manage company sales, and analyze profitability.

CORRECTING SALES INVOICES

This topic explains voiding and deleting invoices and correcting errors on **unpaid** invoices. *(Note: Refer to the instructions in Appendix B if correcting a paid invoice.)*

Open the **Customer Center** and select the **Customers & Jobs** tab. Highlight John Chester's account and select the options shown in Figure 4:19.

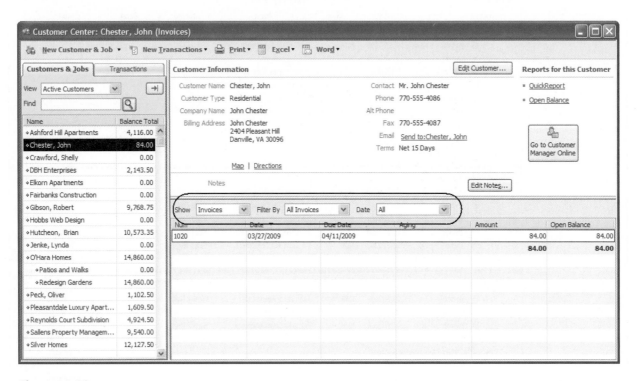

Figure 4:19

Double click the listed invoice to reopen it. ***Do not make any changes to the invoice*** but note that after reopening, you can void the invoice by selecting ***Edit>>Void Invoice*** on the main menu and delete it by selecting ***Edit>>Delete Invoice***. You can also modify the invoice and repost it by clicking **Save & Close**.

Later in the chapter you will learn to invoice customers for employee time and job materials. QBP will not reinstate invoiced time and materials after deleting or voiding this type of invoice. Therefore, you should print a copy of the invoice before deleting or voiding so you can manually reenter service items to reinvoice the customer.

Keep this transaction open for the topic that follows.

QUICKBOOKS EMAIL FEATURES

You will now use QBP's email features to send John's invoice to your email account. With the invoice open, click ⬛Send ▾. Click **Close** if a pop-up appears describing QBP's interaction with Microsoft's Outlook. *(Note: You must be connected to the Internet to use this feature.)*

A message appears using your default email program as shown in Figure 4:20.

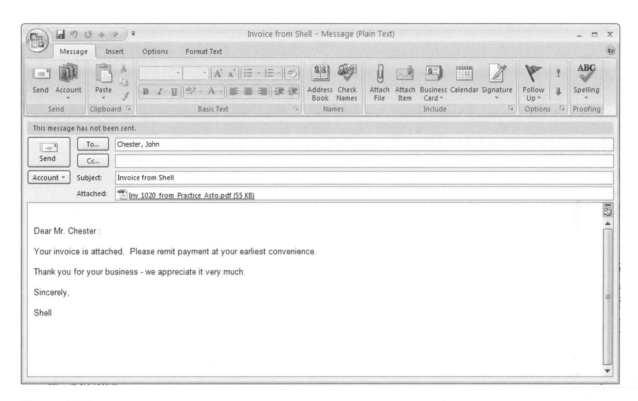

Figure 4:20

Enter your email address in the **To** field and, in **Subject**, replace the text "Invoice from Shell" with "Seasonal maintenance invoice". You can edit text in the body of the message when needed.

The invoice is attached as a PDF file. Click **Send.** You may get the message shown in Figure 4:21 and can turn off this message in the future by checking the Do not display this message in the future box. Click **OK** to close the message.

Figure 4:21

Check your email later to verify delivery. Click **X** to close John's invoice.

CUSTOMER AND JOB ACCOUNTS

This topic explains creating, editing, and deleting customers and jobs. The customer account contains job information used for implementing job costing. You must use the **Customer Center** to manage customer and job accounts. Open this center if not still open from the previous topic, select the **Customers & Jobs** tab, and double click **Chester, John** to open his account. Now follow the next series of illustrations as we describe the tabs of the customer account.

Address Info Tab

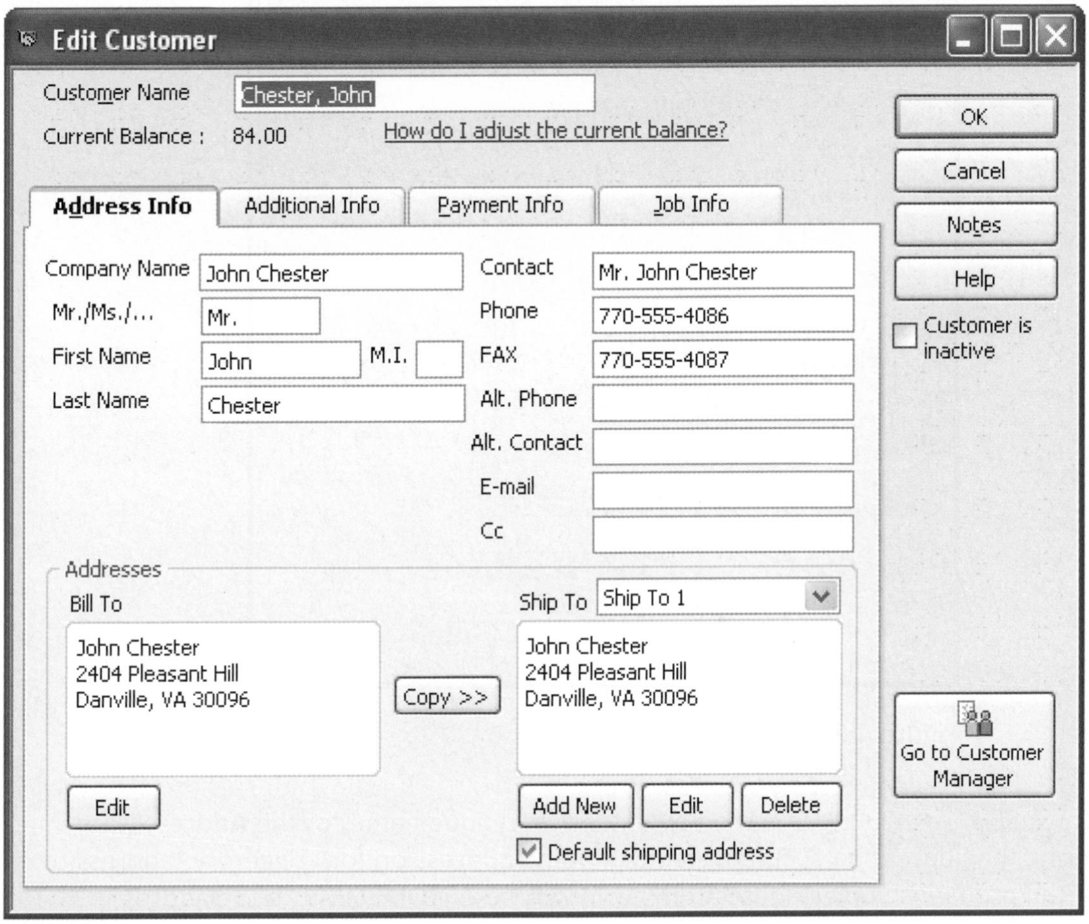

Figure 4:22

The **Address Info** tab stores basic customer information such as address, phone numbers, and email address. The **Bill To** address can be copied to the **Ship To** address by clicking the **Copy** button.

The **Ship To** address is important for companies shipping merchandise to customers because some customers may have one address for receiving invoices (Bill To) and another address for receiving orders (Ship To). When the customer has multiple locations, **Add New** opens the window illustrated in Figure 4:23 to enter additional addresses.

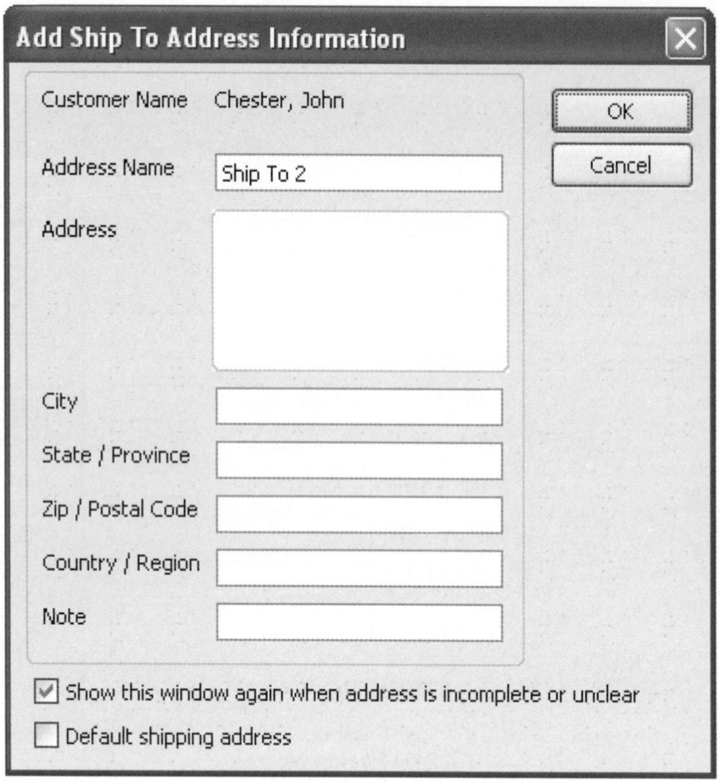

Add Ship To Address Information   ☒

Customer Name   Chester, John   ⟨ OK ⟩

Address Name   Ship To 2   ⟨ Cancel ⟩

Address

City

State / Province

Zip / Postal Code

Country / Region

Note

☑ Show this window again when address is incomplete or unclear

☐ Default shipping address

Figure 4:23

The window in Figure 4:23 is completed by entering a unique name for the **Address Name** and then entering the address data. The **Default shipping address** option triggers an address to appear as the primary shipping address on invoices. Clicking **OK** will store the address.

Additional Info Tab

Edit Customer

Customer Name   Chester, John

Current Balance :   84.00   How do I adjust the current balance?

| Address Info | **Additional Info** | Payment Info | Job Info |

OK

Cancel

Notes

Help

☐ Customer is inactive

Categorizing and Defaults

Type
Residential ⌄

Terms
Net 15 Days ⌄

Rep
⌄

Preferred Send Method
Mail ⌄

Custom Fields

Referral   Shelley Crawford

Special Note

Define Fields

Sales Tax Information

Tax Code   Tax Item
Tax ⌄   VA SALES TAX ⌄

Resale Number

Go to Customer Manager

Figure 4:24

This tab stores customer defaults used during transaction entry. Defaults include the **Preferred Send Method** for invoices, customer payment **Terms**, and the **Tax Code** applied to sales transactions. The **Rep** field assigns an employee sales representative for tracking sales commissions and sales performance.

The **Type** field is optional and can be used to differentiate sales by customer characteristics. Astor uses the types of Commercial and Residential.

Click the dropdown list on **Terms** to open the terms illustrated in Figure 4:25.

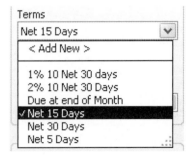

Terms
Net 15 Days ⌄
< Add New >

1% 10 Net 30 days
2% 10 Net 30 Days
Due at end of Month
✓ Net 15 Days
Net 30 Days
Net 5 Days

Figure 4:25

Terms establish invoice due dates and customer early payment discounts. The Net 15 Days terms make an invoice due 15 days from the invoice date. The 2% 10 Net 30 Days terms make the invoice due 30 days from the invoice date but grants a 2 percent discount when paying the total invoice within 10 days. *(Note: Discounts do not apply to sales tax.)*

Payment Info Tab

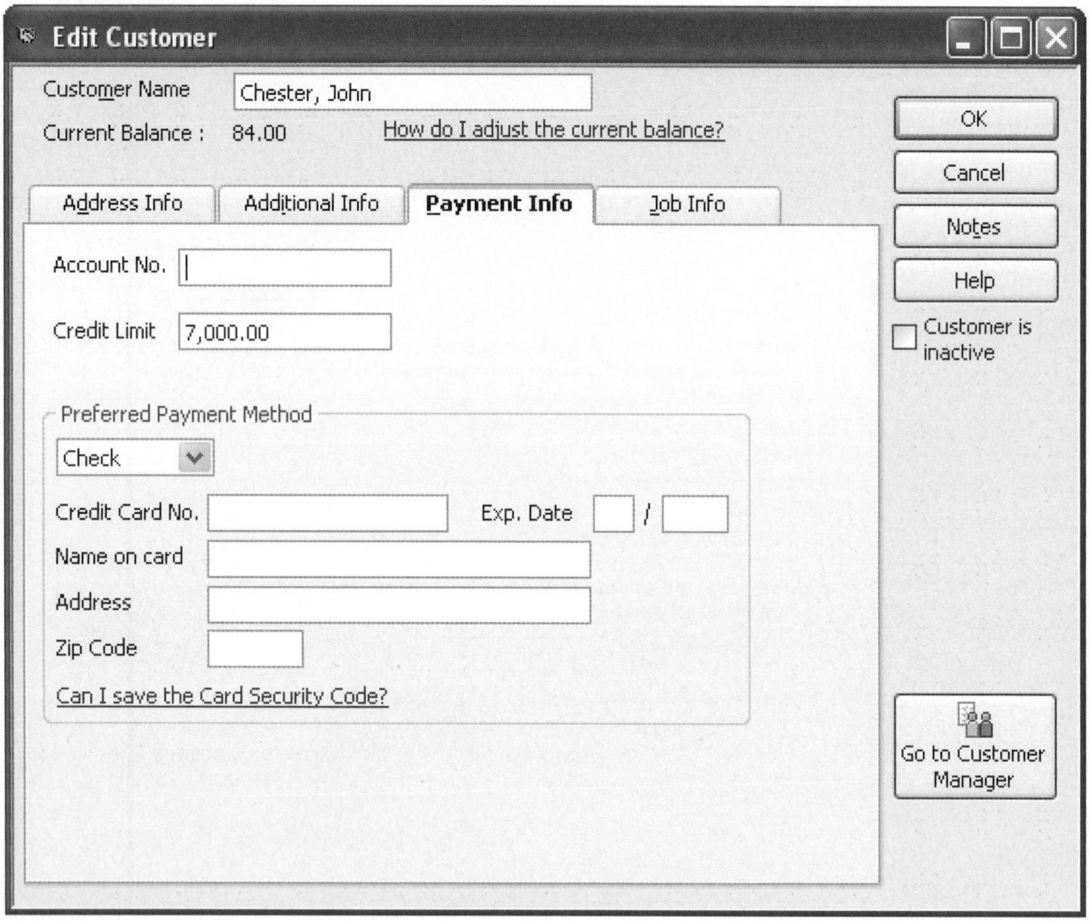

Figure 4:26

This tab stores a customer's **Credit Limit** and **Preferred Payment Method**. Setting a credit limit is important to managing bad debt. QBP will warn when saving a new invoice causes the customer's account balance to exceed the credit limit.

Job Info Tab

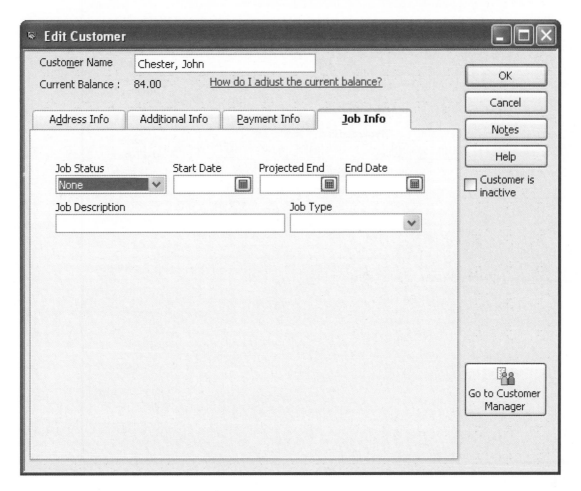

Figure 4:27

This tab implements customer job costing. By creating a job, you can track job revenue and costs such as vendor purchases and employee time. *(Note: Tracking job costs will be illustrated in Chapters 5 and 6.)* To implement job costing means that companies can analyze job profitability.

You can implement job costing without assigning a job to every customer. Sometimes the nature of the service will be short-term or nominal and the company does not find job costing beneficial. For instance, John's account does not have a job because his transaction involved a one-time service for seasonal maintenance.

Click **X** to close John's account and then double click Ashford Hill Apartments. Click the **Job Info** tab (Figure 4:28).

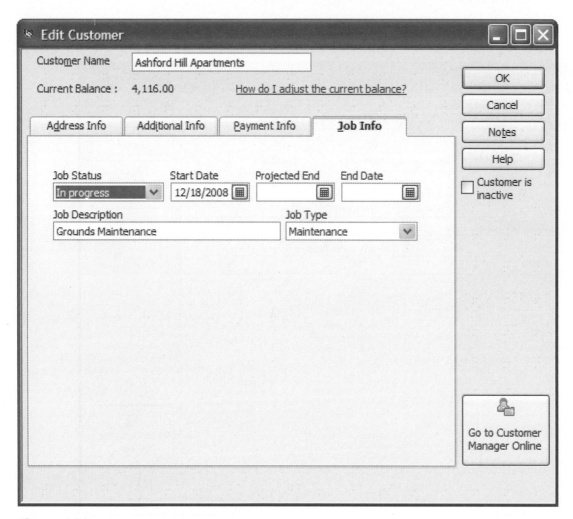

Figure 4:28

Ashford Hill does have a job and it is named "Grounds Maintenance." This Job is "In progress" and started on 12/18/2008. In addition, there is no projected end date because the service is ongoing grounds maintenance.

You can use the **Job Status** to monitor the progress on a job. The dropdown list for this field is shown in Figure 4:29.

Figure 4:29

After completing a job, the accountant sets the job status to Closed and enters an End Date. When the job also contains a Projected End, the company can use this date to analyze how well it met the projection.

Job Type is optional but can improve analysis because different types of services often require different resources. Astor has created the job types of Construction, Design, Landscaping, and Maintenance.

Close Ashford Hill's account and double click **O'Hara Homes**. This account does not have a Job Info tab (Figure 4:30) but that does not mean there is not a customer job.

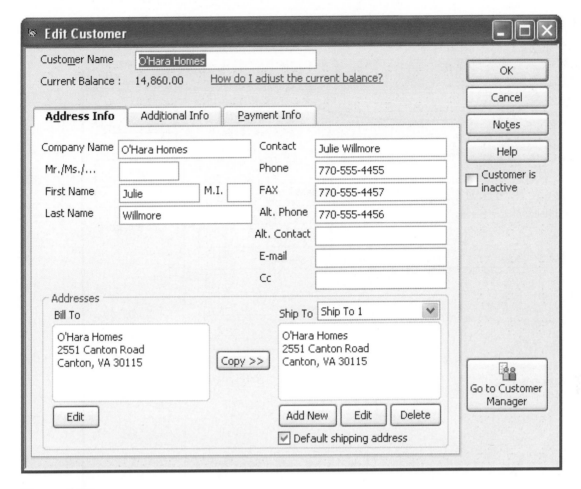

Figure 4:30

Close this account and look at the customer list on the left. There are two subitems beneath O'Hara Homes (Figure 4:31).

◆O'Hara Homes	14,860.00
◆Patios and Walks	0.00
◆Redesign Gardens	14,860.00

Figure 4:31

These subitems are the customer's jobs. When a customer has only one job, the job information is stored on the **Job Info** tab of the customer account. However, after adding more than one job, QBP removes the Job Info tab from the customer account and creates separate job accounts.

Double click **Patios and Walks** to open this job. Job accounts have the same tabs as a customer account and job information is entered on the **Job Info** tab (not illustrated). Close the Patios and Walks job.

Right click O'Hara Homes and select **Add Job**. In **Job Name**, enter "Test Job" (Figure 4:32).

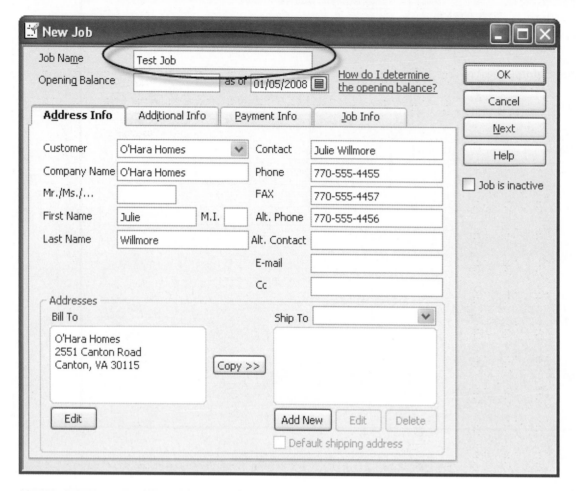

Figure 4:32

Customer account information has transferred to the job account so all you need to do is enter information on the Job Info tab. Click **OK** to save the job and it is placed beneath the Redesign Gardens job (Figure 4:33).

⬥ O'Hara Homes	14,860.00
⬥ Patios and Walks	0.00
⬥ Redesign Gardens	14,860.00
⬥ Test Job	0.00

Figure 4:33

Now highlight **Test Job** and select *Edit>>Delete Customer:Job* on the main menu. Click **OK** to confirm and the job is removed.

You have just created and deleted a job account. The next exercise walks through editing a customer account.

STEPS TO EDIT CUSTOMER ACCOUNT INFORMATION

1. You will be editing Ashford Hill's credit terms so open this account and click the **Additional Info** tab.

2. The accountant wants to offer Ashford an early payment discount of 2/10 net 30. Using the **Terms** dropdown list, select "2% 10 Net 30 Days" (Figure 4:34).

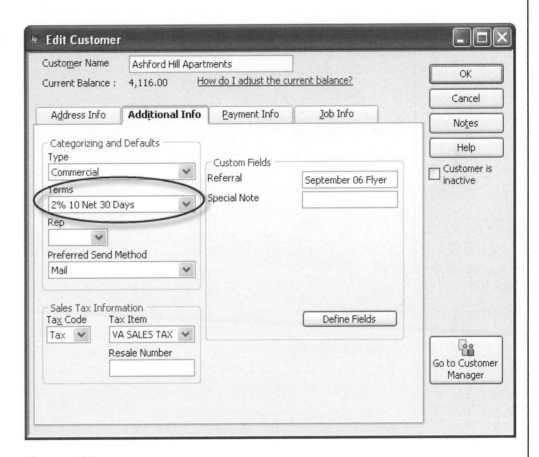

Figure 4:34

These terms mean that Ashford will receive a 2 percent discount on future invoices when paying the invoice in full within 10 days of the invoice date. Regardless, the invoice must be paid in full within 30 days.

3. Click **OK** to save the changes. Click **Yes** if QBP warns about modifying the account because this change does not affect previously posted transactions.

You will now add a new customer account.

STEPS TO CREATE A CUSTOMER ACCOUNT

1. From the Customers & Jobs tab, click **New Customer & Job** and select **New Customer**.

2. Now enter the information illustrated in Figure 4:35.

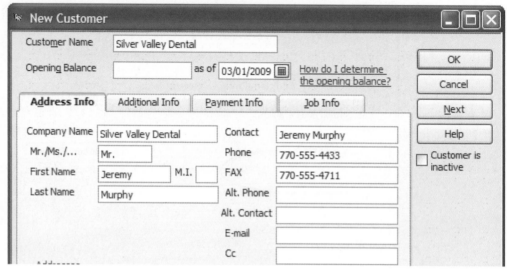

Figure 4:35

3.   Click **Edit** on the **Bill To** field and enter the information illustrated in Figure 4:36. Click **OK**.

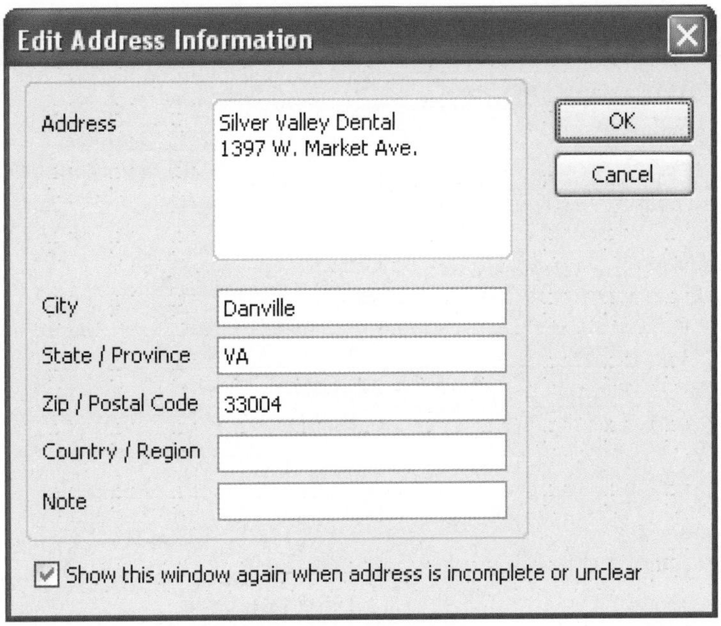

Figure 4:36

4. Click **Copy** to copy the **Bill To** address to the **Ship To** address. Click **OK** on the
    window that opens. The completed **Address Info** tab is shown in Figure 4:37.

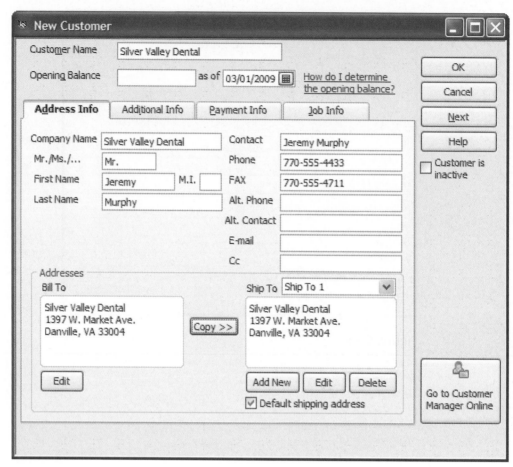

Figure 4:37

5. Click **Additional Info** and enter the information shown in Figure 4:38.

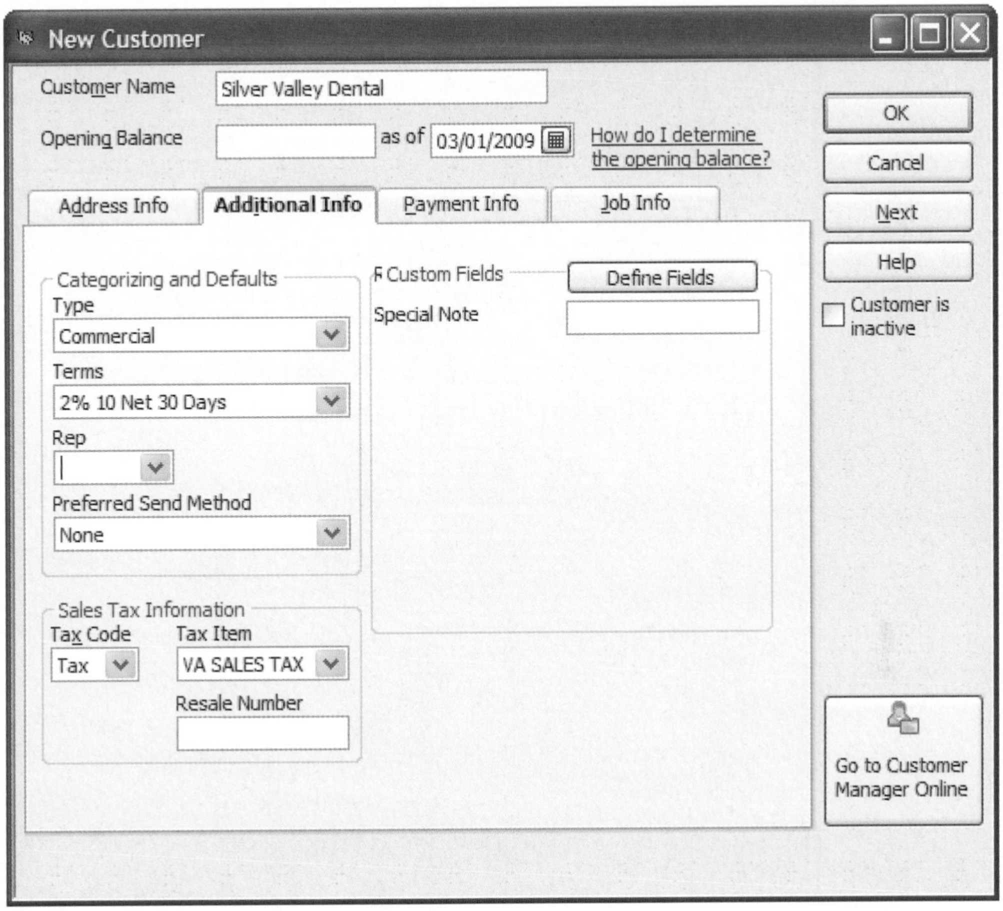

New Customer

Customer Name: Silver Valley Dental

Opening Balance: _____ as of 03/01/2009 📅   How do I determine the opening balance?

| Address Info | **Additional Info** | Payment Info | Job Info |

Categorizing and Defaults

Type
Commercial ▼

Terms
2% 10 Net 30 Days ▼

Rep
| ▼

Preferred Send Method
None ▼

Custom Fields   Define Fields

Special Note _____

Sales Tax Information

Tax Code   Tax Item
Tax ▼   VA SALES TAX ▼

Resale Number
_____

OK
Cancel
Next
Help

☐ Customer is inactive

Go to Customer Manager Online

Figure 4:38

6. On the **Payment Info** tab enter "18,000.00" as the **Credit Limit**.

7. Enter the information shown in Figure 4:39 as the **Job Info**.

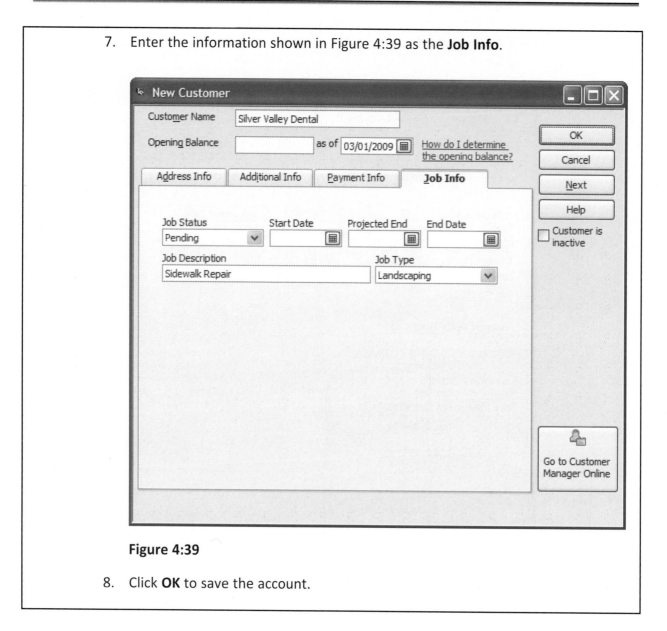

Figure 4:39

8. Click **OK** to save the account.

What happens when you try to delete an account with transaction history?

Highlight **Ashford Hill Apartments** and select ***Edit>>Delete Customer:Job*** on the main menu. QBP prompts, stating that it cannot delete an account with transaction history but can make it inactive. (See Figure 4:40.) Inactivating the account denies future transactions while retaining account history. Click **Cancel**.

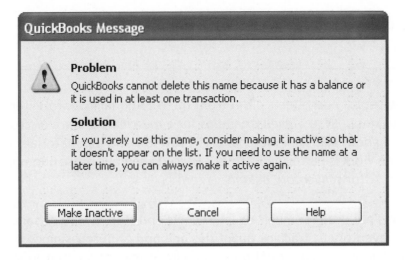

Figure 4:40

Now create a new account on your own.

CREATE A NEW CUSTOMER ACCOUNT

On March 1, 2009, Astor needs to create a new commercial customer with the following information.

Graphic Printing Services   Phone: 701 555-1515
127 Technology Way   Fax: 701 555-1518
Arlington, VA 30097   Contact: Jeffrey Davis
                                 Email: davis@graphic.net

Credit Limit: $5,000.00
Preferred Payment Method: Check

The customer pays VA sales tax and will be offered the terms of 2/10 Net 30 Days. The Preferred Send Method is Mail.

Job information: Pending Grounds Maintenance job, Maintenance job type.

Create this account.

UNDERSTANDING SERVICE AND NON-INVENTORY PART ITEMS

Service and non-inventory part items differ from the traditional inventory items used by a merchandising business. *(Note: Inventory items for a merchandiser are discussed in Chapter 8.)* Unlike goods sold by a merchandiser, services and job materials are not purchased until the work is performed. Thus, service based businesses do not hold inventory. *(Note: Notice that Astor's inventory balance is zero.)*

QBP's service items are used for invoicing labor costs and storing service sales price and do not interact with inventory by tracking quantities on hand or purchasing costs. This also means that cost of goods sold does not post when invoicing. Recall that John Chester's invoice traced in a previous exercise recorded only sales revenue. Since cost of goods sold does not post at the time of sale, Astor must post these costs through another activity, namely the employee or vendor activities discussed in subsequent chapters.

QBP's non-inventory part items are used for invoicing job material purchases. Again, these items do not interact with inventory by tracking quantities on hand or purchasing costs and cost of goods sold does not post when invoicing. Cost of goods sold posts only after recording a vendor receipt or bill for material purchases.

It is important to understand the posting of cost of goods sold; otherwise you might prepare financial statements that do not match revenues with expenses. The following table explains the inventory, non-inventory part, and service items used in this text. After reviewing this table you will better understand when an item class interacts with inventory and when the item posts cost of goods sold at the time of sale.

Item Class	Purpose
Inventory Part	Used to track goods purchased and held for resale. Tracks quantities and purchasing costs. Cost of goods sold posts at the time of invoicing. Cost of goods sold is calculated using the Average costing method. *(Note: QBP does not accommodate the LIFO and FIFO inventory costing methods.)*
Non-inventory Part	Used for job materials purchased but not tracked in inventory. Cost of goods sold posts when posting vendor bills or receipts for material purchases.
Service	Used for service labor costs provided by company employees or subcontractors. When provided by subcontractors, cost of goods sold posts when paying the contractor. When provided by employees, cost of goods sold posts when paying employees.
Sales Tax Item	Used to calculate sales tax for a single taxing agency.
Other Charge	Used for miscellaneous charges such as delivery and photocopying fees. Cost of goods sold posts when reimbursing the employee expense or paying a vendor.

Now look at the service and non-inventory part items used by Astor. Click **Item** on the toolbar to open the **Item List** illustrated in Figure 4:41. *(Note: You can also select **Lists>>Item List** on the main menu.)* Pay particular attention to the **Type** column.

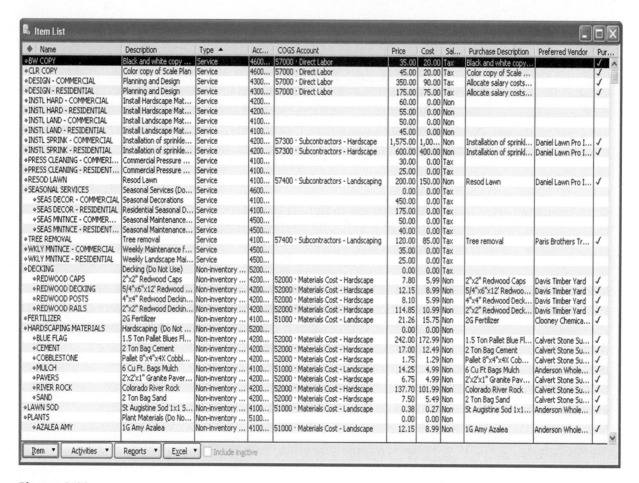

Figure 4:41

We will now review a few of these items.

Service Items

Click to select **SEAS MNTNCE - RESIDENTIAL** and then double click to open the item illustrated in Figure 4:42.

While reviewing this item refer back to the *Entering Sales Invoices* topic where you invoiced John Chester for 2 units of this item. Also refer back to the *Behind the Keys of a Posted Sales Invoice* topic where you traced entries made after posting John's invoice.

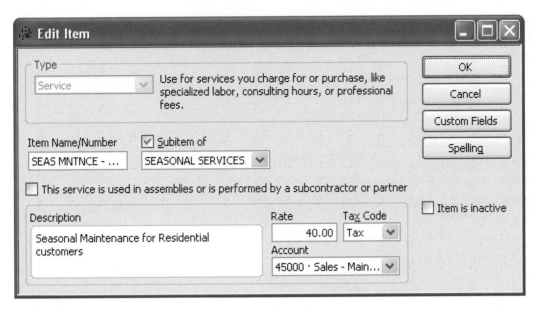

Figure 4:42

This item is for service labor costs provided by company employees. In addition, the item is a **Subitem of** SEASONAL SERVICES meaning it will be grouped with this category.

Rate is the fee charged customers for this service, explaining why John was invoiced $80.00 for 2 units.

Tax Code shows that these services are taxable. However, QBP also looks to the tax default assigned to the customer account before charging sales tax.

Account is the general ledger account used to post sales revenue for this item, explaining why John's invoice posted to 45000 Sales – Maintenance Services.

Notice that the item does not list a cost of goods sold or inventory general ledger account because services are not inventoried and cost of goods sold does not post at the time of sale. This explains why John's invoice posted only revenue entries.

Click **X** to close this item and then open **DESIGN-COMMERCIAL**. (See Figure 4:43.)

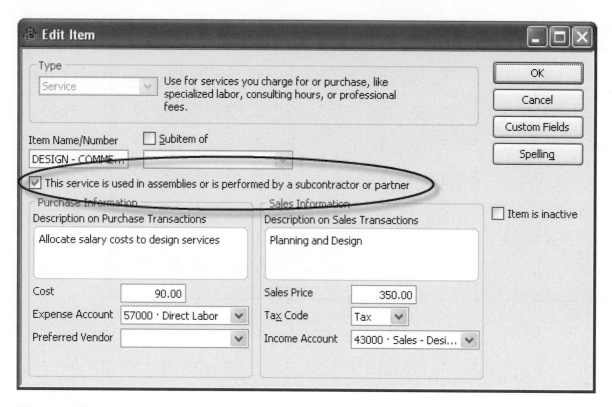

Figure 4:43

This is another labor service provided by employees. The item **Sales Price** is $350.00 and
sales are taxable. Sales revenue for this item will post to **Income Account** 43000-Sales
Design Services.

However, these services are provided by salaried employees so the option circled in Figure 4:43
is marked. This option opens fields for entering standard costs or vendor purchase costs. In
Chapter 5 you will use the $90.00 standard cost on this item to allocate salary expense for this
service to the cost of goods sold **Expense Account** 57000-Direct Labor.

Close this item and open **INSTL SPRINK – COMMERCIAL**. (See Figure 4:44.)

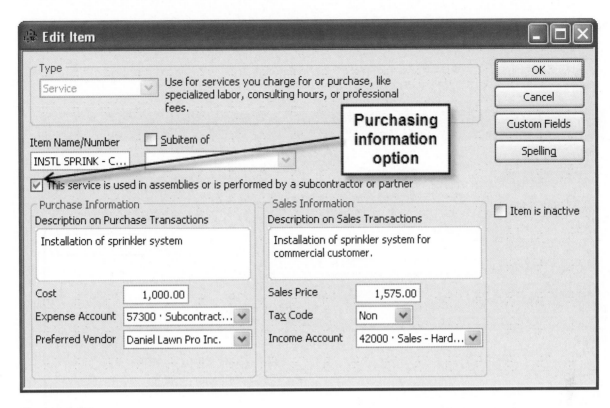

Figure 4:44

This is a subcontractor labor service item purchased from **Preferred Vendor**, Daniel Lawn Pro Inc. Thus, the option for entering purchasing information is selected and the cost of goods sold **Expense Accoun**t is entered. Cost of goods sold posts to "57300 Subcontractors - Hardscape" when recording a vendor bill for this item.

Charge Items

Close the preceding item and open **DELIVERY CHARGES**.

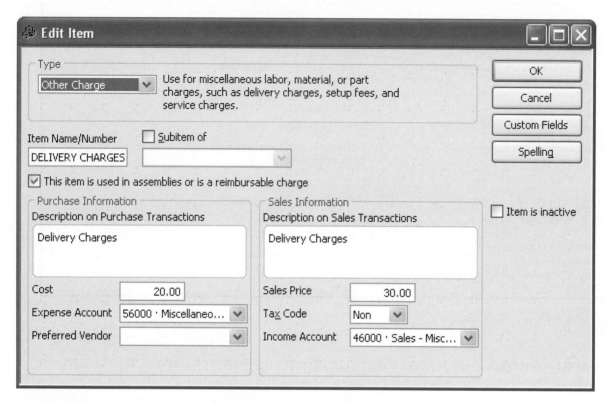

Figure 4:45

This charge item looks like the service item previously viewed; however, cost of goods sold for this item will post to an **Expense Account** when reimbursing employee expenses.

Non-inventory Part

Close the preceding item and open **REDWOOD CAPS.**

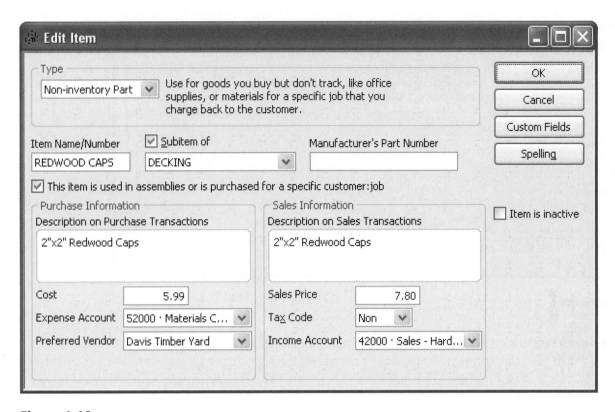

Figure 4:46

This is an item for job material purchases. Astor buys these caps from Davis Timber Yard, who charges $5.99 each. Astor then charges the customer $7.80 each.

Sales revenue for this item posts to 42000 Sales – Hardscape. Davis's bills and receipts for the item post to the costs of goods sold **Expense Account** 52000 Materials Cost – Hardscape.

Sales Tax Item

Close the preceding item and open **VA SALES TAX**.

Edit Item

Type			OK
Sales Tax Item ▾	Use to calculate a single sales tax at a specific rate that you pay to a single tax agency.		Cancel
			Spelling

Sales Tax Name

VA SALES TAX

☐ Item is inactive

Description

Sales Tax

Tax Rate (%)   Tax Agency (vendor that you collect for)

5.0%   VA Sales Tax Department ▾

Figure 4:47

This item sets 5 percent as the sales tax rate for taxable items.

Close this item and the Item List and then move on to invoicing customer jobs.

 # INVOICING CUSTOMER JOBS

Earlier in the chapter you created an invoice for John Chester before recording the costs associated with performing the service. However, service based businesses normally bill customers for the time and materials involved with the job. In other words, invoices are created by transferring job material and labor costs.

The drawback to invoicing job costs is that costs must be recorded before invoicing can occur. Thus, it is important to record accounting transactions in a timely manner so that invoicing can occur as soon as possible. The earlier a company invoices the customer the quicker the cash is collected.

Let's now look at the steps used to invoice job costs. On March 31, 2009, Astor invoiced Silver Homes for job costs incurred to date. Complete the steps that follow to prepare this invoice.

STEPS TO INVOICING JOBS

1. Open a new sales invoice using the Home page icon and select "Silver Homes" as the **Customer:Job**. QBP prompts that this invoice will exceed the customer's credit limit. Click **OK**. You now see how the customer credit limit interacts with sales invoicing.

2. QBP next prompts that the customer has billable job costs (Figure 4:48). Mark the first option and the preference option and click **OK**.

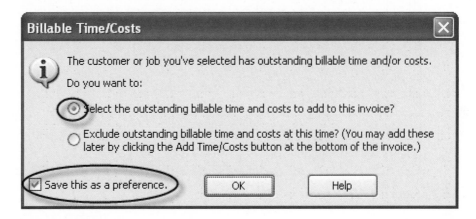

Figure 4:48

3. The Choose Billable Time and Costs window opens for you to select costs to invoice. Following Figure 4:49 is an explanation of the costs stored on each tab.

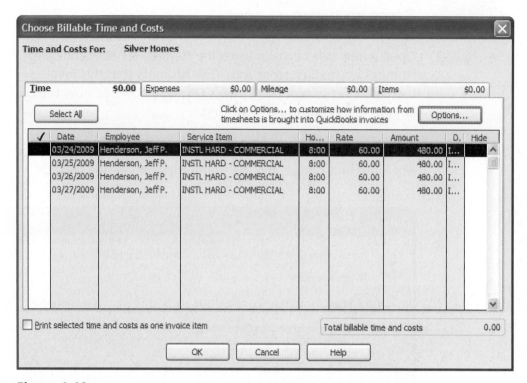

Figure 4:49

Time
Employee time ticket hours assigned to the customer's job.

Expenses
Employee reimbursable expense tickets assigned to the customer's job.

Mileage
Employee mileage charges assigned to the customer's job.

Items
Vendor materials and subcontract labor purchases assigned to the customer's job.

In Chapter 5 you will learn to assign vendor invoices to jobs. In Chapter 6 you will learn to assign employee time and expenses to jobs. For now, remember to check each tab to make sure that you select all costs to be invoiced.

4. Select the **Time** tab and click **Options**. Before transferring employee time, make sure that the **Combine** option illustrated in Figure 4:50 is selected so that hours will be combined for similar activities. Click **OK**.

Figure 4:50

5. Click **Select All** to mark all time for invoicing. *(Note: You can also click individual costs to select the item.)*

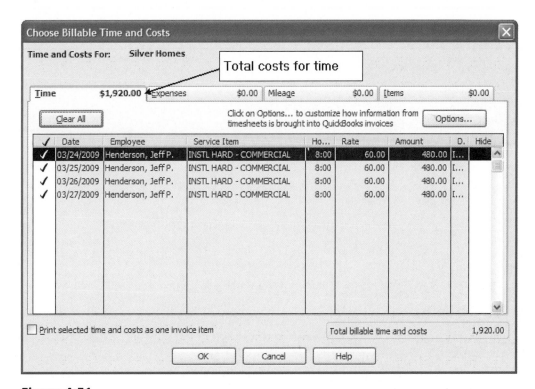

Figure 4:51

6. Select the **Items** tab and click **Select All**.

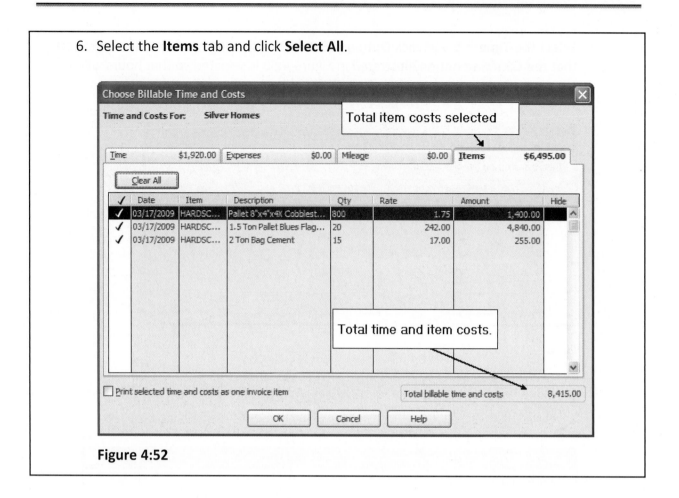

Figure 4:52

7. Click **OK**. Change the invoice date to 3/31/2009 and verify that the **Invoice #** is 1021. Figure 4:53 shows the completed invoice.

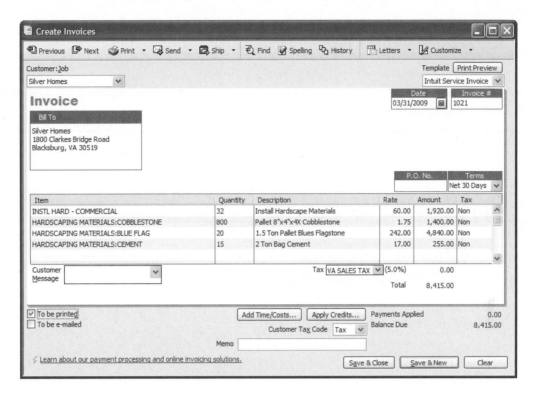

Figure 4:53

If you find a mistake on selecting billable costs then click **Add Time/Costs** to change your selections.

A word of caution: After saving this invoice, you cannot transfer these costs again, even if you delete the invoice. So make sure that the totals are correct before moving to the next step.

8. Print the invoice.

9. Click **Save & Close** and click **Yes** when the credit limit warning appears.

Let's spend a few minutes discussing the importance of invoice dates. QBP posts entries to the general ledger using the date on the invoice. This date is also called the posting date. It is important to use correct dates so that transactions post to the proper accounting period; otherwise, financial statements will be misstated. In addition, invoice dates affect due dates and due dates affect the number of days an invoice is outstanding, which then affects a customer's early payment discount period and credit history. **Always pay careful attention to dates when entering transactions in QBP.**

INVOICE A CUSTOMER FOR JOB COSTS

On March 27, 2009, Astor invoices DBH Enterprises for the 8 hours worked on March 23, 2009. Prepare and print this invoice using invoice number 1022.

JOB REPORTING

After reading this topic you will understand preparing and analyzing job cost reports. Follow the next instructions to prepare a job report.

STEPS TO USING JOB REPORTS

1. Select **Reports>>Report Center** on the main menu and choose the **Jobs, Time & Mileage** category. The Report Center provides a description for each job report (Figure 4:54).

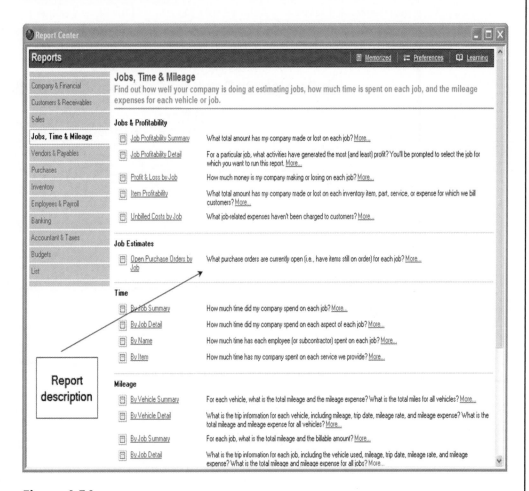

Figure 4:54

2. Click **Job Profitability Detail** and select **Fairbanks Construction** when
    prompted. Enter the date range of **From 1/1/2009** and **To 1/31/2009**.

    The report shows actual cost and actual revenue for this customer. You can
    double click on a number to open transactions behind it.

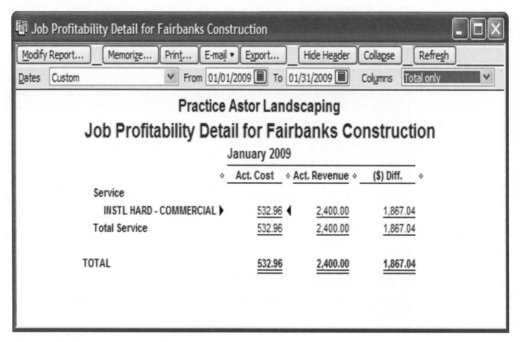

Figure 4:55

3. Click **Modify Report** and select the **Filters** tab. Under **Current Filter Choices**, highlight **Name** and use the dropdown list to the left of Current Filter Choices to select **O'Hara Homes Patios and Walk** job.

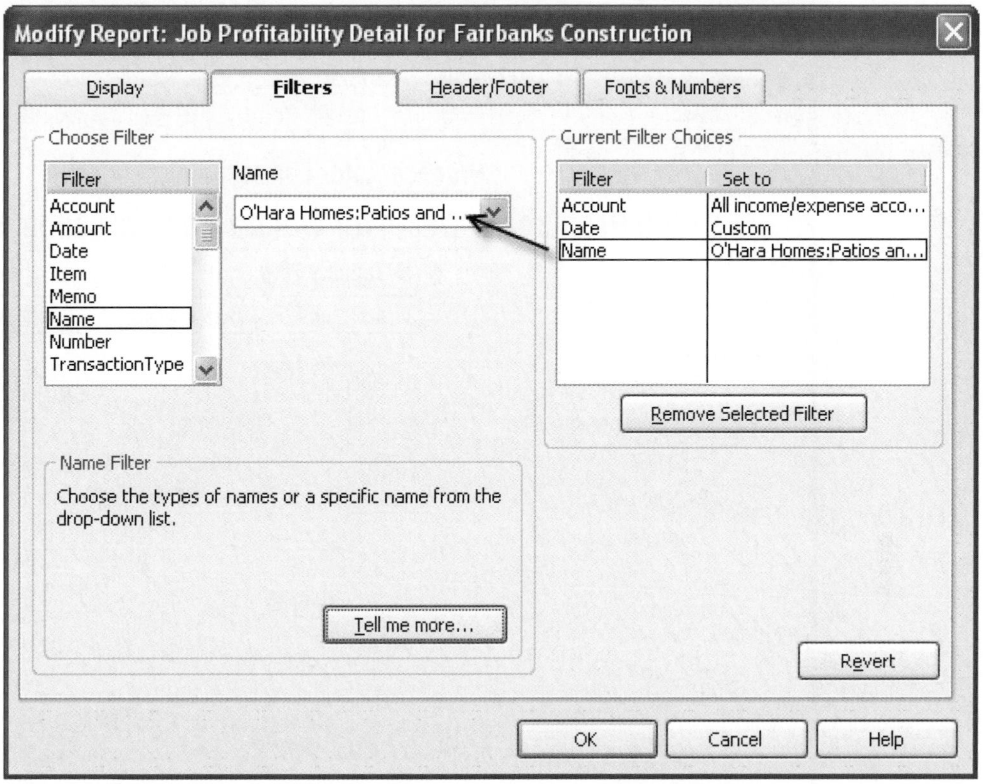

Figure 4:56

4. Click **OK** and the report redisplays as shown in Figure 4:57. Close the report without saving changes.

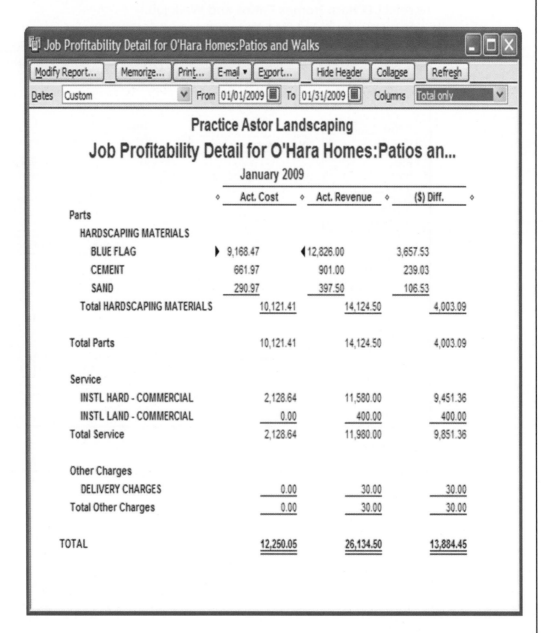

Figure 4:57

5. From the **Report Center** now open the **Unbilled Costs by Job** report. This report lists vendor bills that need to be invoiced to customers (Figure 4:58). Close the report.

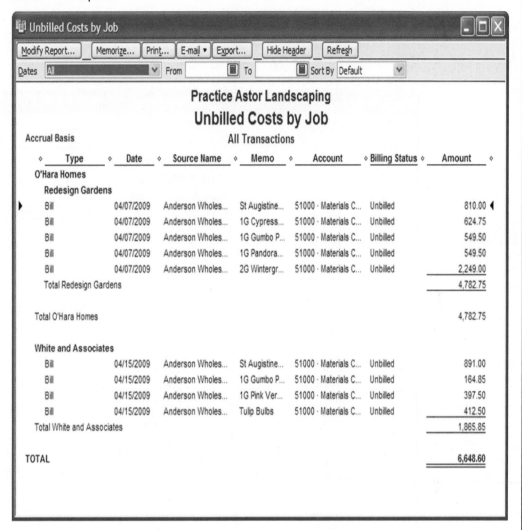

Figure 4:58

6. Click **Item Profitability** and enter the date range of **From 01/01/2009** and **To 03/31/2009**. Click **Modify Report** and use the **Display** tab to add the **% Difference** column. Click **OK**.

This report shows the profit made on each item. Close the report without saving changes.

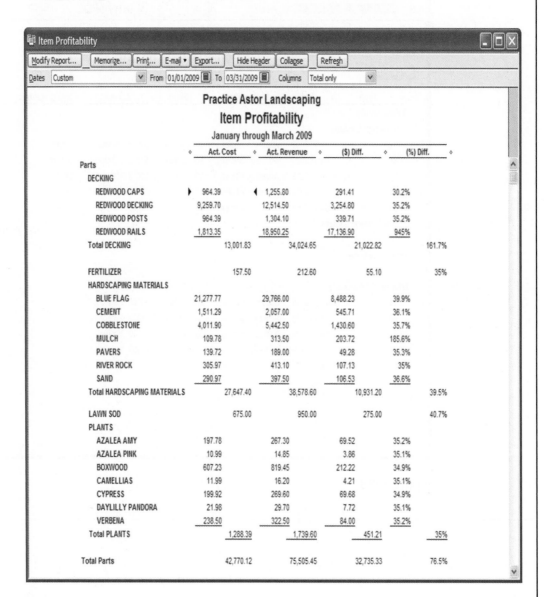

Figure 4:59

CREATE A JOB REPORT

Prepare the **Time** report named **Time by Job Summary**. Enter 3/1/2009 to 3/31/2009. Click **Modify Report** and use the **Display** tab to select **Unbilled** time.

Print the report and explain how you would use it.

CUSTOMER PAYMENTS

Company sales must be turned into cash before employees and vendors can be paid or the company can invest in the business. This topic focuses on processing customer payments.

On March 31, 2009, Robert Gibson remitted check number 1786 for $9,768.75 paying Invoice 965 in full. Follow the next steps to record this payment.

STEPS TO PROCESS CUSTOMER PAYMENTS

1. On the **Home** page, click **Receive Payments**. *(Note: Click No Thanks if QBP prompts on integrated payment processing.)* In **Received From**, select Gibson, Robert and then click the unpaid invoice listed at the bottom. You will receive a message that is explained in the next step.

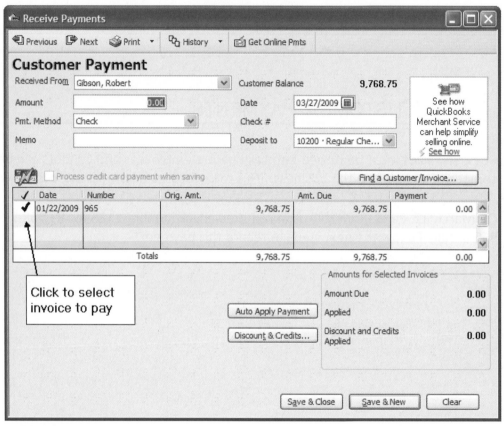

Figure 4:60

2. Because you did not enter an Amount first, QBP prompts to tell you that it can calculate the amount based on invoices selected. Mark the option to turn off future messages and click **Yes** (Figure 4:61).

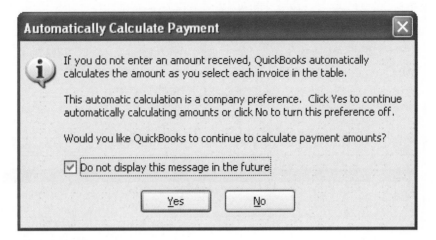

Automatically Calculate Payment

If you do not enter an amount received, QuickBooks automatically calculates the amount as you select each invoice in the table.

This automatic calculation is a company preference. Click Yes to continue automatically calculating amounts or click No to turn this preference off.

Would you like QuickBooks to continue to calculate payment amounts?

☑ Do not display this message in the future

[Yes]   [No]

Figure 4:61

3. Change the **Date** to "3/31/2009" and enter "1786" as the **Check #**.

4. The completed entry is shown in Figure 4:62.

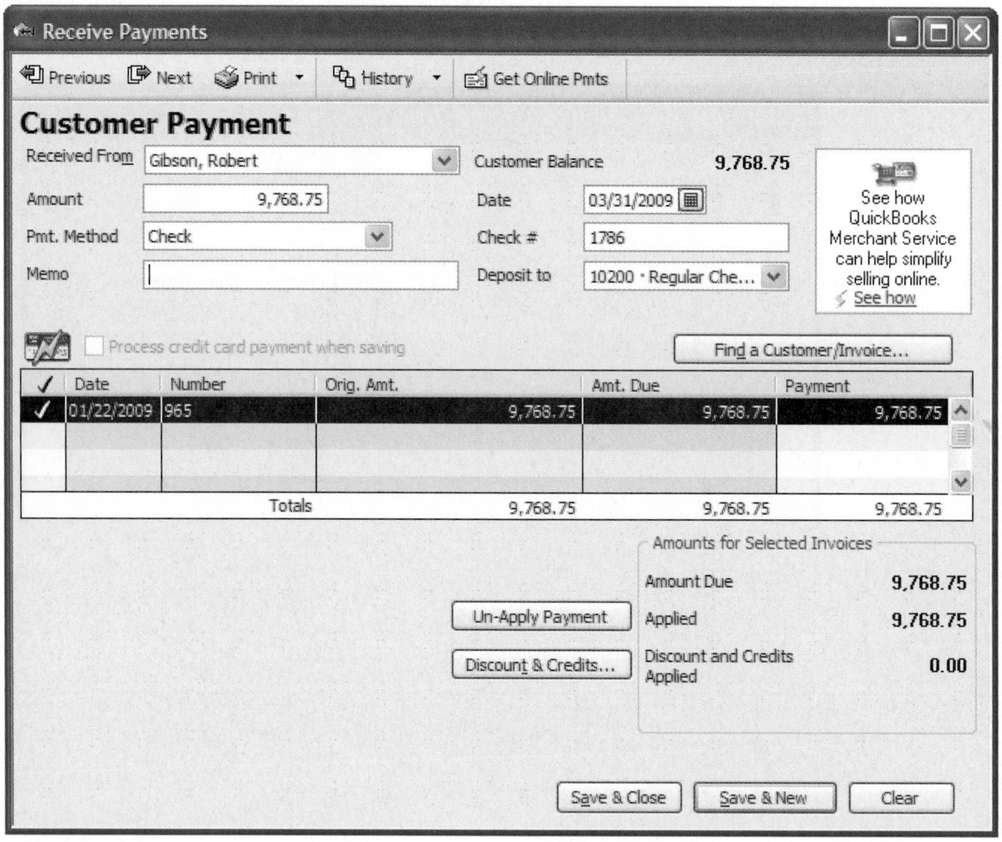

Figure 4:62

Notice that the payment will post (i.e., debit) to **10200 Regular Checking** account. Also the **Pmt Method** has defaulted to **Check**.

If needed, the **Un-Apply Payment** button at the bottom is a quick way to clear selected invoices. You can also click an invoice to clear its selection.

5. Click **Save & Close** to post the payment.

BEHIND THE KEYS OF A POSTED CUSTOMER PAYMENT

Now that you have posted a customer payment, trace the audit trail for the transaction. Recall that in the *MAPS* topic at the beginning of the chapter we explained that a customer's payment is recorded on the Cash Receipts Journal and then posted to the customer's account and general ledger accounts.

So let's begin by opening the Cash Receipts Journal. On the main menu, select **Reports>> Memorized Reports>>Accounting Journals>>Cash Receipts Journal**. Enter the date range of **From** 3/31/2009 and **To** 3/31/2009. The refreshed report is shown in Figure 4:63.

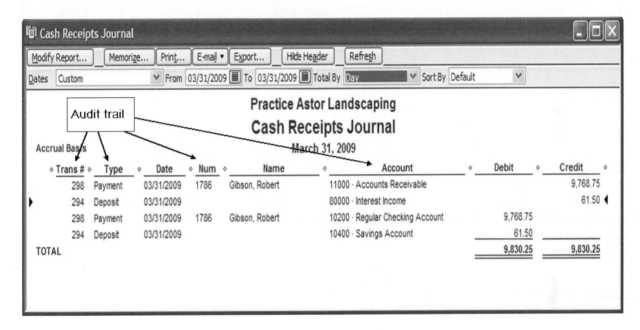

Figure 4:63

The report displays customer payments and other bank deposits. Note the **Trans #** and **Type** for Robert's payment.

Close this report, discarding changes. On the main menu, select **Reports>>Customers & Receivables>>Transaction List by Customer**.

Enter the date range of **From** 3/31/2009 and **To** 3/31/2009. Click **Modify Report** and select **Trans #** under **Columns**. Click **OK**.

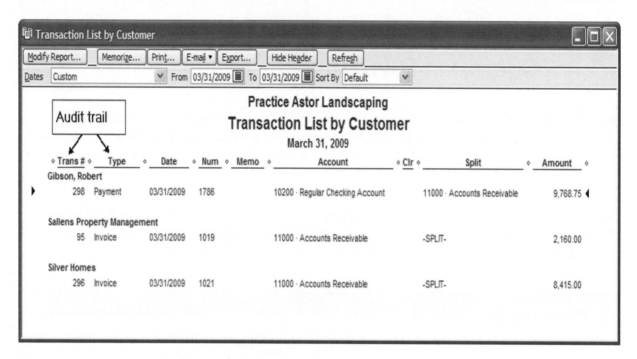

Figure 4:64

Figure 4:64 illustrates the report. Scroll down and locate Robert Gibson's payment. The entry shows the same **Trans #** and **Type** as displayed on the Cash Receipts Journal.

Close this report and complete tracing entries by opening the memorized report named **General Ledger Detail Report**. Locate your entries made to general ledger accounts 10200 Regular Checking and 11000 Accounts Receivable (not illustrated).

CUSTOMER PAYMENTS WITH A DISCOUNT AND SALES RECEIPTS

In this topic, you continue posting customer payments, but this time the customer is paying within the discount period. You will also learn to record customer payments at the time of sale.

On March 31, 2009, Sycamore Homes remitted check number 9832 for $21,389.48 paying Invoice 1012. Record this transaction.

STEPS TO PROCESS CUSTOMER PAYMENT WITH A DISCOUNT

1. On the **Home** page, click **Receive Payments** and select **Sycamore Homes**. Change the **Date** to "3/31/09" and enter "9832" as the **Check #**.

2. Enter "21,389.48" in **Amount** and then select Invoice 1012. Notice that Figure 4:65 shows an underpayment of $436.52 on the invoice.

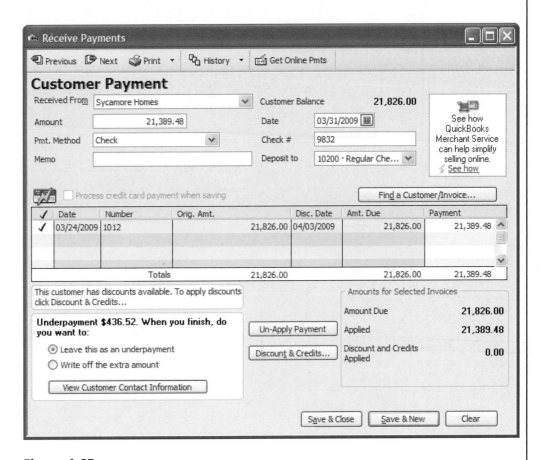

Figure 4:65

3. Click the **Discount and Credits** button to open the window illustrated in Figure 4:66. You see that the invoicing being paid carries the payment terms of 2% 10 Net 30. Select the **Discount Account** shown and click **Done**.

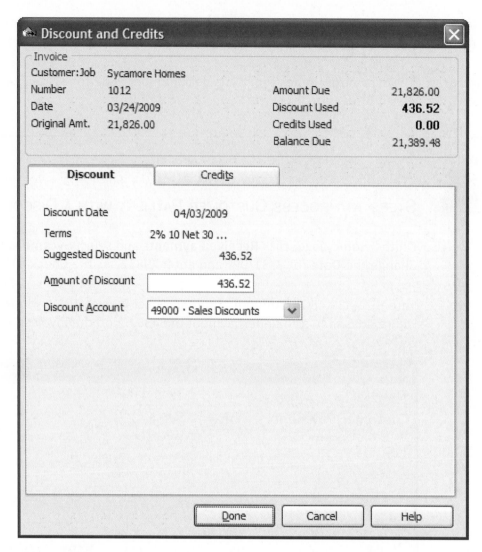

Figure 4:66

4. The completed entry is shown in Figure 4:67. Click **Save & Close**.

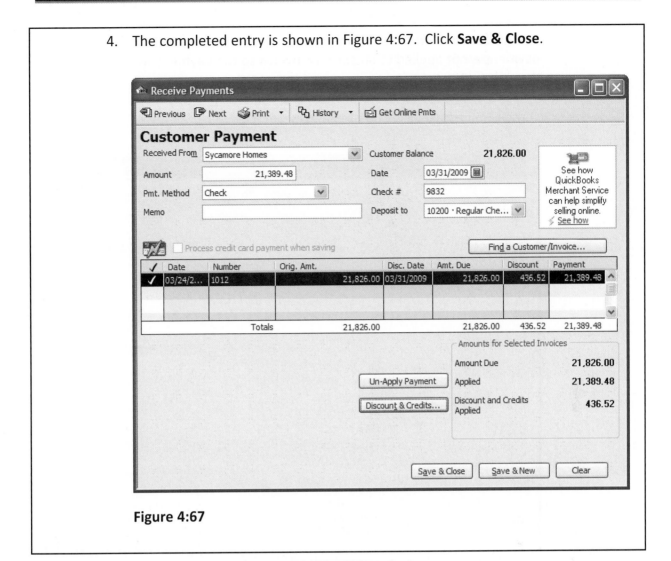

Figure 4:67

5. You will now record a miscellaneous cash sale to Elkorn Apartments. This payment is not applied to an existing invoice so the payment will be recorded through a different window.

On the **Home** page, click **Create Sales Receipts**.

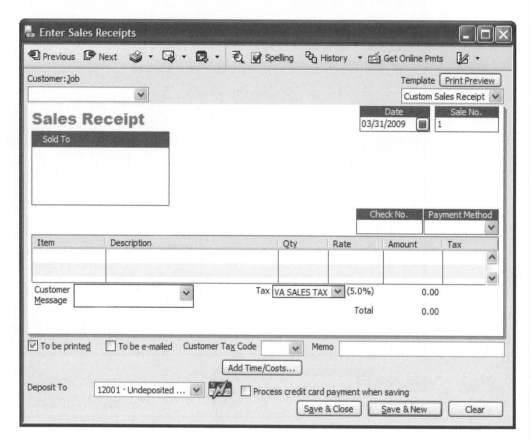

Figure 4:68

6. Select **Elkhorn Apartments** as the customer and enter the **Date** of "3/31/2009" and **Check No.** of "736".

7. Place your cursor in the **Item** field and enter "MISC SALES" in the space provided. Press Tab and QBP prompts to create the item. Click **Yes**.

Complete the item window as illustrated in Figure 4:69. You will not enter a Rate because this item will be used to record miscellaneous sales and the rate varies. Click **OK**.

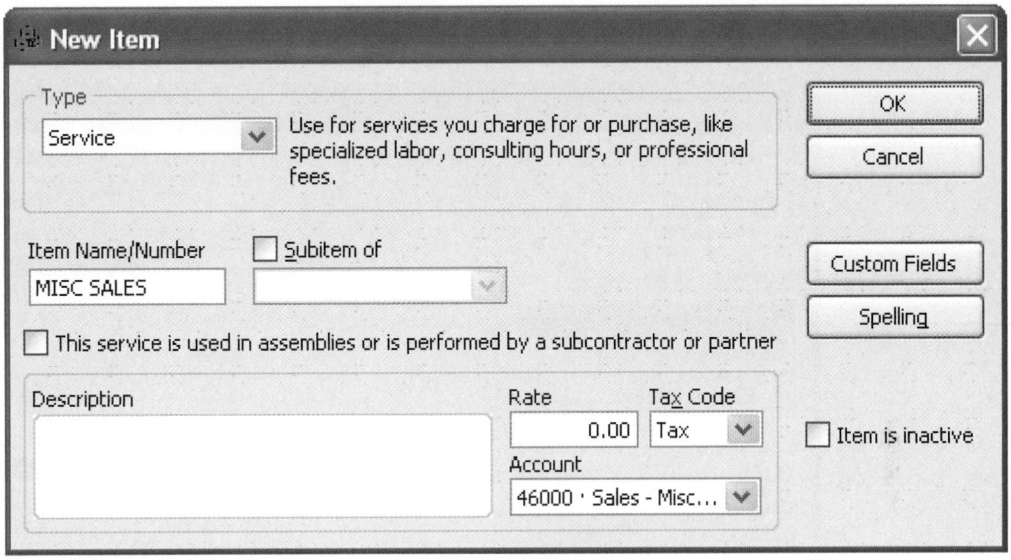

Figure 4:69

8. Return to the Enter Sales Receipts window and enter "Spot treatment for rose disease" as the **Description**. Enter "1" as the **Qty** and 150.00 as the **Rate**. Change the **Deposit To** field to "10200 Regular Checking".

The completed entry is shown in Figure 4:70. This entry will appear in the Cash Receipts Journal as a $157.50 debit to 10200 Regular Checking, a $150.00 credit to 46000 Sales Miscellaneous, and a $7.50 credit to 2200 Sales Tax Payable.

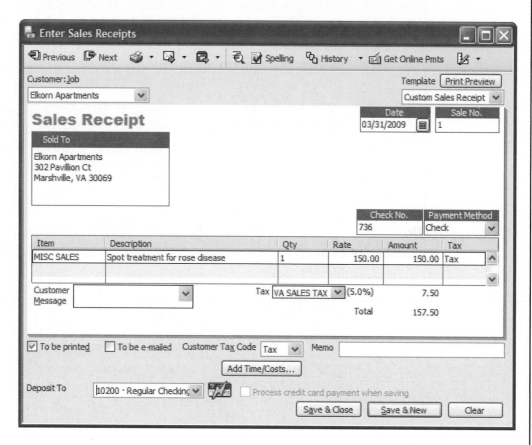

Figure 4:70

9. Click **Save & Close**.

CORRECTING CUSTOMER PAYMENTS

QBP permits editing and deleting customer payments and the next steps show how to correct a customer payment.

1. Using the Customer Center, locate the payment on the customer's account.

2. Double click the payment to reopen.

3. Edit the payment and then click Save & Close to post the changes.

To delete, you would follow steps 1 and 2 and then select **Edit>>Delete Payment** on the main menu. However, you should be careful when deleting payments after reconciling the bank statement. See Appendix B for an explanation on the effect of deleting deposits after reconciling bank statements.

RECORD CUSTOMER PAYMENTS

On March 28, 2009, the following customer payments were received. Post the payments.

Ashford Hill Apartments, check number 78565 for $1,764.00 paying Invoices 985 and 991.

O'Hara Homes check number 1092 for $1,000.00 paying Invoice 993. The customer is not paying the invoice in full so leave the remaining balance as an underpayment.

Print the Cash Receipts Journal filtering the report for the date range of 03/28/2009.

CUSTOMER CREDITS

Occasionally Astor may need to issue a credit against a customer invoice. In the exercise that follows, Astor is issuing a credit to O'Hara Homes for three hours of labor billed on Invoice 1008.

STEPS TO ENTER A CUSTOMER CREDIT MEMO

1. On the **Home** page, click **Refunds & Credits**.

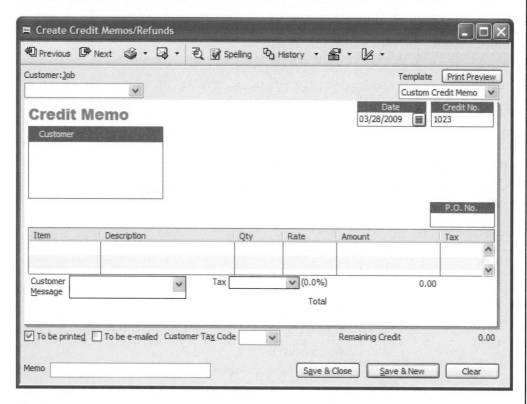

Figure 4:71

2. Select **O'Hara Homes:Redesign Gardens** job and enter "3/28/2009" as the **Date**.

3. In **Item**, select INSTL LAND - COMMERCIAL and enter "3" as the **QTY**. Press Tab and the completed credit is shown in Figure 4:72.

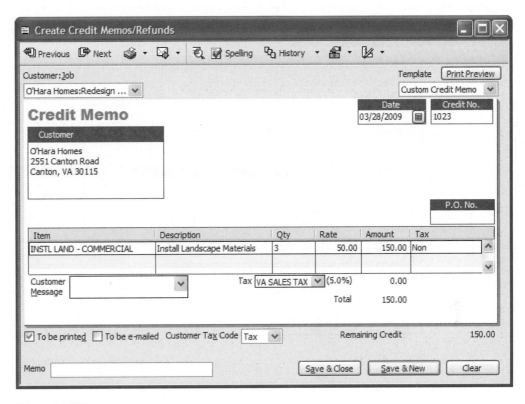

Figure 4:72

4. Click **Save & Close** and QBP prompts to apply the refund to the outstanding invoice. Select the option shown in Figure 4:73 and click **OK**.

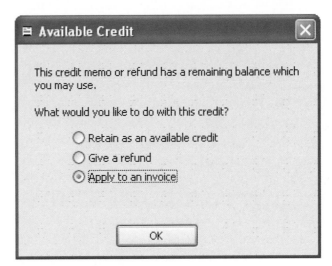

Figure 4:73

5. As shown in Figure 4:74, click **Invoice 993** to deselect it and then click **Invoice 1008** to select it. Click **Done**.

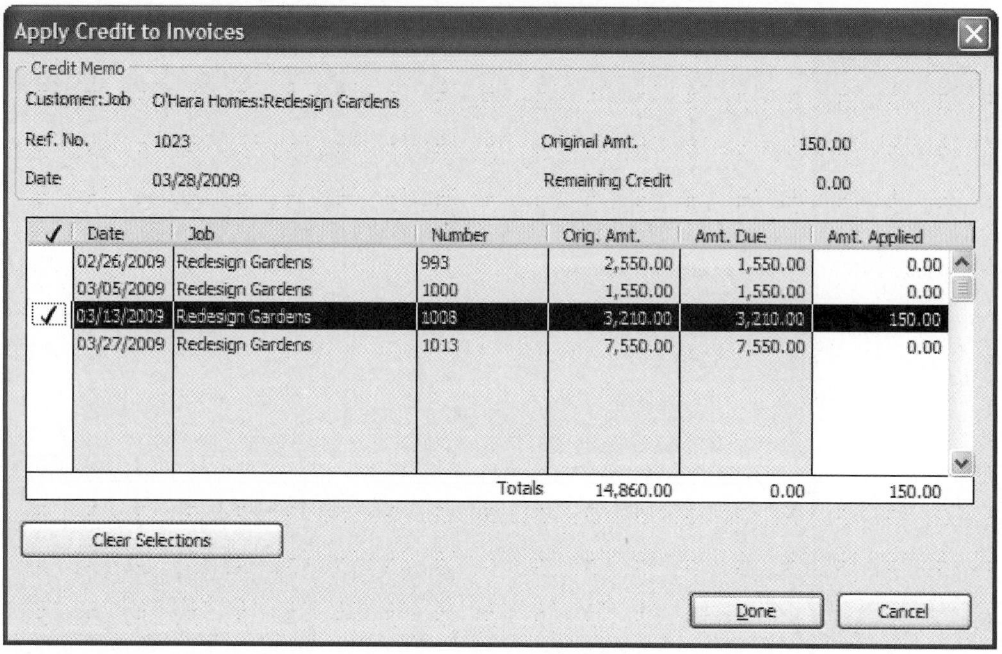

Figure 4:74

CUSTOMER REPORTING AND RECONCILING ACTIVITIES

QBP offers a variety of customer reports and these reports can be viewed from the **Report Center**. Open this center and select the **Customers & Receivables** area.

Click **Summary** in the **A/R Aging** category to open the accounts receivable aging report. Change the date to "3/31/2009". Refresh and the report displays as illustrated in Figure 4:75.

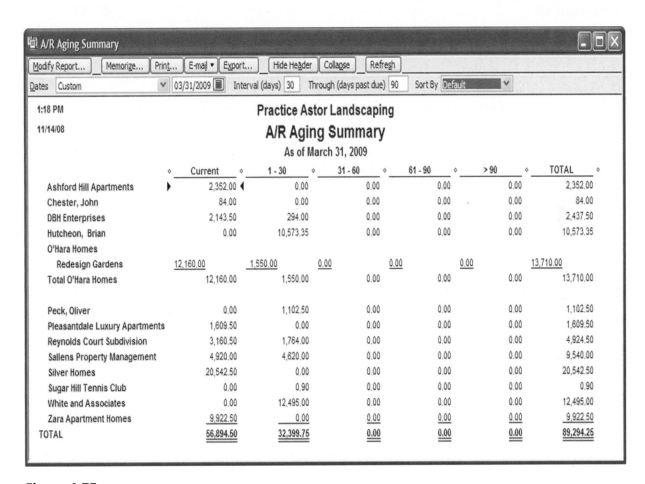

Figure 4:75

This report lists customer outstanding balances by age of the balance. *(Note: Your balances will differ from those illustrated if you have not completed all chapter exercises.)*

The report serves two important purposes. First, Astor uses it to monitor customer payments and manage company cash flow, thus, mitigating the risk of future sales to customers failing to pay.

Second, this report is used to reconcile customer activities with the accounts receivable control account. This task is performed by comparing the report's total amount due with the March ending balance in general ledger account 11000 Accounts Receivable. Close this report.

Now view the balance in accounts receivable. Open the **Trial Balance** report from the **Accountant & Taxes** category in the **Report Center** and filter the report for 3/31/2009 (not illustrated). Scroll down and locate the balance in 11000 Accounts Receivable. The total on the A/R Aging report and the balance in Accounts Receivable on the Trial Balance must agree to verify proper recording of customer activities.

These balances can become out of balance when you improperly correct customer transactions. Therefore, always correct customer transactions by referring to the instructions in Appendix B.

You should reconcile the aged receivables report to the accounts receivable balance at the end of every month and prior to issuing financial reports. Close this report.

Return to the **A/R Aging** category to open the **Detail A/R Aging** report (not illustrated). This report lists invoices by invoice age.

Enter "3/31/2009" as the date. Scroll down to Sugar Hill Tennis Club Invoice 989. This customer has an outstanding balance of $.90 on the invoice. Close the report and the Report Center. You will write off this balance in the next topic.

WRITE OFF A CUSTOMER INVOICE

You will find that customers do not always pay. Furthermore, like Sugar Hill Tennis Club, customers sometimes pay the wrong amount. Instead of calling a payment error to the customer's attention, Astor has decided to write off the invoice balance.

The instructions that follow write off an invoice after posting the payment. The instructions in Chapter 8 illustrate writing off the balance while recording the payment.

STEPS TO WRITE OFF A CUSTOMER'S INVOICE

1. On the **Home** page, click **Receive Payments**. Complete the window as illustrated in Figure 4:76.

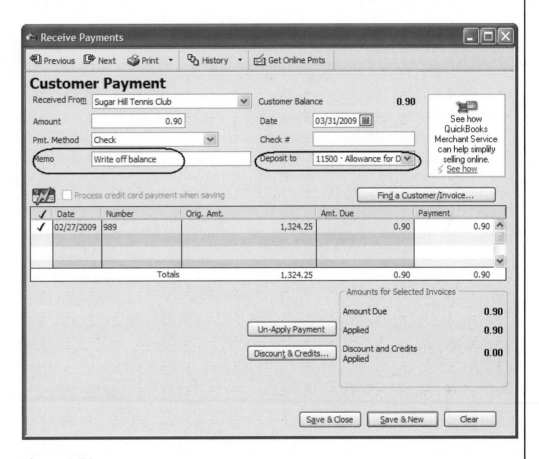

Figure 4:76

Notice that the **Deposit to** account has been changed to 11500 Allowance for Doubtful Accounts. When a company uses the allowance method of accounting for bad debts, bad debt expense is recognized when adjusting the allowance estimate. Actual bad debts are then written off to the estimated allowance.

2. Click **Save & Close**.

CUSTOMER STATEMENTS

Astor mails customer statements once a month. These statements list invoice and payment activity and prompt customers to pay.

Click **Statements** on the **Home** page to open the window illustrated in Figure 4:77. Enter the date and options as illustrated.

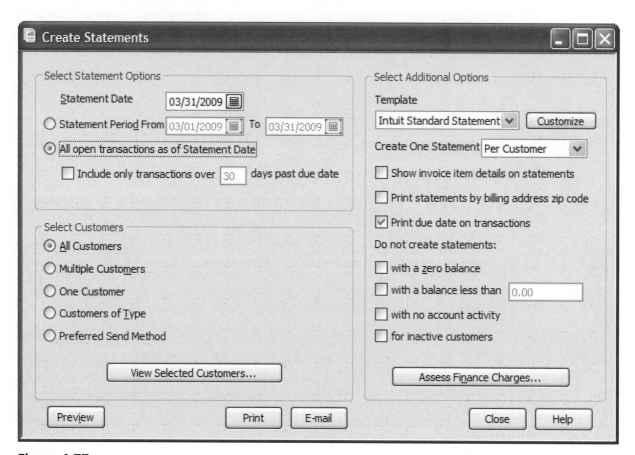

Figure 4:77

Click **Preview** and the first statement is shown in Figure 4:78.

Statement

Practice Astor Landscaping
1505 Pavilion Place, Suite C
Arlington, VA 30093

Date
03/31/2009

To:
Ashford Hill Apartments
3466 Ashford Hill
Danbury, VA 30097

Amount Due	Amount Enc.
$2,352.00	

Date	Transaction	Amount	Balance
03/06/2009	INV #1002. Due 04/05/2009. Orig. Amount $588.00.	588.00	588.00
03/12/2009	INV #1005. Due 04/11/2009. Orig. Amount $882.00.	882.00	1,470.00
03/27/2009	INV #1014. Due 04/26/2009. Orig. Amount $882.00.	882.00	2,352.00

CURRENT	1-30 DAYS PAST DUE	31-60 DAYS PAST DUE	61-90 DAYS PAST DUE	OVER 90 DAYS PAST DUE	Amount Due
2,352.00	0.00	0.00	0.00	0.00	$2,352.00

Figure 4:78

The window indicates that 12 statements will print. Click **Print** and, when prompted to verify that statements printed correctly, click **Yes**.

When QBP prompts to remind you that statements can also be emailed, check the option to turn off future messages and click **OK**.

Click **Close** to exit the window.

You have now completed the chapter. *Make a backup of the Practice Astor Landscaping data file to a backup file named "Practice Astor Landscaping Chpt 4". In the next chapter, you will build on the work completed in this chapter.*

SUMMARY

In this chapter, you learned *MAPS* for posting customer transactions before recording transactions in QBP. By understanding manual entries, you were able to anticipate QBP's *Behind the Keys* postings. Understanding a transaction's effect on financial accounts is critical to posting transactions correctly and to tracing the audit trail of a posted transaction.

After completing this chapter, you are skilled in recording customer invoices, payments, and credit memos for a service based business. You can manage the master accounts linked to transactions (i.e., customer accounts, jobs and service, and non-inventory items). You understand job reporting as well as other reports that let you monitor and document customer activities. With firm knowledge on processing customer activities, you are now ready to take on Astor's vendor activities in the next chapter.

END-OF-CHAPTER QUESTIONS

TRUE/FALSE

_____ 1. The audit trail lets accountants trace entries from the original entry to the general ledger.

_____ 2. Like the manual system, QBP's Sales Journal report will list the general ledger accounts affected by sales transactions.

_____ 3. You can create a sales invoice by entering items or by transferring job costs.

_____ 4. You can customize columns on the Item List using the Item button.

_____ 5. You can create a customer account "on the fly" while entering a sales invoice.

_____ 6. You should reconcile the aged receivables report with the accounts receivable account monthly and before issuing financial statements.

_____ 7. QBP will let you email sales invoices.

_____ 8. You can delete a customer account that has transaction history.

_____ 9. The Item List can be exported to Excel.

_____ 10. You can make corrections to a posted customer payment.

MULTIPLE CHOICE

_____ 1. The _____ will tell you the balance on a customer account.
  a. Customer Center
  b. Customer Balance Summary report
  c. Collections report
  d. All of the above

_____ 2. The _____ report will document individual postings to the accounts receivable account.
  a. General Ledger Detail Trial Balance
  b. Transactions Detail by Account
  c. General Ledger
  d. All of the above

_____ 3. The _____ item type will record cost of goods sold at the time of sale.
      a. Service
      b. Inventory Part
      c. Non-inventory Part
      d. All of the above

_____ 4. Use the _____ icon when recording a customer's payment on an invoice.
      a. Receive Payments
      b. Create Sales Receipts
      c. Both a and b
      d. None of the above

_____ 5. An accounts receivable aging report _____.
      a. monitors the age of customer invoices
      b. reconciles customer activities with the general ledger
      c. manages cash flow
      d. all of the above

_____ 6. Customer statements may be printed using the _____.
      a. Home page
      b. Customers menu
      c. Both a and b
      d. None of the above

_____ 7. When Astor sells Fertilizer, QBP will post revenue to the general ledger account
      _____.
      a. entered in the sales invoice window
      b. stored on the item
      c. Both a and b
      d. None of the above

PRACTICE SET

In this practice set, you will be using the **Graded Astor Landscaping** company file customized with your initials at the end of Chapter 1. *If the company file is not loaded on your computer then restore it using the Graded Astor Landscaping Chpt 1.QBB backup file created in the Practice Set at the end of Chapter 1.*

1.   Open **Graded Astor Landscaping** and enter Astor's April customer activities that follow.

When transferring job costs to an invoice use the **Options** button to select *"Combine activities with the same service items."*

Unless instructed otherwise, do not change the default tax code.

Transactions and reports are printed in Step 2, so make sure that invoices are marked *"To be printed."*

<u>2009</u>

Apr 2   Received check number 1087 for $21,389.48 from Sycamore Homes paying Invoice 1012 within the discount period. Discount is posted to 49000 Sales Discounts.

(Note: If you selected the invoice before entering the payment amount, then click Yes and select the option to turn off future messages.)

Apr 3   Create Invoice 1021 to O'Hara Homes for Redesign Gardens job for $5,600.00. Transfer 96 hours from time tickets dated March 23 to March 30, 2009.

Apr 7   Create the following invoices.

Invoice 1022 to Reynolds Court Subdivision for $1,120.00 plus tax. Transfer 32 hours from time tickets dated March 24 to March 27, 2009.

Invoice 1023 to White and Associates for $1,440.00. Transfer 24 hours from time tickets dated March 25 to March 27, 2009. Click **Yes** to exceed the customer's credit limit.

Apr 9   Received the following checks.

Check number 763 for $4,100.00 from O'Hara Homes paying Invoices 993 and 1000.

Check number 3253 for $4,620.00 from Sallens Property Management paying Invoice 994.

Apr 10   Received check number 7577 for $3,234.00 from Ashford Hill Apartments paying Invoices 985, 991, 1002, and 1005.

Apr 17   Prepare the following invoices.

Invoice 1024 to Ashford Hill Apartments for $1,960.00 plus tax. Transfer 56 hours from all time tickets on file.

Invoice 1025 to DBH Enterprises for $1,680.00 plus tax. Transfer 48 hours from all time tickets on file.

Invoice 1026 to Reynolds Court Subdivision for $1,120.00 plus tax. Transfer 32 hours from all time tickets on file. Click OK to exceed the customer's credit limit.

Apr 23   Received the following checks:

Check number 23463 for $1,261.50 from DBH Enterprises paying Invoices 995, 1001, 1007, and 1011.

Check number 67825 for $10,573.35 from Brian Hutcheon paying Invoice 1006.

Check number 7345 for $10,760.00 from O'Hara Homes paying Invoices 1008 and 1013.

Apr 24   Prepare the following invoices.

Invoice 1027 to O'Hara Homes for Redesign Gardens job for $9,702.50. Transfer 64 hours from all remaining time tickets on file and transfer all item costs. If the spell check window opens, click Ignore All.

Invoice 1028 to Sugar Hill Tennis Club for $560.00 plus tax. Transfer 16 hours from all time tickets on file.

Apr 28   Received the following checks:

                Check number 9099 for $7,276.50 from Reynolds Court Subdivision paying all
                invoices on account.

                Check number 7350 for $15,108.45 from O'Hara Homes paying Invoices 1021
                and 1027 with a discount.

                Create the following customer.
                    Jordan Industries
                    575 N. Main Street
                    Arlington, VA 30022
                    (701) 555-8723
                    Contact: April Raines
                    Customer Type: Commercial
                    Payment Terms: Net 30
                    Tax Code: Tax
                    Credit Limit: $10,000

                Create the following new job for the customer.
                    Description is New deck
                    Status is Awarded
                    Start 5/1/2009 and Projected End 5/15/2009
                    Job Type is Construction

                Post the down payment deposited on the job to Regular Checking. *(Use Create
                Sales Receipts and **print receipt** after entering.)*
                    Check number: 725
                    Item: INSTL HARD - COMMERCIAL
                    Qty: 25
                    Amount: $1,500.00

2. Print the following.

    a. Invoices 1021 through 1028. You can print by using **File>>Print Forms>>Invoices** on the main menu. If you do not have eight invoices totaling $23,504.50 then verify that all invoices are marked *To be printed.*

    b. Cash Receipts Journal for April 1 to April 30, 2009.

    c. Sales Journal for April 1 to April 30, 2009.

    d. Job Profitability Summary for January 1 to April 30, 2009.

    e. A/R Aging Detail report at April 30, 2009.

    f. Customer statement dated April 30, 2009 for DBH Enterprises showing all open transactions. *(Note: Use the One Customer option under Select Customers.)*

3. ***Back up the Graded Astor Landscaping data file to a backup file named "Graded Astor Landscaping Chpt 4". The Practice Set for the next chapter will build on the work completed in this chapter.***

CHAPTER 5   VENDOR ACTIVITIES FOR A SERVICE BASED BUSINESS

LEARNING OBJECTIVES

This chapter works with the Practice Astor Landscaping data file containing the tasks completed in Chapter 4. *If this company is not loaded on your computer then restore it using the Practice Astor Landscaping Chpt 4.QBB backup file created after reading Chapter 4.*

In this chapter you process Astor's vendor activities. Such activities include placing orders for goods and services, entering vendor bills for goods and services, and remitting vendor payments. While learning to perform these activities, you will do the following:

1. Review the *MAPS* for recording vendor transactions before posting transactions in QBP
2. Learn to use the Vendor Center to manage vendor activities
3. Record vendor purchase orders and assign purchases to jobs
4. Learn to correct purchase order transactions
5. Record vendor bills and receipts for items on purchase orders
6. Go *Behind the Keys* to view posted bills and receipts and learn to correct these transactions
7. Record vendor bills for previously posted receipts
8. Learn to manage vendor accounts
9. Record vendor bills for expenses and memorize vendor bills
10. Pay vendors
11. Go *Behind the Keys* to view vendor payments and learn to correct these transactions
12. Learn to write checks without recording a vendor bill
13. Pay sales tax and enter vendor credits
14. Prepare and analyze vendor reports
15. Reconcile vendor activities to the general ledger

Launch QBP and open **Practice Astor Landscaping**.

MANUAL ACCOUNTING PROCEDURES

As in the previous chapter, you begin by learning the manual accounting procedures *(MAPS)* for posting vendor activities before posting transactions in QBP. These procedures help you to understand QBP transaction posting.

Before continuing it helps to explain that Astor sometimes uses a purchase order (PO) to order job materials. POs authorize purchases and document quantities ordered and vendor prices. An Astor employee with authorization to order materials creates and signs the PO before sending it to the vendor. Thereafter, an employee either picks up the materials at the vendor's location or the vendor delivers the materials to a job site.

The vendor's bill is normally included with the materials. This bill is then forwarded to the accounting department. Before recording the bill, the accountant matches it with the PO. This matching process verifies that the purchase was authorized and confirms that billed quantities and prices equal PO terms.

On March 20, 2009, Seth Ruland issues a PO for materials to be used on John Chester's job created in Chapter 4. He manually prepares the document, signs it, and then faxes it to Clooney Chemical Supply. A copy of the PO is sent to Judy in accounting, who files the document for matching with the vendor bill. POs do not trigger accounting recognition because the liability does not occur until receipt of the materials.

On March 24, 2009, Jeff Henderson picks up the materials with the vendor bill. At the end of the day, the bill is dropped off to Judy in accounting. Judy matches the PO with the bill illustrated in Figure 5:1.

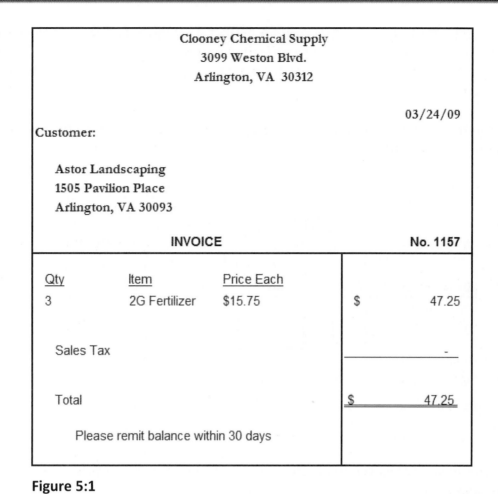

Figure 5:1

Judy then records the transaction on the March 24 Purchases Journal illustrated in Figure 5:2.

Astor Landscaping						
Date: 3/24/2009			Purchases Journal			Page 5
Vendor	Post Ref	Description	Accounts Payable (Credit)	Materials Cost Landscape (Debit)	Office Supplies Expense (Debit)	Utilities Expense (Debit)
Clooney Chemical	CLOO001	Maintenance Job INV 1157	47.25	47.25		
Georgia Gas Co.	GEOR002	March Utilities	143.17			143.17
Office Maxters	OFFI001	Office Supplies INV 7631	237.25		237.25	
Totals:			$ 427.67	$ 47.25	$ 237.25	$ 143.17
Acct Ref:			(20000)	(51000)	(63000)	(71100)

Audit Trail

Figure 5:2

Like the procedures used to enter transactions in the Sales Journal in Chapter 4, Judy totals journal columns and cross-foots totals to verify that entries balance (i.e., debits equal credits). Judy then posts each invoice to the vendor's account and posts column totals to the general ledger accounts listed at the bottom.

Judy's entry to Clooney's account is illustrated in Figure 5:3. *(Note: Entries for other vendor accounts are not illustrated.)*

Clooney Chemical Supply 3099 Weston Blvd. *Audit Trail* Arlington, Va 30312				Acct No: CLOO001	
Date	Description	Post Ref	Debit	Credit	Balance
03/01/09	Beginning Balance				0.00
03/24/09	John Chester Maintenance Job INV 1157	PJ 5		47.25	47.25

Figure 5:3

Judy's entries to general ledger accounts are illustrated in Figure 5:4. *(Note: The entry for utilities is not shown.)*

General Ledger

Accounts Payable   Account No. 20000

Date	Description	Post Ref	Debit	Credit	Balance
03/23/09	Balance Forward				18,158.82
03/24/09		PJ 5		427.67	18,586.49

Audit Trail

General Ledger

Materials Cost - Landscape   Account No. 51000

Date	Description	Post Ref	Debit	Credit	Balance
03/23/09	Balance Forward				1,250.12
03/24/09		PJ 5	47.25		1,297.37

Audit Trail

General Ledger

Office Supplies Expense   Account No. 63000

Date	Description	Post Ref	Debit	Credit	Balance
03/23/09	Balance Forward				253.40
03/24/09		PJ 5	237.25		490.65

Figure 5:4

On a different day Judy reviews vendor bills and prepares checks for bills that are due. Judy also prepares a check to buy postage. These checks are recorded in the Cash Disbursements Journal illustrated in Figure 5:5.

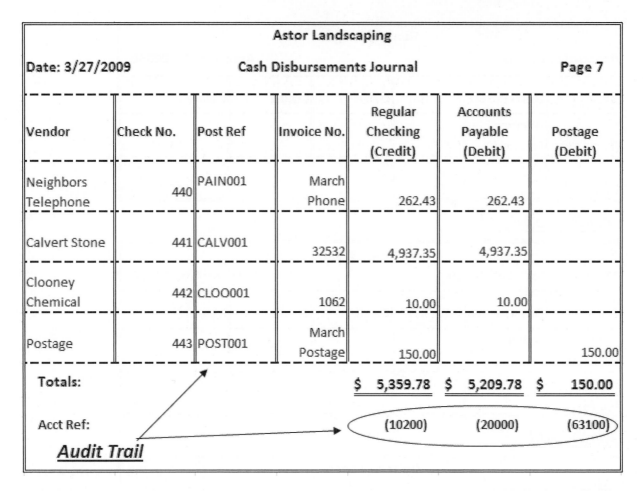

Astor Landscaping

Date: 3/27/2009 — Cash Disbursements Journal — Page 7

Vendor	Check No.	Post Ref	Invoice No.	Regular Checking (Credit)	Accounts Payable (Debit)	Postage (Debit)
Neighbors Telephone	440	PAIN001	March Phone	262.43	262.43	
Calvert Stone	441	CALV001	32532	4,937.35	4,937.35	
Clooney Chemical	442	CLOO001	1062	10.00	10.00	
Postage	443	POST001	March Postage	150.00		150.00
Totals:				$ 5,359.78	$ 5,209.78	$ 150.00
Acct Ref:				(10200)	(20000)	(63100)

Audit Trail

Figure 5:5

Like in the Purchases Journal, columns are totaled and cross-footed. Each check is then posted to a vendor account and column totals are posted to general ledger accounts. This time, Judy will use CDJ (Cash Disbursements Journal) along with the page number as the posting reference. *(Note: These postings are not illustrated.)*

As discussed in Chapter 4, the manual method is fraught with opportunities for making posting errors. Judy could enter an amount incorrectly, post an entry backwards, or forget to post it altogether.

With an understanding of *MAPS* for vendor activities, you are now ready to use QBP for recording vendor transactions. The topic that follows will introduce you to the center focused on these activities.

VENDOR CENTER

The Vendor Center focuses on vendor activities. Click **Vendors** on the **Home** page to open this center (Figure 5:6) and set the options illustrated so we can discuss the center's purpose.

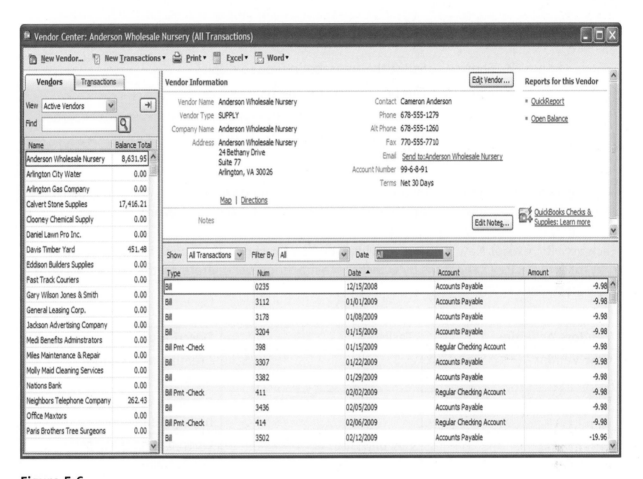

Figure 5:6

The **Vendors** tab lists transactions by vendor account. Astor's vendor accounts and balances appear to the left. The tab's **View** option contains selections for viewing All Vendors, Active Vendors, or Vendors with Open Balances. You are currently viewing Active Vendors.

This button hides the Vendor Information pane shown to the right. After hiding, this button is located on the far right for redisplaying the information pane.

The **Vendor Information** pane displays transactions for the account highlighted on the left. This account is currently Anderson Wholesale Nursery.

The **Edit Vendor** button edits Anderson's account information and the **Edit Notes** button is for entering account notes. There are also hyperlinks for creating **Reports for this Vendor**.

Anderson's transactions are listed at the bottom of its account information. The filtering options of **Show**, **Filter By**, and **Date** determine the transactions listed. Click ⌄ to access an option's dropdown list for changing selections. You are currently viewing **All Transactions** for **All Dates**. *(Note: Remember, if using fiscal year as the date then this is based on your computer date.)*

Filtering options work as follows:

❖   Show: Select the transaction type to display

❖   Filter By: Filtering criteria for the type

❖   Date: List all transactions for the type or only transactions recorded as of a specific date or range of dates

Now turn your attention to activities that can be performed while the Vendor tab is active. These activities are **New Vendor**, **New Transactions**, **Print**, **Excel**, and **Word**.

Each activity, except New Vendor, has this ▪ button for choosing a specific task. The table that follows discusses the tasks by activity. Most actions will operate on the vendor account highlighted on the left.

Vendors Activities	Tasks	Description
New Vendor		Create a new vendor account.
New Transactions	Enter Bills	Record a vendor bill for the highlighted vendor.
	Pay Bills	Open a window to select vendor bills to pay.
	Purchase Orders	Create a purchase order for the highlighted vendor.
	Receive Items and Enter Bill	Enter a receipt accompanied by a bill for items on a PO issued to the highlighted vendor.
	Receive Items	Enter a receipt for items on a PO issued to the high-lighted vendor.
	Enter Bill for Received Items	Enter a bill for a receipt from the highlighted vendor.

Vendors Activities	Tasks	Description
Print	Vendor List	Print a vendor list with balances. The report cannot be customized so you should consider using the Reports menu to print this information.
	Vendor Information	Print account information and notes for the high-lighted vendor. The report cannot be customized so you should consider using the Reports menu to print this information.
	Vendor Transaction List	Print the highlighted ven-dor's transactions for the current fiscal year. The report cannot be customized so you should consider using the Reports menu to print this information.
Excel	Export Vendor List	Create an Excel workbook or comma separated values (.csv) file containing all ven-dor information along with account balances.
	Export Transactions	Create an Excel workbook or comma separated values (.csv) file containing current fiscal year transactions for the highlighted vendor.
	Import from Excel	Import vendor information and/or transactions from an Excel workbook or comma separated values (.csv) file.
Word		Create form letters for com-municating with a vendor.

Next turn your attention to the **Transactions** tab, which lists transactions by type instead of transactions by vendor. Click to activate the tab illustrated in Figure 5:7.

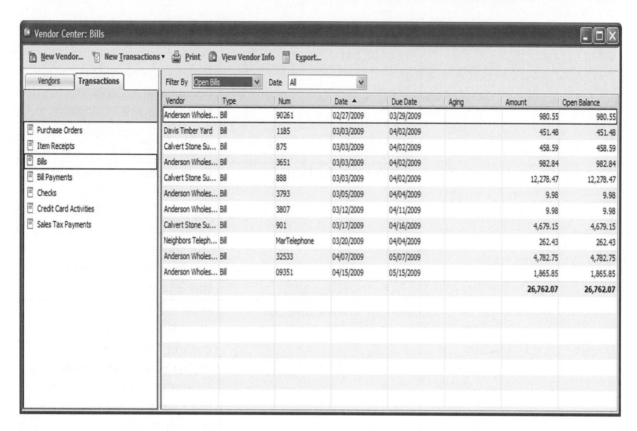

Figure 5:7

Transaction types are chosen on the left. Click **Bills** and then use the dropdown list on **Filter By** to select **Open Bills** and the dropdown on **Date** to select **All**. Your center now matches the illustration in Figure 5:7. You can sort the list by clicking a column name.

Activities that can be performed from this tab are different from activities performed on the previous tab. First, only the New Transactions activity offers multiple tasks so, clicking other activities immediately opens the task. The following table discusses activities on this tab.

Transactions Activities	Description
New Vendor	Create a new vendor account.
New Transactions	Contains the same tasks as the Vendors tab but the user must select the customer.
Print	Print the transactions listed to the right.
View Vendor Info	Edit the vendor account associated with the transaction highlighted on the right.
Export	Create an Excel workbook or comma separated values (.csv) file containing transactions listed on the right.

This illustrates that you can perform a variety of activities from the **Vendor Center**. You can initiate transactions, locate posted transactions, manage accounts, and create new accounts. Close the Vendor Center.

In contrast, the **Vendors** section (Figure 5:8) of the **Home** page only initiates transactions, but offers quick access to such tasks. In addition, you can always use the *Vendors* menu to perform vendor activities.

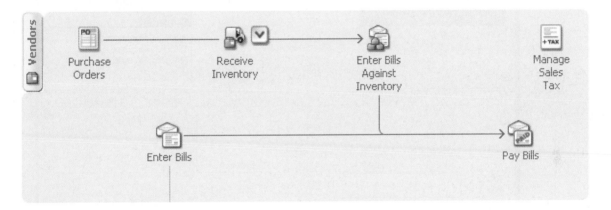

Figure 5:8

Now that you are familiar with locating vendor activities, let's begin recording vendor transactions. Close the Vendor Center.

PURCHASE ORDERS

As previously discussed, POs authorize vendor purchases. Recall from the *MAPS* topic that Seth created a PO for John Chester's landscape maintenance job. Follow the next steps to capture the transaction in QBP.

STEPS TO CREATE A PURCHASE ORDER

1. On the **Home** page, click the **Purchase Orders** icon to open Figure 5:9.

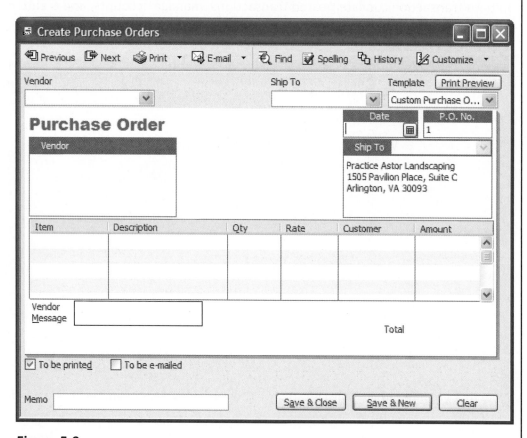

Figure 5:9

2. In **Vendor**, look up and select "Clooney Chemical Supply." Leave **Ship To** empty because an Astor employee will pick up the order. In **Date**, enter "3/20/2009". In **P.O. No.**, enter "180".

3. In **Item**, look up and select "Fertilizer." Tab to **Qty** and enter "3". For **Customer**, look up and select "Chester, John" to assign this cost to the job. Finally, in **Vendor Message** type "Will pick up order."

Figure 5:10 shows the completed PO.

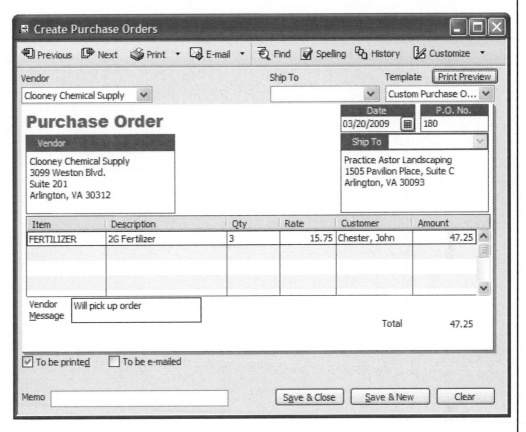

Figure 5:10

4. Click the lookup on **Print** and select **Print Preview**. When prompted with information on shipping labels, select the option to turn off future messages and click **OK**.

Figure 5:11 shows the previewed PO.

Figure 5:11

5. Click **Print** to send the order to the default printer.

    Note: When you want to select a different printer, click Close to exit the preview window and click Print on the transaction window.

6. Click **Save & New** and click **Yes** to save the changes. *(Note: The change occurred because QBP removed the checkmark from To be printed.)*

7. Enter the information shown in Figure 5:12.

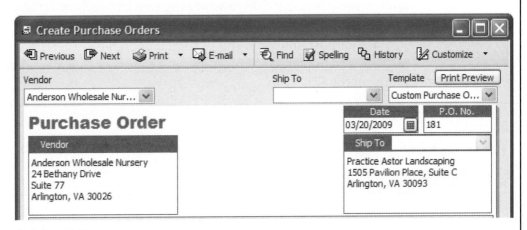

Figure 5:12

8. In **Item**, look up and select "Pavers." In **Qty**, enter "50". In **Customer**, select "O'Hara Homes: Redesign Gardens." When a customer has multiple jobs, you select the customer and job account. Figure 5:13 shows the completed PO.

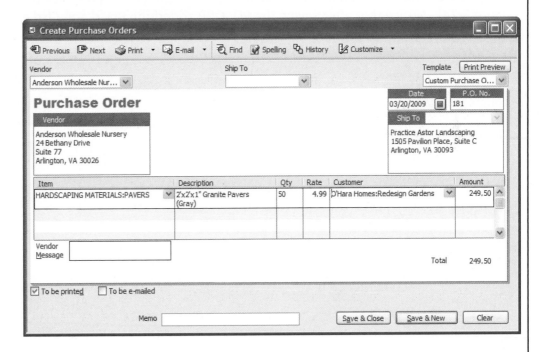

Figure 5:13

9. Click **Print**, select a printer, and click **Print** again.

10. Click **Save & Close** and click **Yes** to save the changes. *(Note: The PO changed after printing because QBP removed the checkmark from To be printed.)*

POs do not post entries to the general ledger because POs are merely commitments to purchase. Accounting recognition occurs after receiving the items on the PO.

CORRECTING A PURCHASE ORDER

You can correct information on a saved PO as long as Astor has not received items on the order.

First, locate the PO using the **Vendor Center**. Click **Vendors** on the **Home** page to open the center.

Next, select the **Transactions** tab and click **Purchase Orders** on the left.

Finally, locate **Clooney Chemical's** transaction on the right and double click to reopen (Figure 5:14). Notice that after saving the PO, QBP added the **Rcv'd** and **Clsd** columns.

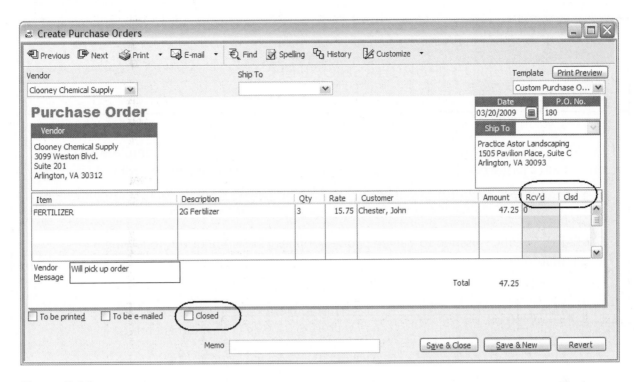

Figure 5:14

The **Rcv'd** field stores the quantity received for each line item. When all quantities ordered for a line item have been received then QBP marks the line item as **Clsd**.

Notice that there is also a **Closed** option for the entire PO located at the bottom. QBP marks this option after receiving all line items in full.

As long as all line items remain open, you can change information and even delete the PO. If needed, POs are deleted by using **Edit>>Delete Purchase Order** on the main menu.

Click **X** to exit the PO window. Now try the next exercise.

ENTER PURCHASE ORDERS

On March 25, 2009, Astor issued the following POs for items needed to complete Sugar Hill Tennis Club's landscape job. Two POs were required because items were ordered from separate vendors. Enter the POs and then exit the transaction window. Remember to use correct transaction dates and verify that POs are marked **To be printed**.

PO 182 for $199.60 is issued to Calvert Stone Supplies consisting of the following billable materials.

Item	Qty	Rate	Customer
Mulch	40	$ 4.99	Sugar Hill Tennis Club

PO 183 for $764.60 is issued to Southern Garden Wholesale consisting of the following billable materials.

Item	Qty	Rate	Customer
Boxwood	30	$ 22.49	Sugar Hill Tennis Club
Azalea Amy	10	$ 8.99	Sugar Hill Tennis Club

Print the POs by selecting *File>>Print Forms>>Purchase Orders* on the main menu. When the window illustrated in Figure 5:15 opens, POs are selected and ready for printing. Click **OK**, choose a printer, and then click **Print**.

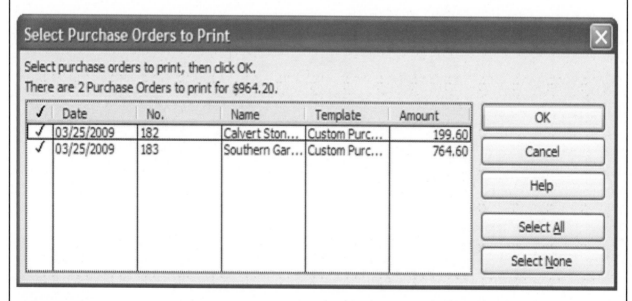

Figure 5:15

VENDOR BILLS AND RECEIPTS FOR PURCHASE ORDERS

From the *MAPS* topic, you will recall that Jeff picked up the chemicals along with the vendor bill from Clooney Chemical Supply on March 24. Jeff then turned the bill over to Judy, who matched it with the PO before posting the bill to the Purchases Journal.

Judy now performs this matching process as she enters the vendor bill. Follow the next instructions to record the bill from Clooney Chemical Supply.

STEPS TO RECORD A VENDOR BILL FOR ITEMS ON A PURCHASE ORDER

1. On the **Home** page, click **Receive Inventory**. You will be offered two choices. Select **Receive Inventory with Bill** to open Figure 5:16.

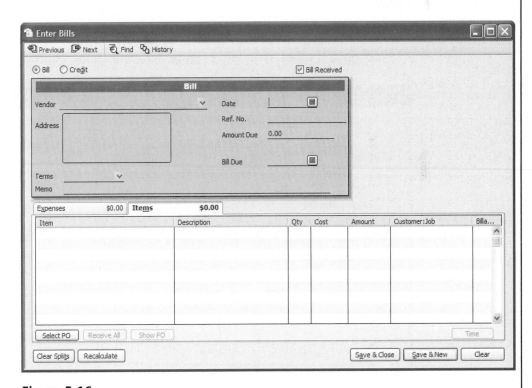

Figure 5:16

Notice that there are two tabs. The **Expenses** tab is used to record non-inventory purchases such as utility and insurance bills. The **Items** tab is for recording inventory purchases.

2. In **Vendor**, look up and select "Clooney Chemical Supply." Click **Yes** when QBP prompts to receive against the PO.

3. In the window that opens (Figure 5:17), click **PO No 180** and click **OK**.

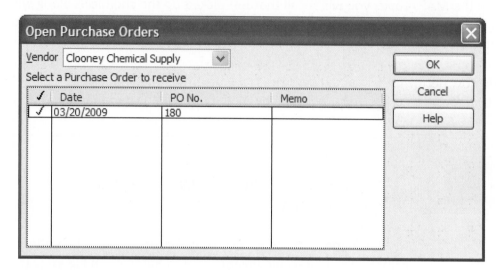

Figure 5:17

4. Change the **Date** to March 24, 2009. Enter Clooney's invoice number "78265" into the **Ref. No.** field. Figure 5:18 shows the bill thus far.

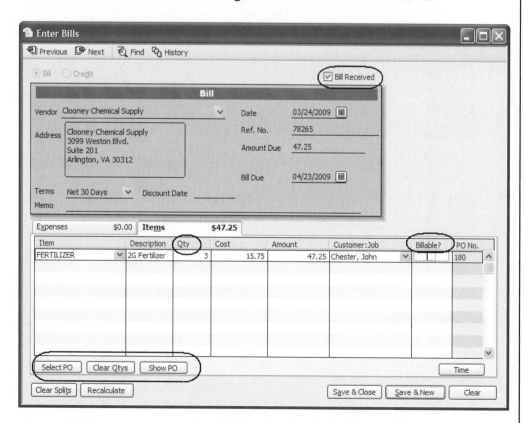

Figure 5:18

5. Before saving, review the following fields on this transaction.

Bill Received, when marked, means that this transaction records a vendor bill for the PO. In the next exercise, you will unmark this field to record a vendor receipt.

Qty stores the number of items received.

Billable marks this bill for invoicing to the customer. However, recall in Chapter 4 that you already invoiced John Chester. So **click** the **Billable option** to turn off the selection.

Select PO reopens the window to change the selected PO.

Clear Qtys deletes values in the Qty field.

Show PO opens the original PO transaction.

6. Click **Save and Close**.

We will cover one last thing before leaving this topic. You may sometimes receive items on a PO prior to receiving a vendor's bill. Remember that the liability occurs upon receipt of the goods because this is when the obligation to pay arises. Therefore, you need to have the ability to recognize the liability by posting a receipt of materials prior to receiving the bill.

The next exercise records a vendor receipt for PO items.

STEPS TO **R**ECORD A **V**ENDOR **R**ECEIPT FOR **I**TEMS ON A
PURCHASE **O**RDER

1. Click **Receive Inventory** and this time select **Receive Inventory without Bill**
   to open Figure 5:19.

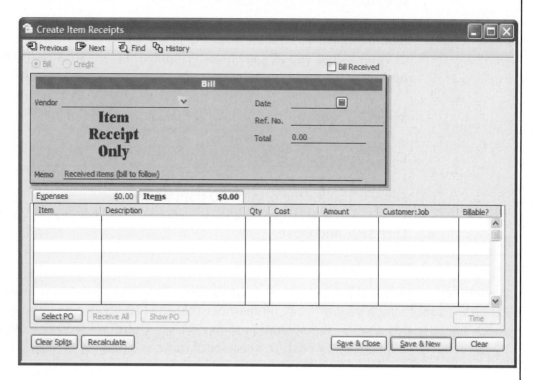

Figure 5:19

You will again find two tabs; however, this time the **Bill Received** option is
not marked and the **Memo** states that this is a receipt with a bill to follow.

2. In **Vendor**, look up and select "Anderson Wholesale Nursery." Click **Yes**
   when QBP prompts to receive against the PO.

3. As shown in Figure 5:20 click **PO No 181** and then click **OK**.

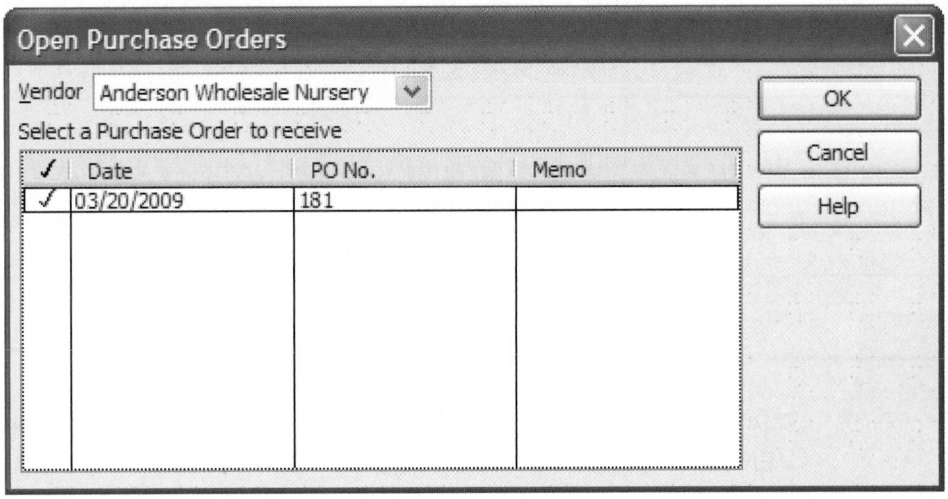

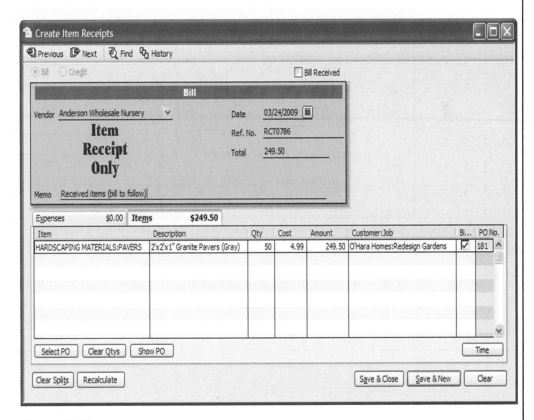

Figure 5:20

4. The **Date** of the receipt is March 24, 2009. For **Ref. No.**, enter receipt number "RCT0786".

Figure 5:21 shows the completed receipt.

Figure 5:21

5. Click **Save and Close**.

BEHIND THE KEYS OF A POSTED VENDOR RECEIPT AND BILL

Transactions in the previous topic posted entries to the Purchases Journal, vendor accounts, and general ledger. Follow the next steps to trace those entries.

STEPS TO TRACE THE ENTRIES FOR A VENDOR BILL AND A VENDOR RECEIPT

1. First, open the Purchases Journal report by selecting **Reports>>Memorized Reports>>Accounting Journals>>Purchases Journal** on the main menu. Enter the date range of **From** "3/24/2009 and **To** "3/24/2009."

   Figure 5:22 shows this report, listing only transactions with the "Bill" **Type**.

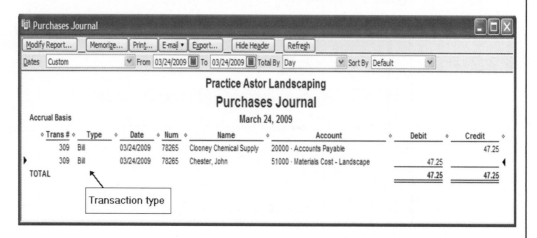

Figure 5:22

Note: The vendor name prints next to the accounts payable entry whereas the customer job name prints next to the cost of goods sold entry. This makes it easier to recognize entries on the general ledger report.

2.   Click **Modify Report** so we can add the "Item Receipt" **Type** to the report. Select the **Filters** tab and click **Transaction Type** under **Filter**.

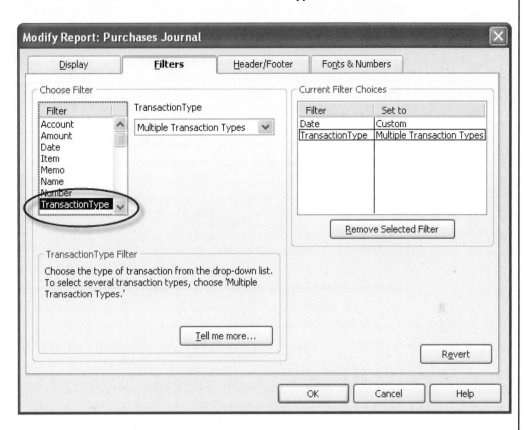

Figure 5:23

Click the dropdown list on **Transaction Type** and click **Multiple Transaction Types**. When the window in Figure 5:24 opens, scroll down and click **Item Receipt** to add it to the report.

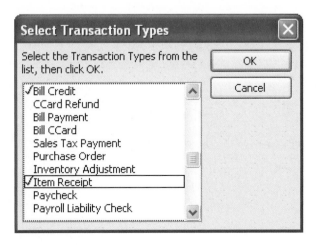

Figure 5:24

3. Click **OK** to close the selection window. Click **OK** on the modify report window and the report refreshes (Figure 5:25). Although Item Receipts posted to accounts payable, you cannot pay receipt transactions until the bill is posted.

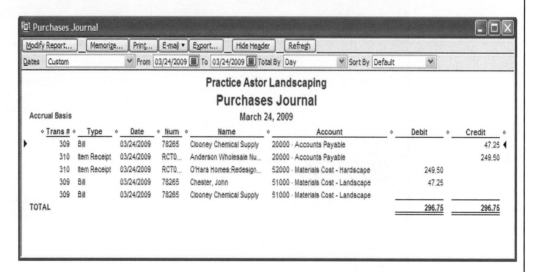

Figure 5:25

Notice that in our example the Clooney bill added an extra transaction line without a financial amount. We created this situation on purpose. Although this does not create a problem, it can be confusing if you cannot identify the source of the entry. We now explain why this occurred.

4. When we double click our Clooney transaction to reopen it and look at the
    Expenses tab, we find account 51000 Materials Cost – Landscape under
    Account. *(Note: This is for illustrative purposes only. Your transaction will
    not have this account present.)*

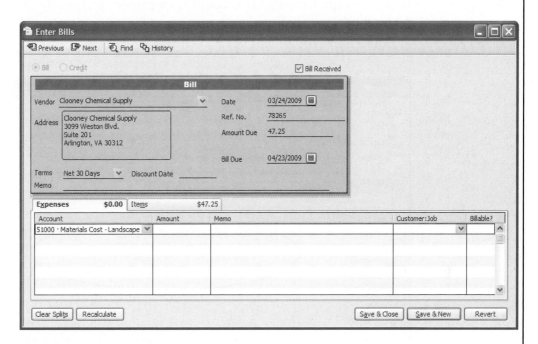

Figure 5:26

You will see later in the chapter that this tab is used to enter vendor
expense bills. QBP will sometimes remember the general ledger accounts
previously used on this tab. It is the presence of this account that caused a
transaction line to post with a zero amount.

To remove this line you need only highlight the account and press **Delete** on the keyboard. Click **Save & Close** and then **Yes** to change the transaction. The Purchases Journal refreshes with the extra transaction line removed.

Note: You can turn off the account "remember" feature by selecting **Edit>>Preferences** *on the main menu and turning off the option illustrated in Figure 5:27. You do not need to do this.*

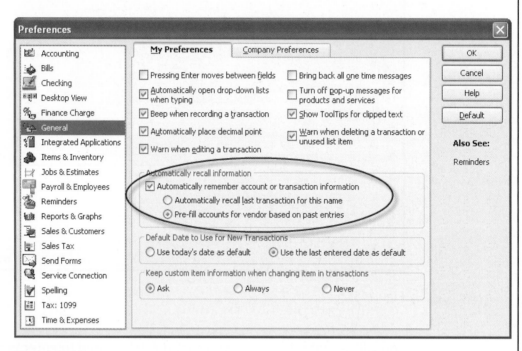

Figure 5:27

Before closing the Purchases Journal, click **Memorize** and click **Replace** to save the modified report. Click **X** to close the Purchases Journal.

5. Now trace entries posted to the vendor accounts.

    Select **Reports>>Vendors & Payables>>Transaction List by Vendor** on the main menu.

    Enter the date range of **From** "3/24/2009" and **To** "3/24/2009" and **Refresh** the report.

    Click **Modify Report** and add the **Trans #** column. Click **OK**.

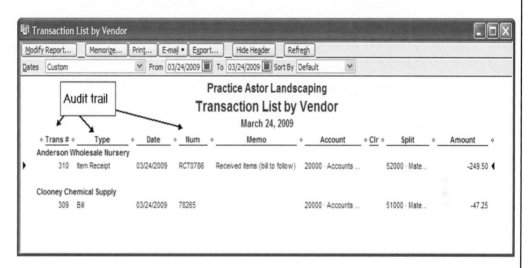

Figure 5:28

Notice that the **Trans#** and **Type** audit trail codes cross-reference to the **Trans#** and **Type** codes on the **Purchases Journal**.

Close this report.

6. Finally, verify QBP's entries to the general ledger.

Select ***Reports>>Memorized Reports>>Accounting Journals>>General Ledger Detail Report*** on the main menu. Enter the March 24, 2009 as the date range and refresh the report.

Practice Astor Landscaping
General Ledger Detail Report

Accrual Basis   March 24, 2009

Trans #	Type	Date	Num	Name	Memo	Debit	Credit
11000 · Accounts Receivable							
99	Invoice	03/24/2009	1012	Sycamore Homes		21,826.00	
Total 11000 · Accounts Receivable						21,826.00	0.00
20000 · Accounts Payable							
309	Bill	03/24/2009	78265	Clooney Chemical Supply			47.25
310	Item Receipt	03/24/2009	RCT0786	Anderson Wholesale Nursery	Received ite...		249.50
Total 20000 · Accounts Payable						0.00	296.75
22000 · Sales Tax Payable							
99	Invoice	03/24/2009	1012	VA Sales Tax Department	Sales Tax	0.00	
Total 22000 · Sales Tax Payable						0.00	0.00
40000 · Sales							
42000 · Sales - Hardscape							
99	Invoice	03/24/2009	1012	Sycamore Homes	Install Hards...		4,800.00
99	Invoice	03/24/2009	1012	Sycamore Homes	Pallet 8"x4"x...		4,025.00
99	Invoice	03/24/2009	1012	Sycamore Homes	1.5 Ton Palle...		12,100.00
99	Invoice	03/24/2009	1012	Sycamore Homes	2 Ton Bag C...		901.00
Total 42000 · Sales - Hardscape						0.00	21,826.00
Total 40000 · Sales						0.00	21,826.00
50000 · Materials Cost of Goods Sold							
51000 · Materials Cost - Landscape							
309	Bill	03/24/2009	78265	Chester, John	2G Fertilizer	47.25	
Total 51000 · Materials Cost - Landscape						47.25	0.00
52000 · Materials Cost - Hardscape							
310	Item Receipt	03/24/2009	RCT0786	O'Hara Homes:Redesign Garde...	2'x2'x1" Gra...	249.50	
Total 52000 · Materials Cost - Hardscape						249.50	0.00
Total 50000 · Materials Cost of Goods Sold						296.75	0.00
TOTAL						22,122.75	22,122.75

Audit trail

Figure 5:29

In Figure 5:29, you finally see cost of goods sold entries. Recall that when explaining service and non-inventory items in Chapter 4 we stated that service based businesses post cost of goods sold when paying employees and posting vendor bills and receipts.

Close the report when finished.

CORRECTING A VENDOR RECEIPT OR BILL

QBP permits modifying and deleting vendor receipts and bills. Use the **Vendor Center** to locate transactions.

Open this center and, on the **Vendors** tab, highlight **Anderson Wholesale Nursery**. Filter to **Show Item Receipts** for **All** dates (Figure 5:30).

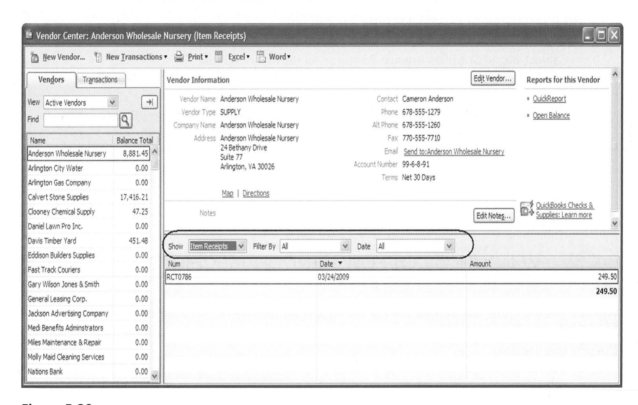

Figure 5:30

After reopening a receipt or bill, you can modify it and save the changes. You can also delete bills and receipts using *Edit* on the main menu. After deleting, QBP will reinstate POs used to create the transaction so you can receive items again.

Caution: You should not modify or delete paid bills because the payment will no longer match the bill. Instead, void the payment and then delete the bill. We will show you how to void payments later in the chapter.

Remember Appendix B provides a complete set of instructions on correcting QBP transactions.

ENTER VENDOR RECEIPTS AND BILLS FOR PURCHASE ORDERS

On March 27, 2009, items were received on the following POs. Post these transactions and click **Yes** if prompted to exceed a vendor's credit limit.

Calvert Stone Supplies Invoice 2346 for all items on PO 182.

Southern Garden Wholesale Receipt RCT5132 for 30 Boxwoods on PO 183.

Print the Purchases Journal for March 27 and list both Bills and Item Receipts.

VENDOR BILLS FOR VENDOR RECEIPTS

You still need to post the vendor bill for Anderson Wholesale Nursery's receipt recorded on March 24. The following instructions show you the steps to turn a receipt into a bill so you can pay the vendor.

STEPS TO RECORD A VENDOR BILL FOR A RECEIPT

1. On the **Home** page, click **Enter Bills Against Inventory**. As shown in Figure 5:31 look up and select **Anderson Wholesale Nursery**.

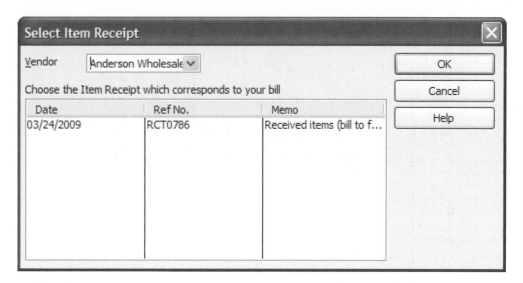

Figure 5:31

2. Highlight the receipt and click **OK**. Change **Date** to "3/26/2009" and **Ref. No.** to "8213". Click **Save & Close** and then click **Yes** to change the transaction.

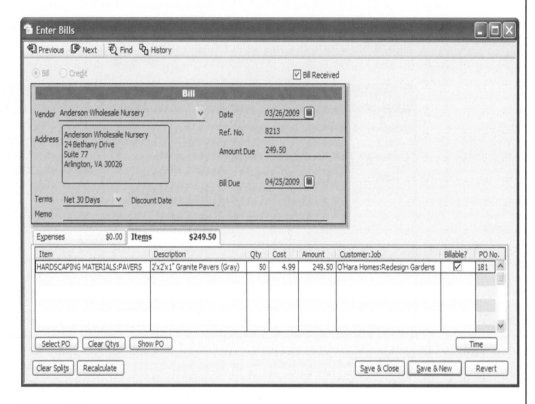

Figure 5:32

ENTER VENDOR BILL FOR VENDOR RECEIPT

On March 30, 2009, Invoice 7631 for $683.69 arrives from Southern Garden Wholesale for RCT5132. One of the Amy Azaleas on PO 183 was received since recording the vendor receipt so use Select PO on the Bill window to reopen the original PO and add this item to it before recording the invoice. Print the Purchases Journal for March 30.

VENDOR ACCOUNTS

This topic explains creating, editing, and deleting vendor accounts. Open the **Vendor Center**, select the **Vendors** tab, and double click **Anderson Wholesale Nursery** to open the account. Now follow below as we describe tabs on the vendor account.

Address Info Tab

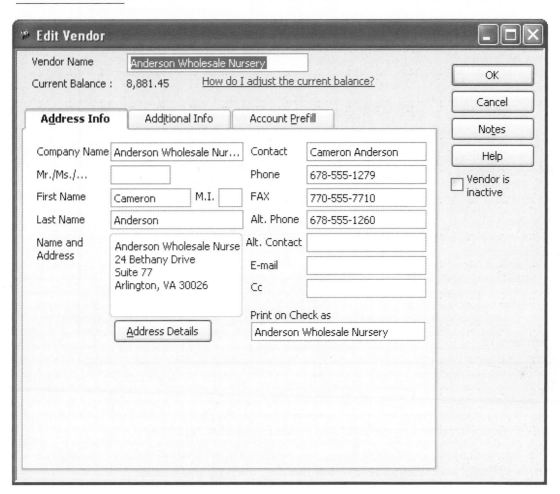

Figure 5:33

This tab stores basic vendor information such as address, phone numbers, and contacts.

Additional Info Tab

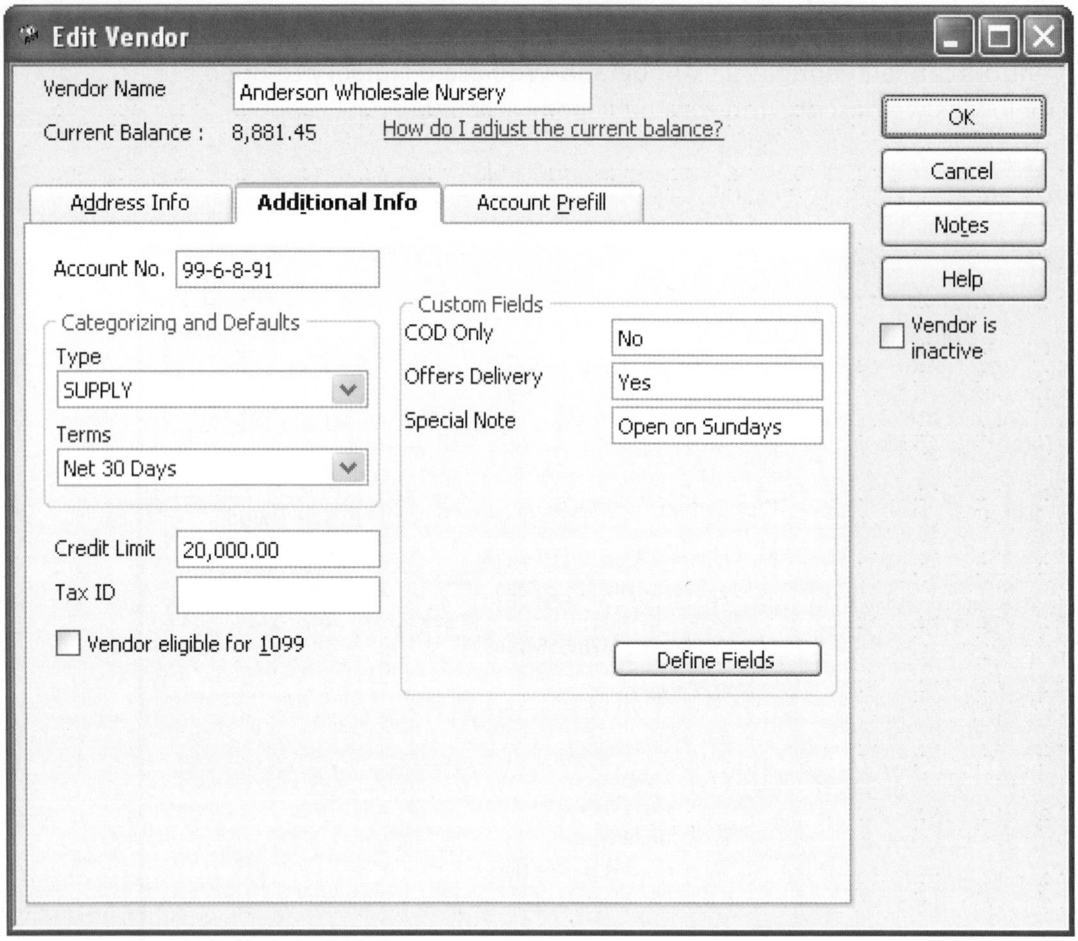

Figure 5:34

This tab stores vendor transaction defaults and fields for vendor reporting.

Account No. is optional and stores the account number used by the vendor.

Type is optional and is used to group reports by vendor characteristics. You can click the dropdown list to view the types used by Astor.

Terms on the vendor serve the same role as terms on the customer by controlling vendor bill due dates and early payment discounts.

Credit Limit on the vendor serves the same function as on the customer by controlling vendor purchases.

Vendor eligible for 1099 triggers a vendor for IRS tax reporting. When selected, QBP tracks annual payments for reporting on Form 1099. The IRS requires the annual filing of Form 1099 for subcontractor payments that exceed $600. Information on 1099 reporting requirements is available at www.irs.gov.

Tax ID stores a vendor's social security number or federal ID number for Form 1099 reporting.

Account Prefill Tab

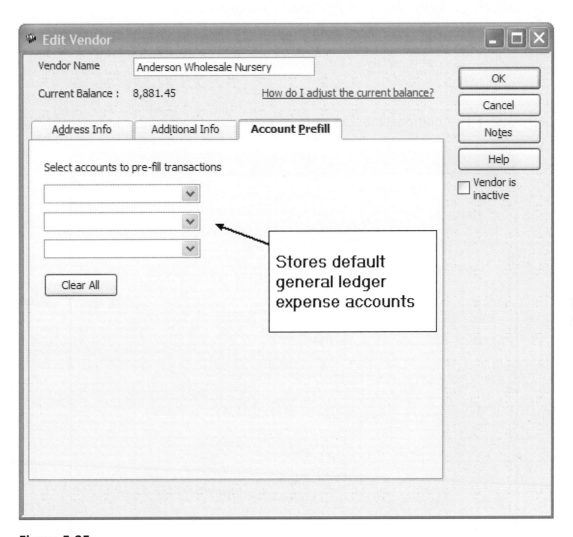

Figure 5:35

This tab assigns multiple default general ledger expense accounts. If a vendor has prefilled accounts then QBP will automatically enter the accounts on the Expenses tab of the Enter Bills window.

Anderson Wholesale Nursery does not have prefill accounts because it is a supplier of inventory so purchases from this vendor use the default account assigned to the inventory item. You can open the Petty Cash vendor if you want to view prefilled accounts.

Click **X** to close the account. Now practice editing vendor accounts by completing the next exercise.

STEPS TO EDIT VENDOR ACCOUNT INFORMATION

1. Open Davis Timber Yard's account. You will change the account terms to calculate a 1 percent discount when paying invoices within 10 days of the invoice date.

2. Select the **Additional Info** tab and look up the terms illustrated in Figure 5:36.

Figure 5:36

3. Click **OK** and click **Yes** if QBP issues a warning about affecting previously posted transactions. This change applies only to future transactions.

You can delete vendors by highlighting a vendor account and selecting *Edit>>Delete Vendor* on the main menu. Like customers, you cannot delete accounts with transaction history, so use the **Vendor is inactive** option if you need to deny future transactions.

Adding vendors is similar to adding customers. Practice creating a new vendor in the exercise that follows.

CREATE A NEW VENDOR ACCOUNT

On March 27, Astor opened an account with the following vendor. Create the vendor account.

Jackson Hyland Tax Service
P.O. Box 8276
Arlington, VA 30010

Phone: 701 555-8723
Contact:Sam Calper, CFO
Fax:701 555-9073
Email:Calper@jacksonhyland.net

Vendor Type:OFFICE
Terms:Net 30 Days
Credit Limit:$5,000
Prefill Account:Legal & Professional Expense

VENDOR BILLS FOR EXPENSES

Astor also receives vendor bills for expenses not originating on a PO and not involving inventory. These bills are normally for expenses such as office supplies, utilities, and insurance.

On March 24, Astor receives a bill for office supplies. Complete the next exercise to record this transaction.

STEPS FOR ENTERING VENDOR BILLS FOR EXPENSES

1. On the **Home** page, click **Enter Bills**. In **Vendor**, look up and select "Office Maxtors." Change the **Date** to "3/24/2009" and click the **Expenses** tab. (See Figure 5:37.)

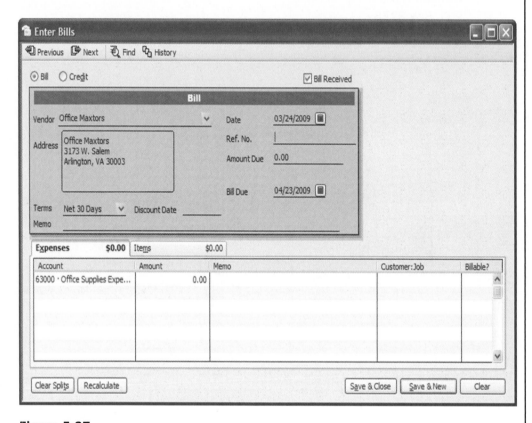

Figure 5:37

You now see the advantage to assigning prefilled accounts because 63000 Office Supplies Expense is already present.

2. Enter "575" as the **Ref. No.**

3. In **Amount**, enter "125.76". Tab to **Memo** and type "Paper supplies". These bills are not usually assigned to a **Customer:Job** so the completed transaction is shown in Figure 5:38.

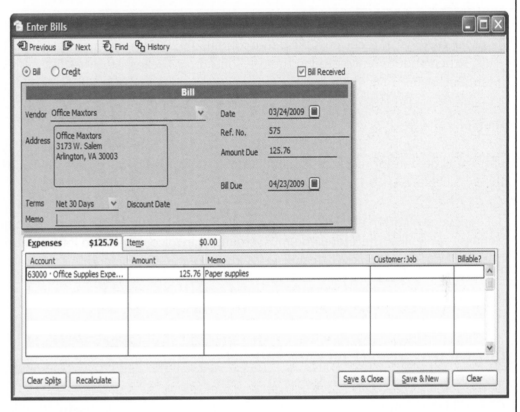

Figure 5:38

4. Click **Save & Close** to post the bill.

The exercise that follows provides more practice on entering vendor bills for expenses.

ENTER VENDOR BILLS FOR EXPENSES

On March 27 Astor received a bill dated March 20, 2009 from Jackson Hyland Tax Service. This is the vendor you created in the previous *You Try* exercise. The bill is for $762.00 for first quarter tax advice. Record this entry.

Hints:
There are a couple of points to this exercise. First, the transaction date is always the invoice date, not the date of receiving the bill. Generally, you will not receive bills on the same day as the invoice date.

Second, you will often encounter bills without an invoice number, particularly utility and professional service bills. Therefore, you must create an invoice number to let you later identify the transaction. For instance, you can use "MarElec" as the invoice number for March electricity.

MEMORIZED VENDOR BILLS

QBP will let you memorize vendor bills. This feature is especially useful for bills that repeat. You can memorize while creating a new bill or you can open a posted bill and memorize it.

The accountant received a bill for monthly advertising. In the following exercise, you will create and memorize this recurring bill.

STEPS TO CREATE A MEMORIZED VENDOR BILL

1. Click **Enter Bills** on the Home page and enter the information illustrated in Figure 5:39.

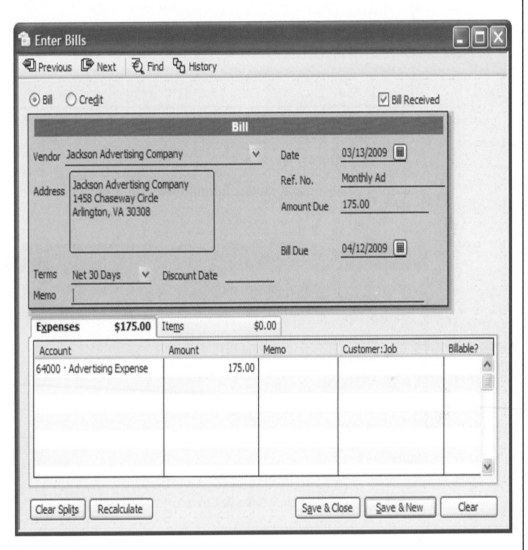

Figure 5:39

2. On the main menu, select **Edit>>Memorize Bill** to open Figure 5:40.

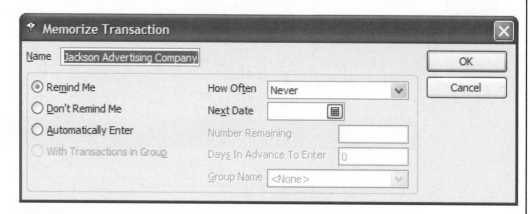

Figure 5:40

You can instruct QBP to remind you to post the bill or tell the software to automatically post it. Select **Remind Me** and then complete remaining fields as illustrated in Figure 5:41.

Figure 5:41

Click **OK** and then click **Save & Close** on the March bill.

3. You will now locate this memorized transaction. Select *Lists>>Memorized Transaction List* on the main menu to open the Memorized Transaction List (Figure 5:42).

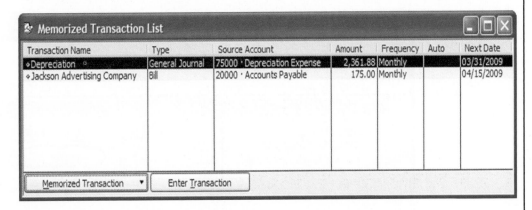

Figure 5:42

Astor has two memorized transactions. The first posts a monthly general journal entry for depreciation and the other is your vendor bill for advertising. You can also memorize sales invoices and POs.

4. You can modify the scheduling of a memorized transaction. Highlight **Jackson's** bill, click the **Memorized Transaction** button and select **Edit Memorized Transaction** to reopen the scheduling window. Click **Cancel**.

5. You will now post the April bill for Jackson. Double click the bill to open it and enter the invoice number as "April Ad". (See Figure 5:43.) Click **Save & Close**.

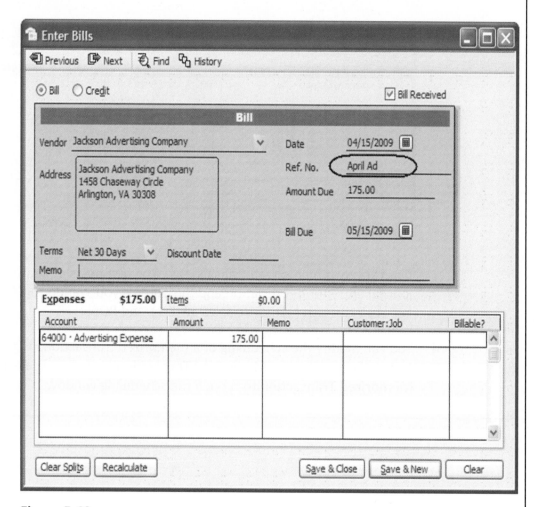

Figure 5:43

6. Notice that the **Next Date** on the Memorized Transaction List advanced to May. Click **X** to close the list.

VENDOR PAYMENTS

You are now ready to pay vendor bills. In the following exercise you create checks dated March 28, 2009 to pay vendor bills due by April 4, 2009.

STEPS TO PAY VENDORS

1. Before cutting checks, Judy prepares an aged payables report to review bill
    due dates. Create this report by selecting *Reports>>Vendors &
    Payables>>A/P Aging Detail* on the main menu. Change the date to
    April 4, 2009 to view bills due by this date. (See Figure 5:44.)

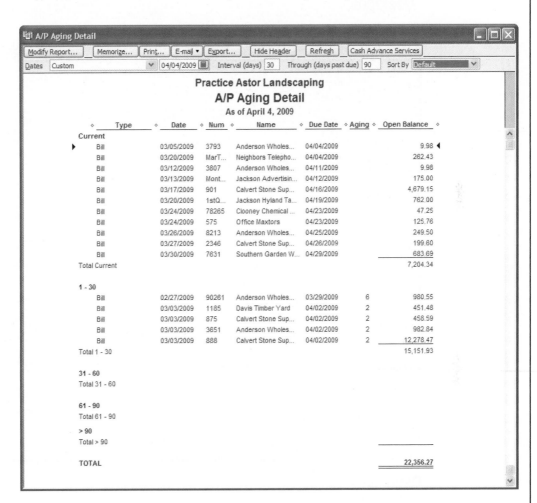

Figure 5:44

The report gives you an idea of the bills that will be selected for payment.
Close the report.

2. Click **Pay Bills** on the Home page. Enter the option illustrated in Figure 5:45 to display all bills due on or before 04/04/2009.

    Note: You cannot use this option to select bills with discounts expiring by April 4; instead you must individually select bills by referring to the Disc. Date column.

    Verify that **To be printed** is selected and change the **Payment Date** to 3/28/2009.

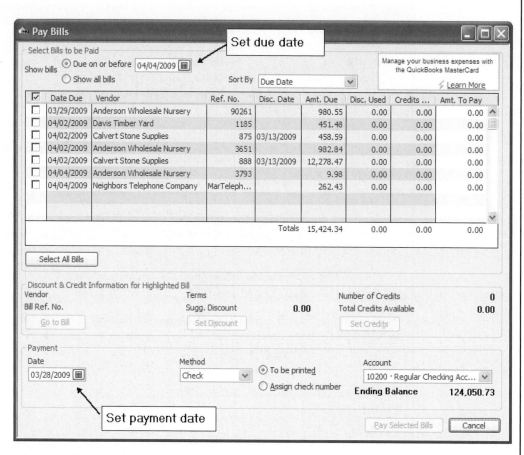

Figure 5:45

Before continuing, note that these checks will post to (credit) 10200 Regular Checking Account.

3. Click **Select All Bills** and then click to deselect the Neighbors Telephony Company bill as illustrated in Figure 5:46.

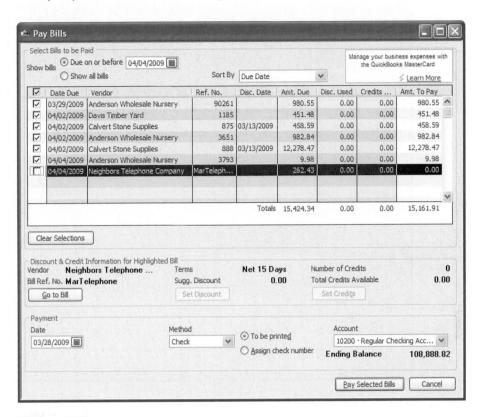

Figure 5:46

You can reduce a payment to a vendor by adjusting the **Amt. To Pay**. After printing checks, the transaction credits the regular checking account and debits the accounts payable account.

Review the **Disc. Date** column to find two discounts lost because bills are being paid after the discount date. If paying bills with a discount then the discount amount is credited to 59500 Purchase Discounts. This account is set under Company Preferences for Bills as illustrated in Figure 5:47.

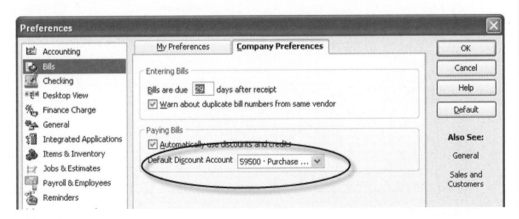

Figure 5:47

4. Click **Pay Selected Bills** to open the window illustrated in Figure 5:48.

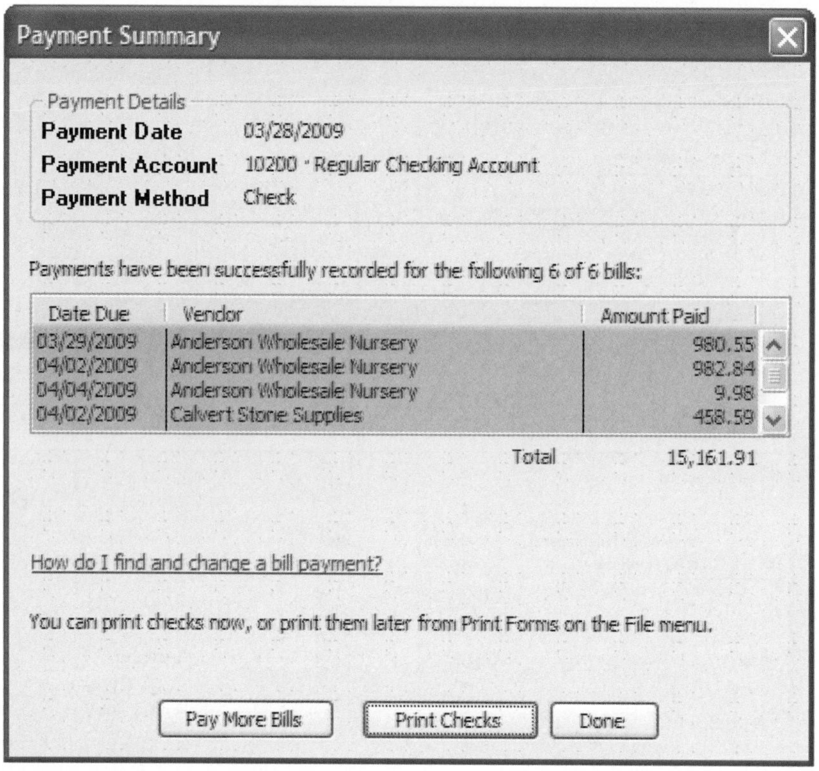

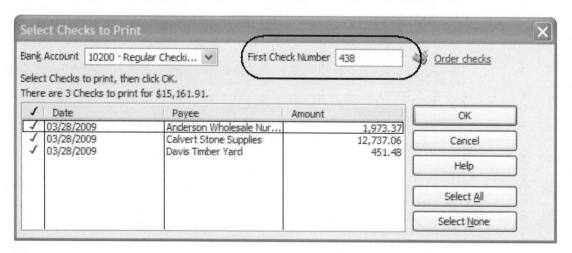

Figure 5:48

Note: You can click Done and return to printing later using the Print Checks icon on the Home page.

5. Click **Print Checks** and Figure 5:49 opens. Enter "438" as the check number.

    Notice that QBP has combined vendor bills so that only three checks will be used to pay six bills.

Figure 5:49

6. Click **OK** and the printer selection window opens. Select a printer and click **Print**. Figure 5:50 shows the first check printed.

03/28/2009

Anderson Wholesale Nursery   **1,973.37

One Thousand Nine Hundred Seventy-Three and 37/100**

Anderson Wholesale Nursery
24 Bethany Drive
Suite 77
Arlington, VA 30026

99-6-8-91

			Anderson Wholesale Nursery		03/28/2009		
Date	Type	Reference		Original Amt.	Balance Due	Discount	Payment
02/27/2009	Bill	90261		980.55	980.55		980.55
03/03/2009	Bill	3651		982.84	982.84		982.84
03/05/2009	Bill	3793		9.98	9.98		9.98
						Check Amount	1,973.37

Regular Checking Acc 99-6-8-91   1,973.37

			Anderson Wholesale Nursery		03/28/2009		
Date	Type	Reference		Original Amt.	Balance Due	Discount	Payment
02/27/2009	Bill	90261		980.55	980.55		980.55
03/03/2009	Bill	3651		982.84	982.84		982.84
03/05/2009	Bill	3793		9.98	9.98		9.98
						Check Amount	1,973.37

Figure 5:50

Note: This check illustrates printing on a two-part check where Astor can send the top portion to the vendor and attach the bottom portion to the paid bill.

7. QBP next confirms check printing (Figure 5:51). If checks did not print properly then click **Select All** and click **OK** so you can reprint the checks.

Click **OK**.

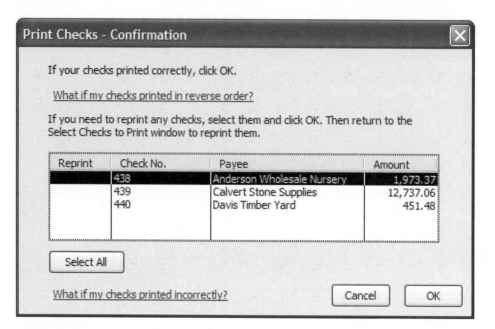

Figure 5:51

BEHIND THE KEYS OF A POSTED VENDOR PAYMENT

Now trace the audit trail for the checks printed in the previous topic. On the main menu, select **Reports>>Memorized Reports>>Accounting Journals>>Cash Disbursement Journal**. Change the date range to "3/28/2009." Note QBP's audit trail under the **Trans #** and **Type** columns. Close the report. (See Figure 5:52.)

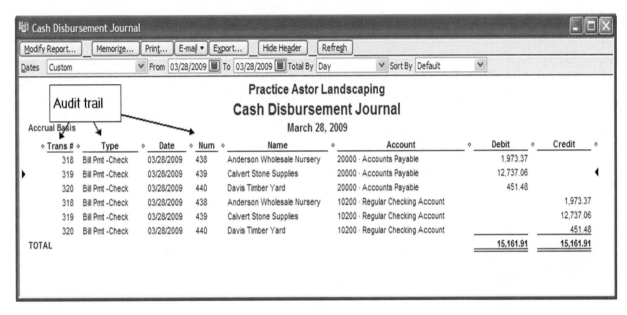

Figure 5:52

Select **Reports>>Vendors & Payables>>Transaction List by Vendor** to open the report listing transactions posted to vendor accounts. Enter "3/28/2009" as the date range and modify the report to add the **Trans #** column. (See Figure 5:53.)

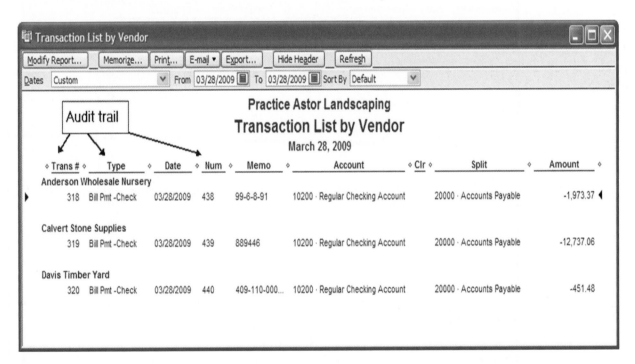

Figure 5:53

The audit trail of **Trans #** and **Type** on this report matches the audit trail in the **Cash Disbursements Journal**. Close this report and complete tracing entries by opening the **General Ledger Detail Report**. Locate your entries in accounts 10200 Regular Checking and 20000 Accounts Payable (not illustrated). Close the report.

WRITE CHECKS WITHOUT A VENDOR BILL

QBP can write checks without entering a vendor bill first. This is useful if you need to write a check to a vendor that requests cash upon delivery. Sometimes the vendor account will also be new so you can add it "on the fly." *(Note: Remember "on the fly" means creating a new account while entering a transaction.)*

Complete the next exercise that records a check for office party food.

STEPS TO ADD A VENDOR ON THE FLY WHILE WRITING A CHECK WITHOUT A VENDOR BILL

1. Click **Write Checks** under the **Banking** section of the **Home** page. Change the **No** field to "441," which is the check number. Enter "3/28/2009" as the **Date**.

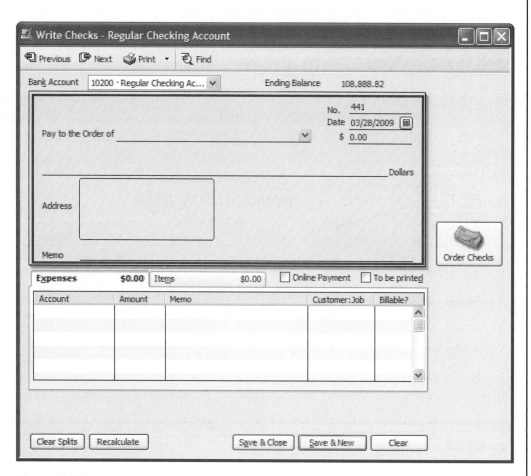

Figure 5:54

---

2. The vendor is not on file so place your cursor in **Pay to the Order of** and type "Joe's Grocery".

    Press Tab. When QBP prompts to create the account (Figure 5:55), click **Set Up**.

Figure 5:55

Next, choose **Vendor** and click **OK**.

Figure 5:56

3. Use information in the next series of figures to create the vendor account.

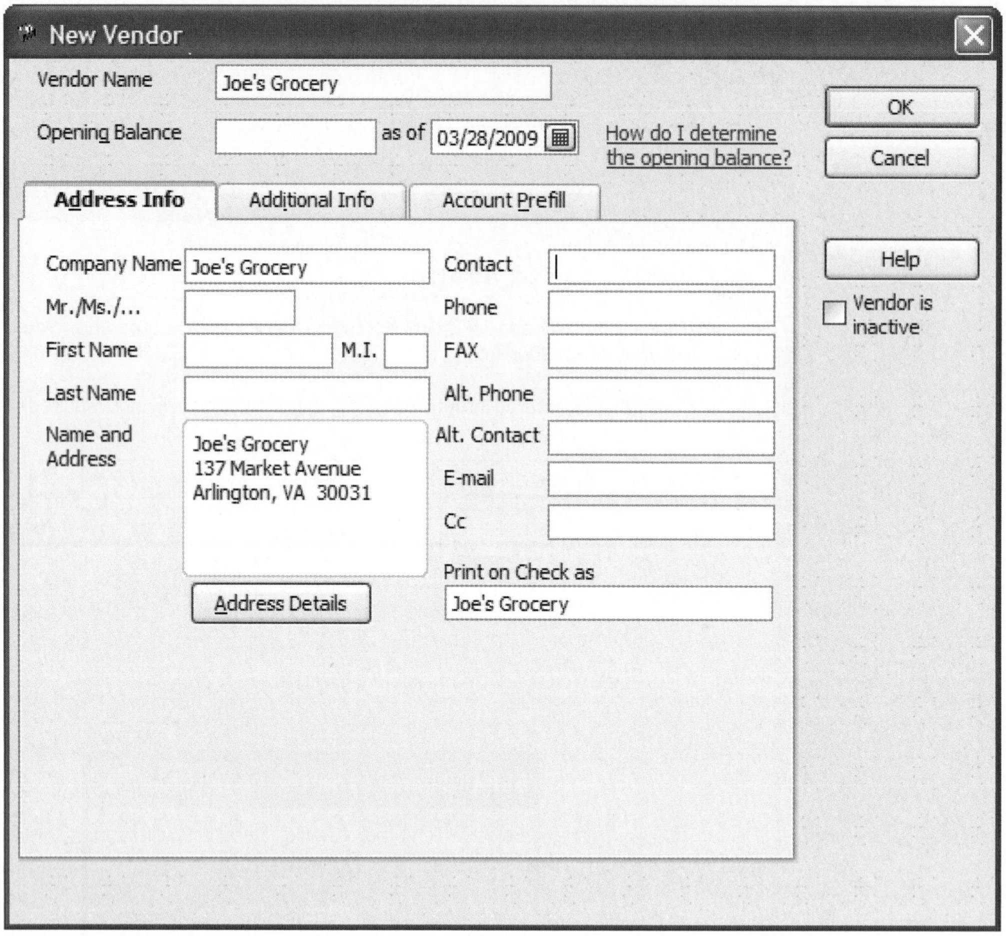

Figure 5:57

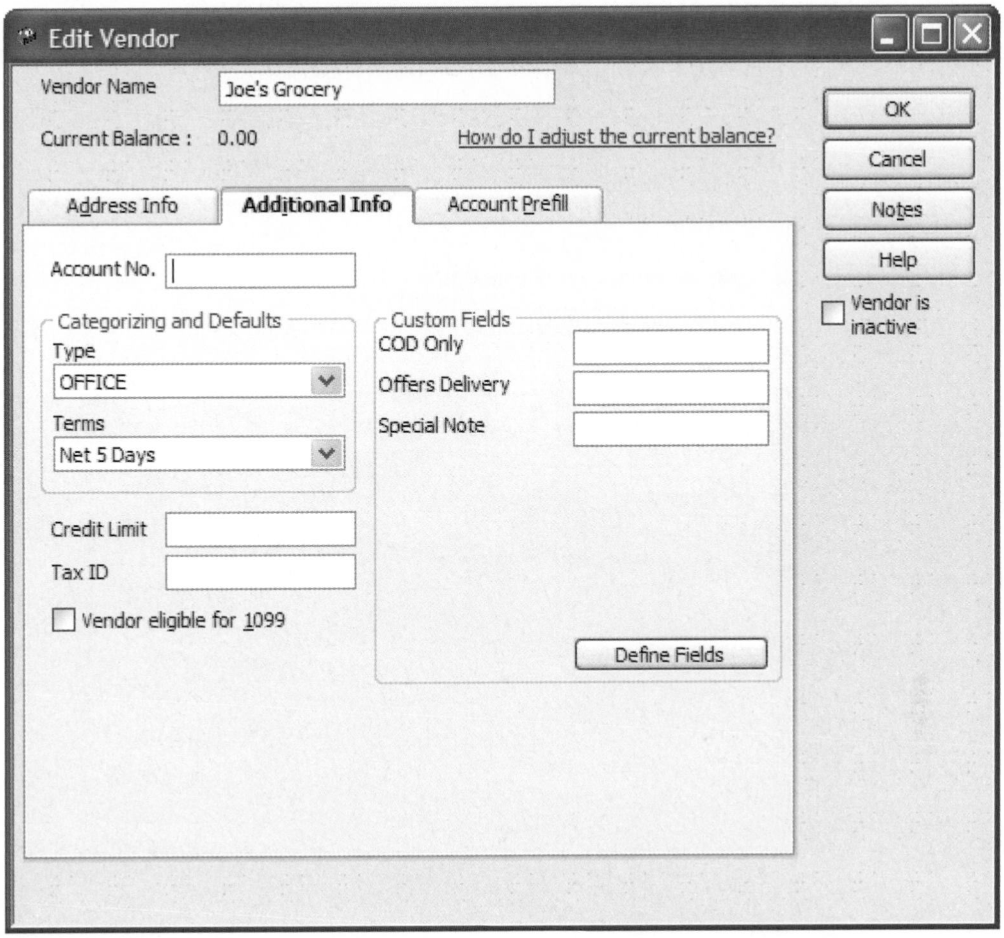

Figure 5:58

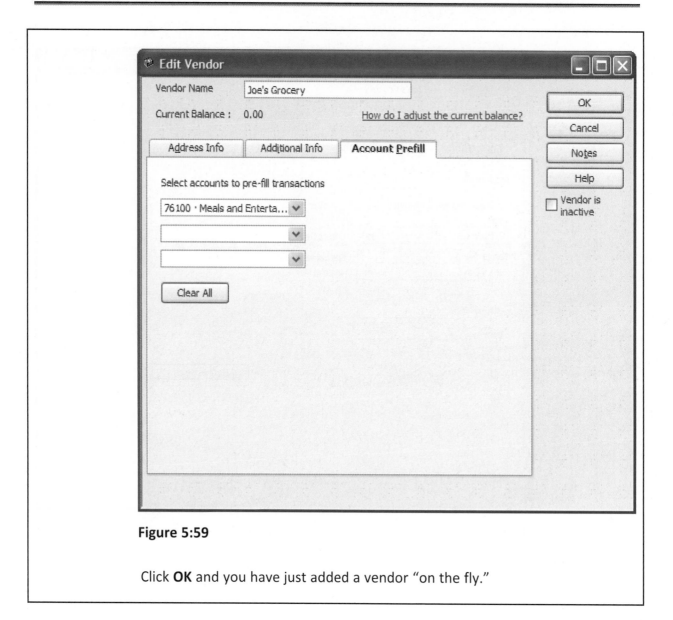

Figure 5:59

Click **OK** and you have just added a vendor "on the fly."

4. Now complete the check as shown in Figure 5:60. Notice that the expense account prefills based on the information entered on the vendor account.

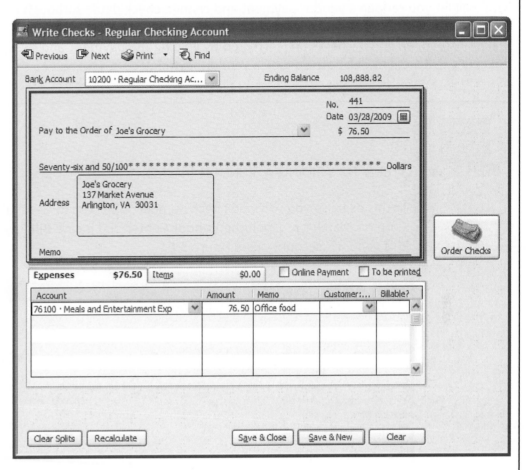

Figure 5:60

5. Click **Print** and confirm the check number of "441." Click **Print** again and then click **OK** to confirm that the check printed correctly.

6. Click **Save & Close**.

VOIDING VENDOR PAYMENTS

QBP will let you reopen a vendor payment and change check data. Although this changes data in the software, the printed check remains incorrect; therefore you should not alter check data. Instead, errors on checks are corrected by voiding the payment and reissuing it. The following instructions illustrate voiding a vendor payment.

STEPS TO VOIDING A VENDOR PAYMENT

1. In this exercise you will void check number "433" cut to General Leasing Corp on March 12. Open the **Vendor Center** and locate **Bill Payments** for this vendor's account. (See Figure 5:61.)

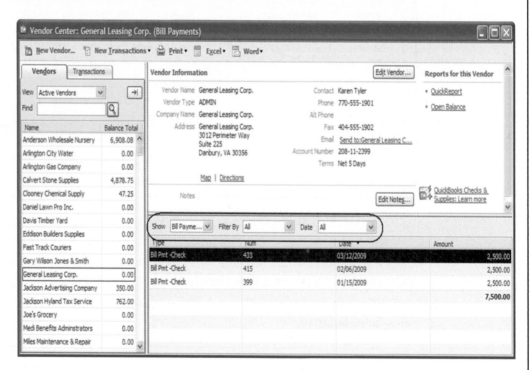

Figure 5:61

2. Double click to reopen the check. On the main menu, select ***Edit>>Void Bill Pmt – Check***.

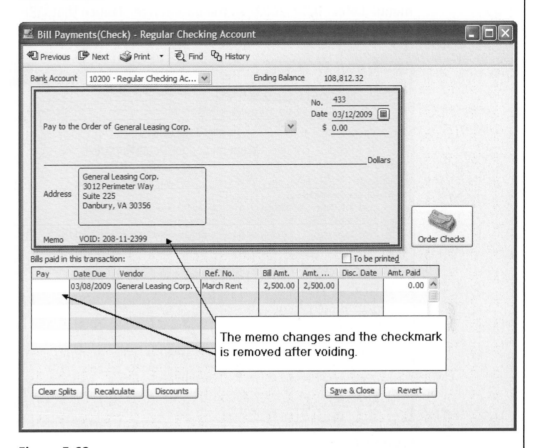

Figure 5:62

You want to be very careful when voiding checks. QBP will always post the entry for a voided check as of the check date. If voiding a check written in a closed accounting period then QBP will prompt to post the entry to the closed period. Unfortunately, there is no option for posting the entry to a selected date. You must permit the entry to backdate to the closed period and then record a general journal entry to reclassify the amount to the open accounting period.

3. Click **Save & Close**. When prompted (Figure 5:63), click **Yes**.

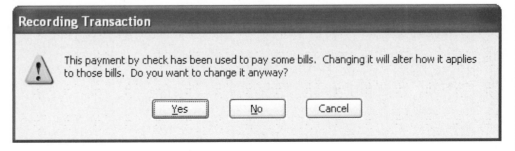

Figure 5:63

4. View the results of your action. Select **Reports>>Memorized Reports>>Accounting Journals>>General Ledger Detail Report** on the main menu. Enter "3/12/2009" as the date range. Notice that QBP voided the check as of the check date (Figure 5:64). Close the report.

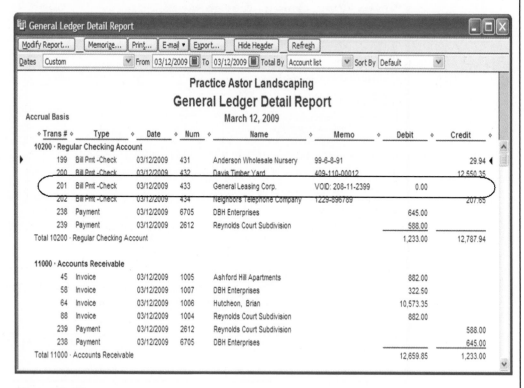

Figure 5:64

5. Return to the vendor's account and view **Bills**. The March bill has an open balance so it can be reselected for payment. You will pay this bill in the next exercise.

Close the **Vendor Center**.

You Try

PAY VENDORS

Create vendor checks dated April 6, 2009. Individually select bills to pay based on the following.
    All bills with a due date on or before 4/16/2009
    All bills with a discount date on or before 4/16/2009

Reduce Calvert Stone Supplies' payment on Invoice 901 to $3,000.00.

Payments will total $6,819.87. Print the checks using "442" as the first check number. *(Note: If you select the wrong bills and have not yet printed then delete the unprinted checks by opening them from the Bill Payments section of the Vendor Center. Then return to selecting bills.)*

Select **Reports>>Banking>>Check Detail** to document the payments. Enter 4/6/2009 as the date range and print the report.

PAYING SALES TAX

At the end of every month, Astor must remit sales tax collected from customers. QBP tracks sales tax collections and the following shows you how to remit it.

STEPS TO PAYING SALES TAX

1. Click **Manage Sales Tax** in the Vendors section of the **Home** page to open the window in Figure 5:65.

Figure 5:65

2. Click **Sales Tax Preferences**. Figure 5:66 shows that Astor collects Virginia sales tax, owes the tax after the customer pays the invoice, and remits sales tax monthly.

    Click **Cancel** to exit.

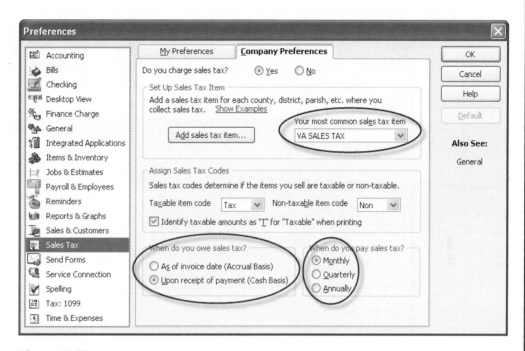

Figure 5:66

3. On the **Manage Sales Tax** window, click the **Sales Tax Liability** link to view a report showing the current sales tax owed.

    Enter the date range of **From** "3/1/2009" and **To** "3/31/2009." Close the report after noting the amount to pay under Sales Tax Payable (Figure 5:67).

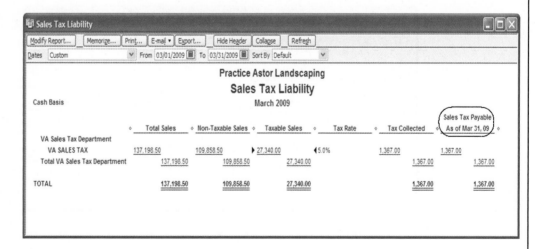

Figure 5:67

4. Click the **Pay Sales Tax** button. Enter the **Check Date** of 04/06/2009 and **Show sales tax due through** date of 03/31/2009. Click **Pay All Tax** and click **To be printed**.

The **Amt. Due** in Figure 5:68 matches the amount due on the previous report.

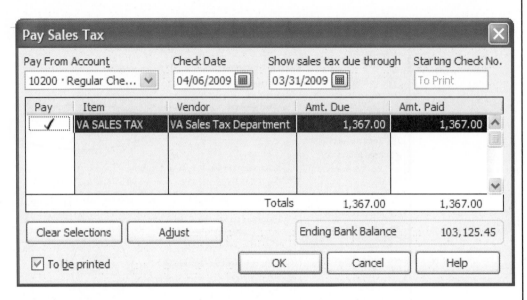

Figure 5:68

5. Click **OK** and then click **Close** to exit the Pay Sales Tax window.

6. You will now print the check. Click **Print Checks** under the **Banking** section of the Home page.

Confirm that "448" is the check number and then click **OK**. Click **Print** in the Print Checks window. Click **OK** in the confirmation window.

Figure 5:69

VENDOR CREDITS

Just as Astor issues credits to customers, vendors issue credits to Astor. Follow the next steps to record a credit for returning 10 granite pavers to Anderson Wholesale Nursery billed on Invoice 8213.

STEPS TO ENTER A VENDOR CREDIT MEMO

1. Click **Enter Bills** on the Home page. Select the **Credit** option and select the **Items** tab.

    Now enter the information shown on Figure 5:70.

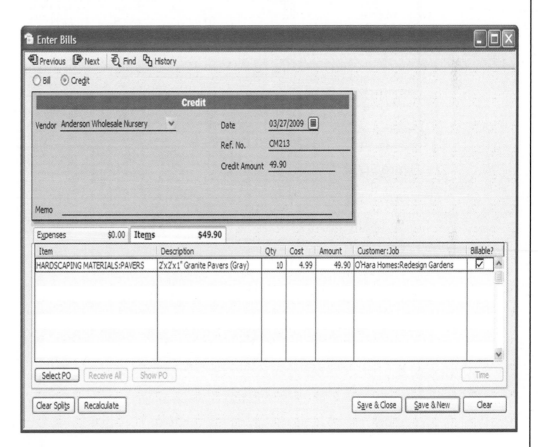

Figure 5:70

2. Click **Save & Close**.

3. Open the **Vendor Center** and view all transactions for Anderson's account. You should see the credit memo shown in Figure 5:71.

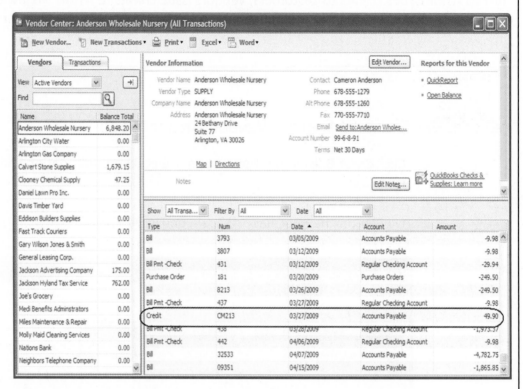

Figure 5:71

4. Now see what happens the next time you pay Anderson. Click the **New Transactions** button on the Vendor Center and select **Pay Bills**.

Highlight any bill from Anderson and the window will display an available credit of $49.90 (Figure 5:72).

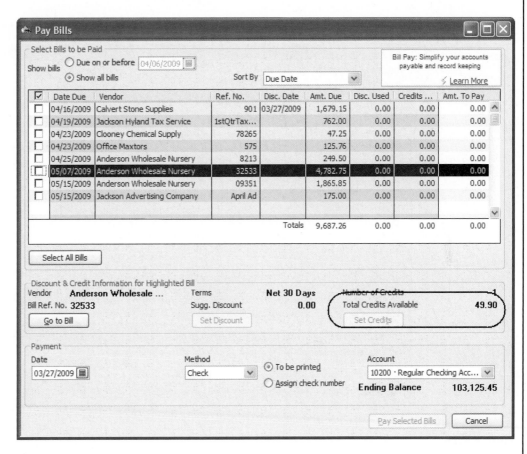

Figure 5:72

Now click to select Anderson's Invoice 8213. The credit will be applied to the bill selected and the amount applied will appear in the **Credits Used** column. *(Note: You can apply the credit to any bill.)*

Click **Cancel** and close the Vendor Center.

VENDOR REPORTING AND RECONCILING ACTIVITIES

QBP offers a variety of purchasing and vendor reports on the **Report Center**. Open the **Report Center** using the icon on the toolbar and select the **Vendors & Payables** category. You have already opened many of these reports using the Reports menu.

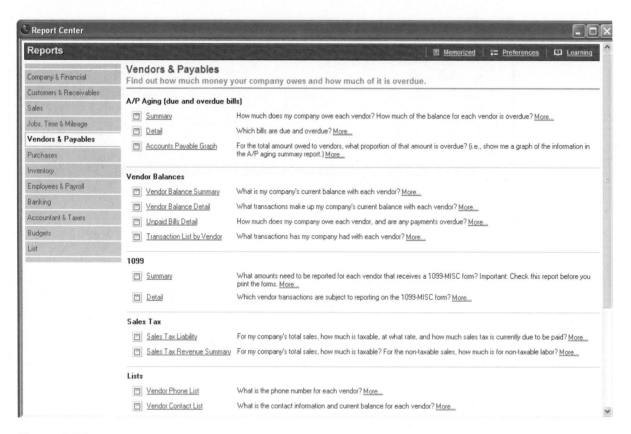

Figure 5:73

We will begin with **A/P Aging** reports. Click **Summary** and change the date to "3/31/2009." Refresh the report (Figure 5:74).

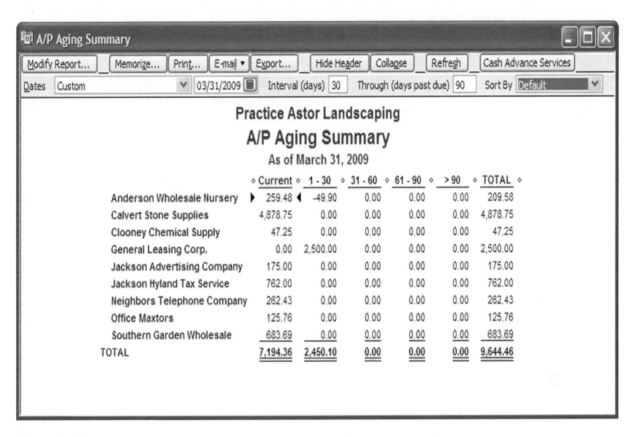

Figure 5:74

This report lists outstanding vendor balances by age of the balance. *(Note: Your balances will differ from those illustrated if you have not completed all chapter exercises.)* The report serves two important purposes.

First, Astor uses it to monitor vendor payments and to manage company cash flow. Second, the report is used to reconcile vendor balances with the accounts payable control account. This task is performed by comparing the aging report total with the March ending balance in general ledger account 20000 Accounts Payable.

Now view the balance in accounts payable. Select **Reports>>Accountant & Taxes>>Trial Balance** on the main menu and filter the report for 3/31/2009. Scroll down and locate the balance in 20000 Accounts Payable. The total on the A/P Aging report and the balance in Accounts Payable must agree to ensure proper recording of vendor activities.

These amounts will not reconcile when you improperly correct vendor transactions. Therefore, you should always refer to the instructions in Appendix B when correcting transactions. You should reconcile the aged payables report to the accounts payable account at the end of every month and prior to issuing financial reports.

Close all open reports and then open the **Detail A/P Aging** report. Change the date to "3/31/2009" and refresh the report. This report (Figure 5:75) lists invoices by invoice age.

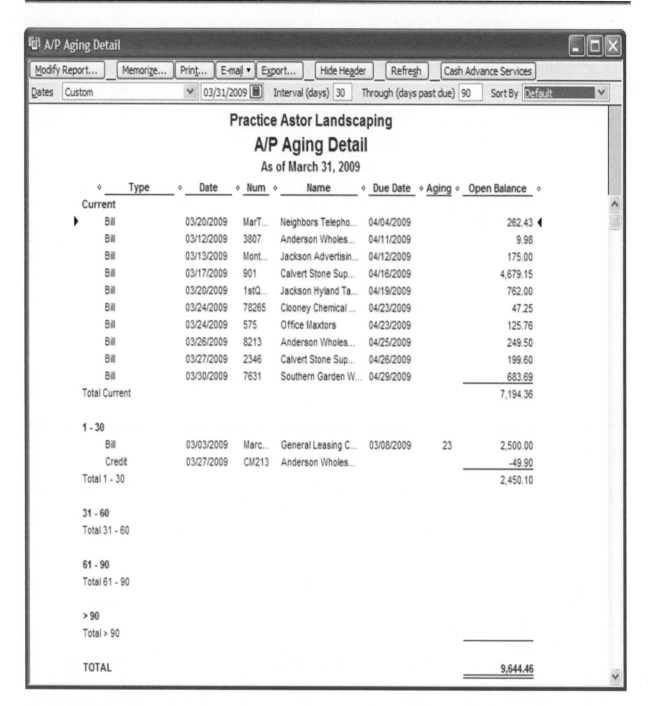

Figure 5:75

Close the Detail A/P Aging report and open the **Summary** report under **1099**. (See Figure 5:76.)

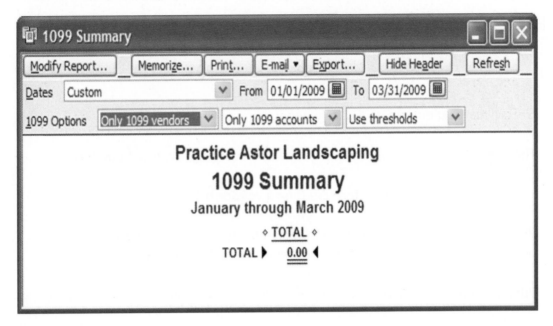

Figure 5:76

This report will list payments to vendors receiving 1099s when payments equal or exceed the $600 reporting threshold. Remember 1099 reporting requirements are set by the IRS.

Close all open reports and the Report Center.

You have now completed the chapter. ***Make a backup of the Practice Astor Landscaping data file to a backup file named "Practice Astor Landscaping Chpt 5". In the next chapter, you will build on the work completed in this chapter.***

SUMMARY

You began the chapter by learning to post transactions in a manual accounting system. You then posted *MAPS* transactions in QBP. You also learned to use the Vendor Center to manage vendor activities.

You have recorded POs and receipts of items on a PO. You posted vendor bills for receipts and vendor bills for expenses. You also paid vendors, voided payments, and recorded vendor credits.

Finally, you reconciled vendor transactions to the general ledger and worked with a variety of accounts payable reports that analyze activities. You are now ready to focus on the payroll activities covered in Chapter 6.

END-OF-CHAPTER QUESTIONS

TRUE/FALSE

_____ 1. QBP will let you enter a void date when voiding a vendor payment.

_____ 2. The Expenses tab on a vendor bill is used for recording inventory purchases.

_____ 3. You must first enter a PO before creating a vendor bill.

_____ 4. Vendor bills assigned to a customer job can be invoiced to the customer after posting the bill. *(Note: Relies on knowledge gained in Chapter 4.)*

_____ 5. Purchase orders are used to verify items on a vendor's bill.

_____ 6. QBP marks a PO "Closed" when all items have been received.

_____ 7. QBP will let you email POs and payments to vendors.

_____ 8. You can delete a vendor account with transaction history.

_____ 9. The Purchases Journal report will list vendor payments.

_____ 10. QBP will let you make changes to a posted vendor payment.

MULTIPLE CHOICE

_____ 1. Which icon(s) initiate a new vendor transaction?
   a. Purchase Orders
   b. Receive Inventory
   c. Enter Bills
   d. Both a and c

_____ 2. The Manage Sales Tax icon will let you _____.
   a. create a report for reviewing sales tax liability
   b. create a check for sales tax owed
   c. view sales tax setup information
   d. all of the above

_____ 3. Reconciling vendor activities means that the balance on the aged payables report equals the balance(s) in the _____.
         a. Accounts Payable account
         b. Accrued Liabilities account
         c. Both a and b
         d. None of the above

_____ 4. Which report lets you analyze all transactions for a vendor account?
         a. Vendor Balance Summary
         b. Transaction List by Vendors
         c. Vendor Balance Detail
         d. Both b and c

_____ 5. Payments to vendors can be reduced in the _____ window.
         a. Enter Bills
         b. Pay Bills
         c. Enter Bills Against Inventory
         d. Both a and b

_____ 6. Which report ages by vendor account balances?
         a. A/P Aging Summary
         b. A/P Aging Detail
         c. Both a and b
         d. None of the above

_____ 7. Clicking _____ will create checks without a vendor bill.
         a. Pay Bills
         b. Receive Inventory
         c. Write Checks
         d. Enter Bills

PRACTICE SET

In this practice set you will be using the **Graded Astor Landscaping** company file with the Practice Set completed in Chapter 4. **If the company file is not loaded on your computer then restore it using the Graded Astor Landscaping Chpt 4.QBB backup file created after completing the Chapter 4 Practice Set.**

1.   Enter Astor's April vendor activities that follow. All transactions, except the PO issued on April 17, will be printed in Step 2. Unless otherwise instructed, accept transaction defaults assigned from the vendor account.

2009

Apr 2   Post Safe State Insurance Company bill for six months of prepaid insurance, $1,200.00.

Apr 3   Add the following Non-inventory Part.

Item name:	ARBORVITAE
Subitem of:	PLANTS
Purchase description:	2G Arborvitae
Purchase cost:	$40.00
Expense account:	51000 Materials Cost - Landscape
Preferred vendor:	Anderson Wholesale Nursery
Sales description:	2G Arborvitae
Sales price:	$52.00
Tax code:	Tax
Income account:	41000 Sales - Landscape

Record the following vendor bills for job materials:

Anderson Wholesale Nursery Invoice 7383 dated April 2, $2,318.00, for O'Hara Homes Redesign Gardens job.

Qty	Item	Cost
20	Verbena	$ 15.90
50	Arborvitae	$ 40.00

Paris Brothers Tree Surgeons Invoice 4263 dated April 2, $1,020.00 for O'Hara Homes Redesign Gardens job.

Qty	Item	Cost
12	Tree removal	$ 85.00

Apr 9   Post Davis Timber Yard's Invoice 9033 dated April 7, $3,775.70 for White and Associates job.

Qty	Item	Cost
400	Redwood Decking	$ 8.99
15	Redwood Posts	$ 5.99
15	Redwood Caps	$ 5.99

Apr 10   Pay $21,133.47 to vendors for bills with a due date or discount date before April 20. First check number is 450.

Apr 16   Post Miles Maintenance & Repair Invoice 1762 for $275.00 dated April 14 for auto repairs. Verify the account number for the transaction.

Apr 17   Issue PO 176 for $449.50 to Davis Timber Yard containing the following item for the White and Associates job. **Print the PO.**

Qty	Item	Cost
50	Redwood Decking	$ 8.99

Post Anderson Wholesale Nursery Invoice 3766 for $9.98 dated April 16 for the DBH Enterprises job.

Qty	Item	Cost
2	Mulch	$ 4.99

Apr 20   Post the following bills for expenses dated April 20.

Arlington City Water	April water	$110.00
Neighbors Telephone Co.	April phone	$230.00
Arlington Gas Company	April gas	$175.80
Southern Power Co.	April electric	$162.50

Apr 21   Write and print check number 455 to Postmaster for postage expense $150.00.

Post Davis Timber Yard Invoice 6261, $449.50, dated April 20 for all items on PO 176.

Apr 22   Add the following new vendor.
                    Metropolitan Supplies
                    672 N. Main Street
                    Arlington, VA 30010
                    (701) 555-7023
                        Contact: Shannon Wilson
                        Vendor Type: OFFICE
                        Payment terms: Net 30
                        Expense Account: Office Supplies Expense

                Post Metropolitan Supplies Invoice 6565 dated April 21 for office supply
                expense $137.20.

Apr 28   Post Anderson Wholesale Nursery Credit memo CM7383, $80.00, dated April 22
                for returning 2 Arborvitae on Invoice 7383 for the O'Hara Homes Redesign
                Garden job.

Apr 30   Pay $4,116.30 to vendors for bills with a due date or discount date before
                May 4, 2009. First check number is 456.

                Write check number 462 for $1,648.25 for April sales tax.

2.   Print the following reports.

    a. Purchases Journal for April transactions.

    b. Cash Disbursements Journal for April transactions. Modify report to add Check and
        Sales Tax Payment to the existing transaction types.

    c. Open Purchase Orders report for April transactions. Modify report's Received filter
        to include Either.

    d. A/P Aging Detail report for April 30, 2009.

    e. Job Profitability Summary report for April transactions

    f. Unbilled Costs by Job report with the Dates option set to All.

3.   *Back up the Graded Astor Landscaping data file to a backup file named "Graded Astor
        Landscaping Chpt 5". The Practice Set for the next chapter will build on the work
        completed in this chapter.*

CHAPTER 6 PAYROLL ACTIVITIES FOR A SERVICE BASED BUSINESS

LEARNING OBJECTIVES

This chapter works with the Practice Astor Landscaping data file containing the tasks completed in Chapter 5. *If this company is not loaded on your computer then restore it using the Practice Astor Landscaping Chpt 5.QBB backup file created after reading Chapter 5.*

In this chapter you process Astor's payroll and do the following:

1. Learn the *MAPS* for recording employee paychecks before processing paychecks in QBP
2. Review payroll items to understand their impact on posting payroll transactions
3. Learn to use the Employee Center to manage employees and paycheck transactions
4. Record employee time and print time reports
5. Pay employees
6. Go *Behind the Keys* of posted paychecks and learn to correct these transactions
7. Allocate salaried employee wages to jobs
8. Remit payroll tax liabilities to government taxing agencies
9. Create and interpret payroll reports, including Form 941 and W-2s

Launch QBP and open **Practice Astor Landscaping**.

 MANUAL ACCOUNTING PROCEDURES

Astor pays employees biweekly (every two weeks). Employees are paid either an hourly wage or an annual salary. Salaried employees are paid the same amount each pay period. Hourly employees are paid for the total hours worked during the pay period and document these hours on timesheets that note the hours related to jobs so Astor can invoice customers.

You will soon learn that payroll in a manual accounting system is tedious and time consuming. First, you must calculate gross pay for hourly and salaried employees. For hourly employee, gross pay is calculated by totaling timesheet hours for the pay period and multiplying total hours by the hourly pay rate. For salaried employees, gross pay remains the same each pay period and is calculated by dividing the annual salary by the number of pay periods in the year. The number of pay periods in the year is 26 for Astor.

After calculating gross pay, you next calculate net pay. Net pay equals gross pay minus total payroll tax withholdings and total voluntary deductions. The following tables explain payroll tax withholdings and voluntary deductions.

Employee Tax Withholdings	Description
Federal Income Tax	Employee federal income taxes withheld on taxable wages. Taxable wages exclude employee contributions to a 401K or IRA retirement plan. IRS Circular E sets the guidelines for withholding federal income taxes (explained later).
Social Security (FICA)	Employee taxes withheld on gross wages and paid to the federal government to fund Social Security retirement. Gross wages include employee contributions to a 401K or IRA retirement plan. The IRS currently taxes gross wages at 6.2 percent (0.062) until wages paid during the year exceed an annual cap. For 2008, the annual cap was $102,000. This cap is increased each year and the 2009 cap was not available at the time of publishing the text.
Medicare (FICA)	Employee taxes withheld on gross wages and paid to the federal government to fund Medicare health insurance. Gross wages include employee contributions to a 401K or IRA retirement plan. The IRS taxes gross wages at 1.45 percent (0.0145) and there is no annual wage cap.
State Income Tax	Employee state income taxes withheld on taxable wages (i.e., gross wages minus contributions to a 401K or IRA retirement plan). Each state publishes guidelines for withholding state income taxes. **Astor withholds 3 percent (0.03) of gross wages.**

Employee Voluntary Deductions	Description
Retirement Plans	Employee voluntary contributions to an employer-sponsored retirement plan. Retirement plans include 401K and IRA plans. These contributions are deducted from gross wages to determine federal and state taxable wages. ***Aster does not sponsor a retirement plan.***
Health Insurance	Health insurance premiums deducted from pay when the employer requires its employees to pay for a portion of health insurance costs. ***Astor does not require employees to share this cost.***
Contributions	Deductions from net pay for charitable contributions made by the employee.

Astor also pays taxes on employee compensation and provides additional compensation by providing health insurance. The next tables explain typical employer tax liabilities and other forms of employee compensation.

Employer Payroll Taxes	Description
Social Security (FICA) and Medicare (FICA)	Employer portion of Social Security and Medicare taxes paid on gross wages. The employer tax equals the tax paid by employees.
Federal Unemployment (FUTA)	Employer tax on gross wages paid to the federal government for subsidizing state unemployment compensation funds. Typically, employers pay 0.08 percent (0.008) on the first $7,000 of annual gross wages paid to each employee.
State Unemployment (SUTA)	Employer tax on gross wages paid to the state for funding compensation for unemployed workers. Typically the tax rate is based on an employer's unemployment history and/or business type and will be capped after reaching an annual limit on gross wages. *For Astor the rate is 1.5 percent (0.015) of the first $8,000 of annual wages paid to each employee.*
Worker's Compensation	Employer tax paid to the state to fund compensating injured workers. Typically, states set the tax rates based on risk factors in an employee's job. *The text does not illustrate worker's compensation tax.*

Additional Compensation	Description
Retirement Plans	Employer contributions to a company-sponsored 401K or IRA retirement plan. Typically companies match contributions based on employee participation in the plan. *Astor does not sponsor a retirement plan.*
Health Insurance	Employer premiums for health insurance. Employers may pay all premiums or require employees to share in this cost. *Astor pays all health insurance premiums for employees eligible to participate in the plan.*

Each pay period the accountant prepares an Excel spreadsheet called the Payroll Register to calculate employee net pay. The register illustrated in Figure 6:1 covers the pay period of February 23 to March 8, 2009.

	A	B	C	D	E	F	G	H	I	J	K	L	M	N
1	Astor Landscaping													
2	Pay Period 2/23/2009 thru 3/08/2009													
3														
4	Check No.	Employee	Filing Status	Allow.	Pay Type	Pay Rate	Regular Hrs	O.T. Hours	Gross Pay	Federal Income Tax	Soc. Sec. (FICA) Tax	Medicare Tax	VA State Tax	Net Pay
5	721	Dillion, Roy J.	Single	1	Hourly Wage	12.00	80.00		996.00	98.00	61.75	14.44	29.88	791.93
6	722	Folse, Jan B.	Single	1	Hourly Office	10.00	80.00		800.00	71.00	49.60	11.60	24.00	643.80
7	723	Greene, Kellie I.	Married	1	Salary	2,346.15			2,346.15	256.00	145.46	34.02	70.38	1,840.29
8	724	Hardman, Alan	Single	2	Hourly Wage	12.00	78.00		1,044.00	87.00	64.73	15.14	31.32	845.81
9	725	Hayes, Mike E	Single	1	Hourly Wage	12.00	32.00		384.00	15.00	23.81	5.57	11.52	328.10
10	726	Henderson, Jeff P.	Married	1	Hourly Wage	12.00	80.00		960.00	53.00	59.52	13.92	28.80	804.76
11	727	Murray, Monica D.	Single	1	Salary	1,211.54			1,211.54	131.00	75.12	17.57	36.35	951.50
12	728	Ramez, Victor M.	Single	0	Hourly Wage	10.00	75.00		750.00	83.00	46.50	10.88	22.50	587.12
13	729	Ruland, Seth N.	Married	0	Salary	3,103.85			3,103.85	429.00	192.44	45.01	93.12	2,344.28
14	730	White, Judy O.	Married	2	Salary	2,084.62			2,084.62	295.00	129.25	30.23	62.54	1,567.60
15														
16		Totals					425.00	0.00	13,680.16	1,518.00	848.18	198.38	410.41	10,705.19
17														
18		Tax Basis								Circular E	6.20%	1.45%	3.00%	
19														
20		G/L Accounts							57000 / 60000	23400	23400	23400	23600	10300

Figure 6:1

The Payroll Register shows that Kellie Greene claims the Married (M) federal filing status with one withholding allowance. To calculate Kellie's federal income tax withholding for this pay period look to the 2008 IRS Circular E tax table in Figure 6:2. *(Note: IRS tables for 2009 were not available at the time of publishing the text. The 2008 tables are also provided in Appendix D.)*

MARRIED Persons—BIWEEKLY Payroll Period
(For Wages Paid in 2008)

If the wages are—		And the number of withholding allowances claimed is—										
At least	But less than	0	1	2	3	4	5	6	7	8	9	10
		The amount of income tax to be withheld is—										
$1,380	$1,400	$132	$112	$92	$72	$54	$41	$27	$14	$1	$0	$0
1,400	1,420	135	115	95	75	56	43	29	16	3	0	0
1,420	1,440	138	118	98	78	58	45	31	18	5	0	0
1,440	1,460	141	121	101	81	61	47	33	20	7	0	0
1,460	1,480	144	124	104	84	64	49	35	22	9	0	0
1,480	1,500	147	127	107	87	67	51	37	24	11	0	0
1,500	1,520	150	130	110	90	70	53	39	26	13	0	0
1,520	1,540	153	133	113	93	73	55	41	28	15	1	0
1,540	1,560	156	136	116	96	76	57	43	30	17	3	0
1,560	1,580	159	139	119	99	79	59	45	32	19	5	0
2,280	2,300	267	247	227	207	187	166	146	126	106	86	66
2,300	2,320	270	250	230	210	190	169	149	129	109	89	69
2,320	2,340	273	253	233	213	193	172	152	132	112	92	72
2,340	2,360	276	256	236	216	196	175	155	135	115	95	75
2,360	2,380	279	259	239	219	199	178	158	138	118	98	78
2,380	2,400	282	262	242	222	202	181	161	141	121	101	81
2,400	2,420	285	265	245	225	205	184	164	144	124	104	84
2,420	2,440	288	268	248	228	208	187	167	147	127	107	87
2,440	2,460	291	271	251	231	211	190	170	150	130	110	90
2,460	2,480	294	274	254	234	214	193	173	153	133	113	93
2,480	2,500	297	277	257	237	217	196	176	156	136	116	96
2,500	2,520	300	280	260	240	220	199	179	159	139	119	99
2,520	2,540	303	283	263	243	223	202	182	162	142	122	102
2,540	2,560	306	286	266	246	226	205	185	165	145	125	105
2,560	2,580	309	289	269	249	229	208	188	168	148	128	108
2,580	2,600	312	292	272	252	232	211	191	171	151	131	111
2,600	2,620	315	295	275	255	235	214	194	174	154	134	114
2,620	2,640	318	298	278	258	238	217	197	177	157	137	117
2,640	2,660	321	301	281	261	241	220	200	180	160	140	120
2,660	2,680	324	304	284	264	244	223	203	183	163	143	123
2,680	2,700	327	307	287	267	247	226	206	186	166	146	126

$2,700 and over   Use Table 2(b) for a **MARRIED person** on page 38. Also see the instructions on page 36.

Figure 6:2

Figure 6:2 is the IRS table for employees paid biweekly and claiming the Married (M) filing status. There are separate IRS tables for employees claiming the Single (S) filing status and separate tables for married and single employees paid on a weekly or monthly basis. You can also withhold extra taxes as Judy White does.

Kellie's $256.00 federal income tax withholding amount is found at the point where her taxable pay of $2,346.15 intersects with her one claimed withholding allowance. Because Kellie does not contribute to a 401K or IRA retirement plan, her taxable pay equals her gross pay.

Kellie's Social Security tax withholding of $145.46 equals her gross pay times 6.2 percent (0.062). Her Medicare tax withholding of $34.02 equals gross pay times 1.45 percent (0.0145).

The state tax withholding of $70.38 is 3 percent (0.03) of her taxable pay.

Kellie has no deductions for health insurance premiums, retirement plan contributions, or charitable contributions. In fact, premiums are not deducted from any employee's paycheck because Astor pays the full cost of health insurance. There are no deductions for retirement plans because Astor does not sponsor a plan. Finally, there are no employees making charitable contributions through payroll.

Accordingly, Kellie's net pay of $1,840.29 equals her gross pay minus the sum of her total tax withholdings.

The accountant has also computed the employer payroll tax liabilities for the pay period, illustrated in Figure 6:3.

	P	Q	R	S	T	U
1	**Astor Landscaping**					
2	**Employer Costs for Period 2/23/2009 thru 3/08/2009**					
3						
4	**Employee**	**ER Soc Sec FICA**	**ER Medicare**	**ER FUTA**	**ER SUTA**	**Health Insurance**
5	Dillion, Roy J.	61.75	14.44	7.97	14.94	0.00
6	Folse, Jan B.	49.60	11.60	6.40	12.00	60.00
7	Greene, Kellie I.	145.46	34.02	0.00	0.00	60.00
8	Hardman, Alan	64.73	15.14	8.35	15.66	0.00
9	Hayes, Mike E	23.81	5.57	5.51	5.76	0.00
10	Henderson, Jeff P.	59.52	13.92	7.68	14.40	0.00
11	Murray, Monica D.	75.12	17.57	9.69	18.17	60.00
12	Ramez, Victor M.	46.50	10.88	6.00	11.25	0.00
13	Ruland, Seth N.	192.44	45.01	0.00	0.00	60.00
14	White, Judy O.	129.25	30.23	0.00	0.00	60.00
15						
16	Totals	848.18	198.38	51.60	92.18	300.00
17						
18	Tax Basis	6.20%	1.45%	0.8%	1.50%	
19						
20	G/L Accounts	23400 / 61000	23400 / 61000	23500 / 61000	23700 / 61000	23800 / 60600

Figure 6:3

After computing employee pay and employer payroll tax liabilities, the accountant creates paychecks and records the general journal entries illustrated in Figure 6:4. *(Note: General ledger accounts are listed on the worksheets. The expense recorded to 57000 Direct Labor is the gross pay for employees paid by Hourly Wage.)*

Astor Landscaping
Audit Trail General Journal   Page 5

Date	Account Post Ref	Description	Debit	Credit
03/09/09	57000	Direct Labor	4,134.00	
	60000	Salaries Expense	9,546.16	
	23400	Federal Payroll Tax Liabilities		2,564.56
	23600	State Payroll Taxes Payable		410.41
	10300	Payroll Checking Account		10,705.19

To record employee paychecks

Date	Account Post Ref	Description	Debit	Credit
03/09/09	61000	Payroll Tax Expense	1,190.34	
	60600	Employee Benefit Exp.	300.00	
	23400	Federal Payroll Tax Liabilities		1,046.56
	23500	FUTA Tax Payable		51.60
	23700	SUTA Tax Payable		92.18
	23800	Medical Insurance Payable		300.00

To record employer payroll tax expense

Figure 6:4

The journal entries are then posted to the general ledger accounts affected by the transactions (Figure 6:5). *(Note: Only two general ledger accounts are illustrated.)*

General Ledger

Payroll Checking Account   **Account No. 10300**

Date	Description	Post Ref	Debit	Credit	Balance
03/08/09	Balance Forward				15,574.80
03/09/09		GJ 5		10,705.19	4,869.61

Audit Trail

General Ledger

Federal Payroll Tax Liabilities   **Account No. 23400**

Date	Description	Post Ref	Debit	Credit	Balance
03/08/09	Balance Forward				-
03/09/09		GJ 5		2,564.56	2,564.56
03/09/09		GJ 5		1,046.56	3,611.12

Figure 6:5

As explained in previous chapters, the audit trail is recorded while posting to general ledger accounts.

With an understanding of *MAPS* for paycheck activities, you are now ready to perform these activities in QBP.

UNDERSTANDING PAYROLL ITEMS

A series of setup steps is performed before a company can use QBP for processing payroll. The accountant has already completed these steps; however, it will help for you to understand payroll setup.

Begin by opening the Payroll Item List. Select **Lists>>Payroll Item List** on the main menu to open the window illustrated in Figure 6:6.

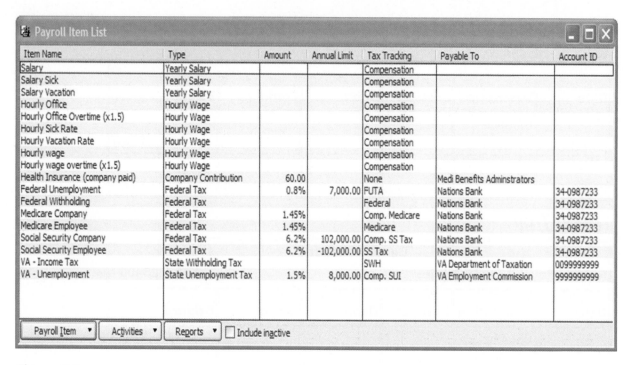

Figure 6:6

Figure 6:6 shows the payroll items for tracking compensation, payroll tax withholdings, and payroll tax liabilities. Salary and wage types track employee compensation whereas federal and state types track employee tax withholdings and employer tax liabilities.

Next, you will add columns to the list so that general ledger accounts are displayed for each item. Click **Payroll Item** at the bottom of the list and select **Customize Columns**.

Highlight **Expense Account** under **Available Columns** and click **Add**. Do the same for **Liability Account**. (See Figure 6:7.)

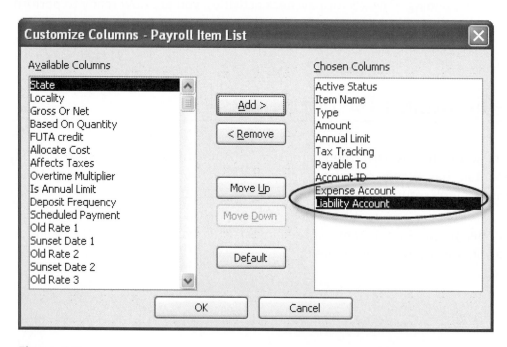

Figure 6:7

Click **OK** to view the list with the added columns (Figure 6:8). You have to resize columns to view all information.

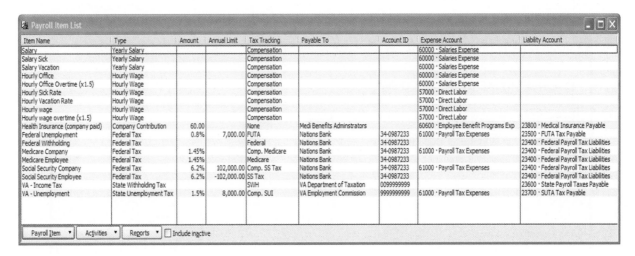

Figure 6:8

Refer to these accounts as we go through the setup of payroll items.

Double click the **Salary** item. The window in Figure 6:9 is used to define the item's name or to inactivate an item. Click **Next**.

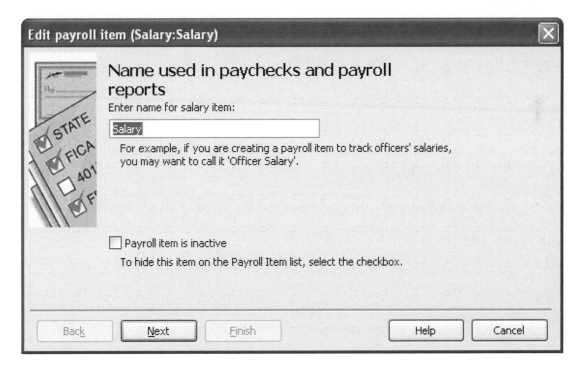

Figure 6:9

This window in Figure 6:10 sets the default general ledger account used when posting a salaried employee's gross pay. The account displayed matches the expense account listed on the Payroll Item List. Click **Cancel**.

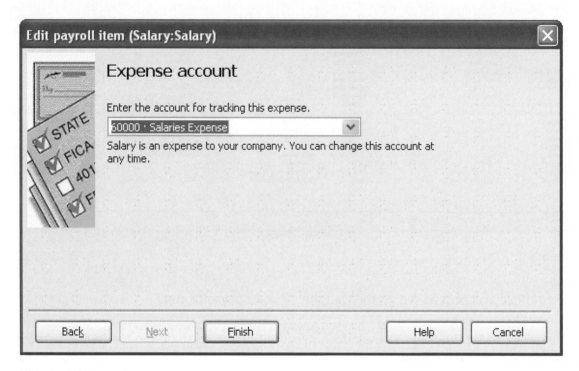

Figure 6:10

Return to the **Payroll Item List** and note that Astor has three categories of wage compensation.

Salary items are for employees paid an annual salary. Gross pay for this item posts to 60000 Salaries Expense.

Hourly office items are for employees paid an hourly wage, but these employees do not work on customer jobs. Gross pay for this item also posts to 60000 Salaries Expense.

Hourly wage items are for employees paid an hourly wage for work performed on customer jobs. Astor will bill customers for these hours. Gross pay for this item will post to 57000 Direct Labor (i.e., a cost of goods sold account).

Double click **Federal Unemployment** to open the item. Once again, the first screen names the item so click **Next**.

Recall from the previous topic that FUTA tax is an employer payroll tax expense. Therefore, the screen in Figure 6:11 selects the vendor for remitting taxes as well as the expense and liability accounts used when posting FUTA taxes.

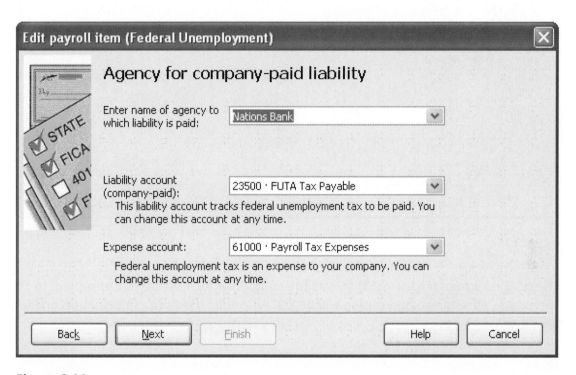

Figure 6:11

Click **Next**. This screen (Figure 6:12) sets the tax rate. Like Astor, most companies use the 0.8% (0.008) rate.

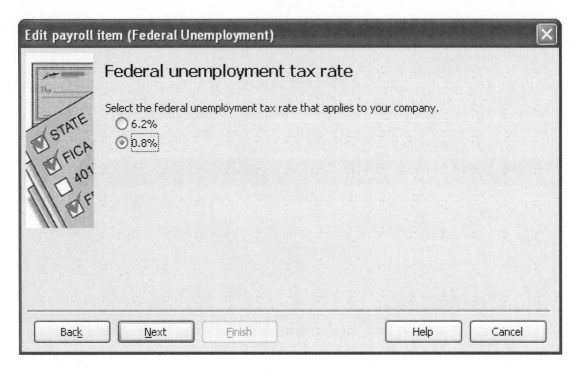

Figure 6:12

Click **Next**. This screen (Figure 6:13) selects the compensation items that are subject to FUTA tax. Generally, all wage compensation will be FUTA taxable. For more information on FUTA taxes, visit www.irs.gov.

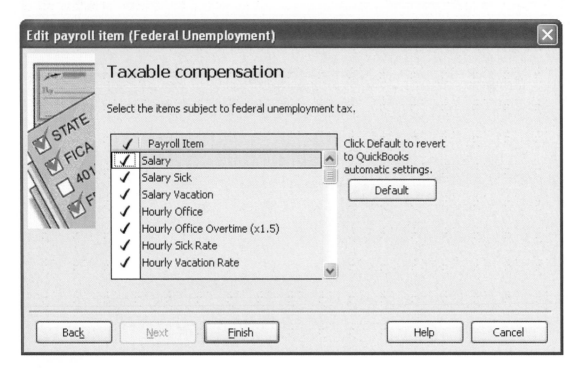

Figure 6:13

Click **Cancel**.

Now open **Medicare Company**.   This screen (Figure 6:14) names two items. Recall that Medicare is paid by both the employee and the employer.

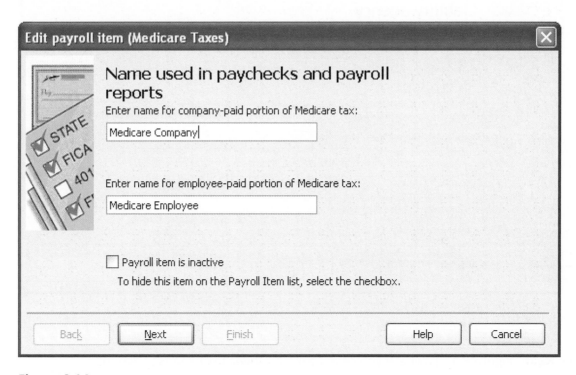

Figure 6:14

Click **Next**. Once again, you find a screen (Figure 6:15) for setting the general ledger posting accounts as well as the vendor for remitting payment. However, this time the screen sets only liability accounts for employer taxes and employee withholdings.

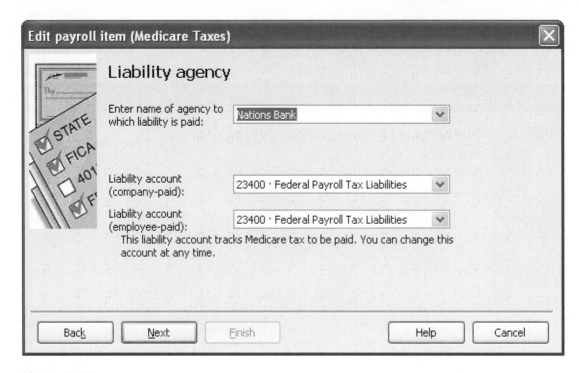

Figure 6:15

Click **Next**. Figure 6:16 is where you select the employer tax expense account.

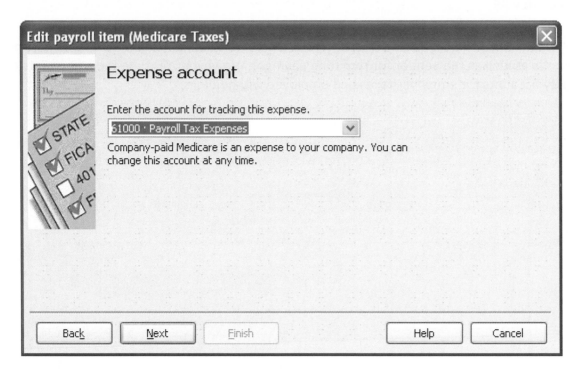

Figure 6:16

Click **Cancel**.

Notice that you were unable to set the tax rate on the previous item. In fact, you are unable to set tax rates for any Federal Tax types, other than FUTA, or State Withholding Taxes. QBP sets these rates when downloading online payroll tax tables and access to these tables requires a paid subscription.

There is one last item to review before moving to the next topic. Open **Health Insurance**. This item (Figure 6:17) tracks company health insurance premiums paid by the employer. Notice that you can also choose to track this expense by job.

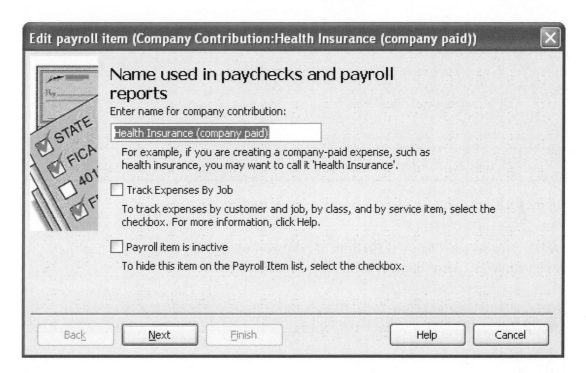

Figure 6:17

Click **Next**. Again, we see the screen (Figure 6:18) for selecting a vendor and general ledger posting accounts.

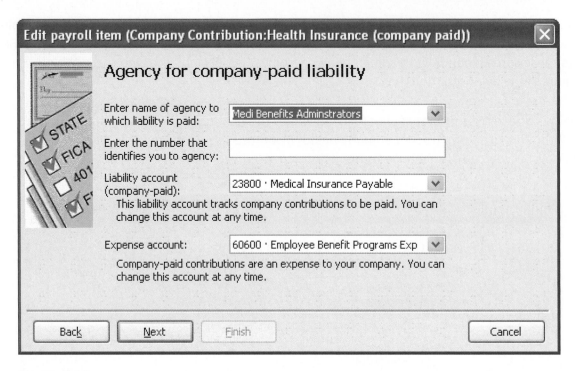

Figure 6:18

Click **Next**. This screen (Figure 6:19) opts to print company contributions for health insurance on employee W-2s. Astor has elected not to print this information.

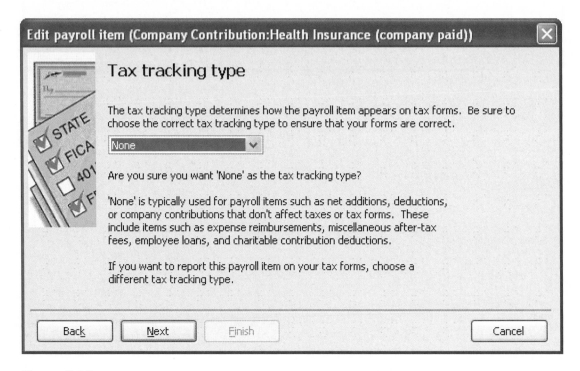

Figure 6:19

Click **Next**. This screen (Figure 6:20) determines when a company-paid benefit is subject to employer and/or employee payroll taxes. Remember, these benefits are deemed additional compensation, which may or may not be taxable. Typically, employer-paid health insurance premiums are not subject to tax.

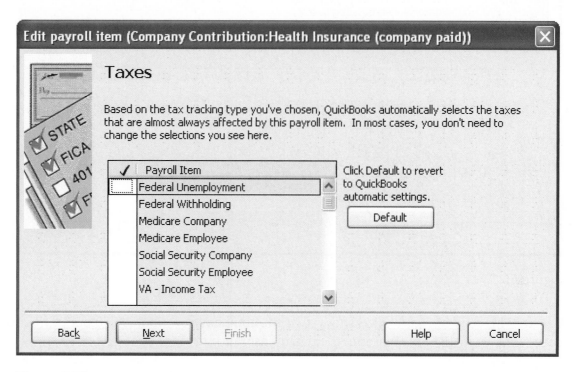

Figure 6:20

Click **Next**. In Figure 6:21 you choose whether a company-paid benefit will be based on a quantity such as hours, a percentage, or a flat amount.

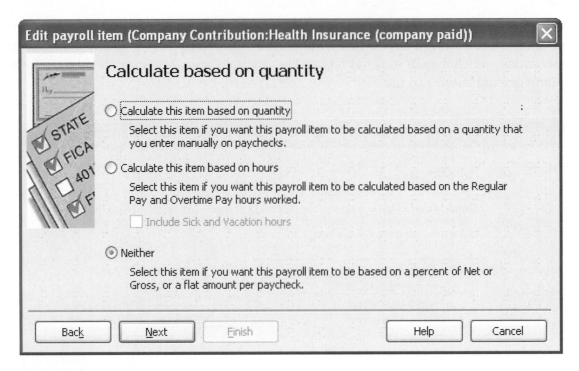

Figure 6:21

Click **Next**. This screen (Figure 6:22) shows that the company contributes $60 per pay period for each employee who participates in the health insurance plan.

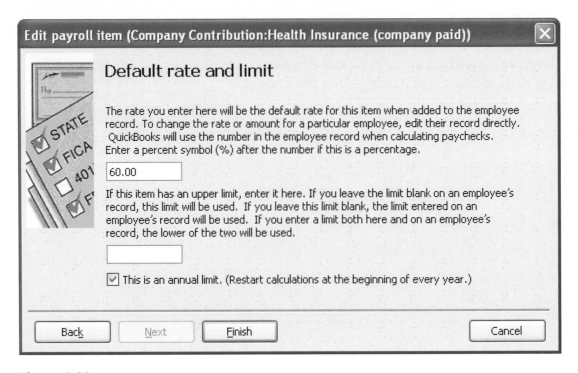

Figure 6:22

Click **Cancel** and then close the Payroll Item List.

With all the complexities just illustrated, you can see why many companies outsource payroll. Now that you understand the purpose of payroll items you will next learn to manage the employee accounts linked to these items.

EMPLOYEE CENTER

In this topic you use the Employee Center to manage employee accounts and locate payroll transactions. Click the **Employee Center** icon on the toolbar and select the **Employees** tab. Set the options illustrated in Figure 6:23.

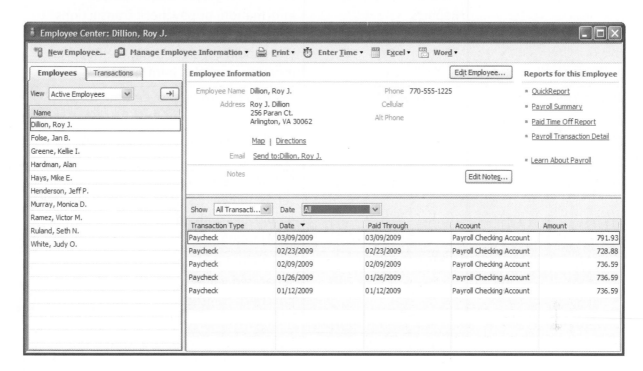

Figure 6:23

The **Transactions** tab serves the same purpose as served on other centers. The table that follows explains activities and tasks on the **Employees** toolbar. Remember that actions are performed on the account highlighted to the left.

Employees Activities	Task	Description
New Employee		Create a new employee account.
Manage Employee Information	Add/Edit Sales Rep	Manage existing employee accounts.
	Change New Employee Default Settings	Create employee defaults that will be assigned to new employee accounts.
Print	Print Paychecks	Print calculated paychecks.
	Print/Email Paystubs	Print only pay stubs. This is used when checks are deposited directly to employee bank accounts.
	Print Other Employee Reports	Print an employee list, employee information, or paycheck transactions. These reports cannot be customized so you should consider using the Reports menu to print this information.
Enter Time	Use Weekly Timesheet	Used to record employee time for an entire week.
	Time/Enter Single Activity	Used to record time for single days or single activities.
Excel	Export Employee List	Create an Excel workbook or comma separated values (.csv) file containing all employees with address and contact information.
	Export Transactions	Create an Excel workbook or comma separated values (.csv) file containing paycheck transactions for the highlighted employee.
	Summarize Payroll Data in Excel	Extract payroll data from QBP for analysis in Excel.
Word		Create form letters for communicating with employees.

The Employee Center is helpful for managing employees and the next topic will walk you through this activity.

MANAGING EMPLOYEES

Double click Roy Dillion's account to open it. *(Note: You can also click the Edit Employee button to the right.)*

An employee account contains tabs for three categories of information. These categories are **Personal Info**, **Payroll and Compensation Info**, and **Employment Info**. (See Figure 6:24.) Tab categories are changed by selecting a different category from the **Change tabs** dropdown list.

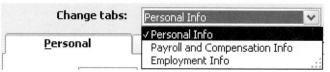

Figure 6:24

Select the **Personal Info** tab and you will find subtabs for information in this category. The following explains the information stored on subtabs in the **Personal Info** category.

Personal Tab

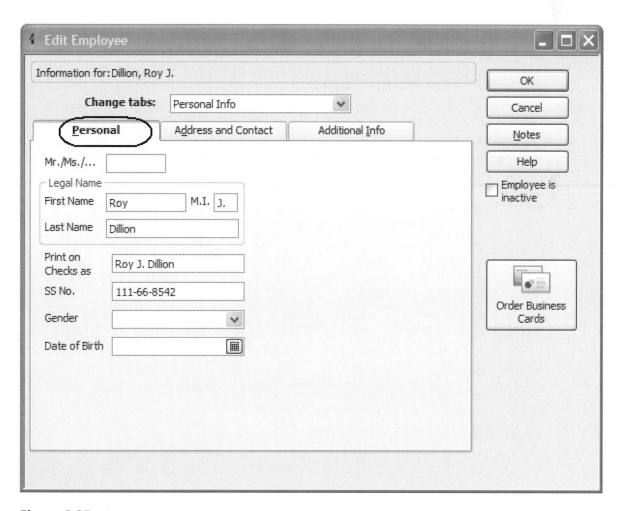

Figure 6:25

This tab stores employee social security number and birth date.

Address and Contact Tab

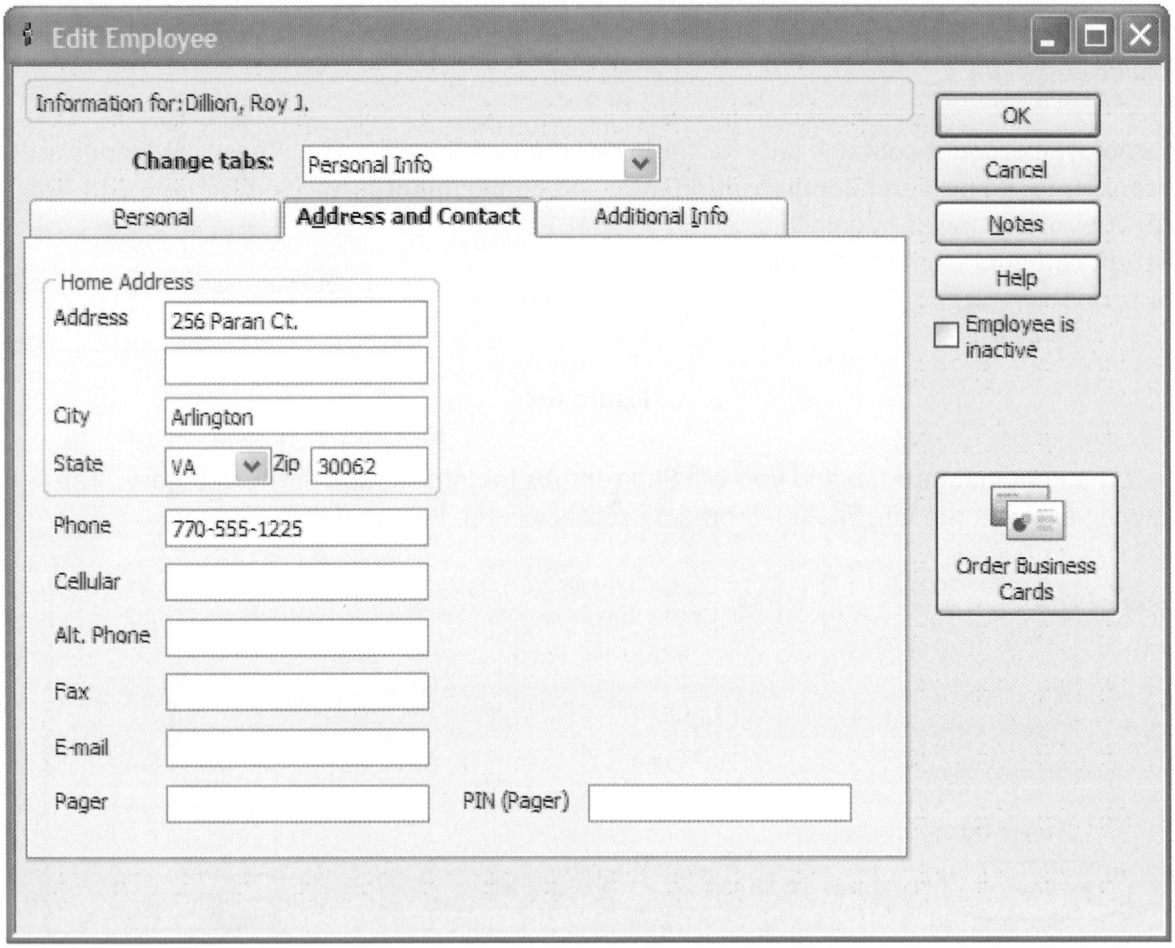

Figure 6:26

This tab stores basic contact information for the employee.

Additional Info Tab

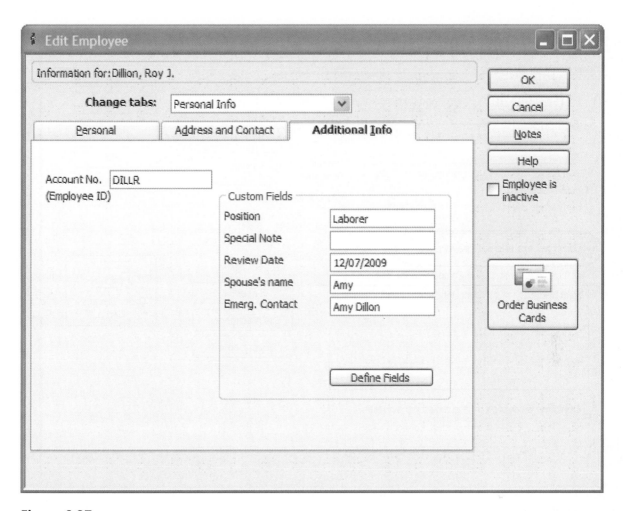

Figure 6:27

This tab stores miscellaneous information such as job position.

Now change the category to **Payroll and Compensation Info**.

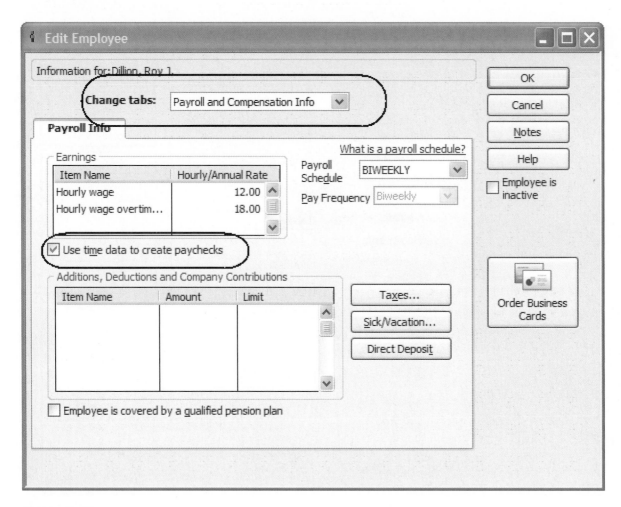

Figure 6:28

Figure 6:28 is where QBP looks to gather pay rates and pay schedule frequency. Notice that Roy is paid biweekly at $12.00 per hour for regular time and $18.00 per hour for overtime.

Also note that time data must be entered to create Roy's paycheck. This option is checked on hourly paid employees so that compensation will be based on the number of hours worked.

Now focus on **Item Name**. Click **Hourly Wage** and open the dropdown list. Figure 6:29 shows Astor's pay codes.

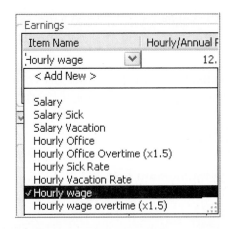

Figure 6:29

You find the compensation payroll items discussed in the Payroll Items topic.

Roy's account has been assigned to **Hourly** wage so you know that his compensation will post to 57000 Direct Labor and that Astor will bill his hours to customers.

Click the **Taxes** button to open the window illustrated in Figure 6:30.

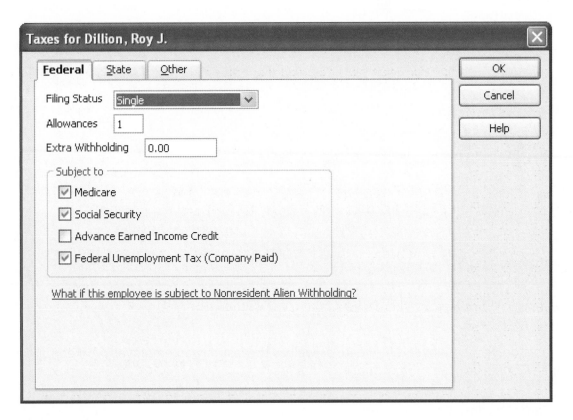

Figure 6:30

QBP looks to this tab to obtain federal and state filing statuses and withholding allowances. The **Federal** tab above shows that Roy's federal **Filing Status** is **Single** with one withholding **Allowance**.

At the bottom you see that Roy's wages are subject to Medicare and Social Security tax withholdings. Wages are also subject to employer Medicare, Social Security, and FUTA taxes.

The **State** tab on this window is used for entering state tax withholding information. The **Other** tab is used when employees also pay city or local taxes.

Click **Cancel** to exit the tax window.

Finally, change the category to **Employment Info**.

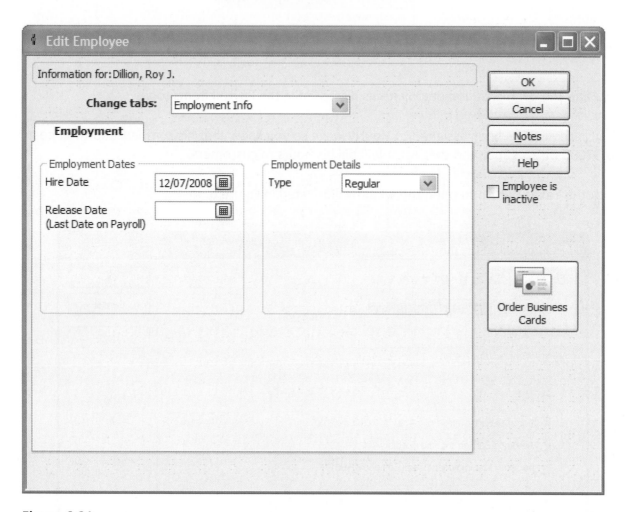

Figure 6:31

This tab stores an employee's hire date as well as the last day an employee worked for the company.

Click **Cancel** to close Roy's account.

Before leaving this topic, open Kellie Greene's account to view pay information for a salaried employee. After opening, change the tab category to **Payroll and Compensation Info**.

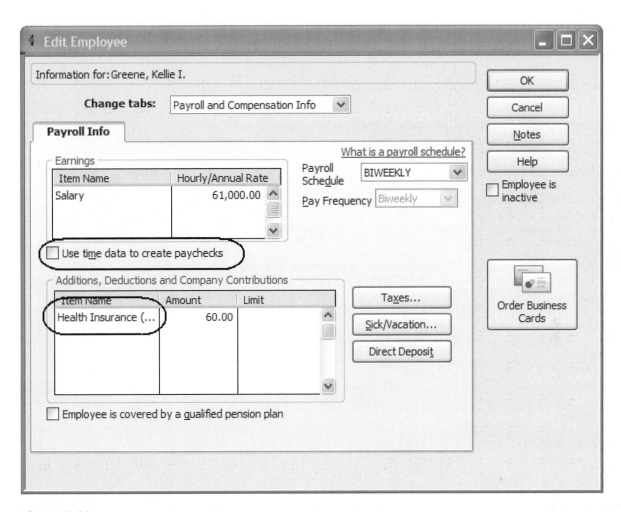

Figure 6:32

Salaried employee pay rates are entered as annual compensation. For Kellie, the annual salary is $61,000. Also notice that Kelly is paid BIWEEKLY, so she will receive 26 paychecks during the year (52 weeks per year / 2 weeks per pay period). Based on this information, QBP will calculate Kellie's gross pay for each pay period as $61,000 / 26.

Furthermore, Kellie's account does not require time data because salaried employees paychecks are not based on the number of hours worked.

Kellie also participates in the company's health insurance plan, so the Health Insurance payroll item is assigned to her account.

Click **Cancel** to exit Kellie's account.

You are now ready to create a new employee. Click the **New Employee** button on the Employee Center.

Astor hired Jack Zickefoose to work as a laborer on customer jobs. Follow the next steps to create the account.

Enter his **Personal** information as shown on Figure 6:33.

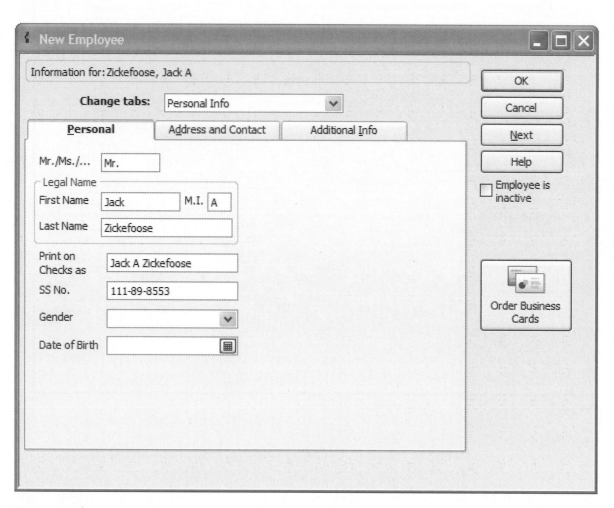

Figure 6:33

Click **Address and Contact** and enter the information shown in Figure 6:34.

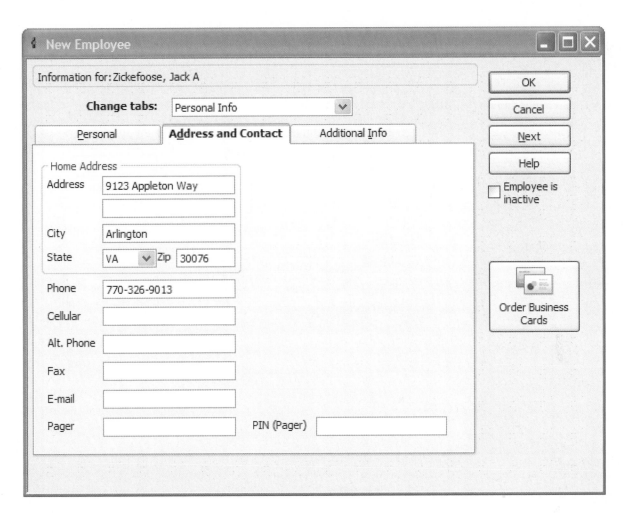

Figure 6:34

Click **Additional Info** and enter the information shown in Figure 6:35.

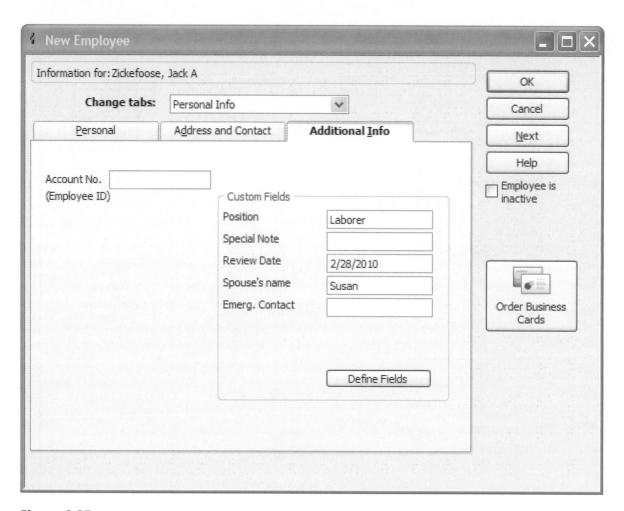

Figure 6:35

Now look up and change the category to **Payroll and Compensation Info**. (See Figure 6:36.)

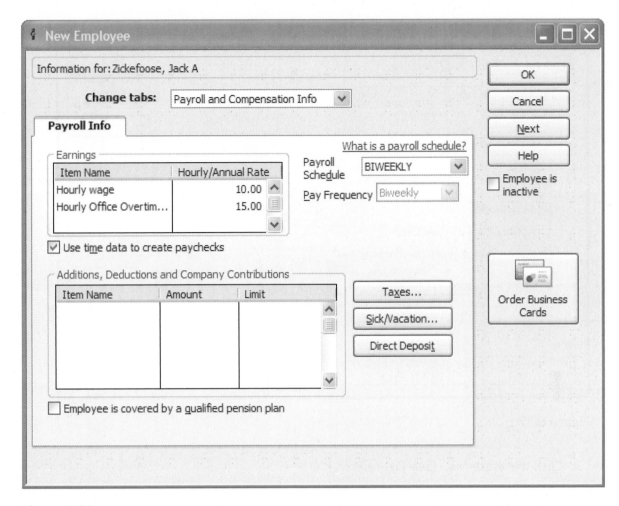

Figure 6:36

Enter Jack's salary information by following the next steps.

1. Place your cursor in **Item Name** and look up **Hourly Wage**.
2. Tab to **Hourly/Annual Rate** and enter 10.00.
3. Place your cursor in the next row for **Item Name** and select **Hourly wage overtime**. QBP will fill in the rate of 15.00.
4. Use your cursor and select **BIWEEKLY** in the **Payroll Schedule**.
5. Verify that **Use time data to create paychecks** is selected.

Click the **Taxes** button and use the following steps to enter Jack's federal and state withholding information.

1. On the **Federal** tab shown in Figure 6:37, look up and select **Married** as the **Filing Status**.

2. Enter "1" in **Allowances**.

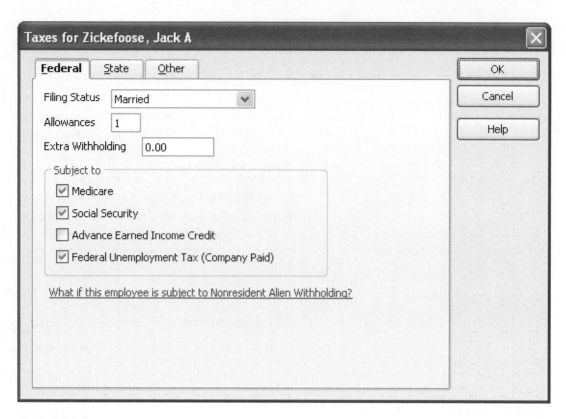

Figure 6:37

3. Click the **State** tab. (See Figure 6:38.)

4. In **State Worked** look up **VA** for **State**. Leave the **SUI (Company Paid)** option
   unchanged. (Note: This option calculates Astor's state unemployment tax expense.)

5. In **State Subject to Withholding**, look up **VA** for **State**. (Note: This state will vary
   when an employee lives in one state but works in a different state.)

6. When finished, click **OK**.

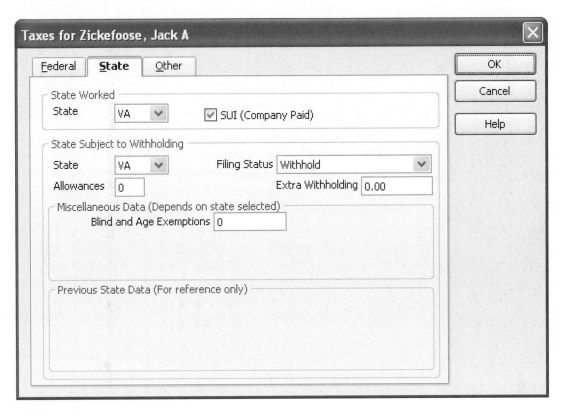

Figure 6:38

Now change the category to **Employment Info** and enter Jack's hire date. (See Figure 6:39.)

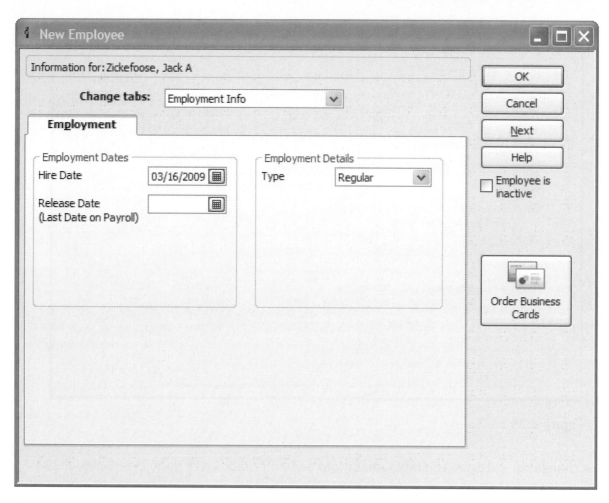

Figure 6:39

Click **OK** to save Jack's account. If prompted to setup local taxes and sick/vacation time, click **Leave As Is**.

Close the Employee Center.

Besides creating employees, you also need to know how to terminate an employee.   You cannot delete an employee account with paycheck history. Instead, you enter a termination date under **Release Date** on the **Employment** tab and mark the **Employee is inactive** option.

Now that you understand managing employee accounts, you are ready to begin entering time data for hourly employees.

EMPLOYEE TIME

Remember at the beginning of the chapter that we explained billable employee time is turned in on timesheets and these sheets list hours along with customer jobs. Also recall in Chapter 4 that you invoiced customers by selecting employee hours for a job. It helps to know that QBP will invoice customers for employee time before actually paying employees. Therefore, you should always enter time data as soon as possible to speed up invoicing.

There is another reason for entering time data as soon as possible. You cannot create an hourly paid employee's paycheck until hours for the pay period have been entered. Astor's next pay date is March 23, 2009, covering the two weeks beginning Monday, March 9 and ending Sunday, March 22.

Before the accountant enters timesheets, Seth verifies these sheets, reviewing for accuracy. Seth then gives the timesheets to Judy who has already entered most of the time data for this pay period. In the next exercise and the *You Try* exercise that follows, you will finish entering time for this pay period.

STEPS TO RECORDING EMPLOYEE TIME DATA

1. On the Home page, click **Enter Time** and select **Use Weekly Timesheet**. In **Name**, look up Hardman, Alan. Using the calendar 🗓, scroll through and select March 16, 2009 (i.e., the day that begins the pay week).

   Figure 6:40 shows Alan's hours already entered for the week. Notice that columns for hours are headed by day and date.

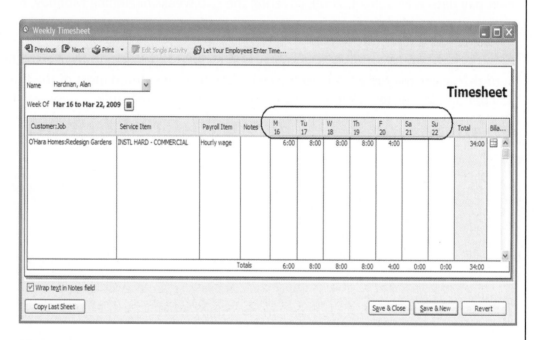

Figure 6:40

2. Alan worked 6 additional hours on Friday for a different customer job. Place your cursor in **Customer:Job** on the second line and look up **Ashford Hill Apartments.**

3. Tab to **Service Item** and look up the inventory service item of **WKLY MNTNCE – COMMERCIAL**. This will assign the time to the job's service item.

4. The **Payroll Item** remains **Hourly wage**. *(Note: You select Hourly wage overtime (x1.5) when employee hours are for overtime.)*

5. Place your cursor in the Friday column (**F**) and enter "6". *(Note: Alan has no overtime hours despite working 10 hours on Friday because he still worked only 40 hours for the pay week.)*

Press Tab and Alan's timesheet for the week is complete (Figure 6:41). Notice that the hours you added are **Billable** to the customer.

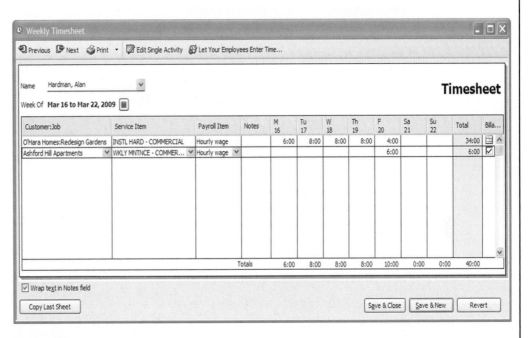

Figure 6:41

6. Click **Save & New** so you can enter a timesheet for Jack Zickefoose for the same work week. Refer to the following information and verify that all hours are marked Billable.

    Line 1:
    Customer:Job: O'Hara Homes:Redesign Gardens
    Service Item: INSTL LAND – COMMERCIAL
    Payroll Item: Hourly wage
    M through F: Enter 8 for each day

    Line 2:
    Customer:Job: O'Hara Homes:Redesign Gardens
    Service Item: INSTL LAND – COMMERCIAL
    Payroll Item: Hourly wage overtime (x1.5)
    Friday, 21:   2

    Figure 6:42 shows the completed timesheet.

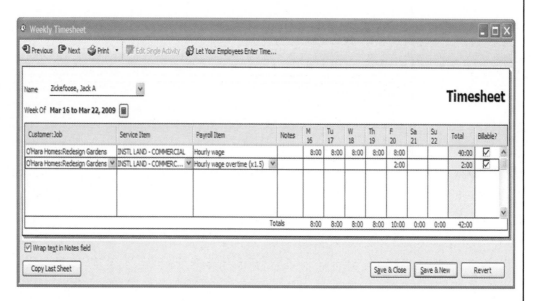

Figure 6:42

We want to point out other information before leaving this window.

The **Previous** and **Next** buttons scroll though an employee's recorded timesheets.

The **Copy Last Sheet** button transfers information from the most recent timesheet onto a new timesheet. This can save data entry time.

You can delete a timesheet in the window by selecting ***Edit>>Delete Timesheet*** on the main menu. You should not delete time that has been invoiced to the customer, meaning a time entry that shows this ▦ symbol in the Billable column.

7. Click **Save & Close**.

WORKING WITH TIMESHEETS

In this exercise, you complete Astor's time data for the payroll period covering March 9 to March 22, 2009.

Roy Dillion had 2 additional regular time hours for his existing timesheet covering March 16 to March 22, 2009. Add these hours to Friday and bill to the White and Associates job. The billing item is INSTL LAND – COMMERCIAL.

Jan Folse turned in her timesheet for the two-week pay period of March 9 to March 15 and March 16 to March 22. Create Jan's timesheet. She worked 8 hours, Monday through Friday. Jan works in the office so her hours are not billable to customer job. ***Hint: Create Jan's timesheet for March 9 to March 15 and then change to the next pay week to use the Copy Last Sheet button.***

EMPLOYEE TIME REPORTS

After recording employee time, Judy prints an employee time report to verify that hours and job information were entered correctly. Follow the next steps to create this report.

STEPS TO CREATE AN EMPLOYEE TIME REPORT

1. Select **Reports>>Jobs, Time & Mileage>>Time by Name** on the main menu. Enter the date range of 3/9/2009 to 3/22/2009 (i.e., the biweekly pay period). (See Figure 6:43.)

Practice Astor Landscaping
Time by Name
March 9 - 22, 2009

◇ Mar 9 - 22, 09 ◇

Dillion, Roy J.
O'Hara Homes:Redesign Gardens ▶ 73:00 ◀
White and Associates 2:00
Total Dillion, Roy J. 75:00

Folse, Jan B.
No job assigned 80:00
Total Folse, Jan B. 80:00

Hardman, Alan
Ashford Hill Apartments 6:00
O'Hara Homes:Redesign Gardens 72:00
Total Hardman, Alan 78:00

Hays, Mike E.
DBH Enterprises 24:00
Reynolds Court Subdivision 30:00
Total Hays, Mike E. 54:00

Henderson, Jeff P.
Ashford Hill Apartments 16:00
Reynolds Court Subdivision 16:00
Sycamore Homes 40:00
Total Henderson, Jeff P. 72:00

Ramez, Victor M.
Ashford Hill Apartments 8:00
DBH Enterprises 8:00
O'Hara Homes:Redesign Gardens 22:00
Sycamore Homes 40:00
Total Ramez, Victor M. 78:00

Ruland, Seth N.
O'Hara Homes:Redesign Gardens 16:00
Total Ruland, Seth N. 16:00

Figure 6:43

Notice that Seth Ruland has 16 hours; however, Seth is a salaried employee so these hours will not be used to calculate his paycheck. Instead, his hours are used to invoice the customer. Also remember that Seth's pay code posts gross pay to 60000 Salaries Expense so cost of goods sold will not be recognized for the time spent on this job. To overcome this, you must allocate the cost of Seth's time to the job. In a subsequent topic you will learn to allocate these costs.

Close the Time by Name report. You are now ready to pay employees.

 # PAYING EMPLOYEES

With employee time tickets entered and verified it is now time to pay employees. Unfortunately, you will not be able to take advantage of QBP's automatic tax calculation for creating paychecks because you have not downloaded the online payroll tax tables. *(Remember that there is a fee for these tables.)*

Instead you are going to create paychecks by entering information calculated in Excel. Although this takes additional time, there are benefits to knowing this method because some companies will not subscribe to QBP's payroll tax service.

Figure 6:44 shows the Excel paycheck register for the pay period ended March 22, 2009. Notice that the total number of hours for hourly paid employees is 479 (regular hours of 477 plus 2 hours of overtime). To reconcile this total to the Time by Name report created earlier, subtract Seth Ruland's 16 hours from the total report hours because Seth is a salaried employee.

Astor Landscaping
Pay Period 3/09/2009 thru 3/22/2009

Check No.	Employee	Filing Status	Allow.	Pay Type	Pay Rate	Regular Hrs	O.T. Hours	Gross Pay	Federal Income Tax	Soc. Sec. (FICA) Tax	Medicare Tax	VA State Tax	Net Pay
731	Dillion, Roy J.	Single	1	Hourly Wage	12.00	75.00		900.00	86.00	55.80	13.05	27.00	718.15
732	Folse, Jan B.	Single	1	Hourly Office	10.00	80.00		800.00	71.00	49.60	11.60	24.00	643.80
733	Greene, Kellie I.	Married	1	Salary	2,346.15			2,346.15	256.00	145.46	34.02	70.38	1,840.29
734	Hardman, Alan	Single	2	Hourly Wage	12.00	78.00		936.00	69.00	58.03	13.57	28.08	767.32
735	Hayes, Mike E	Single	1	Hourly Wage	12.00	54.00		648.00	47.00	40.18	9.40	19.44	531.98
736	Henderson, Jeff P.	Married	1	Hourly Wage	12.00	72.00		864.00	43.00	53.57	12.53	25.92	728.98
737	Murray, Monica D.	Single	1	Salary	1,211.54			1,211.54	131.00	75.12	17.57	36.35	951.50
738	Ramez, Victor M.	Single	0	Hourly Wage	10.00	78.00		780.00	89.00	48.36	11.31	23.40	607.93
739	Ruland, Seth N.	Married	0	Salary	3,103.85			3,103.85	429.00	192.44	45.01	93.12	2,344.28
740	White, Judy O.	Married	2	Salary	2,084.62			2,084.62	295.00	129.25	30.23	62.54	1,567.60
741	Zickefoose, Jack A.	Married	1	Hourly Wage	10.00	40.00	2.00	430.00	0.00	26.66	6.24	12.90	384.20
	Totals					477.00	2.00	14,104.16	1,516.00	874.47	204.53	423.13	11,086.03
	Tax Basis								Circular E	6.20%	1.45%	3.00%	
	G/L Accounts							57000 / 60000	23400	23400	23400	23600	10300

Figure 6:44

Figure 6:45 shows the Excel payroll register for employer costs.

Astor Landscaping
Employer Costs For Period 3/09/2009 thru 3/22/2009

Employee	ER Soc Sec FICA	ER Medicare	ER FUTA	ER SUTA	Health Insurance
Dillion, Roy J.	55.80	13.05	7.20	13.50	0.00
Folse, Jan B.	49.60	11.60	6.40	12.00	60.00
Greene, Kellie I.	145.46	34.02	0.00	-	60.00
Hardman, Alan	58.03	13.57	7.49	14.04	0.00
Hayes, Mike E	40.18	9.40	5.18	9.72	0.00
Henderson, Jeff P.	53.57	12.53	6.91	12.96	0.00
Murray, Monica D.	75.12	17.57	7.55	18.17	60.00
Ramez, Victor M.	48.36	11.31	6.24	11.70	0.00
Ruland, Seth N.	192.44	45.01	0.00	-	60.00
White, Judy O.	129.25	30.23	0.00	-	60.00
Zickefoose, Jack A.	26.66	6.24	3.44	6.45	0.00
Totals	874.47	204.53	50.41	98.54	300.00
Tax Basis	6.20%	1.45%	0.8%	1.50%	
G/L Accounts	23400 / 61000	23400 / 61000	23500 / 61000	23700 / 61000	23800 / 60600

Figure 6:45

Now follow the next steps to create employee paychecks using the Excel data.

STEPS TO CREATE EMPLOYEE PAYCHECKS

1. Click **Pay Employees** on the **Home** page.

    Set the **Pay Period Ends** date to 3/22/2009 and click **Yes** when prompted to fill
    in hours for this pay period. Set the **Check Date** to 3/23/2009 and verify that
    the **Bank Account** is 10300 Payroll Checking. (See Figure 6:46.)

    Review the hours in the window and note that these hours match the hours
    shown on the worksheet.

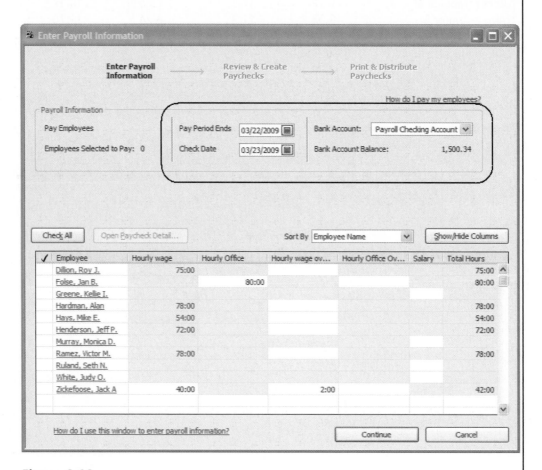

Figure 6:46

Do not worry that the payroll checking balance does not show enough to
cover payroll. Companies normally do not carry large balances in the
payroll account. Instead, funds are transferred on payday to cover the
amount of payroll. In the next chapter, you will transfer funds from the
regular checking account into this account.

2. Click **Check All** to select all employees and then click **Continue**.

Verify that the **Print paychecks from QuickBooks** option is selected (Figure 6:47).

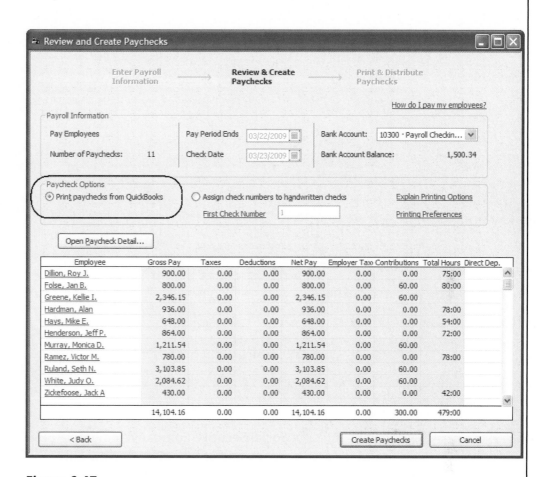

Figure 6:47

Preliminary check totals appear at the bottom. Notice that the total for **Gross Pay** agrees with gross pay on the worksheet.

No tax tables are loaded in the software so no totals are displayed for taxes and deductions. You will now manually enter taxes.

3.   Click **Dillion, Roy J** or highlight his account and click **Open Paycheck Detail** to open paycheck details. Step 4 illustrates entering information into the fields circled in Figure 6:48. *(Note: The information entered is gathered from the payroll spreadsheets.)*

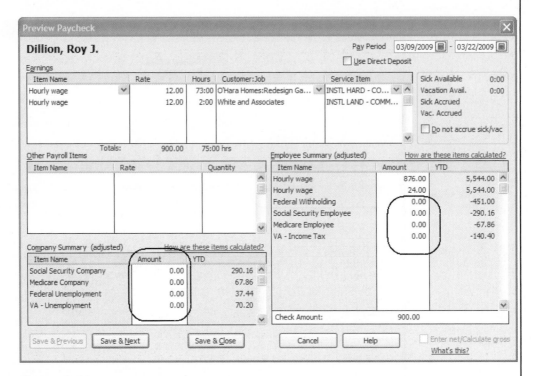

Figure 6:48

4.   Place your cursor in **Social Security Company** and enter "55.80". Tab to **Medicare Company** and enter "13.05". Now enter these remaining employer taxes:

Federal Unemployment (FUTA)   7.20
VA-Unemployment (SUTA)   13.50

5.   Next tab to employee withholdings and enter the amounts on the worksheet. *(Note: You can enter positive amounts and QBP will convert the amount to negative numbers.)*

Federal Withholding   86.00
Social Security Employee   55.80
Medicare Employee   13.05
VA – Income Tax   27.00

6. Figure 6:49 shows Roy's completed paycheck. His check amount agrees with the net pay amount on the worksheet.

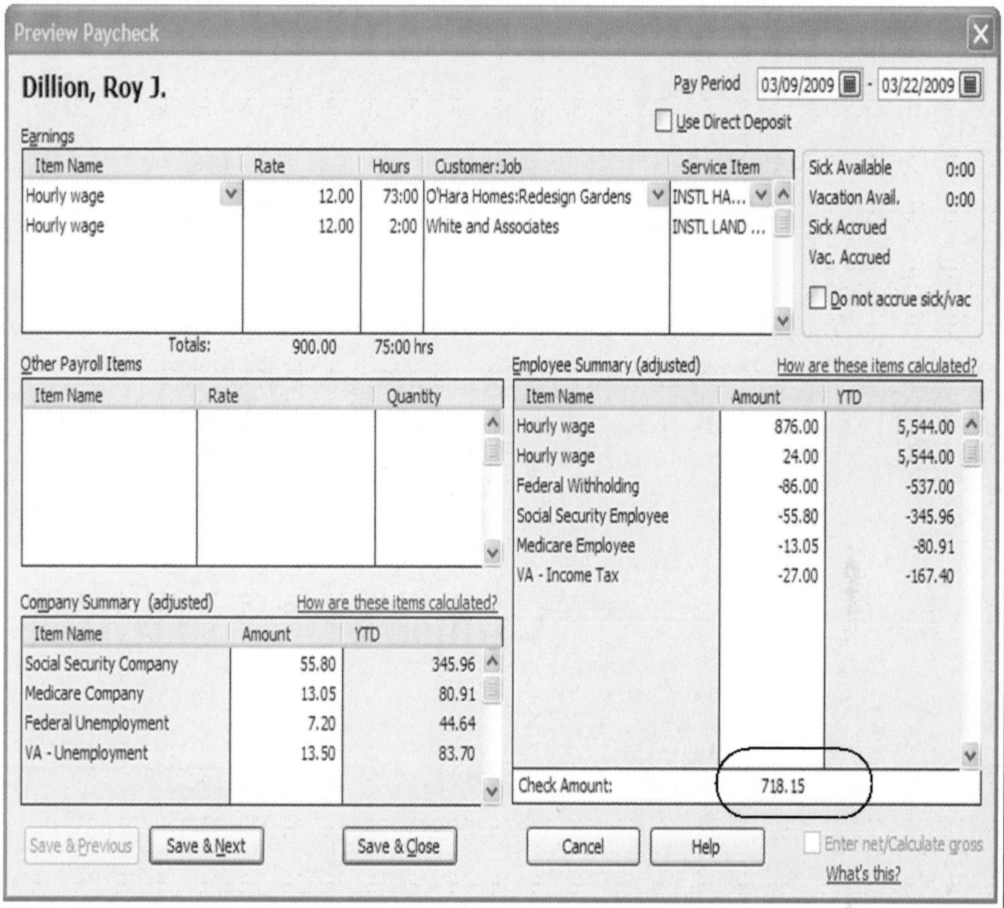

Figure 6:49

7. Click **Save & Next** and enter the following paycheck information for **Jan Folse**.

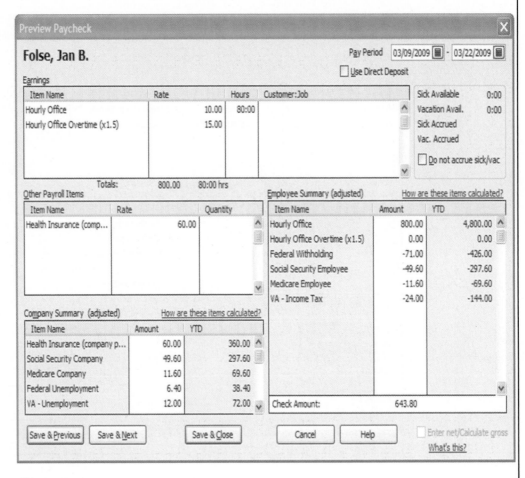

Figure 6:50

8. Continue to click **Save & Next** until you have entered the following paychecks.

Greene, Kellie I.

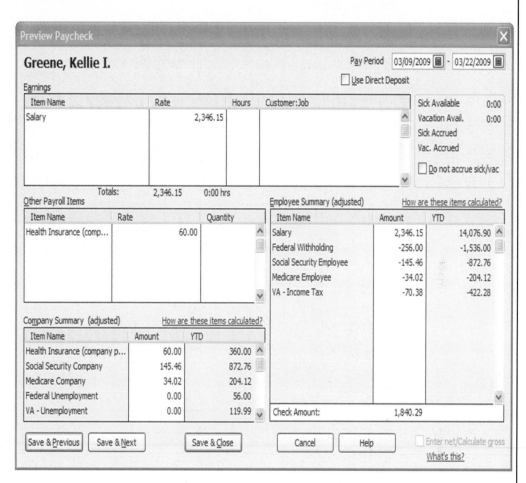

Figure 6:51

(Notice that unemployment taxes for this check are zero because Kellie's year-to-date wages exceed the taxable limit for this year.)

Hardman, Alan

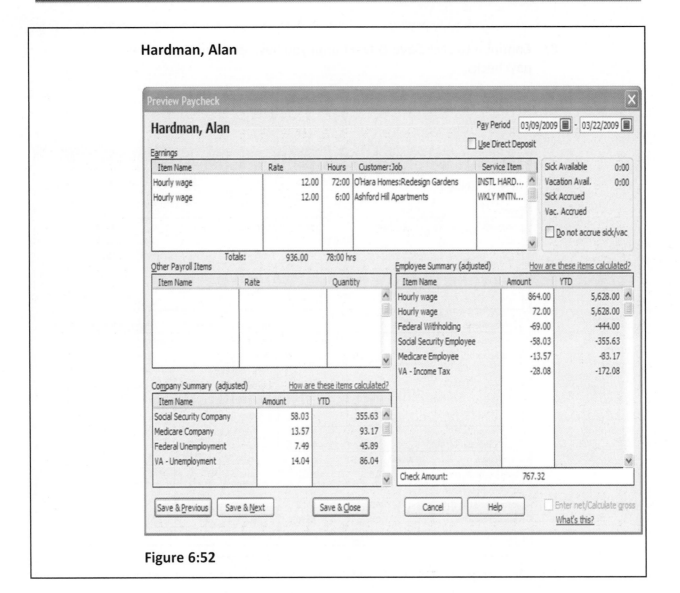

Figure 6:52

Hays, Mike E.

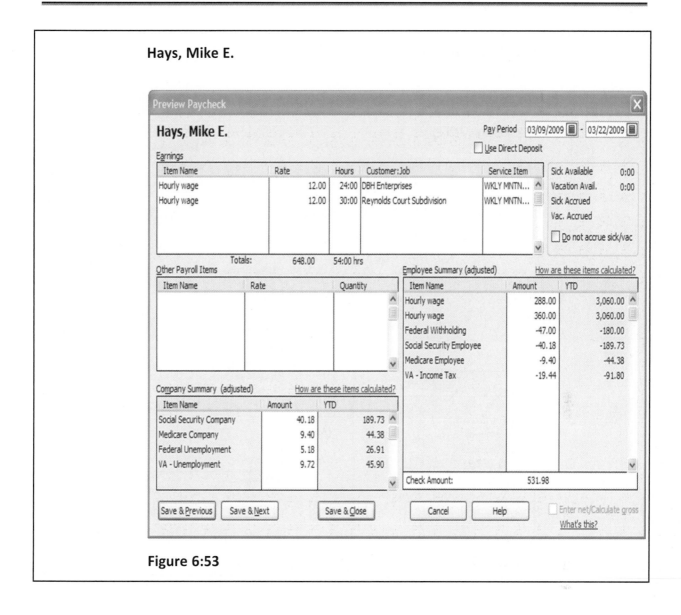

Figure 6:53

Henderson, Jeff P.

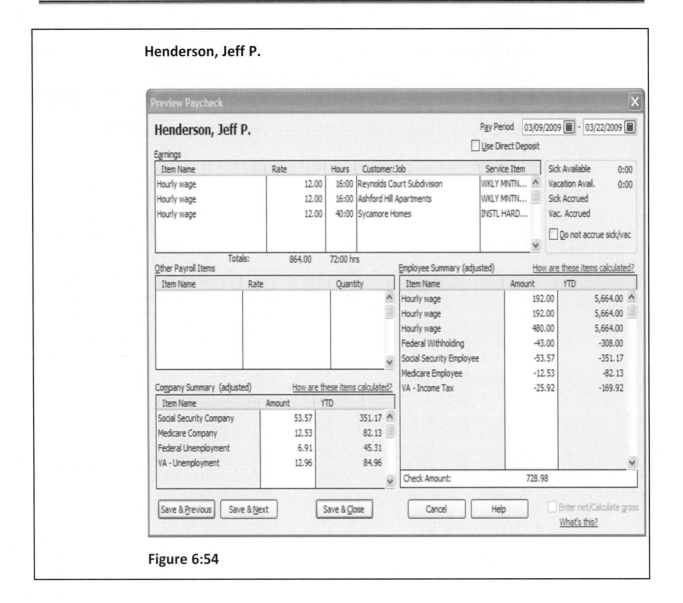

Figure 6:54

Murray, Monica D

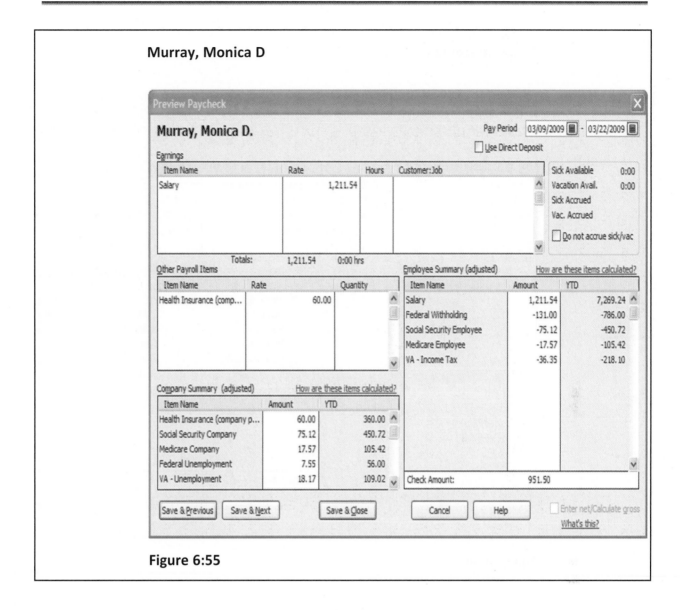

Figure 6:55

Ramez, Victor M

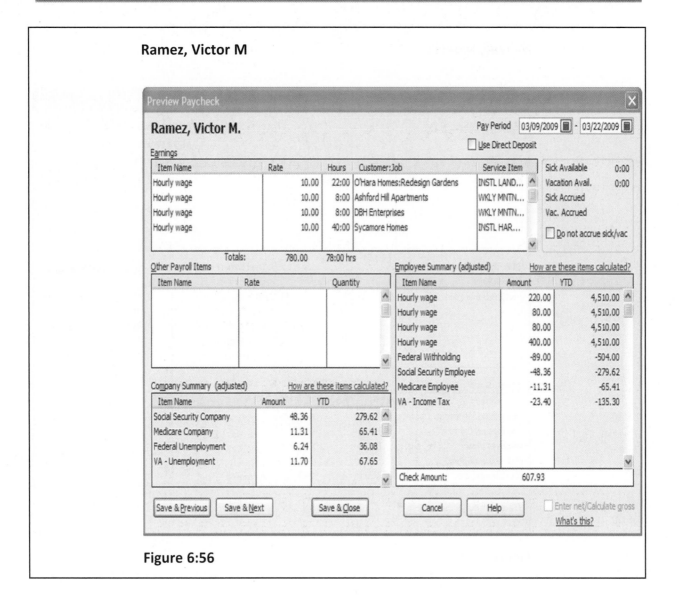

Figure 6:56

Ruland, Seth N.

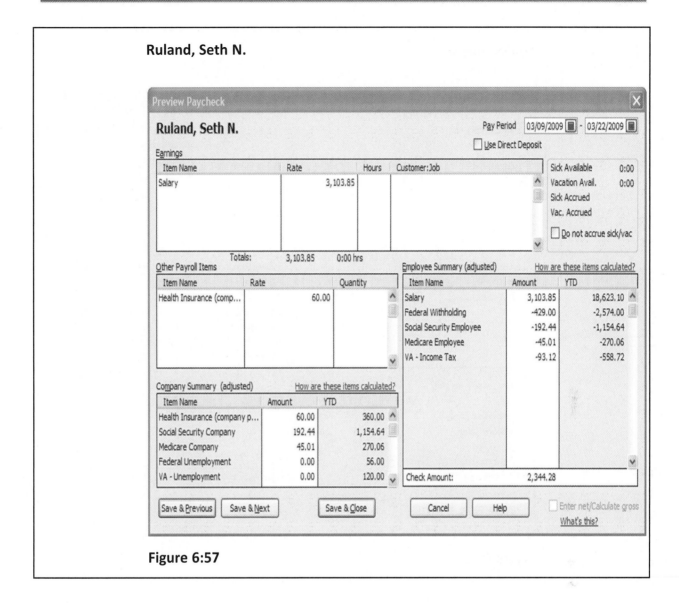

Figure 6:57

White, Judy O.

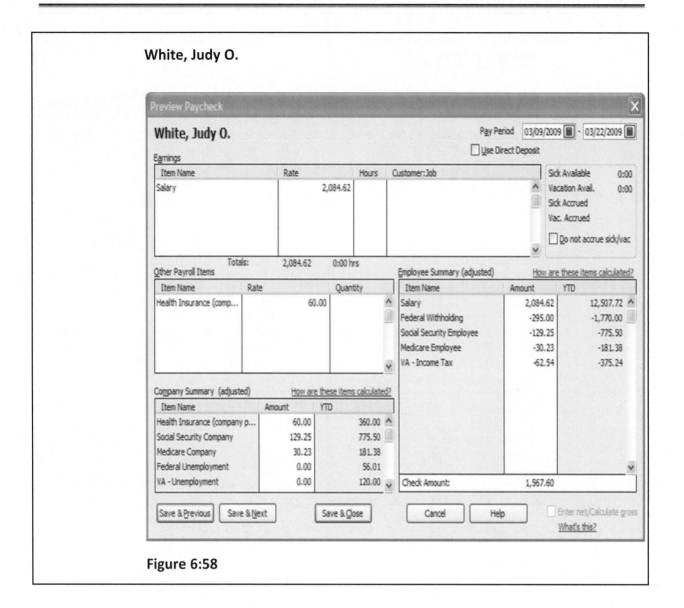

Figure 6:58

Zickefoose, Jack A.

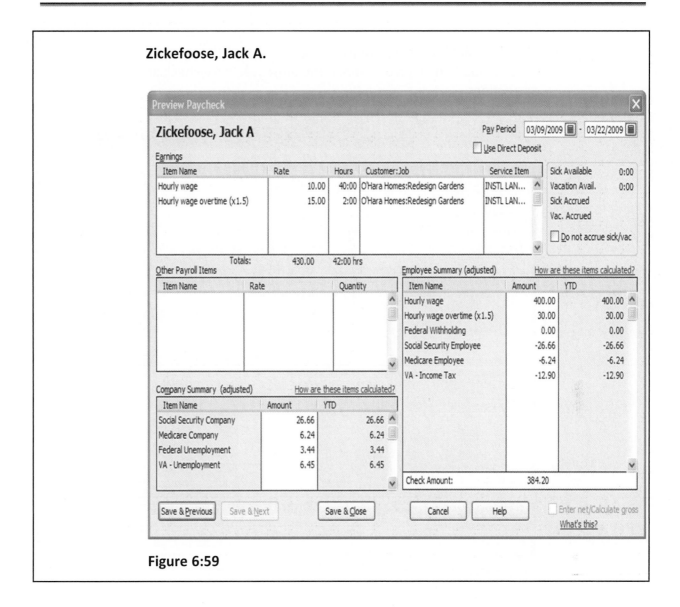

Figure 6:59

9. Click **Save & Close**. Your totals should agree with those shown in Figure 6:60. If you find an error, reopen the employee's paycheck and make corrections.

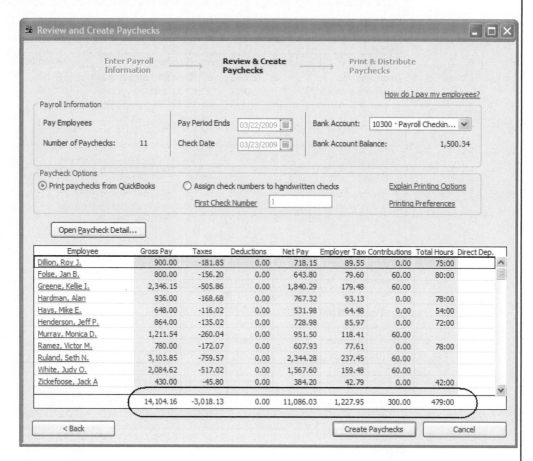

Figure 6:60

10. Click **Create Paychecks** and QBP informs you that 11 paychecks have been created and are ready for printing.

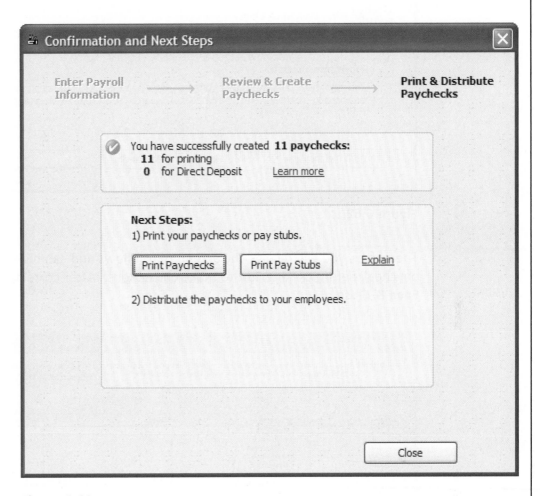

Figure 6:61

Note: If you find a mistake after clicking Create Paychecks DO NOT click Print Paychecks on the window illustrated in Figure 6:61. Instead, click Close and return to Step 1 to reenter the pay ending and check dates. Click Check All and QBP will prompt as shown in Figure 6:62. Click Find Existing Paychecks.

If there are no mistakes then proceed to Step 11.

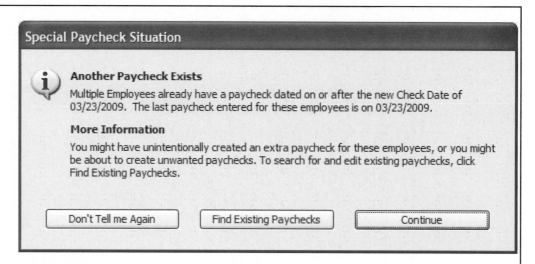

Figure 6:62

Thereafter, you will receive the screen that follows and can highlight a paycheck before clicking **Edit** to make corrections. After correcting, click **Save & Close**.

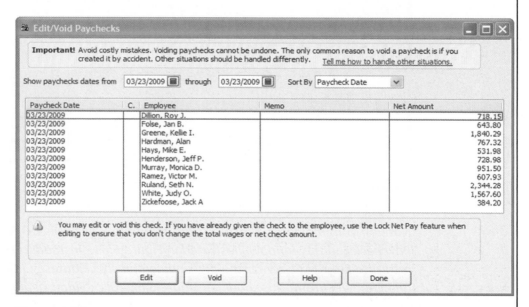

Figure 6:63

To then print the paychecks, you will reopen a check in the window by clicking **Edit**. After reopening, click the dropdown menu on **Print** and select **Print Batch**. You can then complete the following steps to finalize printing.

11. Click **Print Paychecks**. The first check number should be 731 and all the checks should be marked for printing.

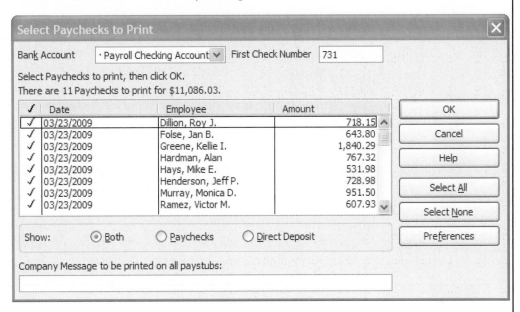

Figure 6:64

12. Click **OK**. Select a printer and then click **Print**. Figure 6:65 shows the first paycheck.

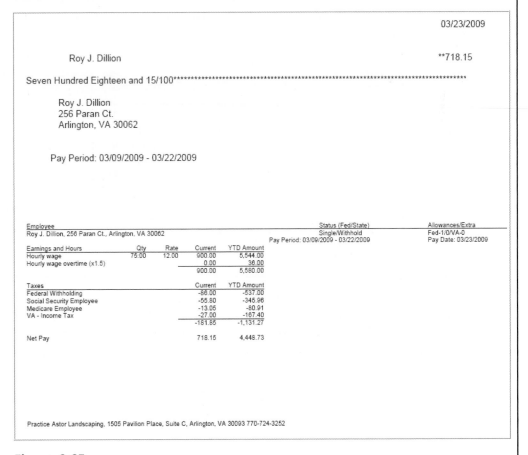

Figure 6:65

---

13. After printing, QBP confirms that checks printed correctly. Click **OK**. Then click **Close** in the confirmation window.

You have just printed paychecks. Now trace the entries that posted.

BEHIND THE KEYS OF A POSTED PAYCHECK

You will now trace entries made after printing paychecks by following the next steps.

STEPS TO TRACING PAYCHECK ENTRIES

1. Click **Report Center** on the Icon bar. Select the **Employees & Payroll** category and open the **Payroll Transaction Detail** report. Enter 3/23/2009 as the date range.

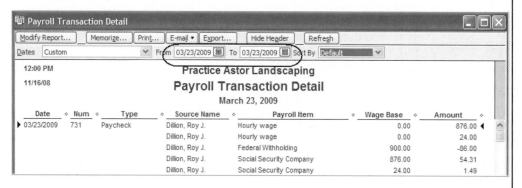

Figure 6:66

2. Now customize the report to show additional information. Click **Modify Report** and

On the Display tab:
   Add columns: Trans #, Account, Debit, Credit
   Remove columns: Wage Base, Amount

On the Filters tab, under Current Filter Choices:
   Click **Detail Level** and remove the filter
   Click **Payroll Item** and remove the filter

On the Header/Footer tab:
   Type "Payroll Journal" as the **Report Title** and click **OK**.

Figure 6:67 shows the modified report listing all accounts affected by an employee's paycheck. Notice that the accounts affected match payroll item settings discussed in the *Payroll Items* topic. You also see the audit trail code under **Tran #** and **Type**.

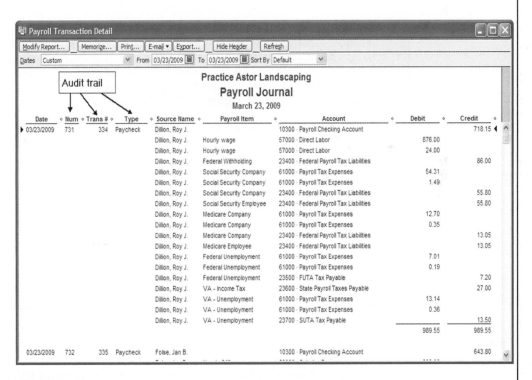

Figure 6:67

Click **Memorize** to enter the information in Figure 6:68 and click **OK**. Close the report.

Figure 6:68

3. To view a report looking something like our payroll register in Excel, open the **Employee Earnings Summary** report. Enter 3/23/2009 as the date range.

    Use the scroll bars to view additional information. This report should reconcile to the Excel payroll register.

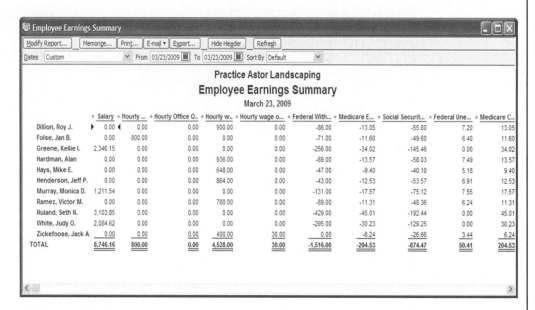

Figure 6:69

4. Remember that you complete tracing entries to the general ledger by displaying the *Reports>>Memorized Reports>>Accounting Journals>>General Ledger Detail Report*.

5. Close all open reports and the Report Center.

CORRECTING EMPLOYEE PAYCHECKS

We told you how to correct a paycheck before printing it while you were entering paycheck data. But what happens when you find an error after printing? Well, you must then void the paycheck and issue a replacement.

Practice voiding a printed paycheck by voiding and reissuing Roy Dillion's March 23 paycheck in the steps that follow.

STEPS TO VOIDING A PRINTED PAYCHECK

1. Select **Employees>>Edit/Void Paychecks** on the main menu. Enter the date range of 3/23/2009 to 3/23/2009. You now see the paychecks issued on this date (Figure 6:70).

   Highlight Roy's check and click **Void**.

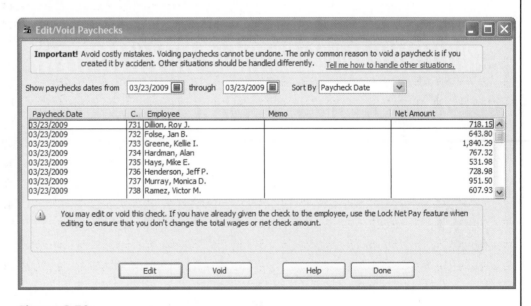

Figure 6:70

2. The void paychecks window updates, showing Roy's paycheck as void. Click
    Done.

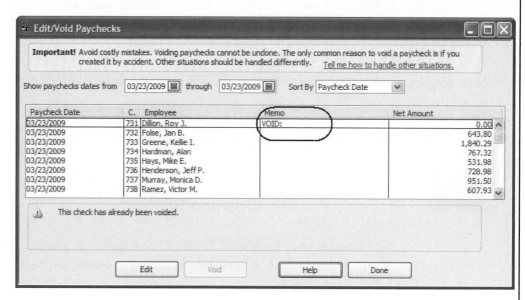

Figure 6:71

3. You will now reissue Roy's check. Click **Pay Employees** on the Home page and enter the dates shown in Figure 6:72. Click to select Roy Dillion.

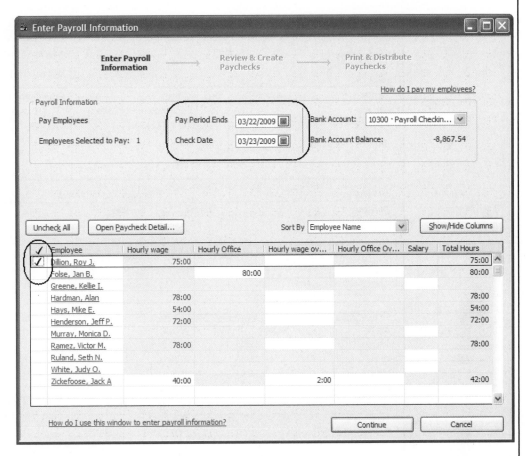

Figure 6:72

4. Click **Continue**. Click to open Roy's paycheck and enter his paycheck information again. (See Figure 6:73.)

Preview Paycheck

Dillion, Roy J. Pay Period 03/09/2009 - 03/22/2009

☐ Use Direct Deposit

Earnings

Item Name	Rate	Hours	Customer:Job	Service Item
Hourly wage	12.00	73:00	O'Hara Homes:Redesign Gardens	INSTL HARD...
Hourly wage	12.00	2:00	White and Associates	INSTL LAND ...

Sick Available 0:00
Vacation Avail. 0:00
Sick Accrued
Vac. Accrued
☐ Do not accrue sick/vac

Totals: 900.00 75:00 hrs

Other Payroll Items

Item Name	Rate	Quantity

Employee Summary (adjusted) — How are these items calculated?

Item Name	Amount	YTD
Hourly wage	876.00	5,544.00
Hourly wage	24.00	5,544.00
Federal Withholding	-86.00	-537.00
Social Security Employee	-55.80	-345.96
Medicare Employee	-13.05	-80.91
VA - Income Tax	-27.00	-167.40

Company Summary (adjusted) — How are these items calculated?

Item Name	Amount	YTD
Social Security Company	55.80	345.96
Medicare Company	13.05	80.91
Federal Unemployment	7.20	44.64
VA - Unemployment	13.50	83.70

Check Amount: 718.15

Save & Previous | Save & Next | Save & Close | Cancel | Help
☐ Enter net/Calculate gross
What's this?

Figure 6:73

5. Click **Save & Close** and Figure 6:74 shows Roy's updated check.

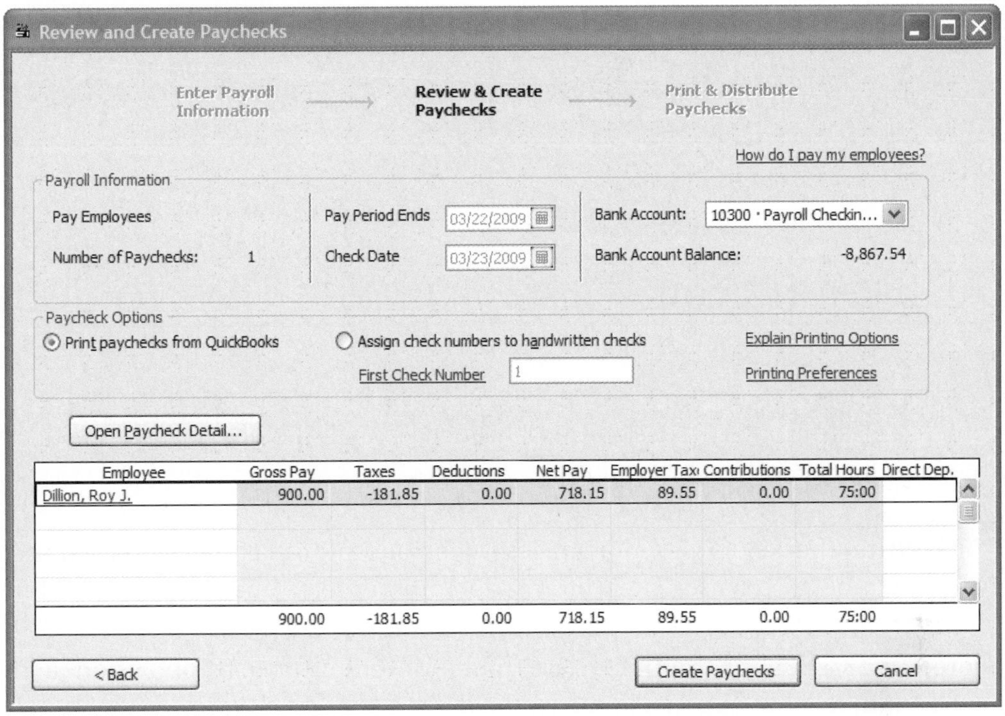

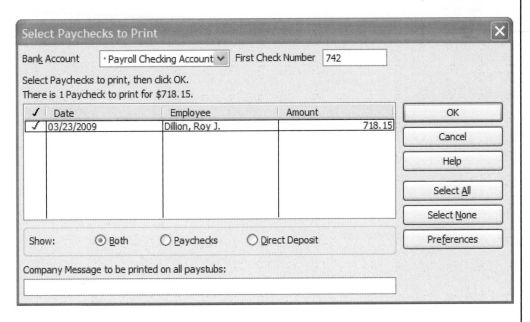

Figure 6:74

6. Click **Create Paychecks** and then click **Print Paychecks**. The first check number should be 742. Click **OK**, select a printer, and click **Print**.

Figure 6:75

7. Click **OK** in the print confirmation window and then **Close** the print confirmation window.

    (Note: If you receive a message to subscribe to payroll tax tables, select No and turn off pop-up messages for products and services.)

ALLOCATING SALARIED EMPLOYEE TIME TO JOBS

As promised earlier, we will now show allocating Seth's salary cost for the 16 hours worked on the O'Hara Homes Redesign Gardens job. To analyze job profitability it is important to match job costs with job revenues.

Click **Write Checks** on the Home page. When allocating salaries, you do not enter a payee or a check number. You also enter information on the Items and the Expenses tabs.

Enter "3/13/2009" as the **Date**, click **To be Printed** to turn off the option, and then delete the check number that appears in the **No** field.

Now enter the information shown on Figure 6:76 onto the **Items** tab. *Note: The Design-Commercial service item has been created to allocate salary costs.* (See Figure 6:77.)

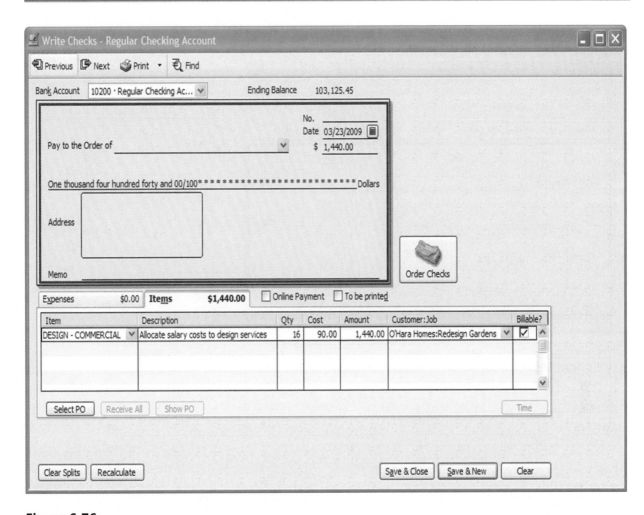

Figure 6:76

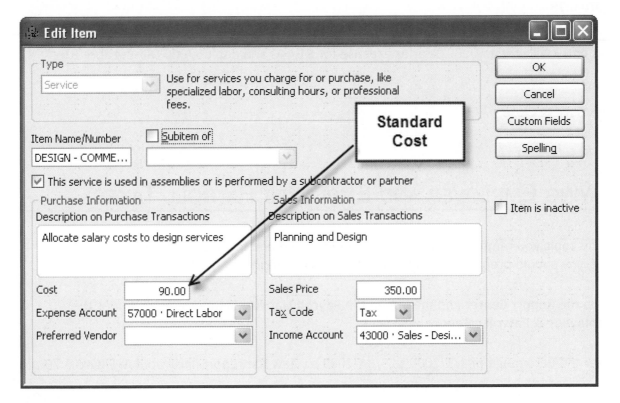

Figure 6:77

Click the **Expenses** tab and enter the information shown in Figure 6:78.

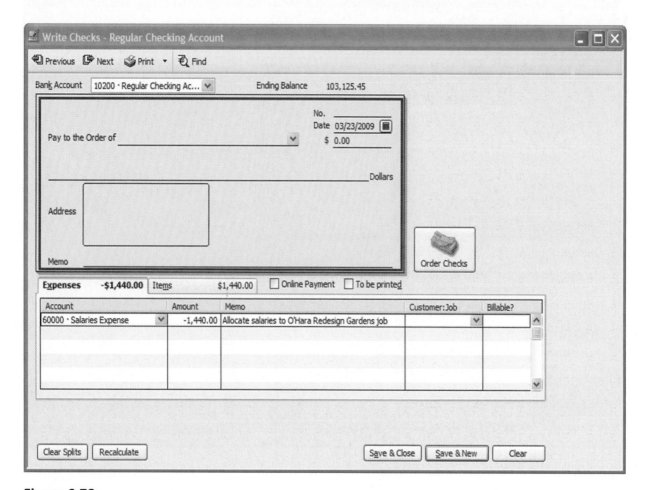

Figure 6:78

This entry will credit 60000 Salaries expense for $1,440 and debit 57000 Direct Labor for $1,440.

Click **Save & Close**.

PAYING EMPLOYER AND EMPLOYEE PAYROLL TAXES

In this topic you remit employee tax withholdings and employer payroll taxes. But before that, you should prepare a Payroll Liability Balances report.

Open the **Report Center** and then open the **Payroll Liability Balances** report under the **Employees & Payroll** category.

Enter the date range of 1/1/2009 to 3/31/2009 to view the report illustrated in Figure 6:79.

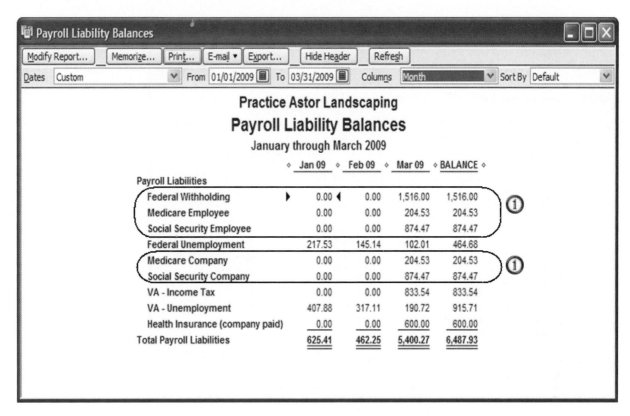

Figure 6:79

Payroll taxes are due on the dates set by taxing agencies. Normally federal tax, FICA, and Medicare taxes are due within three days of paying employees. State income tax for the current month is normally due the first of the next month. Federal and state unemployment taxes are due at the end of every quarter.

The report shows that Astor owes $3,674.00 for federal tax liabilities (i.e., items marked 1 in Figure 6:79). The report lists other payroll liabilities.

Now verify that report totals reconcile with balances in the general ledger accounts. Press **Ctrl + A** on the keyboard to open the chart of accounts. (See Figure 6:80.)

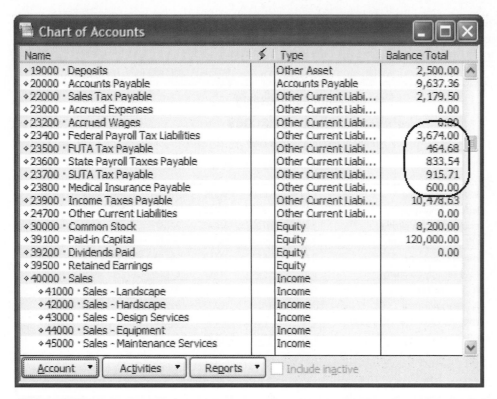

Figure 6:80

Scroll down to 23400 Federal Payroll Tax Liabilities to find that the account balance equals the report balance. You can also compare other payroll liability balances to the report.

Close the report, the Report Center, and the Chart of Accounts.

After reconciling balances, you are ready to pay these taxes. The March 23 payroll previously recorded means that federal taxes are due by March 26. This is also the last pay date in March, so state taxes are due, and the last pay date in the quarter, so FUTA and SUTA taxes are due.

In the next exercise you will create a check paying federal tax, FICA, and Medicare withholdings and employer taxes for FICA and Medicare.

STEPS TO PAYING PAYROLL TAXES

1. Click **Pay Liabilities** on the **Home** page. Enter the date range of 1/1/2009 to 3/31/2009 to view all liabilities for the quarter and then click **OK**.

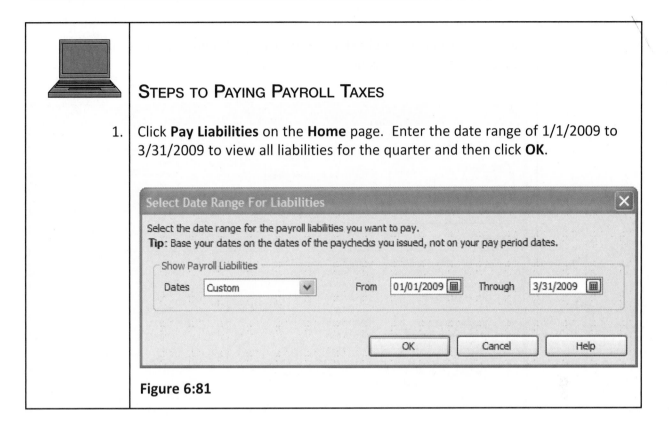

Figure 6:81

2. Enter 3/26/2009 as the **Check Date**. Verify that **To be printed** is marked and that 10200 Regular Checking is the **Bank Account**.

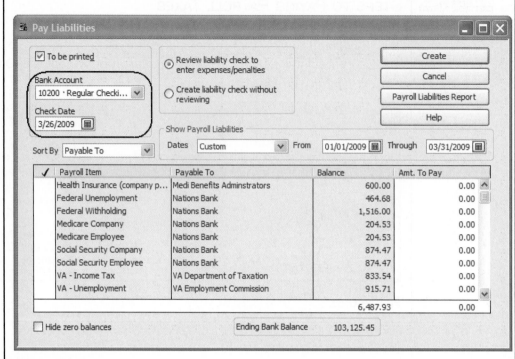

Figure 6:82

This window lists vendor accounts with balances. You now see why vendors were entered on payroll tax and company benefit items.

Also notice that you can print payroll liability reports from this window by clicking the **Payroll Liabilities Report** button.

3. You will next select the taxes to pay. Only federal withholdings, FICA, and Medicare taxes are due by March 26 so choose only these taxes.

The company has also received the health insurance bill so mark that item.

The total payments are listed under the **Amt. To Pay** column.

Before creating the checks notice that the **Review** option is selected in Figure 6:83.

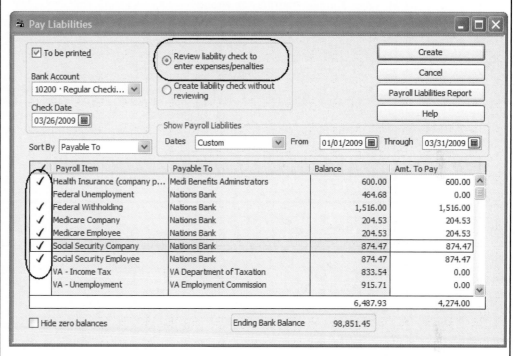

Figure 6:83

4. Click **Create**. The warning in Figure 6:84 is issued because the check date of 3/26/2009 falls before the Through date of 3/31/2009 on Figure 6:83. However, notice that the message states this can be appropriate, especially when prepaying a liability.

Click **Continue**.

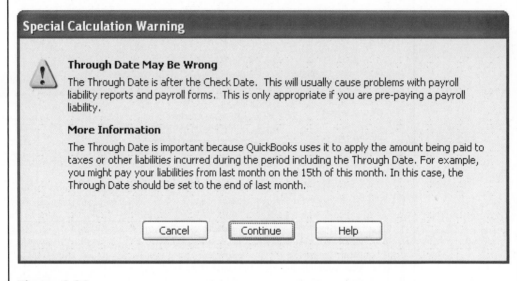

Figure 6:84

5. | The check opens (Figure 6:85) for you to review the amount and enter additional information because the Review option was marked on the previous window. Should the health insurance bill contain other fees, you can add the amount to the Expenses tab.

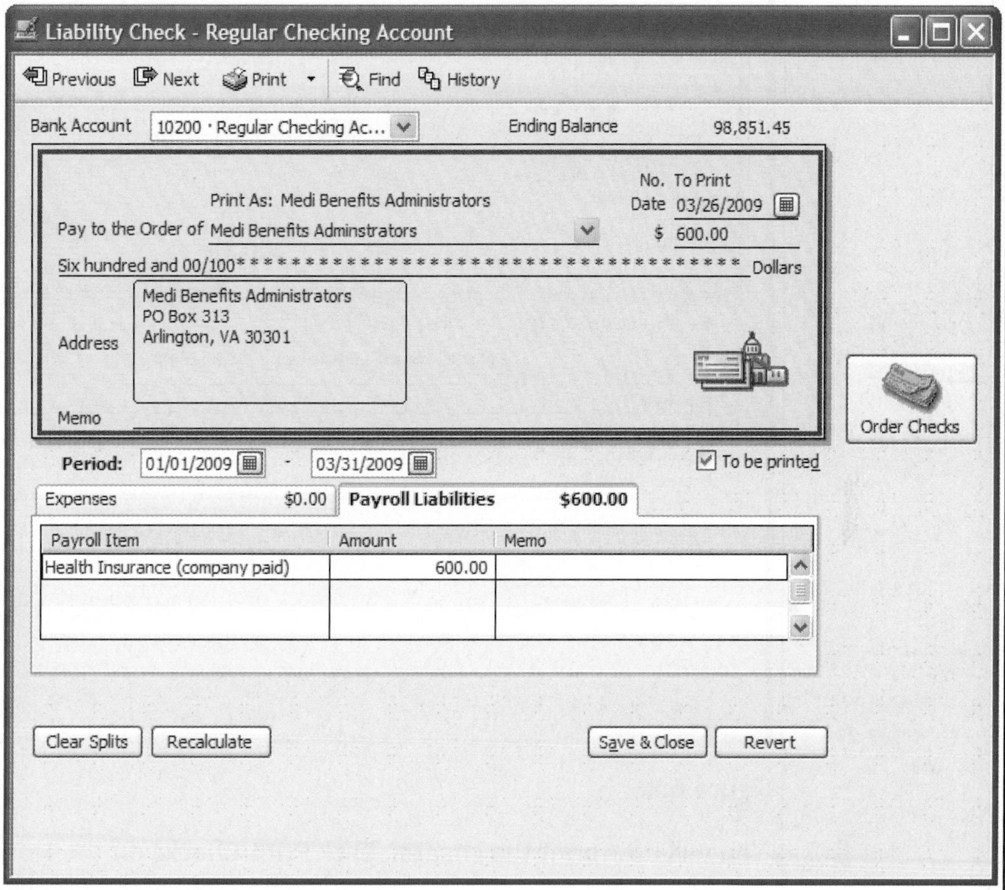

Figure 6:85

6. Click **Next** and the second check opens. Click **Save & Close**.

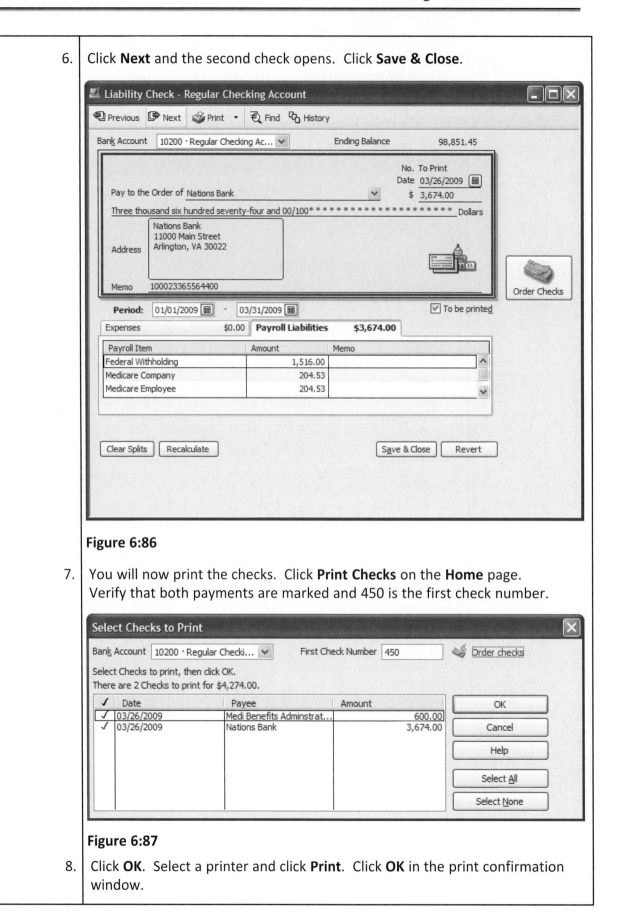

Figure 6:86

7. You will now print the checks. Click **Print Checks** on the **Home** page.
Verify that both payments are marked and 450 is the first check number.

Figure 6:87

8. Click **OK**. Select a printer and click **Print**. Click **OK** in the print confirmation window.

Now complete the next exercise to finish paying tax liabilities for March and the first quarter of 2009.

CREATE CHECKS FOR PAYROLL TAXES

Reopen the Pay Liabilities window and enter the date range of 1/1/2009 to 3/31/2009.

Create checks dated 4/1/2009 for FUTA, VA-Income Tax, and VA-Unemployment taxes.

Print the checks using the first check number of 452. The checks will total $2,213.93.

Print the Check Detail report for April 1, 2009.

QUARTERLY AND YEAR-END PAYROLL REPORTING

At the end of each quarter, Astor prepares payroll tax reports for each taxing agency. These reports list employee wages and reconcile employee tax withholdings and employer tax liabilities with taxes paid during the quarter.

For federal taxes, the quarterly report is called Form 941. We will now show you how to prepare this report based on information from QBP.

Open the **Report Center** and run the **Employee Earnings Summary** for 1/1/2009 to 3/31/2009. (See Figure 6:88.) Print and close the report.

Practice Astor Landscaping
Employee Earnings Summary
January through March 2009

	Salary	Hourly Office	Hourly Office Ov...	Hourly wage	Hourly wage overtime (x...	Federal Withholding
Dillion, Roy J.	0.00	0.00	0.00	5,544.00	36.00	-537.00
Folse, Jan B.	0.00	4,800.00	0.00	0.00	0.00	-426.00
Greene, Kellie I.	14,076.90	0.00	0.00	0.00	0.00	-1,536.00
Hardman, Alan	0.00	0.00	0.00	5,628.00	108.00	-444.00
Hays, Mike E.	0.00	0.00	0.00	3,060.00	0.00	-180.00
Henderson, Jeff P.	0.00	0.00	0.00	5,664.00	0.00	-308.00
Murray, Monica D.	7,269.24	0.00	0.00	0.00	0.00	-786.00
Ramez, Victor M.	0.00	0.00	0.00	4,510.00	0.00	-504.00
Ruland, Seth N.	18,623.10	0.00	0.00	0.00	0.00	-2,574.00
White, Judy O.	12,507.72	0.00	0.00	0.00	0.00	-1,770.00
Zickefoose, Jack A	0.00	0.00	0.00	400.00	30.00	0.00
TOTAL	52,476.96	4,800.00	0.00	24,806.00	174.00	-9,065.00
	①	①		①	①	②

	Medicare Employee	Social Security Employee	Federal Unemployment	Medicare Company	Social Security Company
Dillion, Roy J.	-80.91	-345.96	44.64	80.91	345.96
Folse, Jan B.	-69.60	-297.60	38.40	69.60	297.60
Greene, Kellie I.	-204.12	-872.76	56.00	204.12	872.76
Hardman, Alan	-83.17	-355.63	45.89	93.17	355.63
Hays, Mike E.	-44.38	-189.73	26.91	44.38	189.73
Henderson, Jeff P.	-82.13	-351.17	45.31	82.13	351.17
Murray, Monica D.	-105.42	-450.72	56.00	105.42	450.72
Ramez, Victor M.	-65.41	-279.62	36.08	65.41	279.62
Ruland, Seth N.	-270.06	-1,154.64	56.00	270.06	1,154.64
White, Judy O.	-181.38	-775.50	56.01	181.38	775.50
Zickefoose, Jack A	-6.24	-26.66	3.44	6.24	26.66
TOTAL	-1,192.82	-5,099.99	464.68	1,202.82	5,099.99
	④	③		④	③

	VA - Income Tax	VA - Unemploym...	Health Insurance (...	TOTAL
Dillion, Roy J.	-167.40	83.70	0.00	5,003.94
Folse, Jan B.	-144.00	72.00	360.00	4,700.40
Greene, Kellie I.	-422.28	119.99	360.00	12,654.61
Hardman, Alan	-172.08	86.04	0.00	5,261.85
Hays, Mike E.	-91.80	45.90	0.00	2,861.01
Henderson, Jeff P.	-169.92	84.96	0.00	5,316.35
Murray, Monica D.	-218.10	109.02	360.00	6,790.16
Ramez, Victor M.	-135.30	67.65	0.00	3,974.43
Ruland, Seth N.	-558.72	120.00	360.00	16,026.38
White, Judy O.	-375.24	120.00	360.00	10,898.49
Zickefoose, Jack A	-12.90	6.45	0.00	426.99
TOTAL	-2,467.74	915.71	1,800.00	73,914.61

Figure 6:88

Next run the **Payroll Transactions by Payee** for 1/1/2009 to 3/31/2009, listing the total federal tax payments for the first quarter. (See Figure 6:89.) Print and close the report.

Payroll Transactions by Payee

Modify Report... | Memorize... | Print... | E-mail ▾ | Export... | Hide Header | Refresh

Dates Custom From 01/01/2009 To 03/31/2009 Sort By Default

Practice Astor Landscaping

Payroll Transactions by Payee

January through March 2009

Date	Name	Num	Type	Memo	Account	Amount
Medi Benefits Adminstrators						
01/30/2009	Medi Benefits Adm...	408	Liability Check		10200 · Regular Ch...	-600.00
02/26/2009	Medi Benefits Adm...	402	Liability Check		10200 · Regular Ch...	-600.00
03/26/2009	Medi Benefits Adm...	450	Liability Check		10200 · Regular Ch...	-600.00
Total Medi Benefits Adminstrators						-1,800.00
Nations Bank						
01/15/2009	Nations Bank	397	Liability Check	1000233655...	10200 · Regular Ch...	-3,557.16
01/30/2009	Nations Bank	409	Liability Check	1000233655...	10200 · Regular Ch...	-3,624.38
02/12/2009	Nations Bank	418	Liability Check	1000233655...	10200 · Regular Ch...	-3,626.50
02/26/2009	Nations Bank	403	Liability Check	1000233655...	10200 · Regular Ch...	-3,567.46
03/11/2009	Nations Bank	449	Liability Check	1000233655...	10200 · Regular Ch...	-3,611.12
03/26/2009	Nations Bank	451	Liability Check	1000233655...	10200 · Regular Ch...	-3,674.00
Total Nations Bank						-21,660.62
VA Department of Taxation						

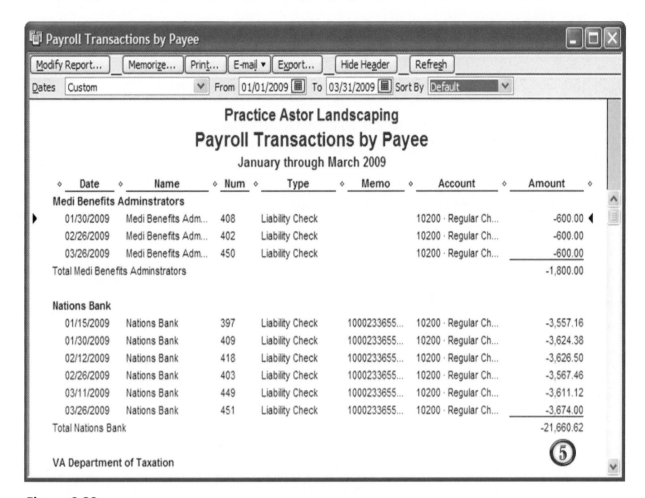

Figure 6:89

You will next plug numbers from these reports onto Form 941. For purposes of this example, we downloaded a Form 941 from the Internal Revenue Service website (www.irs.gov).

The top of Form 941 (Figure 6:90) contains basic company information such as EIN, Business name, Business address and the reporting quarter.

Form **941 for 2008: Employer's QUARTERLY Federal Tax Return** 950108

(Rev. January 2008) Department of the Treasury — Internal Revenue Service OMB No. 1545-0029

(EIN) Employer identification number 3 4 — 0 9 8 7 2 3 3

Name *(not your trade name)* Practice Astor Landscaping

Trade name *(if any)*

Address 1505 Pavilion Place

Number Street Suite or room number

Arlington VA 30093

City State ZIP code

Report for this Quarter of 2008 (Check one.)

- [x] 1: January, February, March
- [ ] 2: April, May, June
- [ ] 3: July, August, September
- [ ] 4: October, November, December

Read the separate instructions before you fill out this form. Please type or print within the boxes.

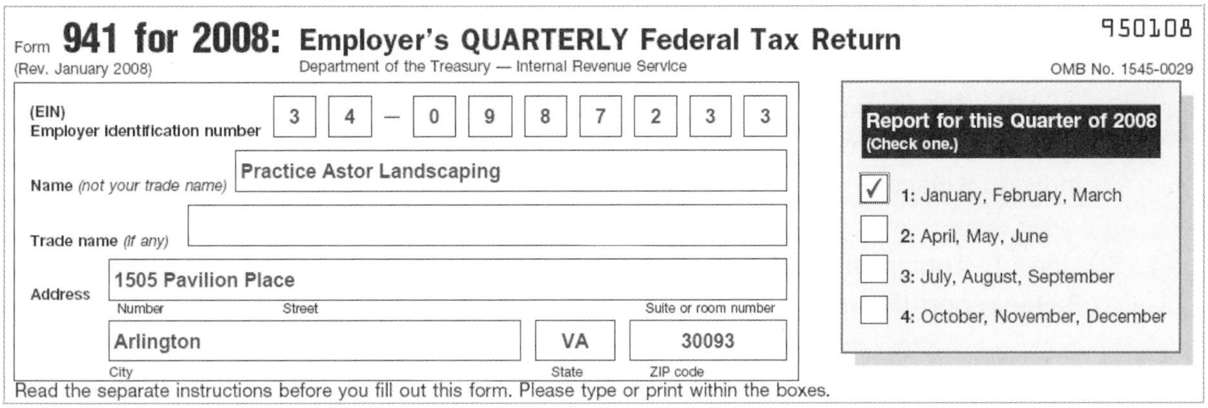

Figure 6:90

Part I of Form 941 (Figure 6:91) reports gross wages, tax liabilities and tax payments during the quarter. You enter information in this section using the next steps.

1. Line 1: Total employees receiving wages in the reporting quarter.

2. Line 2: Total gross wages for the quarter calculated by totaling the columns labeled number 1 on the **Employees Earnings Summary** report shown in Figure 6:88.

3. Line 3: Total federal tax withholdings calculated from the column labeled number 2 on the **Employees Earnings Summary** report.

4. Line 5a:
   a. Column 1: Gross wages from Form 941 Line 2 minus wages over the social security annual limit. Recall that taxes stop after wages exceed the annual taxable limit.
   b. Column 2: Calculated by multiplying Column 1 wages by the percentage provided. The 12.4 percent (0.124) rate represents the employee rate of 6.2 percent (.062) plus the employer rate of 6.2 percent (0.062). This amount should equal the total for columns labeled number 3 on the **Employees Earnings Summary** report, disregarding any rounding differences in the cents.

5. Line 5c:
   a. Column 1: Gross wages from Form 941 Line 2.
   b. Column 2: Calculated by multiplying Column 1 wages by the percentage provided. The 2.9 percent (0.029) rate represents the employee rate of 1.45 percent (.0145) plus the employer rate of 1.45 percent (0.0145). This amount should equal the total for columns labeled number 4 on the **Employees Earnings Summary** report, disregarding any rounding differences in the cents. *(Note: The report is $10.00 higher than the amount calculated on Form 941 and we will illustrate correcting this error later in the chapter.)*

6. Line 5d: The total of Lines 5a plus 5c, column 2. This is the total FICA and Medicare taxes due this quarter.

7. Line 7a: The rounding difference that occurs when Form 941 calculates FICA and Medicare as a percentage of total wages whereas paychecks calculate these taxes on individual wages.

8. Line 11: Total payroll tax payments labeled number 5 on the **Payroll Transactions by Payee** report (Figure 6:89).

Part 1: Answer these questions for this quarter.

1 Number of employees who received wages, tips, or other compensation for the pay period including: *Mar. 12* (Quarter 1), *June 12* (Quarter 2), *Sept. 12* (Quarter 3), *Dec. 12* (Quarter 4)   1 | **11**

2 Wages, tips, and other compensation   2   ① | **82,256 . 96**

3 Total income tax withheld from wages, tips, and other compensation   3   ② | **9,065 . 00**

4 If no wages, tips, and other compensation are subject to social security or Medicare tax . .   ☐ Check and go to line 6.

5 Taxable social security and Medicare wages and tips:

	Column 1		Column 2
5a Taxable social security wages	① **82,256 . 96**	× .124 =	**10,199 . 86**
5b Taxable social security tips	**.**	× .124 =	**.**
5c Taxable Medicare wages & tips	① **82,256 . 96**	× .029 =	**2,385 . 45**

5d Total social security and Medicare taxes (*Column 2*, lines 5a + 5b + 5c = line 5d) . . 5d | **21,650 . 31**

6 Total taxes before adjustments (lines 3 + 5d = line 6) . . . . 6 | **.**

7 **TAX ADJUSTMENTS** (read the instructions for line 7 before completing lines 7a through 7g):

7a Current quarter's fractions of cents . . . . | **0 . 31**

7b Current quarter's sick pay . . . . | **.**

7c Current quarter's adjustments for tips and group-term life insurance | **.**

7d Current year's income tax withholding (attach Form 941c) . . . | **.**

7e Prior quarters' social security and Medicare taxes (attach Form 941c) | **.**

7f Special additions to federal income tax (attach Form 941c) . . . | **.**

7g Special additions to social security and Medicare (attach Form 941c) | **.**

7h **TOTAL ADJUSTMENTS** (combine all amounts: lines 7a through 7g) . . . . 7h | **0 . 31**

8 Total taxes after adjustments (combine lines 6 and 7h) . . . . 8 | **21,650 . 00**

9 Advance earned income credit (EIC) payments made to employees . . . . 9 | **.**

10 Total taxes after adjustment for advance EIC (line 8 – line 9 = line 10) . . . . 10 | **21,650 . 00**

11 Total deposits for this quarter, including overpayment applied from a prior quarter . . . 11   ⑤ | **21,660 . 00**

12 **Balance due** (If line 10 is more than line 11, write the difference here.) . . . . 12 | **.**
For information on how to pay, see the instructions.

13 **Overpayment** (If line 11 is more than line 10, write the difference here.) | **10 . 00**   Check one ☑ Apply to next return. ☐ Send a refund.

▶ You **MUST** fill out both pages of this form and **SIGN** it.   Next ➡

For Privacy Act and Paperwork Reduction Act Notice, see the back of the Payment Voucher.   Cat. No. 17001Z   Form **941** (Rev. 1-2008)

Figure 6:91

After completing Part 1, you complete Parts 2 through 5 using the next instructions. (See Figure 6:92.)

1. Part 2:
    a. Line 14: The code for the state where the company makes tax deposits.
    b. Line 15: Check the box that the company was a semiweekly depositor for the quarter. This also means that Schedule B must be completed and attached to Form 941. (See Figure 6:93.)

2. Part 5: Sign and date.

Name *(not your trade name)*

Practice Astor Landscaping

Employer identification number (EIN)

34-0987233

Part 2: Tell us about your deposit schedule and tax liability for this quarter.

If you are unsure about whether you are a monthly schedule depositor or a semiweekly schedule depositor, see *Pub. 15 (Circular E)*, section 11.

14 | V | A | Write the state abbreviation for the state where you made your deposits OR write "MU" if you made your deposits in *multiple* states.

15 Check one: ☐ Line 10 is less than $2,500. Go to Part 3.

☐ You were a monthly schedule depositor for the entire quarter. Fill out your tax liability for each month. Then go to Part 3.

Tax liability: Month 1 [   ] .

Month 2 [   ] .

Month 3 [   ] .

Total liability for quarter [   ] .   Total must equal line 10.

☑ You were a semiweekly schedule depositor for any part of this quarter. Fill out *Schedule B (Form 941): Report of Tax Liability for Semiweekly Schedule Depositors,* and attach it to this form.

Part 3: Tell us about your business. If a question does NOT apply to your business, leave it blank.

16 If your business has closed or you stopped paying wages . . . . ☐ Check here, and

enter the final date you paid wages [/   /   ] .

17 If you are a seasonal employer and you do not have to file a return for every quarter of the year . .☐ Check here.

Part 4: May we speak with your third-party designee?

Do you want to allow an employee, a paid tax preparer, or another person to discuss this return with the IRS? (See the instructions for details.)

☐ Yes. Designee's name [   ]

Select a 5-digit Personal Identification Number (PIN) to use when talking to IRS. ☐ ☐ ☐ ☐ ☐

☐ No.

Part 5: Sign here. You MUST fill out both pages of this form and SIGN it.

Under penalties of perjury, I declare that I have examined this return, including accompanying schedules and statements, and to the best of my knowledge and belief, it is true, correct, and complete.

✗ Sign your name here [   ]

Print your name here [   ]

Print your title here [   ]

Date [/   /   ]

Best daytime phone (   )   -

Figure 6:92

Finally, Schedule B (Figure 6:93) is completed when a company makes semi-weekly deposits. The information for this form is gathered from the **Payroll Transactions by Payee** report (Figure 6:89).   The IRS will use this information to verify that employers pay all taxes by the due date. Astor is required to pay tax liabilities within 3 days of paying employees. You should know that failure to pay taxes by the due date will result in IRS-imposed penalties and interest.

Schedule B (Form 941):

Report of Tax Liability for Semiweekly Schedule Depositors

(Rev. January 2006)   Department of the Treasury — Internal Revenue Service

990306

OMB No. 1545-0029

(EIN)
Employer identification number   3 4 — 0 9 8 7 2 3 3

Name *(not your trade name)*   **Practice Astor Landscaping**

Calendar year   2 0 0 9   (Also check quarter)

Report for this Quarter ...
(Check one.)

[✓] 1: January, February, March

[ ] 2: April, May, June

[ ] 3: July, August, September

[ ] 4: October, November, December

Use this schedule to show your **TAX LIABILITY** for the quarter; **DO NOT** use it to show your deposits. You must fill out this form and attach it to Form 941 (or Form 941-SS) if you are a semiweekly schedule depositor or became one because your accumulated tax liability on any day was $100,000 or more. Write your daily tax liability on the numbered space that corresponds to the date wages were paid. See Section 11 in *Pub. 15 (Circular E), Employer's Tax Guide,* for details.

Month 1

						Tax liability for Month 1
1	9	17	25			
2	10	18	26	3,625 . 88		7,173 . 04
3	11	19	27			
4	12	3,547 . 16	20	28		
5	13	21	29			
6	14	22	30			
7	15	23	31			
8	16	24				

Month 2

						Tax liability for Month 2
1	9	3,624 . 38	17	25		
2	10	18	26			7,191 . 84
3	11	19	27			
4	12	20	28			
5	13	21	29			
6	14	22	30			
7	15	23	3,567 . 46	31		
8	16	24				

Month 3

						Tax liability for Month 3
1	9	3,611 . 12	17	25		
2	10	18	26			7,285 . 12
3	11	19	27			
4	12	20	28			
5	13	21	29			
6	14	22	30			
7	15	23	3,674 . 00	31		
8	16	24				

Fill in your total liability for the quarter (Month 1 + Month 2 + Month 3) = Total tax liability for the quarter ▶

Total must equal line 10 on Form 941 (or line 8 on Form 941-SS).

Total liability for the quarter

21,650 . 00

For Paperwork Reduction Act Notice, see separate instructions.   Cat. No. 11967Q   Schedule B (Form 941) Rev. 1-2006

Figure 6:93

Now that we have illustrated preparing Form 941, you will fix the $10.00 error on Medicare taxes. *(Note: Rounding differences are not fixed in the software.)* The error occurred when recording Alan Hardman's paycheck number 684 on January 12, 2009. Employer Medicare was reported as $23.40 and should have been $13.40.

This error is located by returning to the **Employees Earnings Summary** report and double clicking Alan Hardman's hourly wage amount to open the **Transactions by Payroll Item** report. Modify the **Payroll Item** filter to show only **Medicare Company** and **Medicare Employee**. (See Figure 6:94.)

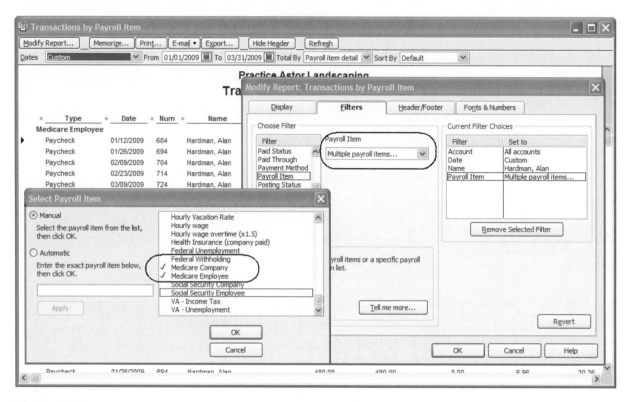

Figure 6:94

Click **OK** after setting the filter and the report refreshes as shown in Figure 6:95.

Transactions by Payroll Item

Modify Report... | Memorize... | Print... | E-mail | Export... | Hide Header | Refresh

Dates Custom | From 01/01/2009 | To 03/31/2009 | Total By Payroll item detail | Sort By Default

Practice Astor Landscaping

Transactions by Payroll Item

January through March 2009

Type	Date	Num	Name	Income Subject To Tax	Wage Base	Wage Base (Tips)	Amount	Balance
Medicare Employee								
Paycheck	01/12/2009	684	Hardman, Alan	924.00	924.00	0.00	-13.40	-13.40
Paycheck	01/26/2009	694	Hardman, Alan	960.00	960.00	0.00	-13.92	-27.32
Paycheck	02/09/2009	704	Hardman, Alan	912.00	912.00	0.00	-13.22	-40.54
Paycheck	02/23/2009	714	Hardman, Alan	960.00	960.00	0.00	-13.92	-54.46
Paycheck	03/09/2009	724	Hardman, Alan	1,044.00	1,044.00	0.00	-15.14	-69.60
Paycheck	03/23/2009	734	Hardman, Alan	936.00	936.00	0.00	-13.57	-83.17
Total Medicare Employee				5,736.00	5,736.00	0.00	-83.17	-83.17
Medicare Company								
Paycheck	01/12/2009	684	Hardman, Alan	156.00	156.00	0.00	3.95	3.95
Paycheck	01/12/2009	684	Hardman, Alan	288.00	288.00	0.00	7.29	11.24
Paycheck	01/12/2009	684	Hardman, Alan	480.00	480.00	0.00	12.16	23.40
Paycheck	01/26/2009	694	Hardman, Alan	480.00	480.00	0.00	6.96	30.36
Paycheck	01/26/2009	694	Hardman, Alan	480.00	480.00	0.00	6.96	37.32
Paycheck	02/09/2009	704	Hardman, Alan	840.00	840.00	0.00	12.18	49.50
Paycheck	02/09/2009	704	Hardman, Alan	72.00	72.00	0.00	1.04	50.54
Paycheck	02/23/2009	714	Hardman, Alan	480.00	480.00	0.00	6.96	57.50
Paycheck	02/23/2009	714	Hardman, Alan	480.00	480.00	0.00	6.96	64.46
Paycheck	03/09/2009	724	Hardman, Alan	516.00	516.00	0.00	7.49	71.95
Paycheck	03/09/2009	724	Hardman, Alan	192.00	192.00	0.00	2.78	74.73
Paycheck	03/09/2009	724	Hardman, Alan	336.00	336.00	0.00	4.87	79.60
Paycheck	03/23/2009	734	Hardman, Alan	864.00	864.00	0.00	12.53	92.13
Paycheck	03/23/2009	734	Hardman, Alan	72.00	72.00	0.00	1.04	93.17
Total Medicare Company				5,736.00	5,736.00	0.00	93.17	93.17
TOTAL				11,472.00	11,472.00	0.00	10.00	10.00

Figure 6:95

You must now check the Medicare calculation to determine whether the employee or the employer tax is incorrect. Multiplying $924 by the tax rate of 0.0145 shows that $13.40 is the correct amount. *Note: You also find the $10.00 difference at the bottom of the report.*

You will now record an adjustment. Again, select ***Employees>>Payroll Taxes and Liabilities>>Adjust Payroll Liabilities*** on the main menu.

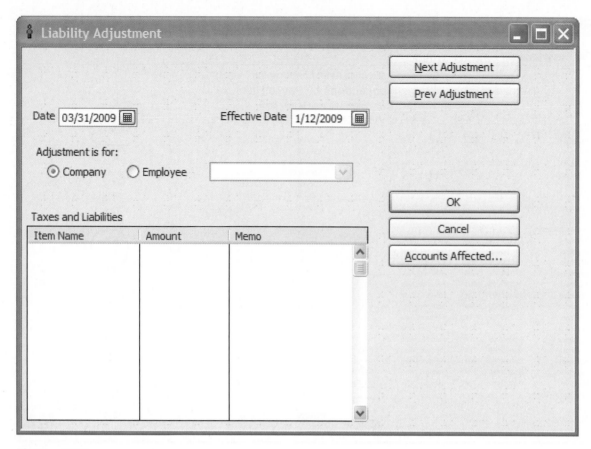

Figure 6:96

We want the adjustment to post in March so enter the **Date** of 3/31/2009. Enter 1/12/2009 in the **Effective Date** because this is the date the error occurred.

Although the error occurred on the company's Medicare liability, you still want to adjust the paycheck so select **Employee** and look up **Hardman, Alan**.

Place your cursor in **Item Name** and select **Medicare Company**. Tab to **Amount** and enter "-10.00" in the space provided. You entered the adjustment as a negative amount so that the tax will be decreased.

Click the **Accounts Affected** button and verify that **Affect liability and expense accounts** is selected so that the adjustment decreases the Medicare liability and posts a debit to the liability account on the general ledger. Click **OK** to exit the window.

Figure 6:97 shows the completed adjustment. Click **OK** to post it.

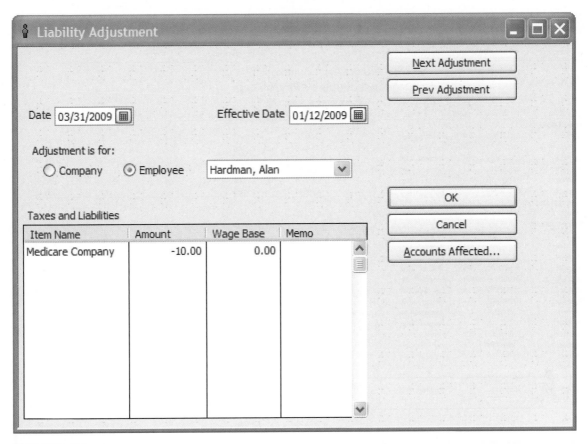

Figure 6:97

Return to the **Transactions by Payroll Item** report and notice that the entry posted to the general ledger as of 3/31/2009 (Figure 6:98). If you had entered 1/12/2009 in the Date field the change would have been made as of the paycheck date; however, this would also cause the entry to backdate to a closed period. Remember that you do not want to post entries to a closed accounting period because it changes reported financial results. The Effective Date will adjust the liability amount on Form 941 as of January.

Finally, you could have selected the Company option instead of Employee to make the adjustment. However, you would not be able to see that the adjustment was related to Alan's paycheck.

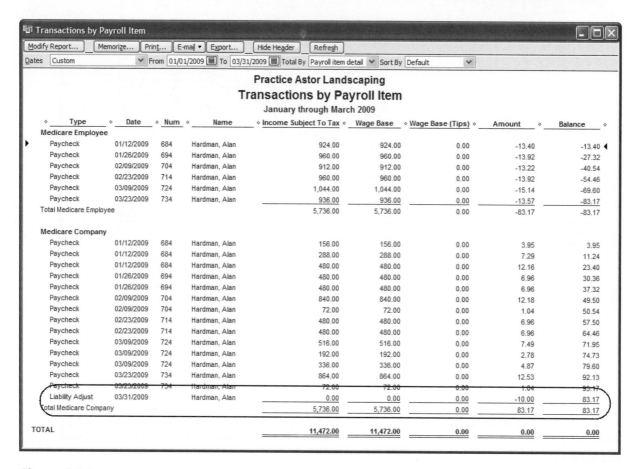

Figure 6:98

Close all open reports and the Report Center.

We just illustrated preparing one quarterly report. There are also quarterly reporting requirements for state tax withholdings and state unemployment tax that were not illustrated.

Besides quarterly reports, Astor files annual reports in January. Form 940 reporting FUTA taxes must be prepared and submitted to the IRS. In addition, W-2s must be printed and distributed to employees by January 31.

Figure 6:99 shows an uncompleted W-2 and Figure 6:100 shows the W-3 that serves to reconcile W-2s by summarizing total wages and taxes.

When you subscribe to QBP's payroll tax service you can then prepare quarterly and annual tax reports in the software.

22222	Void ☐	a Employee's social security number	For Official Use Only ▶ OMB No. 1545-0008		
b Employer identification number (EIN)				1 Wages, tips, other compensation	2 Federal income tax withheld
c Employer's name, address, and ZIP code				3 Social security wages	4 Social security tax withheld
				5 Medicare wages and tips	6 Medicare tax withheld
				7 Social security tips	8 Allocated tips
d Control number				9 Advance EIC payment	10 Dependent care benefits
e Employee's first name and initial	Last name		Suff.	11 Nonqualified plans	12a See instructions for box 12
				13 Statutory employee ☐ Retirement plan ☐ Third-party sick pay ☐	12b
				14 Other	12c
					12d
f Employee's address and ZIP code					
15 State Employer's state ID number	16 State wages, tips, etc.	17 State income tax	18 Local wages, tips, etc.	19 Local income tax	20 Locality name

Form **W-2** Wage and Tax Statement

2008

Department of the Treasury—Internal Revenue Service
For Privacy Act and Paperwork Reduction Act Notice, see back of Copy D.

Copy A For Social Security Administration — Send this entire page with Form W-3 to the Social Security Administration; photocopies are not acceptable.

Cat. No. 10134D

Do Not Cut, Fold, or Staple Forms on This Page — Do Not Cut, Fold, or Staple Forms on This Page

Figure 6:99

DO NOT STAPLE

33333	a Control number	For Official Use Only ▶ OMB No. 1545-0008		

b Kind of Payer	941 ☐ Military ☐ 943 ☐ 944 ☐	1 Wages, tips, other compensation	2 Federal income tax withheld
	CT-1 ☐ Hshld. emp. ☐ Medicare govt. emp. ☐ Third-party sick pay ☐	3 Social security wages	4 Social security tax withheld
c Total number of Forms W-2	d Establishment number	5 Medicare wages and tips	6 Medicare tax withheld
e Employer identification number (EIN)		7 Social security tips	8 Allocated tips
f Employer's name		9 Advance EIC payments	10 Dependent care benefits
		11 Nonqualified plans	12 Deferred compensation
		13 For third-party sick pay use only	
		14 Income tax withheld by payer of third-party sick pay	
g Employer's address and ZIP code			
h Other EIN used this year			
15 State Employer's state ID number		16 State wages, tips, etc.	17 State income tax
		18 Local wages, tips, etc.	19 Local income tax
Contact person		Telephone number ( )	For Official Use Only
Email address		Fax number ( )	

Under penalties of perjury, I declare that I have examined this return and accompanying documents, and, to the best of my knowledge and belief, they are true, correct, and complete.

Signature ▶   Title ▶   Date ▶

Form **W-3** Transmittal of Wage and Tax Statements   **2008**   Department of the Treasury
Internal Revenue Service
Send this entire page with the entire Copy A page of Form(s) W-2 to the Social Security Administration.

Figure 6:100

You have now completed the chapter. *Make a backup of the Practice Astor Landscaping data file to a backup file named "Practice Astor Landscaping Chpt 6". In the next chapter, you will build on the work completed in this chapter.*

Summary

You began this chapter with an overview of payroll processing in a manual system. We first explained the types of employee withholdings and voluntary deductions as well as the types of employer payroll taxes and additional forms of compensation. You also learned to calculate payroll taxes and withholdings.

You next looked at the different types of payroll items in QBP. This helped you to understand how payroll items track wages, employee withholdings, and employer taxes. You also saw that payroll items determine the general ledger account used when posting paychecks.

You then worked with the Employee Center to manage employee accounts and view payroll transactions. You created a new employee and learned the procedures for terminating an employee.

You were then ready to begin processing payroll. You first entered employee time and then prepared a report to verify the accuracy of the data entered. After that you entered data to create paychecks and printed the checks. You even allocated salary expense to a job.

Finally you printed checks for payroll tax liabilities and reviewed quarterly and annual tax filing requirements. You learned to prepare Form 941 and reviewed W-2 and W-3 forms.

In the next chapter you focus on finalizing Astor's March accounting period by recording adjusting entries, printing financial statements, and closing the accounting period.

END-OF-CHAPTER QUESTIONS

TRUE/FALSE

_____ 1. The IRS provides separate withholding tax tables for paying employees monthly and for paying employees biweekly.

_____ 2. Only employees pay Social Security and Medicare taxes.

_____ 3. The Federal Tax payroll item will track FUTA tax liabilities.

_____ 4. You can modify hours on an employee's timesheet as long as you have not paid the employee for the hours.

_____ 5. After voiding a paycheck, you can reissue it using the same timesheet hours.

_____ 6. Unemployment taxes are paid by employees.

_____ 7. You delete an employee account to stop paying the employee.

_____ 8. An employee's net pay will equal the gross pay minus payroll tax withholdings and voluntary deductions.

MULTIPLE CHOICE

_____ 1. The _____ report is used to complete Form 941.
   a. Employee Earnings Summary
   b. Payroll Liability Balances
   c. Payroll Transactions by Payee
   d. Both a and c

_____ 2. You can locate the check number for an employee's paycheck on the _____.
   a. Employee Center
   b. Payroll Transaction Detail report
   c. Check Detail report
   d. All of the above

_____ 3. An employee's withholding for Social Security tax is _____ of an employee's gross pay.
   a. 1.45 percent
   b. 6.2 percent
   c. 7.65 percent
   d. Employees do not pay Social Security taxes.

_____ 4. Per the IRS tax table, the withholding amount for a biweekly paid employee with gross wages of $960 claiming the Married filing status with four allowances will be _____. (Note: See Appendix D for complete payroll tax withholding tables.)
   a. $10
   b. $12
   c. $35
   d. $32

_____ 5. An employee with gross pay of $830 will have a net pay of _____. Assume the employee is paid biweekly, claims Married with three allowances, and pays state taxes of 2 percent of gross pay.
   a. $712.90
   b. $739.90
   c. $737.90
   d. $715.90

PRACTICE SET

In this Practice Set you will be using the **Graded Astor Landscaping** data file containing the Practice Set completed in Chapter 5. *If the company file is not loaded on your computer, restore it using the Graded Astor Landscaping Chpt 5.QBB backup file created after completing the Chapter 5 Practice Set.*

1. Open **Graded Astor Landscaping**. Complete the March and April payroll activities that follow.

2009

Mar 23   Enter the following weekly timesheets for Jan Folse.

Employee ID: Folse, Jan	Mar 9 to Mar 15, 2009											
Customer:Job	Service Item	Payroll Item	M 9	Tu 10	W 11	Th 12	F 13	Sa 14	Su 15	Total	Billable
			8.00	8.00	8.00	8.00	8.00			40.00	No

Employee ID: Folse, Jan	Mar 16 to Mar 22, 2009											
Customer:Job	Service Item	Payroll Item	M 16	Tu 17	W 18	Th 19	F 20	Sa 21	Su 22	Total	Billable
			8.00	8.00	8.00	8.00	8.00			40.00	No

Mar 23   Create the following paychecks for the pay period ending 3/22/2009. Click Yes if prompted to update hours.

Astor Landscaping

Pay Period 3/09/2009 thru 3/22/2009

Check No.	Employee	Filing Status	Allow	Pay Type	Pay Rate	Reg Hrs	OT Hrs	Gross Pay	Federal Income Tax	Soc. Sec. (FICA) Tax	Medicare Tax	VA State Tax	Net Pay
731	Dillion, Roy J.	Single	1	Hrly Wage	12.00	73.00		876.00	80.00	54.31	12.70	26.28	702.71
732	Folse, Jan B.	Single	1	Hrly Office	10.00	80.00		800.00	71.00	49.60	11.60	24.00	643.80
733	Greene, Kellie I.	Married	1	Salary	2,346.15			2,346.15	256.00	145.46	34.02	70.38	1,840.29
734	Hardman, Alan	Single	2	Hrly Wage	12.00	72.00		864.00	60.00	53.57	12.53	25.92	711.98
735	Hayes, Mike E	Single	1	Hrly Wage	12.00	54.00		648.00	47.00	40.18	9.40	19.44	531.98
736	Henderson, Jeff P.	Married	1	Hrly Wage	12.00	72.00		864.00	43.00	53.57	12.53	25.92	728.98
737	Murray, Monica D.	Single	1	Salary	1,211.54			1,211.54	131.00	75.12	17.57	36.35	951.50
738	Ramez, Victor M.	Single	0	Hrly Wage	10.00	78.00		780.00	89.00	48.36	11.31	23.40	607.93
739	Ruland, Seth N.	Married	0	Salary	3,103.85			3,103.85	429.00	192.44	45.01	93.12	2,344.28
740	White, Judy O.	Married	2	Salary	2,084.62			2,084.62	295.00	129.25	30.23	62.54	1,567.60
	Totals					429.00	0.00	13,578.16	1,501.00	841.86	196.90	407.35	10,631.05
	Tax Basis								Circular E	6.20%	1.45%	3.00%	
	G/L Accounts								23400	23400	23400	23600	10300

Astor Landscaping

Employer Costs for 3/09/2009 thru 3/22/2009

Employee	ER Soc Sec FICA	ER Medicare	ER FUTA	ER SUTA	Health Insurance
Dillion, Roy J.	54.31	12.70	7.01	13.14	0.00
Folse, Jan B.	49.60	11.60	6.40	12.00	60.00
Greene, Kellie I.	145.46	34.02	0.00	0.00	60.00
Hardman, Alan	53.57	12.53	6.91	12.96	0.00
Hayes, Mike E	40.18	9.40	5.18	9.72	0.00
Henderson, Jeff P.	53.57	12.53	6.91	12.96	0.00
Murray, Monica D.	75.12	17.57	7.55	18.17	60.00
Ramez, Victor M.	48.36	11.31	6.24	11.70	0.00
Ruland, Seth N.	192.44	45.01	0.00	0.00	60.00
White, Judy O.	129.25	30.23	0.00	0.00	60.00
Totals	841.86	196.90	46.20	90.65	300.00
Tax Basis	6.20%	1.45%	0.8%	1.50%	
G/L Accounts	23400 / 61000	23400 / 61000	23500 / 61000	23700 / 61000	23800 / 60600

The next illustration shows totals after entering the paychecks. Print the paychecks on first check number 731.

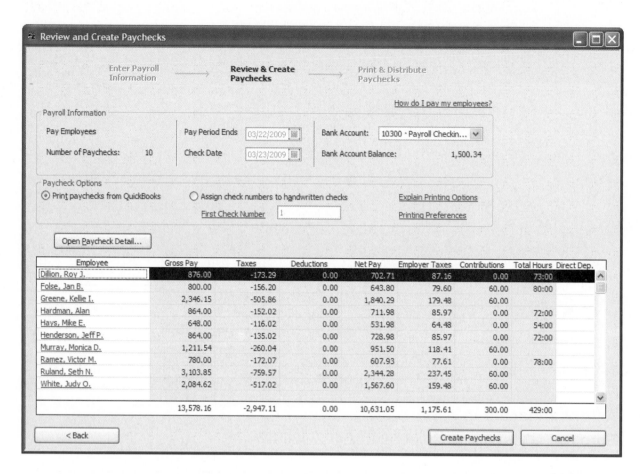

Mar 23   Print check number 463 to Nations Bank for $3,578.52 for federal withholding and Medicare and Social Security taxes for the liability period of 1/1/2009 to 3/31/2009.

2009

Apr 2   Print checks for the following payroll liabilities from 1/1/2009 to 3/31/2009. First
         check number is 464 and checks total $2,786.05.

Medi Benefits Administrators for health insurance	$600.00
Nations Bank for FUTA taxes	$460.47
VA Department of Taxation for VA income tax	$817.76
VA Employment Commission for SUTA taxes	$907.82

Apr 6   Enter the following timesheet for Alan Hardman.

Employee ID: Hardman, Alan   Mar 30 to Apr 5, 2009

Customer:Job	Service Item	Payroll Item	M 30	Tu 31	W 1	Th 2	F 3	Sa 4	Su 5	Total	Billable
O'Hara Homes: Redesign Gardens	INSTL HARD - COMMERCIAL	Hourly Wage	8.00	8.00	8.00	8.00	8.00			40.00	Yes
O'Hara Homes: Redesign Gardens	INSTL HARD - COMMERCIAL	Hourly Wage Overtime	2.00							2.00	Yes
		Totals	10.00	8.00	8.00	8.00	8.00			42.00	

Apr 6   Create the following paychecks for the pay period ending 4/5/2009.

Astor Landscaping
Pay Period 3/23/2009 thru 4/05/2009

Check No.	Employee	Filing Status	Allow.	Pay Type	Pay Rate	Reg Hrs	OT Hrs	Gross Pay	Federal Income Tax	Soc. Sec. (FICA) Tax	Medicare Tax	VA State Tax	Net Pay
741	Dillion, Roy J.	Single	1	Hrly Wage	12.00	80.00		960.00	95.00	59.52	13.92	28.80	762.76
742	Folse, Jan B.	Single	1	Hrly Office	10.00	80.00		800.00	71.00	49.60	11.60	24.00	643.80
743	Greene, Kellie I.	Married	1	Salary	2,346.15			2,346.15	256.00	145.46	34.02	70.38	1,840.29
744	Hardman, Alan	Single	2	Hrly Wage	12.00	80.00	2.00	996.00	78.00	61.75	14.44	29.88	811.93
745	Hayes, Mike E	Single	1	Hrly Wage	12.00	80.00		960.00	95.00	59.52	13.92	28.80	762.76
746	Henderson, Jeff P.	Married	1	Hrly Wage	12.00	80.00		960.00	53.00	59.52	13.92	28.80	804.76
747	Murray, Monica D.	Single	1	Salary	1,211.54			1,211.54	131.00	75.12	17.57	36.35	951.50
748	Ramez, Victor M.	Single	0	Hrly Wage	10.00	64.00		640.00	47.00	39.68	9.28	19.20	524.84
749	Ruland, Seth N.	Married	0	Salary	3,103.85			3,103.85	429.00	192.44	45.01	93.12	2,344.28
750	White, Judy O.	Married	2	Salary	2,084.62			2,084.62	295.00	129.25	30.23	62.54	1,567.60
	Totals					464.00	2.00	14,062.16	1,550.00	871.86	203.91	421.87	11,014.52
	Tax Basis								Circular E	6.20%	1.45%	3.00%	
	G/L Accounts								23400	23400	23400	23600	10300

Astor Landscaping
Employer Costs for 3/23/2009 thru 4/05/2009

Employee	ER Soc Sec FICA	ER Medicare	ER FUTA	ER SUTA	Health Insurance
Dillion, Roy J.	59.52	13.92	7.68	14.40	0.00
Folse, Jan B.	49.60	11.60	6.40	12.00	60.00
Greene, Kellie I.	145.46	34.02	0.00	0.00	60.00
Hardman, Alan	61.75	14.44	7.97	14.94	0.00
Hayes, Mike E	59.52	13.92	7.68	14.40	0.00
Henderson, Jeff P.	59.52	13.92	7.68	14.40	0.00
Murray, Monica D.	75.12	17.57	0.00	10.98	60.00
Ramez, Victor M.	39.68	9.28	5.12	9.60	0.00
Ruland, Seth N.	192.44	45.01	0.00	0.00	60.00
White, Judy O.	129.25	30.23	0.00	0.00	60.00
Totals	871.86	203.91	42.53	90.72	300.00
Tax Basis	3.00%	0.00%	0.8%	1.50%	
G/L Accounts	23400 / 61000	23400 / 61000	23500 / 61000	23700 / 61000	23800 / 60600

The next illustration shows the totals after entering paychecks. Print the paychecks on first check number 741.

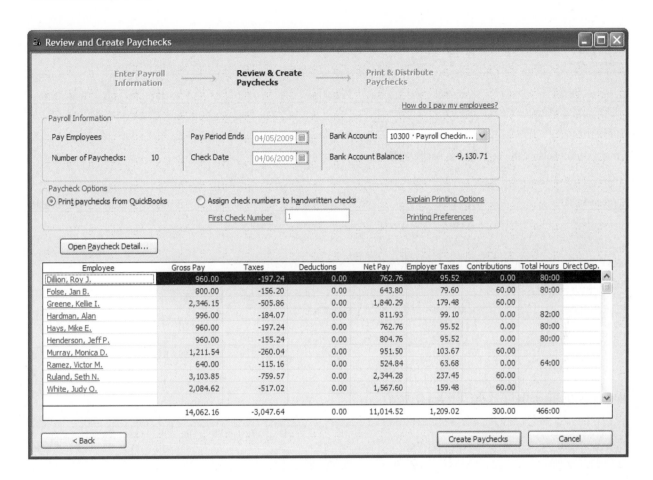

Apr 6   Print check number 468 to Nations Bank for $3,701.54 for federal withholding
             and Medicare and Social Security taxes for the payroll liability period of 1/1/2009
             to 4/6/2009.

Apr 13   Enter the following timesheets. Print a Time by Name report to verify entries.
              Total hours equal 230.

Employee ID: Dillion, Roy   Apr 6 to Apr 12, 2009

Customer/JobID	Service Item	Payroll Item	M 6	Tu 7	W 8	Th 9	F 10	Sa 11	Su 12	Total	Billable
O'Hara Homes: Redesign Gardens	INSTL LAND - COMMERCIAL	Hourly Wage	8.00	8.00	8.00	8.00	8.00			40.00	Yes

Employee ID: Folse, Jan   Apr 6 to Apr 12, 2009

Customer/JobID	Service Item	Payroll Item	M 6	Tu 7	W 8	Th 9	F 10	Sa 11	Su 12	Total	Billable
		Hourly Wage	8.00	8.00	8.00	8.00	6.00			38.00	No

Employee ID: Hardman, Alan Apr 6 to Apr 12, 2009

Customer/JobID	Service Item	Payroll Item	M 6	Tu 7	W 8	Th 9	F 10	Sa 11	Su 12	Total	Billable
Sugar Hill Tennis Club	WKLY MNTNCE - COMMERCIAL	Hourly Wage	8.00			8.00				16.00	Yes
Reynolds Court Subdivision	WKLY MNTNCE - COMMERCIAL	Hourly Wage		8.00	8.00		8.00			24.00	Yes
		Totals	8.00	8.00	8.00	8.00	8.00			40.00	

Employee ID: Hays, Mike   Apr 6 to Apr 12, 2009

Customer/JobID	Service Item	Payroll Item	M 6	Tu 7	W 8	Th 9	F 10	Sa 11	Su 12	Total	Billable
White and Associates	INSTL LAND - COMMERCIAL	Hourly Wage	8.00	8.00	8.00	8.00	8.00			40.00	Yes

Employee ID: Henderson, Jeff Apr 6 to Apr 12, 2009

Customer/JobID	Service Item	Payroll Item	M 6	Tu 7	W 8	Th 9	F 10	Sa 11	Su 12	Total	Billable
Silver Homes	INSTL HARD - COMMERCIAL	Hourly Wage	8.00	8.00	8.00	8.00				32.00	Yes

Employee ID: Ramez, Victor   Apr 6 to Apr 12, 2009

Customer/JobID	Service Item	Payroll Item	M 6	Tu 7	W 8	Th 9	F 10	Sa 11	Su 12	Total	Billable
Ashford Hill Apartments	WKLY MNTNCE - COMMERCIAL	Hourly Wage	8.00	8.00						16.00	Yes
DBH Enterprises	WKLY MNTNCE - COMMERCIAL	Hourly Wage			8.00	8.00	8.00			24.00	Yes
		Totals	8.00	8.00	8.00	8.00	8.00			40.00	

Apr 13   Add the following new employee.

                Name: David R. Bellows
                Address: 873 Trumpet St, Arlington, VA 30026
                Telephone: 777-325-0909
                Soc Sec: 111-00-3232

                Position: Laborer
                Hired: 4/13/2009

                Pay Info: Biweekly pay schedule
                                Hourly Wage: $12.00
                                Hourly Overtime: $18.00
                Tax Info: Federal: Single, 0 Allowances
                                State: VA for worked and withholding

Apr 20   Terminate Alan Hardman. Release date is April 20, 2009.

Apr 20   Enter the following timesheets. Print a Time by Name report to verify entries.
            Total hours equal 235.

Employee ID: Bellows, David   Apr 13 to Apr 19, 2009

Customer/JobID	Service Item	Payroll Item	M 13	Tu 14	W 15	Th 16	F 17	Sa 18	Su 19	Total	Billable
Sugar Hill Tennis Club	WKLY MNTNCE - COMMERCIAL	Hourly Wage	8.00	8.00	8.00					24.00	Yes
Reynolds Court Subdivision	WKLY MNTNCE - COMMERCIAL	Hourly Wage				8.00	8.00			16.00	Yes
		Totals	8.00	8.00	8.00	8.00	8.00			40.00	

Employee ID: Dillion, Roy   Apr 13 to Apr 19, 2009

Customer/JobID	Service Item	Payroll Item	M 13	Tu 14	W 15	Th 16	F 17	Sa 18	Su 19	Total	Billable
O'Hara Homes: Redesign Gardens	INSTL LAND - COMMERCIAL	Hourly Wage	8.00	8.00	8.00	8.00	8.00			40.00	Yes

Employee ID: Folse, Jan   Apr 13 to Apr 19, 2009

Customer/JobID	Service Item	Payroll Item	M 13	Tu 14	W 15	Th 16	F 17	Sa 18	Su 19	Total	Billable
			8.00	8.00	8.00	8.00	8.00			40.00	No

Employee ID: Hays, Mike   Apr 13 to Apr 19, 2009

Customer/JobID	Service Item	Payroll Item	M 13	Tu 14	W 15	Th 16	F 17	Sa 18	Su 19	Total	Billable
White and Associates	INSTL HARD - COMMERCIAL	Hourly Wage	8.00	8.00	8.00	8.00	5.00			37.00	Yes

Employee ID: Henderson, Jeff   Apr 13 to Apr 19, 2009

Customer/JobID	Service Item	Payroll Item	M 13	Tu 14	W 15	Th 16	F 17	Sa 18	Su 19	Total	Billable
Silver Homes	INSTL HARD - COMMERCIAL	Hourly Wage	8.00	8.00	8.00	8.00	8.00			40.00	Yes

Employee ID: Ramez, Victor   Apr 13 to Apr 19, 2009

Customer/JobID	Service Item	Payroll Item	M 13	Tu 14	W 15	Th 16	F 17	Sa 18	Su 19	Total	Billable
Ashford Hill Apartments	WKLY MNTNCE - COMMERCIAL	Houly Wage	8.00	8.00						16.00	Yes
DBH Enterprises	WKLY MNTNCE - COMMERCIAL	Houly Wage			8.00	6.00	8.00			22.00	Yes
		Totals	8.00	8.00	8.00	6.00	8.00			38.00	

Apr 20   Create the following paychecks for the pay period ending 4/19/2009. Note: You must manually change Jan Folse's paycheck hours to 78 because her account does not use time data to create paychecks. Without this, QBP will pay her 80 hours per biweekly pay period.

Astor Landscaping
Pay Period 4/6/2009 thru 4/19/2007

Check No.	Employee	Filing Status	Allow.	Pay Type	Pay Rate	Reg Hrs	OT Hrs	Gross Pay	Federal Income Tax	Soc. Sec. (FICA) Tax	Medicare Tax	VA State Tax	Net Pay
751	Bellows, David R	Single	0	Hrly Wage	12.00	40.00		480.00	43.00	29.76	6.96	14.40	385.88
752	Dillion, Roy J.	Single	1	Hrly Wage	12.00	80.00		960.00	95.00	59.52	13.92	28.80	762.76
753	Folse, Jan B.	Single	1	Hrly Office	10.00	78.00		780.00	68.00	48.36	11.31	23.40	628.93
754	Greene, Kellie I.	Married	1	Salary	2,346.15			2,346.15	256.00	145.46	34.02	70.38	1,840.29
755	Hardman, Alan	Single	2	Hrly Wage	12.00	40.00		480.00	11.00	29.76	6.96	14.40	417.88
756	Hayes, Mike E	Single	1	Hrly Wage	12.00	77.00		924.00	89.00	57.29	13.40	27.72	736.59
757	Henderson, Jeff P.	Married	1	Hrly Wage	12.00	72.00		864.00	43.00	53.57	12.53	25.92	728.98
758	Murray, Monica D.	Single	1	Salary	1,211.54			1,211.54	131.00	75.12	17.57	36.35	951.50
759	Ramez, Victor M.	Single	0	Hrly Wage	10.00	78.00		780.00	68.00	48.36	11.31	23.40	628.93
760	Ruland, Seth N.	Married	0	Salary	3,103.85			3,103.85	429.00	192.44	45.01	93.12	2,344.28
761	White, Judy O.	Married	2	Salary	2,084.62			2,084.62	295.00	129.25	30.23	62.54	1,567.60
	Totals					465.00	0.00	14,014.16	1,528.00	868.89	203.22	420.43	10,993.62
	Tax Basis								Circular E	6.20%	1.45%	3.00%	
	G/L Accounts								23400	23400	23400	23600	10300

Astor Landscaping
Employer Costs for 4/6/2009 thru 4/19/2009

Employee	ER Soc Sec (FICA)	ER Medicare	ER FUTA	ER SUTA	Health Insurance
Bellows, David R	29.76	6.96	3.84	7.20	0.00
Dillion, Roy J.	59.52	13.92	7.68	14.40	0.00
Folse, Jan B.	48.36	11.31	0.00	11.70	60.00
Greene, Kellie I.	145.46	34.02	0.00	0.00	60.00
Hardman, Alan	29.76	6.96	2.72	7.20	0.00
Hayes, Mike E	57.29	13.40	7.39	13.86	0.00
Henderson, Jeff P.	53.57	12.53	3.01	12.96	0.00
Murray, Monica D.	75.12	17.57	0.00	0.00	60.00
Ramez, Victor M.	48.36	11.31	6.24	11.70	0.00
Ruland, Seth N.	192.44	45.01	0.00	0.00	60.00
White, Judy O.	129.25	30.23	0.00	0.00	60.00
Totals	868.89	203.22	30.88	79.02	300.00
Tax Basis	6.20%	1.45%	0.8%	1.50%	
G/L Accounts	23400 / 61000	23400 / 61000	23500 / 61000	23700 / 61000	23750 / 60300

The next illustration shows totals after entering the paychecks. Print the paychecks using first check number 751.

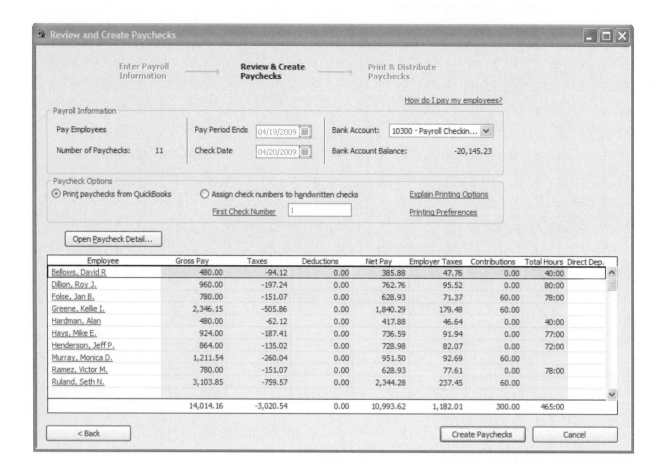

Apr 20   Print check number 469 to Nations Bank for $3,672.22 for federal withholding and Medicare and Social Security taxes for the payroll liability period of 1/1/2009 to 4/20/2009.

Apr 30   Print checks for the following payroll liabilities from 1/1/2009 to 4/30/2009. First check number is 470 and checks total $1,442.30.

Medi Benefits Administrators for health insurance	$600.00
VA Department of Taxation for VA income tax	$842.30

2. Print the following reports to document activities.

    a. Payroll Transactions by Payee filtered for 3/23/2009 to 4/30/2009.

    b. Payroll Liability Balances report filtered for 1/1/2009 to 4/30/2009.

3. *Back up the Graded Astor Landscaping data file to a backup file named "Graded Astor Landscaping Chpt 6". The Practice Set for the next chapter will build on the work completed in this chapter.*

CHAPTER 7   CLOSE THE ACCOUNTING PERIOD FOR A SERVICE BASED BUSINESS

LEARNING OBJECTIVES

This chapter works with the Practice Astor Landscaping data file containing the tasks completed in Chapter 6. *If this company is not loaded on your computer then restore it using the Practice Astor Landscaping Chpt 6.QBB backup file created after reading Chapter 6.*

In this chapter you complete Astor's accounting transactions for March 2009. You will:

1. Analyze transactions posted in March and review a preclosing checklist
2. Post adjusting entries
3. Reconcile bank accounts
4. Print financial statements
5. Close the accounting period

Launch QBP and open **Practice Astor Landscaping**.

ANALYZE TRANSACTIONS

In Chapter 3 you learned to post general journal entries. You will use journal entries in this chapter to adjust account balances and accrue expenses. You will then print financial statements for March and close the accounting period.

It is important to analyze posted transactions before closing an accounting period. You begin this analysis by reviewing the **General Ledger** report that follows.

Open the report by selecting *Reports>>Accountant and Taxes>>General Ledger* on the main menu. Enter the date range of 3/1/2009 to 3/31/2009. (See Figure 7:1.)

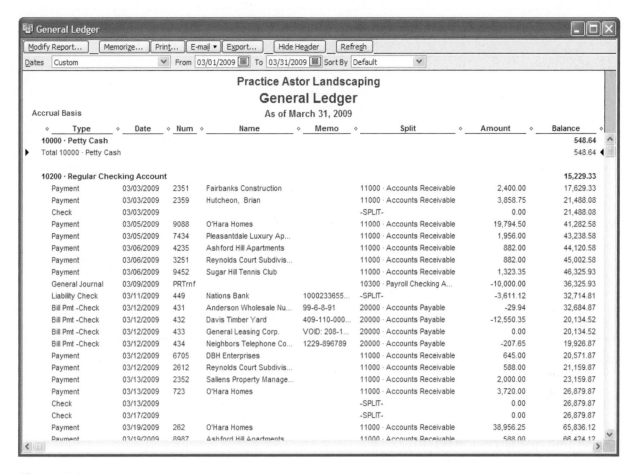

Figure 7:1

This report differs from the General Ledger Detail Report you have been using to document the audit trail because it also lists beginning and ending account balances.

Modify this report so that transactions appear in debit and credit columns. Click **Modify Report** and add the **Debit** and **Credit** columns and remove the **Amount** column. Click **OK**.

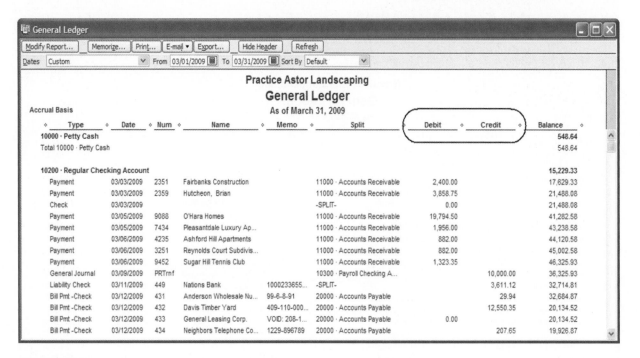

Figure 7:2

Remember that the Split column lists corresponding accounts used on a transaction. If the term "SPLIT" appears then multiple accounts were involved. What follows are the steps performed to analyze the report.

First, scroll through the report to look for transactions that may indicate a posting error. In particular, scroll to account 71100 Utilities Expense and notice that the March telephone bill for $262.43 posted to utilities instead of posting to account 71200 Telephone Expense.

You will now reclassify the expense. Double click the entry to reopen it and use the lookup for **Account** to select 71200 Telephone Expense. (See Figure 7:3.)

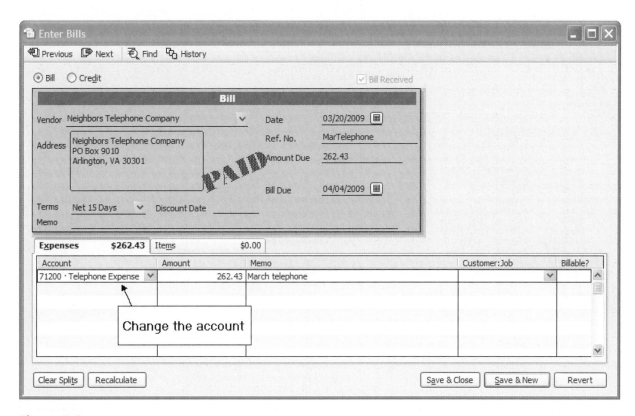

Figure 7:3

Click **Save & Close** and click **Yes** when QBP prompts to confirm changing a posted transaction. That is how easy it is to reclassify a posting error for expenses.

The next step is to review the report for missing transactions. In particular, scroll to account 10300 Payroll Checking to find that the March 23 bank transfer covering payroll checks has not been recorded. (See Figure 7:4.)

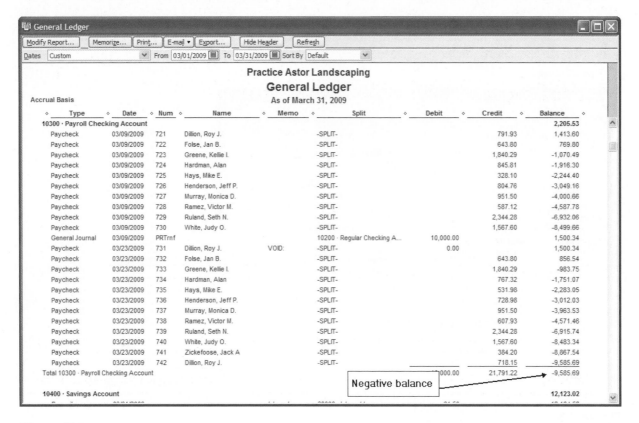

Figure 7:4

You will record this correcting entry in the exercise that follows.

Now scroll down to 14000 Prepaid Expenses. The accountant has already posted the adjusting entry recognizing this month's expired prepaid insurance. Double click the $400 entry to open the transactions. (See Figure 7:5.)

*(Note: If a message appears letting you know that QBP can automatically assign journal entry numbers, click the option to turn off future messages and click **OK**.)*

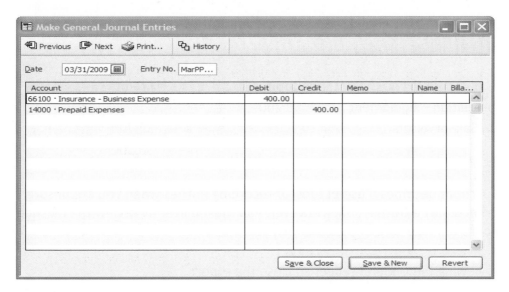

Figure 7:5

Figure 7:5 illustrates recording an adjusting entry for prepaid expense. Click **X** to close the entry.

As you scroll past prepaid expenses, look for March entries to accumulated depreciation. These entries have not been recorded so you will record them in the exercise that follows.

Now is a good time to talk about using a suspense account. Scroll to the bottom of the General Ledger report and locate the **99999 Suspense** account. This account is used when you need to post an entry but do not have all the information necessary to complete it.

For instance, assume the company sold equipment costing $15,000 and received $8,500 in cash. You cannot delay recording cash on the sale; however, you do not have final depreciation on the equipment to finalize gain or loss on the sale. This is where the entry can be posted using the suspense account. The following illustrates the journal entry to post the transaction using the suspense account.

	Debit	**Credit**
10200 Regular Checking Account	$8,500	
99999 Suspense	$6,500	
15100 Equipment		$15,000

When you later calculate that $8,000 was previously posted to the accumulated equipment depreciation account and that final depreciation is $9,200, the following journal entry records the depreciation adjustment.

	Debit	**Credit**
75000 Depreciation Expense	$1,200	
15110 Accum. Depreciation – Equipment		$ 1,200

You are now ready to reclassify the earlier suspense account entry by recording the next journal entry.

		Debit	Credit
15110	Accum. Depreciation – Equipment	$9,200	
90000	Gain/Loss on Sale of Assets		$2,700
99999	Suspense		$6,500

Thus, the suspense account becomes a useful tool for recording entries when you are unsure of all the accounts affected by a transaction. However, you must diligently review the balance in the suspense account to make sure entries are finalized.

You have finished reviewing the General Ledger so close the report.

There are a variety of procedures to be followed before closing an accounting period. Some of these were explained in previous chapters. Additional procedures vary based on a company's accounting transactions. It is not possible to simulate the variety of reconciling procedures you may encounter in practice. Instead, we have prepared the following preclosing checklist to help guide you in the future.

Preclosing Checklist	
Review Pending Transactions	Review pending sales to verify all sales income has been recognized.
	Review pending purchases to verify all expenses have been recognized.
	Review payroll tax liability accounts to ensure timely payment.
Reconciliation Procedures	Reconcile all bank statements.
	Reconcile the A/R aging report to the accounts receivable control account. (Performed in Chapters 4 and 8.)
	Reconcile the inventory valuation report to the inventory control account. (Performed in Chapter 8.)
	Reconcile fixed asset reports to fixed asset control accounts Often fixed asset costs and depreciation will be tracked outside the software. QBP can track fixed asset costs and depreciation but this feature is not illustrated.
	Reconcile the A/P aging report to the accounts payable control account. (Performed in Chapter 5 and 9.)
Adjusting Entries	Post petty cash transactions.
	Review prepaid expenses for expired costs.
	Review accrued liability accounts such as wages and taxes payable.
	Review expenses in the prior period to identify expenses that need to be recognized in the current period. For example, missing utility bills or recurring rent transactions.
	Review posted expenses for prepaid costs and for fixed assets expensed to office supplies.

ADJUSTING ENTRIES

In this topic you post Astor's remaining adjusting entries for March. The accountant has already posted entries for expired prepaid expense and recurring rent. This means that you need to post entries transferring funds to payroll checking, replenishing petty cash and recognizing depreciation and accrued wage expense.

In the exercise that follows you post the bank transfer and depreciation entries. In the *You Try* exercise that follows you post an entry for accrued wages expense and print a check for petty cash.

When posting depreciation, keep in mind that this is an estimate of expense based on ending assets held in the prior year. The estimate may be revised during the year for current year acquisitions or dispositions and any difference between estimated and actual expense is recorded at the end of the fiscal year.

STEPS TO ENTER ADJUSTING ENTRIES

1. You will record the payroll transfer first. Select ***Banking>>Transfer Funds*** on the main menu and enter the information illustrated in Figure 7:6. Click **Save & Close**.

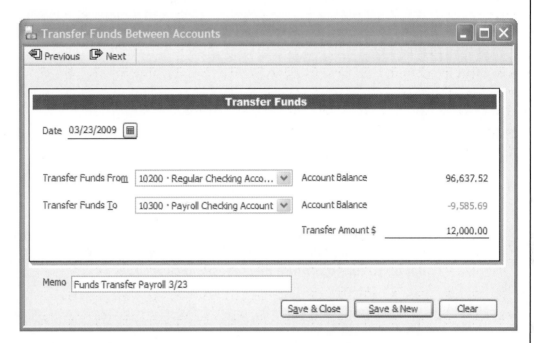

Figure 7:6

2. Adjusting entries are often saved as memorized transactions, especially when such transactions repeat every month. Check to see if the accountant has created a memorized entry for accumulated depreciation.

   Select **Lists>>Memorized Transactions List** on the main menu to find a memorized depreciation transaction. You also find the memorized transaction you created in Chapter 5.

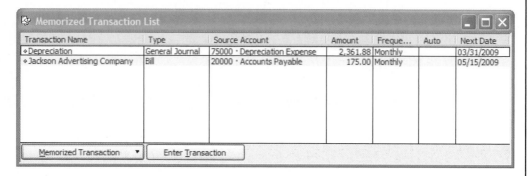

Figure 7:7

3. Double click to open the depreciation transaction (Figure 7:8). *(Note: If prompted about automatically assigning numbers to journal entries, mark the option to turn off future messages and click OK.)*

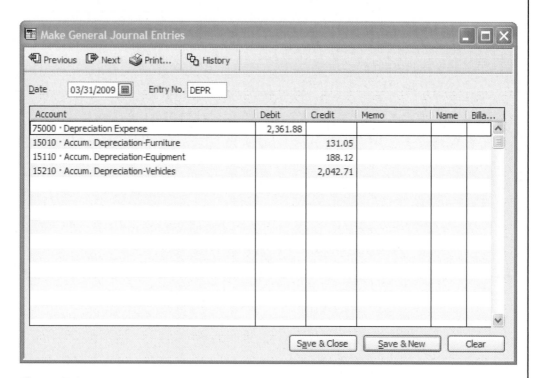

Figure 7:8

4. The accountant wants to revise the estimate for furniture depreciation.

    Change the **Debit** for 75000 Depreciation Expense to 2,370.83.

    Change the **Credit** for 15010 Accum. Depreciation-Furniture to 140.00.

5. Before you post this entry replace the existing memorized transaction.

    Click ***Edit>>Memorize General Journal*** on the main menu. When QBP prompts, select Replace.

6. Now click **Save & Close**. *(Note: You can turn off future messages on fixed assets.)*

    When you return to the Memorized Transaction List, the Next Date for the depreciation entry is scheduled for 4/30/2009.

    Close the Memorized Transaction List.

FINISH RECORDING MARCH ADJUSTING ENTRIES

You will be recording accrued wages for March and printing a check to replenish petty cash.

Print check number 455 on March 31 to Petty Cash for $376.26. The check is expensed as follows.

Travel Expense	$103.76
Meals and Entertainment Expense	$108.67
Office Supplies Expense	$163.83

To post accrued wages you must first calculate the accrual amount using the following steps.

a. Open the Employee Earnings Summary report to determine average weekly wage expense. Enter 2/23/09 to 3/22/09 as the date range (i.e., the last two pay dates, covering four weeks). Total the salary, hourly office, and hourly wage amounts without overtime and divide by 4. The weekly average is $6,767.08 computed as (17,492.32 + 1,600.00 + 7,976.00) / 4.

b. Next, compute a daily average wage by dividing the weekly average by 5 working days. The daily average is $1,353.42.

c. Finally, multiply the daily average by the number of days to accrue. For March, this is 7 days because the last pay period ended March 22. The accrual amount is $9,473.94.

Now post a journal entry for Astor's March accrued wages to 60000 Salaries Expense and 23200 Accrued Wages.

RECONCILE BANK ACCOUNTS

After posting adjusting entries, you are ready to reconcile Astor's bank accounts. The accountant has already reconciled the savings account. The steps that follow help you reconcile the regular checking account. Thereafter, you reconcile the payroll checking account in the *You Try* exercise that follows.

On the Home page, click **Reconcile** under **Banking**. The reconciliation process begins by selecting the bank account.

Note: The Begin Reconciliation window always opens to the first bank account on the Chart of Accounts; therefore, you need to choose the account after opening the window. (See Figure 7:9.)

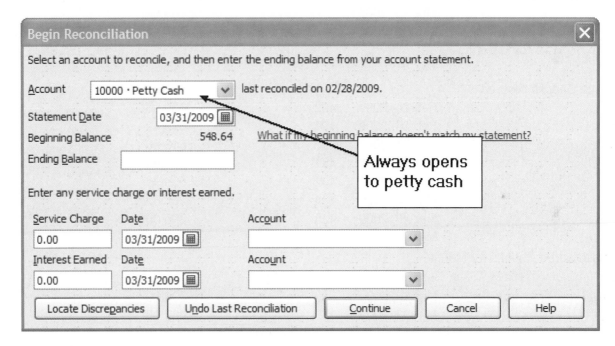

Figure 7:9

Use the **Account** dropdown list to select **10400 Savings Account** and you will find this account already reconciled for March.

Astor has received the March bank statement for the regular checking account. The next exercise walks through reconciling this account to the bank statement illustrated next.

Astor Landscaping
Bank Statement March 31, 2009

Beginning Balance from February Statement				$ 17,266.25
March Deposits				
	Mar 3, 2009		6,258.75	
	Mar 5, 2009		21,750.50	
	Mar 6, 2009		3,087.35	
	Mar 12, 2009		1,233.00	
	Mar 13, 2009		5,720.00	
	Mar 19, 2009		39,544.25	
	Mar 20, 2009		11,258.50	
	Mar 27, 2009		15,196.00	
	Mar 28, 2009		2,764.00	
	Mar 31, 2009		31,315.73	
Total Deposits for March				138,128.08
March Checks Cleared				
	Feb 26, 2009	402	600.00	
	Feb 26, 2009	404	818.42	
	Feb 27, 2009	430	618.50	
	Mar 12, 2009	431	29.94	
	Mar 12, 2009	432	12,550.35	
	Mar 12, 2009	434	207.65	
	Mar 20, 2009	435	300.00	
	Mar 20, 2009	436	97.64	
Total Cleared Checks for March				15,222.50
Less Bank Transfers	Mar 9, 2009		10,000.00	
	Mar 23, 2009		12,000.00	
Total March Transfers				22,000.00
March Service Charges				67.50
Ending Bank Balance March 31, 2009				$ 118,104.33

Figure 7:10

STEPS TO RECONCILE THE CHECKING ACCOUNT

1. Select **10200 Regular Checking** as the Account to reconcile.

    Referring to the bank statement, enter the **Ending Balance**, **Date**, and **Service Charge** as shown in Figure 7:11. Verify that service charges will post to 73000 Bank Charges.

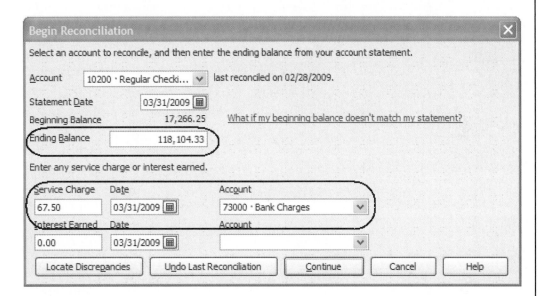

Figure 7:11

2. Click **Continue** to proceed to the screen where you select deposits and checks clearing the March bank statement.

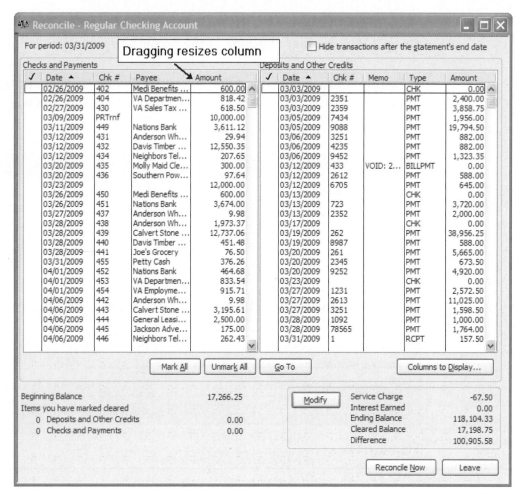

Figure 7:12

3. We will now explain using this window.

    Modify reopens the Begin Reconciliation window illustrated in Step 1 to change entries.

    Outstanding checks and bank transfers are listed on the left. On the right are deposits and void checks. Notice that the check you voided in Chapter 5 is already marked as cleared.

    Click a check or deposit to mark the item as cleared. *(Note: You can also click the Mark All button and then click individual checks and deposits that have not cleared.)*

    You can double click a check or deposit to reopen it.

    The **Columns to Display** button customizes data displayed in the columns.

4. Click the option that hides all transactions after the statement's end date (i.e., top right of window) to remove April checks and deposits from the window.

5. Click **Mark All** and then refer to the totals listed at the bottom of the window. (See Figure 7:13.) The total for **Deposits** and **Other Credits** will equal total cleared deposits on the bank statement. You will now work on the checks.

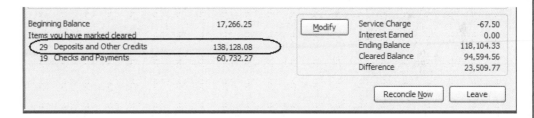

Figure 7:13

6. Refer back to the bank statement and click to deselect checks in the Reconcile window that have not cleared the statement. When finished, your results will compare to the results illustrated in Figure 7:14.

    The total for **Checks**, **Payments** and **Service Charges** will equal the sum of bank transfers, service charges, and cleared checks on the bank statement.

    You cannot complete the next step until the **Difference** equals zero.

    If you have difficulty reconciling an account, the **Leave** button saves your work and closes the reconciliation window. You can return later to complete the reconciliation.

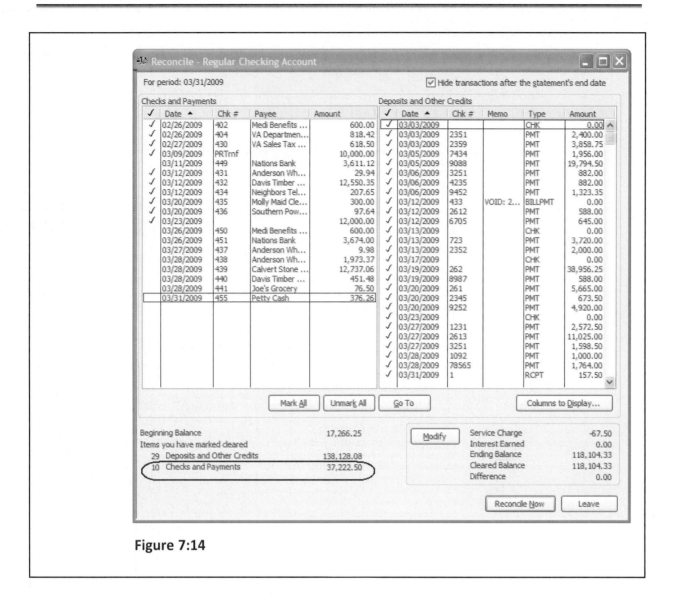

Figure 7:14

7. Click **Reconcile Now** and Figure 7:15 opens. Keep the option of **Both** and click **Display**. *(Note: Turn off future messages when QBP prompts with information about reports.)*

Select Reconciliation Report

Congratulations! Your account is balanced. All marked items have been cleared in the account register.

Select the type of reconciliation report you'd like to see.

- ○ Summary
- ○ Detail
- ◉ Both

To view this report at a later time, select the Report menu, display Banking and then Previous Reconciliation.

[Display] [Print...] [Close]

Figure 7:15

8. Figure 7:16 shows the **Reconciliation Summary** report. The **Cleared Balance** agrees with the ending balance on the March bank statement. You will not print this statement because there is no information on individual items so close the report.

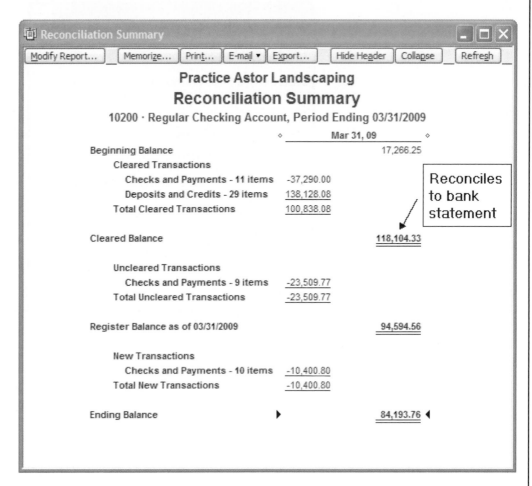

Figure 7:16

9. You now see the **Reconciliation Detail** report, which was located behind the summary report. You will always want to print this report because it provides information on individual transactions.

    Scroll down to where the report lists the **Cleared Balance**. Again, this amount will agree with the ending balance on the March bank statement. Beneath this are transactions that should clear the April bank statement.

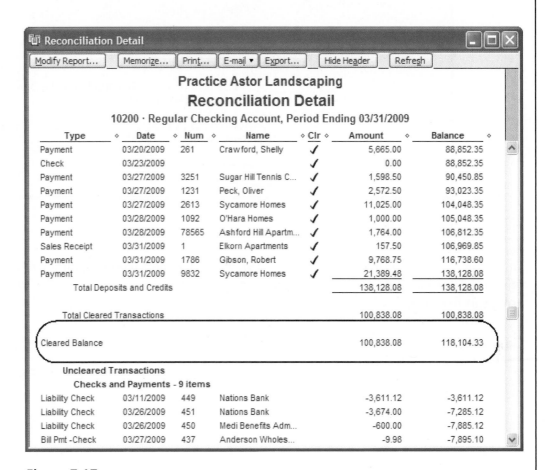

Figure 7:17

10. Click the **Print** button on the report. Select a printer and click **Print**. You can now close the report.

You can reprint reconciliation reports by selecting *Reports>>Banking>>Previous Reconciliation* on the main menu. You then choose the options illustrated in Figure 7:18 and click **Display**.

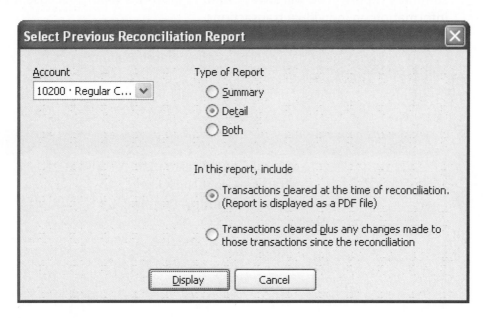

Figure 7:18

The report opens in PDF format (Figure 7:19), which can be saved to your local hard drive by selecting *File>>Save As* on the PDF menu. You can only print the most recent reconciliation using this method.

Close the report.

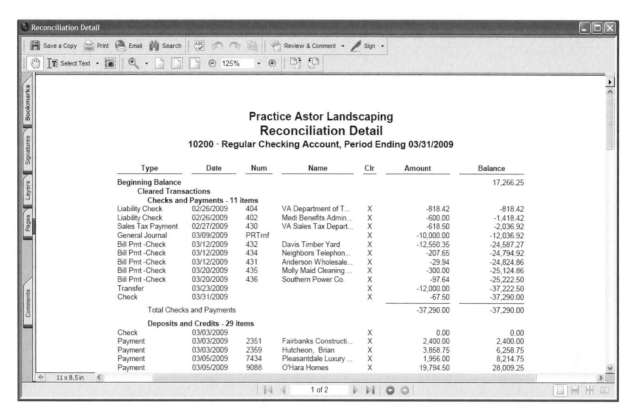

Figure 7:19

RECONCILE THE PAYROLL CHECKING ACCOUNT

The March bank statement for the payroll checking account has arrived. All paychecks and deposits have cleared. Bank charges for March are $28.30 and the ending bank statement balance is $2,386.01.

Reconcile the account and print the Detail Reconciliation report.

FINANCIAL REPORTS

You have now completed the preclosing checklist and are ready to print the trial balance and financial statements.

The trial balance is printed first so you can perform one final check of account balances. Select *Reports>>Accountant and Taxes>>Trial Balance* on the main menu and enter 3/31/2009 as the date range. (See Figure 7:20.)

Practice Astor Landscaping
Trial Balance
As of March 31, 2009

	Mar 31, 09 Debit	Credit
10000 · Petty Cash	548.64	
10200 · Regular Checking Account	94,594.56	
10300 · Payroll Checking Account	2,386.01	
10400 · Savings Account	12,184.52	
11000 · Accounts Receivable	89,293.35	
11500 · Allowance for Doubtful Accounts		4,999.10
14000 · Prepaid Expenses	400.00	
15000 · Furniture and Fixtures	11,007.96	
15010 · Accum. Depreciation-Furniture		1,980.31
15100 · Equipment	35,802.41	
15110 · Accum. Depreciation-Equipment		16,366.78
15200 · Vehicles	102,562.64	
15210 · Accum. Depreciation-Vehicles		22,469.81
19000 · Deposits	2,500.00	
20000 · Accounts Payable		9,644.46
22000 · Sales Tax Payable		3,546.50
23200 · Accrued Wages		9,473.94
23400 · Federal Payroll Tax Liabilities	10.00	
23500 · FUTA Tax Payable		464.68
23600 · State Payroll Taxes Payable		833.54
23700 · SUTA Tax Payable		915.71
23800 · Medical Insurance Payable	0.00	
23900 · Income Taxes Payable		10,478.63
30000 · Common Stock		8,200.00
39100 · Paid-in Capital		120,000.00
39500 · Retained Earnings		70,160.90
41000 · Sales - Landscape		26,270.70
42000 · Sales - Hardscape		135,039.75
43000 · Sales - Design Services		58,100.00
45000 · Sales - Maintenance Services		23,370.00
46000 · Sales - Miscellaneous		210.00
49000 · Sales Discounts	436.52	
51000 · Materials Cost - Landscape	3,161.21	
52000 · Materials Cost - Hardscape	40,739.05	
57000 · Direct Labor	43,880.00	
57400 · Subcontractors - Landscaping	3,000.00	
60000 · Salaries Expense	47,850.90	
60600 · Employee Benefit Programs Exp	1,800.00	
61000 · Payroll Tax Expenses	7,673.20	
63000 · Office Supplies Expense	542.99	
63100 · Postage Expense	282.83	
64000 · Advertising Expense	175.00	
65000 · Legal and Professional Expense	762.00	
66100 · Insurance - Business Expense	800.00	
66200 · Insurance - Auto Expense	822.10	
71000 · Rent Expense	7,500.00	
71100 · Utilities Expense	743.44	
71200 · Telephone Expense	746.26	
72300 · Repairs - Auto Expenses	1,416.56	
72500 · Cleaning Expense	900.00	
73000 · Bank Charges	290.22	
75000 · Depreciation Expense	7,094.59	
76000 · Travel Expense	383.58	
76100 · Meals and Entertainment Exp	413.57	
80000 · Interest Income		179.30
TOTAL	522,704.11	522,704.11

Figure 7:20

In a manual accounting system this report was critical to proving that debits equaled credits before preparing financial statements. You will recall the manual sales journal entries illustrated in Chapter 4 and how this journal was cross-footed before posting entries to customer and general ledger accounts. You also remember the manual purchasing entries in Chapter 5 and the manual payroll entries in Chapter 6. Now you understand why this report is called a "trial" balance. Imagine the number of trials it took before the books balanced because of the number of errors that could occur in a manual system. In fact, an unadjusted trial balance was prepared before posting adjusting entries and then an adjusted closing trial balance was prepared before preparing financial statements.

Today the trial balance still verifies that accounts balance; however, it more likely functions as a tool for reconciling account balances to external source documents and reports. In fact, you used the report to tie the balance on the A/R aging report back to the balance in Accounts Receivable and to tie other report balances back to the general ledger.

Close the trial balance so we can next focus on financial statements.

Open the **Report Center**. As shown in Figure 7:21, QBP refers to the Income Statement as the Profit & Loss Statement.

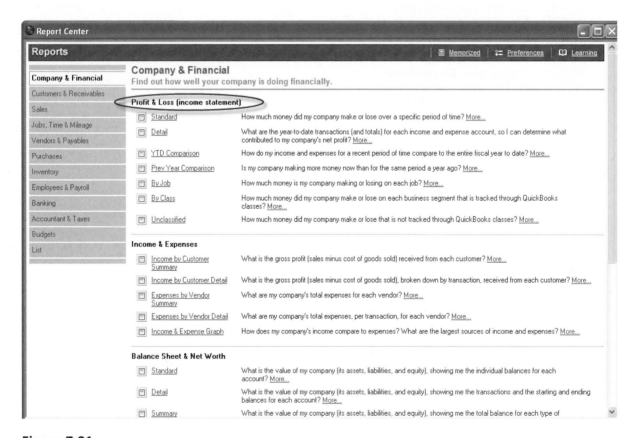

Figure 7:21

Open the **Standard** statement and enter the date range of 1/1/2009 to 3/31/2009. (See Figure 7:22.)

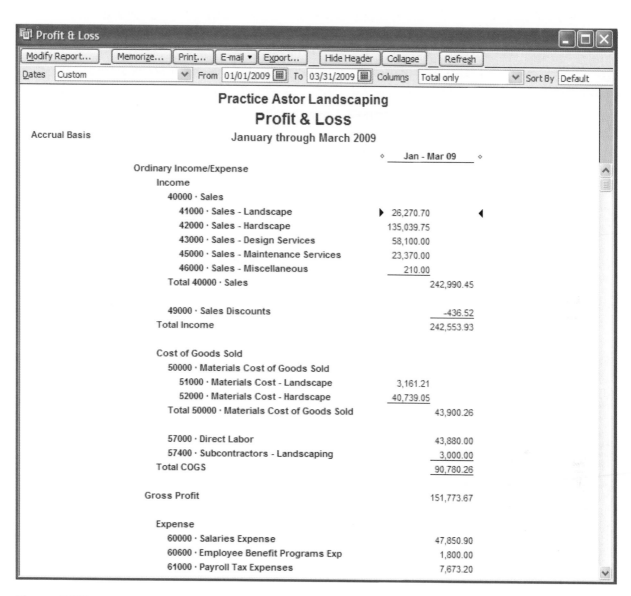

Figure 7:22

Scroll to the bottom and locate year-to-date net income of $71,755.73.

Close this report and open the **Detail** report. Again enter the date range of 1/1/2009 to 3/31/2009.

The report in Figure 7:23 lists individual transactions affecting Income Statement accounts. Close this report.

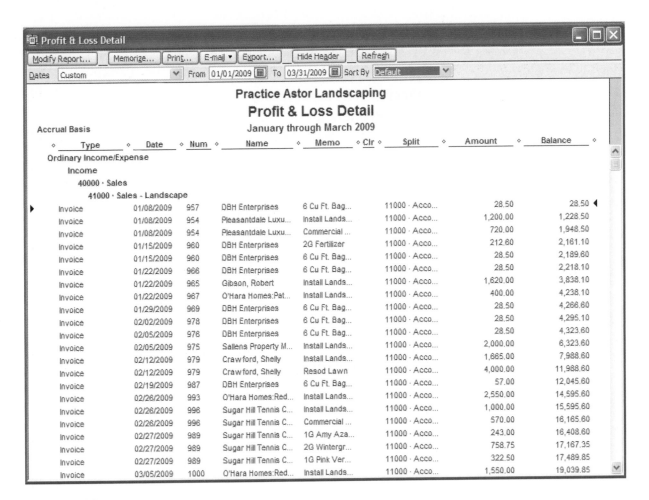

Figure 7:23

Now open the **YTD Comparison** report. This time enter the date range of 3/1/2009 to 3/31/2009 and scroll to the bottom of the report.

Practice Astor Landscaping
Profit & Loss YTD Comparison
March 2009

	Mar 09	Jan - Mar 09
Ordinary Income/Expense		
Income		
40000 · Sales		
41000 · Sales - Landscape	8,780.85	26,270.70
42000 · Sales - Hardscape	50,789.00	135,039.75
43000 · Sales - Design Services	22,050.00	58,100.00
45000 · Sales - Maintenance Services	7,290.00	23,370.00
46000 · Sales - Miscellaneous	150.00	210.00
Total 40000 · Sales	89,059.85	242,990.45
49000 · Sales Discounts	-436.52	-436.52
Total Income	88,623.33	242,553.93
Cost of Goods Sold		
50000 · Materials Cost of Goods Sold		
51000 · Materials Cost - Landscape	1,933.34	3,161.21
52000 · Materials Cost - Hardscape	18,067.29	40,739.05
Total 50000 · Materials Cost of Goods Sold	20,000.63	43,900.26
57000 · Direct Labor	15,982.00	43,880.00
57400 · Subcontractors - Landscaping	0.00	3,000.00
Total COGS	35,982.63	90,780.26
Gross Profit	52,640.70	151,773.67
Expense		
60000 · Salaries Expense	21,276.26	47,850.90
60600 · Employee Benefit Programs Exp	600.00	1,800.00
61000 · Payroll Tax Expenses	2,408.29	7,673.20
63000 · Office Supplies Expense	289.59	542.99
63100 · Postage Expense	0.00	282.83
64000 · Advertising Expense	175.00	175.00
65000 · Legal and Professional Expense	762.00	762.00
66000 · Insurance Expense		
66100 · Insurance - Business Expense	400.00	800.00
66200 · Insurance - Auto Expense	0.00	822.10
Total 66000 · Insurance Expense	400.00	1,622.10
71000 · Rent Expense	2,500.00	7,500.00
71100 · Utilities Expense	97.64	743.44
71200 · Telephone Expense	262.43	746.26
72000 · Repairs and Maintenance Expense		
72300 · Repairs - Auto Expenses	0.00	1,416.56
Total 72000 · Repairs and Maintenance Expense	0.00	1,416.56
72500 · Cleaning Expense	300.00	900.00
73000 · Bank Charges	95.80	290.22
75000 · Depreciation Expense	2,370.83	7,094.59
76000 · Travel Expense	103.76	383.58
76100 · Meals and Entertainment Exp	185.17	413.57
Total Expense	31,826.77	80,197.24
Net Ordinary Income	20,813.93	71,576.43
Other Income/Expense		
Other Income		
80000 · Interest Income	61.50	179.30
Total Other Income	61.50	179.30
Net Other Income	61.50	179.30
Net Income	20,875.43	71,755.73

Figure 7:24

The **YTD Comparison** report compares March income to year-to-date income. As you know, the Income Statement paints a company's financial picture over a period of time and this report informs Astor's owners that approximately thirty percent of year-to-date income was generated in March.

QBP creates the Income Statement using general ledger account types. You will recall setting types when creating general ledger accounts in Chapter 3. You will now see these types mapped to the Income Statement.

Press **Ctrl + A** on the keyboard to open the **Chart of Accounts**. Refer to the **YTD Comparison** report and the **Type** column on the **Chart of Accounts** as we explain type mapping on the Income Statement.

Income account types appear under the Income category on the statement; **Cost of Goods Sold** account types under Cost of Goods Sold, and so forth. Within these categories, account balances are listed individually.

Types serve the same purpose on the Balance Sheet. Close the Income Statement and open the **Standard Balance Sheet**. (See Figure 7:25.) This statement reports a company's financial position on a specific date. Enter 3/31/2009 as the date. Take the time to scroll through accounts on the Balance Sheet and compare the placement of accounts to types on the Chart of Accounts.

Practice Astor Landscaping
Balance Sheet
As of March 31, 2009

	Mar 31, 09
ASSETS	
Current Assets	
Checking/Savings	
10000 · Petty Cash	548.64
10200 · Regular Checking Account	94,594.56
10300 · Payroll Checking Account	2,386.01
10400 · Savings Account	12,184.52
Total Checking/Savings	109,713.73
Accounts Receivable	
11000 · Accounts Receivable	89,293.35
Total Accounts Receivable	89,293.35
Other Current Assets	
11500 · Allowance for Doubtful Accounts	-4,999.10
14000 · Prepaid Expenses	400.00
Total Other Current Assets	-4,599.10
Total Current Assets	194,407.98
Fixed Assets	
15000 · Furniture and Fixtures	11,007.96
15010 · Accum. Depreciation-Furniture	-1,980.31
15100 · Equipment	35,802.41
15110 · Accum. Depreciation-Equipment	-16,366.78
15200 · Vehicles	102,562.64
15210 · Accum. Depreciation-Vehicles	-22,469.81
Total Fixed Assets	108,556.11
Other Assets	
19000 · Deposits	2,500.00
Total Other Assets	2,500.00
TOTAL ASSETS	305,464.09
LIABILITIES & EQUITY	
Liabilities	
Current Liabilities	
Accounts Payable	
20000 · Accounts Payable	9,644.46
Total Accounts Payable	9,644.46
Other Current Liabilities	
22000 · Sales Tax Payable	3,546.50
23200 · Accrued Wages	9,473.94
23400 · Federal Payroll Tax Liabilities	-10.00
23500 · FUTA Tax Payable	464.68
23600 · State Payroll Taxes Payable	833.54
23700 · SUTA Tax Payable	915.71
23900 · Income Taxes Payable	10,478.63
Total Other Current Liabilities	25,703.00
Total Current Liabilities	35,347.46
Total Liabilities	35,347.46
Equity	
30000 · Common Stock	8,200.00
39100 · Paid-in Capital	120,000.00
39500 · Retained Earnings	70,160.90
Net Income	71,755.73
Total Equity	270,116.63
TOTAL LIABILITIES & EQUITY	305,464.09

Figure 7:25

Close the Balance Sheet and the Chart of Accounts.

Next open the **Statement of Cash Flows** and enter the date range of 3/1/2009 to 3/31/2009.

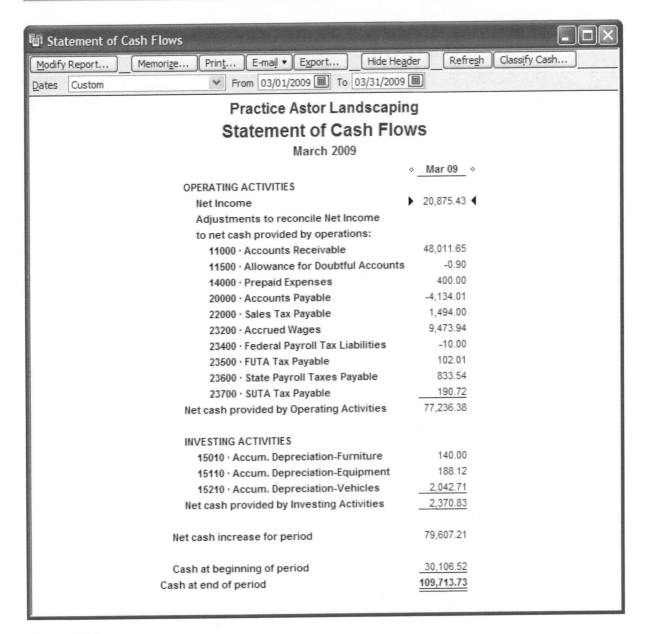

Figure 7:26

This may be your first exposure to the Statement of Cash Flows so we will spend some time explaining its importance.

This statement reports cash activities by operations, investing, and financing. Operating cash is generated by day-to-day activities of the business such as collecting on accounts receivable and reducing accounts payable. Investing is the cash effect of buying or selling company assets such as equipment or buildings. Finally, financing is the cash effect of borrowing or repaying loans. *(Note: Astor does not have any financing activities for this year.)*

After reviewing the report, the accountant notices that accumulated depreciation accounts are appearing under investing activities when these accounts should appear under operating activities because depreciation is a noncash activity added back to net income. Follow the next steps to correct the reporting of these accounts.

Select **Edit>>Preferences** on the main menu or click the [Classify Cash...] button on the Statement of Cash Flows. When the **Preferences** window opens, click the **Classify Cash** button on the **Company Preferences** tab for the **Reports and Graphs** category. (See Figure 7:27.)

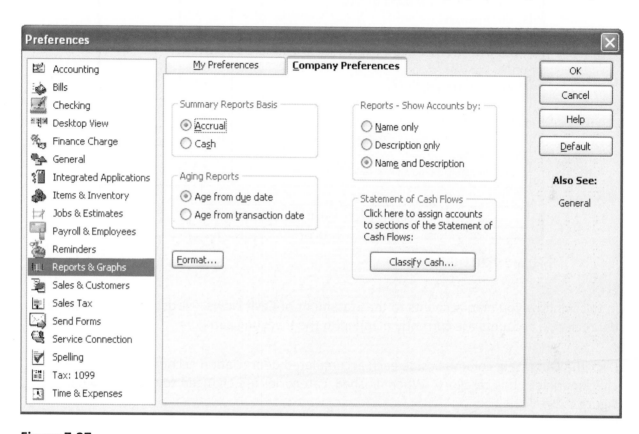

Figure 7:27

After clicking **Classify Cash** the window in Figure 7:28 opens.

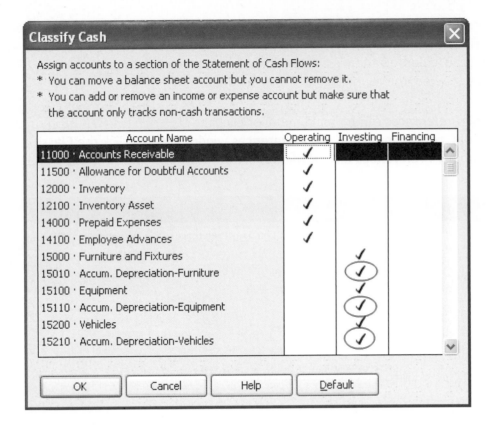

Figure 7:28

In this window you map accounts to the Statement of Cash Flows. Notice that accumulated depreciation accounts are currently mapped to the Investing category.

Click the **Operating** column beside each accumulated depreciation account to move the checkmark into this category. When finished, categories are changed to those shown in Figure 7:29.

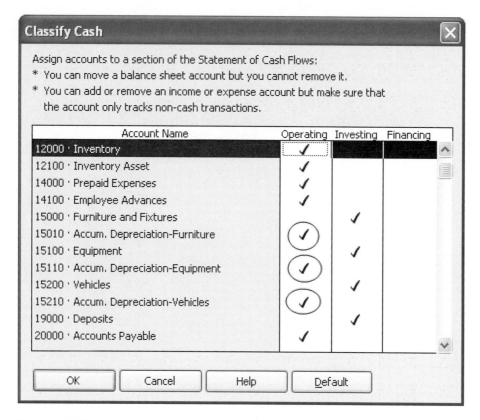

Figure 7:29

Before saving the changes, scroll down and notice that you do not map Income Statement accounts to the Statement of Cash Flows. Instead, these accounts already appear in the Net Income line of the statement.

Click **OK** to save these changes and click **OK** to close the Preferences window.

Return to the Statement of Cash Flows and note the changes. (See Figure 7:30.)

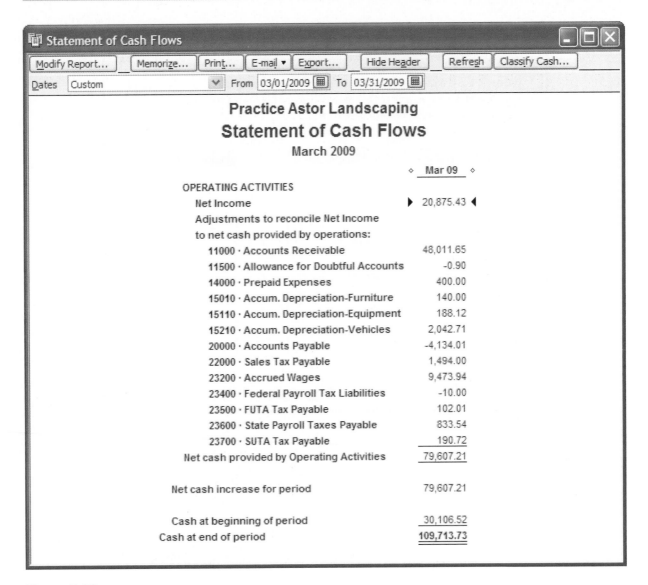

Figure 7:30

We now focus on interpreting this statement. The statement begins with **Net Income** from the March Income Statement and adjusts this number to arrive at net income on a cash basis.

Noncash items, such as depreciation, are added back and the cash changes for operating asset and liability accounts are calculated to obtain the **Net cash provided by Operating Activities**. Net positive cash from operations is a critical point of analysis. Companies that continually fail to generate cash from operations will eventually need to borrow to fund day-to-day activities, such as paying employees and vendors.

Net cash flow from operations is then adjusted for cash changes from investing and financing activities to arrive at the **Net cash increase for period**. *(Note: This could be a net cash decrease.)*

Focus now on the bottom section of the report. **Cash at beginning of period** equals the February 28 total for all cash accounts on the **Balance Sheet**. (See Figure 7:31.)

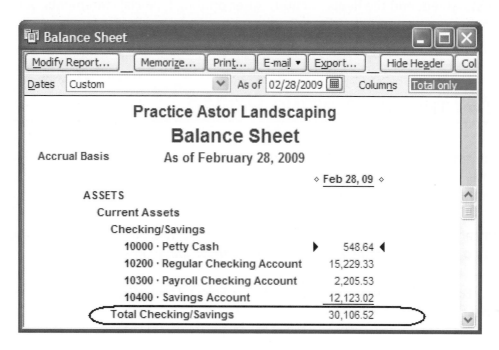

Figure 7:31

Cash at end of Period equals the total for all cash accounts on the March 31 Balance Sheet shown in Figure 7:32.

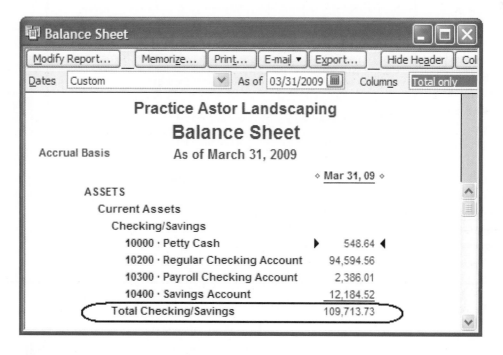

Figure 7:32

The difference between these amounts matches the **Net cash increase for period**.

Close this statement and the Report Center. After printing financial statements, you are ready to close the accounting period.

CLOSING THE ACCOUNTING PERIOD

Closing the period is important to prevent posting transactions that affect issued financial statements. You do not want to send March financial statements to owners or the bank and subsequently have an entry erroneously posted to March.

You should always back up a data file before closing the period so create a ***backup of Astor's data file to a backup file named "Practice Astor Landscaping Chpt 7".***

Now select ***Edit>>Preferences*** on the main menu. Select **Accounting** and click the **Company Preferences** tab. (See Figure 7:33.)

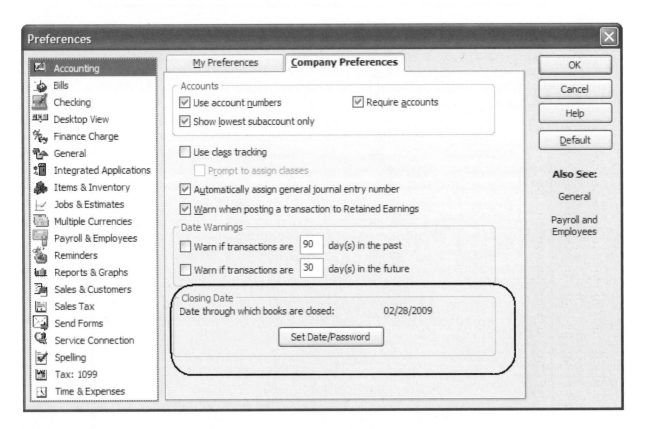

Figure 7:33

This window shows that the books are closed through February 28, 2009. Click **Set Date/Password** and enter 3/31/2009 as illustrated in Figure 7:34.

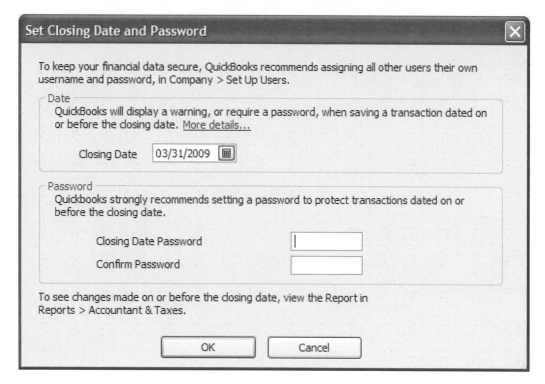

Figure 7:34

In practice, you should set a closing date password to prevent accidentally backdating transactions to a closed period but leave these fields blank for now and click **OK**. Click **No** when QBP reminds you to set a password.

The Closing Date on the preference window updates to 3/31/2009. Click **OK** to close the window.

SUMMARY

In this chapter, you finalized Astor's March accounting period. You reviewed the General Ledger report for missing transactions and posting errors. You corrected posting errors and posted adjusting entries. You then reconciled bank statements and printed financial statements.

Finally, you backed up the Practice Astor Landscaping data file and closed the March accounting period.

Congratulations! You have completed an entire accounting cycle for a service based business. The next chapter presents a comprehensive project for a service based business. Thereafter, Chapters 8 through 11 illustrate the activities completed in Chapters 4 through 7 for a merchandising business.

END-OF-CHAPTER QUESTIONS

TRUE/FALSE

_____ 1. Closing the accounting period prevents posting to a closed month.

_____ 2. The Statement of Cash Flows ties back to the sum of cash account balances on the Balance Sheet.

_____ 3. QBP will track fixed asset costs and calculate monthly depreciation.

_____ 4. Depreciation journal entries are usually posted by using memorized transactions.

_____ 5. The General Ledger report will let you analyze transaction details posted for the month.

MULTIPLE CHOICE

_____ 1. A company's Net Income/Net Loss will be listed on the _____ report.
   a. Statement of Cash Flows
   b. Income Statement
   c. Statement of Retained Earnings
   d. All of the above

_____ 2. The Cash Flow Statement will report changes in cash by _____.
   a. Operations
   b. Financing
   c. Investing
   d. All of the above

_____ 3. Which financial statement is a "snapshot" of financial position at a point in time?
   a. Balance Sheet
   b. Income Statement
   c. Statement of Retained Earnings
   d. Both b and c

_____ 4. To accrue utility expense, you would _____.
   a. post a journal entry that debited accrued expense and credited utility expense
   b. post a journal entry that credited accrued expense and debited utility expense
   c. post a journal entry that debited accounts payable and credited utility expense
   d. none of the above

_____ 5. Which of the following is part of preclosing procedures?
     a. Review pending transactions
     b. Post adjusting entries
     c. Reconcile account balances
     d. All of the above

PRACTICE SET

In this practice set you will be using the **Graded Astor Landscaping** data file with the Practice Set completed in Chapter 6. *If the company file is not loaded on your computer then restore it using the Graded Astor Landscaping Chpt 6.QBB backup file created after completing the Chapter 6 Practice Set.*

1. Open **Graded Astor Landscaping** and perform the following activities that close the March accounting period.

2009

Mar 23   Transfer $11,000.00 from regular checking to payroll checking.

Mar 31   Reconcile the Regular Checking Account for March 31 using the statement that follows. *(Note: This statement is different from the statement illustrated in the chapter.)* Print the Detail Reconciliation report.

                Reconcile the Payroll Checking Account for March 31. The ending statement balance is $1,842.29. All March checks and deposits have cleared and the monthly bank charge is $27.00. Print the Detail Reconciliation report. *(Remember that April paychecks are in this account.)*

                Post the memorized depreciation entry using the depreciation estimates on the transaction.

                Accrue $6,500.00 for Salaries expense.

                Print the Standard Balance Sheet, Standard Profit & Loss, and Statement of Cash Flows for March.

Create a backup file named "Graded Astor Landscaping March Close" and then close the March accounting period.

Astor Landscaping
Bank Statement March 31, 2009

Beginning Balance from February Statement				$ 17,266.25
March Deposits				
	Mar 3, 2009		6,258.75	
	Mar 5, 2009		21,750.50	
	Mar 6, 2009		3,087.35	
	Mar 12, 2009		1,233.00	
	Mar 13, 2009		5,720.00	
	Mar 19, 2009		39,544.25	
	Mar 20, 2009		11,258.50	
	Mar 27, 2009		15,196.00	
Total Deposits for March				104,048.35
March Checks Cleared				
	Feb 26, 2009	402	600.00	
	Feb 26, 2009	404	818.42	
	Feb 27, 2009	430	618.50	
	Mar 12, 2009	431	29.94	
	Mar 12, 2009	432	12,550.35	
	Mar 12, 2009	433	2,500.00	
	Mar 12, 2009	434	207.65	
	Mar 20, 2009	435	300.00	
	Mar 20, 2009	436	97.64	
Total Cleared Checks for March				17,722.50
Less Bank Transfers				
	Mar 9, 2009		10,000.00	
	Mar 23, 2009		11,000.00	
Total March Transfers				21,000.00
March Service Charges				73.20
Ending Bank Balance March 31, 2009				$ 82,518.90

2. Perform the following activities that close the April accounting period.

2009

Apr 1   Reverse the March 31 journal entry for accrued salaries of $6,500.00.

Apr 6   Transfer $10,000.00 from regular checking to payroll checking to cover paychecks printed on April 6.

Apr 20   Transfer $12,000.00 from regular checking to payroll checking to cover paychecks printed on April 20.

Apr 24   Post a journal entry for the following equipment sale.
            Equipment cost: $2,300.00
            Accumulated Depreciation on equipment: $ 1,100.00
            Cash deposited to regular checking: $750.00

Apr 30   Post the following adjusting journal entries.
            Accrue 9 days of Salaries $12,635.00
            Expense prepaid business insurance $200.00
            Expense prepaid auto insurance $400.00

            Post the memorized depreciation entry after revising equipment depreciation to $178.12. Replace the previous memorized transaction.

            Write and print check 472 out of regular checking to Petty Cash for $150.00 to replenish fund for meals and entertainment expense spent in April.

            Reconcile the Regular Checking Account for April using the statement that follows. Print the Detail Reconciliation report.

            Reconcile the Payroll Checking Account for April. The ending statement balance is $1,807.65. All checks and deposits have cleared and the monthly bank charge is $26.50. Print the Detail Reconciliation report.

            Print the Standard Balance Sheet, Standard Profit & Loss, and Statement of Cash Flows for April.

            Create a backup file named "Graded Astor Landscaping April Close" and then close the April accounting period.

Astor Landscaping
Bank Statement April 30, 2009

Beginning Balance from April Statement			$	82,518.90
April Deposits				
	Apr 2, 2009		21,389.48	
	Apr 9, 2009		8,720.00	
	Apr 10, 2009		3,234.00	
	Apr 23, 2009		22,594.85	
	Apr 24, 2009		750.00	
	Apr 28, 2009		23,884.95	
Total Deposits for April				80,573.28
April Checks Cleared				
	Mar 27, 2009	437	9.98	
	Mar 11, 2009	449	3,611.12	
	Apr 10, 2009	450	1,983.35	
	Apr 10, 2009	451	17,416.21	
	Apr 10, 2009	452	451.48	
	Apr 10, 2009	453	262.43	
	Apr 10, 2009	454	1,020.00	
	Apr 21, 2009	455	150.00	
	Mar 23, 2009	463	3,578.52	
	Apr 2, 2008	464	600.00	
	Apr 2, 2008	465	460.47	
	Apr 2, 2008	466	817.76	
	Apr 2, 2008	467	907.82	
	Apr 6, 2009	468	3,701.54	
	Apr 20, 2009	469	3,672.22	
Total Cleared Checks for April				38,642.90
Less Bank Transfers				
	Apr 6, 2009		10,000.00	
	Apr 20, 2009		12,000.00	
Total April Transfers				22,000.00
April Service Charges				83.20
Ending Bank Balance April 30, 2009			$	102,366.08

PROJECT 1

COMPREHENSIVE EXAM FOR A SERVICE BASED BUSINESS

You begin this exam by downloading the **Eragon Electrical Contracting Project** company file from the website *http://www.pearsonhighered.com/brunsdon/*. Add your initials to the **Company Name** and **Legal Name** after opening the company by selecting **Company>> Company Information** on the main menu and clicking **OK** to save the changes.

The following are February 2009 transactions for Eragon Electrical Contracting. This is a service based business that designs and installs electrical systems for new construction and older buildings under renovation. Eragon focuses primarily on commercial buildings although it will also perform residential work on large projects. You will be entering all transactions for the month of February, including month-end adjusting entries.

All checks received on account are deposited into the Regular Checking Account.

Feb 2	Issue and print the following Purchase Orders (POs).

PO 1803 to Parcells Electric for $797.40 for the following items.

Qty	Item	Rate	Job
2	Switch 30 Amp	218.95	Alamo
10	Breaker 30 Amp	35.95	Red Bird

PO 1804 to RJM Electric for $1,678.00 for the following item.

Qty	Item	Rate	Job
40	Wire 100 Ft.	41.95	Fox and Hound

PO 1805 to Spade Hardware for $244.40 for following items.

Qty	Item	Rate	Job
5	Timer Outdoor	18.96	Mendez
10	Timer Air Condition	14.96	Mendez

Enter a bill for $1,100.00 to Brays Property Management for February office and warehouse rental. Print the rent check on check number 1214.

Feb 3	Received bills for the following job materials.

Received bills for the following job materials.

All items on PO 1800 to Parcells Electric. Invoice 8901 for $1,408.75 dated Feb. 2.

All items on PO 1801 to RJM Electrical Supplies. Invoice 23890 for $582.75 dated Feb. 2.

Only five rolls of wire on PO 1802 to Spade Hardware. Invoice 109 for $209.75 dated Feb. 2.

Received the remaining job materials on PO 1802 to Spade Hardware. Invoice 121 for $209.75 dated Feb. 2.

Issue and print PO 1806 to RJM Electric for $ 2,517.00 for the following item.

Qty	Item	Rate	Job
60	Wire 100 Ft.	41.95	Wellington

Received the following checks. *(Note: Verify that checks will post to the Regular Checking Account.)*

Check number 1395 for $839.00 from Fox and Hound Apartments paying Invoice 1205.

Check number 151 for $6,700.26 from Jessie Johnson paying Invoice 1203.

Pay all bills due on or before Feb. 13. Print the checks starting on check number 1215.

Hired the following electrician on February 2, 2009, who is paid biweekly with hourly time ticket hours.

James Munson
321 Park Springs Blvd.
Arlington, TX 76017
SS# 111-08-0754
Filing statuses: Federal is Married with two allowances and State is Texas
Pay rate: $35.00 per hour for regular time, $52.50 per hour for overtime

Feb 4	Issue and print the following POs.
	PO 1807 to Spade Hardware for $674.55 for following items.

Qty	Item	Rate	Job
20	Switch Beach	14.99	Mendez
25	Switch Granite	14.99	Mendez

PO 1808 to Parcells Electric for $1,148.50 for following items.

Qty	Item	Rate	Job
10	Breaker 50 Amp	42.95	Alamo
20	Breaker 30 Amp	35.95	Alamo

Create invoices for all customers with activity during the week of Jan 26 to Feb 1. Perform the following steps to identify customers for billing.

   a. For labor hours, print the **Time by Job Detail** report. Modify the report to add the **Billing Status** filter and set the filter to Unbilled.
   b. For material costs, print the **Unbilled Costs** by Job report.

Before creating invoices, verify that the invoice template is set to **Eragon Electrical Invoice Template**. In addition, when transferring employee time, select the option to **Combine activities with the same service items.**

Print these invoices using starting invoice number 1215.

Feb 6	Received bills for the following job materials.

All items on PO 1804 to RJM Electric. Invoice 24803 for $1,678.00 dated Feb. 6.
All items on PO 1805 to Spade Hardware. Invoice 137 for $244.40 dated Feb. 5
All items on PO 1803 to Parcells Electric. Invoice 8975 for $797.40 dated Feb. 6.

Feb 9	Record credit memo CM8975 for $359.50 from Parcells Electric dated Feb. 6 for the return of 10 items of Breaker 30 Amp on Invoice 8975 for Red Bird job.

Enter James Munson's time ticket for the week of Feb. 2 to Feb. 8. All hours are for regular time and are billable.

Service Item	Job	Hours
Residential Remodel	Mendez	8 hours Wed. through Fri.

Add the following hours to Vu Tran's time ticket for the week of Feb. 2 to Feb. 8. Hours are billable.

Service Item	Job	Hours
Commercial Installation	Fox and Hound	4 hours of overtime on Sunday

Prepare a **Time by Name** report for Jan. 26 to Feb. 8. Verify that 24 hours is listed for James Munson, 4 overtime hours for Vu Tran, and total time equals 348 hours.

Create paychecks for the biweekly pay period of Jan. 26 to Feb. 8 by referring to the spreadsheets that follow. *(Hint: Enter 2/8/2009 as the **Pay Period Ends Date**.)*

Confirm that the hours selected for payment equal the hours on the Time by Name report. Print the paychecks on beginning check number 847.

Create checks for payroll liabilities. Pay the liabilities from 1/01/2009 to 2/9/2009. Pay employee Federal Withholding, Medicare, and Social Security taxes and company Medicare and Social Security taxes. Print on check number 1219 from the Regular Checking Account.

Transfer $12,300.00 from the Regular Checking Account to the Payroll Checking Account to cover payroll.

Eragon Electrical Contracting
Pay Period 1/26/2009 thru 2/08/2009

Employee	Filing Status	Allow	Pay Type	Pay Rate	Regular Hrs	OT Hrs	Gross Pay	Federal Income Tax	Soc. Sec. (FICA) Tax	Medicare Tax	Net Pay
Eragon, Ernest	Married	5	Salary	3,000.00			3,000.00	443.00	186.00	43.50	2,327.50
Hardisty, Warren	Married	2	Salary	2,500.00			2,500.00	260.00	155.00	36.25	2,048.75
Jameson, Mike	Married	2	Hourly	25.75	80.00		2,060.00	194.00	127.72	29.87	1,708.41
Munson, James	Married	2	Hourly	35.00	24.00		840.00	27.00	52.08	12.18	748.74
Rodriguez, Jamie	Married	3	Hourly	25.75	80.00		2,060.00	174.00	127.72	29.87	1,728.41
Tran, Vu	Single	1	Hourly	35.00	80.00	4.00	3,010.00	685.00	186.62	43.65	2,094.73
Wilson, Chuck	Single	1	Hourly	28.00	80.00		2,240.00	450.00	138.88	32.48	1,618.64
Totals					344.00	4.00	15,710.00	2,233.00	974.02	227.80	12,275.18
Tax Basis								Circular E	6.20%	1.45%	
G/L Accounts								57000 / 60000	23400	23400	23400	10300

Eragon Electrical Contracting
Employer Costs for Period 1/26/2009 thru 2/08/2009

Employee	ER Soc. Sec. (FICA)	ER Medicare	ER FUTA	ER SUTA
Eragon, Ernest	186.00	43.50	16.00	90.00
Hardisty, Warren	155.00	36.25	20.00	75.00
Jameson, Mike	127.72	29.87	16.48	61.80
Munson, James	52.08	12.18	6.72	25.20
Rodriguez, Jamie	127.72	29.87	16.48	61.80
Tran, Vu	186.62	43.65	24.08	90.30
Wilson, Chuck	138.88	32.48	17.92	67.20
Totals	974.02	227.80	117.68	471.30
Tax Basis	6.20%	1.45%	0.8%	3.0%
G/L Accounts	23400 / 61000	23400 / 61000	23500 / 61000	23700 / 61000

Feb 9	Received the following checks.
	Check number 1087 for $2,280.00 from River Run Housing paying Invoice 1206.
	Check number 131 for $10,104.00 from TAM Apartments paying Invoice 1204.
	Check number 803 for $960.00 from Fred Thompson paying Invoice 1202.
	Pay all bills due on or before Feb. 20. Print checks on beginning check number 1220.
Feb 11	Received check number 3247 for $10,915.30 from TMI Properties paying Invoices 1200 and 1201.
	Issue and print PO 1809 to Spade Hardware for $149.90 for following item.

Qty	Item	Rate	Job
10	Switch Beach	14.99	Fox and Hound

	Create invoices for customers with activity during the week of Feb. 2 to Feb. 8. Identify customers for invoicing by printing the reports previously illustrated.
	After checking with the owner for approval, you allow Fox and Hound to exceed its credit limit.
	Print these invoices using starting invoice number 1219.

Feb 13	Received bills for the following job materials.
	   All items on PO 1806 to RJM Electric. Invoice 24897 for $2,517.00 dated Feb. 12.
	   All items on PO 1807 to Spade Hardware. Invoice 135 for $674.55 dated Feb. 13.

	Issue and print PO 1810 to RJM Electric for $629.25 for following item.

Qty	Item	Rate	Job
15	Wire 100 Ft.	41.95	Red Bird

	Create the following vendor.
	   Bart's Automotive
	   3318 Pioneer Parkway
	   Arlington, TX 76019
	   Terms: Net 30
	   Account Prefill: 72300 Repairs – Auto Expenses

	Enter bill number 5663 dated Feb. 13 for $573.95 from Bart's Automotive for auto repairs.

Feb 17	Enter James Munson's time ticket for the week of Feb. 9 to Feb 15. All hours are for regular time and are billable.

Service Item	Job	Hours
Residential Remodel	Mendez	8 hours, Mon. through Fri.

Received all items on PO 1810 to RJM Electric. Invoice 25002 for $629.25 dated Feb. 17.

Create invoices for customers with activity during the week of Feb. 9 to Feb. 15. Identify customers for invoicing by printing the reports previously provided.

After checking with the owner for approval, you allow Jackson Property Management to exceed its credit limit.

Print these invoices using starting invoice number 1226.

Feb 20	Received check number 1192 for $7,323.95 from River Run Housing paying Invoice 1211.

Signed a contract for a new residential remodeling job for David White to begin on March 1.

Create a customer using the following information.
David White
3851 Southpark Drive
Arlington, TX 76011
Type: RESID
Terms: Net 30

Create a job using the following information.
Job Name: White Residential Remodel

Feb 23	Enter the following timesheets for the week of Feb. 16 to Feb. 22. All hours are billable.

Employee	Service Item	Job	Hours
Mike Jameson	Design Labor	Wellington	8 hours Mon. through Fri.
Jamie Rodriguez	Commercial Remodel	Red Bird	8 hours Mon. through Thur.
	Commercial Installation	Wellington	8 hours on Fri.
Vu Tran	Commercial Installation	River Run	8 hours Mon. through Fri.
Chuck Wilson	Commercial Installation	Fox and Hound	8 hours Mon. through Fri.
James Munson	Residential Remodel	Mendez	8 hours Mon. through Fri.

Prepare a Time by Name report for Feb. 9 to Feb. 22. Verify that all employees worked 80 hours and total time equals 400 hours.

Create paychecks for the biweekly pay period ending on Feb. 22 by referring to the spreadsheets that follow.

Confirm that the hours selected for payment equal the hours on the Time by Name report. Print the paychecks on beginning check number 854.

Create checks for payroll liabilities for the date range of 1/01/2009 to 2/23/2009. Pay employee Federal Withholding, Medicare, and Social Security taxes and company Medicare and Social Security taxes. Print on check number 1222 from the Regular Checking Account.

Transfer $13,500.00 from the Regular Checking Account to the Payroll Checking Account to cover payroll.

Eragon Electrical Contracting
Pay Period 2/09/2009 thru 2/22/2009

Employee	Filing Status	Allow	Pay Type	Pay Rate	Regular Hrs	OT Hrs	Gross Pay	Federal Income Tax	Soc. Sec. (FICA) Tax	Medicare Tax	Net Pay
Eragon, Ernest	Married	5	Salary	3,000.00			3,000.00	443.00	186.00	43.50	2,327.50
Hardisty, Warren	Married	2	Salary	2,500.00			2,500.00	260.00	155.00	36.25	2,048.75
Jameson, Mike	Married	2	Hourly	25.75	80.00		2,060.00	194.00	127.72	29.87	1,708.41
Munson, James	Married	2	Hourly	35.00	80.00		2,800.00	460.00	173.60	40.60	2,125.80
Rodriguez, Jamie	Married	3	Hourly	25.75	80.00		2,060.00	174.00	127.72	29.87	1,728.41
Tran, Vu	Single	1	Hourly	35.00	80.00		2,800.00	623.00	173.60	40.60	1,962.80
Wilson, Chuck	Single	1	Hourly	28.00	80.00		2,240.00	450.00	138.88	32.48	1,618.64
Totals					400.00	0.00	17,460.00	2,604.00	1,082.52	253.17	13,520.31
Tax Basis								Circular E	6.20%	1.45%	
G/L Accounts							57000 / 60000	23400	23400	23400	10300

Eragon Electrical Contracting
Employer Costs for Period 2/09/2009 thru 2/22/2009

Employee	ER Soc. Sec. (FICA)	ER Medicare	ER FUTA	ER SUTA
Eragon, Ernest	186.00	43.50	0.00	0.00
Hardisty, Warren	155.00	36.25	4.00	45.00
Jameson, Mike	127.72	29.87	0.27	61.80
Munson, James	173.60	40.60	22.40	84.00
Rodriguez, Jamie	127.72	29.87	16.48	61.80
Tran, Vu	173.60	40.60	1.84	36.90
Wilson, Chuck	138.88	32.48	17.92	67.20
Totals	1,082.52	253.17	62.91	356.70
Tax Basis	6.20%	1.45%	0.8%	3.0%
G/L Accounts	23400 / 61000	23400 / 61000	23500 / 61000	23700 / 61000

Feb 23	Pay all bills due on or before March 7. Print checks on beginning check number 1223.

Feb 25	Received the following checks.
	    Check number 3302 for $1,397.50 from TMI Properties paying Invoice 1214.
	    Check number 842 for $4,800.00 from Fred Thompson paying invoice 1213.
	    Check number 181 for $2,880.00 from Jessie Johnson paying Invoice 1210.

	The owner asks that you increase the credit limits for Jackson Property Management to $40,000.00 and for River Run Housing and Fox and Hound Apartments to $30,000.00.
	Create invoices for customers with activity during the week of Feb. 16 to Feb. 22. Identify customers for invoicing by printing the reports previously illustrated. You have received approval for any customers that will exceed the credit limit. Print these invoices using starting invoice number 1231.

Feb 26	Received the following checks.
	    Check number 6387 for $9,768.75 from Jackson Property Management paying Invoices 1208 and 1209.
	
	    Check number 1237 for $8,918.00 from Fox and Hound paying Invoice 1207.

	Enter the following bills dated Feb. 26. Arlington Utilities Feb Water $265.00 Southwestern Bell Telephone Feb Phone $450.00 TXU Electric Feb Elect $775.00

EOM	Prepare the following end of month adjusting entries.
	Refer to the Jan. 31 entry and record February depreciation expense.
	Refer to the Jan. 31 entry and adjust prepaid expenses for expired February insurance.
	Accrue five days of wages. Calculate the accrual amount using the gross pay from the last pay period. Reverse this entry on Mar. 1.
	Write and print check number 1226 to Cash for $141.40 to replenish petty cash fund for the following expenses. Office Supplies Expense $38.95 Meals and Entertainment $84.50 Postage $17.95
	Prepare the following bank reconciliations and print the detail reconciliation report.
	Regular Checking Account statement provided next.
	Payroll Checking Account statement balance is $159.51. Monthly service charge is $25.00. All checks and transfers have cleared.
	Print a February Trial Balance report and review for accuracy.
	Print the Aged Receivables and Aged Payables reports and reconcile Accounts Receivable and Accounts Payable account balances to the trial balance.
	Print the Payroll Liability Report. Reconcile report totals to the appropriate payroll liability accounts on the trial balance.
	Print the Job Profitability Summary for February.
	Print the following February financial statements. Profit & Loss Standard Balance Sheet Standard Statement of Cash Flows

Backup the company data file using the backup file name of **Eragon Proj1**.

Eragon Electrical Contracting
Bank Statement February 28, 2009

Beginning Balance from January Statement				$ 89,159.00
February Deposits				
	Feb 3, 2009		839.00	
	Feb 3, 2009		6,700.26	
	Feb 9, 2009		960.00	
	Feb 9, 2009		2,280.00	
	Feb 9, 2009		10,104.00	
	Feb 11, 2009		10,915.30	
	Feb 20, 2009		7,323.95	
	Feb 25, 2009		1,397.50	
	Feb 25, 2009		2,880.00	
	Feb 25, 2009		4,800.00	
	Feb 26, 2009		8,918.00	
	Feb 26, 2009		9,768.75	
Total Deposits for February				66,886.76
February Checks Cleared				
	Jan 29, 2009	1205	499.65	
	Jan 29, 2009	1206	2,127.25	
	Jan 29, 2009	1207	1,679.45	
	Jan 29, 2009	1208	789.46	
	Jan 30, 2009	1209	100.00	
	Jan 30, 2009	1210	450.00	
	Jan 30, 2009	1211	750.00	
	Jan 30, 2009	1212	300.00	
	Jan 30, 2009	1213	173.85	
	Feb 2, 2009	1214	1,100.00	
	Feb 3, 2009	1215	372.25	
	Feb 3, 2009	1216	1,048.65	
	Feb 3, 2009	1217	1,048.75	
	Feb 3, 2009	1218	3,145.00	
	Feb 9, 2009	1219	4,636.64	
	Feb 9, 2009	1220	3,404.75	
	Feb 9, 2009	1221	1,243.95	
	Feb 23, 2009	1222	5,275.38	
	Feb 23, 2009	1223	1,048.75	
Total Cleared Checks for February				29,193.78
Less Bank Transfers				
	Feb 9, 2009		12,300.00	
	Feb 23, 2009		13,500.00	
Total February Transfers				25,800.00
February Service Charges				75.00
Ending Bank Balance February 28, 2009				$ 100,976.98

CHAPTER 8   CUSTOMER ACTIVITIES FOR A MERCHANDISING BUSINESS

LEARNING OBJECTIVES

This chapter works with the Practice Baxter Garden Supply data file from Chapter 2. *If this file is not loaded on your computer then restore it using the Practice Baxter Garden Supply Chpt 2.QBB backup file created after reading Chapter 2.*

The chapter focuses on using QBP to process customer activities for a merchandising business. The chapter covers the following:

1. The manual accounting procedures (*MAPS*) used to record customer transactions
2. Using the Customer Center to perform customer tasks
3. Recording sales invoices
4. Going *Behind the Keys* of a posted sales invoice and learning to correct posting errors
5. Emailing a sales invoice
6. Managing customers
7. Understanding inventory items and pricing levels
8. Preparing inventory reports and using reports to conduct a physical inventory
9. Entering inventory adjustments
10. Recording sales receipts
11. Handling sales of out-of-stock inventory
12. Recording basic customer payments
13. Going *Behind the Keys* to view posted payments
14. Recording customer payments carrying a discount
15. Correcting errors after posting customer payments
16. Recording customer credits
17. Reporting on and reconciling customer activities
18. Writing off customer invoices
19. Preparing customer statements

Launch QBP and open **Practice Baxter Garden Supply**.

The following is background information on Baxter's business operations. Baxter is a corporation selling garden supplies to retail and wholesale customers. The company uses QBP to track inventory and invoice customers. The current accounting period is March 2009.

MANUAL ACCOUNTING PROCEDURES

Before illustrating QBP sales transactions we want to cover the accounting procedures for a manual accounting system so you will better understand processing these transactions in the software. Manual accounting procedures (*MAPS*) for processing a customer sales transaction begin at the point where a customer initiates a transaction.

On March 20, 2009, Knight Brothers Nurseries contacts Baxter salesperson, Brandee Nunnley, requesting shipment of 10 Bell-Gro hose end sprayers and 15 Bell-Gro fan head sprayers. Brandee quoted Knight a total sales price of $384.35.

In a manual system, Brandee writes up a sales order and sends a copy of the order to the customer and the company accountant, Melvin Frost. She also sends a picking ticket to Al Duke in the company warehouse. Al then fills and ships the order, indicating the quantities filled on the picking ticket.

Al filled Knight's order on March 24 and forwarded the picking ticket to Melvin. Melvin matches the ticket with the sales order and prepares the invoice illustrated in Figure 8:1.

Baxter Garden Supply
1305 Maple Ave
Arlington, VA 23523

Date: 3/24/2009

Customer:

Knight Brothers
5682 Main Street
Arlington, VA 30004

INVOICE	No. 10346

Qty	Description		
10	Bell-Gro Hose End Sprayers	$	129.50
15	Bell-Gro Fan End Sprayers		254.85
Subtotal			384.35
Sales Tax			-
Total		$	384.35

Terms: Net 30

Figure 8:1

Melvin next records the invoice, along with other invoices issued that day, in the Sales Journal for March 24 (Figure 8:2).

Baxter Garden Supply					
Date: 3/24/2009		Sales Journal			**Page 8**
Customer	Post Ref	Description	Accounts Receivable (Debit)	Sales Equipment (Credit)	Sales Tax Payable (Credit)
Knight Brothers	KNIG001	Invoice 10346	384.35	384.35	
Cummings Construction	CUMM001	Invoice 10347	3,768.25	3,504.47	263.78
Dash Business Systems	DASH001	Invoice 10348	4,326.00	4,023.18	302.82
Totals:			$ 8,478.60	$ 7,912.00	$ 566.60
Acct Ref:			(11000)	(40003)	(23100)
Audit Trail					

Figure 8:2

Melvin entered Knight's invoice as a debit to accounts receivable and as a credit to equipment sales. At day's end, Melvin totals Sales Journal columns and cross-foots the totals to verify that entries balance (i.e., debits equal credits). He then posts each invoice to the customer's account and posts column totals to the general ledger accounts noted at the bottom.

Melvin's entry to Knight's customer account is illustrated in Figure 8:3. *(Note: Entries for other customer accounts are not illustrated.)*

Knight Brothers 5682 Main Street Arlington, VA 30004		*Audit Trail*		Acct No:	KNIG001	
Date	Description	Post Ref	Debit	Credit	Balance
03/01/09	Beginning Balance				0.00
03/24/09	Invoice 10346	SJ 8	384.35		384.35

Figure 8:3

Melvin's entries to general ledger accounts are shown in Figure 8:4.

General Ledger

Accounts Receivable   **Account No. 11000**

Date	Description	Post Ref	Debit	Credit	Balance
03/21/09	Balance Forward				75,792.58
03/24/09		SJ 8	8,478.60		84,271.18

Audit Trail

General Ledger

Sales Equipment   **Account No. 40003**

Date	Description	Post Ref	Debit	Credit	Balance
03/21/09	Balance Forward				60,952.30
03/24/09		SJ 8		7,912.00	68,864.30

Audit Trail

General Ledger

Sales Tax Payable   **Account No. 23100**

Date	Description	Post Ref	Debit	Credit	Balance
03/21/09	Balance Forward				4,570.55
03/24/09		SJ 8		566.60	5,137.15

Figure 8:4

As Melvin posts, he is also entering the posting references that form the audit trail. An audit trail documents entries from the Sales Journal to general ledger accounts, from the Sales Journal to customer accounts, and vice versa. You can imagine the posting errors that could occur in a manual system. Melvin could record an entry backwards (e.g., enter a debit as a credit), record an out-of-balance entry, omit an entry, or forget to enter the audit trail.

Notice that Melvin did not post an entry for costs of goods sold and inventory when recording Knight's invoice because he does not know the specific cost for the items sold. In a manual system, inventory purchases are recorded to the purchases account instead of the inventory account. Only after conducting a physical inventory count to determine the cost of quantities on hand does the accountant post a general journal entry to adjust the inventory and purchases accounts. The example that follows illustrates calculating an inventory adjusting entry.

1/1/2008	Beginning Inventory	$ 17,856.00
	Purchases in 2008	+ 30,765.00
	Total Inventory Available	$ 48,621.00
12/31/2008	Ending Inventory	– $ 16,375.00
12/31/2008	COGS	$ 32,246.00

The above calculation shows that a credit of $1,481.00 ($17,856 minus $16,375) needs to be posted to the inventory account to adjust inventory to the physical count taken on December 31, 2008. Figure 8:5 illustrates the adjusting entry that will be recorded in the general journal.

Baxter Garden Supply
General Journal   **Page 17**

Date	Account Post Ref	Description	Debit	Credit
12/31/2008	45100	Purchases	1,481.00	
	13000	Inventory		1,481.00
To record COGS				

Figure 8:5

After reading the inventory topic, you will discover that QBP automatically posts inventory and cost of goods sold entries at the time of sale (i.e., when saving an invoice).

On the same day as posting sales invoices, Melvin posts customer payment receipts on outstanding invoices. These transactions are recorded on the Cash Receipts Journal shown in Figure 8:6.

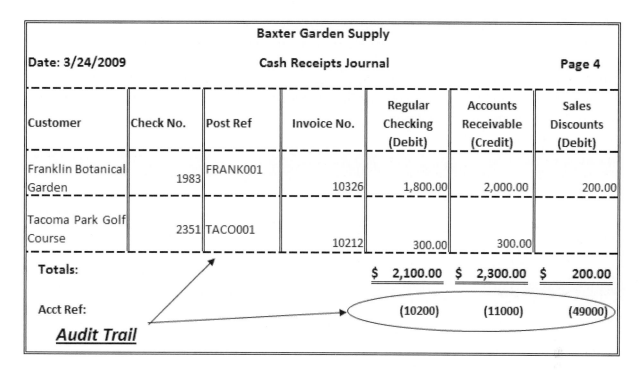

Figure 8:6

As with the Sales Journal, Melvin posts each check to a customer account and column totals to general ledger accounts. This time he will use the posting reference of CRJ (Cash Receipts Journal) along with the page number. *(Note: These postings are not illustrated.)*

With QBP most of the posting errors are eliminated. You will see in subsequent topics that sales invoices and customer payments are posted when saving. In addition, QBP posts entries recorded in the Sales and Cash Receipts Journals to the customer's account and general ledger accounts. QBP also enters the audit trail and will not post entries that are out of balance.

We next focus your attention on processing customer transactions in QBP.

CUSTOMER CENTER

The **Customer Center** (Figure 8:7) focuses on customer activities. Click **Customers** on the **Home** page to open the center so we can discuss its purpose. *(Note: If the invoices illustrated are not listed, change the Date to All.)*

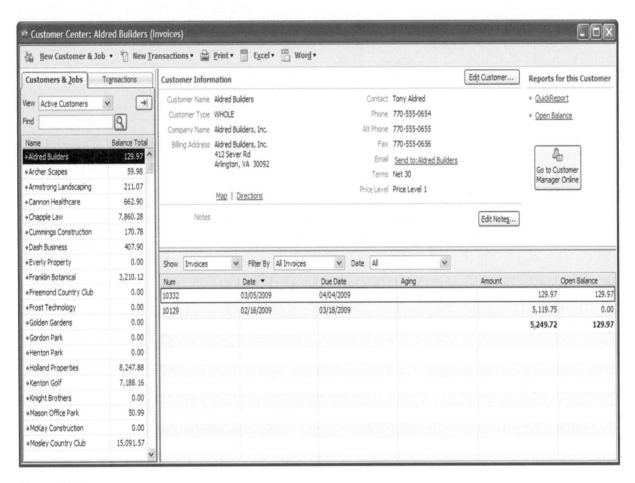

Figure 8:7

The **Customers & Jobs** tab lists transactions by customer account. Baxter's customer accounts and balances appear to the left. The **View** option will toggle accounts for viewing All Customers, Active Customers, or Customers with Open Balances. You are currently viewing Active Customers.

This ⊡ button hides the Customer Information pane shown to the right. After hiding, this ⊡ button appears on the far right for redisplaying the pane.

The **Customer Information** pane displays transactions for the account highlighted on the left. This account is currently Aldred Builders.

The **Edit Customer** button opens the account for editing customer information and the **Edit Notes** button lets you enter account notes. There are also hyperlinks for creating **Reports for this Customer**.

Aldred's transactions are listed at the bottom of the account information. The filter options of **Show, Filter By**, and **Date** determine the transactions displayed. Click ⌄ to access an option's dropdown list for changing selections. You are currently viewing **Invoices** that are **All Invoices** recorded on **All** dates. *(Remember that selecting the fiscal year option uses your computer system date.)*

Filter options work as follows:

     ❖ Show: Select the transaction type to list
     ❖ Filter By: Criteria based on transaction type
     ❖ Date: List all transactions for the type or only transactions recorded as of a specific date or range of dates

Now turn your attention to the task buttons for activities that can be performed while displaying the Customers & Jobs tab. These activities are **New Customer & Job**, **New Transactions**, **Print**, **Excel**, and **Word**.

Each activity has this ⌄ dropdown symbol, meaning the activity contains multiple tasks. The next table discusses task choices by activity. Most actions perform the task on the customer account highlighted on the left.

Customers & Jobs Activities	Task	Description
New Customer & Job	New Customer	Create a new customer account.
	Add Job	Create a new job for the highlighted customer.
New Transactions	Invoices	Create a sales invoice for the highlighted customer.
	Sales Receipts	Record a sales transaction for the highlighted customer. Used when the customer is paying in full at the time of sale. Do not use this activity when the customer is making a sales deposit. Instead, use Invoices.
	Statement Charges	Open the highlighted customer's register and enter charges that will print on a statement. This is an alternate method for billing customers that bypasses creating an invoice. It can also be used to record finance charges. The text will not illustrate this method.
	Receive Payments	Record payment receipt from the highlighted customer.
	Credit Memos/Refunds	Issue a credit to the highlighted customer or refund a customer overpayment.

Customers & Jobs Activities	Task	Description
Print	Customer & Job List	Print a customer list with balances. The report cannot be customized so you should consider using the Reports menu to print this information.
	Customer & Job Information	Print account information and notes for the highlighted customer. The report cannot be customized so you should consider using the Reports menu to print this information.
	Customer & Job Transaction List	Print the highlighted customer's transactions for the current fiscal year. The report cannot be customized so you should consider using the Reports menu to print this information.
Excel	Export Customer List	Create an Excel workbook or comma separated values (.csv) file containing account information for all customers along with account balances.
	Export Transactions	Create an Excel workbook or comma separated values (.csv) file containing current fiscal year transactions for the highlighted customer.
	Import from Excel	Import customer information and/or transactions from an Excel workbook or comma separated values (.csv) file.
Word	Customer communications	Create form letters for customers.

Next turn your attention to the **Transactions** tab, which lists transactions by type instead of transactions by customer. Click to activate the tab and select the options illustrated next.

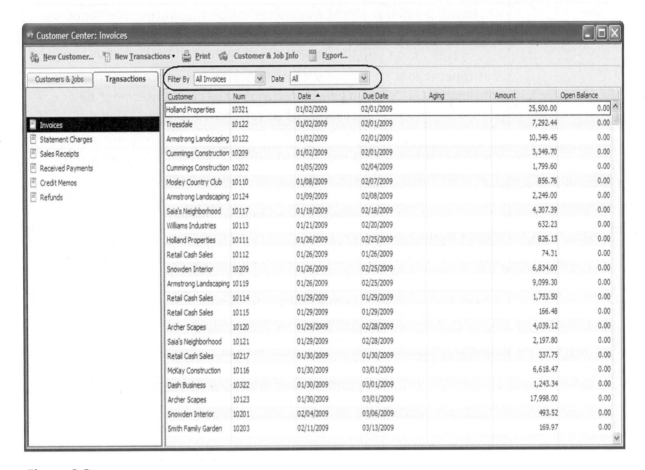

Figure 8:8

Transaction types are chosen on the left. **Invoices** is the type currently highlighted and the information displayed on the right lists **All Invoices** for **All** dates. Once again, you filter transactions by selecting an option from the filtering options. You can also sort the list by clicking a column header.

Activities that can be performed while this tab is active are different from activities performed on the previous tab. First, not all activities have an additional task symbol so clicking an activity immediately opens the task. The next table discusses activities for the **Transactions** tab.

Transactions Activities	Description
New Customer	Create a new customer account. Additional jobs must be added by using the first tab.
New Transactions	Contains the same tasks found on the Customers & Jobs tab but this time the user selects the customer.
Print	Print transactions listed to the right.
Customer & Job Info	Edit customer and job information for the transaction highlighted on the right.
Export	Create an Excel workbook or comma separated values (.csv) file containing transactions listed on the right.

As illustrated, you can perform a variety of customer activities from the Customer Center. You can initiate transactions, locate posted transactions, manage accounts, and create new accounts. Close the Customer Center.

In contrast, the customer section of the Home page (Figure 8:9) only initiates transactions but offers quicker access to such tasks. In addition, you can always use the **Customers** menu to perform customer activities.

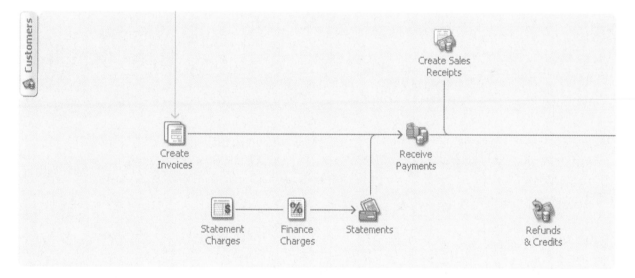

Figure 8:9

Now that you are familiar with locating customer activities, let's begin recording customer transactions.

ENTERING SALES INVOICES

You will now return to Knight Brothers' transaction illustrated in the *MAPS* topic and record the invoice in QBP. Read the data entry tips before performing the exercise that follows.

Data Entry Tips

Tip 1:   The **Customer:Job** field links the transaction to a customer's account. The **Item** field links inventory items to the transaction. Customer accounts and items are also called master records. You will recognize a master record field because it contains lookups for selecting a record.

Tip 2:   You can either click the dropdown list on the **Customer:Job** or **Item** field to select a record or begin typing the name of the customer account or item to make a selection.

Tip 3:   If you select the wrong customer or item then return to the field and change the selection. Click **Edit** on the main menu when you want to add or delete invoice line items.

Tip 4:   QBP will create new master records "on the fly," meaning a new customer or item can be created while entering a transaction. Example: A new customer can be added by typing a customer name in the **Customer:Job** field and pressing tab. QBP will then prompt with the following:

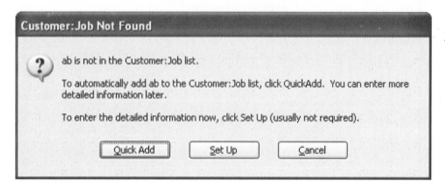

Figure 8:10

Clicking **Set Up** opens the New Customer window for entering all information on the new account. Clicking **Cancel** returns you to the Customer:Job field for selecting an existing customer. Clicking **Quick Add** creates the new account without opening the New Customer window. You will not want to use this option because it does not allow you to enter address or other information for the new account.

Tip 5:   Figure 8:11 illustrates toolbar icons on the invoice window and a description of relevant icons follows the illustration.

Figure 8:11

Previous and **Next** scroll through posted invoices. QBP will prompt to save a new or modified transaction before moving to another transaction.

Print sends the current invoice to a printer. The dropdown list for this icon contains an option for previewing an invoice before printing it and an option for printing multiple invoices.

Send emails an invoice. The dropdown list for this icon contains options for emailing multiple invoices.

STEPS FOR ENTERING A SALES INVOICE

1. On the **Home** page, click **Create Invoices** to open the invoice transaction window.

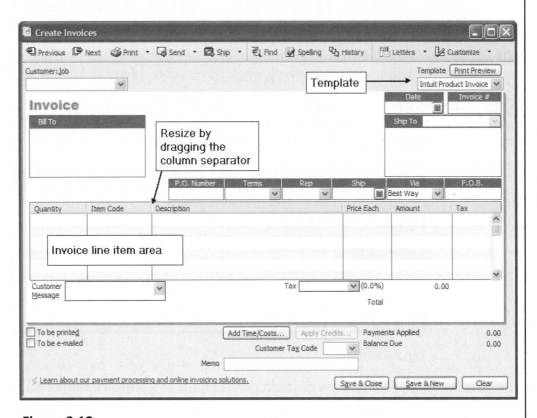

Figure 8:12

Make sure that the form template reads Intuit Product Invoice. You change the template using the dropdown list. The product invoice template sets the columns for line items and other fields displayed on the form.

To resize the window, drag the edges using the mouse. To resize line item columns, drag the column separators.

2. Place your cursor in **Customer:Job** and look up to select "Knight Brothers." The **Bill To**, **Ship To**, **Terms**, and **Rep** information transfers from the customer account.

3. Place your cursor in **Date**. Type "3/24/2009" because this is the day that the order was filled and shipped. *(Note: You can also select the date using the field's calendar icon.)*

   (Note: The first time you open a transaction window QBP sets the transaction date to your computer date. **BE CAREFUL** *and remember to always check transaction dates before saving.)*

4. Tab to **Invoice #** and enter "10346".

5. Place your cursor in **Quantity** on the first line item and enter "10".

6. Tab to **Item Code** and look up to select "EQFF-13130." Turn off future information on assigning sales taxes and click **OK**.

   (Note: The lookup on Item Code signals this as a master record.)

7. Tab to **Quantity** on the second line item and enter "15". Tab to the next **Item Code** and look up to select "EQWT-15150."

8. The completed invoice appears in Figure 8:13.

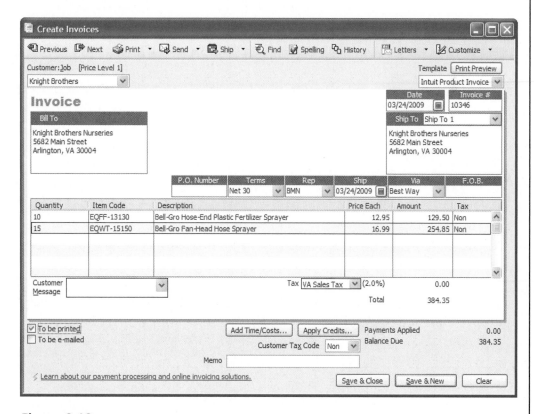

Figure 8:13

Before saving, review remaining fields in the window. You will normally not need to change data in these fields.

- ❖ **Description** and **Price Each** defaults from the inventory item selected.
- ❖ **Amount** equals the **Quantity** times **Price Each**.
- ❖ The **Tax** field on a line item shows whether sales tax is normally charged on the item. You can mix taxable line items with nontaxable line items.
- ❖ Tax on the form (i.e., **VA Sales Tax**) is the sales tax rate applied to taxable line items. This rate code defaults from the customer account.
- ❖ **Customer Tax Code** shows when sales to a particular customer are taxable. If the customer is not taxable then the invoice will not compute sales tax even when line items are taxable.
- ❖ *To be printed* flags an invoice for printing. *To be e-mailed* flags it for email delivery.
- ❖ The **Apply Credits** button is used when applying outstanding customer credit memos and overpayments to the invoice.
- ❖ Text in the **Customer Message** field will appear on the printed invoice whereas text in the **Memo** field stores internal notes.

9. Click [Print Preview] to view the invoice before sending it to the printer (Figure 8:14).

(Note: If prompted about shipping labels, select the option that turns off future messages and click OK.)

Scroll to the bottom of the invoice to view the total. You can click on the invoice to enlarge it.

Click **Close** to return to the invoice transaction.

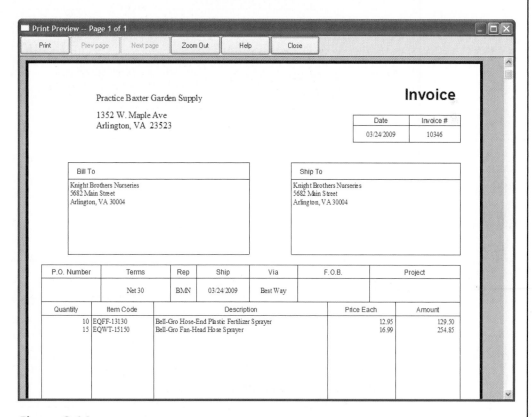

Figure 8:14

10. Click **Print** and QBP saves the invoice and opens a window to choose the printer (Figure 8:15). Use the dropdown list on **Printer name** if you need to select a different printer.

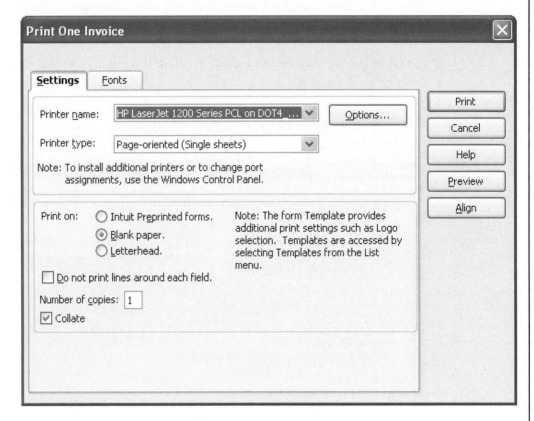

Figure 8:15

11. Click **Print** to send the invoice to the printer.

12. Click **Save & Close**. *(Note: Save & New will post a transaction and remain in the window so you can enter the next transaction.)*

In this exercise you entered a single invoice and then printed it. Normally you will enter several invoices before printing. To print multiple invoices, click the dropdown list on the Print icon and select Print Batch. QBP will then print every invoice with this option ☑ To be printed selected.

You do not have to recheck the *To be printed* option to reprint a posted invoice. Just reopen the invoice and click Print.

BEHIND THE KEYS OF A POSTED SALES INVOICE

In this topic you will trace QBP's audit trail by locating the entries made when posting Knight Brothers' invoice. Remember that the audit trail in the manual system referenced the Sales Journal and the page number. Let's see how that compares with QBP's audit trail.

TRACE THE AUDIT TRAIL OF A POSTED SALES INVOICE

1. First, open the Sales Journal by selecting **Reports>>Memorized Reports>>Accounting Journals>>Sales Journal** on the main menu.

2. Enter the date range of **From** 3/24/2009 **To** 3/24/2009. Click **Modify Report** and select the **Filters** tab. Under **Choose Filter**, select **Name** and then look up Knight Brothers' account. Click **OK**.

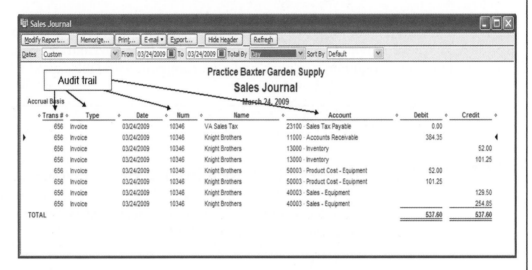

Figure 8:16

Recall that manual sales journal entries debited 11000 Accounts Receivable for $384.35 and credited 40003 Sales - Equipment for $384.35. Although QBP recorded sales entries to the same accounts, it posted each line item as a separate sales entry. QBP also posted cost of goods sold and inventory entries for the items sold.

Note the audit trail codes under **Type** and **Tran #** because we will refer to them later. (*Note: Your Trans # may differ because numbers are assigned based on activity in the software.*)

Close this report without saving changes.

(Hint: You can reopen the original invoice by double clicking any of the entries shown on the report.)

As explained in the *MAPS* topic, cost of goods sold entries are not recorded in a manual system because companies do not have the resources to identify inventory costs at the time of sale. Instead, cost of goods sold is recorded after taking a physical count of quantities on hand. Furthermore, companies using a manual system do not have immediate access to accurate on hand inventory.

You will see in the inventory topic to follow that QBP tracks item cost and quantities on hand. As a result, companies have more timely financial information because cost of goods sold posts and quantities on hand adjust when invoicing.

3. Recall in the *MAPS* topic that after posting an invoice to the Sales Journal the invoice was then posted to the customer's account. You will now locate QBP's entries to Knight Brothers' customer account.

   Click *Reports>>Customers & Receivables>>Transaction List by Customer* on the main menu.

   Enter the date range of **From** 3/24/2009 and **To** 3/24/2009.

4. Click **Modify Report**. Select **Trans #** under **Columns** to print this audit trail code (Figure 8:17). Scroll down and click **Split** to uncheck this column. Click **OK** and the report displays. (See Figure 8:18.)

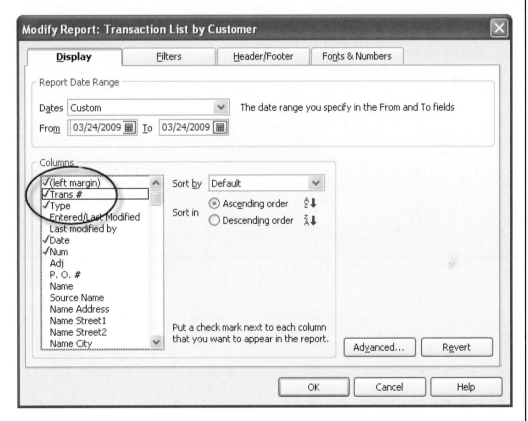

Figure 8:17

5. Notice that the **Trans #** and **Type** on Knight Brothers' account match the **Trans #** and **Type** on the Sales Journal. Close this report without saving changes.

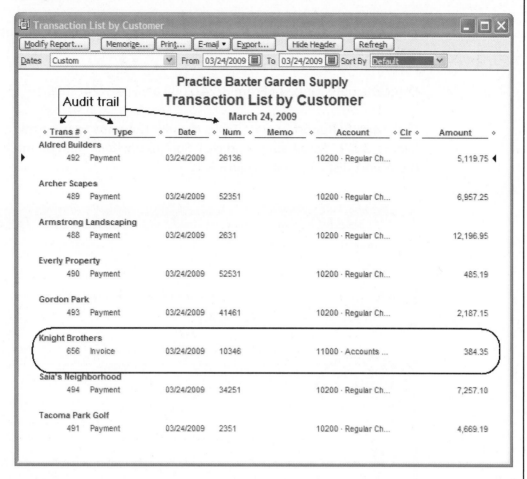

Figure 8:18

6. All that remains is tracing entries in the general ledger. Select **Reports>> Memorized Reports>>Accounting Journals>>General Ledger Detail Report** on the main menu. Enter the date range of From 3/24/2009 and To 3/24/2009 and the report redisplays as illustrated in Figure 8:19.

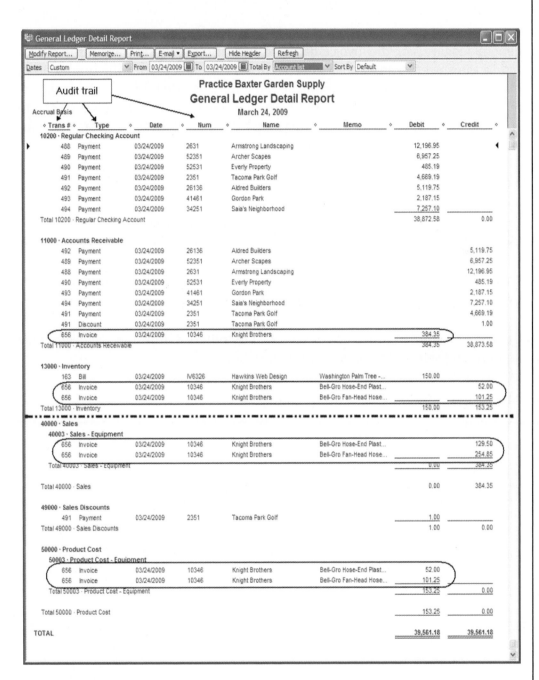

Figure 8:19

Once again you see that the **Trans #** and **Type** on Knight Brothers' entries match the Sales Journal audit trail. Scroll down and locate the cost of goods sold entries to 50003 Product Cost – Equipment and then close this report without saving changes.

You have now followed QBP's audit trail and can see the advantages to using a computerized accounting system. You were able to capture a sales invoice and QBP posted entries to the Sales Journal, customer account, and general ledger when saving it. In addition, the accountant is better equipped to answer customer inquiries, provide customer support, manage company sales, and analyze profitability.

Let's spend a few minutes discussing the importance of invoice dates. QBP posts entries to the general ledger using the invoice date, which is also called the transaction date. It is important to use the correct transaction date so that transactions post to the proper accounting period; otherwise, financial statements will be misstated. In addition, invoice dates affect due dates and due dates affect the number of days an invoice is outstanding, which can then affect the customer's credit history and early payment discount. **Always pay careful attention to dates when entering transactions in QBP.**

 ## CORRECTING SALES INVOICES

This topic explains voiding and deleting invoices and correcting errors on **unpaid** invoices. *(Note: Refer to the instructions in Appendix B if correcting a paid invoice.)*

Open the **Customer Center** and select the **Customers & Jobs** tab. Highlight Knight Brothers' account and select the options shown in Figure 8:20.

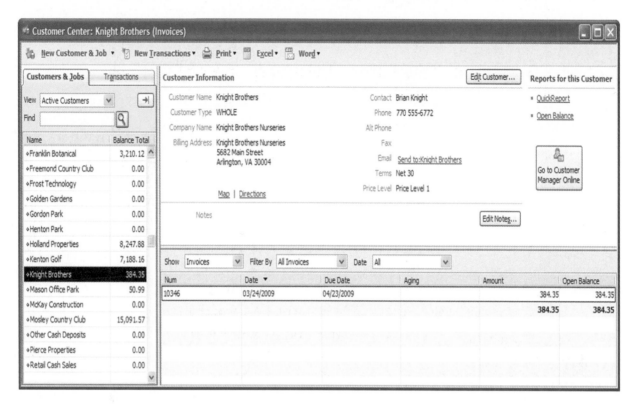

Figure 8:20

Double click the listed invoice to reopen it. ***Do not make any changes to the invoice*** but note that after reopening, you can void the invoice by selecting ***Edit>>Void Invoice*** on the main menu and delete it by selecting ***Edit>>Delete Invoice***. You can also modify the invoice and repost it by clicking **Save & Close**.

Keep this transaction open for the topic that follows.

QUICKBOOKS EMAIL FEATURES

You will now use QBP's email features to send Knight Brothers' invoice to your email account.

With the invoice open, click ⬚ Send ▾. ***(Note: You must be connected to the Internet to use this feature.)***

A message appears using your default email program as shown in Figure 8:21.

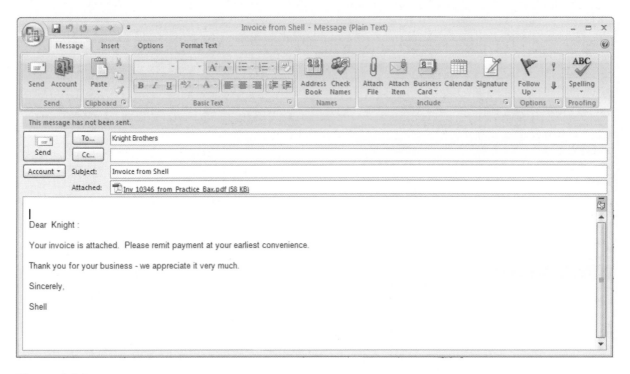

Figure 8:21

Enter your email address in the **To** field and, in **Subject**, replace the text "Invoice from Shell" with "Merchandise invoice". Change the body's salutation to "Dear Knight Brothers".

The invoice is attached as a PDF file. Click **Send.** You may get the message shown in Figure 8:22 and can turn off this message in the future by checking the Do not display this message in the future box and clicking OK to close the message.

Figure 8:22

Check your email later to verify delivery. Click **X** to close Knight's invoice.

CUSTOMER ACCOUNTS

This topic explains creating, editing, and deleting customer accounts for a merchandising company, which means you will not use the Job Info tab. (*Note: Chapter 4 illustrates using this tab*). *The customer account contains job information used for implementing job costing.* You use the **Customer Center** to manage customer accounts. Open this center if it is not still open from the previous topic, select the **Customers & Jobs** tab, and double click **Knight Brothers** to open the account. Now follow below as we describe the tabs of the customer account.

Address Info Tab

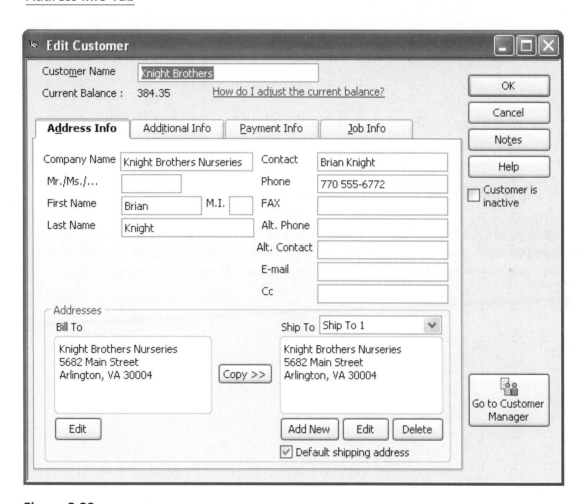

Figure 8:23

The **Address Info** tab stores basic customer information such as address, phone numbers, and email address. The **Bill To** address can be copied to the **Ship To** address by clicking the **Copy** button.

The **Ship To** address is important for companies shipping merchandise to customers because some customers may have one address for receiving invoices (Bill To) and another address for receiving orders (Ship To). When the customer has multiple locations, **Add New** opens the window illustrated in Figure 8:24 to enter additional addresses.

Figure 8:24

The window in Figure 8:24 is completed by entering a unique name for the **Address Name** and then entering the address data. The **Default shipping address** option triggers an address to appear as the primary shipping address on invoices. Clicking **OK** will store the address.

Additional Info Tab

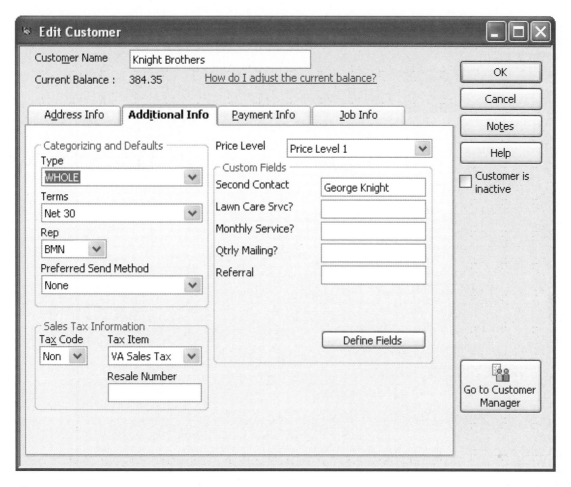

Figure 8:25

This tab stores customer defaults used during transaction entry. Defaults include the **Preferred Send Method** for invoices, customer payment **Terms** and the **Tax Code** applied to sales transactions. The **Rep** field assigns an employee sales representative for tracking sales commissions and sales performance.

The **Type** field is optional and can be used to differentiate sales by customer characteristics. Baxter uses the types of Retail and Whole.

Click the dropdown list on **Terms** to open the terms illustrated in Figure 8:26.

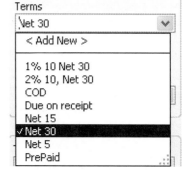

Figure 8:26

Terms establish invoice due dates and customer early payment discounts. The Net 15 terms make an invoice due 15 days from the invoice date. The 2% 10, Net 30 terms make the invoice due 30 days from the invoice date but grants a 2 percent discount when paying the total invoice within 10 days. *(Note: Discounts do not apply to sales tax.)*

Payment Info Tab

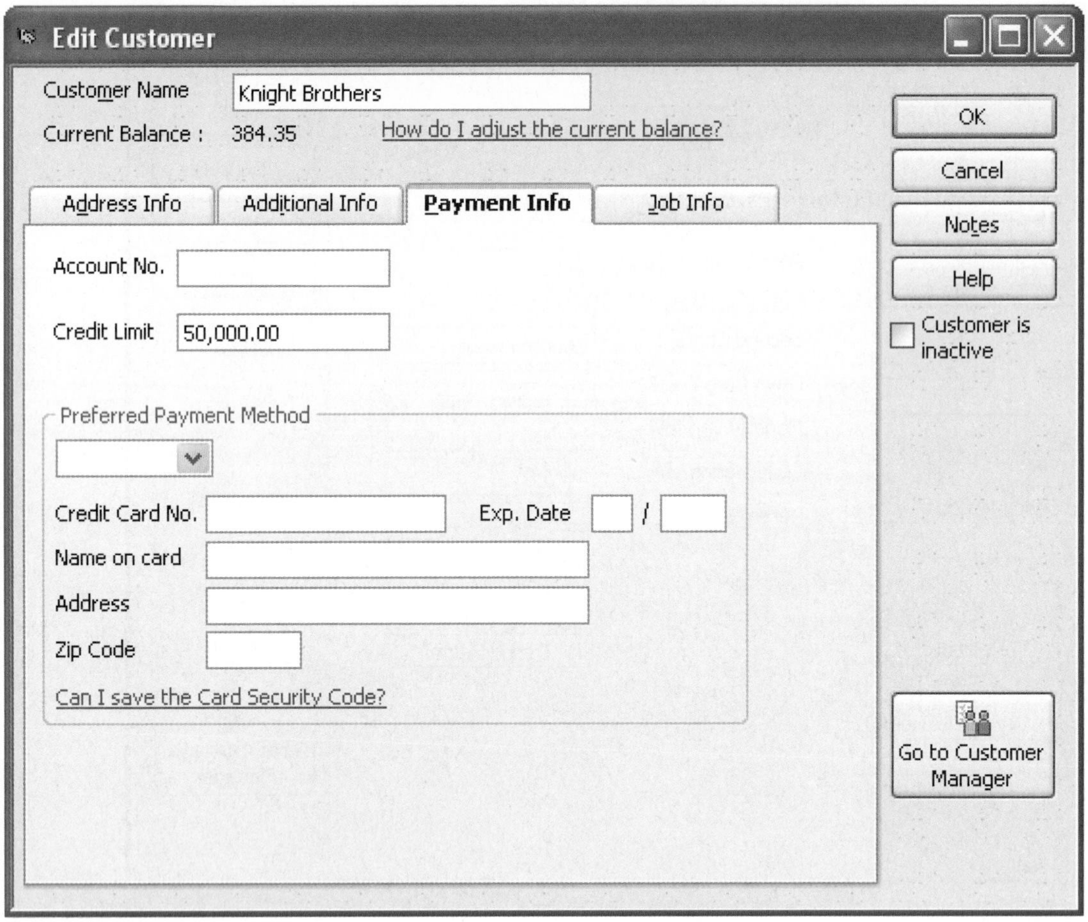

Figure 8:27

This tab stores a customer's **Credit Limit** and **Preferred Payment Method**. Setting a credit limit is important to managing bad debt. QBP will warn when saving a new invoice causes the customer's account balance to exceed the credit limit.

Job Info Tab

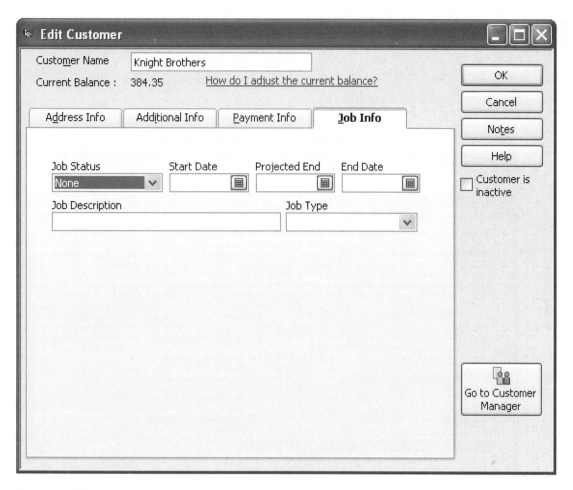

Figure 8:28

This tab implements QBP job costing and is discussed in Chapter 4. Baxter, as a merchandiser, does not use job costing.

Click **X** to close Knight's account.

The next exercise walks through editing a customer account.

STEPS TO EDIT CUSTOMER ACCOUNT INFORMATION

1. You will be editing Aldred Builders' sales representative, so open this account and click the **Additional Info** tab.

2. Brandee Nunnley is replacing Dorothy Beck as the customer sales representative. Using the dropdown list on **Rep**, look up and select "BMN."

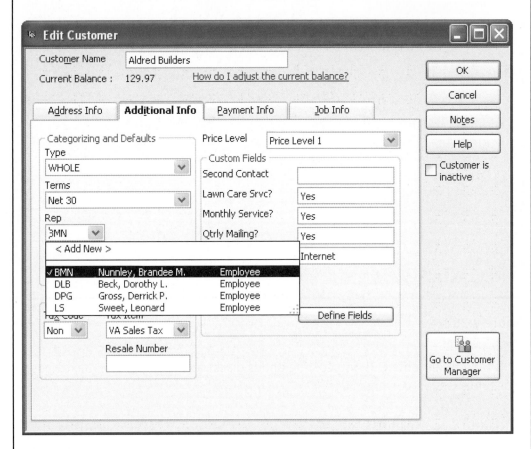

Figure 8:29

3. Click **OK** to save the changes. Click **Yes** on if QBP warns about modifying the account because this change only affects future transactions.

You will now add a new customer account.

Steps to Create a Customer Account

1. From the Customers & Jobs tab, click **New Customer & Job** and select **New Customer**.

2. Enter the information illustrated in Figure 8:30.

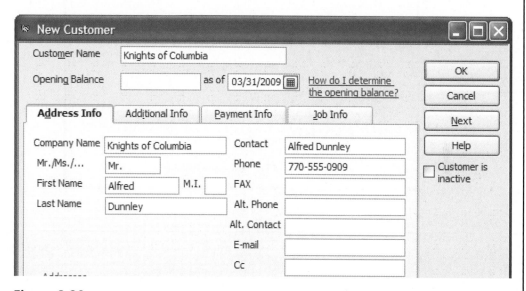

Figure 8:30

3.   Click **Edit** on the **Bill To** field and enter the following information. Click **OK**.

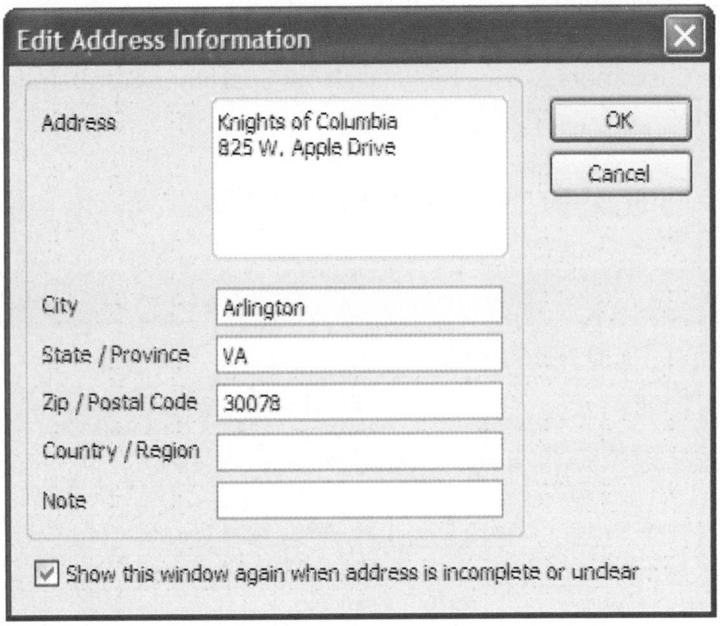

Edit Address Information

Address	Knights of Columbia 825 W. Apple Drive
City	Arlington
State / Province	VA
Zip / Postal Code	30078
Country / Region	
Note	

OK

Cancel

☑ Show this window again when address is incomplete or unclear

Figure 8:31

4. Click **Copy** to insert the **Bill To** address into the **Ship To** address. Click **OK** on the window that opens. The completed **Address Info** tab is shown in Figure 8:32.

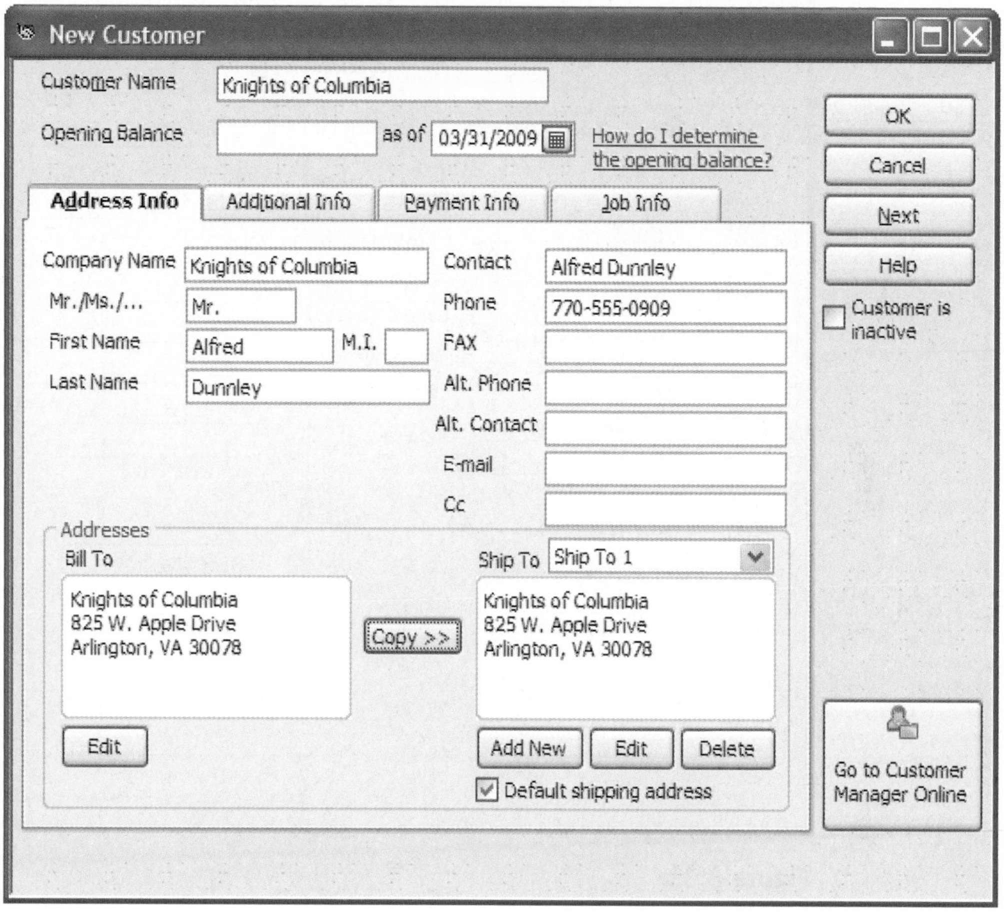

Figure 8:32

5. Click **Additional Info** and enter the information in Figure 8:33.

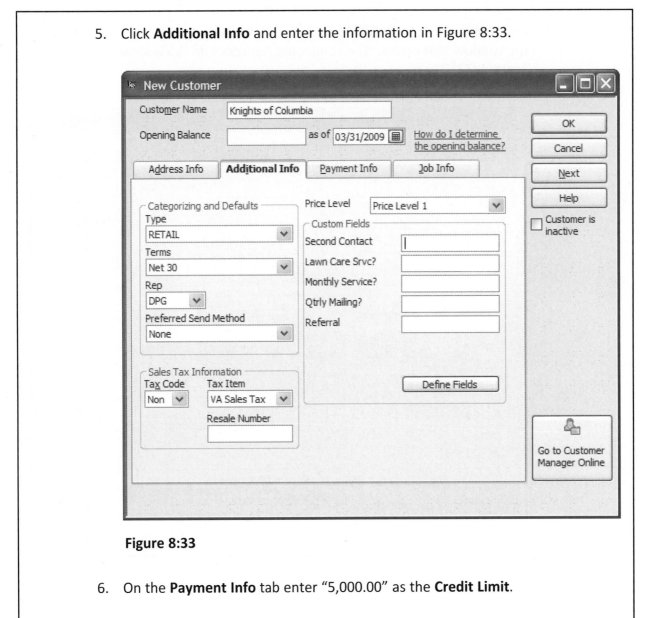

Figure 8:33

6. On the **Payment Info** tab enter "5,000.00" as the **Credit Limit**.

7. Click **OK**.

What happens when you try to delete an account with transaction history?

Highlight **Mosley Country Club** and select *Edit>>Delete Customer:Job* on the main menu. QBP prompts, stating that it cannot delete an account with transaction history but can make it inactive. (See Figure 8:34.) Inactivating the account denies future transactions while retaining account history. Click **Cancel**.

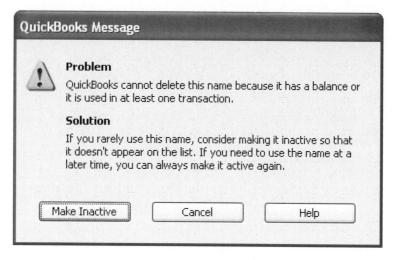

Figure 8:34

Now create a new account on your own.

 CREATE A NEW CUSTOMER ACCOUNT

On March 3, 2009, Baxter needs to create a new wholesale customer with the following information.

Frost Garden Center		Phone:	701 555-1515
127 Frost Avenue		Fax:	701 555-1518
Danville, VA 30765		Contact:	Jeffrey Davis
		Email:	davis@frost.net

Credit Limit:	$15,000.00
Preferred Payment Method:	Check
Sales Rep:	Leonard Sweet
Price Level:	Price Level 1

The customer does not pay sales tax and will be offered the terms of 1/10 Net 30.

UNDERSTANDING INVENTORY ITEMS

Inventory items differ from the service and non-inventory part items discussed in Chapter 4 for a service based businesses. Recall that such businesses do not hold inventory. On the other hand, merchandising businesses do hold inventory because goods are purchased in advance of sale. These businesses need to track the quantities of items on-hand and purchasing costs.

QBP's inventory items store sales prices, quantities on hand, and purchasing costs. The software posts to inventory when purchasing items and cost of goods sold when selling items. Recall that Knight's invoice traced in a previous exercise posted cost of goods sold. QBP calculates the cost of goods sold amount by averaging the item's purchase costs. *(Note: QBP only accommodates the average costing method.)*

It is important to understand the posting of cost of goods sold; otherwise you might prepare financial statements that do not match revenues with expenses. The following table explains the inventory, non-inventory part, and service items used in this text. After reviewing this table, you will better understand when an item class interacts with inventory and when the item posts cost of goods sold at the time of sale.

Item Class	Purpose
Inventory Part	Used to track goods purchased and held for resale. Tracks quantities and purchasing costs. Cost of goods sold posts at the time of invoicing. Cost of goods sold is calculated using the Average costing method. *(Note: QBP does not accommodate the LIFO and FIFO inventory costing methods.)*
Non-inventory Part	Used for job materials purchased but not tracked in inventory. Cost of goods sold posts when posting vendor bills or receipts for material purchases.
Service	Used for service labor costs provided by company employees or subcontractors. When provided by subcontractors, cost of goods sold posts when paying the contractor. When provided by employees, cost of goods sold posts when paying employees.
Sales Tax Item	Used to calculate sales tax for a single taxing agency.
Other Charge	Used for miscellaneous charges such as delivery and photocopying fees. Cost of goods sold posts when reimbursing the employee expense or paying a vendor.

Now look at the inventory items sold by Baxter. Click **Item** on the toolbar to open the Item List illustrated in Figure 8:35. *(Note: You can also select **Lists>>Item List** on the main menu.)* Pay particular attention to the **Type** column.

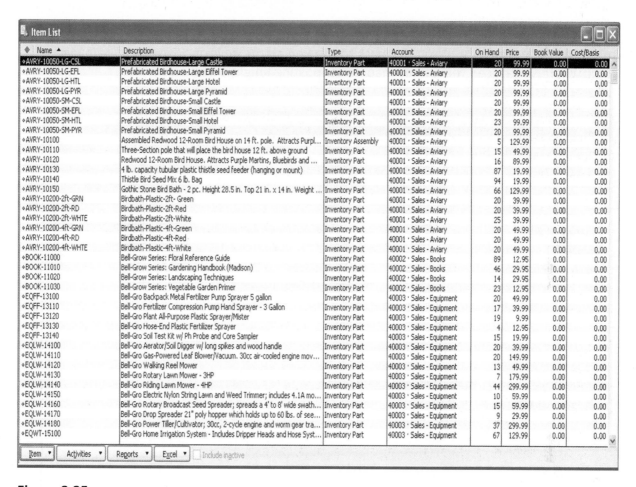

Figure 8:35

The list contains columns for Book Value and Cost/Basis with zero values displayed; however, you will find average cost data on item records.

Now customize the Item List. Click the **Item** button at the bottom and select **Customize Columns**. On the right, highlight **Book Value** and click **Remove**. Use the same procedures to remove the **Cost/Basis** column. On the left, highlight **Preferred Vendor** and click **Add**. Click **OK** and the list refreshes.

We will now review a few of these items.

Inventory Part

Scroll down and highlight **EQFF-13130**. Double click to open the item (Figure 8:36).

While reviewing this item, refer back to the *Entering Sales Invoices* topic where you sold 10 of these to Knight Brothers. Also refer back to the *Behind the Keys of a Posted Sales Invoice* topic where you traced the entries made after posting Knight's invoice.

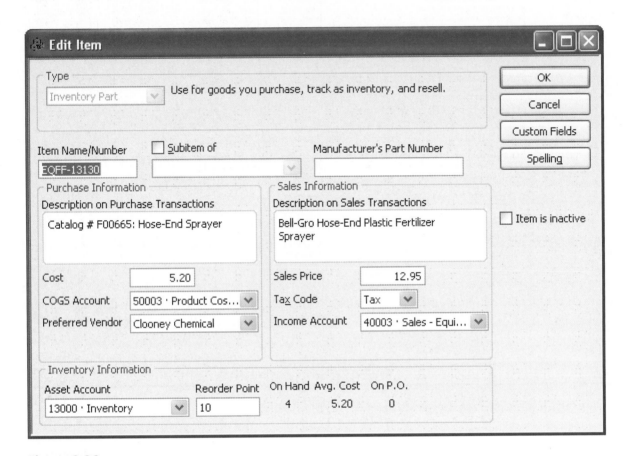

Figure 8:36

Purchase Information describes the item to vendors on purchase orders.

Sales Information is the description that appears on customer invoices.

Cost is the price paid vendors when purchasing the item. In Chapter 9 you will see that this Cost autofills as the purchase price on vendor purchase orders and bills.

COGS Account is the account used for posting cost of goods sold. For this item cost of goods sold posts to account 50003 Product Cost-Equipment and can be verified by reviewing the Sales Journal printed after posting Knight's invoice. *(Note: Click the dropdown list on this field to view the account's full name.)*

Sales Price autofills as the sales price on invoices and explains why Knight's invoice charged $12.95 for this item.

Tax Code shows that sales of this item are normally taxable. However, remember that QBP looks to the tax default on a customer account before charging sales tax.

Income Account is the account used for posting sales revenue, explaining why Knight's invoice posted revenue to 40003 Sales-Equipment.

Next, focus your attention on the **Inventory Information** section.

Purchases of this item debit **Asset Account** 13000 Inventory whereas sales of the item credit this account.

The **Reorder Point** on this item is 10 and the **On Hand** quantity is 4. This information indicates that a purchase order should be issued to restock the item.

Avg. Cost is $5.20, explaining why $52.00 posted to cost of goods sold when Knight's invoice posted the sale of ten of these items. The average cost adjusts as items are purchased.

Finally, there are no items currently on order to vendors (**On P.O.**).

Click **X** to close this item.

Inventory Assembly

Now open **AVRY-10100**.

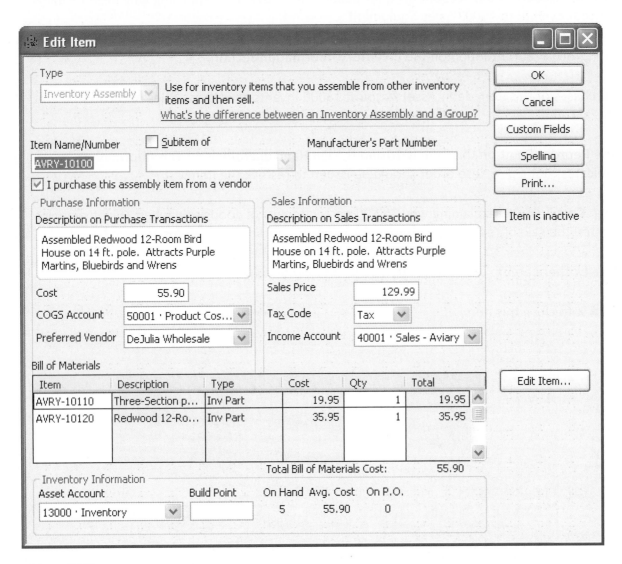

Figure 8:37

This is an assembly item that combines the two individual items listed under **Bill of Materials**. Furthermore, this item is restocked by purchasing the individual items.

Sales Tax Item

Close the previous item and open **VA SALES TAX**.

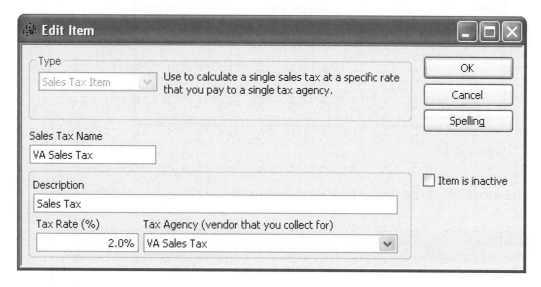

Figure 8:38

This item sets 2 percent as the sales tax rate for taxable items.

Close this item and then close the Item List. We will next discuss inventory pricing and price levels.

INVENTORY PRICING AND PRICE LEVELS

Baxter offers tiered sales pricing, meaning it can offer different sales prices for the same item. This is sometimes called preferred pricing. Companies use this feature when offering different sales prices to preferred customers or customers buying large quantities of an item. You should recall assigning a price level to the customer account created in an earlier exercise.

Baxter's sales price tiers are opened from the Lists menu. Select *Lists>>Price Level List* on the main menu to open the window illustrated in Figure 8:39.

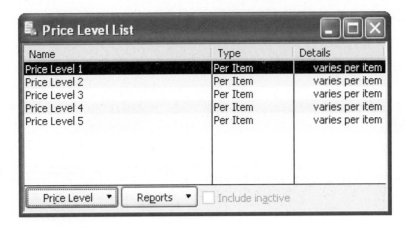

Figure 8:39

Double click **Price Level 1** and the following information opens.

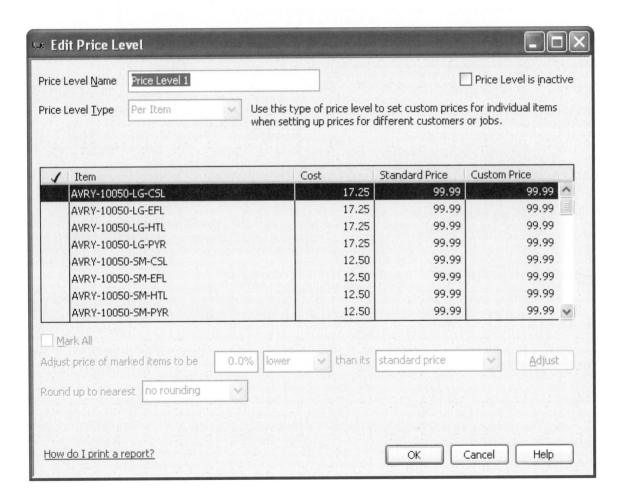

Figure 8:40

Click **Cancel** to close this list and then click **Price Level 2** to open the list illustrated in Figure 8:41.

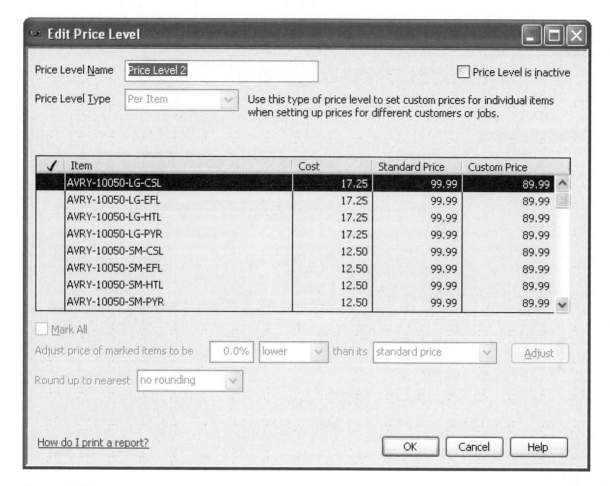

Figure 8:41

Level 2 sells items at a lower price than Level 1. Now look at using price levels on an invoice. *(Note: Keep the Price Level List open.)*

On the **Home** page, click **Create Invoices** and select **Aldred Builders**. Enter "1" in **Quantity** and then select **Item Code** "AVRY-10050-LG-CSL" (i.e., the first item on the inventory list).

Click the dropdown list on **Price Each** to view the sales prices at different levels. (See Figure 8:42.)

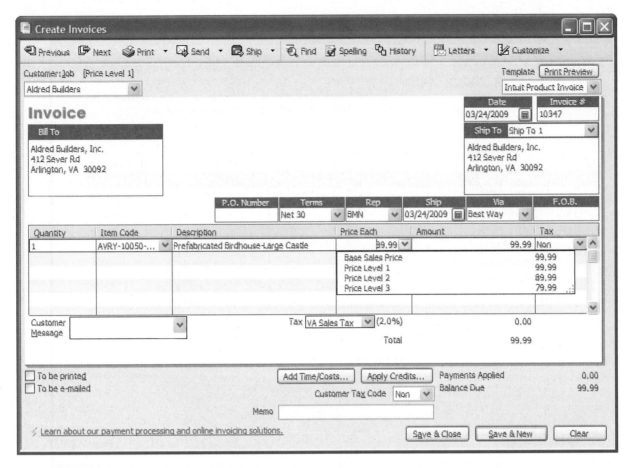

Figure 8:42

Aldred Builders' account is assigned to Price Level 1 so $99.99 defaulted as the Price Each. You can, if needed, override the default by selecting a different price level.

Click **Clear** and then **X** to close the invoice window.

Now look at changing sales prices.

You can change sales prices on individual items by opening each item and entering a new price. However, this method would be time consuming if changing the prices on several items so QBP provides another method.

Return to the Price Level List and click **Price Level** to select **Edit Price Level**. The window illustrated in Figure 8:43 does not permit editing sales prices because these prices were created on a Per Item basis. *(Note: See the Author's Note that follows.)*

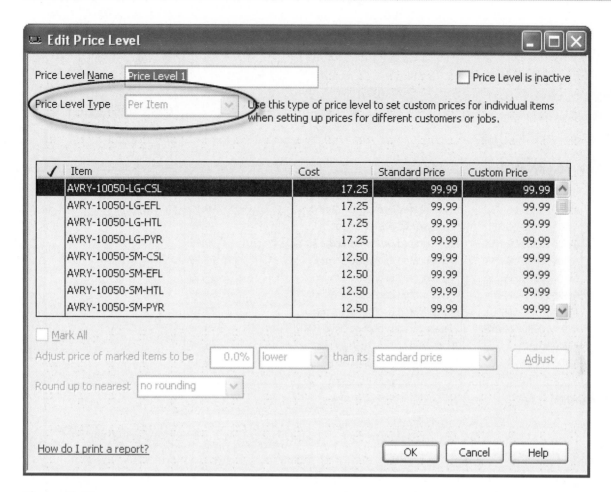

Figure 8:43

> **Author's Note:**
>
> The Baxter Garden Supply data file was created using QuickBooks Premier Edition, which can customize price lists on a per item basis. You are using the QuickBooks Pro Edition, which can only customize sales prices by fixed percentages. With the other edition you lose pricing flexibility and can only adjust Price Level 1 sales prices.
>
> Furthermore, the Pro Edition does not include sales orders. If a company needs to capture customer orders then QuickBooks Premier or a higher edition is required. Accountants often find themselves in charge of choosing the accounting software purchased by a business. From this information you see that it is important to analyze a company's business operations before selecting the software package to ensure that software features meet the needs of the business.

Click **Cancel** to exit the Edit Price Level window and select **Customers>>Change Item Prices** on the main menu so we can illustrate changing Price Level 1 sales prices.

Select **Inventory Part** as the **Item Type** and the Change Item Prices window appears as illustrated in Figure 8:44.

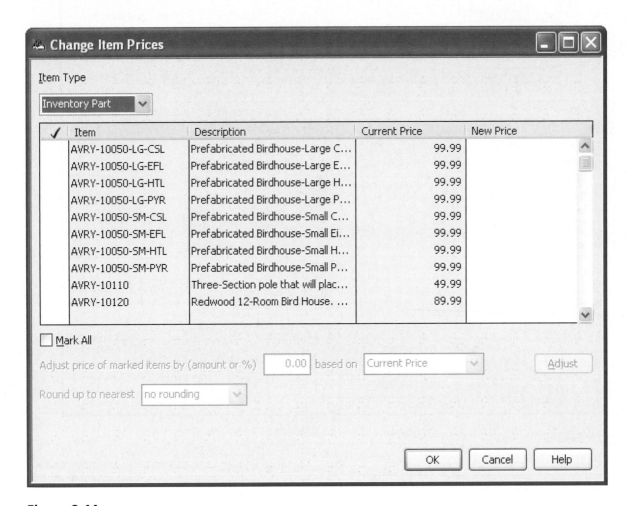

Figure 8:44

To begin changing prices you first select the items to change by clicking individual items or by clicking **Mark All**. Click this [✓] column on the first item. (See Figure 8:45.)

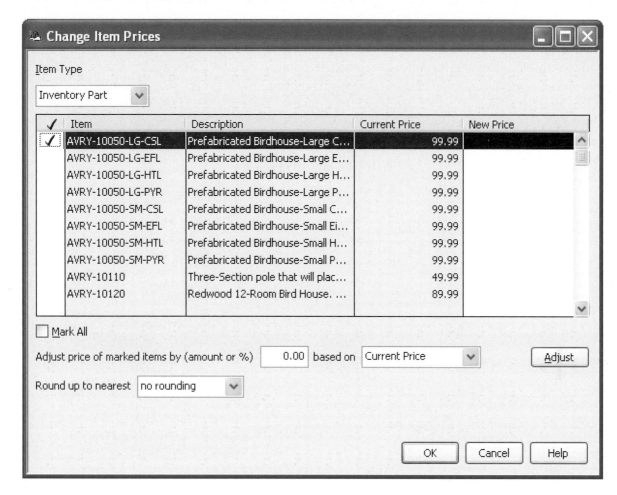

Figure 8:45

You change this item's sales price by entering a new value in the **New Price** column or by entering percentage criteria at the bottom of the window.

You will raise the selected item's price by 10 percent and base this price increase on the **Current Price** so enter the criteria shown in Figure 8:46.

Figure 8:46

Click **Adjust** and QBP enters a new sales price of $109.99.

Let's now round this sales price to the nearest dollar. Click the dropdown list on round and select $1.00. Click **Adjust** and the new price changes to $110.00.

Click **Cancel** and exit the window without adjusting the item's price.

Return to the Price Level List. Before leaving this topic, we want to illustrate other aspects of pricing levels. You add and delete price levels using the Price Level button. Furthermore, price levels are printed using the Reports button.

Click **X** to close the Price Level List.

INVENTORY REPORTING

You will now look at several inventory reports so click **Report Center** on the toolbar and select the **Inventory** area.

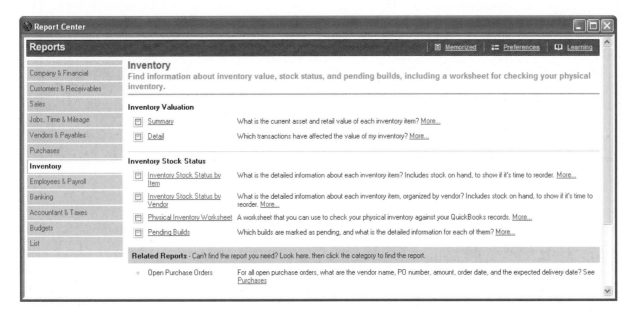

Figure 8:47

Click **Summary** under **Inventory Valuation**. Change the date to "3/31/2009." Scroll to the bottom and locate the total **Asset Value**. (See Figure 8:48.)

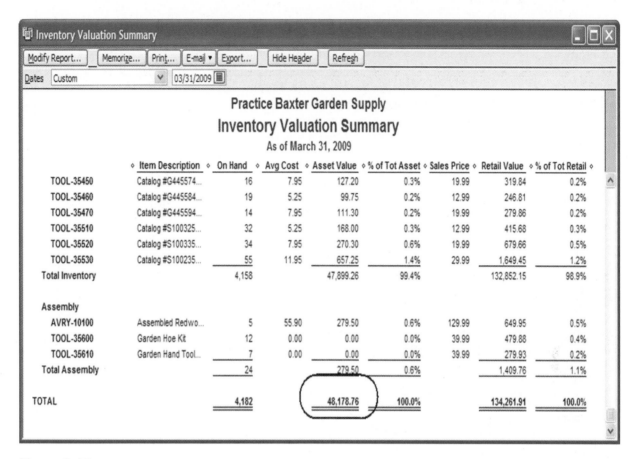

Figure 8:48

The total on this report must equal the total in the general ledger inventory control account. *(Note: Your total will differ when you have not completed previous exercises.)*

Check the balance in your inventory account by selecting **Reports>>Accountants & Taxes>> Trial Balance** on the main menu. Enter "3/31/2009" as the date range and scroll down to account 13000 Inventory. Compare the balance on your Inventory Valuation Summary report with your balance in 13000 Inventory.

This reconciliation procedure makes sure that sales and purchases of inventory have posted to the correct general ledger accounts. The report and general ledger can become "out of balance" when you fail to properly correct transactions. Therefore, always check the steps in Appendix B when correcting a posted transaction.

Close the Trial Balance and return to the inventory report. The amount for the **Retail Value** shows the sales value of on hand inventory.

Close this report and click **Inventory Stock Status by Item**. Enter the date range of **From** 3/31/2009 and **To** 3/31/2009. (See Figure 8:49.)

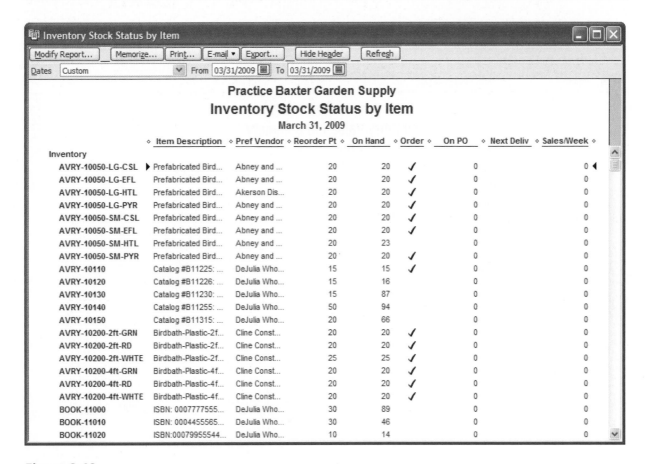

Figure 8:49

This report shows that several items need to be restocked. The order column appears checked when on-hand quantities fall below the reorder point. Recall that the reorder point is set on individual items.

It is important to monitor this report to ensure sufficient stock levels exist to fill customer orders.

Close the report and open the **Physical Inventory Worksheet** illustrated in Figure 8:50. This report is distributed to employees conducting a physical inventory count. To protect the integrity of the count, you should remove On Hand quantities before distributing the report.

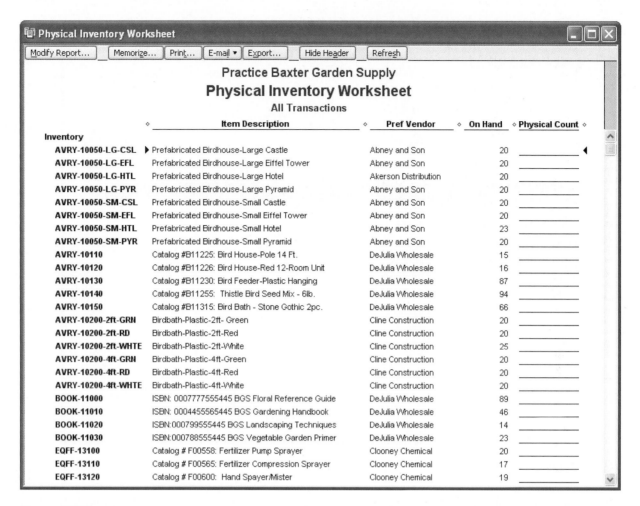

Figure 8:50

Close the report and the Report Center before moving on to the tasks performed after conducting a physical count.

PHYSICAL INVENTORY

Although QBP tracks inventory quantities, Baxter still conducts a physical count to confirm that actual quantities agree with QBP quantities. The Physical Inventory Worksheet previously illustrated is distributed to employees taking a physical count. These employees enter the actual quantities counted and the completed report is returned to the accounting department for comparison with QBP.

On the main menu, select ***Vendors>>Inventory Activities>>Adjust Quantity/Value on Hand*** to open the window illustrated in Figure 8:51. Enter the **Adjustment Date** of 3/31/2009.

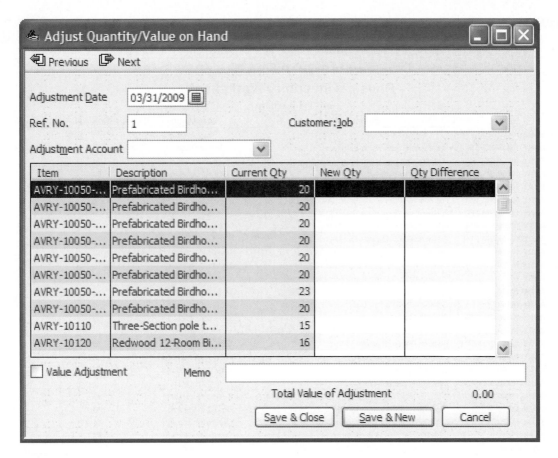

Figure 8:51

The accountant discovered that the actual quantity of AVRY-10140, Thistle Bird Seed is 93 whereas QBP shows 94. It is not unusual for actual quantities to disagree with QBP quantities. Sometimes items are damaged or become obsolete and are discarded. However, large discrepancies in physical counts may indicate a problem with control over inventory and should be investigated.

Record the adjustment for birdseed that is needed to reconcile QBP quantities to on-hand quantities by entering the following data. Be sure to select the **Adjustment Account** indicated.

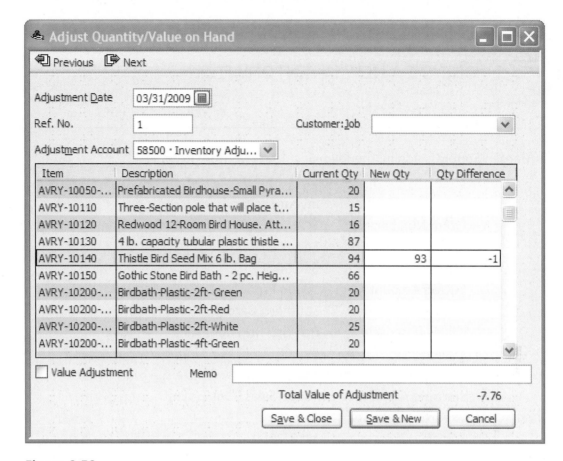

Figure 8:52

Notice that the adjustment will post (as a debit) to Adjustment Account 58500 Inventory Adjustment. Baxter uses this account so it can analyze profits lost to damaged or obsolete inventory.

Click **Save & Close** to post the adjustment.

Now create a new inventory item.

CREATE A NEW INVENTORY ITEM

Baxter Garden Supply is adding the following new inventory item.

Item Type:	Inventory Part
Item Number:	EQWT-15175
Purchase Description:	Sprinkler – Drip
Cost:	$10.50
COGS Account:	50003 Product Cost – Equipment
Preferred Vendor:	Southern Garden
Sales Description:	Bell-Gro Drip Sprinkler
Sales Price:	$22.00
Tax Code:	Tax
Income Account:	40003 Sales - Equipment
Reorder Quantity:	6
As of:	3/10/2009

You will need to determine the Asset Account.

Print an Item Listing filtered to display only the new item. Add the Account, Purchase Description, Asset Account, and COGS Account columns to the report and delete the Quantity on Hand, Quantity on Purchase Orders, and Quantity on Sales Order columns.

STOREFRONT SALE OF MERCHANDISE

On March 26, 2009, Baxter made a storefront sale of merchandise. With these sales, customers usually come into the store and pay for items at the time of sale. Therefore, these transactions are recorded using the **Create Sales Receipts** icon.

Follow the next steps to record this sale.

STEPS TO RECORD A STOREFRONT SALE OF MERCHANDISE

1. On the **Home** page, click **Create Sales Receipts** and enter the following information. *(Note: Click No Thanks if QBP prompts on integrated payment processing.)*

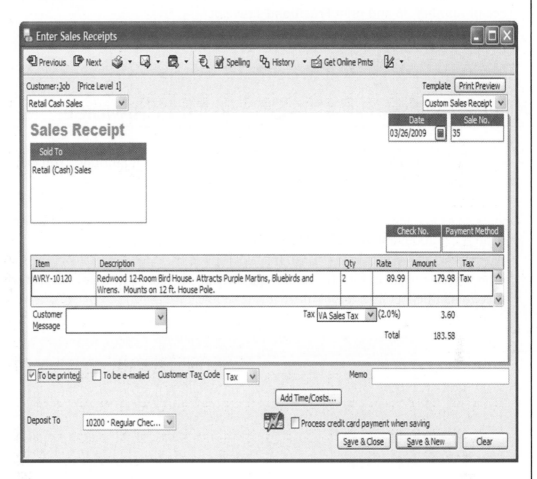

Figure 8:53

2. Click **Print** to give the customer a receipt and then click **Save & Close**.

Note: The debit will post to the regular checking account instead of the accounts receivable account because this is not a sale on account.

ENTER A STOREFRONT SALE OF MERCHANDISE

On March 26, 2009, Freemond Country Club picked up 30 bags of topsoil, item SOIL-34120. The customer paid with check number 8925 at the time of purchase. Record the sale on receipt number 36 and print Freemond's receipt.

INVOICES FOR OUT-OF-STOCK MERCHANDISE

QBP warns when selling an inventory item exceeds on-hand quantities. You can override this warning and save the invoice. We now test the warning.

Open a sales invoice and select Pierce Properties as the customer. Enter the transaction date of March 27, 2009, and use 10347 as the invoice number.

On the first line item, enter "16" as the Quantity and select "NURS-24010" as the item. QBP warns of insufficient stock to fill the invoice. (See Figure 8:54.)

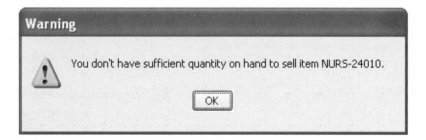

Figure 8:54

Click **OK** and refer to the invoice in Figure 8:55.

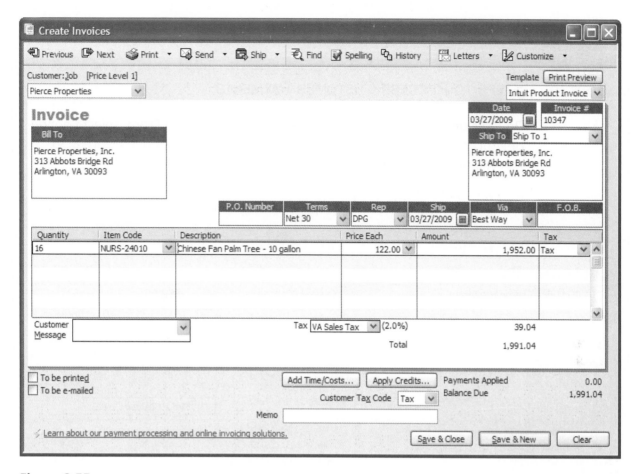

Figure 8:55

Click **Save & Close**.

Normally you will not sell items without sufficient stock. However, if you receive an insufficient quantity message when working end-of-chapter exercises, override the warning and save the invoice.

 ## CUSTOMER PAYMENTS

Companies can have thousands of dollars in sales, but without collecting the cash on the sale, continuing operations are threatened. In other words, sales must be realized in cash before the company can pay employees and vendors or invest in the business. This topic focuses on processing customer payments on account.

On March 27, 2009, Cannon Healthcare Center remitted check number 875 for $662.90, paying Invoices 10321 and 10329 in full. Follow the next steps to record this payment.

STEPS TO PROCESS CUSTOMER PAYMENTS

1. On the **Home** page, click **Receive Payments**. In **Received From**, select Cannon Healthcare and then click the two unpaid invoices illustrated in Figure 8:56. You will receive a message that is explained in the next step.

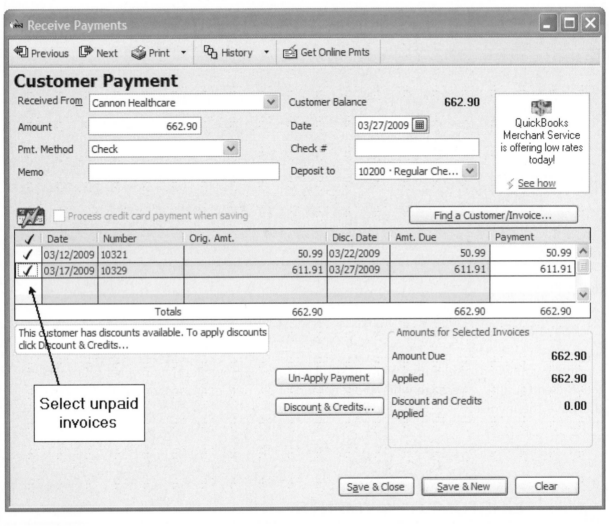

Figure 8:56

2. Because you did not enter an Amount first, QBP prompts to tell you that it can calculate the amount based on the invoices selected. Mark the option to turn off future messages and click **Yes**.

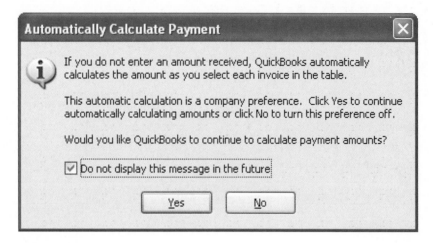

Figure 8:57

3. Change the **Date** to "3/27/2009" and enter "875" as the **Check #**.

4. The completed entry is illustrated in Figure 8:58.

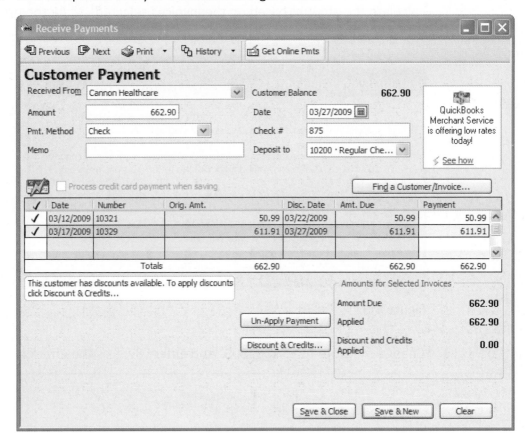

Figure 8:58

Notice that the payment will post (i.e., debit) to **10200 Regular Checking** and the **Pmt Method** defaulted to **Check**.

If needed, the **Un-Apply Payment** button at the bottom is a quick way to clear selected invoices. You can also click an invoice to clear its selection.

5. Click **Save & Close** to post the payment.

BEHIND THE KEYS OF A POSTED CUSTOMER PAYMENT

Now trace the audit trail for the payment posted in the previous topic. Recall that in the *MAPS* topic at the beginning of the chapter we explained that customer payments are recorded on the Cash Receipts Journal and then posted to customer accounts and general ledger accounts.

So let's begin by opening the Cash Receipts Journal. On the main menu, select **Reports>> Memorized Reports>>Accounting Journals>>Cash Receipts Journal**. Enter the date range of **From 3/27/2009** and **To 3/27/2009**. The refreshed report is shown in Figure 8:59.

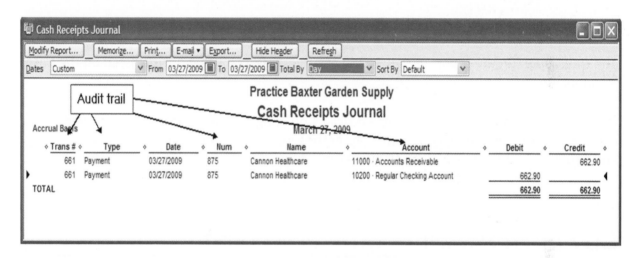

Figure 8:59

Note the **Trans #** and **Type** for Cannon's payment. *(Note: Your Trans # number may vary based on the number of transactions recorded thus far.)* Now trace this entry to the customer's account.

Close the report, discarding any changes. On the main menu, select **Reports>>Customers & Receivables>>Transaction List by Customer**.

Enter the date range of **From** 3/27/2009 and **To** 3/27/2009. Click **Modify Report** and select **Trans #** under **Columns**. Click **OK**.

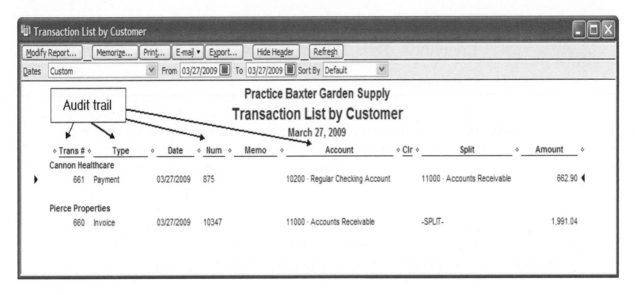

Figure 8:60

The transaction on the report in Figure 8:60 has the same **Trans #** and **Type** listed on the Cash Receipts Journal.

Close this report and complete tracing entries by opening the memorized report named **General Ledger Detail Report**. Locate your entries made to accounts 10200 Regular Checking and 11000 Accounts Receivable (not illustrated).

CUSTOMER PAYMENTS WITH A DISCOUNT

In this topic you continue posting customer payments. This time the customer is paying within the discount period.

On March 25, 2009, Franklin Botanical paid Invoices 10326 and 10328 with check number "1983" for $3,142.68. Record this transaction.

STEPS TO PROCESS CUSTOMER PAYMENT WITH A DISCOUNT

1. On the **Home** page, click **Receive Payments** and select **Franklin Botanical**. Change the **Date** to "3/25/09"and enter "1983" as the **Check #**. Click to select Invoice **10328** and then click the **Discount and Credits** button.

2. The Discount and Credits window shows that the invoice carries discount terms. Select the **Discount Account** illustrated in Figure 8:61 and click **Done**.

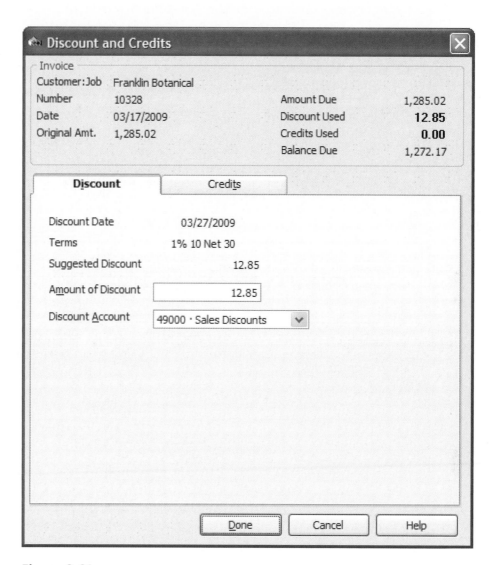

Figure 8:61

3. Now select Invoice **10326** and click the **Discount and Credits** to see that this invoice also carries a discount. Click **Done**.

4. The completed entry is shown in Figure 8:62. Click **Save & Close.**

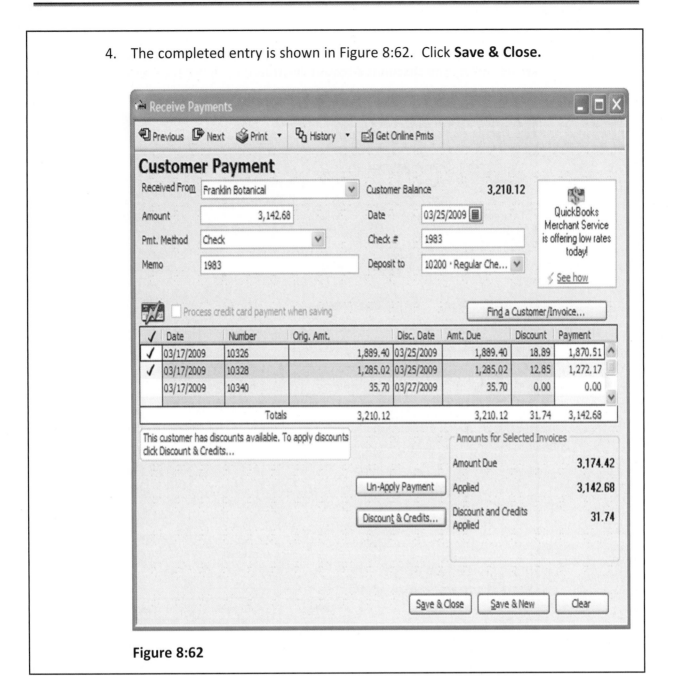

Figure 8:62

5. Companies selling merchandise may wait until the end of the day to post storefront sales as one entry for entire cash sales that day. As illustrated in the *Storefront Sales of Merchandise* topic, these receipts are entered using the **Create Sales Receipts** icon. Click this icon to open the window illustrated in Figure 8:63.

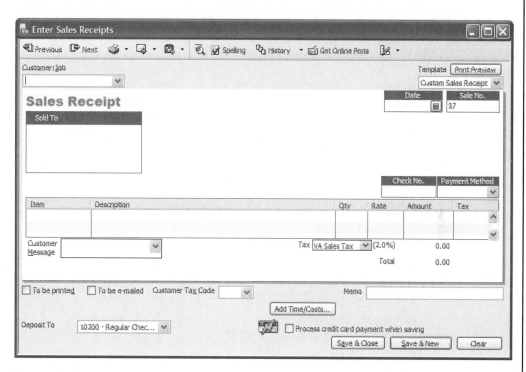

Figure 8:63

6. Select **Retail Cash Sales** as the customer and enter the **Date** of "3/31/2009". In **Payment Method**, look up and select **Cash**.

7. Placing your cursor in the **Item** field, look up and select "AVRY-10050-SM-EFL." Enter "5" as the **Qty**. Verify that the **Deposit To** field is 10200 Regular Checking.

8. The completed entry is shown in Figure 8:64. In theory, the company would continue selecting inventory items until all sales activity for the day is recorded. If a high level of sales activity occurs then this method can be time consuming so it may be better to record each sale as it occurs.

The entry below will post in the Cash Receipts Journal as a debit to 10200 Regular Checking, a debit to 50001 Product Cost-Aviary, a credit to 13000 Inventory, a credit to 23100 Sales Tax Payable, and a credit to 40001 Sales Aviary.

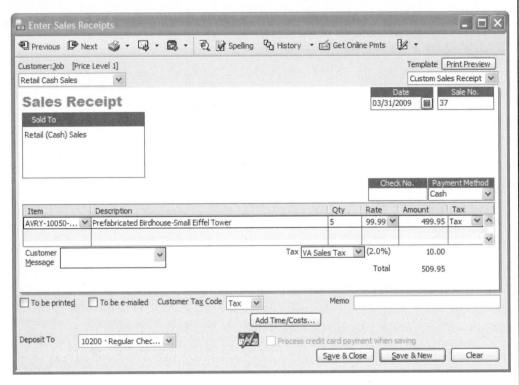

Figure 8:64

9. Click **Save & Close**.

CORRECTING CUSTOMER PAYMENTS

QBP permits editing and deleting customer payments and the next steps show how to correct a customer payment.

1. Using the Customer Center, locate the payment on the customer's account.

2. Double click the payment to reopen.

3. Edit the payment and then click Save & Close to post the changes.

To delete, you would follow steps 1 and 2 and then select **Edit>>Delete Payment** on the main menu. However, you should be careful when deleting payments after reconciling the bank statement. See Appendix B for an explanation on the effect of deleting deposits after reconciling bank statements.

RECORD CUSTOMER PAYMENTS

On March 30, 2009, the following payments were deposited:

Chapple Law Offices check number 8565 for $7,860.28 for Invoices 10313 and 10345

Snyder Securities check number 9092 for $1,000.00 on Invoice 10127

Note: Snyder did not pay the invoice in full so select the underpayment option that will Leave this as an underpayment.

Post these payments. Print the Cash Receipts Journal filtered for the date range of 3/30/2009 to 3/30/2009.

CUSTOMER CREDITS

Occasionally Baxter may need to issue a credit for returned inventory. In the exercise that follows, Baxter issues a credit to Mosley Country Club for the return of three window planter boxes, item "POTS-30200," on Invoice 10342.

STEPS TO ENTER A CUSTOMER CREDIT MEMO

1. On the **Home** page, click **Refunds & Credits**.

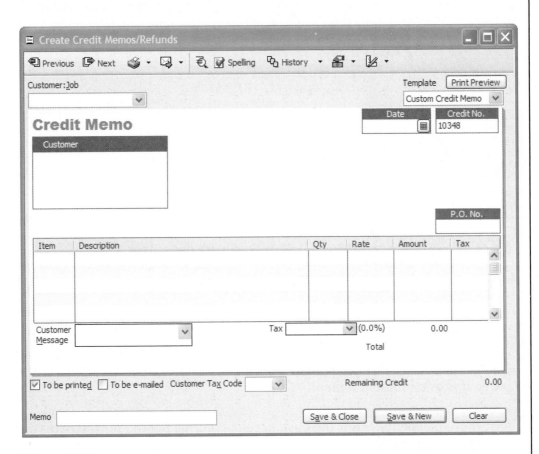

Figure 8:65

2. Select **Mosley Country Club** and enter "3/31/2009" as the **Date**.

3. In **Item**, select "POTS-30200" and enter "3" as the **QTY**. The completed credit is shown in Figure 8:66.

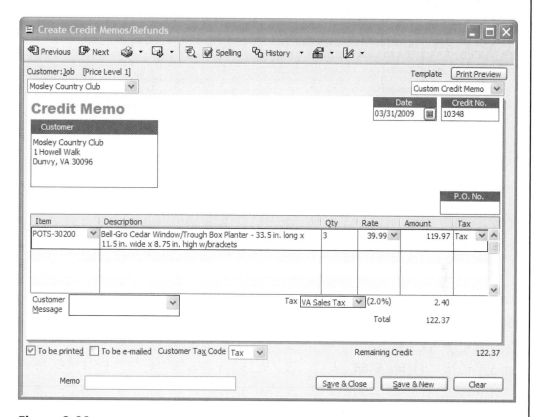

Figure 8:66

4. Click **Save & Close** and QBP prompts for instructions on handling the refund. Select the option illustrated in Figure 8:67 and click **OK**.

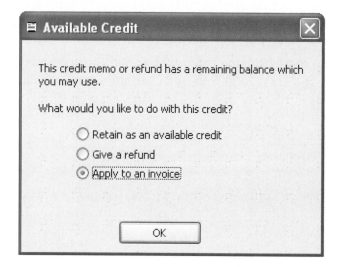

Figure 8:67

5. On the window illustrated in Figure 8:68, click to deselect **Invoice 10108** and then click **Invoice 10342** to select it. Click **Done**.

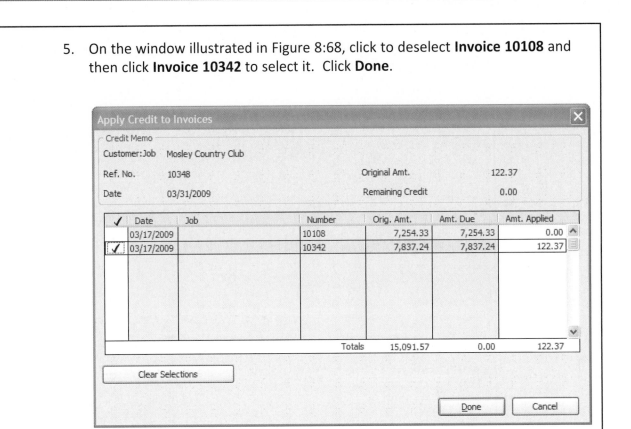

Figure 8:68

CUSTOMER REPORTING AND RECONCILING ACTIVITIES

QBP offers a variety of customer reports and these reports can be viewed from the **Report Center**. Open this center and select the **Customers & Receivables** area.

Click **Summary** in the **A/R Aging** category to open the accounts receivable aging report. Change the date to "3/31/2009." Refresh and the report displays as illustrated in Figure 8:69.

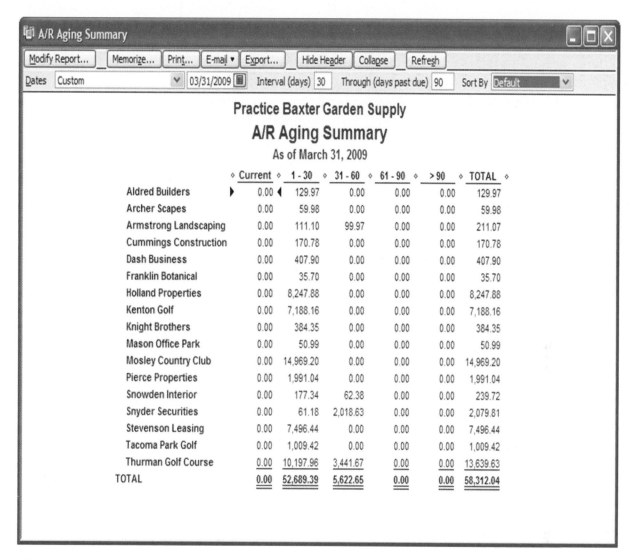

Figure 8:69

This report lists customer outstanding balances by age of the balance. *(Note: Your balances will differ from those illustrated if you have not completed all chapter exercises.)*

The report serves two important purposes. First, Baxter uses it to monitor customer payments and manage company cash flow, thus, mitigating the risk of future sales to customers failing to pay.

Second, this report is used to reconcile customer activities with the accounts receivable control account. This task is performed by comparing the report's total amount due with the March ending balance in general ledger account 11000 Accounts Receivable. Close this report.

Now view the balance in accounts receivable. Open the **Trial Balance** report from the **Accountant & Taxes** category in the **Report Center** and filter the report for 3/31/2009 (not illustrated). Scroll down and locate the balance in 11000 Accounts Receivable. The total on the A/R Aging report and the balance in Accounts Receivable on the Trial Balance must agree to verify proper recording of customer activities.

These balances can become out of balance when you improperly correct customer transactions. Therefore, always correct customer transactions by referring to the instructions in Appendix B.

You should reconcile the aged receivables report to the accounts receivable balance at the end of every month and prior to issuing financial reports. Close this report.

Return to the **A/R Aging** category to open the **Detail A/R Aging** report (not illustrated). This report lists invoices by invoice age. Close this report and the Report Center.

WRITE OFF A CUSTOMER INVOICE

You will find that customers do not always pay. Furthermore, customers sometimes pay the wrong amount. Instead of calling a payment error to the customer's attention, Baxter has decided to write off the invoice balance.

The instructions that follow write off an invoice balance while recording the payment. The instructions in Chapter 4 illustrated writing off the balance after posting the payment.

STEPS TO WRITE OFF A CUSTOMER'S INVOICE

1. On the **Home** page, click **Receive Payments**. Complete the window as illustrated in Figure 8:70.

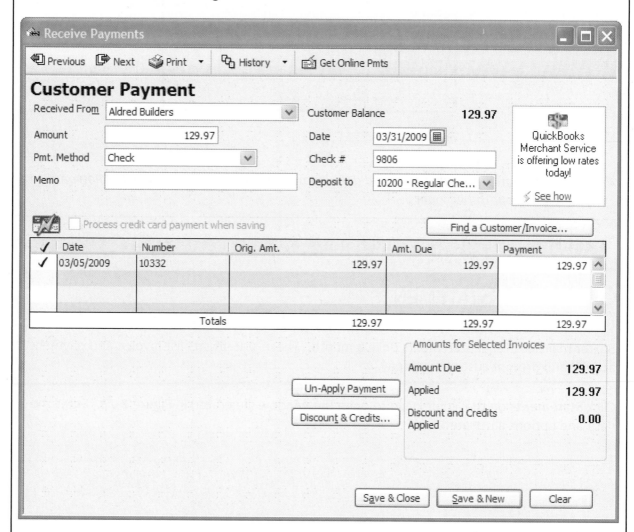

Figure 8:70

2. Now change **Amount** to 129.87 and the window in Figure 8:72 opens. Select the option shown.

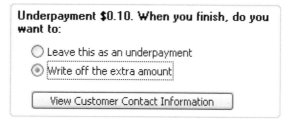

Figure 8:71

3. Click **Save & Close** and the window in Figure 8:73 opens for you to select the write-off posting account. Select the account shown and click **OK**.

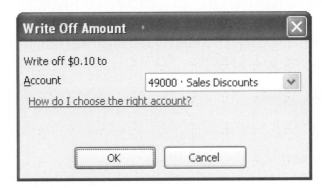

Figure 8:72

Note: If writing off a bad debt invoice then you would use 11100 Allowance for Doubtful Accounts.

CUSTOMER STATEMENTS

Baxter mails customer statements once a month. These statements list invoice and payment activity and prompt customers to pay.

Click **Statements** on the Home page to open the window illustrated in Figure 8:73. Enter the date and options illustrated.

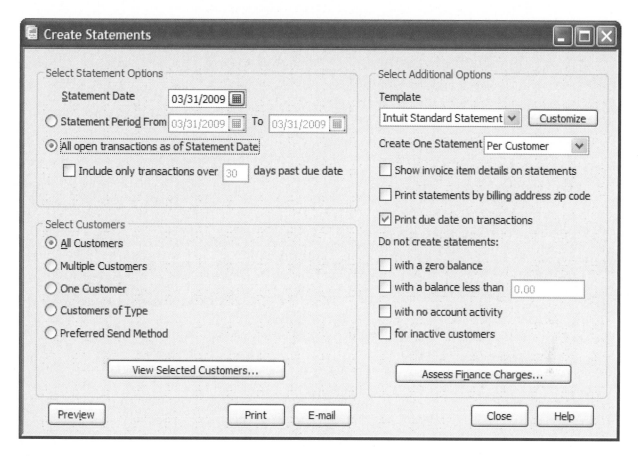

Figure 8:73

Click **Preview** and the first statement appears. (See Figure 8:74)

Statement

Practice Baxter Garden Supply
1352 W. Maple Ave
Arlington, VA 23523

Date
03/31/2009

To:

Archer Scapes and Ponds
778 Oakland Parkway
Arlington, VA 30092

Amount Due	Amount Enc.
$59.98	

Date	Transaction	Amount	Balance
03/05/2009	INV #10329. Due 04/04/2009. Orig. Amount $59.98.	59.98	59.98

CURRENT	1-30 DAYS PAST DUE	31-60 DAYS PAST DUE	61-90 DAYS PAST DUE	OVER 90 DAYS PAST DUE	Amount Due
0.00	59.98	0.00	0.00	0.00	$59.98

Figure 8:74

The window indicates that 16 statements will print.

Click **Print** and, when prompted to verify that statements printed correctly, click **Yes**.

When QBP prompts to remind you that statements can also be emailed, check the option to turn off future messages and click **OK**.

Click **Close** to exit the window.

You have now completed the chapter. *Make a backup of the Practice Baxter Garden Supply data file to a backup file named "Practice Baxter Garden Supply Chpt 8". In the next chapter, you will build on the work completed in this chapter.*

SUMMARY

In this chapter you learned *MAPS* for customer transactions before entering transactions in QBP. By understanding manual entries, you were able to anticipate QBP's *Behind the Keys* entries. Understanding a transaction's effect on financial accounts is critical to posting transactions correctly and to tracing the audit trail of a posted transaction.

After completing this chapter, you are skilled in recording customer invoices, payments, and credit memos for a merchandising business. You can manage the master accounts linked to transactions (i.e., customer accounts and inventory items). You understand the customer, inventory, and sales reports that let you monitor and document customer activities. With firm knowledge on processing customer activities, you are now ready to take on Baxter's vendor activities in the next chapter.

END-OF-CHAPTER QUESTIONS

TRUE/FALSE

_____   1. QBP will post costs of goods sold at the time of saving a sales invoice for merchandise.

_____   2. The Sales Journal report will display customer credit memo transactions.

_____   3. When a customer pays for inventory at the time of sale, QBP posts entries to the inventory account but not to accounts receivable.

_____   4. Adjustments to quantities of on-hand merchandise are posted as journal entries.

_____   5. Companies do not need to conduct a physical inventory because QBP stores on-hand inventory quantities.

_____   6. QBP uses the date entered on a customer payment to determine if a customer has remitted payment within the discount period.

_____   7. QBP will email sales invoices.

_____   8. Customer statements list the age of an invoice.

_____   9. QBP offers the LIFO, FIFO, and average cost methods of valuing inventory.

_____   10. You must delete the original customer payment transaction and reenter it to correct the transaction date.

MULTIPLE CHOICE

_____   1. Saving a sales invoice will post entries to the _____ accounts.
   a. sales and accounts receivable
   b. sales, accounts receivable, and cost of goods sold
   c. sales, accounts receivable, cost of goods sold, and inventory
   d. none of the above

_____   2. Saving a cash sale of merchandise will post entries to the _____ accounts.
   a. cash, accounts receivable, and sales
   b. cash, accounts receivable, inventory, and cost of goods sold
   c. cash, sales, inventory, and cost of goods sold
   d. none of the above

_____ 3. Saving a credit memo posts entries to the _____ accounts.
   a. sales and accounts receivable
   b. sales, accounts receivable, and cost of goods sold
   c. sales, accounts receivable, and inventory
   d. sales, accounts receivable, cost of goods sold, and inventory

_____ 4. Which report will let you analyze the retail value of inventory?
   a. Inventory Valuation Summary
   b. Inventory Valuation Detail
   c. Inventory Stock Status by Item
   d. Both a and b

_____ 5. An inventory valuation report can be used to _____.
   a. view the cost value of an item
   b. reconcile inventory values to the general ledger
   c. see on-hand quantities as of a specific date
   d. all of the above

_____ 6. Reports needed to document the audit trail of a posted sales invoice are the _____.
   a. General Journal and Sales Journal
   b. General Ledger Detail Report, Transaction List by Customer, and Sales Journal
   c. General Ledger, Customer Transaction History, and Cash Receipts Journal
   d. General Journal, Transaction List by Customer, and Sales Journal

_____ 7. The A/R Aging Summary report _____.
   a. is used to reconcile customer balances with the accounts receivable account
   b. lists customer balances by aging categories
   c. both a and b
   d. none of the above

PRACTICE SET

In this practice set you will be using the **Graded Baxter Garden Supply** data file customized with your initials at the end of Chapter 1. *If the company file is not loaded on your computer then restore it using the Graded Baxter Garden Supply Chpt 1.QBB backup file created in the Practice Set at the end of Chapter 1.*

1. Open **Graded Baxter Garden Supply** and enter Baxter's April customer activities listed below.

    Unless instructed otherwise, do not change default terms, tax code, or price level.

    Unless instructed otherwise, transactions will be printed in Step 2 so make sure that invoices are marked *"To be printed."*

2009

Apr 2   Received check number 1077 for $211.07 from Armstrong Landscaping paying Invoices 10326, 10336, and 10339.

Apr 3   Issue Invoice 10346 to Rose University Invoice for $519.88 for the following items.

QTY	Item	Price Each
2	EQLW-14160	$ 59.99
10	EQWT-15120	$ 39.99

Apr 7   Issue Invoice 10347 to Knight Brothers Nurseries for $7,099.20 for the following items.

QTY	Item	Price Each
30	AVRY-10130	$ 19.99
50	EQWT-15100	129.99

Apr 9   Issue Invoice 10348 to Franklin Botanical Gardens for $2,019.42 for the following
               items.

QTY	Item	Price Each
10	EQLW-14110	$ 149.99
8	EQLW-14160	59.99

               Received check number 463 for $7,254.33 from Mosley Country Club paying
               Invoice 10108.

               Received check number 255 for $13,639.63 from Thurman Golf Course Design
               paying Invoices 10119, 10130, and 10343.

Apr 10   Issue Invoice 10349 to Smith Family Garden Center for $13,397.10 for the
               following items.

QTY	Item	Price Each
30	EQLW-14140	$ 299.99
40	NURS-21900	55.95
60	POTS-30200	35.99 (Price Level 2)

Apr 16   Issue Invoice 10350 to Saia's Neighborhood Nursery for $4,499.10 for the
               following items.

QTY	Item	Price Each
60	SOIL-34160	$ 6.99
30	NURS-21810	16.99
30	NURS-23010	119.00

               Post Retail Cash Sales Receipt 38 for $713.80 paid in cash for the following items.
               Print customer receipt.

QTY	Item	Price Each
10	EQWT-15130	$ 19.99
10	TOOL-35300	49.99

Apr 17   Received check number 735 for $5,209.35 from Franklin Botanical Gardens
               paying Invoices 10326, 10328, 10340, and 10348 (with discount). Post discount
               to 49000 Sales Discounts.

Apr 23   Received the following checks:

                Check number 234 for $7,188.16 from Kenton Golf and Tennis Center paying
                Invoices 10338 and 10324.

                Check number 6725 for $7,860.28 from Chapple Law Offices paying Invoices
                10313 and 10345.

Apr 24   Issue Invoice 10351 to Golden Gardens for $13,069.18 for the following items.

QTY	Item	Price Each
30	EQLW-14180	$ 299.99
20	EQWT-15150	16.99
17	EQWT-15170	23.99
35	FERT-16100	8.99
30	NURS-21820	16.99
50	NURS-22000	49.95

Apr 28   Create the following new customer.

                Rose Gardens Supply
                603 W. Arndale Street
                Centerville, VA 30004
                (701) 555-8144

Contact:	Jeffrey Campbell
Customer Type:	WHOLE
Payment Terms:	Net 30
Sales Rep:	Derrick Gross
Tax Code:	Non
Price Level:	Price Level 1
Credit Limit:	$20,000

                Issue Invoice 10352 to the new customer for $149.85 for the following item.

QTY	Item	Price Each
15	EQFF-13120	$ 9.99

2. Print the following.

   a. Invoices 10346 through 10352. You can print using *File>>Print Forms>>Invoices* on the main menu. If you do not have seven invoices, totaling $40,753.73, then check that all invoices are marked "To be printed."

   b. Cash Receipts Journal for April 1 to April 30, 2009.

   c. Sales Journal for April 1 to April 30, 2009.

   d. Inventory Valuation Summary for April 30, 2009. Explain how you would use this report.

   e. A/R Aging Detail report at April 30, 2009. Explain how you would use this report.

   f. Customer statement for Rose Gardens Supply showing all open transactions. *(Note: Use the One Customer option under Select Customers.)*

3. ***Back up the Graded Baxter Garden Supply data file to a backup file named "Graded Graded Baxter Garden Supply Chpt 8". The Practice Set for the next chapter will build on the work completed in this chapter.***

CHAPTER 9   VENDOR ACTIVITIES FOR A MERCHANDISING BUSINESS

LEARNING OBJECTIVES

This chapter works with the **Practice Baxter Garden Supply** data file containing the tasks completed in Chapter 8. *If this company file is not loaded on your computer then restore it using the Practice Baxter Garden Supply Chpt 8.QBB backup file created after reading Chapter 8.*

In this chapter you process Baxter's vendor activities. Such activities include ordering goods, entering vendor bills and receipts of goods, and remitting vendor payments. While performing these activities, you will:

1. Review the *MAPS* for recording vendor transactions before posting transactions in QBP
2. Learn to use the Vendor Center to manage vendor activities
3. Record vendor purchase orders for inventory and learn to correct purchase order transactions
4. Record vendor bills and receipts for items on purchase orders
5. Go *Behind the Keys* to view posted bills and receipts and learn to correct these transactions
6. Record vendor bills for previously posted receipts
7. Learn to manage vendor accounts
8. Record vendor bills for expenses and memorize vendor bills and pay vendors
9. Go *Behind the Keys* to view vendor payments and learn to correct these transactions
10. Learn to write checks without recording a vendor bill, pay sales tax and enter vendor credits
11. Prepare and analyze vendor, purchasing, and inventory reports and reconcile vendor activities to the general ledger

Launch QBP and open **Practice Baxter Garden Supply**.

 ## MANUAL ACCOUNTING PROCEDURES

As in the previous chapter, you begin by learning manual accounting procedures (*MAPS*) for posting vendor activities before using QBP. These procedures help you to understand QBP transaction posting.

Before continuing, it helps to explain that Baxter uses purchase orders (POs) to order inventory. POs authorize inventory purchases and document purchased quantities and prices. A Baxter employee, with authorization to order, creates and signs the PO before sending it to the vendor. Thereafter, the vendor ships the order to Baxter's warehouse, enclosing a packing receipt. This receipt is then forwarded to the accounting department and filed until receiving a vendor bill.

When the bill arrives, the accountant matches it with the PO and receipt. This matching process verifies that the purchase was authorized and that billed quantities and prices agree to PO terms. The accountant then records the transaction.

On March 19, 2009, Sam Prather issues a PO to restock Baxter's supply of drip sprinklers. He orders 20 of EQWT-15100 drip sprinklers at $59.95 each from Southern Garden. Sam manually writes up the PO and then signs and sends it to Southern Garden. A copy of the PO is sent to Melvin in accounting, who files the document for matching with the vendor bill. POs do not trigger accounting recognition because the liability does not occur until receipt of the materials.

The vendor's shipment arrives on March 20. Inventory clerk, Al Duke, inspects the merchandise before placing items on warehouse shelves. Al then sends Southern Garden's packing receipt to Melvin, who files it with the PO until Southern Garden's bill arrives.

On March 24, Melvin receives the following bill.

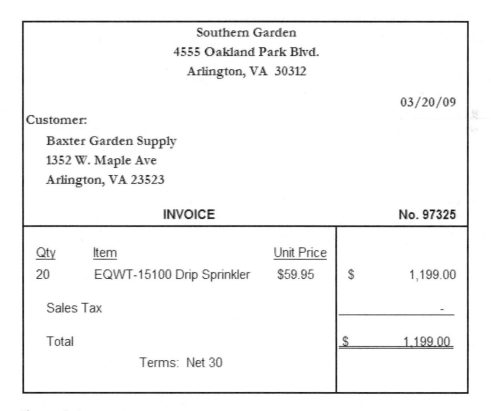

Figure 9:1

Melvin matches the bill with the receipt and the PO and then enters the bill in the Purchases Journal. Melvin's entries to the Purchases Journal for March 24 appear in Figure 9:2.

Note: Technically the liability to Southern Garden was incurred on March 20 (i.e., the day the merchandise was received). However, manual accounting procedures do not accommodate such semantics. It would be tedious to record the receipt and then to record the bill. Instead, bills are recorded to the Purchases Journal on the date of receiving the bill.

Baxter Garden Supply					
Date: 3/24/2009		Purchases Journal			Page 4
Vendor	Post Ref	Description	Accounts Payable (Credit)	Purchases (Debit)	Utilities Expense (Debit)
Southern Garden	SOUT001	Invoice 97325	1,199.00	1,199.00	
Neighbors Telephone	NEIGH001	March Phone	237.05		237.05
Hubbard Wholesale	HUBB001	Invoice 877	677.00	677.00	
Totals:			$ 2,113.05	$ 1,876.00	$ 237.05
Acct Ref:			(20000)	(50000)	(71100)

Audit Trail

Figure 9:2

Like the procedures used to enter transactions in the Sales Journal in Chapter 8, Melvin totals journal columns and cross-foots totals to verify that entries balance (i.e., debits equal credits). He then posts each invoice to the vendor's account and posts column totals to general ledger accounts listed at the bottom.

Melvin's entry to Southern Garden's vendor account is illustrated in Figure 9:3. *(Note: Entries for other vendor accounts are not illustrated.)*

Southern Garden					
4555 Oakland Park Blvd.	*Audit Trail*				
Arlington, Va 30312				Acct No:	SOUT001
Date	Description	Post Ref	Debit	Credit	Balance
03/01/09	Beginning Balance				0.00
03/24/09	Invoice 97325	PJ 4		1,199.00	1,199.00

Figure 9:3

Melvin's entries to general ledger accounts follow. *(Note: The entry for utilities is not shown.)*

General Ledger					
Accounts Payable					Account No. 20000
Date	Description	Post Ref	Debit	Credit	Balance
03/23/09	Balance Forward				51,506.21
03/24/09		PJ 4		2,113.05	53,619.26

Audit Trail

General Ledger					
Purchases					Account No. 50000
Date	Description	Post Ref	Debit	Credit	Balance
03/23/09	Balance Forward				24,668.25
03/24/09		PJ 4	1,876.00		26,544.25

Figure 9:4

The next day, Melvin reviews vendor bills and prepares checks for bills that are due. He also prepares a check to buy postage. Melvin records these checks on the Cash Disbursements Journal shown in Figure 9:5.

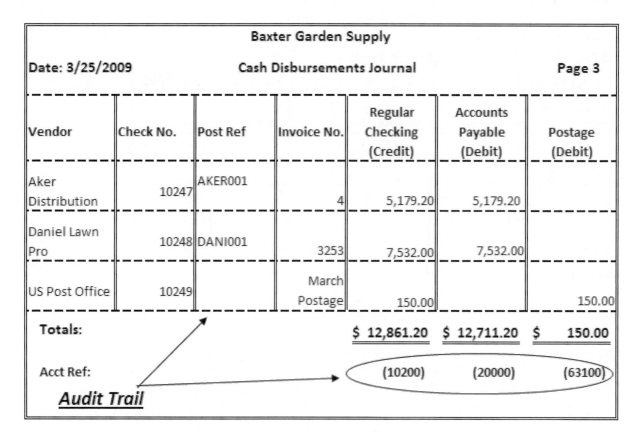

Figure 9:5

Like in the Purchases Journal, Melvin posts each check to a vendor account and column totals to general ledger accounts. He will use the posting reference of CDJ (Cash Disbursements Journal) along with the page number. *(Note: These postings are not illustrated.)*

As discussed in Chapter 8, the manual method is fraught with opportunities to make posting errors. Melvin could enter an amount incorrectly, post an entry backwards, or forget to post it altogether.

With an understanding of *MAPS* for vendor activities, you are now ready to use QBP for processing vendor transactions. The topic that follows will introduce you to the navigation center for these activities.

VENDOR CENTER

The Vendor Center focuses on vendor activities. Click **Vendors** on the **Home** page to open this center and select the options illustrated in Figure 9:6 so we can discuss its purpose.

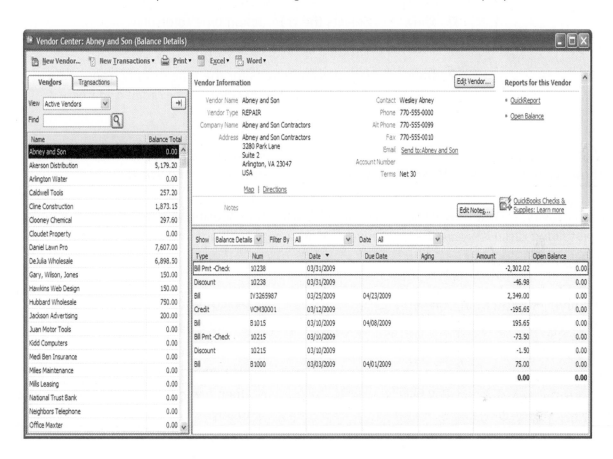

Figure 9:6

The **Vendors** tab lists transactions by vendor account. Baxter's vendor accounts and balances appear to the left. The tab's **View** option contains selections for viewing All Vendors, Active Vendors, or Vendors with Open Balances. You are currently viewing Active Vendors.

This ⇥ button hides the Vendor Information pane shown to the right. After hiding, this ⇤ button is located on the far right for redisplaying the information pane.

The **Vendor Information** pane displays transactions for the account highlighted on the left. This account is currently Abney and Son.

The **Edit Vendor** button edits Abney's account information and the **Edit Notes** button is for entering account notes. There are also hyperlinks for creating **Reports for this Vendor**.

Abney's transactions are listed at the bottom of its account information. The filtering options of **Show**, **Filter By**, and **Date** determine the transactions listed. Click ⌄ to access an option's dropdown list for changing selections. You are currently viewing **All Transactions** for **All Dates**. *(Note: Remember, if using fiscal year as the date then this is based on your computer date.)*

Filtering options work as follows:

❖ Show: Selects the transaction type to display

❖ Filter By: Filtering criteria for the type

❖ Date: List all transactions for the type or only transaction recorded as of a specific date or range of dates

Now turn your attention to activities that can be performed while the Vendor tab is active. These activities are **New Vendor**, **New Transactions**, **Print**, **Excel**, and **Word**.

Each activity, except New Vendor, has this ⌄ button for choosing a specific task. The table that follows discusses the tasks by activity. Most actions will operate on the vendor account highlighted on the left.

Vendors Activities	Tasks	Description
New Vendor		Create a new vendor account.
New Transactions	Enter Bills	Record a vendor bill for the highlighted vendor.
	Pay Bills	Open a window to select vendor bills to pay.
	Purchase Orders	Create a purchase order for the highlighted vendor.
	Receive Items and Enter Bills	Enter a receipt accompanied by a bill for items on a PO issued to the highlighted vendor.
	Receive Items	Enter a receipt for items on a PO issued to the highlighted vendor.
	Enter Bill for Received Items	Enter a bill for a receipt from the highlighted vendor.

Vendors Activities	Tasks	Description
Print	Vendor List	Print a vendor list with balances. The report cannot be customized so you should consider using the Reports menu to print this information.
	Vendor Information	Print account information and notes for the highlighted vendor. The report cannot be customized so you should consider using the Reports menu to print this information.
	Vendor Transaction List	Print the highlighted vendor's transactions for the current fiscal year. The report cannot be customized so you should consider using the Reports menu to print this information.
Excel	Export Vendor List	Create an Excel workbook or comma separated values (.csv) file containing all vendor information along with account balances.
	Export Transactions	Create an Excel workbook or comma separated values (.csv) file containing current fiscal year transactions for the highlighted vendor.
	Import from Excel	Import vendor information and/or transactions from an Excel workbook or comma separated values (.csv) file.
Word		Create form letters for communicating with a vendor.

Next turn your attention to the **Transactions** tab, which lists transactions by type instead of transactions by vendor. Click to activate the tab and select the options illustrated in Figure 9:7.

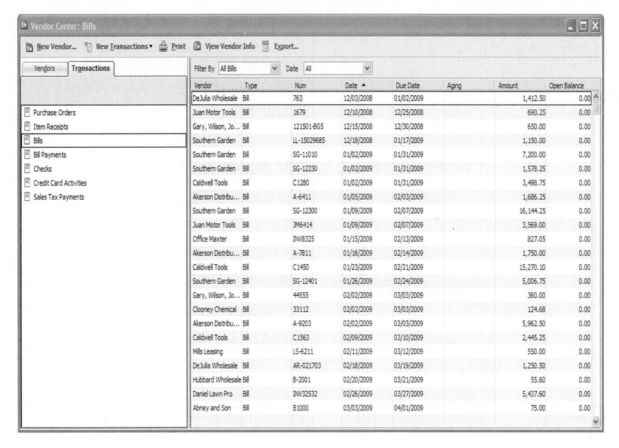

Figure 9:7

Transaction types are chosen on the left. You can sort the list by clicking a column name.

Activities that can be performed from this tab are different from those performed on the previous tab. First, only the New Transactions activity offers multiple tasks so clicking other activities immediately opens the task. The following table discusses activities on this tab.

Transactions Activities	Description
New Vendor	Create a new vendor account.
New Transactions	Contains the same tasks as the Vendors tab but the user must select the customer.
Print	Print the transactions listed to the right.
View Vendor Info	Edit the vendor account associated with the transaction highlighted on the right.
Export	Create an Excel workbook or comma separated values (.csv) file containing transactions listed on the right.

This illustrates that you can perform a variety of activities from the Vendor Center. You can initiate transactions, locate posted transactions, manage accounts, and create new accounts. Close the Vendor Center.

In contrast, the **Vendors** section (Figure 9:8) of the **Home** page only initiates transactions, but offers quick access to such tasks. In addition, you can always use the *Vendors* menu to perform vendor activities.

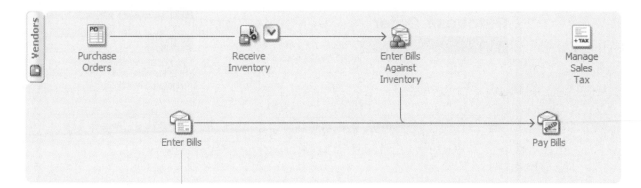

Figure 9:8

Now that you are familiar with locating vendor activities, let's begin recording vendor transactions.

PURCHASE ORDERS

As previously discussed, POs authorize vendor purchases. Recall from the *MAPS* topic that Sam created a PO to restock drip sprinklers. Follow the next steps and capture this transaction in QBP.

STEPS TO CREATE A PURCHASE ORDER

1. On the **Home** page, click the **Purchase Orders** icon to open the window illustrated in Figure 9:9.

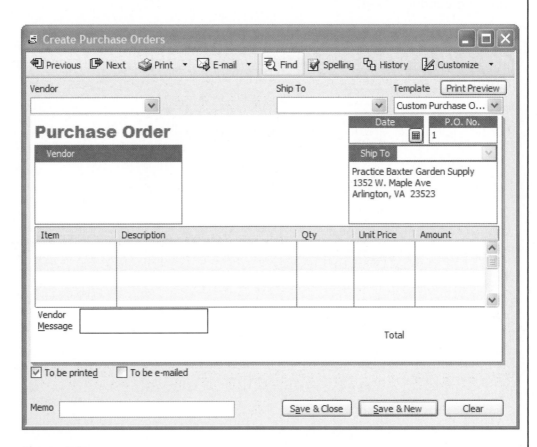

Figure 9:9

2. In **Vendor ID**, look up and select "Southern Garden." In **Date**, enter "3/19/2009". In **P.O. No.**, enter "280".

3. In **Item**, look up and select "EQWT-15100". Tab to **Qty** and enter "20".
    Press Tab again. Figure 9:10 shows the completed PO.

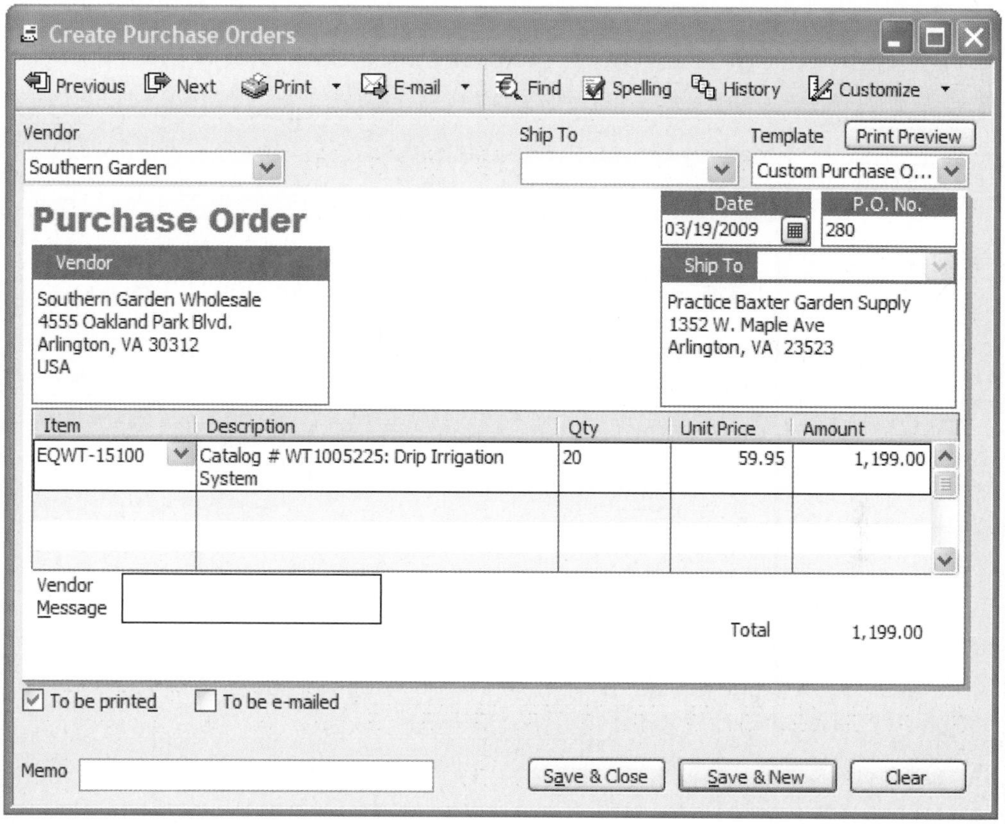

Figure 9:10

4. Click the lookup on **Print** and select **Preview**. If prompted with
    information on shipping labels then select the option to turn off future
    messages and click **OK**.

    Figure 9:11 shows the previewed PO.

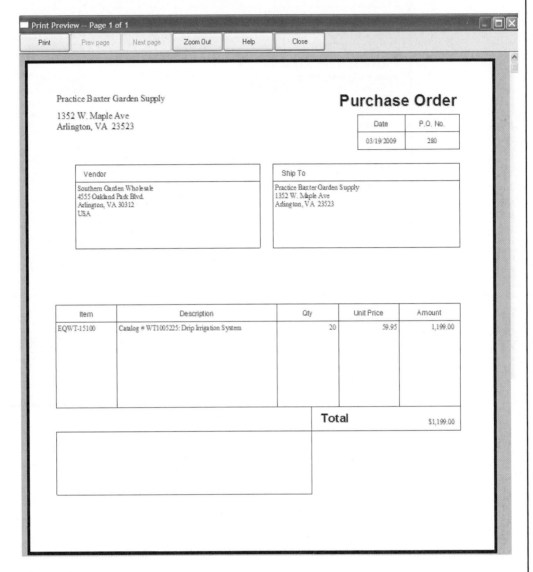

Figure 9:11

5. Click **Print** to send the order to the default printer.

    *Note: If you want to select a different printer then click Close to exit the
    preview window and click Print on the transaction window.*

6. Click **Save & New** and click **Yes** to save the changes. *(Note: The change
    occurred because QBP removed the checkmark from To be printed.)*

7. Enter the information shown in Figure 9:12.

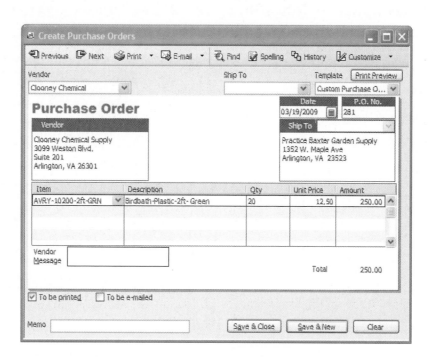

Figure 9:12

8. Click **Print**, make a printer selection, and click **Print** again.

9. Click **Save & Close** and click **Yes** to save the changes.

    Remember that POs do not post because these documents are merely commitments to purchase. Accounting recognition occurs after receiving items on the PO.

CORRECTING A PURCHASE ORDER

You can correct information on a saved PO as long as Baxter has not received items on the order.

First, locate the PO using the **Vendor Center**. Click **Vendors** on the **Home** page to open the center.

Next, select the **Transactions** tab and click **Purchase Orders** on the left.

Finally, locate the **Clooney Chemical** transaction on the right and doubleclick to reopen (Figure 9:13). Notice that after saving the PO, QBP added the **Rcv'd** and **Clsd** columns.

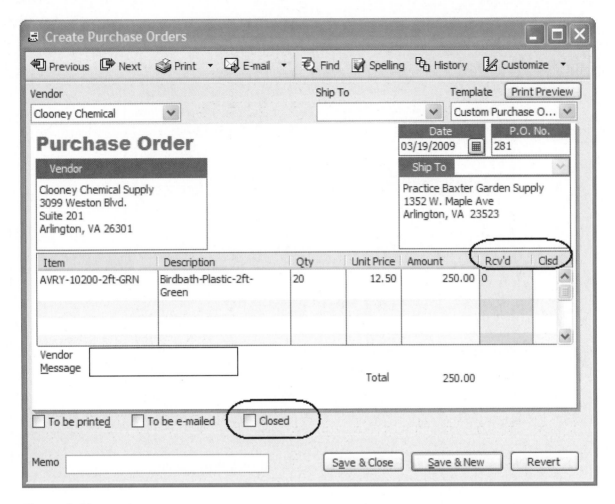

Figure 9:13

The **Rcv'd** field stores the quantity received for each line item. When all quantities ordered for a line item have been received, QBP marks the line item as **Clsd**.

Notice that there is also a **Closed** option for the entire PO located at the bottom. QBP marks this option after receiving all line items in full.

As long as all line items remain open, you can change information and even delete the PO. If needed, POs are deleted by using **Edit>>Delete Purchase Order** on the main menu.

Click **X** to exit the PO window. Now try the next exercise.

ENTER PURCHASE ORDERS

On March 23, 2009, Baxter issued the following POs to restock inventory. Do not print individual POs. You will print them altogether after saving the transactions so verify that *To be printed* is selected.

PO 282 for $719.00 to DeJulia Wholesale Suppliers for the following goods:

Item	Qty	Short Description	Unit Price
AVRY-10120	20	Bird House-Red	$35.95

PO 283 for $431.25 to Abney and Son Contractors for the following goods:

Item	Qty	Short Description	Unit Price
AVRY-10050-LG-EFL	15	Bird House-Large Eiffel	$ 17.25
AVRY-10050-LG-CSL	10	Bird House-Large Castle	$ 17.25

Close the Purchase Order window and print the POs.

To print the POs, select *File>>Print Forms>>Purchase Orders* on the main menu. Verify that both POs are selected and click **OK**. Select a printer and click **Print**.

After printing, click **OK** in the print confirmation window.

VENDOR RECEIPTS AND BILLS FOR PURCHASE ORDERS

From the *MAPS* topic you will recall that vendors ship orders to Baxter's warehouse enclosing a packing receipt with the merchandise. When Southern Garden's order arrived, Al inspected the merchandise and then sent the packing receipt to Melvin in accounting. Melvin filed the receipt until the vendor's bill arrived.

With QBP, Melvin now records the packing receipt as a receipt of inventory. Two benefits flow from immediately recording the receipt. First, inventory assets are recorded when possession takes place and quantities of on-hand inventory are immediately updated. Second, the liability is recognized when the obligation to pay occurs.

Follow the next steps and record Baxter's receipt of Southern Garden's shipment of merchandise ordered on PO 280.

STEPS TO RECORD A VENDOR RECEIPT FOR ITEMS ON A PURCHASE ORDER

1. Click **Receive Inventory** on the Home page and select **Receive Inventory without Bill** to open the window in Figure 9:14.

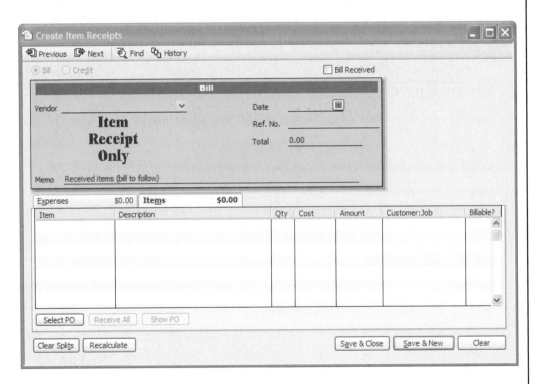

Figure 9:14

Note that there are two tabs. The **Expenses** tab is for recording non-inventory purchases such as utility and insurance bills. The **Items** tab is for recording receipt of inventory items.

On receipt transactions the **Bill Received** option will not be marked and the **Memo** will indicate that this is a receipt transaction with bill to follow.

2. In **Vendor**, look up and select "Southern Garden." Click **Yes** when QBP prompts to receive against the PO.

3.   In the window illustrated in Figure 9:15, click **PO No 280** and then click **OK**.

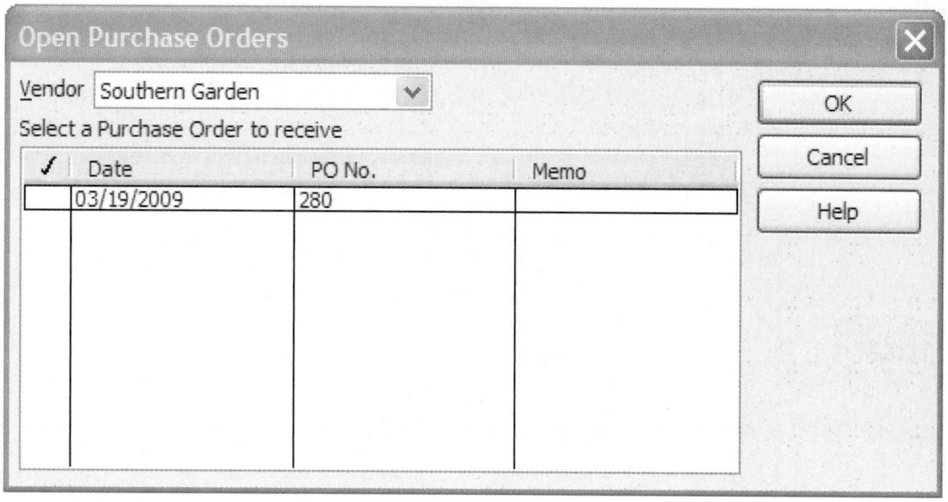

Open Purchase Orders

Vendor Southern Garden ▾

Select a Purchase Order to receive

✓	Date	PO No.	Memo
	03/19/2009	280	

OK

Cancel

Help

Figure 9:15

4. The **Date** of receipt is March 20, 2009. In **Ref. No.** enter the vendor's receipt number of "RCT3217".

Figure 9:16 shows the completed receipt.

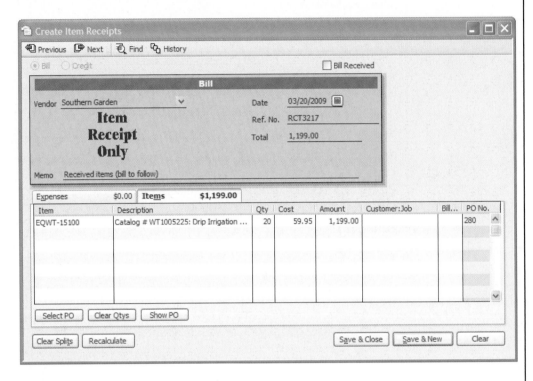

Figure 9:16

Before saving, review the following fields on this transaction.

Qty stores the number of items received.

Customer:Job and **Billable** are job costing fields that were illustrated in Chapter 5 and will not be used in this chapter.

Select PO reopens the window to change the selected PO.

Clear Qtys deletes values in the Qty field.

Show PO opens the original PO transaction.

5. Now click the **Expenses** tab to see if a general ledger account is present. If you ever receive the following message when saving a transaction then check for the Retained Earnings account on the Expenses tab. You can remove this account by highlighting and pressing Delete on the keyboard.

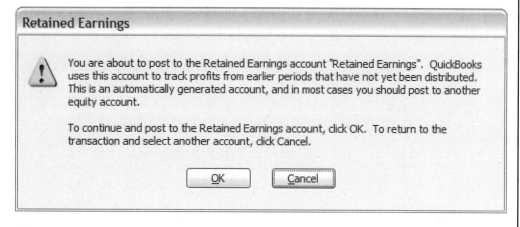

Retained Earnings

⚠ You are about to post to the Retained Earnings account "Retained Earnings". QuickBooks uses this account to track profits from earlier periods that have not yet been distributed. This is an automatically generated account, and in most cases you should post to another equity account.

To continue and post to the Retained Earnings account, click OK. To return to the transaction and select another account, click Cancel.

[OK]   [Cancel]

Figure 9:17

6. Click **Save and Close**.

This transaction posted entries to the inventory and accounts payable accounts. You will trace these entries in the next topic.

Unlike the manual system where the vendor bill was recorded to the Purchases Journal on March 24 (i.e., the day the bill arrived), Baxter now recognizes the transaction on the actual date of incurring the liability (i.e., March 20).

We have one more task before leaving this topic. Vendors will sometimes enclose a bill with the merchandise shipment in place of the packing receipt. When this occurs, you will record the bill and bypass recording the receipt.

The next exercise records a vendor bill for PO items.

STEPS TO RECORD A VENDOR BILL FOR ITEMS ON A PURCHASE ORDER

1. On the **Home** page, click **Receive Inventory** and this time select **Receive Inventory with Bill** to open the window illustrated in Figure 9:18.

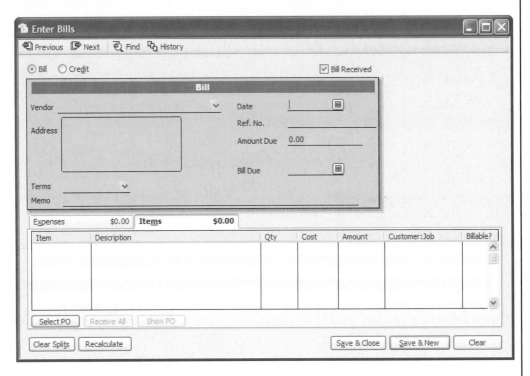

Figure 9:18

2. Look up "Clooney Chemical" as the **Vendor**. Click **Yes** when QBP prompts to receive against the PO.

3. In the next window (Figure 9:19), click **PO No 281** and click **OK**.

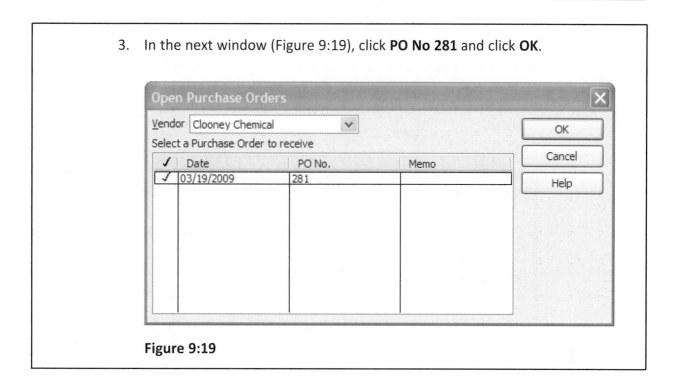

Figure 9:19

4. Baxter also received these goods on March 20, 2009 so enter this as the **Date**. Enter Clooney's invoice number of "1265" in the **Ref. No.** field.

    Figure 9:20 shows the bill you have entered. Notice that **Bill Received** is marked.

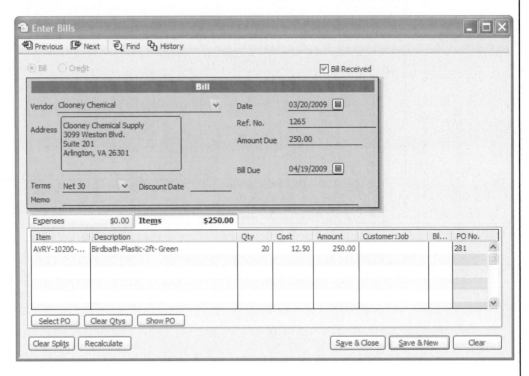

Figure 9:20

5. Click **Save and Close**.

BEHIND THE KEYS OF A POSTED VENDOR RECEIPT AND BILL

Transactions in the previous topic posted entries to the Purchases Journal, vendor accounts, and general ledger accounts. Follow the next steps to trace those entries.

STEPS TO TRACE THE ENTRIES FOR A VENDOR BILL AND A VENDOR RECEIPT

1. First, open the Purchases Journal report by selecting **Reports>>Memorized Reports>>Accounting Journals>>Purchases Journal** on the main menu. Enter the date range of **From** "3/20/2009" and **To** "3/20/2009".

    Figure 9:21 shows the refreshed report, listing both **Bill** and **Item Receipt** transactions. The report contains the transactions posted previously as well as bills from DeJulia Wholesale and Sulley Printing. Note the audit trail codes in **Trans #** and **Type** and then close the report.

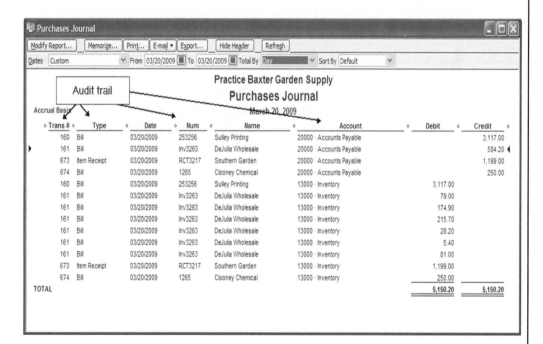

Figure 9:21

2. Now trace the entries to vendor accounts.

    Select **Reports>>Vendors & Payables>>Transaction List by Vendor** on the main menu. Enter the date range of **From** "3/20/2009" and **To** "3/20/2009".

    Click **Modify Report** and add the **Trans #** column. Click **OK** and the report appears as illustrated in Figure 9:22.

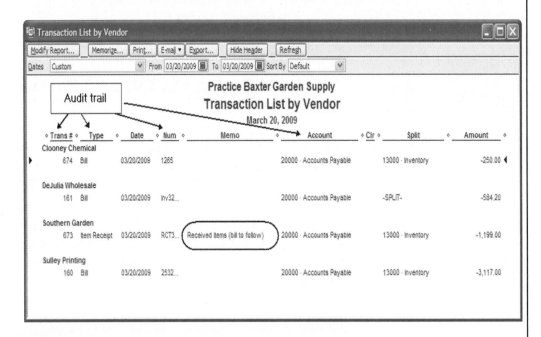

Figure 9:22

Notice that the **Trans #** and **Type** audit trail codes cross-reference to the audit trail codes in the **Purchases Journal**.

Close this report.

3.   Finally, verify QBP's entries to the general ledger.

Select **Reports>>Memorized Reports>>Accounting Journals>>General Ledger Detail Report** on the main menu. Enter March 20, 2009 as the date range.

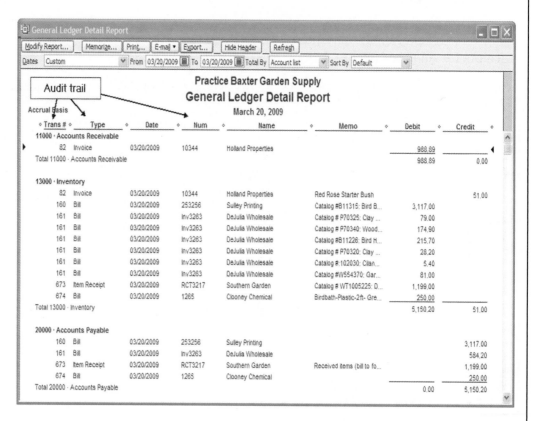

Figure 9:23

You can locate your entries by looking for the audit trail code. Close the report when finished.

CORRECTING A VENDOR RECEIPT OR BILL

QBP permits modifying and deleting vendor receipts and bills. Use the **Vendor Center** to locate transactions.

Open this center and, on the **Vendors** tab, highlight **Southern Garden**. Filter to **Show Item Receipts** for **All** dates (Figure 9:24).

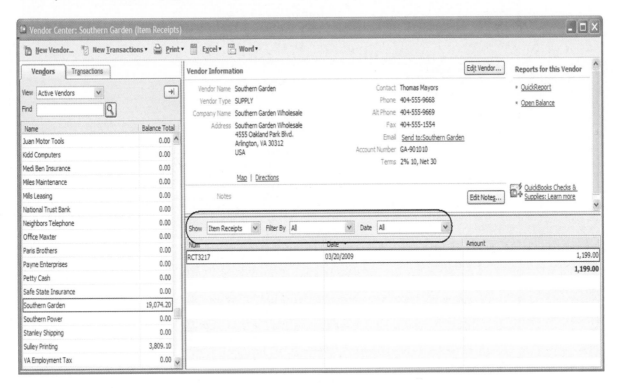

Figure 9:24

After reopening a receipt or bill, you can modify it and save the changes. You can also delete bills and receipts using *Edit* on the main menu. After deleting, QBP will reinstate POs used to create the transaction so you can receive items again.

Caution: You should not modify or delete paid bills because the payment will no longer match the bill. Instead, void the payment and then delete the bill. We will show you how to void payments later in the chapter.

Remember Appendix B provides a complete set of instructions on correcting QBP transactions.

ENTER VENDOR RECEIPTS AND BILLS FOR PURCHASE ORDERS

On March 24, 2009, Baxter receives the following shipments. Record the transactions.

DeJulia Wholesale receipt number RCT0707 for PO 282:

Item	Qty	Unit Price
AVRY-10120	20	$35.95

Abney and Son Contractors bill number 5355 for PO 283:

Item	Qty	Unit Price	
AVRY-10050-LG-EFL	10	$ 17.25	(Not all items received)
AVRY-10050-LG-CSL	10	$ 17.25	

VENDOR BILLS FOR VENDOR RECEIPTS

You still need to post the vendor bill for Southern Garden's receipt recorded on March 20. The following instructions show you the steps to turn a receipt into a bill so you can pay the vendor.

STEPS TO RECORD A VENDOR BILL FOR A RECEIPT

1. On the **Home** page, click **Enter Bills Against Inventory**. As shown in Figure 9:25 look up and select **Southern Garden**.

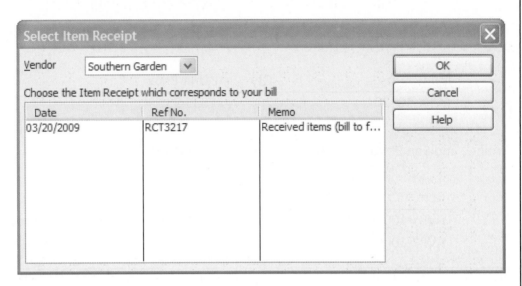

Figure 9:25

2. Highlight the receipt and click **OK**. Change the **Date** to "3/20/2009" and the **Ref. No.** to "97235".

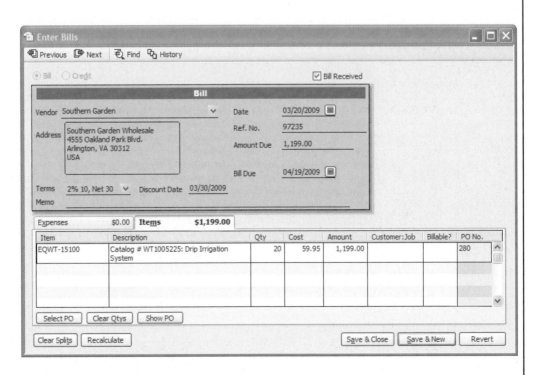

Figure 9:26

3. Click **Save & Close** and then click **Yes** to change the transaction.

ENTER VENDOR BILL FOR VENDOR RECEIPT

On March 31, 2009 Invoice "7631" from DeJulia Wholesale arrives for RCT0707. The bill is dated March 27, 2009. Record this transaction and print the Purchases Journal for March 27.

VENDOR ACCOUNTS

This topic explains creating, editing, and deleting vendor accounts. Open the **Vendor Center**, select the **Vendors** tab, and double click **Southern Garden** to open the account. Now follow below as we describe the tabs of the vendor account.

Address Info Tab

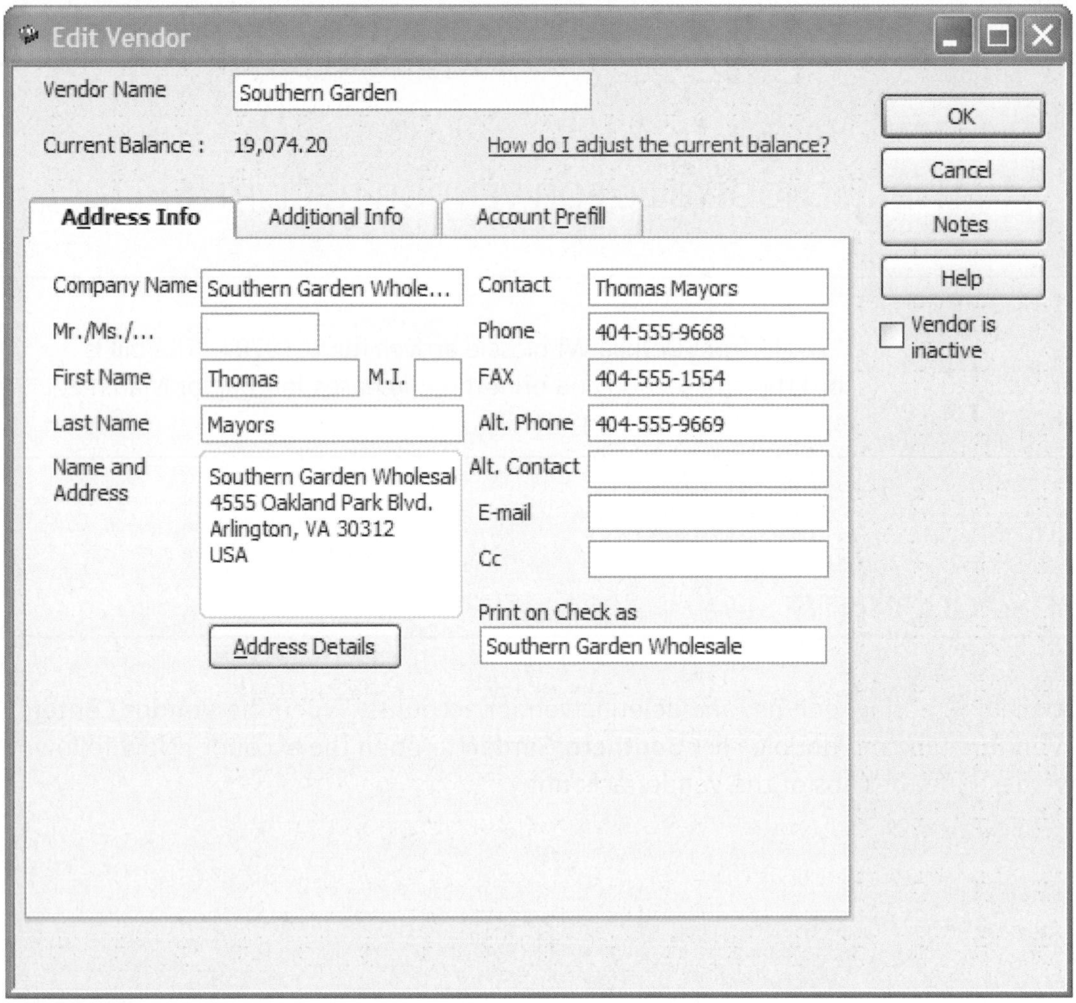

Figure 9:27

This tab stores basic vendor information such as address, phone numbers, and contacts.

Additional Info Tab

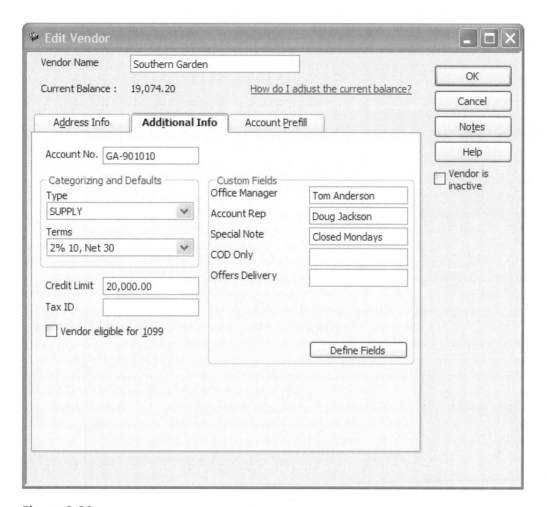

Figure 9:28

This tab stores vendor transaction defaults and fields for vendor reporting.

Account No. is optional and stores the account number used by the vendor.

Type is optional and is used to group reports by vendor characteristics. You can click the dropdown list to view the types used by Baxter.

Terms on the vendor serve the same role as terms on the customer by controlling vendor bill due dates and early payment discounts.

Credit Limit on the vendor serves the same function as on the customer by controlling vendor purchases.

Vendor eligible for 1099 triggers a vendor for IRS tax reporting. When selected, QBP tracks annual payments for reporting on Form 1099. The IRS requires the annual filing of Form 1099 for subcontractor payments that exceed $600. Information on 1099 reporting requirements is available at www.irs.gov.

Tax ID stores a vendor's social security number or federal ID number for Form 1099 reporting.

Account Prefill

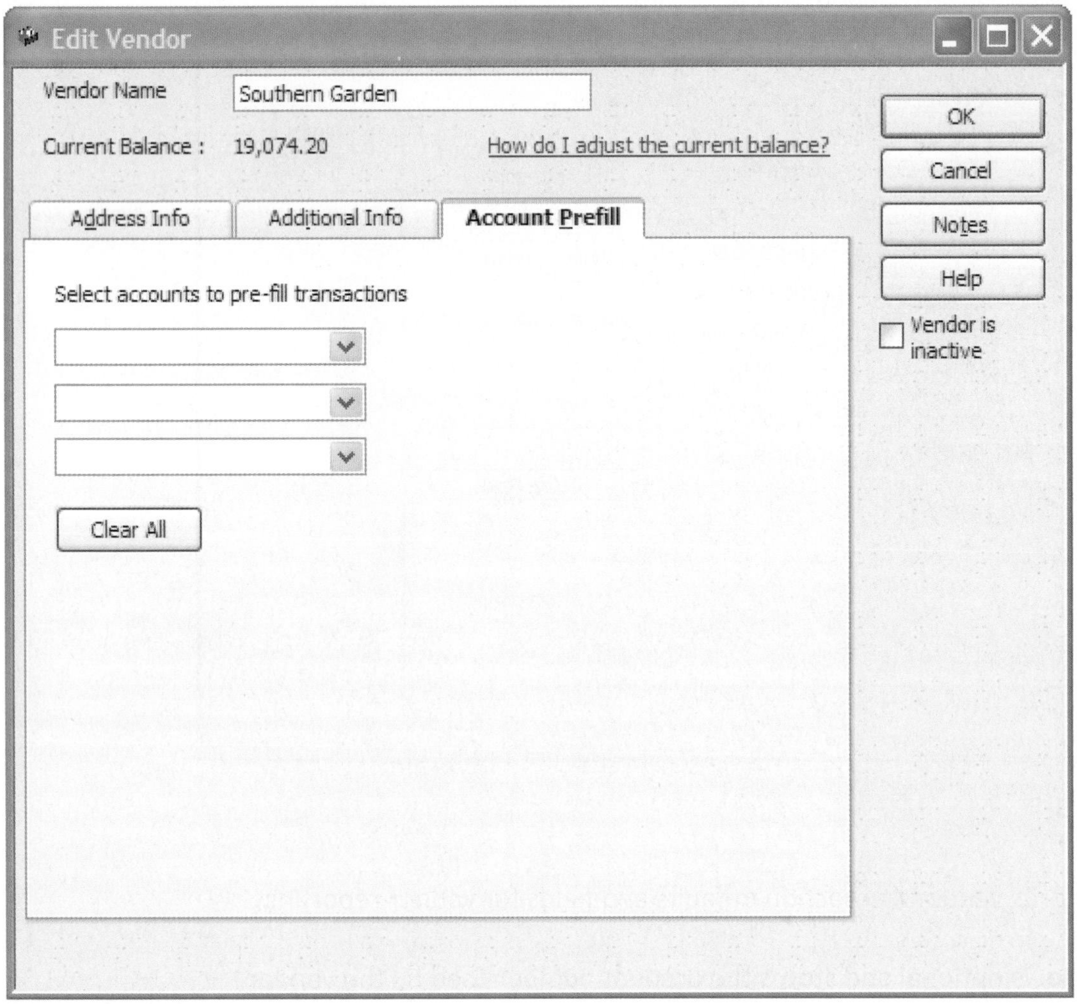

Figure 9:29

This tab assigns multiple default general ledger expense accounts. If a vendor has prefilled accounts then QBP will automatically enter the accounts on the Expenses tab of the Enter Bills window.

Southern Garden does not have prefill accounts because it is a supplier of inventory so purchases from this vendor use the default account assigned to the inventory item. You can open the Petty Cash vendor if you want to view prefilled accounts.

Click **X** to close the account. Now practice editing vendor accounts by completing the next exercise.

STEPS TO EDIT VENDOR ACCOUNT INFORMATION

1. Open the **Daniel Lawn Pro** account. Select the **Additional Info** tab and change the **Type** to **SUBCON**. Notice that the company is a 1099 vendor. (See Figure 9:30.)

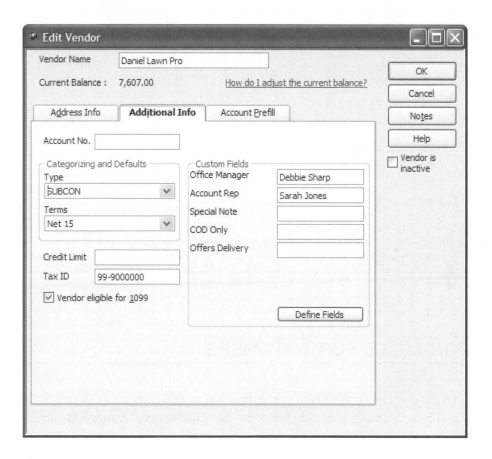

Figure 9:30

2. Click **OK** and click **Yes** if warned about affecting previously posted transactions.

You can delete vendors by highlighting a vendor account and selecting *Edit>>Delete Vendor* on the main menu. Like customers, you cannot delete accounts with transaction history, so use the **Vendor is inactive** option if you need to deny future transactions.

Adding vendors is similar to adding customers. Practice creating a new vendor in the exercise that follows.

 CREATE A NEW VENDOR ACCOUNT

The following lists information for Baxter's new vendor account added on March 6, 2009.

Sullivan Buyer Supplies
P.O. Box 1732
Arlington, VA 30022

Phone:	701 555-6723
Fax:	701 555-8723
Contact:	Susan Calley
Email:	SCalley@bbsupply.com

Vendor Type:	OFFICE
Terms:	Net 30
Account Prefill:	Office Supplies Expense

VENDOR BILLS FOR EXPENSES

Baxter also receives vendor bills for expenses not originating on POs and not involving inventory. These bills are normally for expenses such as office supplies, utilities, and insurance.

On March 30, Baxter receives a bill for advertising expense. Complete the exercise that follows to record this transaction.

STEPS FOR ENTERING VENDOR BILLS FOR EXPENSES

1. On the **Home** page, click **Enter Bills.** In **Vendor**, look up and select "Jackson Advertising." Change the **Date** to "3/30/2009".

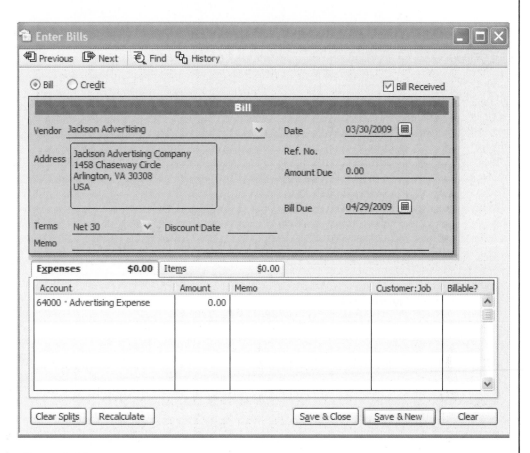

Figure 9:31

2. Enter "6067" as the **Ref. No.**

3. In **Amount**, enter "250.00".

4. Notice that the prefilled account of Advertising Expense automatically filled on the **Expenses** tab and the **Amount** automatically filled after entering $250.00 into **Amount Due**. Tab to **Memo** and type "Advertising flyers".

5. Figure 9:32 shows the completed transaction. Click **Save & Close** to post it.

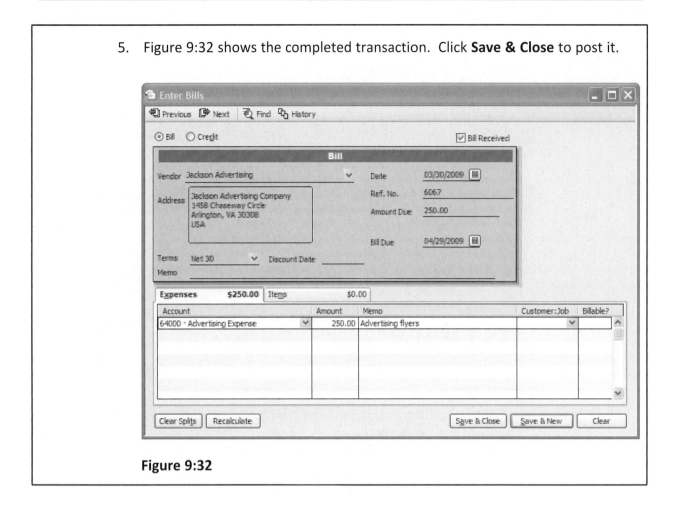

Figure 9:32

The *You Try* exercise that follows provides more practice on entering vendor bills for expenses.

ENTER VENDOR BILLS FOR EXPENSES

On March 31, 2009 Baxter received the following bills.

> Juan Motor Tools Invoice 3434 dated March 30, 2009 for $603.25 for fixing vehicle transmission. Post to auto repairs expense account.

> Neighbors Telephone Company telephone bill dated March 24, 2009 for $216.00 for March telephone. Post to utilities expense account.

Hints:
There are a couple of points to this exercise. First, the transaction date is always the invoice date, not the date of receiving the bill. Generally, you will not receive bills on the same day as the invoice date.

Second, you will often encounter bills without an invoice number, particularly utility and professional service bills. Therefore, you must create an invoice number to let you later identify the transaction. For instance, you can use "MarElec" as the invoice number for March electricity.

MEMORIZED VENDOR BILLS

QBP will let you memorize vendor bills. This feature is especially useful with recurring bills. You can memorize while creating a new bill or you can open a posted bill and memorize it.

The accountant has just signed a contract with Miles Maintenance for monthly office cleaning. In the following exercise you enter the March bill and save it as a memorized bill.

STEPS TO CREATE A MEMORIZED VENDOR BILL

1. Click **Enter Bills** on the Home page and enter the following information.

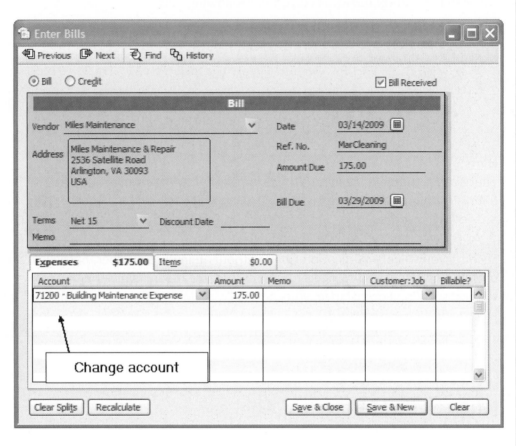

Figure 9:33

2. On the main menu, select ***Edit>>Memorize Bill*** to open the window illustrated in Figure 9:34.

Figure 9:34

You can instruct QBP to remind you to post the bill or tell the software to automatically post it. Select **Remind Me** and then complete remaining fields as illustrated Figure 9:35.

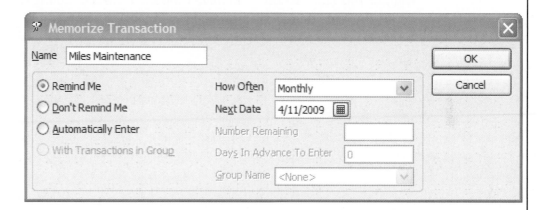

Figure 9:35

Click **OK** and then click **Save & Close** on the March bill.

3. You will now locate this memorized transaction. Select ***Lists>>Memorized Transaction List*** on the main menu to open the Memorized Transaction List (Figure 9:36).

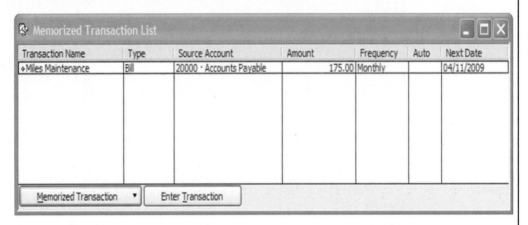

Figure 9:36

4. You can modify the scheduling of a memorized transaction. Highlight the **Miles** bill, click the **Memorized Transaction** button and select **Edit Memorized Transaction**. You have reopened the scheduling window where you reschedule the transaction. Click **Cancel**.

5. You will now record this transaction for April. Double click the memorized bill to Miles. Notice that the transaction date is already provided.

    Type "AprCleaning" in **Ref. No.** and change the **Memo** to "April office cleaning". Click **Save & Close**.

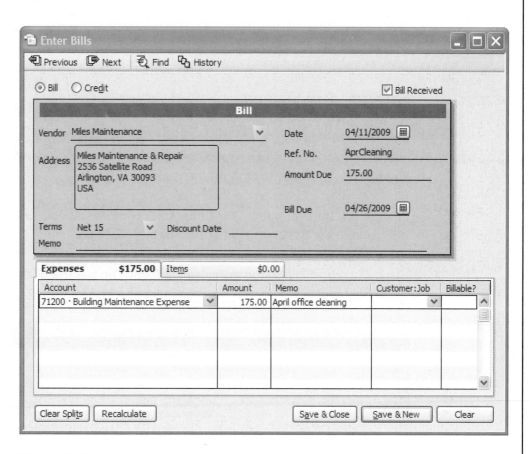

Figure 9:37

6. Notice that the **Next Date** on the Memorized Transaction List updates to May. Click **X** to close the list.

VENDOR PAYMENTS

In this topic you focus on paying vendor bills. In the following exercise, you create checks dated March 27, 2009 for vendor bills due by April 3, 2009.

STEPS TO PAY VENDORS

1. Before cutting checks, Melvin prepares an aged payables report to review bill due dates. Create this report by selecting >**Reports>>Vendors & Payables>>A/P Aging Detail** on the main menu.

    Change the **Date** to March 31, 2009. Click **Modify Report**. On the **Display** tab, change the **Sort by** field to "Due Date." Click **OK**.

    Using the report illustrated in Figure 9:38, you can see the bills due by April 3. Close the report.

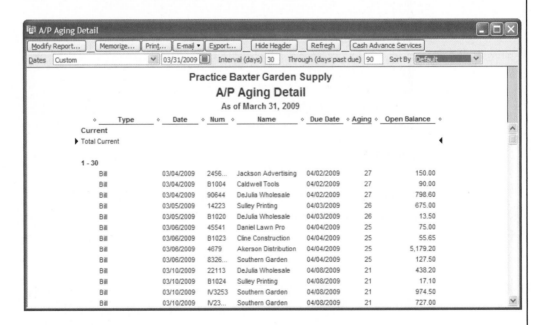

Figure 9:38

2. Click **Pay Bills** on the Home page. We will not use the filtering option because Baxter wants to pay bills due on or before April 3 plus a bill for Daniel Lawn Pro that is not due until April 15.

Select **Show all bills** and mark the bills show in Figure 9.39.

Note: This is also the method to use if you want to pay bills with a date in the Disc. Date column.

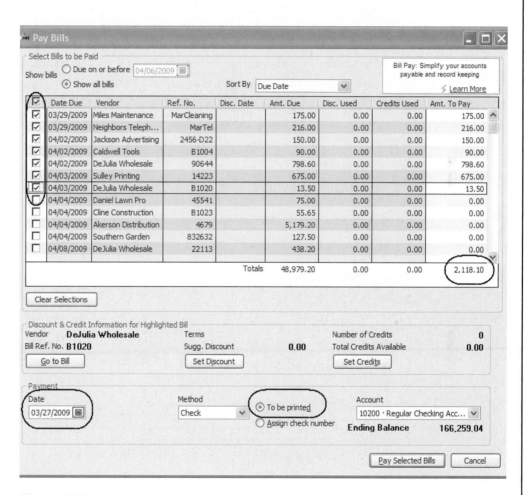

Figure 9:39

Select the **To be printed** option and change the **Payment Date** to 3/27/2009.

Before proceeding, note that these checks will post to (credit) 10200 Regular Checking Account.

3. Next, scroll down and select INV3253 due to Daniel Lawn Pro. Eight bills are now selected, totaling $9,650.10.

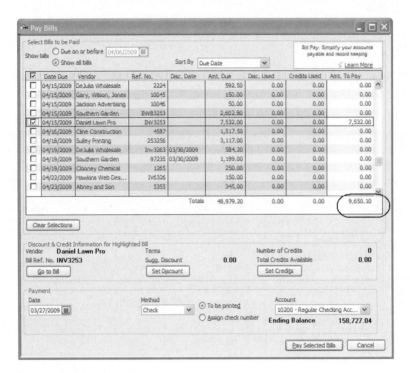

Figure 9:40

You can reduce a payment to a vendor by adjusting the **Amt. To Pay** field. After printing the checks, payments post as a credit to the regular checking account and a debit to accounts payable.

If paying bills with a discount, a discount amount appears in the Disc. Used column and the credit posts to account 59500 Purchase Discounts. This account is set on the Company Preferences options for Bills illustrated in Figure 9:41.

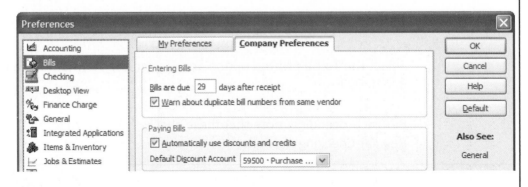

Figure 9:41

4. Click **Pay Selected Bills** to open the window illustrated in Figure 9:42.

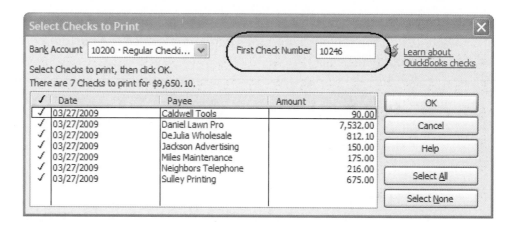

Figure 9:42

Note: You can click Done and return to printing later by using the Print Checks icon on the Home page.

5. Click **Print Checks** and the window in Figure 9:43 opens. Enter "10246" as the **First Check Number**.

Notice that QBP has combined vendor bills so that seven checks will print.

Figure 9:43

6. Click **OK** and the printer selection window opens. Select a printer and click **Print**. Figure 9:44 shows the first check printed.

03/27/2009

Caldwell Tools Company   **90.00

Ninety and 00/100***

Caldwell Tools Company
2356 Steve Reynolds Place
Norpoint, VA 23531
USA

Caldwell Tools Company				03/27/2009		
Date	Type	Reference	Original Amt.	Balance Due	Discount	Payment
03/04/2009	Bill	B1004	90.00	90.00		90.00
					Check Amount	90.00

Regular Checking Acc   90.00

Caldwell Tools Company				03/27/2009		
Date	Type	Reference	Original Amt.	Balance Due	Discount	Payment
03/04/2009	Bill	B1004	90.00	90.00		90.00
					Check Amount	90.00

Figure 9:44

Note: This check illustrates printing on a two-part check where Baxter can send the top portion to the vendor and attach the bottom portion to the paid bill.

7. QBP next confirms check printing (Figure 9:45). If checks did not print properly, you can click Select All and then click Cancel so that QBP will not assign check numbers. You would then return to printing by using the Print Checks icon on the Home page.

Click **OK**.

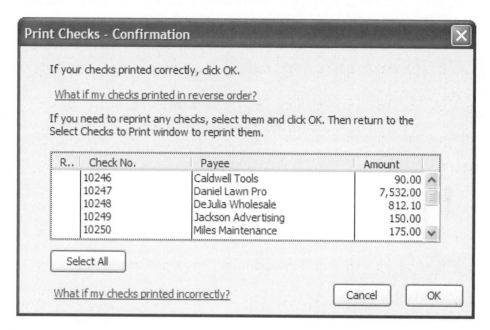

Figure 9:45

BEHIND THE KEYS OF A POSTED VENDOR PAYMENT

Now trace the audit trail for the checks printed in the previous topic. On the main menu, select **Reports>>Memorized Reports>>Accounting Journals>>Cash Disbursement Journal**. Change the date range to "3/27/2009". (See Figure 9:46.)

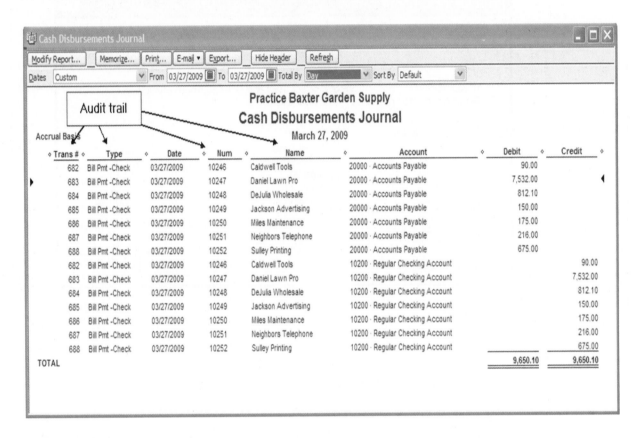

Figure 9:46

The report lists the **Trans #** and **Type** audit trail for each payment. Close the report.

Select **Reports>>Vendors & Payables>>Transaction List by Vendor** to open the report listing transactions to vendor accounts. Enter "3/27/2009" as the date range and **Modify** to add the **Trans #** column. Also add a **Filter** to limit the **Transaction Type** to **Bill Payment**. Click **OK**.

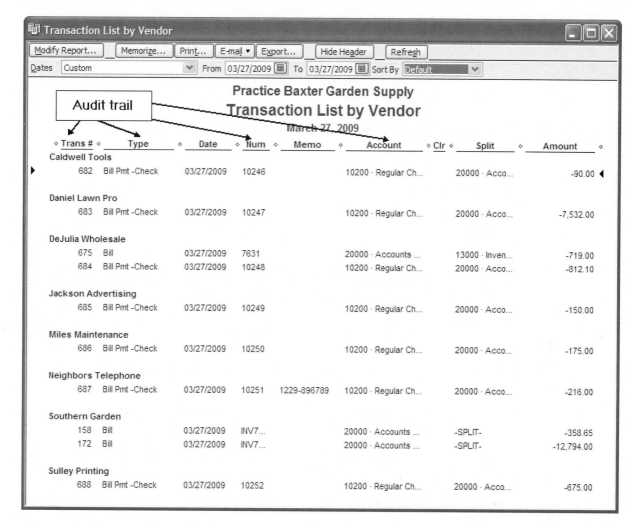

Figure 9:47

The **Trans #** and **Type** in Figure 9:47 match the audit trail in the **Cash Disbursements Journal**.

Close this report and complete tracing entries by opening the **General Ledger Detail Report**. Locate your entries in accounts 10200 Regular Checking and 20000 Accounts Payable (not illustrated).

WRITE CHECKS WITHOUT A VENDOR BILL

QBP will write checks without entering a vendor bill first. This is useful if you need to write a check to a vendor that requests cash upon delivery. Sometimes the vendor account will also be new so you add it "on the fly." *(Note: Remember "on the fly" means creating a new account while entering a transaction.)*

Complete the next exercise to write a check for miscellaneous office supplies.

STEPS TO ADD A VENDOR ON THE FLY WHILE WRITING A CHECK WITHOUT A VENDOR BILL

1. Click **Write Checks** under the **Banking** section of the **Home** page. Change the **No** field to "10253", which is the check number. Enter "3/27/2009" as the **Date**.

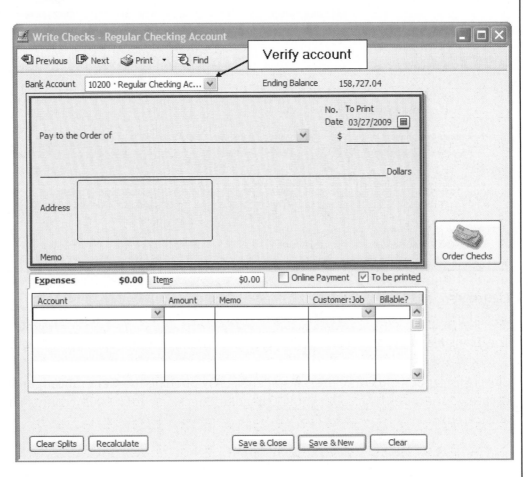

Figure 9:48

2. The vendor is not on file so place your cursor in **Pay to the Order of** and type "Ready Supplies".

    Press Tab. When QBP prompts to create the account (Figure 9:49), click **Set Up**.

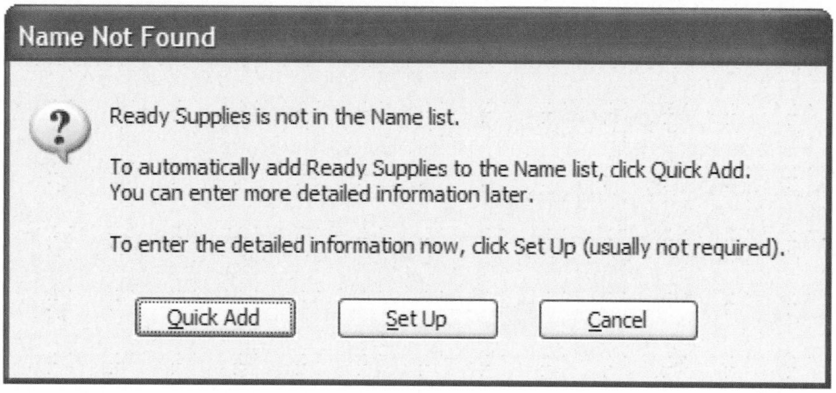

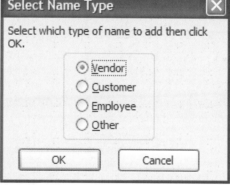

Name Not Found

? Ready Supplies is not in the Name list.

To automatically add Ready Supplies to the Name list, click Quick Add. You can enter more detailed information later.

To enter the detailed information now, click Set Up (usually not required).

[Quick Add]   [Set Up]   [Cancel]

Figure 9:49

Next, choose **Vendor** and click **OK**.

Select Name Type   [X]

Select which type of name to add then click OK.

⦿ Vendor
○ Customer
○ Employee
○ Other

[OK]   [Cancel]

Figure 9:50

3. Use information in the next series of figures to create the vendor account.

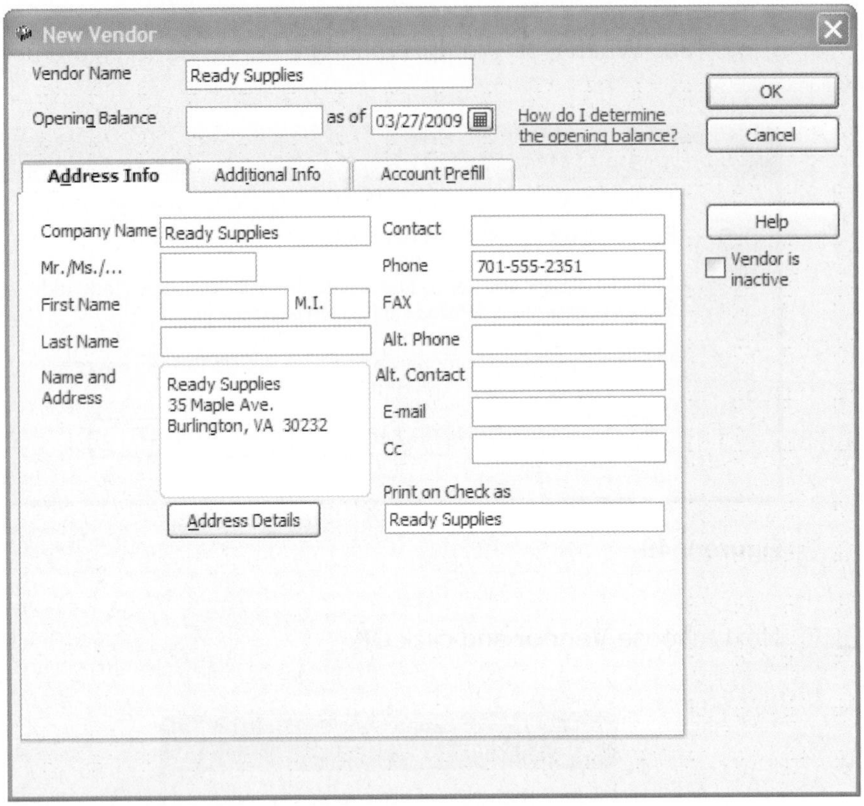

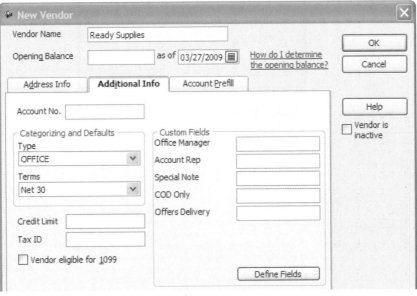

Figure 9:51

Figure 9:52

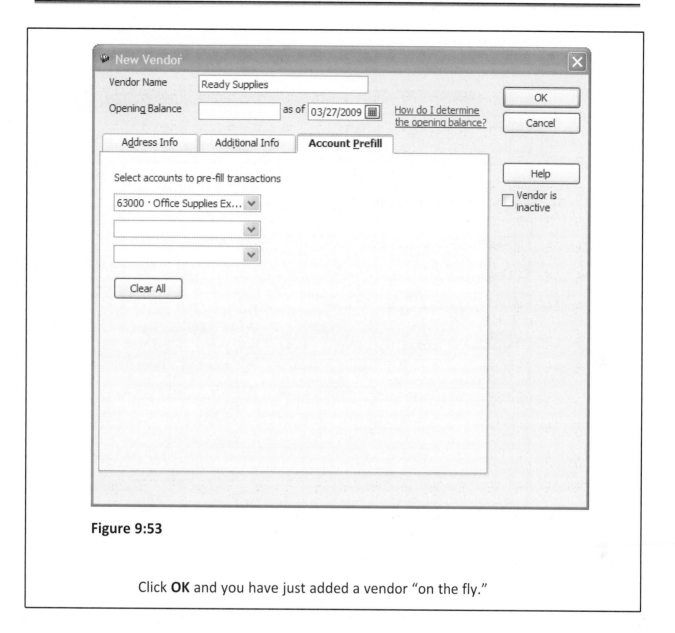

Figure 9:53

Click **OK** and you have just added a vendor "on the fly."

4. Now complete the check as shown in Figure 9:54.

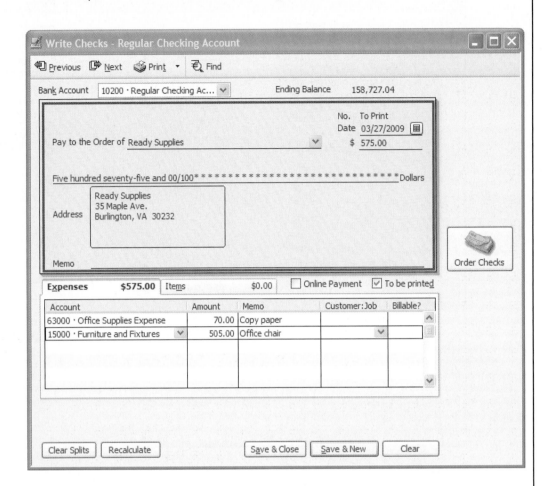

Figure 9:54

You are using two different accounts to record this transaction because office chairs are furniture and fixture assets not office supplies expense.

5. Click **Print** and confirm that the check number is "10253". Click **Print** again in the select printer window. Click **OK** to confirm that the check printed correctly.

6. Click **Save & Close**.

VOIDING VENDOR PAYMENTS

QBP will let you reopen a vendor payment and change check data. Although this changes data in the software, the printed check remains incorrect; therefore you should not alter check data. Instead, errors on checks are corrected by voiding the payment and reissuing it. The following instructions illustrate voiding a vendor payment.

STEPS TO VOIDING A VENDOR PAYMENT

1. In this exercise you will void check number "10231" cut to Juan Motor Tools on March 13. Open the **Vendor Center** and locate **Bill Payments** for this vendor's account. (See Figure 9:55.)

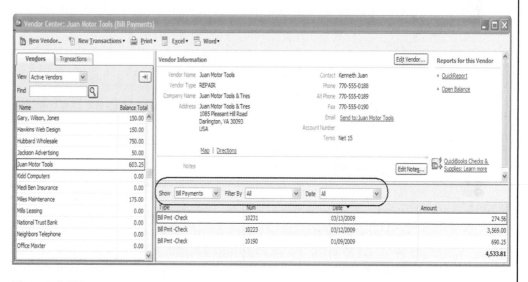

Figure 9:55

2. Double click to reopen the check. On the main menu, select ***Edit>>Void Bill Pmt – Check***.

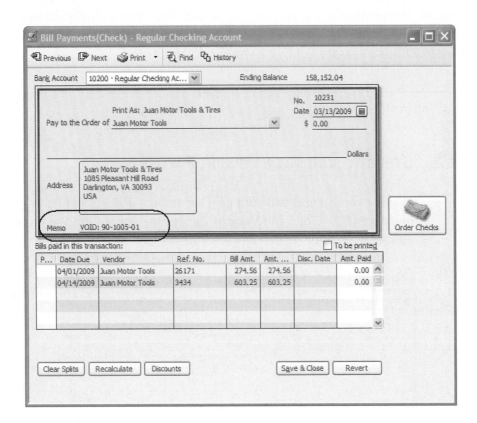

Figure 9:56

You want to be very careful when voiding checks. QBP will always post the entry for a voided check as of the check date. If voiding a check written in a closed accounting period, QBP will prompt to post the entry to the closed period. Unfortunately, there is no workaround for posting the entry to a selected date. You must permit the entry to backdate to the closed period and then record a general journal entry to reclassify the amount to the open accounting period.

3. Click **Save & Close**. When prompted (Figure 9:57), click **Yes**.

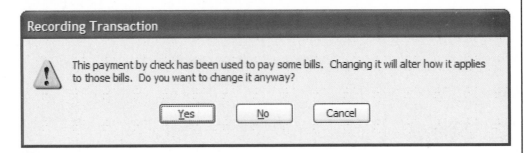

Figure 9:57

4. View the results of your action. Select **Reports>>Memorized Reports>>Accounting Journals>>General Ledger Detail Report** on the main menu. Enter "3/13/2009" as the date range. Notice that QBP voided the check as of the check date (Figure 9:58). Close the report.

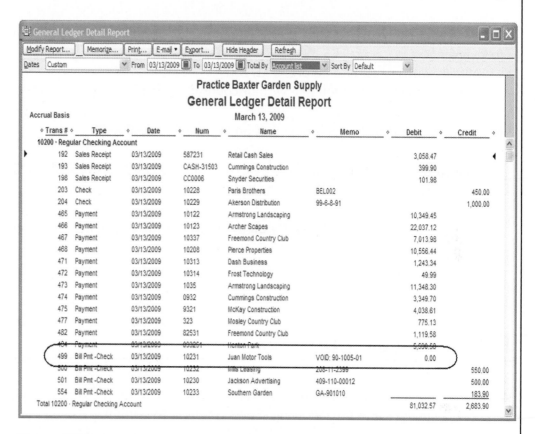

Figure 9:58

5. Return to the vendor's account and view **Bills**. The March bill has an open balance so it can be reselected for payment. You will pay this bill in the next exercise.

    Close the **Vendor Center**.

PAY VENDORS

Create vendor checks dated April 3, 2009. Individually select bills to pay based on the following.

    All bills with a due date before 4/11/2009

    Two bills to DeJulia Wholesale with discount dates expiring by 4/6/2009

Reduce Akerson Distribution's payment on Invoice 4 to $5,000.00.

The selected payments will total $11,693.76. Print the checks using "10254"as the first check number.

Select **Reports>>Banking>>Check Detail** to document the payments. Enter 4/3/2009 as the date range.

PAYING SALES TAX

At the end of every month, Baxter must remit sales tax collected from customers. QBP tracks sales tax collections and the following shows you how to remit it.

STEPS TO PAYING SALES TAX

1. Click **Manage Sales Tax** on the **Home** page to open the window shown in Figure 9:59.

Figure 9:59

2. Click **Sales Tax Preferences**. Figure 9:60 shows that Baxter collects Virginia sales tax, owes the tax after the customer pays the invoice, and remits sales tax monthly.

   Click **Cancel** to exit this window.

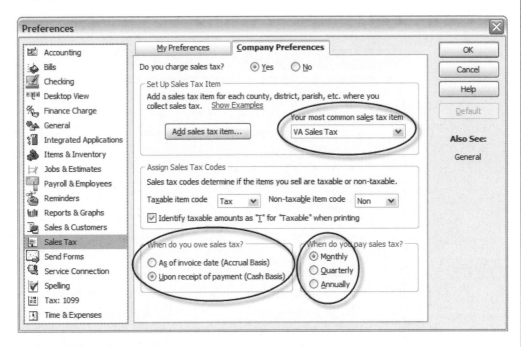

Figure 9:60

3. On the **Manage Sales Tax** window, click the **Sales Tax Liability** link to view a report showing the current sales tax owed.

   Enter the date range of **From** "3/1/2009" and **To** "3/31/2009". Close the report after noting the amount under Sales Tax Payable (Figure 9:61).

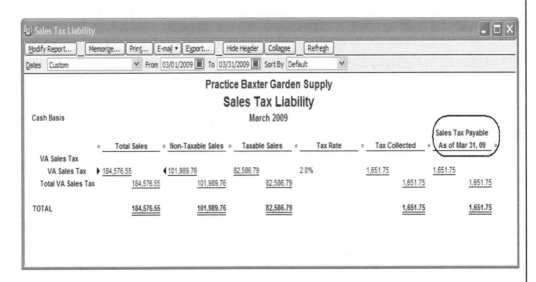

Figure 9:61

4. Click the **Pay Sales Tax** button. Enter the **Check Date** of 04/03/2009 and **Show sales tax due through** date of 03/31/2009. Click **Pay All Tax** and click **To be printed**.

The **Amt. Due** in Figure 9:62 matches the amount due on the previous report.

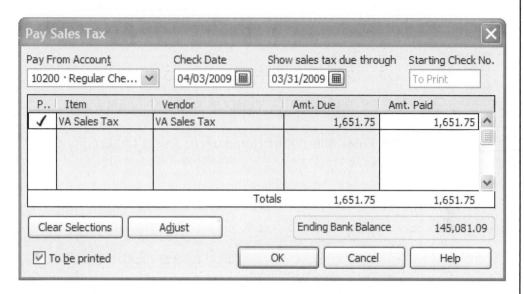

Figure 9:62

5. Click **OK** and then click **Close** to exit the Pay Sales Tax window.

6. You will now print the check. Click **Print Checks** under the **Banking** section of the Home page and select the Regular Checking Account.

Confirm that "10262" is the check number and then click **OK**. Click **Print** in the printer selection window. Click **OK** in the confirmation window.

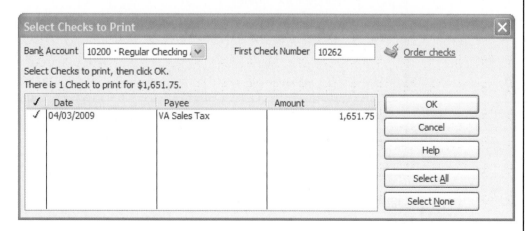

Figure 9:63

VENDOR CREDITS

Just as Baxter issues credits to customers, vendors issue credits to Baxter. Follow the next steps and record a credit for returning five EQWT-15100 Drip Irrigation Systems to Southern Garden billed on Invoice 97325.

STEPS TO ENTER A VENDOR CREDIT MEMO

1. Click **Enter Bills** on the Home page. Select the **Credit** option and select the **Items** tab.

   Now enter the information on Figure 9:64.

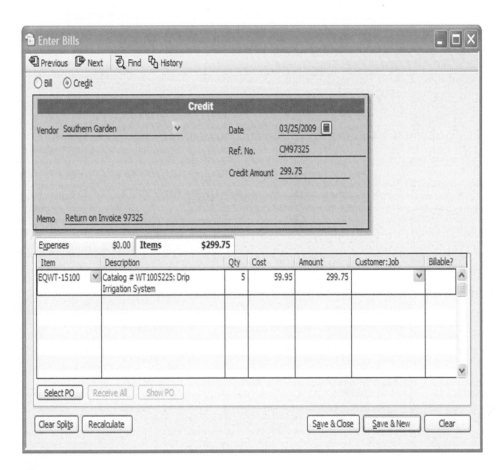

Figure 9:64

2. Click **Save & Close**.

3. Open the **Vendor Center** and view all transactions for Southern Garden's account. The credit memo is circled in Figure 9:65.

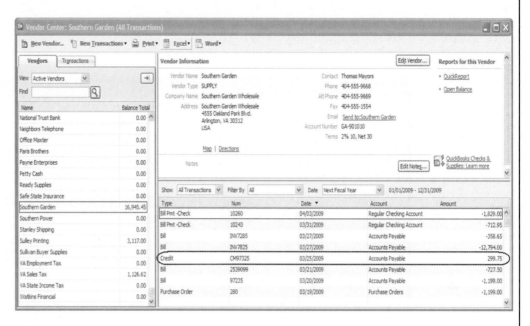

Figure 9:65

4. See what happens the next time you pay Southern Garden. Click the **New Transactions** button on the Vendor Center and select **Pay Bills**.

Highlight any bill due to Southern Garden and the window will display the available credit of $299.75.

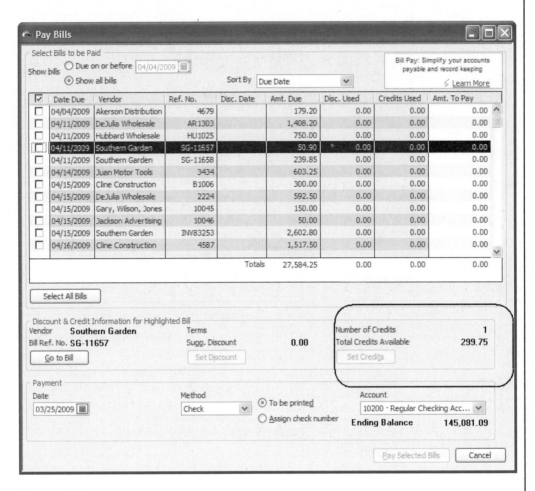

Figure 9:66

Now click to select Southern Garden's Invoice 97325. The credit will be applied to the bill selected and the amount applied will appear in the **Credits Used** column. *(Note: You can apply the credit to any bill.)*

Click **Cancel** on the window above and then close the Vendor Center.

VENDOR REPORTING AND RECONCILING ACTIVITIES

QBP offers a variety of purchasing and vendor reports on the **Report Center**. Open the **Report Center** using the icon on the toolbar and select the **Vendors & Payables** category. You have already opened many of these reports using the Reports menu.

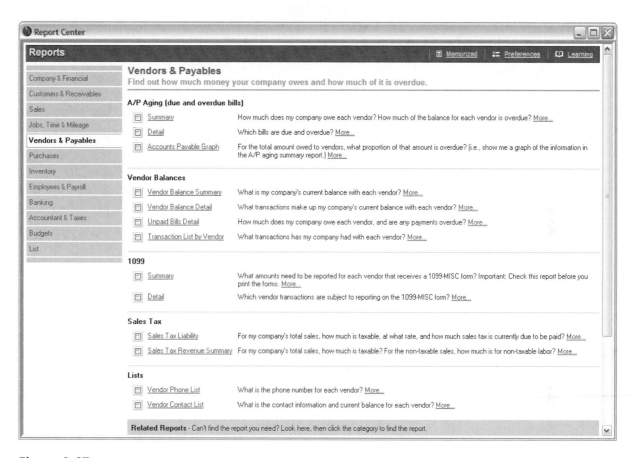

Figure 9:67

We will begin with **A/P Aging** reports. Click **Summary** and change the date to "3/31/2009". Refresh the report (Figure 9:68).

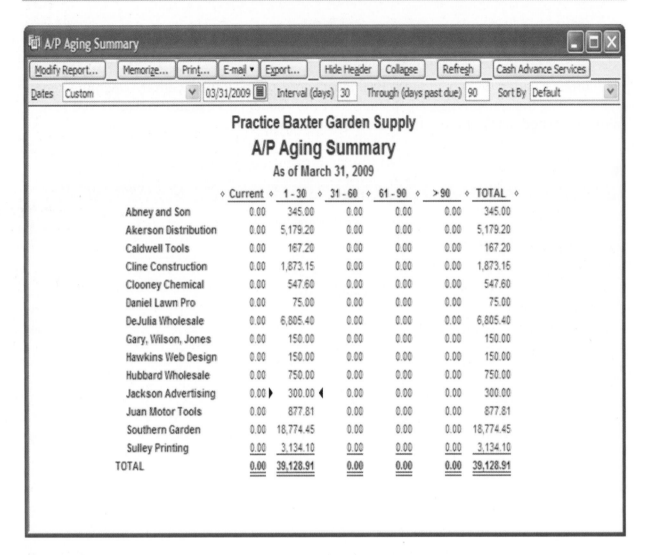

Figure 9:68

This report lists outstanding vendor balances by age of the balance. *(Note: Your balances will differ from those illustrated if you have not completed all chapter exercises.)* The report serves two important purposes.

First, Baxter uses it to monitor vendor payments and to manage company cash flow. Second, the report is used to reconcile vendor balances with the accounts payable control account. This task is performed by comparing the aging report total with the March ending balance in general ledger account 20000 Accounts Payable.

Now view the balance in accounts payable. Select *Reports>>Accountant & Taxes>>Trial Balance* on the main menu and filter the report for 3/31/2009. Scroll down and locate the balance in 20000 Accounts Payable. The total on the A/P Aging report and the balance in Accounts Payable must agree to ensure proper recording of vendor activities.

These amounts will not reconcile when you improperly correct vendor transactions. Therefore, you should always refer to the instructions in Appendix B when correcting transactions. You should reconcile the aged payables report to the accounts payable account at the end of every month and prior to issuing financial reports.

Close all open reports and then open the **Detail A/P Aging** report. Change the date to "3/31/2009". This report (Figure 9:69) lists invoices by invoice age.

Practice Baxter Garden Supply
A/P Aging Detail
As of March 31, 2009

Type	Date	Num	Name	Due Date	Aging	Open Balance
Current						
Total Current						
1 - 30						
Bill	03/03/2009	26171	Juan Motor Tools	04/01/2009	28	274.56
Bill	03/06/2009	45541	Daniel Lawn Pro	04/04/2009	25	75.00
Bill	03/06/2009	B1023	Cline Construction	04/04/2009	25	55.65
Bill	03/06/2009	4679	Akerson Distribution	04/04/2009	25	5,179.20
Bill	03/06/2009	832632	Southern Garden	04/04/2009	25	127.50
Bill	03/10/2009	22113	DeJulia Wholesale	04/08/2009	21	438.20
Bill	03/10/2009	B1024	Sulley Printing	04/08/2009	21	17.10
Bill	03/10/2009	IV3253	Southern Garden	04/08/2009	21	974.50
Bill	03/10/2009	IV23513	Southern Garden	04/08/2009	21	727.00
Bill	03/12/2009	116655	Clooney Chemical	04/10/2009	19	297.60
Bill	03/13/2009	AR1303	DeJulia Wholesale	04/11/2009	18	1,408.20
Bill	03/13/2009	HU1025	Hubbard Wholesale	04/11/2009	18	750.00
Bill	03/13/2009	SG-11657	Southern Garden	04/11/2009	18	50.90
Bill	03/13/2009	SG-11658	Southern Garden	04/11/2009	18	239.85
Bill	03/17/2009	B1006	Cline Construction	04/15/2009	14	300.00
Bill	03/17/2009	2224	DeJulia Wholesale	04/15/2009	14	592.50
Bill	03/17/2009	10045	Gary, Wilson, Jones	04/15/2009	14	150.00
Bill	03/17/2009	10046	Jackson Advertising	04/15/2009	14	50.00
Bill	03/17/2009	INV83253	Southern Garden	04/15/2009	14	2,602.80
Bill	03/18/2009	4587	Cline Construction	04/16/2009	13	1,517.50
Bill	03/20/2009	253256	Sulley Printing	04/18/2009	11	3,117.00
Bill	03/20/2009	Inv3263	DeJulia Wholesale	04/19/2009	11	584.20
Bill	03/20/2009	97235	Southern Garden	04/19/2009	11	1,199.00
Bill	03/20/2009	1265	Clooney Chemical	04/19/2009	11	250.00
Bill	03/24/2009	IV6326	Hawkins Web Design	04/22/2009	7	150.00
Bill	03/24/2009	5355	Abney and Son	04/23/2009	7	345.00
Bill	03/25/2009	9864	Caldwell Tools	04/23/2009	6	167.20
Credit	03/25/2009	CM97325	Southern Garden			-299.75
Bill	03/26/2009	INV3253	DeJulia Wholesale	04/25/2009	5	3,063.30
Bill	03/27/2009	INV7285	Southern Garden	04/25/2009	4	358.65
Bill	03/27/2009	INV7825	Southern Garden	04/25/2009	4	12,794.00
Bill	03/27/2009	7631	DeJulia Wholesale	04/26/2009	4	719.00
Bill	03/30/2009	3434	Juan Motor Tools	04/14/2009	1	603.25
Bill	03/30/2009	6067	Jackson Advertising	04/29/2009	1	250.00
Total 1 - 30						39,128.91
31 - 60						
Total 31 - 60						
61 - 90						
Total 61 - 90						
> 90						
Total > 90						
TOTAL						**39,128.91**

Figure 9:69

Close the **Detail A/P Aging** report and open the **Summary** report under **1099**.

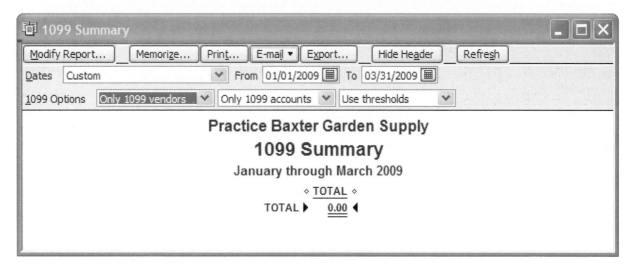

Figure 9:70

This report will list payments to vendors receiving 1099s when payments to the vendor equal or exceed the $600 reporting threshold. Remember 1099 reporting requirements are set by the IRS.

Close this report but keep the Report Center open for the next topic.

PURCHASING AND INVENTORY ACTIVITY REPORTING

Select the **Purchases** area of the **Report Center**. These reports let you analyze vendor purchases and monitor open purchase orders.

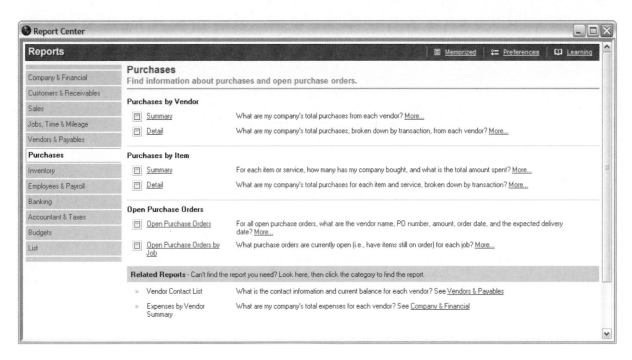

Figure 9:71

Click **Open Purchase Orders** to find the outstanding PO illustrated in Figure 9:72. Companies monitor this report to make sure that inventory is delivered in a timely manner.

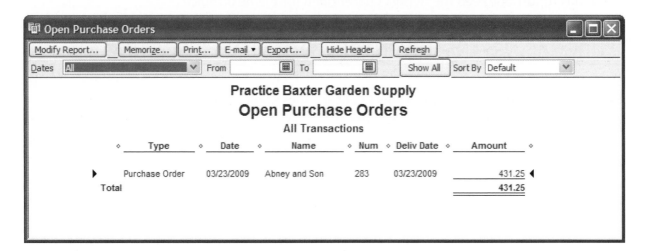

Figure 9:72

Purchases by Vendor reports can help analyze the volume of items purchased from vendors. Upon finding large volumes of purchases with specific vendors, you could possibly negotiate more favorable discount terms or preferred pricing discounts. Close the report.

Now select the **Inventory** category.

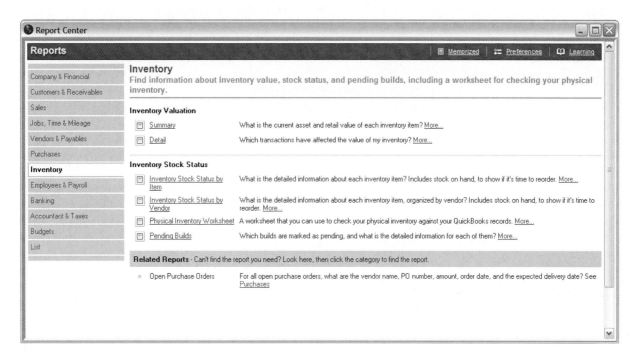

Figure 9:73

Inventory reports let you analyze inventory turnover and stock status and reconcile inventory transactions to the general ledger inventory control account. In Chapter 8, you practiced inventory reconciliation procedures.

Open the **Inventory Stock Status by Item** report and enter the date range of 3/1/2009 to 3/31/2009. (See Figure 9:74.)

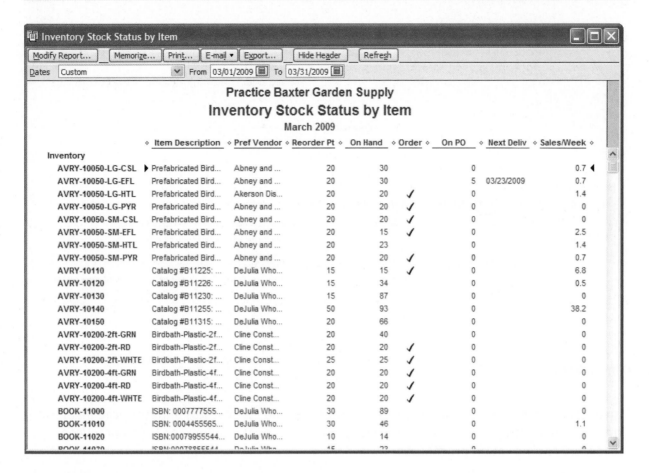

Figure 9:74

This report shows on-hand quantities and quantities on POs. A checkmark in the **Order** column is a quick indicator that an item needs to be ordered. The checkmark appears when the **On Hand** quantity falls below the **Reorder Pt**.

The report also helps analyze sales by item. The **Sales/Week** column lists the average quantity sold in March.

Close this report and the Report Center.

Remember that inventory reports can be exported to Excel. After exporting, you can further analyze transactions such as computing inventory turnover ratios.

The key point is that reports are the basic means for analyzing company performance. Take the time to review other inventory and purchasing reports to see the wide range of information that is available.

You have now completed the chapter. ***Make a backup of the Practice Baxter Garden Supply data file to a backup file named "Practice Baxter Garden Supply Chpt 9". In the next chapter, you will build on the work completed in this chapter.***

SUMMARY

You began the chapter by learning to post transactions in a manual accounting system. You then posted *MAPS* transactions in QBP. You also learned to use the Vendor Center to manage vendor activities.

You have recorded POs and receipts of items on a PO. You posted vendor bills for receipts and vendor bills for expenses. You also paid vendors, voided payments, and recorded vendor credits.

Finally, you reconciled vendor transactions to the general ledger and worked with a variety of accounts payable, purchasing, and inventory reports that analyze activities. You are now ready to focus on the payroll activities covered in Chapter 10.

END-OF-CHAPTER QUESTIONS

TRUE/FALSE

_____ 1. You can locate open POs using the Report Center.

_____ 2. The Enter Bills icon is used to record PO receipts.

_____ 3. QBP will let you change information on a posted vendor payment.

_____ 4. Vendor bills for expenses are entered as vendor receipts.

_____ 5. When entering a vendor bill, QBP prompts to select a PO if the vendor has an open PO.

_____ 6. After recording a vendor bill for receipt of all items on a PO, QBP marks the PO as Received.

_____ 7. When deleting a vendor receipt, QBP will reinstate the PO so that you can receive the items again.

_____ 8. You can reopen a vendor bill using the Vendor Center.

_____ 9. The Write Checks icon will let you pay a vendor without entering a vendor bill.

_____ 10. You must delete a check issued to the wrong vendor.

MULTIPLE CHOICE

_____ 1. QBP will post an item receipt as a _____.
   a. debit to inventory, credit to accounts payable
   b. debit to inventory, credit to accounts payable, debit to cost of goods sold
   c. debit to inventory, credit to accounts receivable
   d. none of the above

_____ 2. QBP posts entries for vendor payments as a _____.
   a. debit to inventory, credit to checking
   b. debit to checking, credit to accounts payable
   c. credit to checking, debit to accounts payable
   d. credit to checking, debit to accounts receivable

_____   3. QBP will post a PO as a _____.
   a. debit to inventory, credit to accounts payable
   b. debit to inventory, credit to accounts payable, debit to cost of goods sold
   c. debit to inventory, credit to accounts receivable
   d. none of the above

_____   4. Which report will display items that need to be reordered?
   a. Physical Inventory Worksheet
   b. Inventory Stock Status by Vendor
   c. Inventory Stock Status by Item
   d. Both b and c

_____   5. Payments to vendors are listed on the _____ report.
   a. Transaction List by Vendor
   b. Check Detail
   c. Vendor Balance Detail
   d. All of the above

_____   6. Which report will age by vendor invoice?
   a. A/P Aging Summary
   b. A/P Aging Detail
   c. Vendor Balance Detail
   d. All of the above

PRACTICE SET

In this practice set you will be using the **Graded Baxter Garden Supply** data file with the Practice Set completed in Chapter 8. *If the company file is not loaded on your computer then restore it using the Graded Baxter Garden Supply Chpt 8.QBB backup file created after completing the Chapter 8 Practice Set.*

1. Open **Graded Baxter Garden Supply**. All transactions, except POs printed on April 3 and April 23, will be printed in Step 2.

2009

Apr 1   Post Mills Leasing Corp bill dated April 1 for office rent, $600.00. Create a memorized bill with a reminder of May 1.

                  Post Safe State Insurance bill dated April 1 for 6 months of vehicle insurance, $600.00. Post to prepaid expenses.

Apr 3   Create the following POs and then print POs 1037 to 1040.

PO 1037 for $602.25 to Cline Construction for the following items.

Item	Short Description	Qty	Unit Price
AVRY-10200-2ft-GRN	Birdbath 2ft Green	25	$ 12.50
AVRY-10200-2ft-WHTE	Birdbath 2ft White	25	$ 11.59

PO 1038 for $1,035.00 to Abney and Son for the following items.

Item	Short Description	Qty	Unit Price
AVRY-10050-LG-CSL	Birdhouse-Large Castle	30	$ 17.25
AVRY-10050-LG-HTL	Birdhouse-Large Hotel	30	$ 17.25

PO 1039 for $557.25 to DeJulia Wholesale for the following items.

Item	Short Description	Qty	Unit Price
TOOL-35520	Hedge Shears	25	$ 7.95
TOOL-35530	Pruning Shears	30	$ 11.95

PO 1040 for $935.00 to Clooney Chemical for the following items.
Note: Prices have increased. Enter new price and click Yes when prompted.

Item	Short Description	Qty	Unit Price
EQFF-13100	Fertilizer Pump Sprayer	20	$ 17.00
EQFF-13110	Fertilizer Comp. Sprayer	35	$ 17.00

Apr 9	Post DeJulia Wholesale receipt number RCT6932, $557.25, for all items on PO 1039 issued April 3.

Post Abney and Son Invoice 871 dated April 7, $1,035.00 for all items on PO 1038 issued April 3.

Apr 10 Post DeJulia Wholesale Invoice 3030 dated April 9, $557.25, for receipt number RCT6932.

Post Clooney Chemical Invoice 2223 dated April 8 $850.00 for the following items received on PO 1040 issued April 3.

Item	Short Description	Qty	Unit Price
EQFF-13100	Fertilizer Pump Sprayer	15	$ 17.00
EQFF-13110	Fertilizer Comp. Sprayer	35	$ 17.00

Post Cline Construction receipt number RCT321, $602.25, for all items on PO 1037 issued April 3.

Apr 14 Post Cline Construction Invoice 1315 dated April 10, $602.25, for receipt number RCT321

Apr 15 Post Clooney Chemical Invoice 2351 dated April 14, $85.00, for remaining 5 items of EQFF-13100 on PO 1040 issued April 3.

Apr 16 Pay vendors for bills with a due date or discount date before April 20. Total for bills selected, $32,723.20. First check number is 10246. Verify that the option *To be printed* is selected.

Post Cline Construction credit memo CM1315 dated April 14, $62.50, for returning 5 AVRY 10200 2ft GRN on Invoice 1315.

Apr 17 Enter bills dated April 18 for the following expenses dated.

Southern Power Co	April electric	$153.00
Neighbors Telephone Co	April telephone	$205.00
National Trust Bank	Line of credit interest expense	$250.00
Arlington Water	April water	$125.00

Apr 21 Write and print check number 10258 to Postmaster for postage expense, $250.00. Add Postmaster account "on the fly" using the following information.

Address:	317 W. Main St, Arlington, VA 23135
Type:	OFFICE
Prefill Account:	Postage Expense

Apr 22   Create the following POs and then print POs 1041 to 1043.

                PO 1041 for $679.50 to Southern Garden for the following items.

Item	Short Description	Qty	Unit Price
EQWT-15120	Garden Hose 75 ft.	20	$ 15.95
EQWT-15130	Hose Hanger-Wall Mount	15	$ 7.95
EQWT-15170	Sprinkler Oscillating	25	$ 9.65

                PO 1042 for $856.50 to Clooney Chemical for the following items.

Item	Short Description	Qty	Unit Price
NURS-21810	Rose – Yellow Seeds	40	$ 5.10
NURS-21820	Rose – White Seeds	25	$ 5.10
NURS-22000	Ginko Tree 14-16 ft.	30	$ 17.50

                PO 1043 for $78.00 to DeJulia Wholesale for the following items.

Item	Short Description	Qty	Unit Price
TOOL-35280	Garden Hand Trowel	15	$ 5.20

Apr 23   Create the following new vendor.

                Wilmort Hotel
                173 E. Rutherford St.
                Newport, RI 32653
                Telephone: (800) 555-1353
                Type: OFFICE
                Payment terms: Net 5
                Prefill Account: Travel Expense

                Enter the following bills dated April 21.

Wilmort Hotel, Invoice 713	April travel expense	$ 225.00
Office Maxter, Invoice 3131	Office supply expense	$ 108.00
Juan Motor Tools, Invoice 137	Auto repairs	$ 325.00
Kidd Computers, Invoice 431	Repair equipment	$ 178.25

Apr 24   Post DeJulia Wholesale receipt number RCT8032, $78.00, for all items on
                PO 1043 issued April 22.

Apr 27   Post Clooney Chemical Invoice 2302 dated April 23, $856.50, for all items on
                PO 1042 issued April 22.

Apr 28   Post Southern Garden Invoice 686 dated April 24, $615.70 for following items on PO 1041 issued April 22. *(Note: If you receive a message about posting to retained earnings, click the Expenses tab and delete the value in the Account field.)*

Item	Short Description	Qty	Unit Price
EQWT-15120	Garden Hose 75 ft.	16	$ 15.95
EQWT-15130	Hose Hanger-Wall Mount	15	$ 7.95
EQWT-15170	Sprinkler Oscillating	25	$ 9.65

Apr 29   Pay vendors for bills with a due date or discount date before May 6. Total for bills selected, $15,631.24. First check number is 10259.

Apr 30   Write and print check number 10268 for $2,211.66 for April sales tax.

2. Print the following reports.

   a. Purchases Journal for April transactions.

   b. Cash Disbursements Journal for April transactions. Modify the report to add Check and Sales Tax Payment to the existing transaction types.

   c. Open Purchase Orders report for All dates.

   d. Detailed A/P Aging report for April 30, 2009.

   e. Inventory Valuation Summary report for April 30, 2009.

Back up the Graded Baxter Garden Supply data file to a backup file named "Graded Baxter Garden Supply Chpt 9". The Practice Set for the next chapter will build on the work completed in this chapter.

CHAPTER 10 PAYROLL ACTIVITIES FOR A MERCHANDISING BUSINESS

LEARNING OBJECTIVES

This chapter works with the **Practice Baxter Garden Supply** data file containing the tasks completed in Chapter 9. *If this company file is not loaded on your computer then restore it using the Practice Baxter Garden Supply Chpt 9.QBB backup file created after reading Chapter 9.*

In this chapter you will process Baxter's payroll and:

1. Learn the *MAPS* for recording employee paychecks before processing paychecks in QBP
2. Review payroll items to understand their impact on posting payroll transactions
3. Learn to use the Employee Center to manage employees and paycheck transactions
4. Pay employees
5. Go *Behind the Keys* of posted paychecks and learn to correct these transactions
6. Remit payroll tax liabilities to government taxing agencies
7. Create and interpret payroll reports, including Form 941 and W-2s

Launch QBP and open **Practice Baxter Garden Supply**.

 ## MANUAL ACCOUNTING PROCEDURES

Baxter pays employees biweekly (every two weeks) so the number of pay periods for the year is 26 (i.e., 52 weeks divided by 2). Employees are paid either an annual salary or an hourly wage. Salaried employees receive the same gross pay amount each pay period, which is calculated by dividing the annual salary by the number of pay periods in the year. Hourly employees are paid for the hours worked during the pay period and these employees turn in timesheets to document those hours.

You will soon learn that payroll in a manual accounting system is tedious and time consuming. You must first calculate each hourly employee's gross pay by totaling timesheet hours for the pay period and multiplying total hours by the hourly pay rate. As explained above, salaried employees receive the same gross pay each pay period.

After calculating gross pay, you then calculate each employee's net pay. Net pay equals gross pay minus total payroll tax withholdings and voluntary deductions. The following tables explain payroll tax withholdings and voluntary deductions.

Employee Tax Withholdings	Description
Federal Income Tax	Employee federal income taxes withheld on taxable wages. Taxable wages exclude employee contributions to a 401K or IRA retirement plan. IRS Circular E sets the guidelines for withholding federal income taxes (explained below).
Social Security (FICA)	Employee taxes withheld on gross wages and paid to the federal government to fund Social Security retirement. Gross wages include employee contributions to a 401K or IRA retirement plan. The IRS currently taxes gross wages at 6.2 percent (0.062) until wages paid during the year exceed an annual cap. For 2008 the annual cap was $102,000. This cap is increased each year and the 2009 cap was not available at the time of publishing the text.
Medicare (FICA)	Employee taxes withheld on gross wages and paid to the federal government to fund Medicare health insurance. Gross wages include employee contributions to a 401K or IRA retirement plan. The IRS taxes gross wages at 1.45 percent (0.0145) and there is no annual wage cap.
State Income Tax	Employee state income taxes withheld on taxable wages (i.e., gross wages minus contributions to a 401K or IRA retirement plan). Each state publishes guidelines for withholding state income taxes. ***Baxter withholds 3 percent (0.03) of gross wages.***

Employee Voluntary Deductions	Description
Retirement Plans	Employee voluntary contributions to an employer-sponsored retirement plan. Retirement plans include 401K and IRA plans. These contributions are deducted from gross wages to determine federal and state taxable wages. ***Baxter sponsors a 401K retirement plan and employees may elect to participate.***
Health Insurance	Health insurance premiums deducted from pay when the employer requires its employees to pay for a portion of health insurance costs. ***Baxter does not require employees to share this cost.***
Contributions	Deductions from net pay for charitable contributions made by the employee.

Baxter also pays taxes on employee compensation and provides additional compensation by paying the full cost of health insurance and matching employee contributions to a company sponsored 401K plan. The next tables explain typical employer tax liabilities and other forms of additional employee compensation.

Employer Payroll Taxes	Description
Social Security (FICA) and Medicare (FICA)	Employer portion of Social Security and Medicare taxes paid on gross wages. The employer tax equals the tax paid by employees.
Federal Unemployment (FUTA)	Employer tax on gross wages paid to the federal government for subsidizing state unemployment compensation funds. Typically, employers pay 0.08 percent (0.008) on the first $7,000 of annual gross wages paid to each employee.
State Unemployment (SUTA)	Employer tax on gross wages paid to the state for funding compensation for unemployed workers. Typically the tax rate is based on an employer's unemployment history and/or business type and will be capped after reaching an annual limit on gross wages. *For Baxter the rate is 1.5 percent (0.015) of the first $8,000 of annual wages paid to each employee.*
Worker's Compensation	Employer tax paid to the state to fund compensating injured workers. Typically, states set the tax rates based on risk factors in an employee's job. *The text does not illustrate worker's compensation tax.*

Additional Compensation	Description
Retirement Plans	Employer contributions to a company-sponsored 401K or IRA retirement plan. Typically companies match contributions based on employee participation in the plan. *Baxter's matches employee 401K contributions $.50 for every dollar contributed by the employee, up to a maximum of 5 percent (0.05) of the employee's annual pay.*
Health Insurance	Employer premiums for health insurance. Employers may pay all premiums or require employees to share in this cost. *Baxter pays all health insurance premiums for employees eligible to participate in the plan.*

Each pay period the accountant prepares this Excel spreadsheet called the **Payroll Register** to calculate employee net pay. The register illustrated in Figure 10:1 covers the pay period of February 23 to March 8, 2009.

	A	B	C	D	E	F	G	H	I	J	K	L	M	N	O	P
1	Baxter Garden Supply															
2	Pay Period 2/23/2009 thru 3/08/2009															
3																
4	Check No.	Employee	Filing Status	Allow	Pay Type	Pay Rate	Regular Hrs	OT Hrs	Gross Pay	Taxable Pay	Federal Income Tax	Soc. Sec. (FICA) Tax	Medicare Tax	VA State Tax	401K Deduc.	Net Pay
5	1180 Barkley, Steve N.		Married	3	Hourly wage	11.00	80.00		880.00	844.80	14.00	54.56	12.76	25.34	35.20	738.14
6	1181 Beck, Dorothy L.		Married	2	Hourly wage	9.00	80.00		720.00	720.00	15.00	44.64	10.44	21.60	0.00	628.32
7	1182 Chester, Amanda W.		Single	1	Hourly wage	14.00	80.00		1,120.00	1,075.20	110.00	69.44	16.24	32.26	44.80	847.26
8	1183 Duke, Al C.		Single	0	Hourly wage	12.50	80.00		1,000.00	1,000.00	122.00	62.00	14.50	30.00	0.00	771.50
9	1184 Frost, Melvin H.		Single	1	Salary	1,461.54			1,461.54	1,373.85	155.00	90.62	21.19	41.22	87.69	1,065.82
10	1185 Gross, Derrick P.		Married	2	Salary	1,000.00			1,000.00	940.00	37.00	62.00	14.50	28.20	60.00	798.30
11	1186 Hecter, Anthony H.		Single	1	Hourly wage	13.00	80.00		1,040.00	1,040.00	107.00	64.48	15.08	31.20	0.00	822.24
12	1187 Nunnley, Brandee M.		Married	1	Salary	1,211.54			1,211.54	1,211.54	85.00	75.12	17.57	36.35	0.00	997.50
13	1188 Prather, Samuel R.		Married	1	Salary	1,584.62			1,584.62	1,489.54	127.00	98.25	22.98	44.69	95.08	1,196.62
14	1189 Sweet, Leonard		Single	0	Hourly wage	9.00	80.00		720.00	720.00	80.00	44.64	10.44	21.60	0.00	563.32
15	1190 Trotter, Mitchell K.		Married	2	Hourly wage	11.00	80.00		880.00	844.80	27.00	54.56	12.76	25.34	35.20	725.14
16																
17		Totals					560.00	0.00	11,617.70		879.00	720.31	168.46	337.80	357.97	9,154.16
18																
19		Tax Basis									Circular E	6.20%	1.45%	3.00%		

Figure 10:1

The Payroll Register shows that Amanda Chester claims the Single (S) federal filing status with one withholding allowance. To calculate Amanda's federal income tax withholding for this pay period look to the 2008 IRS Circular E tax table in Figure 10:2. *(Note: IRS tables for 2009 were not available at the time of publishing the text.)*

					SINGLE Persons—BIWEEKLY Payroll Period						
					(For Wages Paid in 2008)						
If the wages are—		And the number of withholding allowances claimed is—										
At least	But less than	0	1	2	3	4	5	6	7	8	9	10
		The amount of income tax to be withheld is—										
$800	$820	$92	$71	$51	$31	$17	$4	$0	$0	$0	$0	$0
820	840	95	74	54	34	19	6	0	0	0	0	0
840	860	98	77	57	37	21	8	0	0	0	0	0
860	880	101	80	60	40	23	10	0	0	0	0	0
880	900	104	83	63	43	25	12	0	0	0	0	0
900	920	107	86	66	46	27	14	0	0	0	0	0
920	940	110	89	69	49	29	16	2	0	0	0	0
940	960	113	92	72	52	32	18	4	0	0	0	0
960	980	116	95	75	55	35	20	6	0	0	0	0
980	1,000	119	98	78	58	38	22	8	0	0	0	0
1,000	1,020	122	101	81	61	41	24	10	0	0	0	0
1,020	1,040	125	104	84	64	44	26	12	0	0	0	0
1,040	1,060	128	107	87	67	47	28	14	1	0	0	0
1,060	1,080	131	110	90	70	50	30	16	3	0	0	0
1,080	1,100	134	113	93	73	53	33	18	5	0	0	0
1,100	1,120	137	116	96	76	56	36	20	7	0	0	0
1,120	1,140	140	119	99	79	59	39	22	9	0	0	0
1,140	1,160	143	122	102	82	62	42	24	11	0	0	0
1,160	1,180	146	125	105	85	65	45	26	13	0	0	0
1,180	1,200	149	128	108	88	68	48	28	15	1	0	0
1,200	1,220	152	131	111	91	71	51	30	17	3	0	0
1,220	1,240	155	134	114	94	74	54	33	19	5	0	0
1,240	1,260	158	137	117	97	77	57	36	21	7	0	0
1,260	1,280	161	140	120	100	80	60	39	23	9	0	0
1,280	1,300	164	143	123	103	83	63	42	25	11	0	0
1,300	1,320	167	146	126	106	86	66	45	27	13	0	0

Figure 10:2

Figure 10:2 is the IRS table for employees paid biweekly and claiming the Single (S) filing status. There are separate IRS tables for employees claiming the Married (M) filing status and separate tables for married and single employees paid on a weekly or monthly basis

Amanda's $110.00 federal income tax withholding amount is found at the point where her taxable pay of $1,075.20 intersects with her one claimed withholding allowance. Federal income taxes are calculated on taxable pay, which is equal to gross pay minus 401K deductions.

Amanda's Social Security tax withholding of $69.44 equals her gross pay times 6.2 percent (.062). Her Medicare tax withholding of $16.24 equals gross pay times 1.45 percent (.0145). *(Note: 401K contributions are not deducted from FICA and Medicare tax calculations.)*

The state tax withholding amount of $32.26 is based on a state tax rate of 3 percent (.03) of taxable pay. 401K contributions are deducted from gross pay to determine taxable pay for state purposes.

Baxter sponsors a 401K retirement plan that allows employees to elect participation by contributing a percentage of gross pay. Employees can choose to contribute any percentage up to 11 percent of gross pay and Baxter will match contributions by the same percentage up to 5 percent of gross pay. Amanda has chosen to contribute 4 percent (.04) of gross pay each pay period.

Amanda has no deductions for health insurance premiums or charitable contributions. In fact, premiums are not deducted from any employee's paycheck because Baxter pays the full cost of health insurance. Finally, there are no employees making charitable contributions through payroll.

Accordingly, Amanda's net pay of $847.26 equals her gross pay of $1,120.00 minus the sum of her tax withholdings and voluntary deductions.

In addition to preparing the payroll register, the accountant computes the following employer payroll tax liabilities for the pay period.

	R	S	T	U	V	W	X
1	**Baxter Garden Supply**						
2	**Employer Costs for Period 2/23/2009 thru 3/08/2009**						
3							
4	Employee	401K Match	ER Soc. Sec. (FICA)	ER Medicare	ER FUTA	ER SUTA	Health Insurance
5	Barkley, Steve N.	17.60	54.56	12.76	7.04	13.20	125.00
6	Beck, Dorothy L.	0.00	44.64	10.44	5.76	10.80	0.00
7	Chester, Amanda W.	22.40	69.44	16.24	8.96	16.80	90.00
8	Duke, Al C.	0.00	62.00	14.50	8.00	15.00	90.00
9	Frost, Melvin H.	43.85	90.62	21.19	4.58	21.92	125.00
10	Gross, Derrick P.	30.00	62.00	14.50	8.00	15.00	90.00
11	Hecter, Anthony H.	0.00	64.48	15.08	8.32	15.60	90.00
12	Nunnley, Brandee M.	0.00	75.12	17.57	9.69	18.17	125.00
13	Prather, Samuel R.	47.54	98.25	22.98	0.00	23.77	125.00
14	Sweet, Leonard	0.00	44.64	10.44	5.76	10.80	90.00
15	Trotter, Mitchell K.	17.60	54.56	12.76	7.04	13.20	90.00
16							
17	Totals	178.99	720.31	168.46	73.15	174.26	1,040.00
18							
19	Tax Basis	50% Match	6.20%	1.45%	0.8%	1.5%	
20							
21	G/L Accounts	23300 / 60500	23400 / 61000	23400 / 61000	23500 / 61000	23700 / 61000	23750 / 60300
22							

Figure 10:3

After computing employee pay and employer payroll tax expenses, the accountant creates paychecks and records the general journal entries illustrated in Figure 10:4.

Audit Trail	**Baxter Garden Supply** General Journal			**Page 7**
Date	Account Post Ref	Description	Debit	Credit
03/09/09	60000	Salaries and Wages Expense	11,617.70	
	23400	Federal Payroll Taxes Payable		1,767.77
	23600	State Payroll Taxes Payable		337.80
	23300	401K Deductions Payable		357.97
	10300	Payroll Checking Account		9,154.16
To record employee paychecks				
03/09/09	61000	Payroll Tax Expense	1,136.18	
	60500	Employee Benefit Exp.	178.99	
	60600	Employee Benefit Exp.	1,040.00	
	23400	Federal Payroll Taxes Payable		888.77
	23500	FUTA Tax Payable		73.15
	23700	SUTA Tax Payable		174.26
	23300	401K Deductions Payable		178.99
	23750	Health Insurance Payable		1,040.00
To record employer payroll tax expense				

Figure 10:4

These journal entries are then posted to the general ledger accounts illustrated next. *(Note: Only two general ledger accounts are illustrated.)* As explained in previous chapters, the audit trail is recorded while posting to general ledger accounts.

General Ledger

Payroll Checking Account   **Account No. 10300**

Date	Description	Post Ref	Debit	Credit	Balance
03/08/09	Balance Forward				12,097.97
03/09/09		GJ 7		9,154.16	2,943.81

Audit Trail

General Ledger

Federal Payroll Taxes Payable   **Account No. 23400**

Date	Description	Post Ref	Debit	Credit	Balance
03/08/09	Balance Forward				-
03/09/09		GJ 7		1,767.77	1,767.77
03/09/09		GJ 7		888.77	2,656.54

Figure 10:5

With an understanding of *MAPS* for paycheck activities, you are now ready to perform these activities in QBP.

UNDERSTANDING PAYROLL ITEMS

A series of setup steps is performed before a company can use QBP to process payroll. The accountant has already completed these steps; however, it will help for you to understand payroll setup.

Begin by opening the Payroll Item List. Select *Lists>>Payroll Item List* on the main menu to open the window illustrated next.

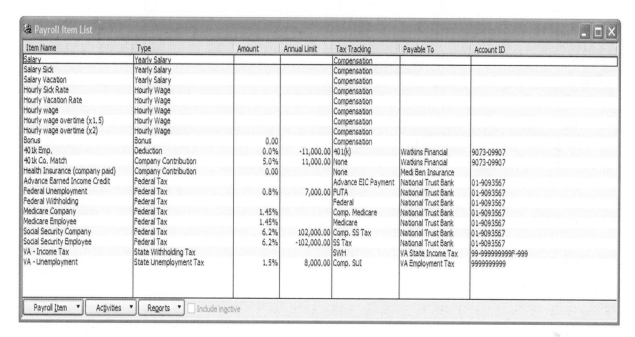

Figure 10:6

This list shows payroll items for tracking compensation, payroll tax withholdings, and payroll tax liabilities. Salary and wage types track employee compensation whereas federal and state types track employee tax withholdings and employer tax liabilities.

You will now add columns to the list so that general ledger accounts display for each item. Click **Payroll Item** at the bottom of the list and select **Customize Columns**. Highlight **Expense Account** under **Available Columns** and click **Add**. Do the same for **Liability Account**. (See Figure 10:7.)

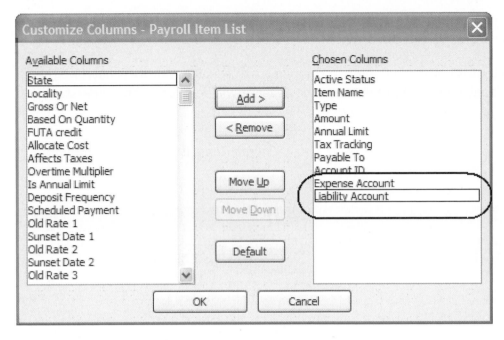

Figure 10:7

Click **OK** to view the list with the new columns (Figure 10:8). You will need to resize columns to view all information.

Item Name	Type	Amount	Annual Limit	Tax Tracking	Payable To	Account ID	Expense Account	Liability Account
Salary	Yearly Salary			Compensation			60000 · Salaries and Wages Expense	
Salary Sick	Yearly Salary			Compensation			60300 · Payroll Expenses	
Salary Vacation	Yearly Salary			Compensation			60300 · Payroll Expenses	
Hourly Sick Rate	Hourly Wage			Compensation			60300 · Payroll Expenses	
Hourly Vacation Rate	Hourly Wage			Compensation			60300 · Payroll Expenses	
Hourly wage	Hourly Wage			Compensation			60000 · Salaries and Wages Expense	
Hourly wage overtime (x1.5)	Hourly Wage			Compensation			60000 · Salaries and Wages Expense	
Hourly wage overtime (x2)	Hourly Wage			Compensation			60000 · Salaries and Wages Expense	
Bonus	Bonus	0.00		Compensation			60100 · Salaries Bonus Expense	
401k Emp.	Deduction	0.0%	-11,000.00	401(k)	Watkins Financial	9073-09907		23300 · 401 K Deductions Payable
401k Co. Match	Company Contribution	5.0%	11,000.00	None	Watkins Financial	9073-09907	60500 · Pension/Profit-Sharing Expense	23300 · 401 K Deductions Payable
Health Insurance (company paid)	Company Contribution	0.00		None	Medi Ben Insurance		60300 · Payroll Expenses	23750 · Health Insurance Payable
Advance Earned Income Credit	Federal Tax			Advance EIC Payment	National Trust Bank	01-9093567		23400 · Federal Payroll Taxes Payable
Federal Unemployment	Federal Tax	0.8%	7,000.00	FUTA	National Trust Bank	01-9093567	61000 · Payroll Tax Expense	23500 · FUTA Tax Payable
Federal Withholding	Federal Tax			Federal	National Trust Bank	01-9093567		23400 · Federal Payroll Taxes Payable
Medicare Company	Federal Tax	1.45%		Comp. Medicare	National Trust Bank	01-9093567	61000 · Payroll Tax Expense	23400 · Federal Payroll Taxes Payable
Medicare Employee	Federal Tax	1.45%		Medicare	National Trust Bank	01-9093567		23400 · Federal Payroll Taxes Payable
Social Security Company	Federal Tax	6.2%	102,000.00	Comp. SS Tax	National Trust Bank	01-9093567	61000 · Payroll Tax Expense	23400 · Federal Payroll Taxes Payable
Social Security Employee	Federal Tax	6.2%	-102,000.00	SS Tax	National Trust Bank	01-9093567		23400 · Federal Payroll Taxes Payable
VA - Income Tax	State Withholding Tax			SWH	VA State Income Tax	99-999999999F-999		23600 · State Payroll Taxes Payable
VA - Unemployment	State Unemployment Tax	1.5%	8,000.00	Comp. SUI	VA Employment Tax	9999999999	61000 · Payroll Tax Expense	23700 · SUTA Tax Payable

Figure 10:8

Refer to these accounts as we go through the setup of payroll items.

Double click to open the **Salary** item. The screen illustrated in Figure 10:9 is used to define an item's name or to inactivate the item.

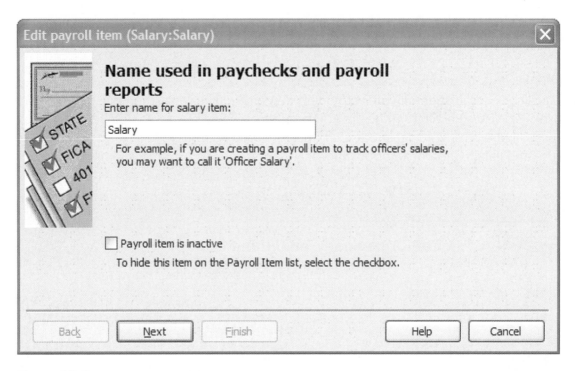

Figure 10:9

Click **Next** to move to the screen illustrated in Figure 10:10. This is where you set the default general ledger account used when posting a salaried employee's gross pay. The account displayed in the window agrees to the expense account for this item on the Payroll Item List.

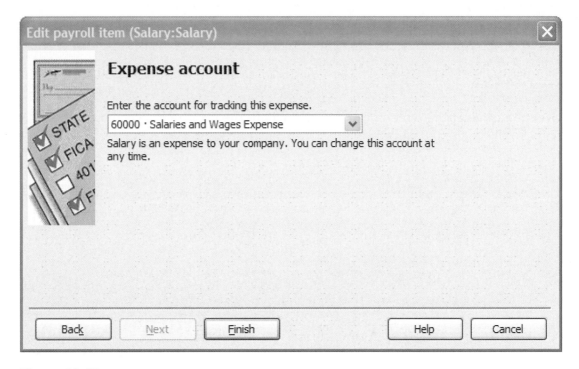

Figure 10:10

Click **Cancel** and now review the **Payroll Item List** to note that Baxter has a separate category for hourly wage compensation.

Salary items are for employees paid an annual salary whereas hourly wage items are for employees paid an hourly wage. Compensation under both items will post to 60000 Salaries and Wages Expense.

Double click **Federal Unemployment** to open the item. Once again, the first screen names the item so click **Next**. Recall from the previous topic that FUTA tax is an employer payroll tax expense. Figure 10:11 is where you select the vendor for remitting taxes to as well as the expense and liability accounts for posting FUTA taxes.

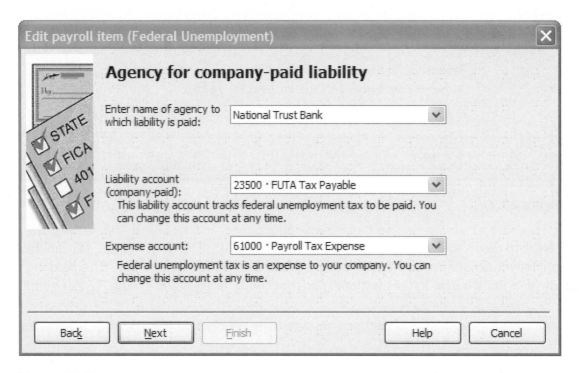

Figure 10:11

Click **Next** to arrive at the screen (Figure 10:12) where the tax rate is selected. Most companies will use the 0.8 percent (0.008) rate.

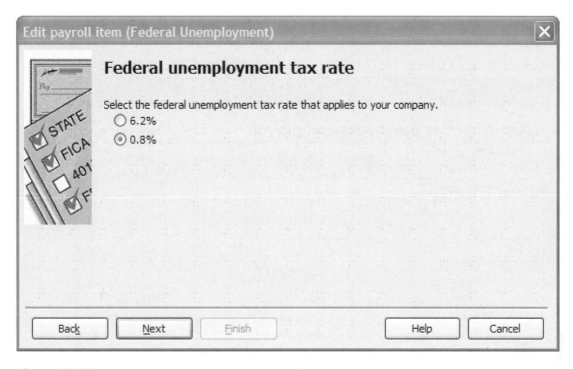

Figure 10:12

Click **Next** and you are at the screen (Figure 10:13) for choosing compensation items that are subject to FUTA tax. Generally, all wage compensation will be FUTA taxable. For more information on FUTA taxes, visit www.irs.gov.

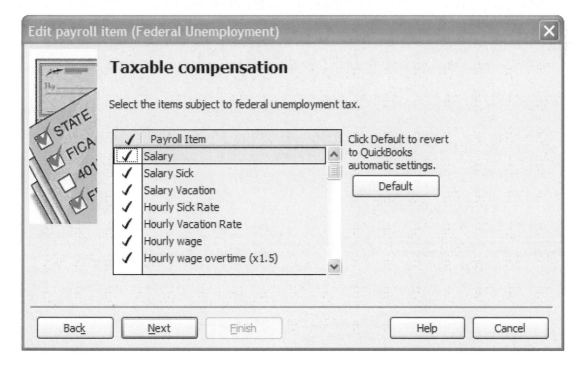

Figure 10:13

Click **Cancel**.

Now open **Medicare Company**. The screen in Figure 10:14 names two items because Medicare is paid by both the employee and the employer.

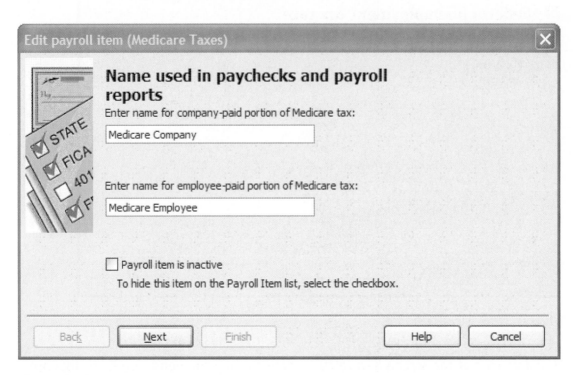

Figure 10:14

Click **Next**. Once again, you find a screen (Figure 10:15) for selecting the general ledger posting accounts as well as the vendor for remitting payment. However, this time the screen sets only liability accounts for employer taxes and employee withholdings.

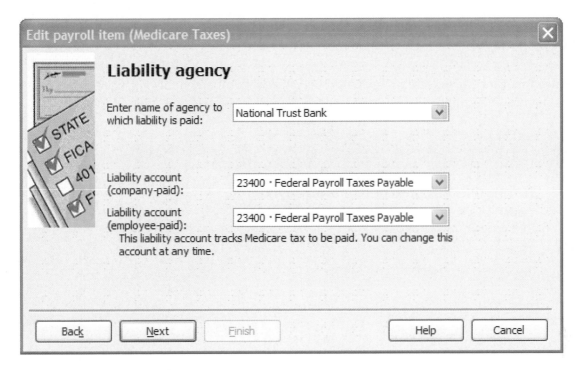

Figure 10:15

Click **Next**. The screen in Figure 10:16 is where you select the employer tax expense account.

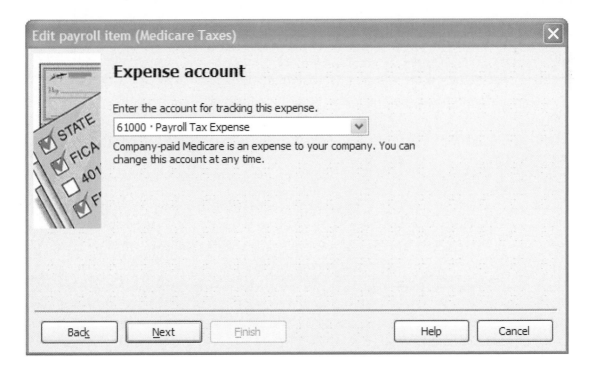

Figure 10:16

Click **Cancel**.

Notice that you were unable to set the tax rate on the previous item. In fact, you will be unable to set tax rates for any Federal Tax types, other than FUTA, or State Withholding Tax types.

QBP sets these rates when downloading the online payroll tax tables that require a paid subscription to download.

Open **Health Insurance**. The screen in Figure 10:17 tracks company health insurance premiums paid by the employer.

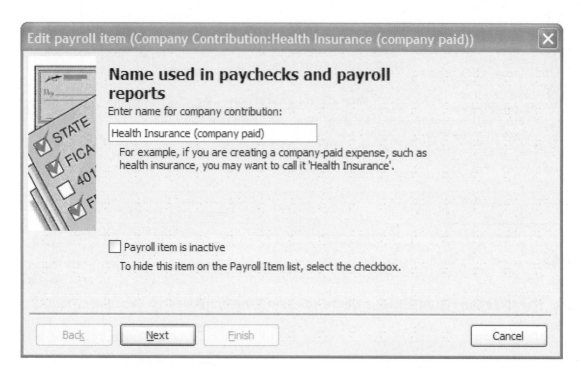

Figure 10:17

Click **Next**. Again, you find the screen (Figure 10:18) for selecting a vendor and general ledger accounts.

Figure 10:18

Click **Next**. On this screen (Figure 10:19) you can opt to print company contributions for health insurance on employee W-2s. Baxter has elected not to print this information.

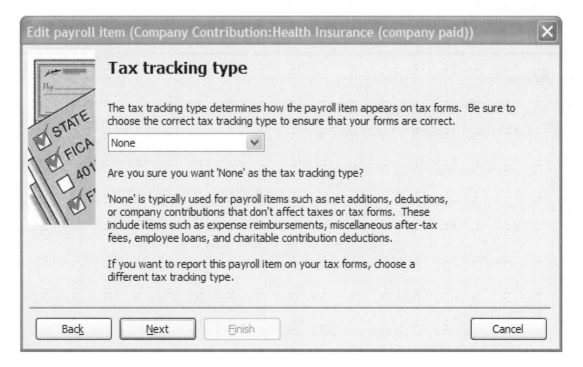

Figure 10:19

Click **Next**. This screen (Figure 10:20) determines when a company-paid benefit is subject to employer and/or employee payroll taxes. Remember, these benefits are deemed additional compensation, which may or may not be taxable. Typically, employer-paid health insurance premiums are not subject to tax.

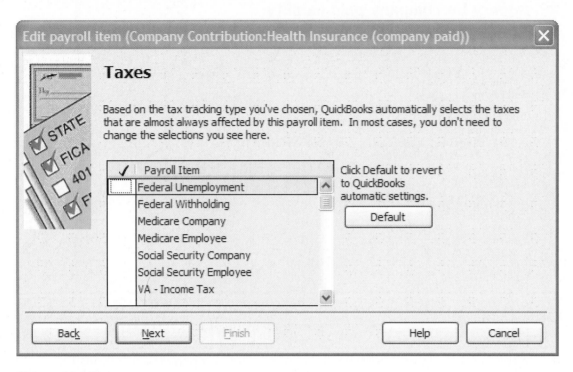

Figure 10:20

Click **Next**. The screen illustrated in Figure 10:21 is where you choose whether to base a company-paid benefit on quantities (e.g., hours worked) or a percentage or flat amount.

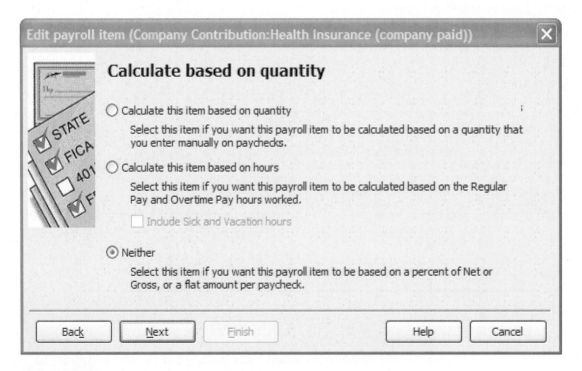

Figure 10:21

Click **Next**. On the screen illustrated in Figure 10:22 the default rate or percentage is set. Baxter has not entered an amount because the amount varies by employee. Instead, the rate will be entered on the employee account.

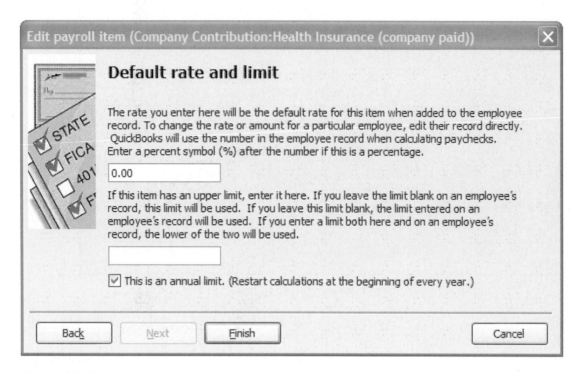

Figure 10:22

Click **Cancel**.

Now open **401k Emp**. This item is for employee 401K contributions. Click **Next** on the screen that names the item and **Next** on the screen that sets the vendor and general ledger account to arrive at the screen (Figure 10:23) that reports the item on W-2s and lists the annual contribution limit.

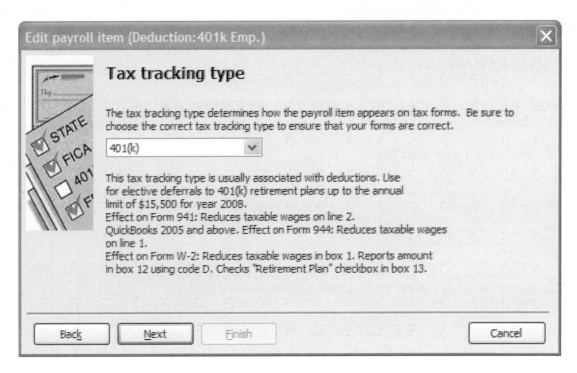

Figure 10:23

Click **Next**. Figure 10:24 shows the tax calculations affected by 401K contributions. Notice that only federal and state income tax withholdings are affected. Gross wages will be reduced by employee 401K contributions before calculating Federal Withholding and VA-Income Tax.

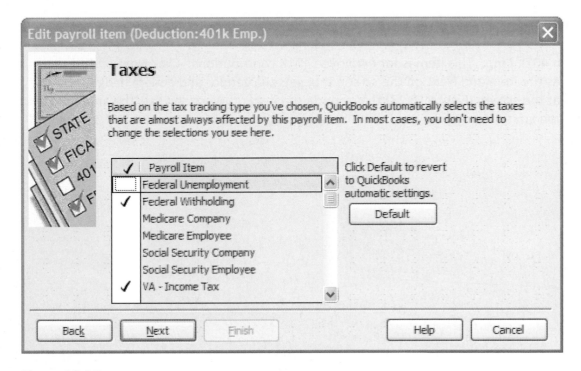

Figure 10:24

Click **Next** and then **Next** on the calculation basis window to arrive at the screen illustrated in Figure 10:25. Baxter has not set a default percentage because employee contribution rates vary. However, this screen shows that 401K calculations will stop after an employee has contributed the annual limit of $11,000. This limit is not up to date, showing that a company needs to make sure to monitor payroll tax items when not subscribing to the on-line payroll service. Information on annual limits for retirement plans is available on the IRS website.

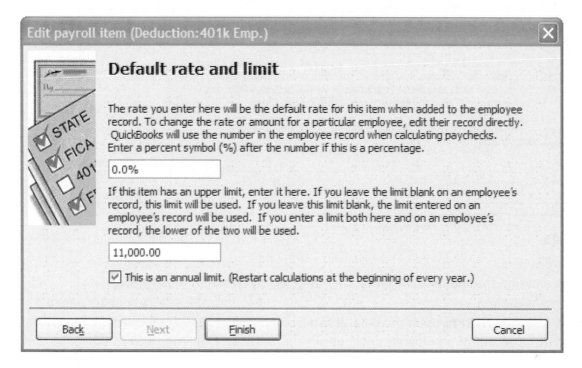

Figure 10:25

Click **Cancel** and you will now open the employer 401K matching contribution item.

Open **401k Co. Match**. Click **Next** and then **Next** to arrive at the screen illustrated in Figure 10:26. Baxter has set this item to not be reported on employee W-2s. Employer contributions are not taxable when paid to an employee because the employee pays tax on contributions after receiving retirement benefits.

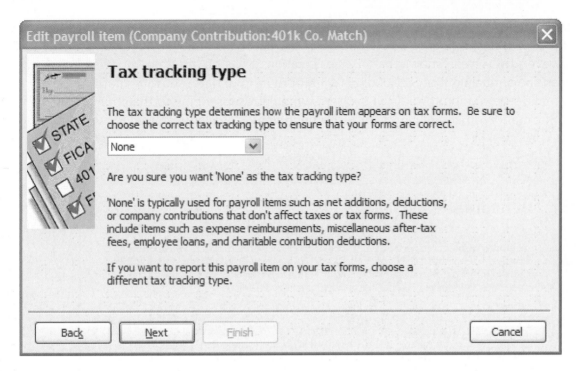

Figure 10:26

Click **Next** and find that no tax calculations are affected by this item (not shown).

Click **Next** and then **Next** to open the default rate screen (Figure 10:27). Baxter will match a maximum of 5 percent of employee contributions up to the annual limit of $11,000.

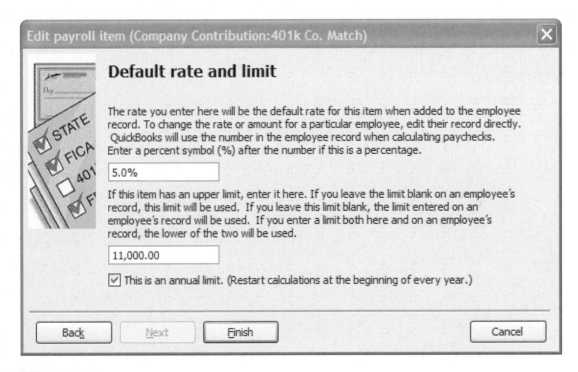

Figure 10:27

Click **Cancel** and then close the Payroll Item List.

With all the complexities just illustrated, you can see why many companies outsource payroll. Now that you understand the purpose of payroll items, you will next learn to manage the employee accounts linked to these items.

EMPLOYEE CENTER

In this topic you use the Employee Center to manage employee accounts and locate payroll transactions.

Click the **Employee Center** icon on the toolbar and it opens with the **Employees** tab active. Click **Amanda Chester** and set the filtering options illustrated in Figure 10:28.

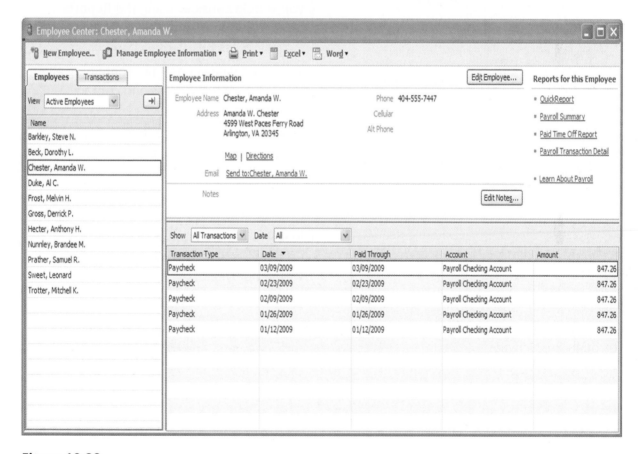

Figure 10:28

The **Transactions** tab serves the same purpose as served on other centers. The table that follows explains activities and tasks on the **Employees** toolbar. Remember that actions are performed on the account highlighted to the left.

Employees Activities	Task	Description
New Employee		Create a new employee account.
Manage Employee Information	Add/Edit Sales Rep	Manage existing employee accounts.
	Change New Employee Default Settings	Create employee defaults that will be assigned to new employee accounts.
Print	Print Paychecks	Print calculated paychecks.
	Print/Email Paystubs	Print only pay stubs. This is used when checks are deposited directly to employee bank accounts.
	Print Other Employee Reports	Print an employee list, account information, or paycheck transactions. These reports cannot be customized so you should consider using the Reports menu to print this information.
Excel	Export Employee List	Create an Excel workbook or comma separated values (.csv) file containing all employees with address and contact information.
	Export Transactions	Create an Excel workbook or comma separated values (.csv) file containing paycheck transactions for the highlighted employee.
	Summarize Payroll Data in Excel	Extract payroll data from QBP for analysis in Excel.
Word		Create form letters for communicating with employees.

The Employee Center is helpful for managing employees and the next topic will walk you through this activity.

MANAGING EMPLOYEES

Double click Amanda Chester's account to open it. *(Note: You can also click the Edit Employee button to the right.)*

An employee account contains tabs for three categories of information. These categories are **Personal Info**, **Payroll and Compensation Info**, and **Employment Info**. (See Figure 10:29.) Tab categories are changed by selecting a different category from the **Change tabs** dropdown list.

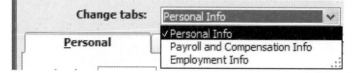

Figure 10:29

Select the **Personal Info** tab and you will find subtabs for information in this category. The following explains the information stored on subtabs in the **Personal Info** category.

Personal Tab

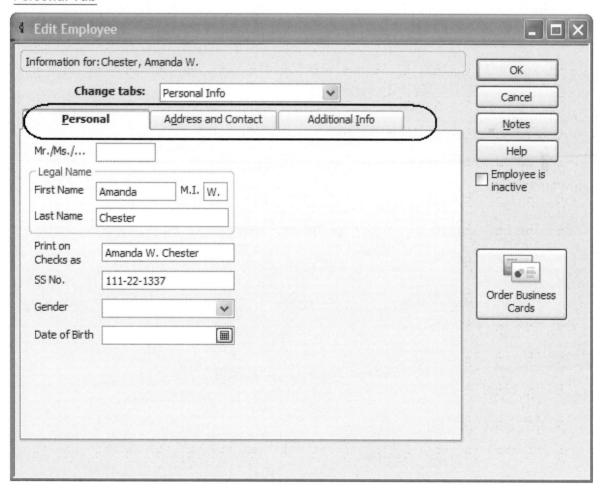

Figure 10:30

This tab stores employee social security number and birth date.

Address and Contact Tab

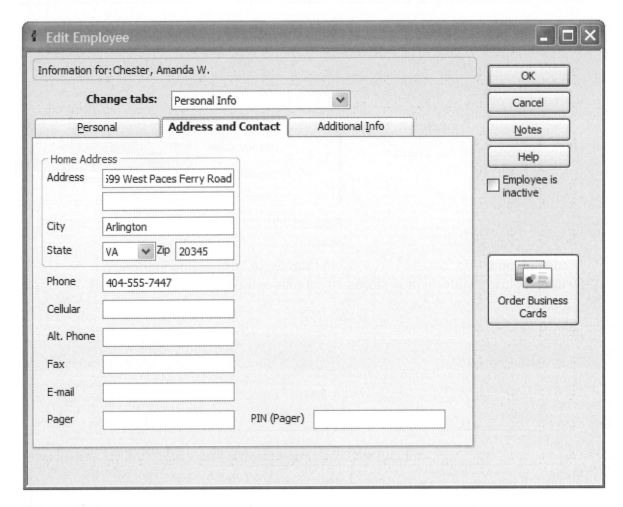

Figure 10:31

This tab stores basic contact information for the employee.

Additional Info Tab

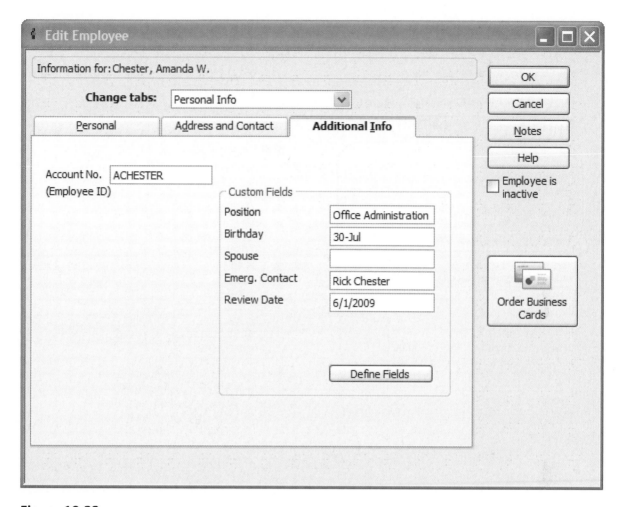

Figure 10:32

This tab stores miscellaneous information such as job position.

Now change the category to **Payroll and Compensation Info**.

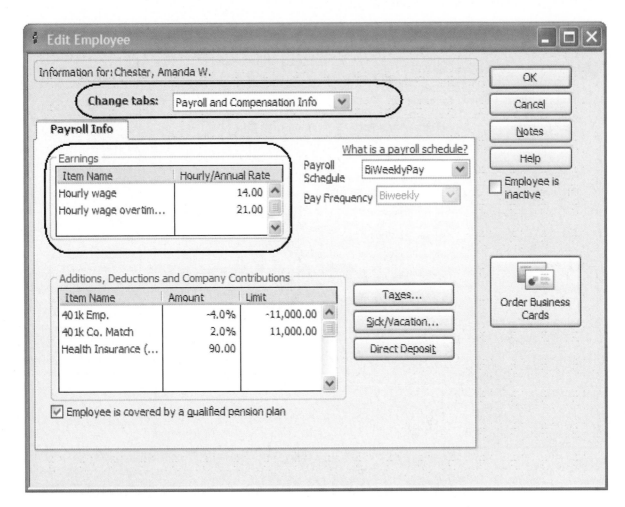

Figure 10:33

Figure 10:33 is where QBP looks to gather pay rates and pay schedule frequency. Notice that Amanda is paid biweekly at $14.00 per hour for regular time and $21.00 per hour for overtime. Also note that the employee is covered by a qualified pension plan.

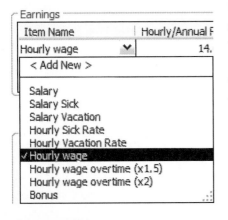

Now focus on **Item Name**. Click **Hourly wage** and open the dropdown list. Figure 10:34 shows Baxter's pay code. You find the compensation payroll items discussed in the Payroll Items topic. Amanda's account has been assigned to Hourly wage, so you know that her compensation is based on hours worked during the pay period.

Figure 10:34

Click the **Taxes** button. QBP looks to the tab illustrated in Figure 10:35 to obtain federal and state filing statuses and withholding allowances.

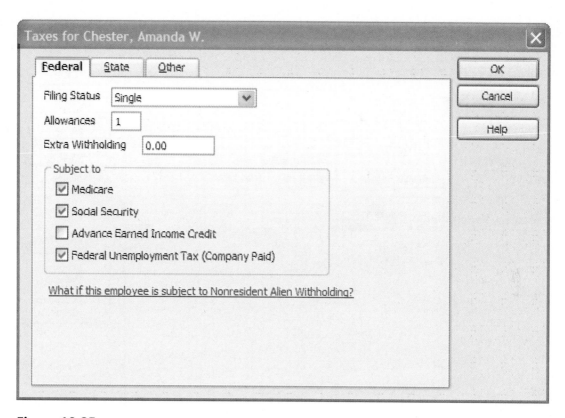

Figure 10:35

The **Federal** tab shows Amanda's federal **Filing Status** as **Single** with one withholding **Allowance**. At the bottom you see that Amanda's wages are subject to Medicare and Social Security tax withholdings. In addition, wages are subject to employer Medicare, Social Security, and FUTA taxes.

The **State** tab is used for entering state withholding information. The **Other** tab is used when employees must also pay city or local taxes.

Click **Cancel** to exit the tax window.

Finally, change the category to **Employment Info**. This tab (Figure 10:36) stores an employee's hire date as well as the last day an employee worked for the company.

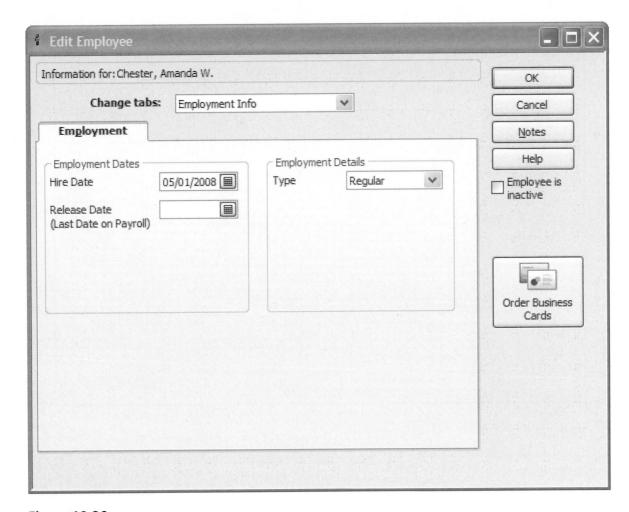

Figure 10:36

Click **Cancel** to close Amanda's account.

Before leaving this topic, open Melvin Frost's account to view pay information for a salaried employee. After opening, change the tab category to **Payroll and Compensation Info**. (See Figure 10:37.)

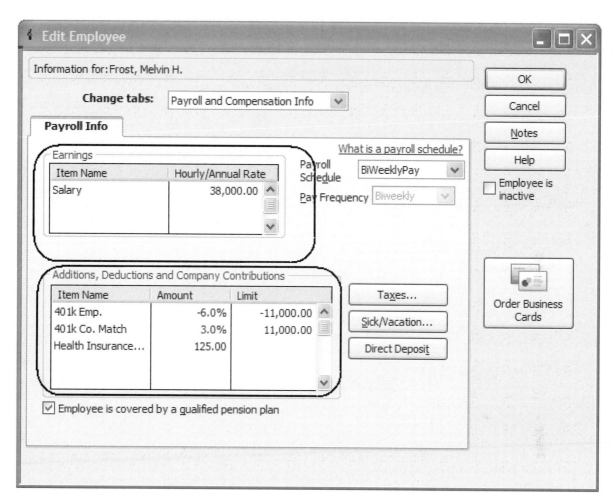

Figure 10:37

Salaried employee pay rates are entered as annual compensation. For Melvin, the annual salary is $38,000. Also notice that Melvin is paid biweekly, so he will receive 26 paychecks during the year (52 weeks per year / 2 weeks per pay period). Based on this information, QBP will calculate Melvin's gross pay for each pay period as $38,000 / 26.

Melvin's account is also linked to other payroll items. Melvin contributes 6 percent to his 401K account and the company matches 3 percent. The company also accrues $125 each pay period for Melvin's health insurance.

Click **Cancel** to exit Melvin's account.

You are now ready to create a new employee. Click the **New Employee** button on the Employee Center. Baxter hired Susan Sharpton to work as a retail clerk so follow the next steps to create her account.

Enter the **Personal** information illustrated in Figure 10:38.

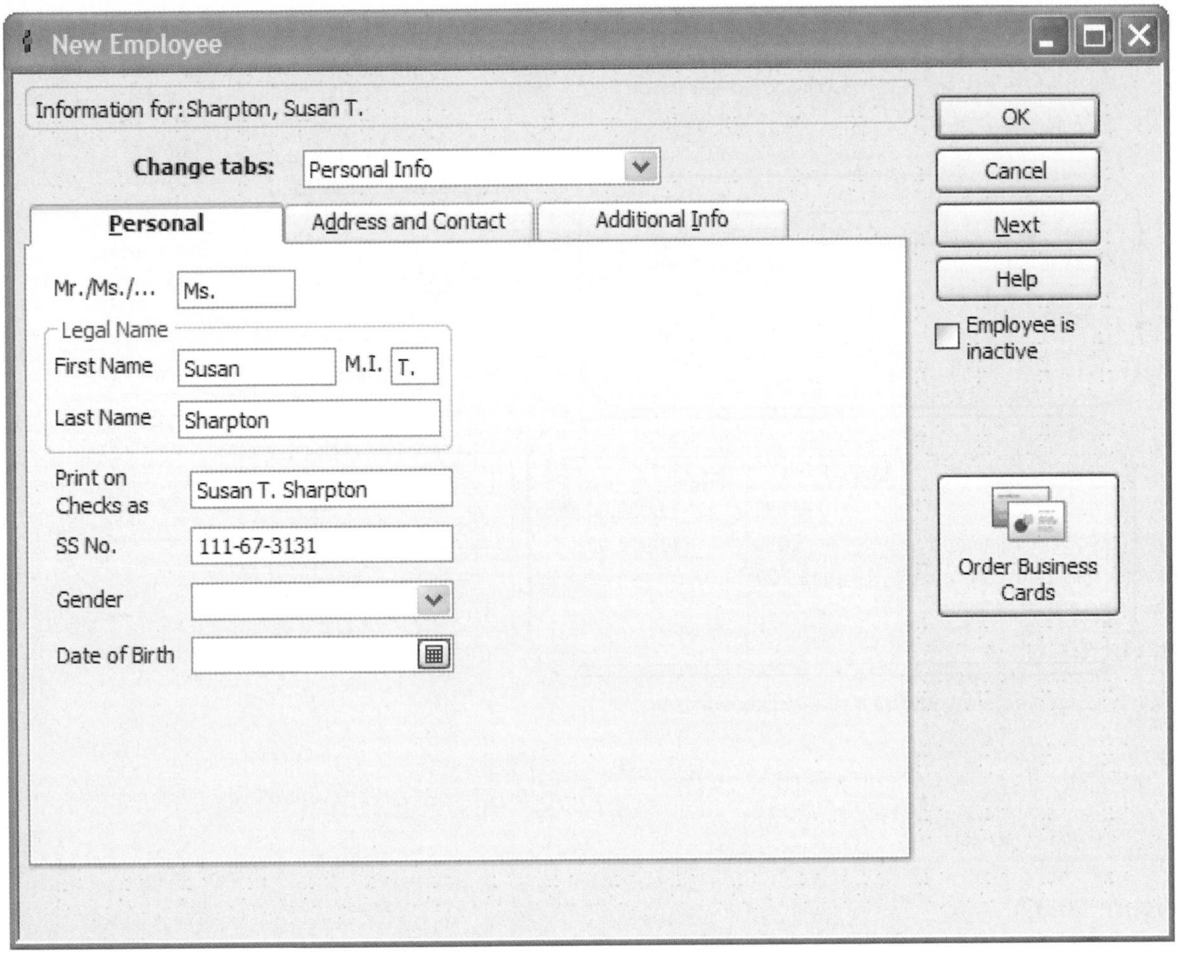

New Employee

Information for: Sharpton, Susan T.

Change tabs: Personal Info

Tabs: Personal | Address and Contact | Additional Info

Buttons: OK, Cancel, Next, Help

Employee is inactive

Mr./Ms./... Ms.

Legal Name
First Name Susan   M.I. T.
Last Name Sharpton

Print on Checks as Susan T. Sharpton
SS No. 111-67-3131
Gender
Date of Birth

Order Business Cards

Figure 10:38

Click **Address and Contact** and enter the information shown in Figure 10:39.

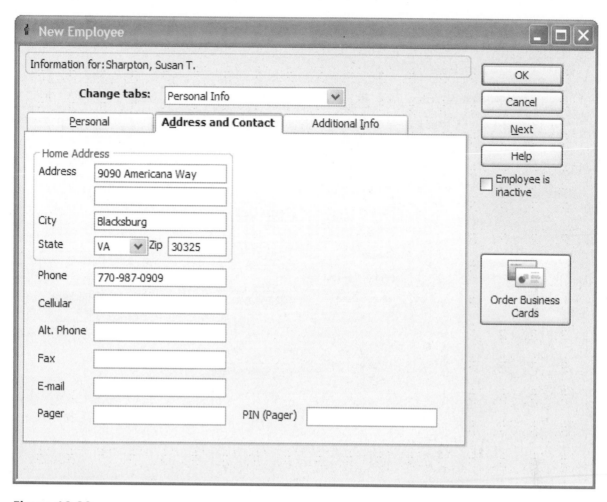

Figure 10:39

Click **Additional Info** and enter the information shown in Figure 10:40.

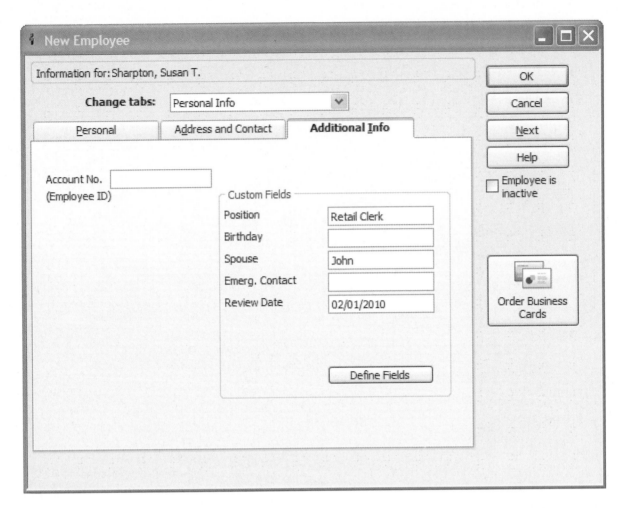

Figure 10:40

Now look up and change the category to **Payroll and Compensation Info**. (See Figure 10:41.)

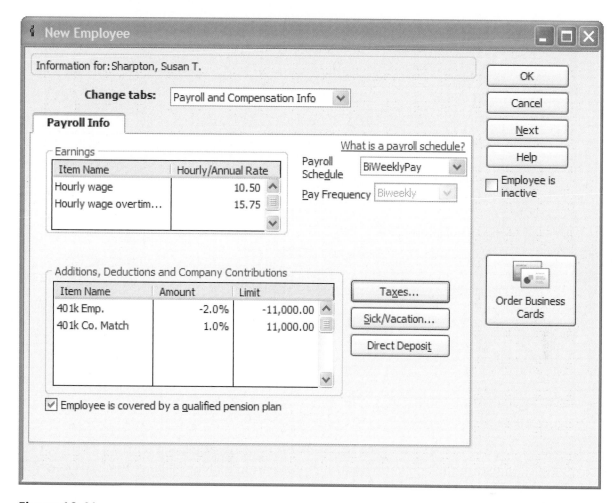

Figure 10:41

Enter Susan's salary information by following the next steps.

1. Place your cursor in **Item Name** and look up **Hourly Wage**.
2. Tab to **Hourly/Annual Rate** and enter 10.50.
3. Place your cursor in the next row for **Item Name** and select **Hourly wage overtime (x1.5)**. QBP will fill in the rate of $15.75.
4. Use your cursor and select **BiWeeklyPay** in the **Payroll Schedule**.
5. At the bottom, look up and select **401k Emp**. Tab to **Amount** and enter "2%".
6. Add the employer match by looking up and selecting **401k Co. Match**. Tab to **Amount** and enter "1%".

Click the **Taxes** button and follow the next steps to enter Susan's federal and state withholding information.

1. On the **Federal** tab illustrated in Figure 10:42, look up and select **Married** as the **Filing Status**.
2. Enter "0" in **Allowances**.

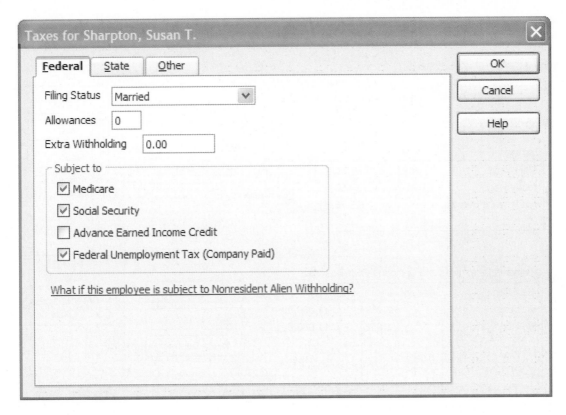

Figure 10:42

3. Click the **State** tab and verify that the information matches Figure 10:43. When finished, click **OK**.

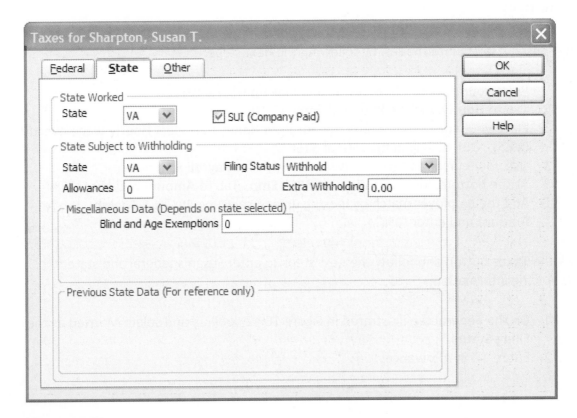

Figure 10:43

Now change the category to **Employment Info** and enter Susan's hire date.

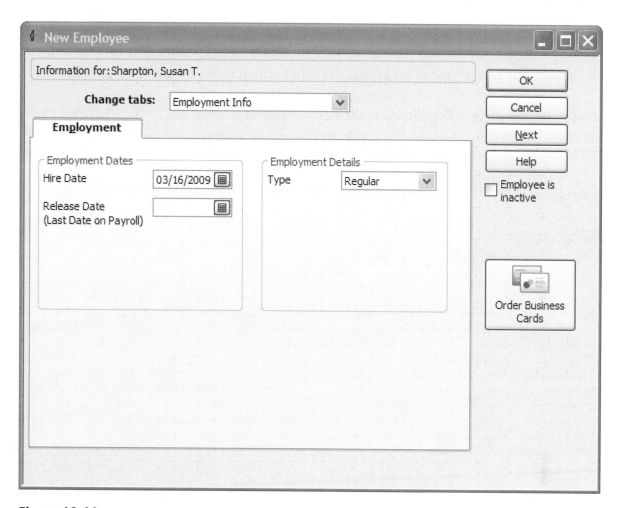

Figure 10:44

Click **OK** to save Susan's account. If prompted to set up local taxes and sick/vacation time, click **Leave As Is**.

Close the Employee Center.

Besides creating employees, you also need to know how to terminate an employee. You cannot delete an employee account with paycheck history. Instead, you enter a termination date under **Release Date** on the **Employment** tab and mark the **Employee is inactive** option.

Now that you understand managing employee accounts, you are ready to pay employees.

Note: In Chapter 4 we covered entering employee time after explaining employee accounts because the company in that chapter was a service based business and time was billed to customers. Baxter is a merchandising business so you do not need to enter timesheets because hours can be entered while paying employees.

PAYING EMPLOYEES

In this topic you prepare Baxter's payroll. Unfortunately, you will not be able to take advantage of QBP's automatic tax calculation for creating paychecks because you have not downloaded the online payroll tax tables. *(Remember that there is a fee for these tables.)*

Instead you are going to create paychecks by entering information calculated in Excel. Although this takes additional time, there are benefits to knowing this method because some companies will not subscribe to QBP's payroll tax service.

Figure 10:45 shows the Excel paycheck register for the pay period ended March 22, 2009.

Baxter Garden Supply
Pay Period 3/9/2009 thru 3/22/2009

Check No.	Employee	Filing Status	Allow	Pay Type	Pay Rate	Regular Hrs	OT Hrs	Gross Pay	Taxable Pay	Federal Income Tax	Soc. Sec. (FICA) Tax	Medicare Tax	VA State Tax	401K Deduc.	Net Pay
1191	Barkley, Steve N.	Married	3	Hourly wage	11.00	80.00	2.00	913.00	876.48	16.00	56.61	13.24	26.29	36.52	764.34
1192	Beck, Dorothy L.	Married	2	Hourly wage	9.00	80.00		720.00	720.00	15.00	44.64	10.44	21.60	0.00	628.32
1193	Chester, Amanda W.	Single	1	Hourly wage	14.00	80.00		1,120.00	1,075.20	110.00	69.44	16.24	32.26	44.80	847.26
1194	Duke, Al C.	Single	0	Hourly wage	12.50	78.00		975.00	975.00	116.00	60.45	14.14	29.25	0.00	755.16
1195	Frost, Melvin H.	Single	1	Salary	1,461.54			1,461.54	1,373.85	155.00	90.62	21.19	41.22	87.69	1,065.82
1196	Gross, Derrick P.	Married	2	Salary	1,000.00			1,000.00	940.00	37.00	62.00	14.50	28.20	60.00	798.30
1197	Hecter, Anthony H.	Single	1	Hourly wage	13.00	80.00		1,040.00	1,040.00	107.00	64.48	15.08	31.20	0.00	822.24
1198	Nunnley, Brandee M.	Married	1	Salary	1,211.54			1,211.54	1,211.54	85.00	75.12	17.57	36.35	0.00	997.50
1199	Prather, Samuel R.	Married	1	Salary	1,584.62			1,584.62	1,489.54	127.00	98.25	22.98	44.69	95.08	1,196.62
1200	Sharpton, Susan T.	Married	0	Hourly wage	10.50	40.00		420.00	411.60	11.00	26.04	6.09	12.35	8.40	356.12
1201	Sweet, Leonard	Single	0	Hourly wage	9.00	80.00		720.00	720.00	80.00	44.64	10.44	21.60	0.00	563.32
1202	Trotter, Mitchell K.	Married	2	Hourly wage	11.00	80.00		880.00	844.80	27.00	54.56	12.76	25.34	35.20	725.14
	Totals					598.00	2.00	12,045.70		886.00	746.85	174.67	350.35	367.69	9,520.14
	Tax Basis									Circular E	6.20%	1.45%	3.00%		
	G/L Accounts							60000		23400	23400	23400	23600	23300	10300

Figure 10:45

Figure 10:46 shows the Excel payroll register for employer costs.

Baxter Garden Supply						
Employer Costs for Period 3/9/2009 thru 3/22/2009						
Employee	401K Match	ER Soc. Sec. (FICA)	ER Medicare	ER FUTA	ER SUTA	Health Insurance
Barkley, Steve N.	18.26	56.61	13.24	7.30	13.70	125.00
Beck, Dorothy L.	0.00	44.64	10.44	5.76	10.80	0.00
Chester, Amanda W.	22.40	69.44	16.24	8.96	16.80	90.00
Duke, Al C.	0.00	60.45	14.14	7.80	14.63	90.00
Frost, Melvin H.	43.85	90.62	21.19	0.00	10.40	125.00
Gross, Derrick P.	30.00	62.00	14.50	8.00	15.00	90.00
Hecter, Anthony H.	0.00	64.48	15.08	8.32	15.60	90.00
Nunnley, Brandee M.	0.00	75.12	17.57	7.55	18.17	125.00
Prather, Samuel R.	47.54	98.25	22.98	0.00	1.15	125.00
Sharpton, Susan T.	4.20	26.04	6.09	3.36	6.30	0.00
Sweet, Leonard	0.00	44.64	10.44	5.76	10.80	90.00
Trotter, Mitchell K.	17.60	54.56	12.76	7.04	13.20	90.00
Totals	183.85	746.85	174.67	69.85	146.55	1,040.00
Tax Basis	50% Match	6.20%	1.45%	0.8%	1.5%	
G/L Accounts	23300 / 60500	23400 / 61000	23400 / 61000	23500 / 61000	23700 / 61000	23750 / 60600

Figure 10:46

Now follow the next steps to create employee paychecks using the Excel data.

STEPS TO CREATE EMPLOYEE PAYCHECKS

1. Click **Pay Employees** on the **Home** page to open the Enter Payroll Information window illustrated in Figure 10:47.

   Set the **Pay Period Ends** date to 3/22/2009; **Check Date** to 3/23/2009; and verify that the **Bank Account** is 10300 Payroll Checking. Click **Check All** to select all employees.

   Baxter does not use timesheets so you must verify that employee hours agree with the hours reported in Figure 10:45. You can enter hours for each employee in this screen.

   Steve Barkley worked 2 hours of overtime so enter "2" in his **Hourly wage overtime (x1.5)** column.

   Al Duke worked only 78 hours so change his **Hourly wage** hours to "78".

   This is the first paycheck for Susan Sharpton so scroll down to Susan's record and enter "40" in the **Hourly wage** column.

   Do not worry that the payroll checking balance does not show enough to cover payroll. Companies normally do not carry large balances in the payroll account. Instead, funds are transferred on payday to cover the amount of payroll. In the next chapter, you will transfer funds from the regular checking account into this account.

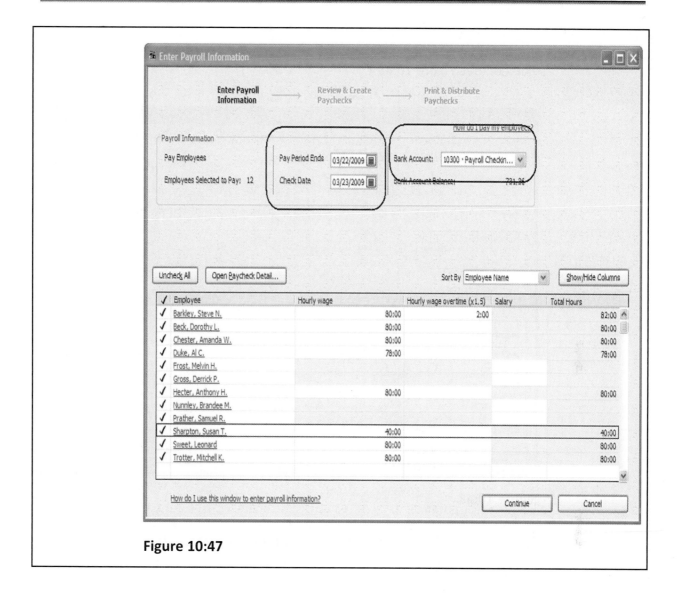

Figure 10:47

2. Click **Continue**. Verify that the **Print paychecks from QuickBooks** option is
    selected. (See Figure 10:48.)

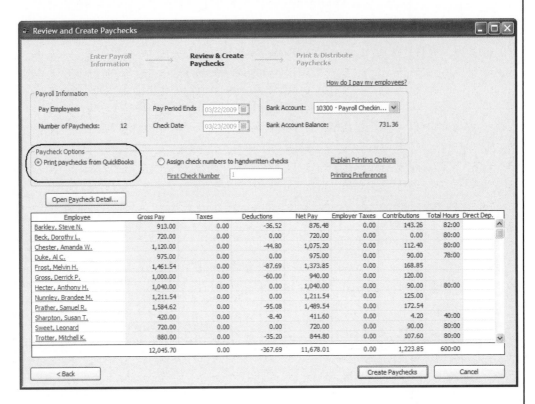

Figure 10:48

Preliminary check totals appear at the bottom. Notice that the total for **Gross
Pay** agrees with gross pay on the worksheet.

No tax tables are loaded in the software so no totals are displayed for taxes
and deductions. You will now manually enter taxes.

3. Click **Barkley, Steven N.** or highlight his account and click **Open Paycheck Detail** to open paycheck details. Step 4 illustrates entering information in the fields circled in Figure 10:49. *(Note: This information is gathered from the payroll spreadsheets.)*

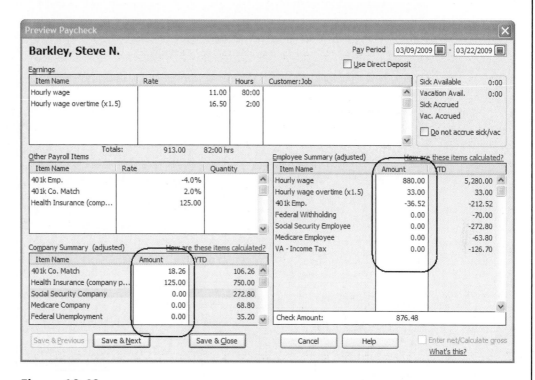

Figure 10:49

4. You do not need to change the 401K and health insurance information because QBP already calculated these amounts.

   Place your cursor in **Social Security Company** and enter "56.61". Tab to **Medicare Company** and enter "13.24". Now enter these remaining employer taxes:

Federal Unemployment (FUTA)	7.30
VA-Unemployment (SUTA)	13.70

5. Next tab to employee withholdings and enter the amounts on the worksheet. *(Note: You can enter positive amounts and QBP will convert the amounts to negative numbers.)*

Federal Withholding	16.00
Social Security Employee	56.61
Medicare Employee	13.24
VA – Income Tax	26.29

6. Steve's completed paycheck is shown in Figure 10:50. His check amount agrees with the net pay amount on the worksheet. *(Note: Scroll down the company taxes to view employer insurance and 401K expense.)*

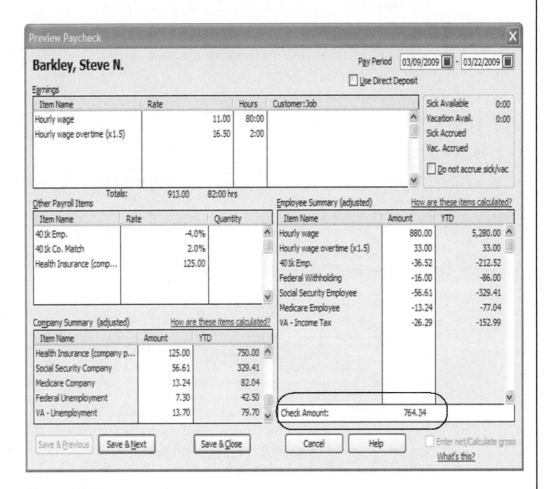

Figure 10:50

7. Click **Save & Next** and enter the following paycheck information for **Dorothy Beck**.

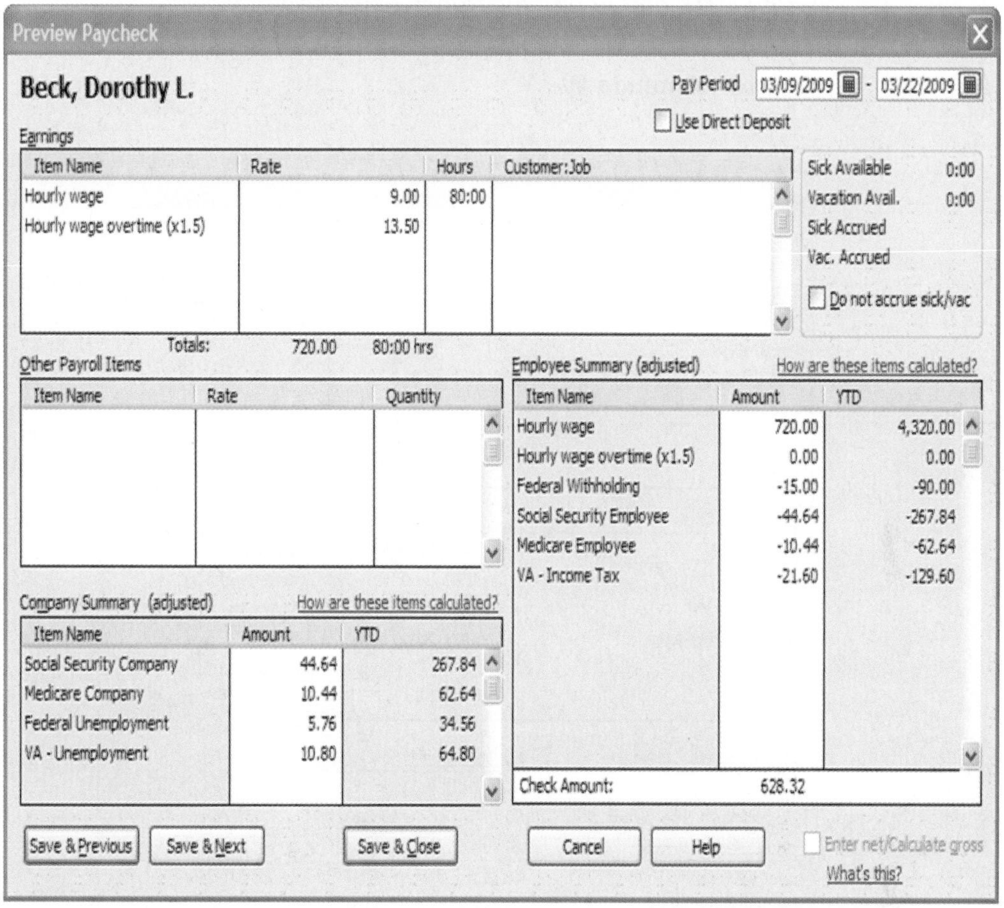

Figure 10:51

8. Continue clicking **Save & Next** until you have entered the remaining paychecks illustrated next. *(Note: Company fields are scrolled to the bottom so you can verify 401K and health insurance expense.)*

Chester, Amanda W.

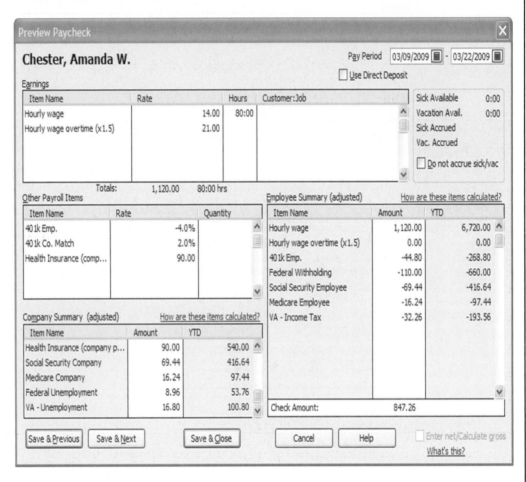

Figure 10:52

Duke, Al C.

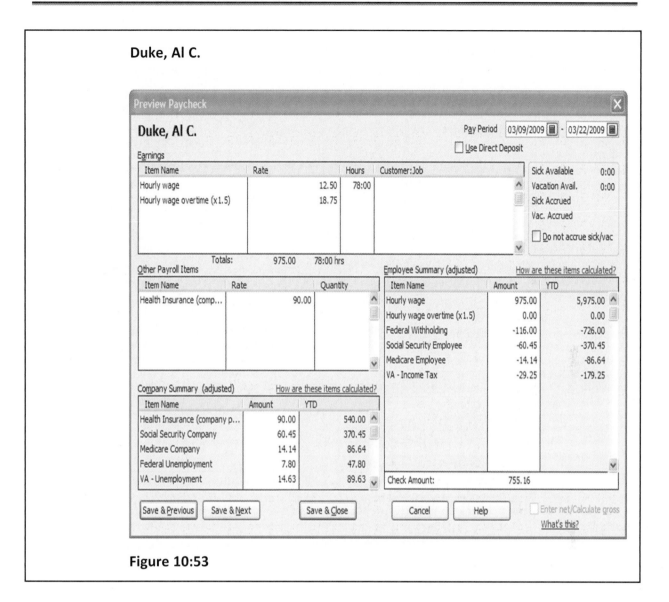

Figure 10:53

Frost, Melvin H.

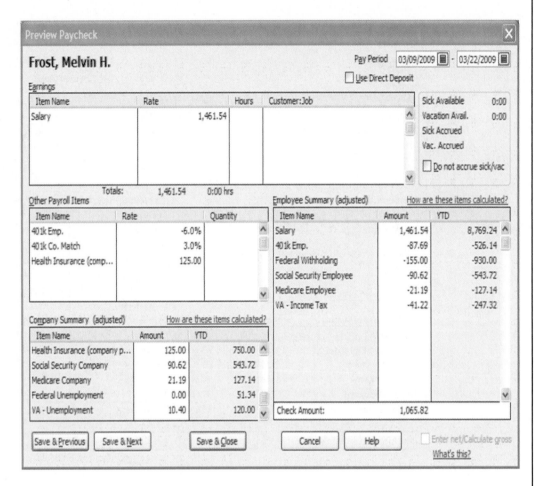

Figure 10:54

(Notice that unemployment taxes are zero on this check because Melvin's year-to-date wages exceed the taxable limit for this year.)

Gross, Derrick P.

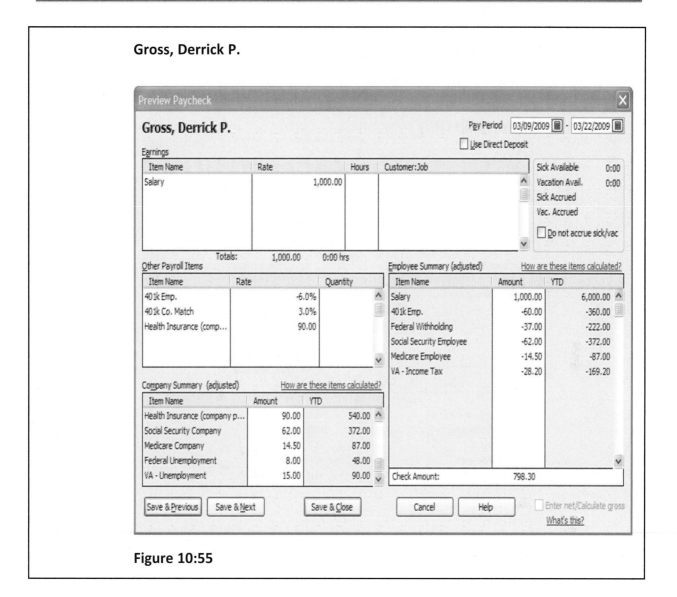

Figure 10:55

Hecter, Anthony H.

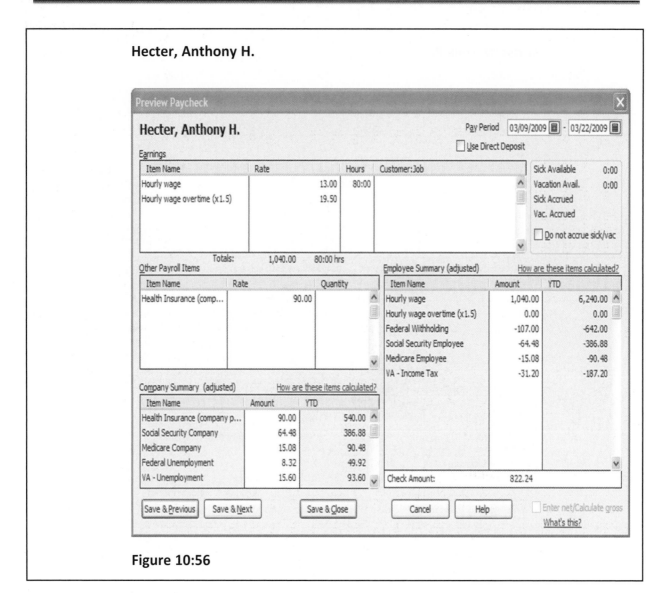

Figure 10:56

Nunnley, Brandee M.

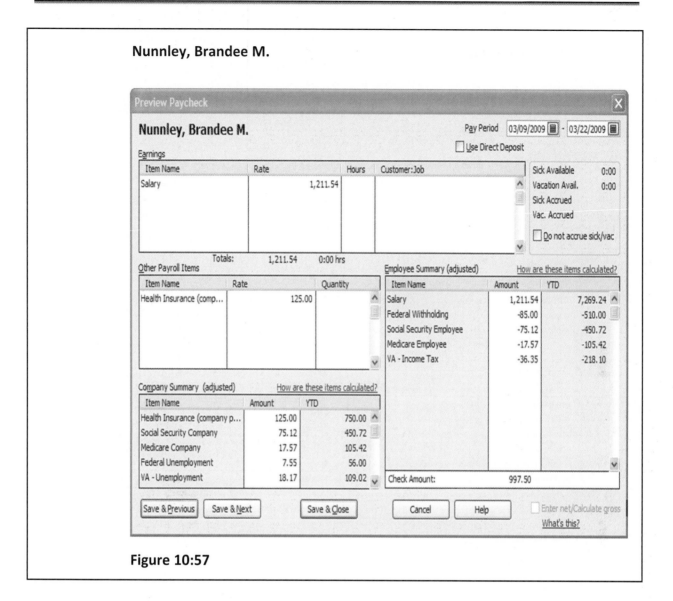

Figure 10:57

Prather, Samuel R.

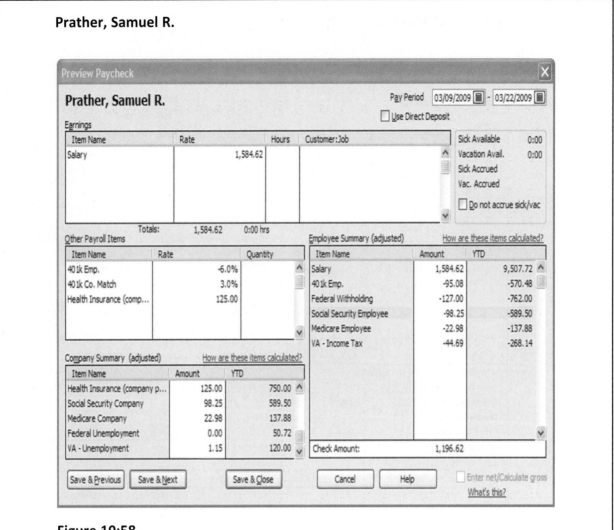

Figure 10:58

Sharpton, Susan T.

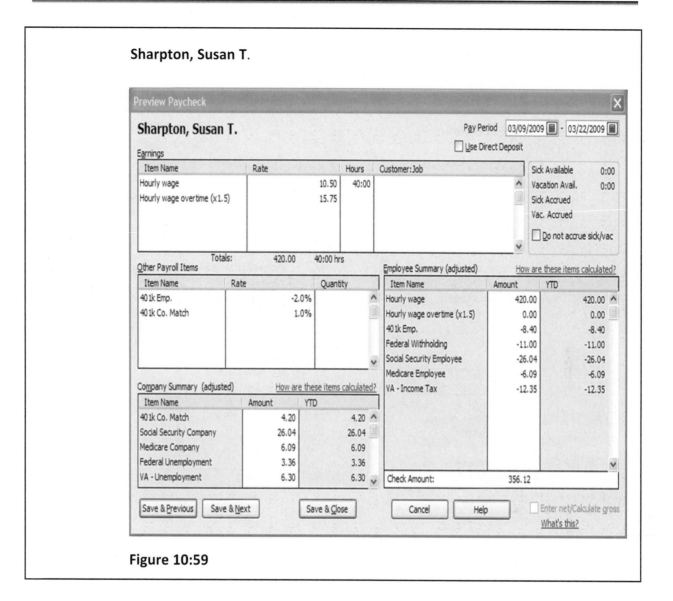

Figure 10:59

Sweet, Leonard

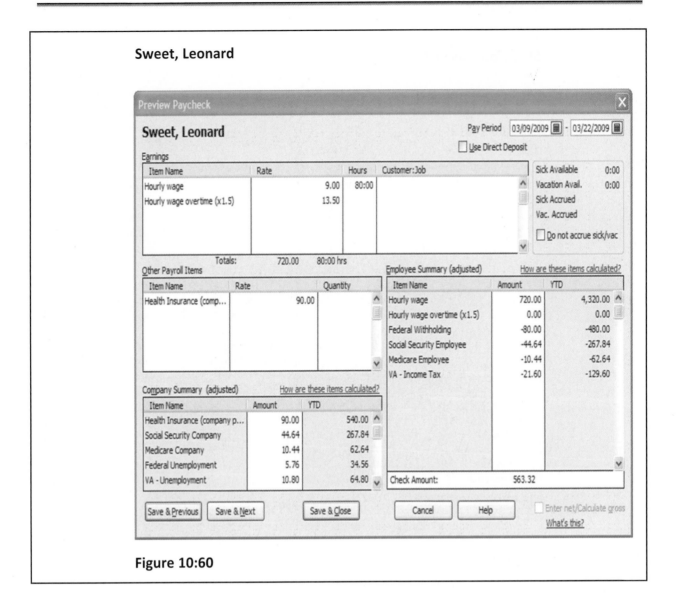

Figure 10:60

Trotter, Mitchell K.

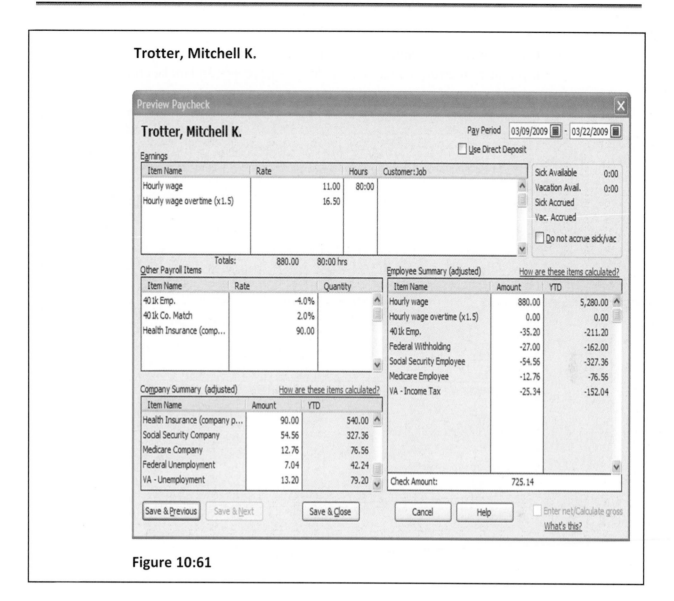

Figure 10:61

9. Click **Save & Close**. Your totals should agree with those illustrated in Figure 10:62. If you find an error, reopen the employee's paycheck and make corrections.

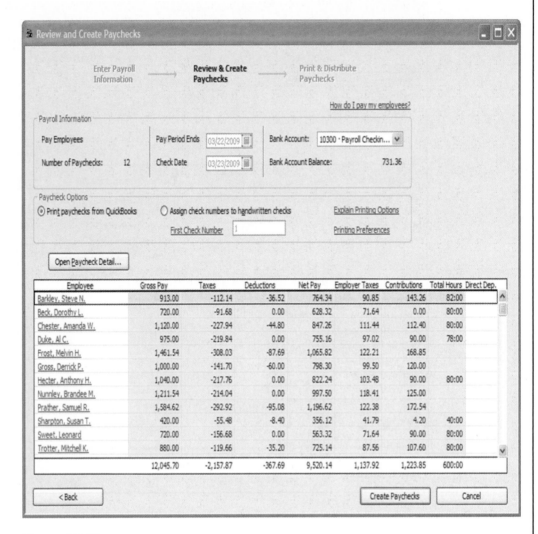

Figure 10:62

10. Click **Create Paychecks** and QBP informs you that 12 paychecks have been created and are ready for printing.

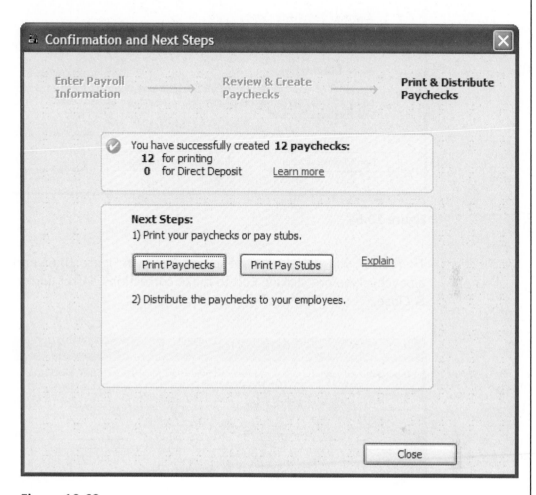

Figure 10:63

Note: If you find a mistake after clicking Create Paychecks DO NOT click Print Paychecks on the window illustrated in Figure 10:63. Instead, click Close and return to Step 1 to reenter the pay ending and check dates. Click Check All and QBP will prompt as shown in Figure 10:64. Click Find Existing Paychecks.

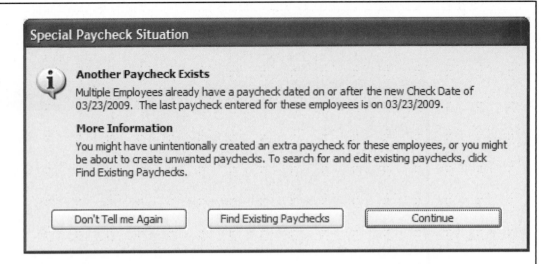

Figure 10:64

Thereafter, you will receive the screen shown in Figure 10:65 and can highlight a paycheck before clicking **Edit** to make corrections. After correcting, click **Save & Close**.

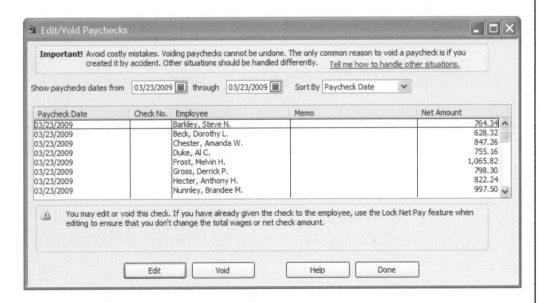

Figure 10:65

To then print the paychecks, you will reopen a check in the window by clicking **Edit**. After reopening, click the dropdown menu on **Print** and select **Print Batch**. You can then complete the remaining steps to follow that finalize printing.

11. Click **Print Paychecks**. The first check number should be 1191 and all the checks should be marked for printing.

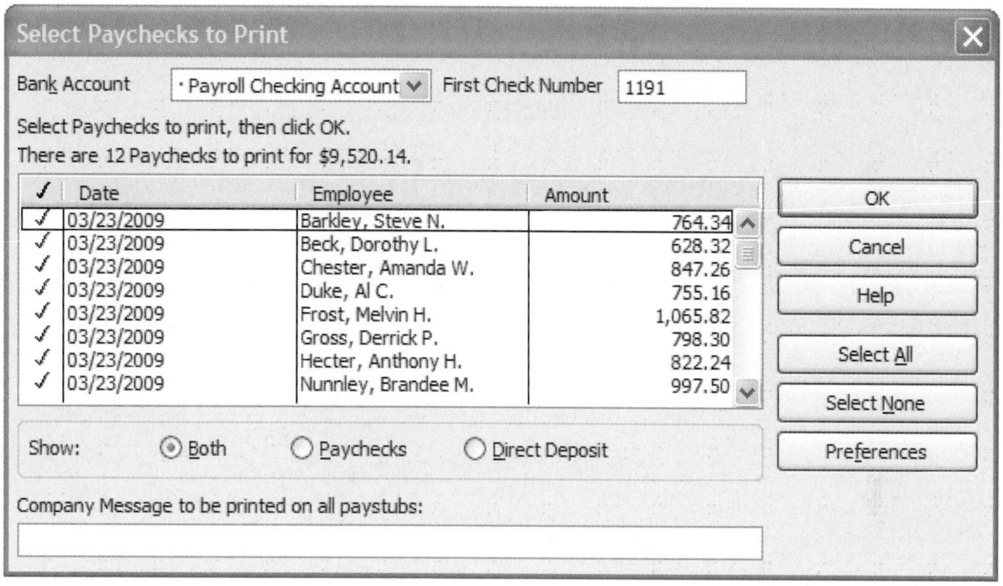

Select Paychecks to Print   ✕

Bank Account   · Payroll Checking Account ⌄   First Check Number   1191

Select Paychecks to print, then click OK.
There are 12 Paychecks to print for $9,520.14.

✓	Date	Employee	Amount
✓	03/23/2009	Barkley, Steve N.	764.34
✓	03/23/2009	Beck, Dorothy L.	628.32
✓	03/23/2009	Chester, Amanda W.	847.26
✓	03/23/2009	Duke, Al C.	755.16
✓	03/23/2009	Frost, Melvin H.	1,065.82
✓	03/23/2009	Gross, Derrick P.	798.30
✓	03/23/2009	Hecter, Anthony H.	822.24
✓	03/23/2009	Nunnley, Brandee M.	997.50

[OK]
[Cancel]
[Help]
[Select All]
[Select None]
[Preferences]

Show: ⦿ Both   ○ Paychecks   ○ Direct Deposit

Company Message to be printed on all paystubs:

[   ]

Figure 10:66

12. Click **OK**. Select a printer and then click **Print**. Figure 10:67 shows the first paycheck.

```
                                                                                                03/23/2009


        Steve N. Barkley                                                                        **764.34

Seven Hundred Sixty-Four and 34/100**************************************************************************

        Steve N. Barkley
        4558 New Hope Court
        Lilburn, VA 23074


        Pay Period: 03/09/2009 - 03/22/2009


Employee                                                          Status (Fed/State)          Allowances/Extra
Steve N. Barkley, 4558 New Hope Court, Lilburn, VA 23074          Married/Withhold             Fed-3/0/VA-0
                                                                  Pay Period: 03/09/2009 - 03/22/2009   Pay Date: 03/23/2009

Earnings and Hours          Qty      Rate    Current   YTD Amount
Hourly wage                80:00     11.00   880.00     5,280.00
Hourly wage overtime (x1.5) 2:00     16.50    33.00        33.00
                                             913.00     5,313.00

Deductions From Gross                        Current   YTD Amount
401k Emp.                                     -36.52     -212.52

Taxes                                        Current   YTD Amount
Federal Withholding                           -16.00      -86.00
Social Security Employee                      -56.61     -329.41
Medicare Employee                             -13.24      -77.04
VA - Income Tax                               -26.29     -152.99
                                             -112.14     -645.44

Net Pay                                       764.34    4,455.04

Non-taxable Company Items                    Current   YTD Amount
401k Co. Match                                 18.26      106.26
Health Insurance (company paid)               125.00      750.00


Practice Baxter Garden, 1352 W. Maple Ave, Arlington, VA  23523 888-999-0909


Employee                                                          Status (Fed/State)          Allowances/Extra
Steve N. Barkley, 4558 New Hope Court, Lilburn, VA 23074          Married/Withhold             Fed-3/0/VA-0
                                                                  Pay Period: 03/09/2009 - 03/22/2009   Pay Date: 03/23/2009

Earnings and Hours          Qty      Rate    Current   YTD Amount
Hourly wage                80:00     11.00   880.00     5,280.00
Hourly wage overtime (x1.5) 2:00     16.50    33.00        33.00
                                             913.00     5,313.00

Deductions From Gross                        Current   YTD Amount
401k Emp.                                     -36.52     -212.52

Taxes                                        Current   YTD Amount
Federal Withholding                           -16.00      -86.00
Social Security Employee                      -56.61     -329.41
Medicare Employee                             -13.24      -77.04
VA - Income Tax                               -26.29     -152.99
                                             -112.14     -645.44

Net Pay                                       764.34    4,455.04

Non-taxable Company Items                    Current   YTD Amount
401k Co. Match                                 18.26      106.26
Health Insurance (company paid)               125.00      750.00


Practice Baxter Garden, 1352 W. Maple Ave, Arlington, VA  23523 888-999-0909
```

Figure 10:67

13. After printing, QBP confirms that checks printed correctly. Click **OK**. Then click **Close** in the confirmation window.

You have just printed paychecks. Now trace the entries that posted.

BEHIND THE KEYS OF A POSTED PAYCHECK

You will now trace the entries made after printing the paychecks by following the next steps.

STEPS TO TRACING PAYCHECK ENTRIES

1. Click **Report Center** on the Icon bar. Select the **Employees & Payroll** category and open the **Payroll Transaction Detail** report. Enter 3/23/2009 as the date range.

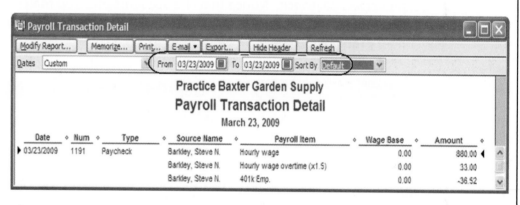

Figure 10:68

2. Now customize the report to show additional information. Click **Modify Report** and

On the Display tab:
  Add columns: Trans #, Account, Debit, Credit
  Remove columns: Wage Base, Amount

On the Filters tab, under Current Filter Choices:
  Click **Detail Level** and remove the filter
  Click **Payroll Item** and remove the filter

On the Header/Footer tab:
  Type "Payroll Journal" as the **Report Title**. Click **OK**.

Figure 10:69 shows the modified report listing all accounts affected by an employee's paycheck. Notice that the accounts affected match payroll item settings discussed in the *Payroll Items* topic. You also see the audit trail code under **Tran #** and **Type**.

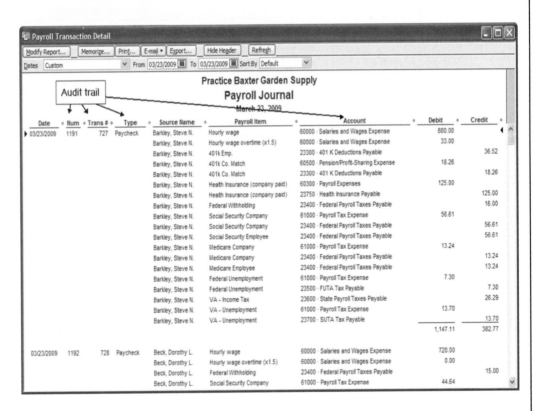

Figure 10:69

Click **Memorize**, enter the following information, and close the report.

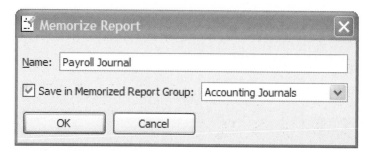

Figure 10:70

3. To view a report that looks something like our payroll register in Excel, open the **Employee Earnings Summary** report. Enter 3/23/2009 as the date range.

    Use the scroll bars to view additional information. This report should reconcile to the Excel payroll register.

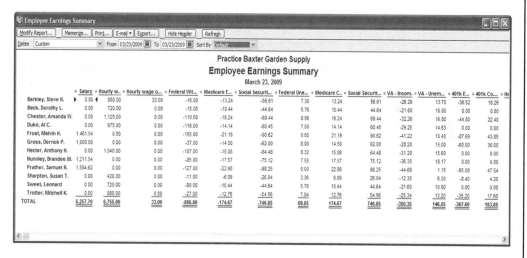

Figure 10:71

4. Remember that you complete tracing entries to the general ledger by displaying the *Reports>>Memorized Reports>>Accounting Journals>>General Ledger Detail Report*.

5. Close all open reports and the Report Center.

CORRECTING EMPLOYEE PAYCHECKS

We told you how to correct a paycheck before printing it while you were entering paycheck data. But what happens when you find an error after printing? Well, you must then void the paycheck and issue a replacement.

Practice voiding a printed check by voiding and reissuing Steve Barkley's March 23 paycheck in the steps that follow.

STEPS TO VOIDING A PRINTED PAYCHECK

1. Select **Employees>>Edit/Void Paychecks** on the main menu. Enter the date range of 3/23/2009 to 3/23/2009. You now see the paychecks issued on this date (Figure 10:72).

    Highlight Steve's check and click **Void**.

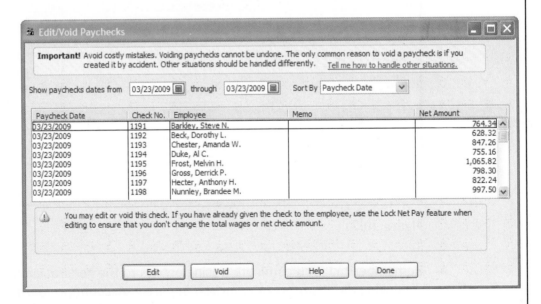

Figure 10:72

2. The void paychecks window updates, showing Steve's paycheck as void. Click **Done**.

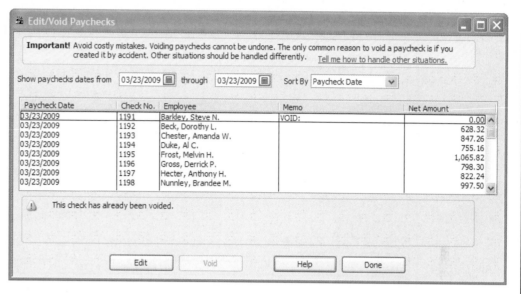

Figure 10:73

3. You will now reissue Steve's check. Click **Pay Employees** on the Home page and enter the dates shown in Figure 10:74. Click to select Barkley, Steve N.

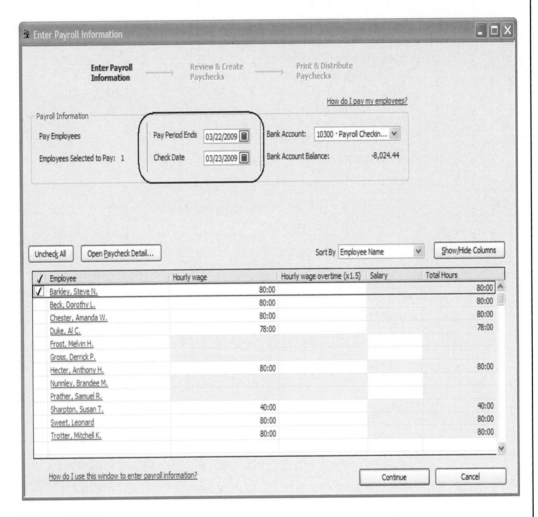

Figure 10:74

4. Click **Continue**. Click to open Steve's paycheck and enter his paycheck information again as illustrated in Figure 10:75. *(Note: You will have to enter 2 hours of overtime.)*

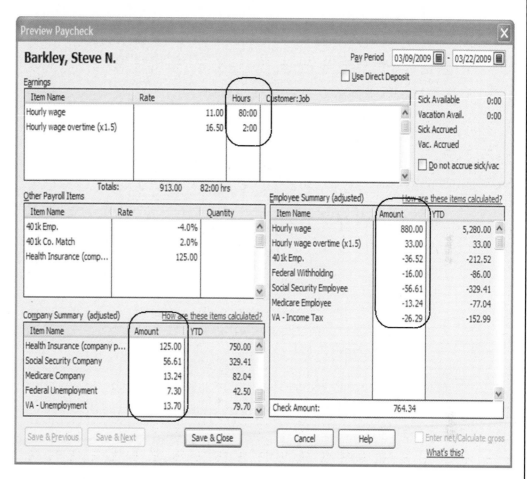

Figure 10:75

5. Click **Save & Close** and Figure 10:76 shows Steve's updated check.

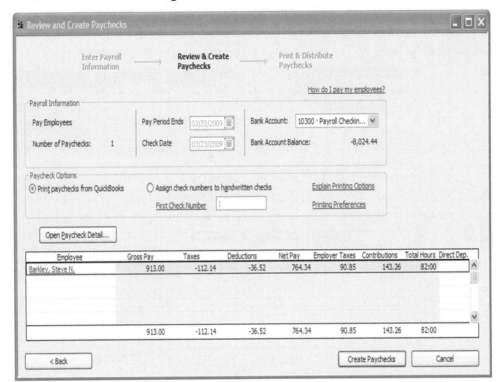

Figure 10:76

6. Click **Create Paychecks** and then click **Print Paychecks**. The first check number
    should be 1203. Click **OK**, select a printer, and click **Print**.

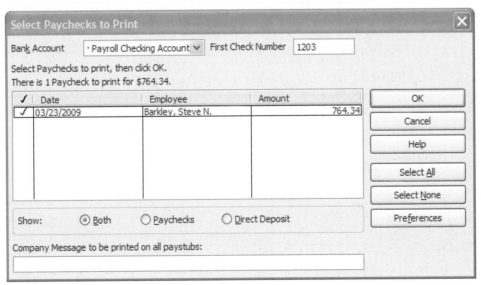

Figure 10:77

7. Click **OK** in the print confirmation window and then **Close** the print
    confirmation window.

    *(Note: If you receive a message to subscribe to payroll tax tables, select No and
    turn off pop-up messages for products and services.)*

PAYING EMPLOYER AND EMPLOYEE PAYROLL TAXES

In this topic you remit employee tax withholdings and employer payroll taxes. But before that, you should prepare a Payroll Liability Balances report.

Open the **Report Center** and then open the **Payroll Liability Balances** report under the **Employees & Payroll** category.

Enter the date range of 1/1/2009 to 3/31/2009 to view the report illustrated in Figure 10:78.

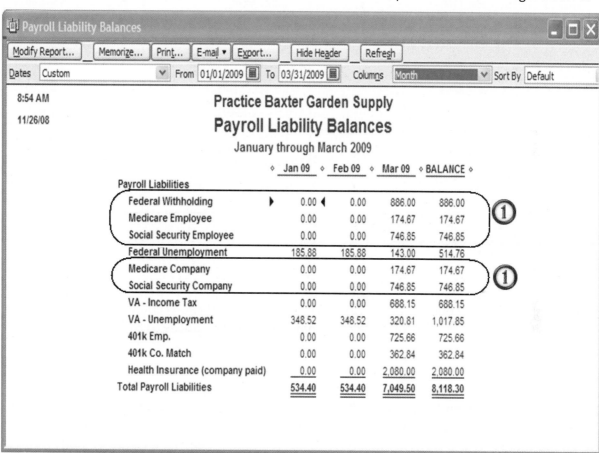

Figure 10:78

Payroll taxes are due on the dates set by taxing agencies. Normally federal tax, FICA, and Medicare taxes are due within three days of paying employees. State income tax for the current month is normally due the first of the next month. Federal and state unemployment taxes are due at the end of every quarter.

The report shows that Baxter owes $2,729.04 for federal tax liabilities (i.e., items marked 1 in Figure 10:78). The report lists other payroll liabilities.

Now verify that report totals reconcile with balances in the general ledger accounts. Press **Ctrl + A** on the keyboard to open the chart of accounts. (See Figure 10:79.)

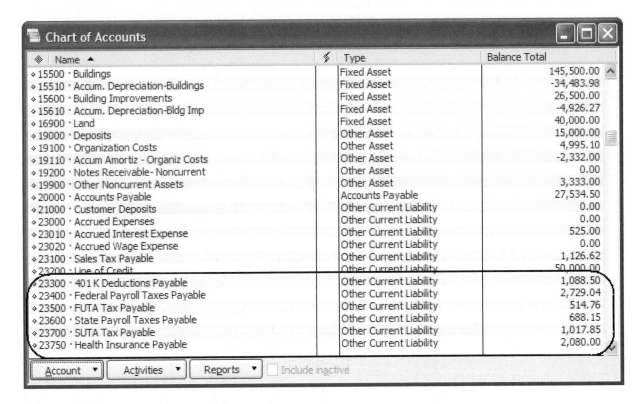

Figure 10:79

Scroll down to 23400 Federal Payroll Tax Liabilities to find that the account balance equals the report balance. You can also compare other payroll liability balances to the report.

Close the report and the Chart of Accounts.

Because March is the end of a quarter it is time to pay FUTA and SUTA taxes. You will now run a report to check those taxes. Return to the **Report Center** and open the **Employee Earnings Summary** report. Enter 1/1/2009 to 3/31/2009 as the date range. (See Figure 10:80.)

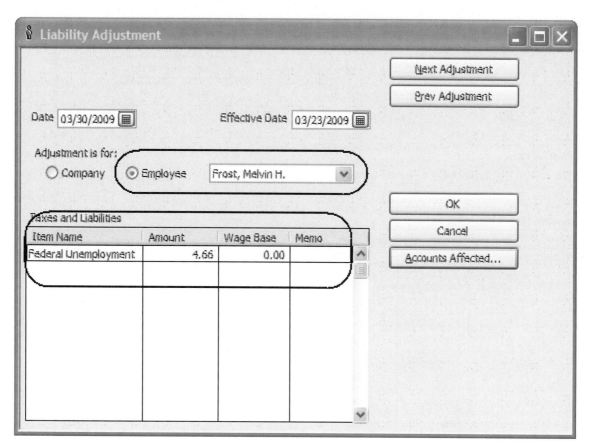

Figure 10:82

Click **Next Adjustment**.

Look up **Prather, Sam** as the employee. Select **Federal Unemployment** as the **Item Name** and, in **Amount**, enter "5.28" (i.e., $56.00 – $50.72). (See Figure 10:83.)

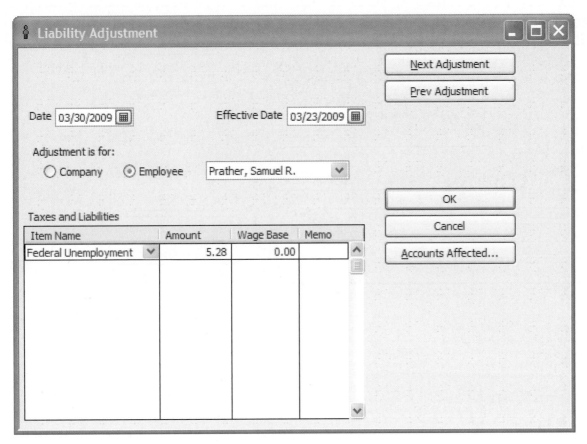

Figure 10:83

Click **OK**.

Return to the **Employee Earnings Summary** report and note that FUTA tax for both employees has increased to $56.00. You can also check the chart of accounts to find that the balance in the liability account now equals the $524.70 shown on the report.

Close the report and the Report Center.

After reconciling balances, you are ready to pay these taxes. The March 23 payroll you previously recorded means that federal taxes are also due. This is also the last pay date for March so state taxes are due and the last pay date for the quarter so FUTA and SUTA taxes are due.

In the next exercise you create a check for employee federal tax, FICA, and Medicare withholdings and employer FICA and Medicare taxes.

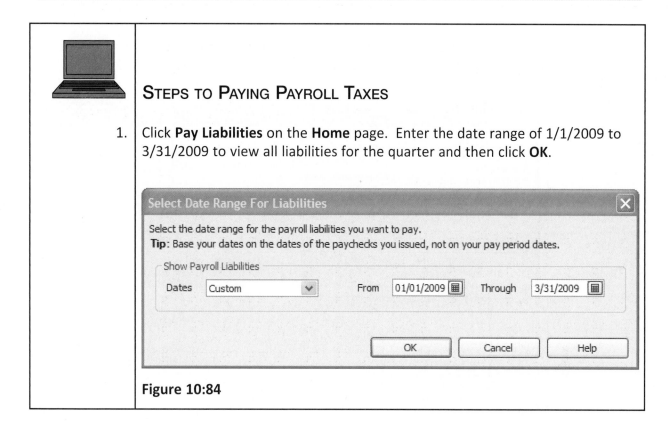

STEPS TO PAYING PAYROLL TAXES

1. Click **Pay Liabilities** on the **Home** page. Enter the date range of 1/1/2009 to 3/31/2009 to view all liabilities for the quarter and then click **OK**.

Figure 10:84

2. Enter 3/23/2009 as the **Check Date**. Verify that **To be printed** is marked and 10200 Regular Checking is the **Bank Account**.

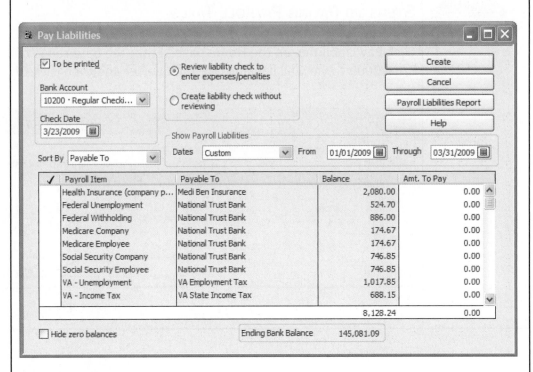

Figure 10:85

This window lists vendor accounts with balances. You now see why vendors were entered on payroll tax and company benefit items.

Also notice that you can print payroll liability reports from this window by clicking the **Payroll Liabilities Report** button.

3. You will now select the taxes to pay. Only federal withholdings, FICA, and Medicare taxes are due by March 26 so choose only these taxes.

The company has also received the health insurance bill, so mark that item. Also mark both 401K liabilities for payment.

The total payments are listed under the **Amt. To Pay** column.

Before creating the checks notice that the Review option is selected in Figure 10:86.

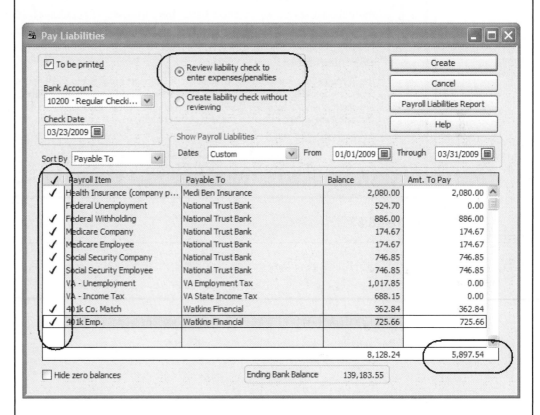

Figure 10:86

4. Click **Create**. The warning in Figure 10:87 is issued because the check date of 3/23/2009 falls before the Through date of 3/31/2009 on Figure 10:86. However, notice that the message states this can be appropriate, especially when prepaying a liability.

Click **Continue**.

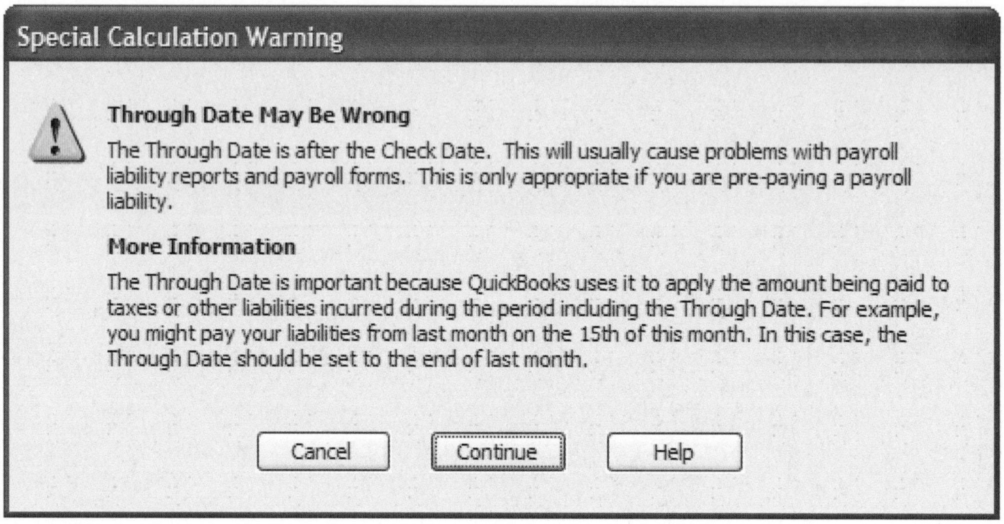

Special Calculation Warning

Through Date May Be Wrong
The Through Date is after the Check Date. This will usually cause problems with payroll liability reports and payroll forms. This is only appropriate if you are pre-paying a payroll liability.

More Information
The Through Date is important because QuickBooks uses it to apply the amount being paid to taxes or other liabilities incurred during the period including the Through Date. For example, you might pay your liabilities from last month on the 15th of this month. In this case, the Through Date should be set to the end of last month.

Cancel   Continue   Help

Figure 10:87

5. The check opens (Figure 10:88) for you to review the amount and enter additional information because the Review option was marked on the previous window. Should the health insurance bill contain other fees, you can add the amount to the Expenses tab.

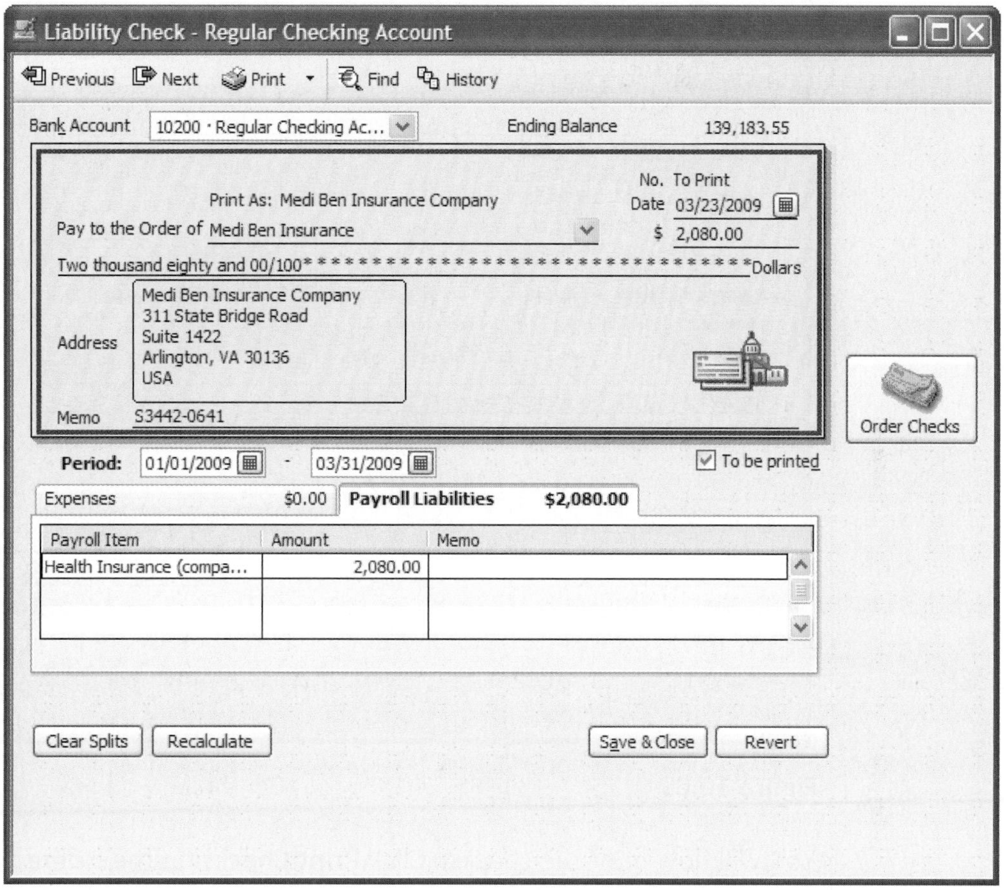

Figure 10:88

6. Click **Next** and the second check opens. Click **Save & Close**.

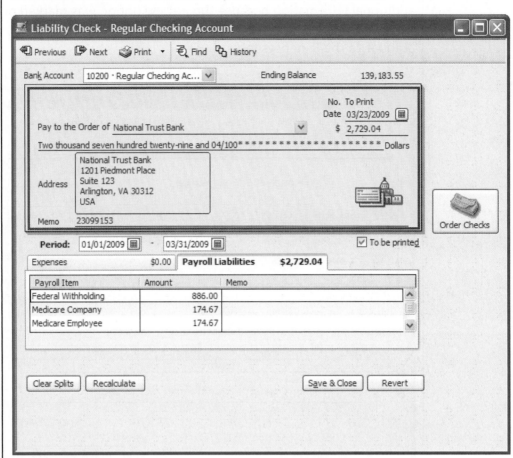

Figure 10:89

7. You will now print the checks. Click **Print Checks** on the **Home** page and verify that the **Bank Account** is the Regular Checking Account. Confirm that three payments are marked and 10263 is the first check number.

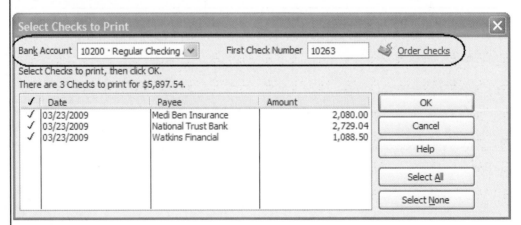

Figure 10:90

8. Click **OK**. Select a printer and click **Print**. Click **OK** in the print confirmation window.

Now complete the next exercise to pay the remaining tax liabilities for March and the first quarter of 2009.

 CREATE CHECKS FOR PAYROLL TAXES

Reopen the Pay Liabilities window and enter the date range of 1/1/2009 to 3/31/2009.

Create checks dated 4/3/2009 for FUTA, VA-Income Tax, and VA-Unemployment taxes.

Print the checks using the first check number of 10266. The checks will total $2,230.70.

Print the Check Detail report for April 3, 2009, modified to filter for the Transaction Type of Payroll Liability Check.

QUARTERLY AND YEAR-END PAYROLL REPORTING

At the end of each quarter, Baxter prepares payroll tax reports for each taxing agency. These reports lists employee wages and reconcile employee tax withholdings and employer tax liabilities with taxes paid during the quarter.

For federal taxes, the quarterly report is called Form 941. We will now show you how to prepare this report based on information from QBP.

Open the **Report Center** and run the **Employee Earnings Summary** for 1/1/2009 to 3/31/2009 (See Figure 10:91.) Print and close the report.

Practice Baxter Garden Supply

Employee Earnings Summary

January through March 2009

	Salary	Hourly wage	Hourly wage overtime...	Federal Withholding	Medicare Employee	Social Security Employee	Federal Unemployment
Barkley, Steve N.	0.00	5,280.00	33.00	-86.00	-77.04	-329.41	42.50
Beck, Dorothy L.	0.00	4,320.00	0.00	-90.00	-62.64	-267.84	34.56
Chester, Amanda W.	0.00	6,720.00	0.00	-660.00	-97.44	-416.64	53.76
Duke, Al C.	0.00	5,975.00	0.00	-726.00	-86.64	-370.45	47.80
Frost, Melvin H.	8,769.24	0.00	0.00	-930.00	-127.14	-543.72	56.00
Gross, Derrick P.	6,000.00	0.00	0.00	-222.00	-87.00	-372.00	48.00
Hecter, Anthony H.	0.00	6,240.00	0.00	-642.00	-90.48	-386.88	49.92
Nunnley, Brandee M.	7,269.24	0.00	0.00	-510.00	-105.42	-450.72	56.00
Prather, Samuel R.	9,507.72	0.00	0.00	-762.00	-137.88	-589.50	56.00
Sharpton, Susan T.	0.00	420.00	0.00	-11.00	-6.09	-26.04	3.36
Sweet, Leonard	0.00	4,320.00	0.00	-480.00	-62.64	-267.84	34.56
Trotter, Mitchell K.	0.00	5,280.00	0.00	-162.00	-76.56	-327.36	42.24
TOTAL	31,546.20	38,555.00	33.00	-5,281.00	-1,016.97	-4,348.40	524.70
	①	①	①	②	④	③	

	Medicare Company	Social Security Company	VA - Income Tax	VA - Unemp...	401k Emp.	401k Co. Match	Health Insurance (...	TOTAL
Barkley, Steve N.	82.04	329.41	-152.99	79.70	-212.52	106.26	750.00	5,844.95
Beck, Dorothy L.	62.64	267.84	-129.60	64.80	0.00	0.00	0.00	4,199.76
Chester, Amanda W.	97.44	416.64	-193.56	100.80	-268.80	134.40	540.00	6,426.60
Duke, Al C.	86.64	370.45	-179.25	89.63	0.00	0.00	540.00	5,747.18
Frost, Melvin H.	127.14	543.72	-247.32	120.00	-526.14	263.10	750.00	8,254.88
Gross, Derrick P.	87.00	372.00	-169.20	90.00	-360.00	180.00	540.00	6,106.80
Hecter, Anthony H.	90.48	386.88	-187.20	93.60	0.00	0.00	540.00	6,094.32
Nunnley, Brandee M.	105.42	450.72	-218.10	109.02	0.00	0.00	750.00	7,456.16
Prather, Samuel R.	137.88	589.50	-268.14	120.00	-570.48	285.24	750.00	9,118.34
Sharpton, Susan T.	6.09	26.04	-12.35	6.30	-8.40	4.20	0.00	402.11
Sweet, Leonard	62.64	267.84	-129.60	64.80	0.00	0.00	540.00	4,349.76
Trotter, Mitchell K.	76.56	327.36	-152.04	79.20	-211.20	105.60	540.00	5,521.80
TOTAL	1,021.97	4,348.40	-2,039.35	1,017.85	-2,157.54	1,078.80	6,240.00	69,522.66
	④	③						

Figure 10:91

Next run the **Payroll Transactions by Payee** for 1/1/2009 to 3/31/2009, listing total federal tax payments for the first quarter. (See Figure 10:92.) Print and close the report.

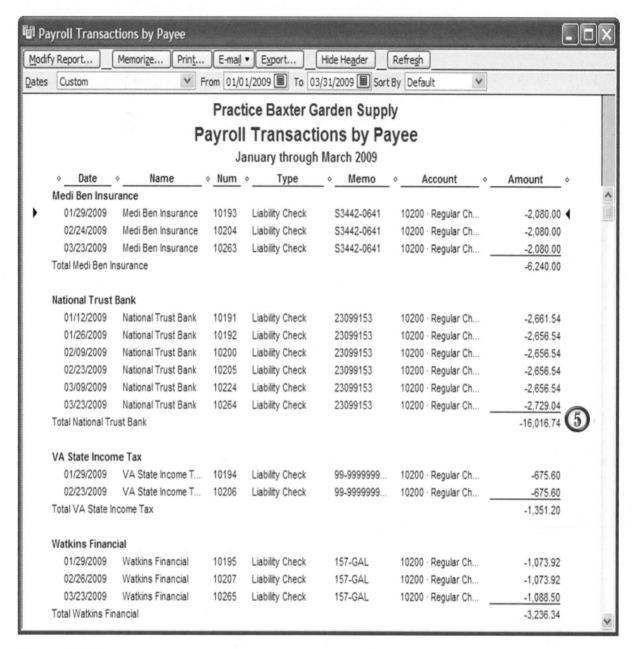

Figure 10:92

You will next plug numbers from these reports onto Form 941. For purposes of this example, we downloaded a Form 941 from the Internal Revenue Service website (www.irs.gov).

The top of Form 941 (Figure 10:93) contains basic company information such as EIN, Business name, Business address and the reporting quarter.

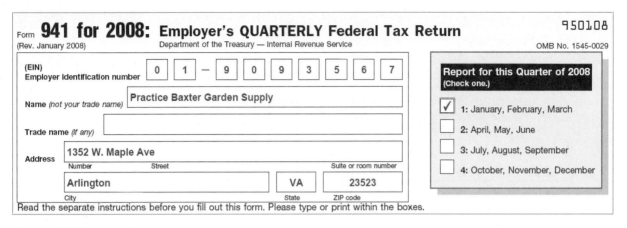

Figure 10:93

Part I of Form 941 (Figure 10:94) reports gross wages, tax liabilities and tax payments during the quarter. You enter information in this section using the following steps.

1. Line 1: Total employees receiving wages in the reporting quarter.
2. Line 2: Total gross wages for the quarter calculated by totaling the columns labeled number 1 on the **Employees Earnings Summary** report shown in Figure 10:91.
3. Line 3: Total federal tax withholdings calculated from the column labeled number 2 on the **Employees Earnings Summary** report.
4. Line 5a:
   a. Column 1: Gross wages from Form 941 Line 2 minus wages over the social security annual limit. Recall that taxes stop after wages exceed the annual taxable limit.
   b. Column 2: Calculated by multiplying Column 1 wages by the percentage provided. The 12.4 percent (0.124) rate represents the employee rate of 6.2 percent (.062) plus the employer rate of 6.2 percent (0.062). This amount should equal the total for columns labeled number 3 on the **Employees Earnings Summary** report, disregarding any rounding differences in the cents.
5. Line 5c:
   a. Column 1: Gross wages from Form 941 Line 2.
   b. Column 2: Calculated by multiplying Column 1 wages by the percentage provided. The 2.9 percent (0.029) rate represents the employee rate of 1.45 percent (.0145) plus the employer rate of 1.45 percent (0.0145). This amount should equal the total for columns labeled number 4 on the **Employees Earnings Summary** report, disregarding any rounding differences in the cents. (Note: The report is $5.00 higher than the amount calculated on Form 941 and we will illustrate correcting this error later in the chapter.)
6. Line 5d: The total of Lines 5a plus 5c, column 2. This is the total FICA and Medicare taxes due this quarter.
7. Line 7a: The rounding difference that occurs when Form 941 calculates FICA and Medicare as a percentage of total wages whereas paychecks calculate these taxes on individual wages.
8. Line 11: The total payroll tax payments labeled number 5 on the **Payroll Transactions by Payee** report (Figure 10:92).

Part 1: Answer these questions for this quarter.

1 Number of employees who received wages, tips, or other compensation for the pay period including: *Mar. 12* (Quarter 1), *June 12* (Quarter 2), *Sept. 12* (Quarter 3), *Dec. 12* (Quarter 4) **1** _____ 12

2 Wages, tips, and other compensation . . . . **2** ① 70,134 . 20

3 Total income tax withheld from wages, tips, and other compensation . . . . **3** ② 5,281 . 00

4 If no wages, tips, and other compensation are subject to social security or Medicare tax . . ☐ Check and go to line 6.

5 Taxable social security and Medicare wages and tips:

	Column 1		Column 2	
5a Taxable social security wages	① 70,134 . 20	× .124 =	8,696 . 64	
5b Taxable social security tips	.	× .124 =	.	
5c Taxable Medicare wages & tips	① 70,134 . 20	× .029 =	2,033 . 89	

5d Total social security and Medicare taxes (*Column 2*, lines 5a + 5b + 5c = line 5d) . . **5d** 10,730 . 53

6 Total taxes before adjustments (lines 3 + 5d = line 6) . . . . **6** 16,011 . 53

7 **TAX ADJUSTMENTS** (read the instructions for line 7 before completing lines 7a through 7g):

7a Current quarter's fractions of cents . . . . 0 . 21

7b Current quarter's sick pay . . . .

7c Current quarter's adjustments for tips and group-term life insurance

7d Current year's income tax withholding (attach Form 941c) . . .

7e Prior quarters' social security and Medicare taxes (attach Form 941c)

7f Special additions to federal income tax (attach Form 941c) . . .

7g Special additions to social security and Medicare (attach Form 941c)

7h **TOTAL ADJUSTMENTS** (combine all amounts: lines 7a through 7g) . . . . **7h** 0 . 21

8 Total taxes after adjustments (combine lines 6 and 7h) . . . . **8** 16,011 . 74

9 Advance earned income credit (EIC) payments made to employees . . . . **9** .

10 Total taxes after adjustment for advance EIC (line 8 – line 9 = line 10) . . . . **10** 16,011 . 74

11 Total deposits for this quarter, including overpayment applied from a prior quarter . . . **11** ⑤ 16,016 . 74

12 **Balance due** (If line 10 is more than line 11, write the difference here.) . . . . **12** .
For information on how to pay, see the instructions.

13 **Overpayment** (If line 11 is more than line 10, write the difference here.) 5 . 00 Check one ☑ Apply to next return.
☐ Send a refund.

▶ You **MUST** fill out both pages of this form and **SIGN** it. Next ➡

For Privacy Act and Paperwork Reduction Act Notice, see the back of the Payment Voucher. Cat. No. 17001Z Form **941** (Rev. 1-2008)

Figure 10:94

After completing Part 1, you complete Parts 2 through 5 using the next instructions. (See Figure 10:95.)

1. Part 2:
   a. Line 14: The code for the state where the company makes tax deposits.
   b. Line 15: Check the box that the company was a semiweekly depositor for the quarter. This also means that Schedule B must be completed and attached to Form 941. (See Figure 10:96.)
2. Part 5: Sign and date.

Name *(not your trade name)*	Employer identification number (EIN)
Practice Baxter Garden Supply	01-9093567

Part 2: Tell us about your deposit schedule and tax liability for this quarter.

If you are unsure about whether you are a monthly schedule depositor or a semiweekly schedule depositor, see *Pub. 15 (Circular E)*, section 11.

14 [V] [A] Write the state abbreviation for the state where you made your deposits OR write "MU" if you made your deposits in *multiple* states.

15 Check one: ☐ Line 10 is less than $2,500. Go to Part 3.

☐ You were a monthly schedule depositor for the entire quarter. Fill out your tax liability for each month. Then go to Part 3.

Tax liability: Month 1 [.   ]

Month 2 [.   ]

Month 3 [.   ]

Total liability for quarter [.   ] Total must equal line 10.

☑ You were a semiweekly schedule depositor for any part of this quarter. Fill out *Schedule B (Form 941): Report of Tax Liability for Semiweekly Schedule Depositors*, and attach it to this form.

Part 3: Tell us about your business. If a question does NOT apply to your business, leave it blank.

16 If your business has closed or you stopped paying wages . . . . ☐ Check here, and

enter the final date you paid wages [/   /   ] .

17 If you are a seasonal employer and you do not have to file a return for every quarter of the year . ☐ Check here.

Part 4: May we speak with your third-party designee?

Do you want to allow an employee, a paid tax preparer, or another person to discuss this return with the IRS? See the instructions for details.

☐ Yes. Designee's name and phone number [   ] (   )   –

Select a 5-digit Personal Identification Number (PIN) to use when talking to IRS. ☐ ☐ ☐ ☐ ☐

☐ No.

Part 5: Sign here. You MUST fill out both pages of this form and SIGN it.

Under penalties of perjury, I declare that I have examined this return, including accompanying schedules and statements, and to the best of my knowledge and belief, it is true, correct, and complete.

X Sign your name here [   ]   Print your name here [   ]

Print your title here [   ]

Date [/   /   ]   Best daytime phone (   )   –

Part 6: For paid preparers only (optional)

Paid Preparer's Signature			
Firm's name (or yours if self-employed)			
Address		EIN	
		ZIP code	
Date / /	Phone ( ) –	SSN/PTIN	
☐ Check if you are self-employed.			

Page **2**   Form **941** (Rev. 1-2008)

Figure 10:95

Finally, Schedule B (Figure 10:96) is completed when a company makes semi-weekly deposits. The information for this form is gathered from the **Payroll Transactions by Payee** report (Figure 10:92).   The IRS will use this information to verify that employers pay all taxes by the due date. Baxter is required to pay tax liabilities within 3 days of paying employees. You should know that failure to pay taxes by the due date will result in IRS-imposed penalties and interest.

Schedule B (Form 941):

Report of Tax Liability for Semiweekly Schedule Depositors

(Rev. January 2006)   Department of the Treasury — Internal Revenue Service

990306

OMB No. 1545-0029

(EIN) Employer identification number: 0 1 – 9 0 9 3 5 6 7

Name (not your trade name): **Practice Baxter Garden Supply**

Calendar year: 2 0 0 9   (Also check quarter)

Report for this Quarter ... (Check one.)

- [✓] 1: January, February, March
- [ ] 2: April, May, June
- [ ] 3: July, August, September
- [ ] 4: October, November, December

Use this schedule to show your TAX LIABILITY for the quarter; DO NOT use it to show your deposits. You must fill out this form and attach it to Form 941 (or Form 941-SS) if you are a semiweekly schedule depositor or became one because your accumulated tax liability on any day was $100,000 or more. Write your daily tax liability on the numbered space that corresponds to the date wages were paid. See Section 11 in *Pub. 15 (Circular E), Employer's Tax Guide,* for details.

Month 1

- 26: 2,656.54
- 12: 2,656.54

Tax liability for Month 1: **5,313.08**

Month 2

- 9: 2,656.54
- 23: 2,656.54

Tax liability for Month 2: **5,313.08**

Month 3

- 9: 2,656.54
- 23: 2,729.04

Tax liability for Month 3: **5,385.58**

Fill in your total liability for the quarter (Month 1 + Month 2 + Month 3) = Total tax liability for the quarter ▶

Total must equal line 10 on Form 941 (or line 8 on Form 941-SS).

Total liability for the quarter: **16,011.74**

Figure 10:96

You can close the **Payroll Transactions by Payee** report. Now that we have illustrated reconciling Form 941, you will fix the $5.00 error that occurred when recording Steven Barkley's paycheck number 1136 on January 12, 2009. *(Note: Rounding differences are not fixed in the software.)* Employer Medicare was reported as $17.76 and should have been $12.76.

This error is located by returning to the **Employees Earnings Summary** report and double clicking Steve Barkley's hourly wage amount to open the **Transactions by Payroll Item** report. Modify the **Payroll Item** filter to show only **Medicare Company** and **Medicare Employee**. (See Figure 10:97.)

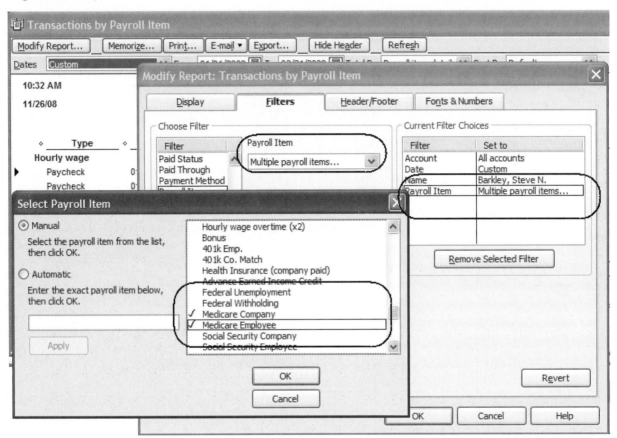

Figure 10:97

Click **OK** after setting the filter and the report refreshes as shown in Figure 10:98.

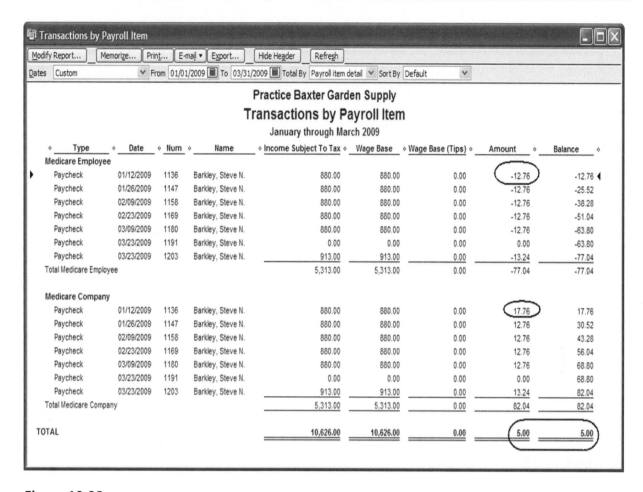

Figure 10:98

You must now check the Medicare calculation to determine whether the employee or the employer tax is incorrect. Multiplying $880 by the tax rate of 0.0145 shows that $12.76 is the correct amount. *Note: You also find the $5.00 difference at the bottom of the report.*

You will now record the adjustment. Again, select **Employees>>Payroll Taxes and Liabilities>>Adjust Payroll Liabilities** on the main menu.

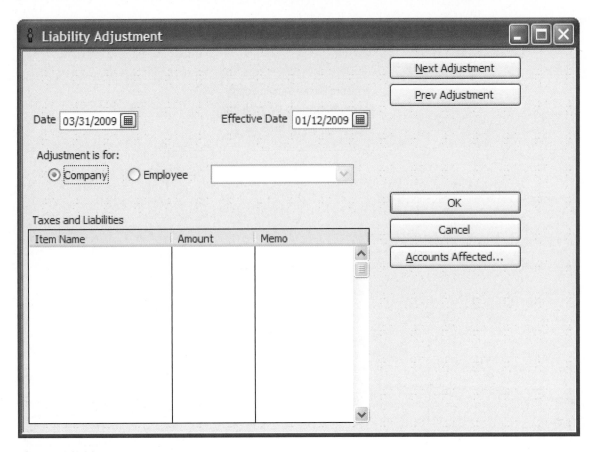

Figure 10:99

We want the adjustment to post in March so enter the **Date** of 3/31/2009. Enter 1/12/2009 in **Effective Date** because this is the date the error occurred.

Although the error occurred on the company's Medicare liability, you still want to adjust the paycheck so select **Employee** and look up **Barkley, Steve**.

Place your cursor in **Item Name** and select **Medicare Company**. Tab to **Amount** and enter "-5.00". You entered the adjustment as a negative amount so that the tax will be decreased.

Click the **Accounts Affected** button and verify that **Affect liability and expense accounts** is selected so that the adjustment decreases the Medicare liability and posts a debit to the liability account on the general ledger. Click **OK** to exit the window.

Figure 10:100 shows the completed entry. Click **OK** to post it.

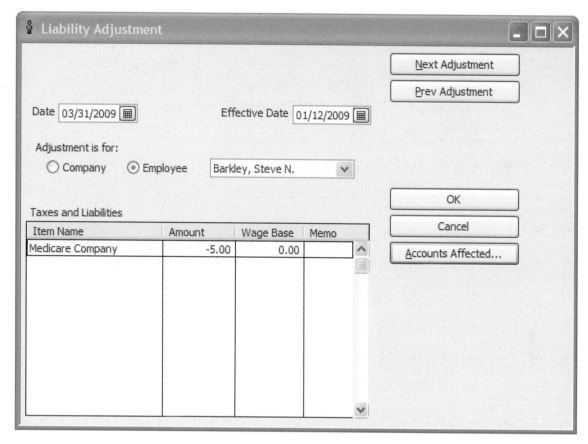

Figure 10:100

Return to the **Transactions by Payroll Item** report and notice that the entry posted to the general ledger as of 3/31/2009 (Figure 10:101). If you had entered 1/12/2009 in the Date field the change would have been made as of the paycheck date; however, this would also cause the entry to backdate to a closed period. Remember that you do not want to post entries to a closed accounting period because it changes reported financial results. The Effective Date will, however, adjust the liability amount on Form 941 as of January.

Finally, you could have selected the Company option instead of Employee to make the adjustment. However, you would not be able to see that the adjustment was related to Steve's paycheck.

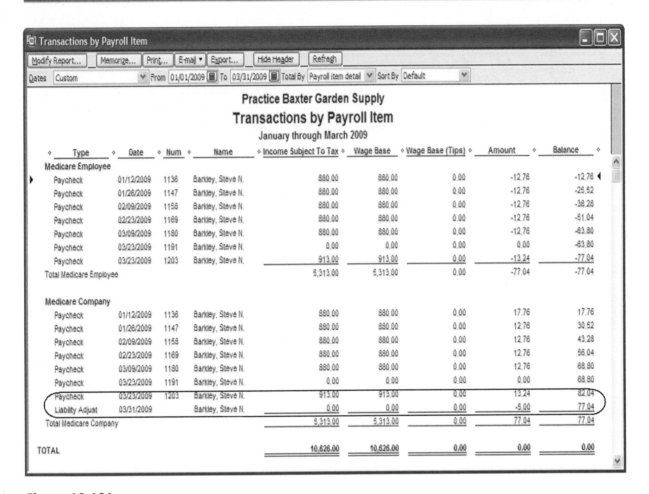

Figure 10:101

Close all open reports and the Report Center.

We just illustrated preparing one quarterly report. There are additional quarterly reporting requirements for state tax withholdings and state unemployment tax that were not illustrated.

Besides quarterly reports, Baxter files annual reports in January. Form 940 reporting FUTA taxes must be prepared and submitted to the IRS. In addition, W-2s must be printed and distributed to employees by January 31.

Figure 10:102 shows an uncompleted W-2 and Figure 10:103 shows the W-3 that serves to reconcile W-2s by summarizing total wages and taxes.

When you subscribe to QBP's payroll tax service you can then prepare quarterly and annual tax reports in the software.

22222	Void ☐	a Employee's social security number		For Official Use Only ▶ OMB No. 1545-0008		

b Employer identification number (EIN)		1 Wages, tips, other compensation	2 Federal income tax withheld
c Employer's name, address, and ZIP code		3 Social security wages	4 Social security tax withheld
		5 Medicare wages and tips	6 Medicare tax withheld
		7 Social security tips	8 Allocated tips
d Control number		9 Advance EIC payment	10 Dependent care benefits

e Employee's first name and initial	Last name	Suff.	11 Nonqualified plans	12a See instructions for box 12
			13 Statutory employee ☐ Retirement plan ☐ Third-party sick pay ☐	12b
			14 Other	12c
				12d
f Employee's address and ZIP code				

15 State	Employer's state ID number	16 State wages, tips, etc.	17 State income tax	18 Local wages, tips, etc.	19 Local income tax	20 Locality name

Form **W-2** Wage and Tax Statement

2008

Department of the Treasury—Internal Revenue Service

Copy A For Social Security Administration — Send this entire page with Form W-3 to the Social Security Administration; photocopies are not acceptable.

For Privacy Act and Paperwork Reduction Act Notice, see back of Copy D.

Cat. No. 10134D

Do Not Cut, Fold, or Staple Forms on This Page — Do Not Cut, Fold, or Staple Forms on This Page

Figure 10:102

DO NOT STAPLE

33333	a Control number	For Official Use Only ▶ OMB No. 1545-0008		

b Kind of Payer	941 ☐ Military ☐ 943 ☐ 944 ☐ CT-1 ☐ Hshld. emp. ☐ Medicare govt. emp. ☐ Third-party sick pay ☐	1 Wages, tips, other compensation	2 Federal income tax withheld
		3 Social security wages	4 Social security tax withheld
c Total number of Forms W-2	d Establishment number	5 Medicare wages and tips	6 Medicare tax withheld
e Employer identification number (EIN)		7 Social security tips	8 Allocated tips
f Employer's name		9 Advance EIC payments	10 Dependent care benefits
		11 Nonqualified plans	12 Deferred compensation
		13 For third-party sick pay use only	
		14 Income tax withheld by payer of third-party sick pay	
g Employer's address and ZIP code			
h Other EIN used this year			
15 State Employer's state ID number		16 State wages, tips, etc.	17 State income tax
		18 Local wages, tips, etc.	19 Local income tax
Contact person		Telephone number ( )	For Official Use Only
Email address		Fax number ( )	

Under penalties of perjury, I declare that I have examined this return and accompanying documents, and, to the best of my knowledge and belief, they are true, correct, and complete.

Signature ▶   Title ▶   Date ▶

Form **W-3** Transmittal of Wage and Tax Statements   **2008**   Department of the Treasury Internal Revenue Service

Send this entire page with the entire Copy A page of Form(s) W-2 to the Social Security Administration.

Figure 10:103

You have now completed the chapter. *Make a backup of the Practice Baxter Garden Supply data file to a backup file named "Practice Baxter Garden Supply Chpt 10". In the next chapter, you will build on the work completed in this chapter.*

SUMMARY

You began this chapter with an overview of payroll processing in a manual system. We first explained the types of employee withholdings and voluntary deductions as well as the types of employer payroll taxes and additional forms of compensation. You also learned to calculate payroll taxes and withholdings.

You next looked at the different types of payroll items in QBP. This helped you to understand how item types track wages, employee withholdings, and employer taxes. You also saw that items determine the general ledger account used when posting paychecks.

You then worked with the Employee Center to manage employee accounts and view payroll transactions. You also created a new employee and learned the procedures for terminating an employee.

With this knowledge, you were ready to begin processing payroll. You entered data to create paychecks and then printed the checks. You also printed checks for payroll tax liabilities and reviewed quarterly and annual tax filing requirements. You learned to prepare Form 941 and reviewed W-2s.

In the next chapter, you will focus on finalizing Baxter's March accounting period by recording adjusting entries, printing financial statements, and closing the accounting period.

END-OF-CHAPTER QUESTIONS

TRUE/FALSE

_____   1. Employee state tax withholdings can be calculated by referring to Circular E.

_____   2. Employers pay Social Security and Medicare taxes equal to employee withholdings for these taxes.

_____   3. Government taxing agencies set the due date for employer tax payments.

_____   4. You must void a paycheck to properly correct errors discovered after printing.

_____   5. Deductions are mandatory employee tax withholdings.

_____   6. Employer tax expense includes unemployment taxes.

_____   7. Gross pay for a salaried employee equals hours worked in the pay period times the pay rate.

_____   8. You should contribute to a 401K plan when possible to reduce your federal and state taxes while saving for future retirement.

MULTIPLE CHOICE

1. The _____ report can be used to reconcile the employer's FUTA tax liability for the quarter. *(Hint: Explore optional fields.)*
    a. Employee State Taxes Detail
    b. Employee Earnings Summary
    c. Payroll Liability Balances
    d. Both b and c

2. Form 940 reports _____ taxes and is filed _____.
    a. FUTA, annually
    b. employee withholdings and employer FICA and Medicare taxes, annually
    c. FUTA, quarterly
    d. employee withholdings and employer FICA and Medicare taxes, quarterly

3. An employee's Medicare taxes equal _____ of an employee's gross pay.
   a. 1.45 percent
   b. 6.2 percent
   c. 7.65 percent
   d. Employees do not pay Medicare taxes.

4. Per the IRS tax table, an employee must withhold _____ for federal taxes when paid biweekly for taxable pay of $960 and claiming Single with 2 allowances. *(Note: See Appendix D for complete payroll tax withholding tables.)*
   a. $72
   b. $75
   c. $37
   d. $39

5. An employee with gross pay of $1,295 will have a net pay of_____. Assume the employee is paid biweekly, claims Single with 0 allowances, contributed $35 to a 401k plan, and pays state taxes at 3 percent of taxable pay.
   a. $965.13
   b. $962.13
   c. $959.13
   d. $1,006.13

PRACTICE SET

In this practice set you will be using the **Graded Baxter Garden Supply** data file with the Practice Set completed in Chapter 9. *If the company file is not loaded on your computer then restore it using the Graded Baxter Garden Supply Chpt 9.QBB backup file created after completing the Chapter 9 Practice Set.*

1. Open **Graded Baxter Garden Supply** and complete the March and April payroll activities that follow.

   <u>**2009**</u>

   Mar 23   Create the following paychecks for the Pay Period ending 3/22/2009.

Baxter Garden Supply

Pay Period 3/9/2008 thru 3/22/2009

Check No.	Employee	Filing Status	Allow	Pay Type	Pay Rate	Regular Hrs	OT Hrs	Gross Pay	Taxable Pay	Federal Income Tax	Soc. Sec. (FICA) Tax	Medicare Tax	VA State Tax	401K Deduc.	Net Pay
1191	Barkley, Steve N.	Married	3	Hourly wage	11.00	80.00		880.00	844.80	14.00	54.56	12.76	25.34	35.20	738.14
1192	Beck, Dorothy L.	Married	2	Hourly wage	9.00	80.00		720.00	720.00	15.00	44.64	10.44	21.60	0.00	628.32
1193	Chester, Amanda W.	Single	1	Hourly wage	14.00	80.00		1,120.00	1,075.20	110.00	69.44	16.24	32.26	44.80	847.26
1194	Duke, Al C.	Single	0	Hourly wage	12.50	80.00		1,000.00	1,000.00	122.00	62.00	14.50	30.00	0.00	771.50
1195	Frost, Melvin H.	Single	1	Salary	1,461.54			1,461.54	1,373.85	155.00	90.62	21.19	41.22	87.69	1,065.82
1196	Gross, Derrick P.	Married	2	Salary	1,000.00			1,000.00	940.00	37.00	62.00	14.50	28.20	60.00	798.30
1197	Hecter, Anthony H.	Single	1	Hourly wage	13.00	80.00	5.00	1,137.50	1,137.50	107.00	70.53	16.49	34.13	0.00	909.35
1198	Nunnley, Brandee M.	Married	1	Salary	1,211.54			1,211.54	1,211.54	85.00	75.12	17.57	36.35	0.00	997.50
1199	Prather, Samuel R.	Married	1	Salary	1,584.62			1,584.62	1,489.54	127.00	98.25	22.98	44.69	95.08	1,196.62
1200	Sweet, Leonard	Single	0	Hourly wage	9.00	80.00		720.00	720.00	80.00	44.64	10.44	21.60	0.00	563.32
1201	Trotter, Mitchell K.	Married	2	Hourly wage	11.00	80.00		880.00	844.80	27.00	54.56	12.76	25.34	35.20	725.14
	Totals					560.00	5.00	11,715.20		879.00	726.36	169.87	340.73	357.97	9,241.27
	Tax Basis									Circular E	6.20%	1.45%	3.00%		
	G/L Accounts							60000		23400	23400	23400	23600	23300	10300

Baxter Garden Supply

Employer Costs for Period 3/9/2009 thru 3/22/2009

Employee	401K Match	ER Soc. Sec. (FICA)	ER Medicare	ER FUTA	ER SUTA	Health Insurance
Barkley, Steve N.	17.60	54.56	12.76	7.04	13.20	125.00
Beck, Dorothy L.	0.00	44.64	10.44	5.76	10.80	0.00
Chester, Amanda W.	22.40	69.44	16.24	8.96	16.80	90.00
Duke, Al C.	0.00	62.00	14.50	8.00	15.00	90.00
Frost, Melvin H.	43.85	90.62	21.19	4.66	10.40	125.00
Gross, Derrick P.	30.00	62.00	14.50	8.00	15.00	90.00
Hecter, Anthony H.	0.00	70.53	16.49	9.10	17.06	90.00
Nunnley, Brandee M.	0.00	75.12	17.57	7.55	18.17	125.00
Prather, Samuel R.	47.54	98.25	22.98	5.28	1.15	125.00
Sweet, Leonard	0.00	44.64	10.44	5.76	10.80	90.00
Trotter, Mitchell K.	17.60	54.56	12.76	7.04	13.20	90.00
Totals	178.99	726.36	169.87	77.15	141.58	1,040.00
Tax Basis	50% Match	6.20%	1.45%	0.8%	1.5%	
G/L Accounts	23300 / 60500	23400 / 61000	23400 / 61000	23500 / 61000	23700 / 61000	23750 / 60600

The next illustration shows your totals after entering the paychecks. Print the paychecks on
first check number 1191.

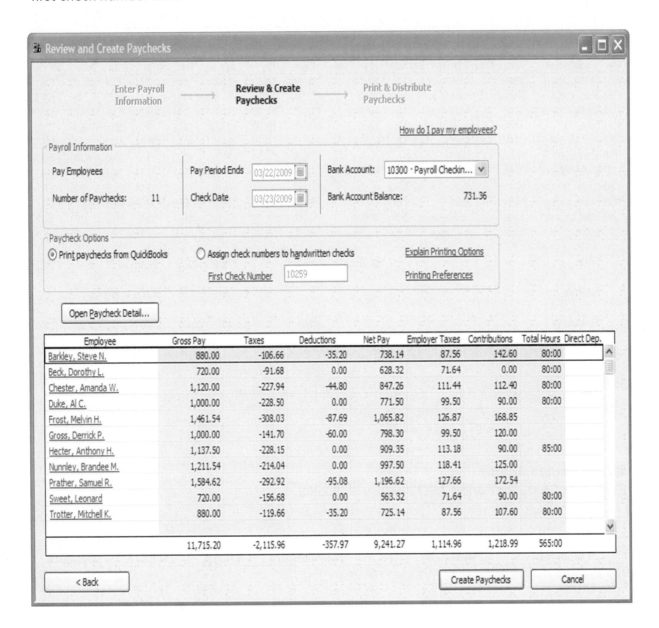

Mar 23   Print check number 10269 to National Trust Bank for $2,671.46 for federal
            withholdings, Medicare, and Social Security taxes for the liability period of
            1/1/2009 to 3/23/2009.

2009

Apr 2   Print the following checks for payroll liabilities from 1/1/2009 to 3/31/2009. First check number is 10270 and checks total $5,367.39.

Medi Ben Insurance for health insurance	$ 2,080.00
National Trust Bank for FUTA taxes	$ 522.06
VA State Income Tax for VA income tax	$ 678.53
VA Employment Tax for unemployment	$ 1,012.88
Watkins Financial for 401K liabilities	$ 1,073.92

Apr 6   Create the following paychecks for the Pay Period ending 4/5/2009.

Baxter Garden Supply
Pay Period 3/23/2009 thru 4/5/2009

Check No.	Employee	Filing Status	Allow	Pay Type	Pay Rate	Regular Hrs	OT Hrs	Gross Pay	Taxable Pay	Federal Income Tax	Soc. Sec. (FICA) Tax	Medicare Tax	VA State Tax	401K Deduc.	Net Pay
1202	Barkley, Steve N.	Married	3	Hourly wage	11.00	80.00		880.00	844.80	14.00	54.56	12.76	25.34	35.20	738.14
1203	Beck, Dorothy L.	Married	2	Hourly wage	9.00	80.00		720.00	720.00	15.00	44.64	10.44	21.60	0.00	628.32
1204	Chester, Amanda W.	Single	1	Hourly wage	14.00	80.00		1,120.00	1,075.20	110.00	69.44	16.24	32.26	44.80	847.26
1205	Duke, Al C.	Single	0	Hourly wage	12.50	80.00		1,000.00	1,000.00	122.00	62.00	14.50	30.00	0.00	771.50
1206	Frost, Melvin H.	Single	1	Salary	1,461.54			1,461.54	1,373.85	155.00	90.62	21.19	41.22	87.69	1,065.82
1207	Gross, Derrick P.	Married	2	Salary	1,000.00			1,000.00	940.00	37.00	62.00	14.50	28.20	60.00	798.30
1208	Hecter, Anthony H.	Single	1	Hourly wage	13.00	80.00		1,040.00	1,040.00	107.00	64.48	15.08	31.20	0.00	822.24
1209	Nunnley, Brandee M.	Married	1	Salary	1,211.54			1,211.54	1,211.54	85.00	75.12	17.57	36.35	0.00	997.50
1210	Prather, Samuel R.	Married	1	Salary	1,584.62			1,584.62	1,489.54	127.00	98.25	22.98	44.69	95.08	1,196.62
1211	Sweet, Leonard	Single	0	Hourly wage	9.00	75.00		675.00	675.00	71.00	41.85	9.79	20.25	0.00	532.11
1212	Trotter, Mitchell K.	Married	2	Hourly wage	11.00	80.00		880.00	844.80	27.00	54.56	12.76	25.34	35.20	725.14
	Totals					555.00	0.00	11,572.70		870.00	717.52	167.81	336.45	357.97	9,122.95
	Tax Basis									Circular E	6.20%	1.45%	3.00%		
	G/L Accounts							60000		23400	23400	23400	23600	23300	10300

Baxter Garden Supply
Employer Costs for Period 3/23/2009 thru 4/5/2009

Employee	401K Match	ER Soc. Sec. (FICA)	ER Medicare	ER FUTA	ER SUTA	Health Insurance
Barkley, Steve N.	17.60	54.56	12.76	7.04	13.20	125.00
Beck, Dorothy L.	0.00	44.64	10.44	5.76	10.80	0.00
Chester, Amanda W.	22.40	69.44	16.24	2.24	16.80	90.00
Duke, Al C.	0.00	62.00	14.50	8.00	15.00	90.00
Frost, Melvin H.	43.85	90.62	21.19	0.00	0.00	125.00
Gross, Derrick P.	30.00	62.00	14.50	8.00	15.00	90.00
Hecter, Anthony H.	0.00	64.48	15.08	5.30	15.60	90.00
Nunnley, Brandee M.	0.00	75.12	17.57	0.00	10.98	125.00
Prather, Samuel R.	47.54	98.25	22.98	0.00	0.00	125.00
Sweet, Leonard	0.00	41.85	9.79	5.40	10.13	90.00
Trotter, Mitchell K.	17.60	54.56	12.76	7.04	13.20	90.00
Totals	178.99	717.52	167.81	48.78	120.71	1,040.00
Tax Basis	50% Match	6.20%	1.45%	0.8%	1.5%	
G/L Accounts	23300 / 60500	23400 / 61000	23400 / 61000	23500 / 61000	23700 / 61000	23750 / 60600

The next illustration shows your totals after entering the paychecks. Print the paychecks on first check number 1202.

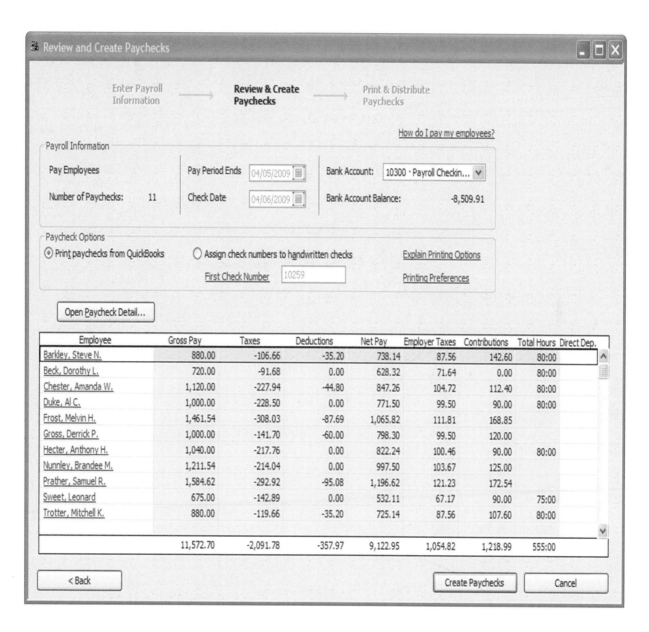

Apr 6   Print check number 10275 to National Trust Bank for $2,640.66 for federal withholding, Medicare, and Social Security taxes for the payroll liability period of 1/1/2009 to 4/6/2009.

Apr 13   Add the following new employee.
              Name: Arthur C. Parker
              Address: 782 Sewickly Blvd, Arlington, VA 30025
              Telephone: 770-987-7109
              Soc Sec: 111-88-0909

              Type: Regular
              Hired: 4/13/2009

              Pay Info: BiWeeklyPay pay schedule
                              Annual salary: $27,690.00
                              401K: 4% with employer match of 2%
              Tax Info: Federal   Single, 0 Allowances
                              State: VA for worked and withholding

              Terminate Brandee M. Nunnley. Termination date is April 19, 2009

Apr 20   Create the following paychecks for the Pay Period ending 4/19/2009. **_Note: You_**
              will have to manually adjust Brandee Nunnley's and Arthur Parker's gross pay
              when editing their checks. QBP will not prorate pay for salaried employees.

Baxter Garden Supply
Pay Period 4/6/2009 thru 4/19/2009

Check No.	Employee	Filing Status	Allow	Pay Type	Pay Rate	Regular Hrs	OT Hrs	Gross Pay	Taxable Pay	Federal Income Tax	Soc. Sec. (FICA) Tax	Medicare Tax	VA State Tax	401K Deduc.	Net Pay
1213	Barkley, Steve N.	Married	3	Hourly wage	11.00	80.00		880.00	844.80	14.00	54.56	12.76	25.34	35.20	738.14
1214	Beck, Dorothy L.	Married	2	Hourly wage	9.00	80.00		720.00	720.00	15.00	44.64	10.44	21.60	0.00	628.32
1215	Chester, Amanda W.	Single	1	Hourly wage	14.00	80.00		1,120.00	1,075.20	110.00	69.44	16.24	32.26	44.80	847.26
1216	Duke, Al C.	Single	0	Hourly wage	12.50	80.00		1,000.00	1,000.00	122.00	62.00	14.50	30.00	0.00	771.50
1217	Frost, Melvin H.	Single	1	Salary	1,461.54			1,461.54	1,373.85	155.00	90.62	21.19	41.22	87.69	1,065.82
1218	Gross, Derrick P.	Married	2	Salary	1,000.00			1,000.00	940.00	37.00	62.00	14.50	28.20	60.00	798.30
1219	Hecter, Anthony H.	Single	1	Hourly wage	13.00	80.00		1,040.00	1,040.00	107.00	64.48	15.08	31.20	0.00	822.24
1220	Nunnley, Brandee M.	Married	1	Salary	605.77			605.77	605.77	17.00	37.56	8.78	18.17	0.00	524.26
1221	Parker, Arthur C.	Married	0	Salary	537.50			537.50	516.00	20.00	33.33	7.79	15.48	21.50	439.40
1222	Prather, Samuel R.	Married	1	Salary	1,584.62			1,584.62	1,489.54	127.00	98.25	22.98	44.69	95.08	1,196.62
1223	Sweet, Leonard	Single	0	Hourly wage	9.00	75.00		675.00	675.00	71.00	41.85	9.79	20.25	0.00	532.11
1224	Trotter, Mitchell K.	Married	2	Hourly wage	11.00	80.00		880.00	844.80	27.00	54.56	12.76	25.34	35.20	725.14
	Totals					565.00	0.00	11,504.43		822.00	713.29	166.81	333.75	379.47	9,089.11
	Tax Basis									Circular E	6.20%	1.45%	3.00%		
	G/L Accounts							60000		23400	23400	23400	23600	23300	10300

Baxter Garden Supply
Employer Costs for Period 4/6/2009 thru 4/19/2009

Employee	401K Match	ER Soc. Sec. (FICA)	ER Medicare	ER FUTA	ER SUTA	Health Insurance
Barkley, Steve N.	17.60	54.56	12.76	6.72	13.20	125.00
Beck, Dorothy L.	0.00	44.64	10.44	5.76	10.80	0.00
Chester, Amanda W.	22.40	69.44	16.24	0.00	2.40	90.00
Duke, Al C.	0.00	62.00	14.50	0.00	15.00	90.00
Frost, Melvin H.	43.85	90.62	21.19	0.00	0.00	125.00
Gross, Derrick P.	30.00	62.00	14.50	0.00	15.00	90.00
Hecter, Anthony H.	0.00	64.48	15.08	0.00	9.34	90.00
Nunnley, Brandee M.	0.00	37.56	8.78	0.00	0.00	125.00
Parker, Arthur C.	10.75	33.33	7.79	4.30	8.06	0.00
Prather, Samuel R.	47.54	98.25	22.98	0.00	0.00	125.00
Sweet, Leonard	0.00	41.85	9.79	5.40	10.13	90.00
Trotter, Mitchell K.	17.60	54.56	12.76	6.72	13.20	90.00
Totals	189.74	713.29	166.81	28.90	97.13	1,040.00
Tax Basis	50% Match	6.20%	1.45%	0.8%	1.5%	
G/L Accounts	23300 / 60500	23400 / 61000	23400 / 61000	23500 / 61000	23700 / 61000	23750 / 60600

The next illustration shows your totals after entering the paychecks. Print the paychecks on first check number 1213.

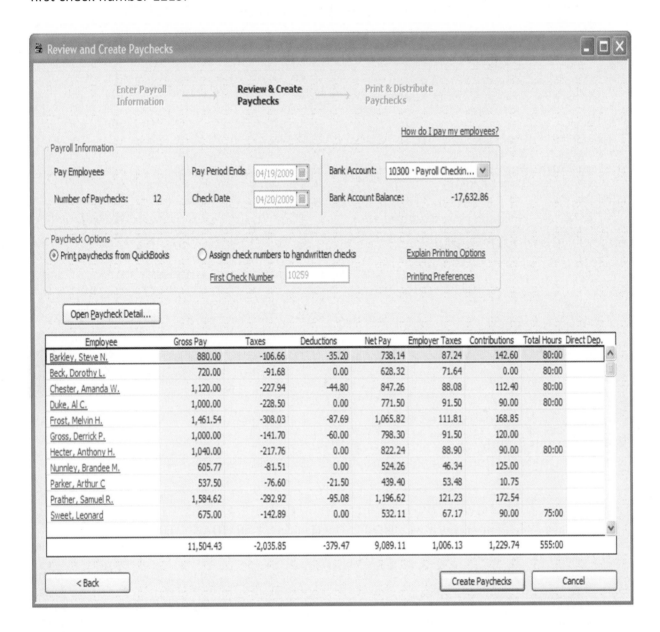

Apr 20   Print check number 10276 to National Trust Bank for $2,582.20 for federal withholdings, Medicare and Social Security taxes for the payroll liability period of 1/1/2009 to 4/20/2009.

Apr 30   Print the following checks for payroll liabilities from 1/1/2009 to 4/30/2009. First check number is 10277 and checks total $3,856.37.

Medi Ben Insurance for health insurance	$ 2,080.00
VA State Income Tax for VA income tax	$ 670.20
Watkins Financial for 401K liabilities	$ 1,106.17

2. Print the following reports to document activities.

    a. Payroll Transactions by Payee filtered for 3/23/2009 to 4/30/2009.

    b. Payroll Liability Balances report filtered for 3/1/2009 to 4/30/2009.

3. ***Back up the Graded Baxter Garden Supply data file to a backup file named "Graded Baxter Garden Supply Chpt 10". The Practice Set for the next chapter will build on the work completed in this chapter.***

CHAPTER 11   CLOSE THE ACCOUNTING PERIOD FOR A MERCHANDISING BUSINESS

LEARNING OBJECTIVES

This chapter works with the **Practice Baxter Garden Supply** data file containing the tasks completed in Chapter 10. *If this company file is not loaded on your computer then restore it using the Practice Baxter Garden Supply Chpt 10.QBB backup file created after reading Chapter 10.*

In this chapter you complete Baxter's accounting transactions for March 2009. You will do the following:

1. Analyze transactions posted in March and review a preclosing checklist
2. Post adjusting entries
3. Reconcile bank accounts
4. Print financial statements
5. Close the accounting period

Launch QBP an open **Practice Baxter Garden Supply**.

ANALYZE TRANSACTIONS

In Chapters 3 and 7 you posted general journal entries. In this chapter, you again use journal entries to adjust account balances and accrue expenses. You will then print financial statements for March and close the accounting period.

It is important to analyze posted transactions before closing an accounting period. You begin this analysis by reviewing the **General Ledger** report that follows.

Open the report by selecting *Reports>>Accountant and Taxes>>General Ledger>* on the main menu. Enter the date range of 3/1/2009 to 3/31/2009.

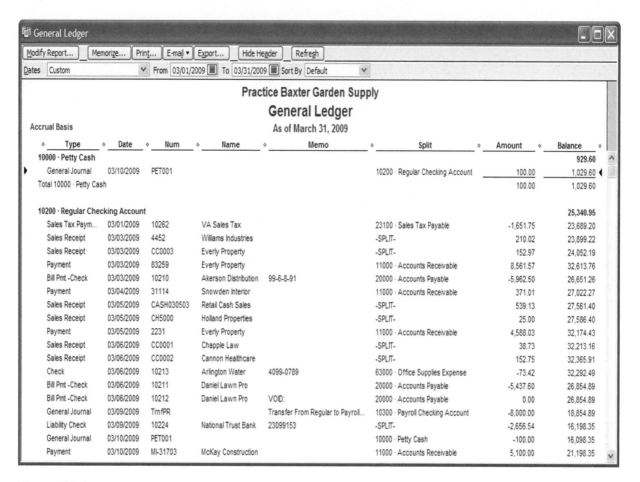

Figure 11:1

This report differs from the General Ledger Detail report you used to document the audit trail because it also lists beginning and ending account balances.

Next, modify the report so that transactions appear in debit and credit columns. Click **Modify Report**, add the **Debit** and **Credit** columns and then remove the **Amount** column. (See Figure 11:2.)

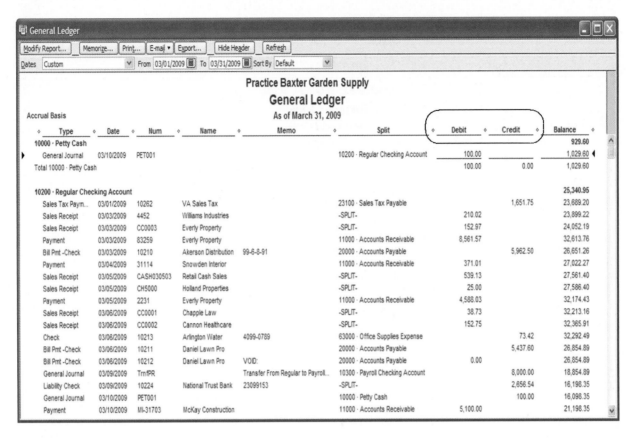

Figure 11:2

Remember that the Split column lists the corresponding account used on the transaction. If the term "SPLIT" appears then multiple accounts were involved. What follows are steps performed to analyze the report.

First, scroll through the report looking for transactions that may indicate a posting error. In particular, scroll to 72100 Repairs - Equipment Expense to locate an entry for shipping. The accountant recalls that this transaction involved shipping a package to a customer and should have posted to 57500 Freight.

You will now reclassify the expense. Double click the entry to reopen it and then use the lookup on **Account** to select 57500 Freight. (See Figure 11:3.)

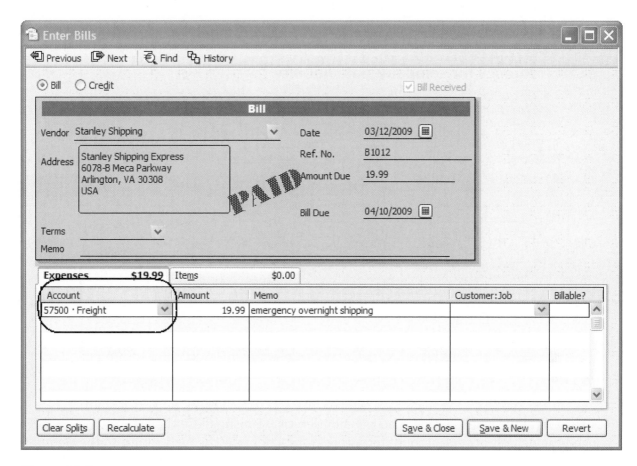

Figure 11:3

Click **Save & Close** and then click **Yes** when QBP prompts to confirm changing a posted transaction. That is how easy it is to reclassify a posting error for expenses.

However, it is not so easy to correct a posting error if the posting account is controlled by another record linked to the transaction, such as an inventory or payroll item. Scroll to 60300 Payroll Expenses, which contains entries for employee health insurance costs. The accountant wanted this expense to post to 60600 Employee Benefits Expense. You cannot simply open each payroll check to change the posting account because this will not correct future posting errors. Instead, you must change the payroll item's default posting account.

To change the default account open the Payroll Item List using *Lists>>Payroll Item List* on the main menu. Double click to open the **Health Insurance** item. Click **Next** and change the **Expense account** as shown in Figure 11:4.

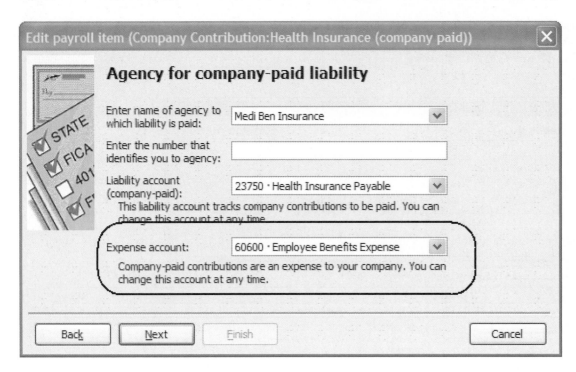

Figure 11:4

Click **Next** until the Finish button is active and then click **Finish**. Close the list. You have just changed the default posting account for future transactions. Moreover, return to the General Ledger report and notice that QBP has reclassified existing transactions into 60600 Employee Benefits Expense, so error correction is complete.

The next step in analyzing the General Ledger involves reviewing the report for missing transactions. In particular, scroll to account 10300 Payroll Checking to find that the March 23 bank transfer covering payroll checks has not been recorded. (See Figure 11:5.)

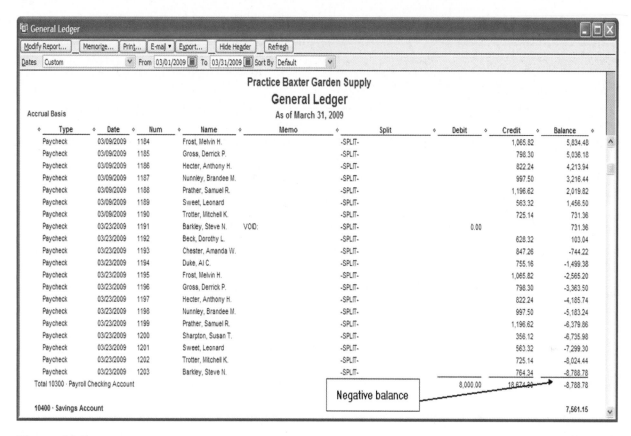

Figure 11:5

Next scroll to 14000 Prepaid Expenses to find that the entry recognizing this month's expired prepaid insurance must also be recorded. You will record these entries in the exercises that follow.

Scroll to 15010 Accum Depreciation – Furniture. The accountant has already posted the entry for March depreciation. Double click the entry to open it. (See Figure 11:6.) *Note: Click* **OK** *if you receive a message on automatically assigning journal entry numbers.*

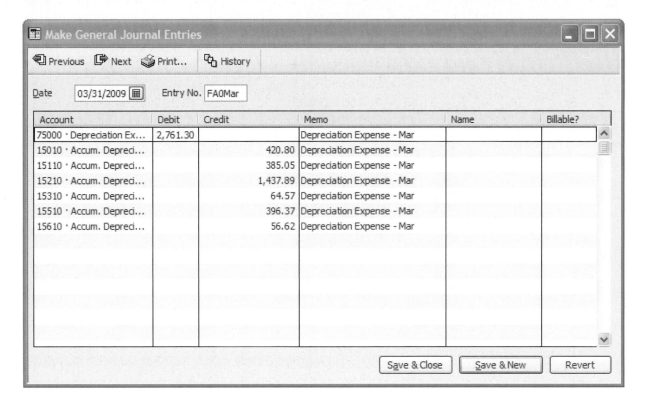

Figure 11:6

Figure 11:6 illustrates recording an adjusting entry for depreciation. Furthermore, adjusting entries are often saved as memorized transactions when the transaction repeats every month. Before closing the entry see if the accountant has created a memorized transaction for depreciation.

Select *Lists>>Memorized Transactions List* on the main menu.

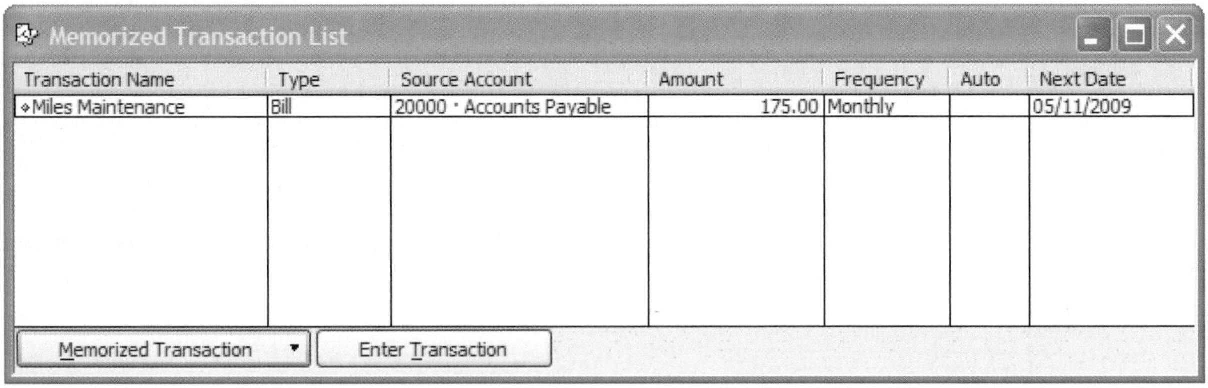

Figure 11:7

The only transaction you find is the entry memorized in Chapter 9. So now you will create a memorized depreciation entry using the existing transaction. Close the list.

Return to the open journal entry and select *Edit>>Memorize General Journal* on the main menu. Next, enter the information shown in Figure 11:8 and click **OK**.

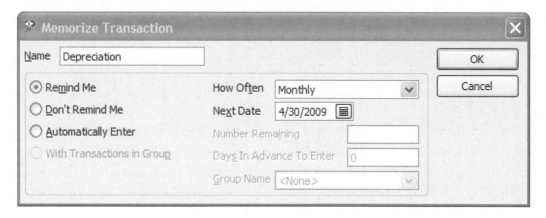

Figure 11:8

Click **X** to close the journal entry window. Return to the Memorized Transaction List and notice your memorized entry before clicking **X** to close the list.

Now is a good time to talk about using a suspense account. Scroll to the bottom of the General Ledger report to locate the **99999 Suspense** account. This account is used when you need to post an entry but do not have all the information necessary to complete it.

For instance, assume the company sold a vehicle costing $3,000 and received $500 in cash. You cannot delay recording cash on the sale; however, you do not have final depreciation on the vehicle to finalize gain or loss on the sale. This is where the entry can be posted using the suspense account. The following illustrates the journal entry to post the transaction using the suspense account.

	Debit	Credit
10200 Regular Checking Account	$ 500	
99999 Suspense	$2,500	
15200 Vehicles		$3,000

When you later calculate that $1,000 was previously recorded to the accumulated vehicle depreciation account and that final depreciation is $1,200, the following journal entry records the depreciation adjustment.

	Debit	Credit
75000 Depreciation Expense	$ 200	
15210 Accum. Depreciation – Vehicles		$ 200

You are now ready to reclassify the earlier suspense account entry by recording the next journal entry.

	Debit	Credit
15210 Accum. Depreciation – Vehicles	$1,200	
90000 Gain/Loss on Sale of Assets	$1,300	
99999 Suspense		$2,500

Thus, the suspense account becomes a useful tool for recording entries when you are unsure of all the accounts affected by a transaction. However, you must diligently review the balance in the suspense account to make sure entries are finalized.

You have finished reviewing the General Ledger report so close it.

There are a variety of procedures to be followed before closing an accounting period. Some of these were explained in previous chapters. Additional procedures vary based on a company's accounting transactions. It is not possible to simulate the variety of reconciling procedures you may encounter in practice. Instead, we have prepared the following preclosing checklist to help guide you in the future.

Preclosing Checklist	
Review Pending Transactions	Review pending sales to verify all sales income has been recognized.
	Review pending purchases to verify all expenses have been recognized.
	Review payroll tax liability accounts to ensure timely payment.
Reconciliation Procedures	Reconcile all bank statements.
	Reconcile the A/R aging report to the accounts receivable control account. (Performed in Chapters 4 and 8.)
	Reconcile the inventory valuation report to the inventory control account. (Performed in Chapter 8.)
	Reconcile fixed asset reports to fixed asset control accounts. Often fixed asset costs and depreciation will be tracked outside the software. QBP can track fixed asset costs and depreciation but this feature is not illustrated.
	Reconcile the A/P aging report to the accounts payable control account. (Performed in Chapter 5 and 9.)
Adjusting Entries	Post petty cash transactions.
	Review prepaid expenses for expired costs.
	Review accrued liability accounts such as wages and taxes payable.
	Review expenses in the prior period to identify expenses that need to be recognized in the current period. For example, missing utility bills or recurring rent transactions.
	Review posted expenses for prepaid costs and for fixed assets expensed to office supplies.

ADJUSTING ENTRIES

In this topic, you post Baxter's remaining adjusting entries for March. The accountant has already posted entries for depreciation expense. When posting depreciation, keep in mind that this is an estimate of expense based on ending assets held in the prior year. Actual depreciation expense is then adjusted at year-end to take into account asset additions and deletions during the year

All that remains are entries recording the transfer of funds from the regular checking account to the payroll checking, the expensing of expired prepaid expense, the accrual of wage expense, and a check that reimburses petty cash. In the next exercise you post accrued wages and petty cash. In the *You Try* exercise that follows you post entries for expired prepaid insurance and the bank transfer.

STEPS TO ENTER ADJUSTING ENTRIES

1. You will be recording accrued wages for March. The steps for calculating the amount to accrue are as follows:

   a. Open the **Employee Earnings Summary** report to determine the average weekly wage expense. Enter 3/9/2009 to 3/23/2009 as the date range (i.e., the last two pay dates). Total the salary and hourly wage amounts and divide by 4. The weekly average, rounded to the nearest dollar) is $5,908 computed as (10,515.40 +13,115.00) / 4.

   b. Next, compute a daily average wage by dividing the weekly average by 5 working days. The daily average, rounded to the nearest dollar, is $1,182.

   c. Finally, multiply the daily average by the number of days to accrue. For March, this is 7 days because the last pay period ended March 22. The accrual amount is $8,274.

2. Close the report and Report Center. Select **Company>>Make General Journal Entries** on the main menu and enter the information illustrated in Figure 11:9. Click **Save & New**.

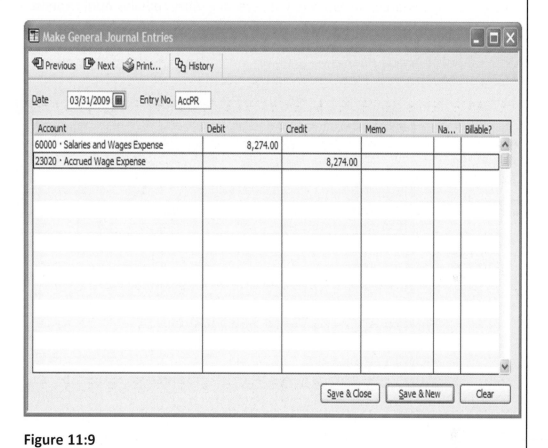

Figure 11:9

3. You will now record an entry on April 1 that reverses the payroll accrued in the previous step. Remember that the 7 days accrued will post as an expense when posting April paychecks covering the remaining days in March. In essence, the reversing entry reduces April expense for the 7 days of expense recognized in March.

    Enter the transaction in Figure 11:10 and click **Save & Close**.

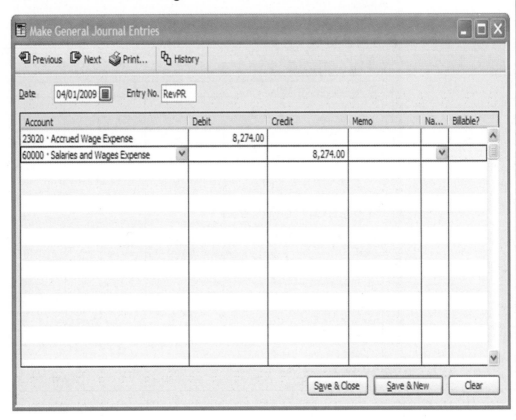

Figure 11:10

4. Now create a check that reimburses petty cash. Click the **Write Checks** icon and complete the check as illustrated in Figure 11:11.

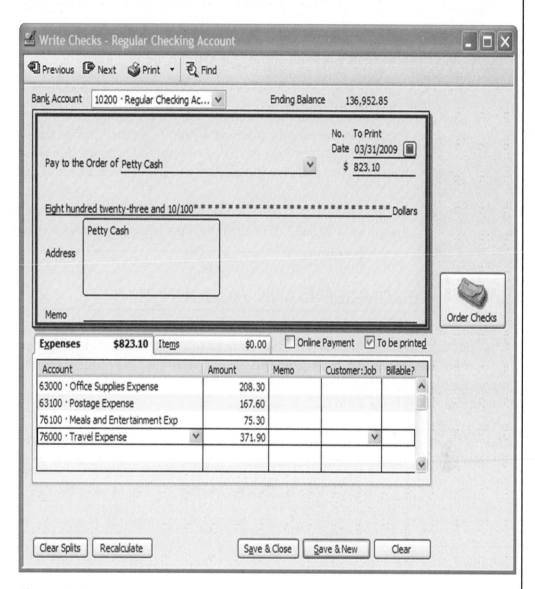

Figure 11:11

5. Click **Print**, verify the next check number of 10269, and click **OK**. Select a printer and then print and confirm that the check printed correctly. When you return to the transaction window notice that the check No. changed to 10269. Click **Save & Close**.

FINISH RECORDING MARCH ADJUSTING ENTRIES

In this exercise you record journal entries for expired prepaid insurance and the bank transfer covering March 23 paychecks.

a. On March 23, the accountant transferred $10,000 from the regular checking account to the payroll checking account. Record this as a journal entry. *(Note: In Chapter 7 we recorded the payroll account deposit as a bank transfer. This exercise shows that you can also record it as a journal entry.)*

b. On March 31, the accountant determined that $400 of prepaid auto insurance and $687 of prepaid business insurance have expired.

RECONCILE BANK ACCOUNTS

After posting adjusting entries, you are ready to reconcile Baxter's bank accounts. The accountant has previously reconciled the savings account. The steps that follow will help you reconcile the regular checking account. Thereafter, you will reconcile the payroll checking account in the *You Try* exercise.

On the Home page, click **Reconcile** under **Banking**. The reconciliation process always begins by selecting the bank account. Furthermore, it will always open to the first bank account on the Chart of Accounts. (See Figure 11:12.)

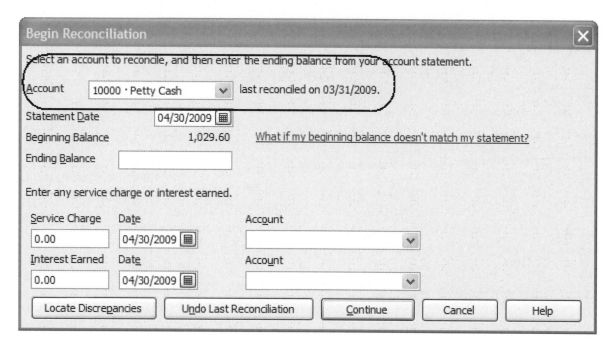

Figure 11:12

Notice that 10000 Petty Cash has been reconciled for March 31. Use the **Account** dropdown list to select **10400 Savings Account**. You will find that the March reconciliation for this account is complete.

Baxter received the March bank statement for the regular checking account. The next exercise walks through reconciling this account to the March bank statement that follows.

Baxter Garden Supply
Bank Statement March 31, 2009

Beginning Balance from February Statement				$ 34,300.94

March Deposits

Mar 3, 2009	8,924.56
Mar 4, 2009	371.01
Mar 5, 2009	5,152.16
Mar 6, 2009	191.48
Mar 10, 2009	5,100.00
Mar 12, 2009	779.10
Mar 13, 2009	81,032.57
Mar 17, 2009	31,930.92
Mar 24, 2009	38,872.58
Mar 25, 2008	3,142.68
Mar 26, 2009	393.28
Mar 27, 2009	662.90
Mar 30, 2009	8,860.28
Mar 31, 2009	639.82

Total Deposits for March: 186,053.34

March Checks Cleared

Date	Check	Amount
Feb 26, 2009	10203	5,006.75
Feb 24, 2009	10204	2,080.00
Feb 23, 2009	10206	675.60
Feb 26, 2009	10207	1,073.92
Feb 27, 2009	10209	123.72
Mar 3, 2009	10210	5,962.50
Mar 6, 2009	10211	5,437.60
Mar 6, 2009	10213	73.42
Mar 10, 2009	10214	1,500.00
Mar 10, 2009	10215	73.50
Mar 10, 2009	10216	23.37
Mar 10, 2009	10217	1,250.50
Mar 10, 2009	10218	2,445.25
Mar 10, 2009	10219	3,090.90
Mar 10, 2009	10220	74.97
Mar 10, 2009	10221	55.60
Mar 12, 2009	10222	124.68
Mar 12, 2009	10223	3,569.00
Mar 12, 2009	10224	2,656.54
Mar 12, 2009	10225	360.00
Mar 12, 2009	10226	550.00
Mar 12, 2009	10227	335.50
Mar 13, 2009	10228	450.00
Mar 13, 2009	10229	1,000.00
Mar 13, 2009	10230	500.00
Mar 13, 2009	10232	550.00
Mar 13, 2009	10233	183.90
Mar 17, 2009	10234	50.00
Mar 17, 2009	10235	50.00
Mar 17, 2009	10236	100.00
Mar 17, 2009	10237	100.00
Mar 26, 2009	10264	2,729.04

Total Cleared Checks for March: 42,256.26

Less Bank Transfers

Mar 9, 2009	8,000.00
Mar 9, 2009	100.00
Mar 23, 2009	10,000.00

Total March Transfers: 18,100.00

March Service Charges: 83.20

Ending Bank Balance March 31, 2009: $ 159,914.82

Figure 11:13

STEPS TO RECONCILE THE CHECKING ACCOUNT

1. Select **10200 Regular Checking** as the **Account**.

    Referring to the bank statement, enter the **Ending Balance**, **Date**, and **Service Charge** as shown in Figure 11:14. Verify that the service charge will post to 73000 Bank Charges.

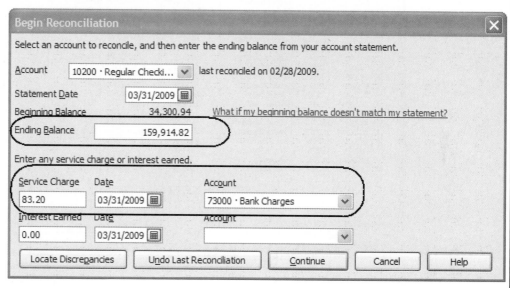

Figure 11:14

2. Click **Continue** to proceed to the screen for selecting deposits and checks clearing the March bank statement.

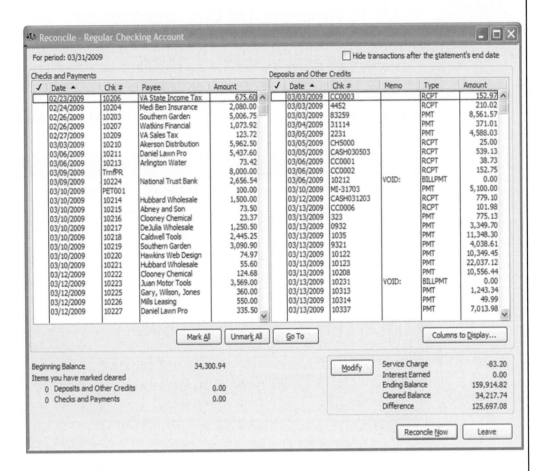

Figure 11:15

3. We will now explain using this window.

Modify reopens the Begin Reconciliation window illustrated in Step 1 to change entries.

Outstanding checks and bank transfers are listed on the left. On the right are deposits and void checks. Notice that the check you voided in Chapter 5 is already marked as cleared.

Click a check or deposit to mark the item as cleared. *(Note: You can also click the Mark All button and then click individual checks and deposits that have not cleared.)*

You can double click a check or deposit to reopen it.

The **Columns to Display** button customizes data displayed in the columns.

4. Click the option that hides all transactions after the statement's end date (i.e., top right of window) to remove April checks and deposits from the window.

5. Click **Mark All** and then refer to the totals listed at the bottom of the window. (See Figure 11:16.) The total for **Deposits** and **Other Credits** will equal total cleared deposits on the bank statement. You will now work on the checks.

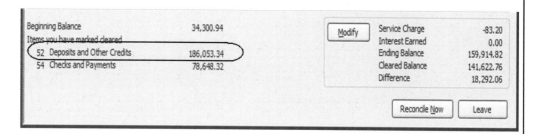

Figure 11:16

6. Refer again to the bank statement and click to deselect checks in the Reconcile window that have not cleared the statement. When finished, your results will compare to the results illustrated in Figure 11:17. *(Hint: Click the Chk # column header on the left to sort by check number.)*

The total for **Checks**, **Payments** and **Service Charges** will equal the sum of bank transfers, service charges, and cleared checks on the bank statement.

You cannot complete the next step until the **Difference** equals zero.

If you have difficulty reconciling an account then the **Leave** button saves your work and closes the reconciliation window. You can return later to complete the reconciliation.

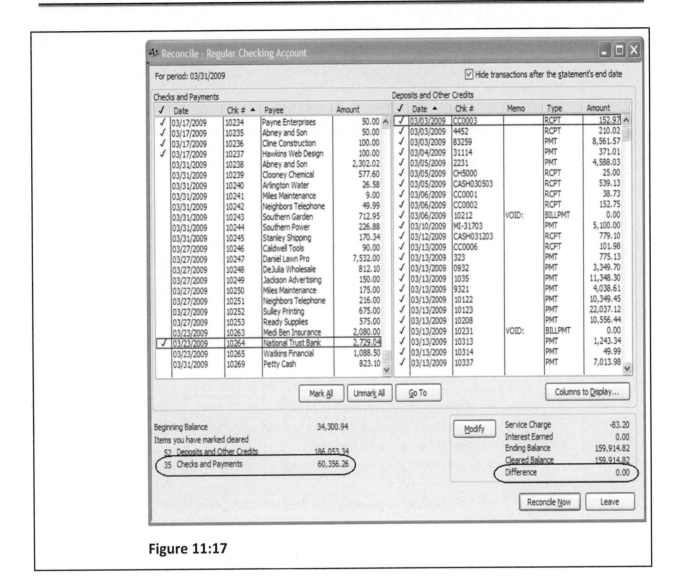

Figure 11:17

7. Click **Reconcile Now** and Figure 11:18 opens. Keep the report option of **Both** and click **Display**. *(Note: Turn off future messages when QBP prompts with information about reports.)*

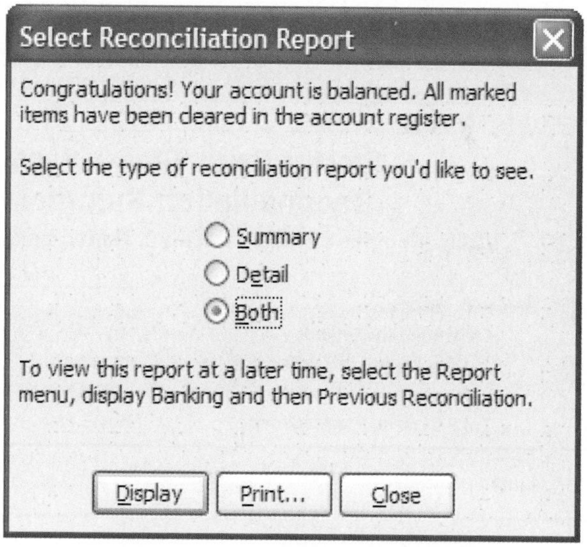

Select Reconciliation Report

Congratulations! Your account is balanced. All marked items have been cleared in the account register.

Select the type of reconciliation report you'd like to see.

- ○ Summary
- ○ Detail
- ◉ Both

To view this report at a later time, select the Report menu, display Banking and then Previous Reconciliation.

[Display] [Print...] [Close]

Figure 11:18

8. Figure 11:19 is the **Reconciliation Summary** report. The **Cleared Balance** agrees with the ending balance on the March bank statement. You will not print this statement because there is no information on individual items, so close it.

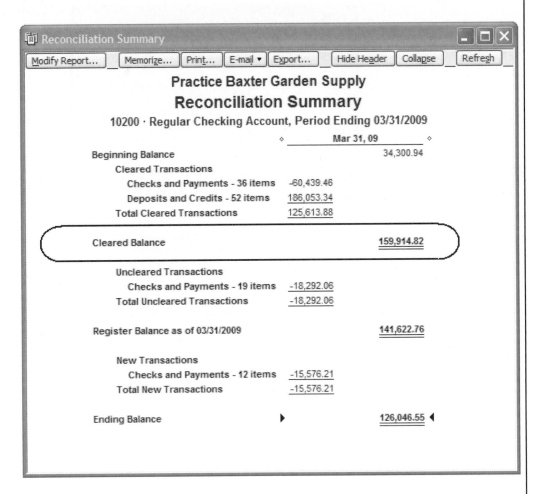

Figure 11:19

9. You now see the **Reconciliation Detail** report, which was located behind the summary report. You will always want to print this report because it provides information on individual transactions.

Scroll down to where the report lists the **Cleared Balance**. Again, this amount will agree with the ending balance on the March bank statement. Beneath this are transactions that should clear the April bank statement.

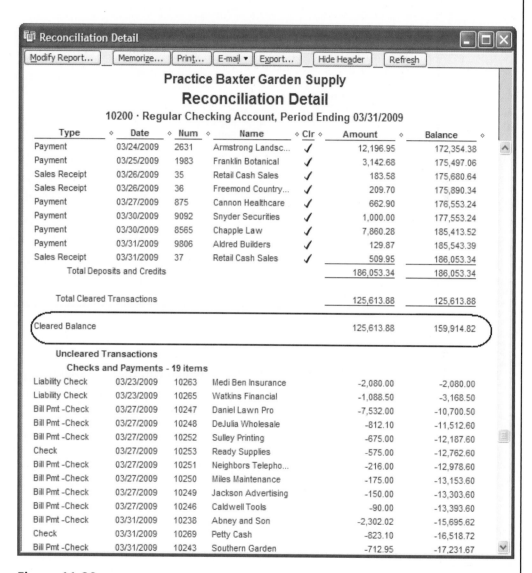

Figure 11:20

---

10. Click the **Print** button on the Reconciliation Detail report. Select a printer and click **Print**. You can now close the report.

You can reprint reconciliation reports by selecting ***Reports>>Banking>>Previous Reconciliation*** on the main menu. Open the window illustrated in Figure 11:21 and choose the options shown. Click **Display**.

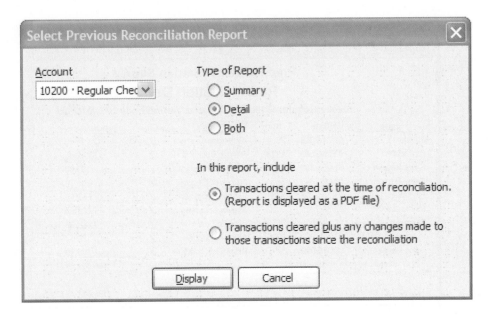

Figure 11:21

The report opens in PDF format (Figure 11:22), which can then be saved to your local hard drive by selecting ***File>>Save As*** on the PDF menu. You can only print the most recent reconciliation using this method.

Close the report.

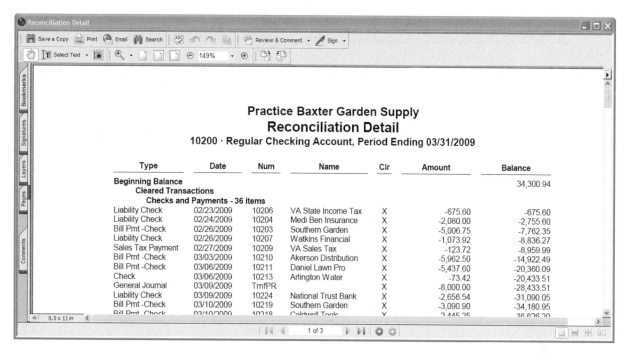

Figure 11:22

RECONCILE THE PAYROLL CHECKING ACCOUNT

The March bank statement for the payroll checking account has arrived. All paychecks and deposits have cleared. Bank charges for March are $32.75 and the ending bank statement balance is $1,178.47.

Reconcile the account and print the Detail Reconciliation report.

FINANCIAL REPORTS

You have now completed the preclosing checklist and are ready to print the trial balance and financial statements.

The trial balance is printed first so you can perform one final check of account balances. Select **Reports>>Accountant and Taxes>>Trial Balance** on the main menu and enter 3/31/2009 as the date range. (See Figure 11:23. This report has been shortened.)

Practice Baxter Garden Supply
Trial Balance
As of March 31, 2009

	Mar 31, 09	
	Debit	Credit
10000 · Petty Cash	1,029.60	
10200 · Regular Checking Account	141,622.76	
10300 · Payroll Checking Account	1,178.47	
10400 · Savings Account	7,592.65	
11000 · Accounts Receivable	58,182.07	
11100 · Allowance for Doubtful Accounts		5,000.00
13000 · Inventory	49,894.00	
14000 · Prepaid Expenses	9,783.00	
14200 · Notes Receivable-Current	0.00	
14210 · Accrued Interest Income	0.00	
15000 · Furniture and Fixtures	63,274.25	
15010 · Accum. Depreciation-Furniture		54,680.61
15100 · Equipment	38,738.33	
15110 · Accum. Depreciation-Equipment		33,138.17
15200 · Vehicles	86,273.40	
15210 · Accum. Depreciation-Vehicles		51,585.26
15300 · Other Depreciable Property	6,200.96	
15310 · Accum. Depreciation-Other		3,788.84
60000 · Salaries and Wages Expense	76,087.90	
60500 · Pension/Profit-Sharing Expense	1,078.80	
60600 · Employee Benefits Expense	6,240.00	
61000 · Payroll Tax Expense	6,907.92	
63000 · Office Supplies Expense	4,205.15	
63100 · Postage Expense	477.32	
64000 · Advertising Expense	1,575.00	
64200 · Dues and Subscriptions Exp	208.01	
65000 · Legal and Professional Expense	450.00	
66001 · Insurance - Auto Expense	1,200.00	
66102 · Insurance - Business Expense	2,061.00	
71110 · Rent - Office	1,650.00	
71100 · Utilities Expense	1,146.75	
71200 · Building Maintenance Expense	650.00	
72000 · Repairs - Building Expense	203.93	
72100 · Repairs - Equipment Expense	546.45	
72300 · Repairs - Auto Expenses	877.81	
73000 · Bank Charges	312.60	
75000 · Depreciation Expense	8,394.00	
75100 · Amortization Expense	249.00	
76000 · Travel Expense	371.90	
76100 · Meals and Entertainment Exp	402.04	
80000 · Interest Income		167.65
85000 · Interest Expense	570.83	
TOTAL	904,868.76	904,868.76

Figure 11:23

In a manual accounting system this report was critical to proving that debits equaled credits before preparing financial statements. You will recall the manual sales journal entries illustrated in Chapter 8 and how this journal was cross-footed before posting entries to customer and general ledger accounts. You also remember the manual purchasing entries in Chapter 9 and the manual payroll entries in Chapter 10. Now you understand why this report is called a "trial" balance. Imagine the number of trials it took before the books balanced because of the number of errors that could occur in a manual system. In fact, an unadjusted trial balance was prepared before posting adjusting entries and then an adjusted closing trial balance was prepared before preparing financial statements.

Today the trial balance still verifies that accounts balance; however, it more likely functions as a tool for reconciling account balances to external source documents and reports. In fact, you used the report to tie the balance on the A/R aging report back to the balance in Accounts Receivable and to tie other report balances back to the general ledger.

Close the trial balance so we can next focus on financial statements.

Open the **Report Center**. As shown in Figure 11:24, QBP refers to the Income Statement as the **Profit & Loss** statement.

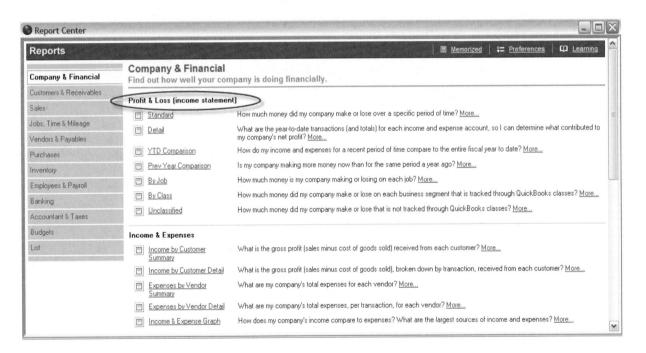

Figure 11:24

Open the **Standard Profit & Loss** statement and enter the date range of 1/1/2009 to 3/31/2009. (See Figure 11:25.)

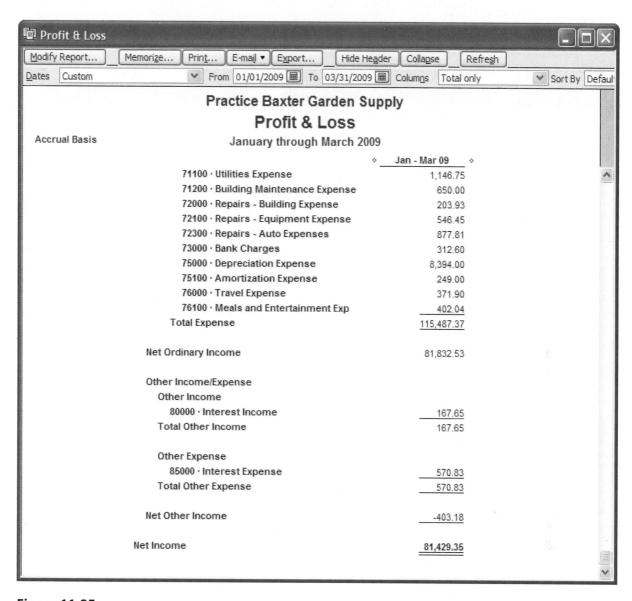

Figure 11:25

Scroll to the bottom and locate year-to-date net income.

Close this report and open the **Detail** report. Again enter the date range of 1/1/2009 to 3/31/2009.

The report in Figure 11:26 lists individual transactions affecting Income Statement accounts. Close this report.

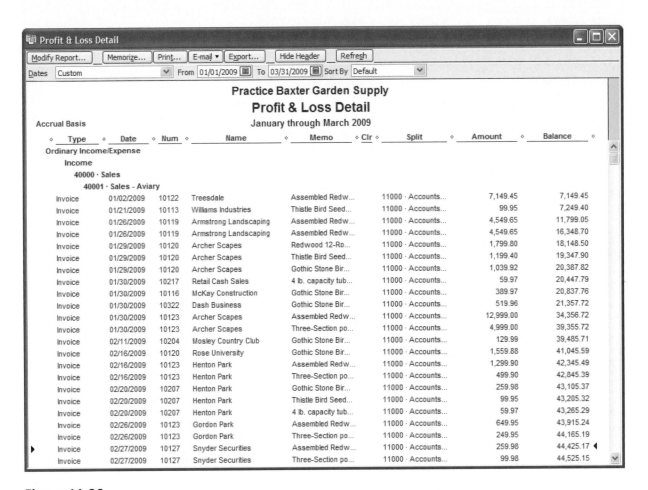

Figure 11:26

Now open the **YTD Comparison** report. This time enter the date range of 3/1/2009 to 3/31/2009 and scroll to the bottom of the report.

Practice Baxter Garden Supply
Profit & Loss YTD Comparison
March 2009

Ordinary Income/Expense	Mar 09	Jan - Mar 09
Income		
40000 · Sales		
40001 · Sales – Aviary	▶ 7,807.64	◀ 52,332.79
40002 · Sales – Books	149.75	7,293.10
40003 · Sales – Equipment	18,963.17	61,316.66
40004 · Sales – Food/Fert	1,006.96	5,204.15
40005 · Sales – Hand Tools	729.67	7,058.12
40006 · Sales – Landscape Services	21,176.44	30,789.52
40007 · Sales – Miscellaneous	2,074.60	27,574.60
40008 · Sales – Nursery	35,496.95	69,339.03
40009 · Sales – Pots	4,507.15	8,071.58
40010 · Sales – Seeds	1,457.43	8,661.39
40011 · Sales – Soil	356.49	8,784.02
40000 · Sales – Other	0.00	0.00
Total 40000 · Sales	93,726.25	286,424.96
49000 · Sales Discounts	-174.96	-184.86
Total Income	93,551.29	286,240.10
Cost of Goods Sold		
50000 · Product Cost		
50001 · Product Cost – Aviary	2,582.10	20,990.35
50002 · Product Cost – Books	14.27	2,361.37
50003 · Product Cost – Equipment	7,903.80	24,660.30
50004 · Product Cost – Food/Fert	398.80	2,060.04
50005 · Product Cost – Hand Tools	274.45	2,801.15
50007 · Product Cost – Miscellaneous	183.90	183.90
50008 · Product Cost – Nursery	7,584.00	13,126.60
50009 · Product Cost – Pots	1,796.80	2,071.80
50010 · Product Cost – Seeds	584.45	3,450.65
50011 · Product Cost – Soil	156.69	3,921.94
50000 · Product Cost – Other	-463.00	-463.00
Total 50000 · Product Cost	21,016.26	75,165.10
57300 · Subcontractors		
57306 · Subcontractors – Landscaping	8,317.50	13,755.10
Total 57300 · Subcontractors	8,317.50	13,755.10
Total COGS	29,333.76	88,920.20
Gross Profit	64,217.53	197,319.90
Expense		
57500 · Freight	273.94	323.94
58500 · Inventory Adjustments	7.76	7.76
59500 · Purchase Discounts	-139.91	-139.91
60000 · Salaries and Wages Expense	27,937.40	76,087.90
60500 · Pension/Profit-Sharing Expense	362.84	1,078.80
60600 · Employee Benefits Expense	2,080.00	6,240.00
61000 · Payroll Tax Expense	2,279.04	6,907.92
63000 · Office Supplies Expense	3,201.72	4,205.15
63100 · Postage Expense	167.60	477.32
64000 · Advertising Expense	1,575.00	1,575.00
64200 · Dues and Subscriptions Exp	0.00	208.01
65000 · Legal and Professional Expense	90.00	450.00
66000 · Insurance Expense		
66001 · Insurance – Auto Expense	400.00	1,200.00
66102 · Insurance – Business Expense	687.00	2,061.00
Total 66000 · Insurance Expense	1,087.00	3,261.00
71000 · Rent Expense		
71110 · Rent – Office	550.00	1,650.00
Total 71000 · Rent Expense	550.00	1,650.00
71100 · Utilities Expense	519.45	1,146.75
71200 · Building Maintenance Expense	650.00	650.00
72000 · Repairs – Building Expense	203.93	203.93
72100 · Repairs – Equipment Expense	0.00	546.45
72300 · Repairs – Auto Expenses	877.81	877.81
73000 · Bank Charges	115.95	312.60
75000 · Depreciation Expense	2,761.30	8,394.00
75100 · Amortization Expense	83.00	249.00
76000 · Travel Expense	371.90	371.90
76100 · Meals and Entertainment Exp	75.30	402.04
Total Expense	45,131.03	115,487.37
Net Ordinary Income	19,086.50	81,832.53
Other Income/Expense		
Other Income		
80000 · Interest Income	31.50	167.65
Total Other Income	31.50	167.65
Other Expense		
85000 · Interest Expense	275.00	570.83
Total Other Expense	275.00	570.83
Net Other Income	-243.50	-403.18
Net Income	18,843.00	81,429.35

Figure 11:27

This **YTD Comparison** report compares March income to year-to-date income. As you know, the Income Statement paints a company's financial picture over a period of time and this report informs Baxter's owners that less than 25 percent of year-to-date income year was generated in March.

QBP creates the Income Statement using general ledger account types. You will recall setting types when creating general ledger accounts in Chapter 3. You will now see these types mapped to the Income Statement.

Press **Ctrl + A** on the keyboard to open the **Chart of Accounts**. Refer to the **YTD Comparison** report and the **Type** column on the **Chart of Accounts** as we explain type mapping on the Income Statement.

Income account types appear under the Income category on the statement; **Cost of Goods Sold** account types under Cost of Goods Sold, and so forth. Within these categories, account balances are listed individually.

Types serve the same purpose on the Balance Sheet. Close the Income Statement and open the **Standard Balance Sheet**. (See Figure 11:28.) This statement reports a company's financial position on a specific date. Enter 3/31/2009 as the date. Take the time to scroll through accounts on the Balance Sheet and compare the placement of accounts to types on the Chart of Accounts.

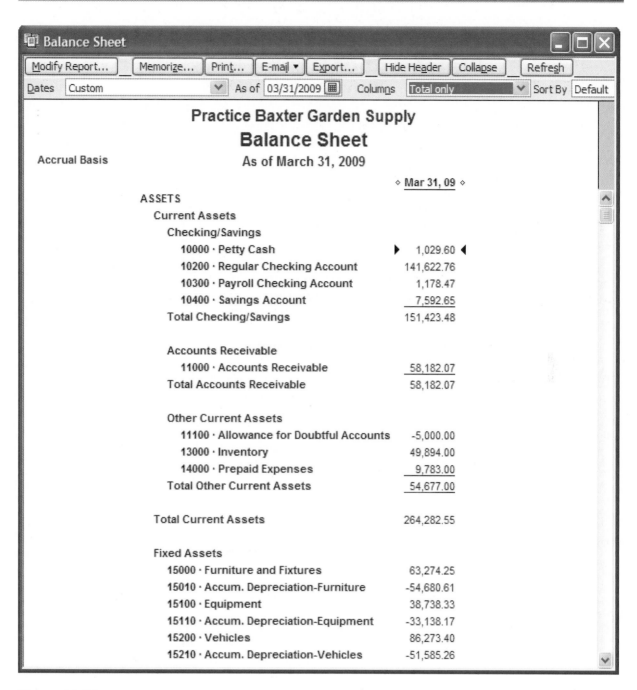

Figure 11:28

Close the Balance Sheet and the Chart of Accounts.

Next open the **Statement of Cash Flows** and enter the date range of 3/1/2009 to 3/31/2009.

Practice Baxter Garden Supply
Statement of Cash Flows
March 2009

	Mar 09
OPERATING ACTIVITIES	
Net Income	18,843.00
Adjustments to reconcile Net Income	
to net cash provided by operations:	
11000 · Accounts Receivable	90,953.26
13000 · Inventory	-24,144.77
14000 · Prepaid Expenses	1,087.00
20000 · Accounts Payable	19,373.78
23100 · Sales Tax Payable	1,548.79
23010 · Accrued Interest Expense	275.00
23020 · Accrued Wage Expense	4,274.00
23400 · Federal Payroll Taxes Payable	-5.00
23500 · FUTA Tax Payable	152.94
23600 · State Payroll Taxes Payable	688.15
23700 · SUTA Tax Payable	320.81
Net cash provided by Operating Activities	113,366.96
INVESTING ACTIVITIES	
15000 · Furniture and Fixtures	-505.00
15110 · Accum. Depreciation-Equipment	385.05
15210 · Accum. Depreciation-Vehicles	1,437.89
15310 · Accum. Depreciation-Other	64.57
15510 · Accum. Depreciation-Buildings	396.37
15610 · Accum. Depreciation-Bldg Imp	56.62
15010 · Accum. Depreciation-Furniture	420.80
19110 · Accum Amortiz - Organiz Costs	83.00
Net cash provided by Investing Activities	2,339.30
Net cash increase for period	115,706.26
Cash at beginning of period	35,717.22
Cash at end of period	**151,423.48**

Figure 11:29

This may be your first exposure to the Statement of Cash Flows so we will spend some time explaining its importance.

This statement reports cash activities by operations, investing, and financing. Operating cash is generated by day-to-day activities of the business such as collecting on accounts receivable and reducing accounts payable. Investing is the cash effect of buying or selling company assets such as equipment or buildings. Finally, financing is the cash effect of borrowing or repaying loans.

After reviewing the report, the accountant notices that accumulated depreciation accounts are appearing under investing activities when these accounts should appear under operating activities because depreciation is a noncash activity added back to net income.   Follow the next steps to correct the reporting of these accounts.

Select **Edit>>Preferences** on the main menu or click the [Classify Cash...] button on the Statement of Cash Flows. When the **Preferences** window opens, click the **Classify Cash** button on the **Company Preferences** tab for the **Reports and Graphs** category. (See Figure 11:30.)

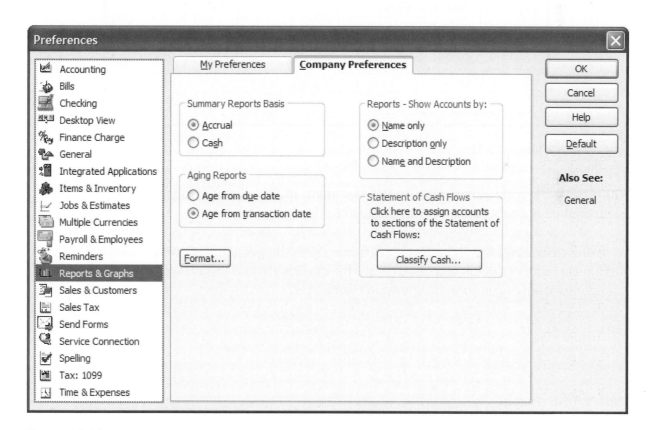

Figure 11:30

After clicking **Classify Cash** the window in Figure 11:31 opens. Scroll down to the accounts indicated.

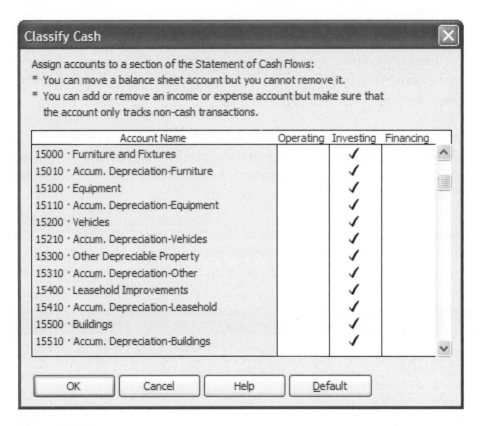

Figure 11:31

In this window you map accounts to the Statement of Cash Flows. Notice that accumulated depreciation accounts are currently mapped to the Investing category.

Click the **Operating** column for the seven accumulated depreciation accounts and the accumulated amortization account to move the checkmark into this category. When finished, categories are changed to those shown in Figure 11:32.

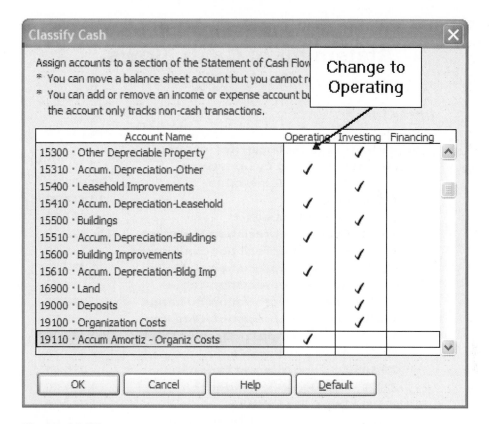

Figure 11:32

Before saving the changes, scroll down and notice that you do not map Income Statement accounts to the Statement of Cash Flows. Instead, these accounts already appear in the Net Income line of the statement.

Click **OK** to save these changes and click **OK** to close the Preferences window.

Return to the Statement of Cash Flows and note the changes. (See Figure 11:33.)

Practice Baxter Garden Supply
Statement of Cash Flows
March 2009

	Mar 09
OPERATING ACTIVITIES	
Net Income	18,843.00
Adjustments to reconcile Net Income	
to net cash provided by operations:	
11000 · Accounts Receivable	90,953.26
13000 · Inventory	-24,144.77
14000 · Prepaid Expenses	1,087.00
15010 · Accum. Depreciation-Furniture	420.80
15110 · Accum. Depreciation-Equipment	385.05
15210 · Accum. Depreciation-Vehicles	1,437.89
15310 · Accum. Depreciation-Other	64.57
15510 · Accum. Depreciation-Buildings	396.37
15610 · Accum. Depreciation-Bldg Imp	56.62
19110 · Accum Amortiz - Organiz Costs	83.00
20000 · Accounts Payable	19,373.78
23010 · Accrued Interest Expense	275.00
23020 · Accrued Wage Expense	4,274.00
23100 · Sales Tax Payable	1,548.79
23400 · Federal Payroll Taxes Payable	-5.00
23500 · FUTA Tax Payable	152.94
23600 · State Payroll Taxes Payable	688.15
23700 · SUTA Tax Payable	320.81
Net cash provided by Operating Activities	116,211.26
INVESTING ACTIVITIES	
15000 · Furniture and Fixtures	-505.00
Net cash provided by Investing Activities	-505.00
Net cash increase for period	115,706.26
Cash at beginning of period	35,717.22
Cash at end of period	**151,423.48**

Figure 11:33

We now focus on interpreting this statement. The statement begins with **Net Income** from the March Income Statement and adjusts this number to arrive at net income on a cash basis.

Noncash items, such as depreciation, are added back and the cash changes for operating asset and liability accounts are calculated to obtain the **Net cash provided by Operating Activities**. Net positive cash from operations is a critical point of analysis. Companies that continually fail to generate cash from operations will eventually need to borrow to fund day-to-day activities, such as paying employees and vendors.

Net cash flow from operations is then adjusted for cash changes from investing and financing activities to arrive at the **Net cash increase for period**. *(Note: This could be a net cash decrease.)*

Focus now on the bottom section of the report. **Cash at beginning of period** equals the February 28 total for all cash accounts on the **Balance Sheet**. (See Figure 11:34.)

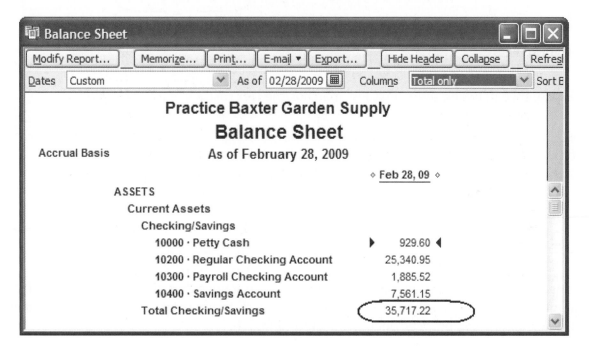

Figure 11:34

Cash at end of Period equals the total for all cash accounts on the March 31 **Balance Sheet** shown in Figure 11:35.

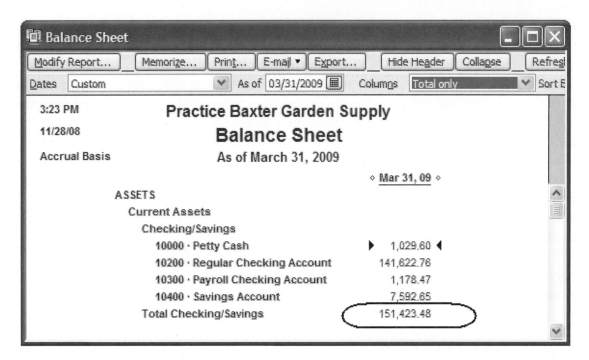

Figure 11:35

The difference between these amounts matches the **Net cash increase for period**.

Close this statement and the Report Center. After printing financial statements, you are ready to close the accounting period.

CLOSING THE ACCOUNTING PERIOD

Closing the period is important to prevent posting transactions that affect issued financial statements. You do not want to send March financial statements to owners or the bank and subsequently have an entry erroneously posted to March.

You should always back up a data file before closing a period so create a ***backup of Baxter's data file to a backup file named "Practice Baxter Garden Supply Chpt 11"***.

Now select ***Edit>>Preferences*** on the main menu. Select **Accounting** and click the **Company Preferences** tab. (See Figure 11:36.)

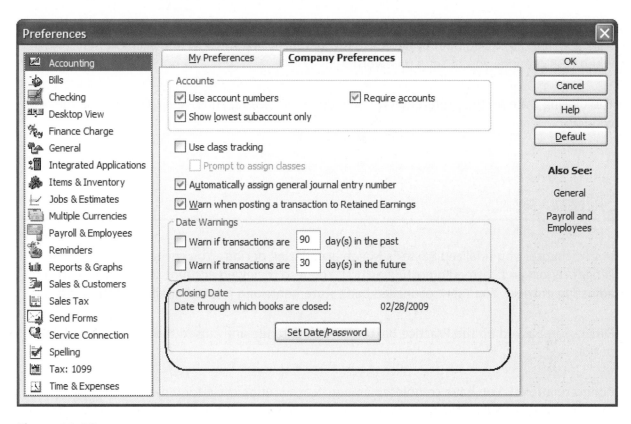

Figure 11:36

This window shows that the books are closed through February 28, 2009. Click **Set Date/Password** and enter 3/31/2009 as illustrated in Figure 11:37.

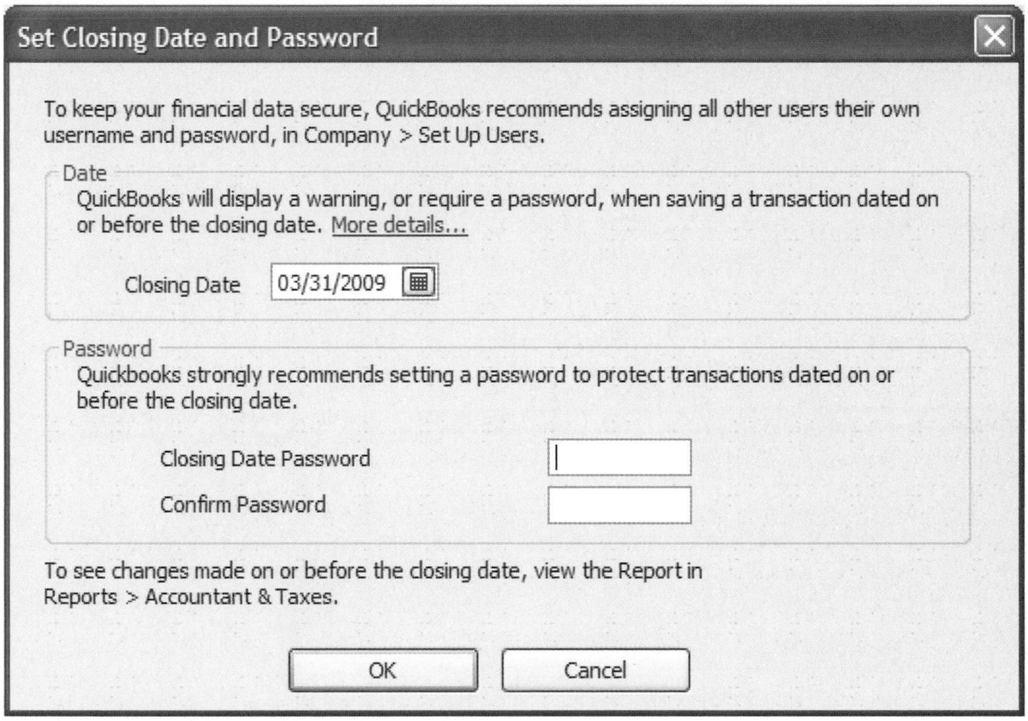

Figure 11:37

In practice, you should set a closing date password to prevent accidentally backdating transactions to a closed period, but leave these fields blank for now and click **OK**. Click **No** when QBP reminds you to set a password.

The Closing Date on the preference window updates to 3/31/2009. Click **OK** to close the window.

SUMMARY

In this chapter you finalized Baxter's March accounting period. You reviewed the General Ledger report and corrected posting errors. You also reviewed account balances and posted adjusting entries. You then reconciled bank statements and printed financial statements.

Finally you backed up the Practice Baxter Garden data file and closed the March accounting period.

Congratulations! You have completed an entire accounting cycle for a merchandising business. The next chapter presents a comprehensive project for a merchandising business. Thereafter, one chapter remains to illustrate creating a new company.

END-OF-CHAPTER QUESTIONS

TRUE/FALSE

_____ 1. The accounting period is closed only at the end of the year.

_____ 2. The Standard Profit & Loss report will report March income compared to year-to-date income.

_____ 3. Accrued wages should be reversed in the following month.

_____ 4. The Balance Sheet date range of 3/1/2009 to 3/31/2009 will report assets, liabilities, and equity for March.

_____ 5. The Cash Flow Statement begins with net income or loss for the period.

MULTIPLE CHOICE

_____ 1. Which statement reports a company's financial position at a specific point in time?
    a. Statement of Cash Flows
    b. Balance Sheet
    c. Statement of Retained Earnings
    d. Income Statement

_____ 2. The owner wants to see cash generated from accounts receivable. Which report(s) would you print?
    a. Cash Receipts Journal
    b. Statement of Cash Flows
    c. Income Statement
    d. Both a and b

_____ 3. Net income/net loss for March will affect the _____ statement(s).
    a. Balance Sheet
    b. Income Statement
    c. Statement of Retained Earnings
    d. All of the above

_____ 4. Which report demonstrates that the inventory general ledger account reconciles to the inventory costs?

      a. Inventory Stock Status by Item report

      b. Inventory Valuation Summary report

      c. Both a and b

      d. None of the above

_____ 5. Which report would you use for spotting missing or out-of-sequence accounts payable checks?

      a. Missing Checks

      b. Check Detail

      c. Cash Disbursements Journal

      d. All of the above

PRACTICE SET

In this practice set you will be using the **Graded Baxter Garden Supply** data file with the Practice Set completed in Chapter 10. *If the company file is not loaded on your computer then restore it using the Graded Baxter Garden Supply Chpt 10.QBB backup file created after completing the Chapter 10 Practice Set.*

1. Open **Graded Baxter Garden Supply**. Perform these accounting activities to close the March accounting period.

2009	
Mar 23	Post the transfer of $10,000.00 from regular checking to payroll checking.
Mar 31	Reconcile the Regular Checking account for March using the statement that follows. *(Note: This statement is different from the statement illustrated in the chapter.)* Print the Detail Reconciliation report.
	Reconcile the Payroll Checking Account for March. The ending statement balance is $1,473.29. All checks and deposits for the month have cleared and the monthly bank charge is $16.80. *(Remember that April transactions are also in this account.)* Print the Detail Reconciliation report.
	Post an entry that expenses the following prepaid expenses. 66001 Insurance - Auto Expense $200.00 66102 Insurance - Business Expense $800.00
	Accrue $5,000.00 for Salaries expense.
	Print the Standard Balance Sheet, Standard Profit & Loss, and Statement of Cash Flows for March.

Create a backup file named "Graded Baxter Garden Supply March Close" and then close the March accounting period.

Baxter Garden Supply
Bank Statement March 31, 2009

Beginning Balance from February Statement				$ 34,300.94

March Deposits

Mar 3, 2009	8,924.56	
Mar 4, 2009	371.01	
Mar 5, 2009	5,152.16	
Mar 6, 2009	191.48	
Mar 10, 2009	5,100.00	
Mar 12, 2009	779.10	
Mar 13, 2009	81,032.57	
Mar 17, 2009	31,930.92	
Mar 24, 2009	38,872.58	
Total Deposits for March		172,354.38

March Checks Cleared

Date	Check	Amount
Feb 26, 2009	10203	5,006.75
Feb 24, 2009	10204	2,080.00
Feb 23, 2009	10206	675.60
Feb 26, 2009	10207	1,073.92
Feb 27, 2009	10209	123.72
Mar 3, 2009	10210	5,962.50
Mar 6, 2009	10211	5,437.60
Mar 6, 2009	10213	73.42
Mar 10, 2009	10214	1,500.00
Mar 10, 2009	10215	73.50
Mar 10, 2009	10216	23.37
Mar 10, 2009	10217	1,250.50
Mar 10, 2009	10218	2,445.25
Mar 10, 2009	10219	3,090.90
Mar 10, 2009	10220	74.97
Mar 10, 2009	10221	55.60
Mar 12, 2009	10222	124.68
Mar 12, 2009	10223	3,569.00
Mar 12, 2009	10224	2,656.54
Mar 12, 2009	10225	360.00
Mar 12, 2009	10226	550.00
Mar 12, 2009	10227	335.50
Mar 13, 2009	10228	450.00
Mar 13, 2009	10229	1,000.00
Mar 13, 2009	10230	500.00
Mar 13, 2009	10231	274.56
Mar 13, 2009	10232	550.00
Mar 13, 2009	10233	183.90
Mar 17, 2009	10234	50.00
Mar 17, 2009	10235	50.00
Mar 17, 2009	10236	100.00
Mar 17, 2009	10237	100.00
Mar 23, 2009	10269	2,671.46
Total Cleared Checks for March		42,473.24

Less Bank Transfers

Mar 9, 2009	8,000.00	
Mar 10, 2009	100.00	
Mar 23, 2009	10,000.00	
Total March Transfers		18,100.00

March Service Charges		76.80
Ending Bank Balance March 31, 2009		$ 146,005.28

2. Perform the following accounting activities that close the April accounting period.

2009

Apr 1   Reverse the March 31 journal entry for $5,000.00 of accrued salaries.

Apr 6   Record a journal entry transferring $8,500.00 from the Regular Checking Account to the Payroll Checking account to cover paychecks printed on April 6.

Apr 20   Record a journal entry transferring $9,000.00 from the Regular Checking Account to the Payroll Checking account to cover paychecks printed on April 20.

Apr 22   Post a journal entry for the following sale of a vehicle.

Vehicle cost	$13,500.00
Accumulated Depreciation on vehicles	$10,700.00
Cash deposited to regular checking	$ 1,000.00

Apr 30   Post the following adjusting journal entries.

Accrue 9 days of wages	$10,385.00
Prepaid auto insurance	$ 200.00
Prepaid business insurance	$ 800.00
Accrued interest expense	$ 300.00

Post April depreciation expense.

Accum Depr Furniture	$ 421.00
Accum Depr Equipment	$ 385.00
Accum Depr Vehicles	$ 1,200.00
Accum Depr Other	$ 65.00
Accum Depr Buildings	$ 400.00
Accum Depr Bldg Imp	$ 60.00

Reconcile the Regular Checking account using the statement that follows. Print the Detail Reconciliation report.

Reconcile the Payroll Checking Account. The ending statement balance is $742.48. All checks and deposits have cleared and the monthly bank charge is $18.75. Print the Detail Reconciliation report.

Reconcile the Savings Account. Interest income is $37.50 and the ending statement balance is $7,630.15. Do not print the reconciliation report.

Print the Standard Balance Sheet, Standard Profit & Loss, and Statement of Cash Flows for April.

Create a backup file named "Graded Baxter Garden Supply April Close" and then close the April accounting period.

Baxter Garden Supply
Bank Statement April 30, 2009

Beginning Balance from March Statement				$ 146,005.28
April Deposits				
	Apr 2, 2009		211.07	
	Apr 9, 2009		20,893.96	
	Apr 16, 2009		713.80	
	Apr 17, 2009		5,209.35	
	Apr 23, 2009		15,048.44	
	Apr 22, 2009		1,000.00	
Total Deposits for April				43,076.62
April Checks Cleared				
	Mar 31, 2009	10238	2,302.02	
	Mar 31, 2009	10239	577.60	
	Mar 31, 2009	10240	26.58	
	Mar 31, 2009	10241	9.00	
	Mar 31, 2009	10242	49.99	
	Mar 31, 2009	10243	712.95	
	Mar 31, 2009	10244	226.88	
	Mar 31, 2009	10245	170.34	
	Apr 16, 2009	10246	5,179.20	
	Apr 16, 2009	10247	90.00	
	Apr 16, 2009	10248	1,873.15	
	Apr 16, 2009	10249	297.60	
	Apr 16, 2009	10250	7,607.00	
	Apr 16, 2009	10251	7,444.60	
	Apr 16, 2009	10252	150.00	
	Apr 16, 2009	10253	750.00	
	Apr 16, 2009	10254	200.00	
	Apr 16, 2009	10255	600.00	
	Apr 16, 2009	10256	4,722.55	
	Apr 16, 2009	10257	3,809.10	
	Apr 21, 2009	10258	250.00	
	Apr 2, 2009	10270	2,080.00	
	Apr 2, 2009	10271	522.06	
	Apr 2, 2009	10272	1,012.88	
	Apr 2, 2009	10273	678.53	
	Apr 2, 2009	10274	1,073.92	
	Apr 6, 2009	10275	2,640.66	
	Apr 23, 2009	10276	2,582.20	
Total Cleared Checks for April				47,638.81
Less Bank Transfers				
	Apr 6, 2009		8,500.00	
	Apr 20, 2009		9,000.00	
Total April Transfers				17,500.00
April Service Charges				87.50
Ending Bank Balance April 30, 2009				$ 123,855.59

PROJECT 2
COMPREHENSIVE EXAM FOR A MERCHANDISING BUSINESS

You begin this exam by downloading the **Olsen Office Furniture Project** company file from the website http://www.pearsonhighered.com/brunsdon/. Add your initials to the **Company Name** and **Legal Name** after opening the company by selecting *Company>>Company Information* on the main menu and clicking **OK** to save the changes.

The following are February 2009 transactions for Olsen Office Furniture. Olsen specializes in selling mid-range office furniture to wholesale distributors and also sells furniture directly to businesses for use in their offices. You will be entering all transactions for the month of February, including month-end adjusting entries.

All checks received on account are deposited into the Regular Checking Account.

Feb 2	Issue and print the following sales invoices.
	Invoice 1790 to Winetraub Office Furniture for $2,999.80.
	Qty Item Unit Price
	20 SmallDesk $149.99
	Invoice 1791 to Anderson & Anderson, Attorneys at Law for $9,523.00.
	Qty Item Unit Price
	10 ChairClothBlack $185.00
	12 ChairLeatherBlack $375.00
	3 ConfTableOak $850.00

	Received the following checks. *(Note: Verify that checks will deposit into the Regular Checking Account.)*
	Check number 1835 for $8,774.88 from Arbrook Office Supply for Invoice 1783.
	Check number 3078 for $30,575.25 from Parker Office Building for Invoice 1784.

	New vendor:
	Pearson Property Management
	3075 W. 7th Street
	Forth Worth, TX 76022
	Terms: Net 3
	Account Prefill: 74000 Rent or Lease Expense
	Enter a rent bill for $800.00 to Pearson Property Management for February office and warehouse rental.

	Print checks for all bills due on or before February 6. First check number is 8938.

Feb 4	Issue and print the following POs. PO 1040 to Brothers Furniture Mfg for $1,875.00 for the following item. Item Qty Price ChairLeatherBlack 25 $75.00 PO 1041 to Planter Interiors for $2,600.00 for the following item. Item Qty Price SmallDesk 40 $65.00
	Received bills for the following inventory that was received. All items on PO 1038 to Tollman Table Manufacturing. Invoice 68534 for $5,500.00 dated Feb. 4. All items on PO 1039 to Willis Office Supplies. Invoice 2378 for $1,910.00 dated Feb. 4.
	Received the following checks. Check number 8053 for $34,595.00 from Ernst Furniture for Invoice 1785. Check number 3478 for $5,403.50 from Poseiden Landscaping for Invoice 1786.

Feb 5	Issue the following sales invoices.
	Invoice 1792 to Arbrook Office Supply for $3,599.78.
	Qty Item Unit Price 15 ChairErgo $169.99 7 SmallDesk $149.99
	Invoice 1793 to Parker Office Building for $12,224.75 with tax. Qty Item Unit Price 8 ConfTableMaple $850.00 5 ExecDeskMaple $925.00
	Issue Credit Memo CM1787 for $4,012.50 with tax to Anderson and Anderson for the return of 10 ChairLeatherBrown on Invoice 1787.
	Received check number 5768 for $4,825.57 from Anderson and Anderson for balance due on Invoice 1787.

Feb 6	Issue and print the following sales invoices.

Invoice 1794 to Wellman and Wellman, CPA for $27,017.50 with tax. *(You checked with Mr. Olsen and he approved exceeding the customer's credit limit.)*

Qty	Item	Unit Price
20	ChairLeatherBrown	$375.00
10	ExecDeskAsh	$925.00
10	ConfTableAsh	$850.00

Invoice 1795 to Ernst Furniture for $11,799.85.

Qty	Item	Unit Price
15	ChairErgo	$169.99
10	ExecDeskOak	$925.00

Issue the following POs.

PO 1042 to Brothers Furniture Mfg for $1,500.00 for the following item.

Item	Qty	Price
ChairLeatherBrown	20	$75.00

PO 1043 to Oregon Oak Furniture for $21,000.00 for the following items.

Item	Qty	Price
ExecDeskAsh	25	$350.00
ExecDeskMaple	15	$350.00
ExecDeskOak	20	$350.00

PO 1044 to Planter Interiors for $700.00 for the following item.

Item	Qty	Price
ChairErgo	20	$35.00

PO 1045 to Tollman Table Manufacturing for $2,500.00 for the following item.

Item	Qty	Price
ConfTableAsh	10	$250.00

Received the following inventory.

Invoice 3479 dated Feb. 5 from Brothers Furniture for $1,125.00 for 15 of the ChairLeatherBlack items on PO 1040.

All items on PO 1041 to Planter Interiors. Invoice not included. Receipt number RCT89007 dated Feb. 5.

| Feb 9 | Prepare payroll for the biweekly pay period ended Feb. 8. Daniel Anderson worked 4 hours of overtime and remaining hourly paid employees worked 80 hours.

Create the paychecks using the spreadsheets that follow. Print the paychecks on beginning check number 1109.

Create checks for payroll liabilities using the date range of 1/01/2009 to 2/9/2009. Pay employee federal withholding, Medicare, and Social Security taxes and company Medicare and Social Security taxes. Print on check number 8943 from the Regular Checking Account.

Transfer $8,500.00 from the Regular Checking Account to the Payroll Checking Account to cover payroll. |
|---|---|
| | Enter Invoice 100378 for $2,600.00 dated Feb. 6 from Planter Interiors for receipt number RCT89007. |

Olsen Office Furniture
Pay Period 1/26/2009 thru 2/08/2009

Employee	Filing Status	Allow	Pay Type	Pay Rate	Regular Hrs	OT Hrs	Gross Pay	Federal Income Tax	Soc. Sec. (FICA) Tax	Medicare Tax	Net Pay
Anderson, Daniel	Married	3	Hourly	15.00	80.00	4.00	1,290.00	56.00	79.98	18.71	1,135.31
Jenkins, Charles	Married	2	Hourly	15.00	80.00		1,200.00	65.00	74.40	17.40	1,043.20
Olsen, David	Married	4	Salary	2,500.00			2,500.00	220.00	155.00	36.25	2,088.75
Olsen James	Married	3	Salary	2,500.00			2,500.00	240.00	155.00	36.25	2,068.75
Vavra, Wesley	Married	4	Hourly	16.00	80.00		1,280.00	44.00	79.36	18.56	1,138.08
Wilson, Brian	Married	4	Hourly	15.00	80.00		1,200.00	36.00	74.40	17.40	1,072.20
Totals					320.00	4.00	9,970.00	661.00	618.14	144.57	8,546.29
Tax Basis								Circular E	6.20%	1.45%	
G/L Accounts								60000	23400	23400	23400	10300

Olsen Office Furniture
Employer Costs for Period 1/26/2009 thru 2/08/2009

Employee	ER Soc. Sec. (FICA)	ER Medicare	ER FUTA	ER SUTA
Anderson, Daniel	79.98	18.71	10.32	38.70
Jenkins, Charles	74.40	17.40	9.60	36.00
Olsen, David	155.00	36.25	20.00	75.00
Olsen James	155.00	36.25	20.00	75.00
Vavra, Wesley	79.36	18.56	10.24	38.40
Wilson, Brian	74.40	17.40	9.60	36.00
Totals	618.14	144.57	79.76	299.10
Tax Basis	6.20%	1.45%	0.8%	3.0%
G/L Accounts	23400 / 60100	23400 / 60100	23500 / 60100	23700 / 60100

Feb 12	Issue and print Invoice 1796 to Baker Hardware for $7,998.25 with tax for the following items.
	
	      <u>Qty</u> <u>Item</u> <u>Unit Price</u>
	      10 ChairClothBlack $185.00
	      15 ChairLeatherBlack $375.00

	Received the following inventory. The remaining items on PO 1040 to Brothers Furniture. Invoice 3501 for $750.00 dated Feb. 12. All items on PO 1044 issued to Planter Interiors. Invoice 100425 for $700.00 dated Feb. 12. All items on PO 1042 issued to Brothers Furniture. Invoice 3502 for $1,500.00 dated Feb. 12.

Feb 13	New vendor:
	     DFW Equipment
	     3300 Camp Bowie Blvd.
	     Fort Worth, TX 76022
	     Terms: Net 3 Days
	     Account Prefill: 74500 Repairs Expense
	
	Enter Invoice 5663 dated Feb. 13 for $859.87 from DFW Equipment for repair of equipment.
	
	Pay bill on check number 8944.

	Received the following inventory. All items on PO 1045 issued to Tollman Tables Manufacturing. Invoice 68578 for $2,500.00 dated Feb. 13. All items on PO 1043 issued to Oregon Oak Furniture. Invoice 98873 for $21,000.00 dated Feb. 13.

Feb 16	Mr. Olsen sent a memo instructing you to raise the credit limit for Art Decoraters and Arbrook Office Supply to $85,000.

Issue and print the following Sales Invoices.

Invoice 1797 to Art Decoraters for $37,824.70.

Qty	Item	Unit Price
30	SmallDesk	$149.99
25	ExecDeskAsh	$925.00
12	ConfTableAsh	$850.00

Invoice 1798 to Arbrook Office Supply for $35,774.80.

Qty	Item	Unit Price
20	ExecDeskOak	$925.00
15	ExecDeskMaple	$925.00
20	ChairErgo	$169.99

Issue the following POs.

PO 1046 to Oregon Oak Furniture for $21,000.00 for the following items.

Item	Qty	Price
ExecDeskAsh	25	$350.00
ExecDeskMaple	15	$350.00
ExecDeskOak	20	$350.00

PO 1047 to Planter Interiors for $3,300.00 for the following items.

Item	Qty	Price
ChairErgo	20	$35.00
SmallDesk	40	$65.00

PO 1048 to Tollman Table Manufacturing for $2,500.00 for the following item.

Item	Qty	Price
ConfTableAsh	10	$250.00

Received the following checks.

Check number 2057 for $5,950.00 from Art Decoraters for Invoice 1788.
Check number 90087 for $2,549.85 from Winetraub Office Furniture for Invoice 1789.

Feb 18	Received the following inventory.
	All items on PO 1046 to Oregon Oak Furniture. Invoice 98899 for $21,000.00 dated Feb. 18. *(Note: The vendor raised the credit limit to $50,000 so make this change on the account.)*
	All items on PO 1047 to Planter Interiors. Invoice 100863 for $3,300.00 dated Feb. 17.

Mr. Olsen sent a memo instructing you to raise the credit limit for Ernst Furniture to $50,000.

Issue and print the following Sales Invoices.

Invoice 1799 to Ernst Furniture for $36,250.00.

Qty	Item	Unit Price
30	ExecDeskAsh	$925.00
10	ConfTableOak	$850.00

Invoice 1800 to Winetraub Office Furniture for $12,749.30.

Qty	Item	Unit Price
20	ChairErgo	$169.99
10	ChairClothBlack	$185.00
50	SmallDesk	$149.99

Feb 20	Received all items on PO 1048 to Tollman Tables Manufacturing. Invoice 68883 for $2,500.00 dated Feb. 20.
	Issue the following POs.

PO 1049 to Brothers Furniture Mfg for $1,300.00 for the following item.

Item	Qty	Price
ChairClothBlack	20	$65.00

PO 1050 to Oregon Oak Furniture for $8,750.00 for the following item.

Item	Qty	Price
ExecDeskAsh	25	$350.00

PO 1051 to Planter Interiors for $3,300.00 for the following items.

Item	Qty	Price
ChairErgo	20	$35.00
SmallDesk	40	$65.00

PO 1052 to Tollman Table Manufacturing for $2,500.00 for the following item.

Item	Qty	Price
ConfTableOak	10	$250.00

| Feb 23 | Prepare payroll for the biweekly pay period ended Feb. 22. All hourly paid employees worked 80 hours.

Create the paychecks using the spreadsheets that follow. Print the paychecks on beginning check number 1115.

Create the checks for payroll liabilities using the date range of 1/01/2009 to 2/23/2009. Pay employee federal withholding, Medicare, and Social Security taxes and company Medicare and Social Security taxes. Print on check number 8945 from the Regular Checking Account.

Transfer $8,500.00 from the Regular Checking Account to the Payroll Checking Account to cover payroll. |
|---|---|
| | Pay all vendor invoices due on or before March 8. Print checks on beginning check number 8946. |

Olsen Office Furniture
Pay Period 2/09/2009 thru 2/22/2009

Employee	Filing Status	Allow	Pay Type	Pay Rate	Regular Hrs	OT Hrs	Gross Pay	Federal Income Tax	Soc. Sec. (FICA) Tax	Medicare Tax	Net Pay
Anderson, Daniel	Married	3	Hourly	15.00	80.00		1,200.00	50.00	74.40	17.40	1,058.20
Jenkins, Charles	Married	2	Hourly	15.00	80.00		1,200.00	65.00	74.40	17.40	1,043.20
Olsen, David	Married	4	Salary	2,500.00			2,500.00	220.00	155.00	36.25	2,088.75
Olsen James	Married	3	Salary	2,500.00			2,500.00	240.00	155.00	36.25	2,068.75
Vavra, Wesley	Married	4	Hourly	16.00	80.00		1,280.00	44.00	79.36	18.56	1,138.08
Wilson, Brian	Married	4	Hourly	15.00	80.00		1,200.00	36.00	74.40	17.40	1,072.20
Totals					320.00	0.00	9,880.00	655.00	612.56	143.26	8,469.18
Tax Basis								Circular E	6.20%	1.45%	
G/L Accounts							60000	23400	23400	23400	10300

Olsen Office Furniture
Employer Costs for Period 2/09/2009 thru 2/22/2009

Employee	ER Soc. Sec. (FICA)	ER Medicare	ER FUTA	ER SUTA
Anderson, Daniel	74.40	17.40	9.60	36.00
Jenkins, Charles	74.40	17.40	9.60	36.00
Olsen, David	155.00	36.25	4.00	45.00
Olsen James	155.00	36.25	4.00	45.00
Vavra, Wesley	79.36	18.56	10.24	38.40
Wilson, Brian	74.40	17.40	9.60	36.00
Totals	612.56	143.26	47.04	236.40
Tax Basis	6.20%	1.45%	0.8%	3.0%
G/L Accounts	23400 / 60100	23400 / 60100	23500 / 60100	23700 / 60100

Feb 25	Received the following checks. Check number 90133 for $2,999.80 from Winetraub Office Furniture for Invoice 1790. Check number 5773 for $9,523.00 from Anderson & Anderson for Invoice 1791.
Feb 26	Received the following inventory. 20 ExecDeskAsh items on PO 1050 to Oregon Oak Furniture. Invoice 98903 for $7,000.00 dated Feb. 26. All items on PO 1051 to Planter Interiors. Invoice 100984 for $3,300.00 dated Feb. 26. All items on PO 1052 to Tollman Table Manufacturing. Invoice 68885 for $2,500.00 dated Feb. 25.
	Pay February sales tax liability due through March 1 to Texas Comptroller and print on check number 8950.
	Write check number 8951 for $625.00 to Reliant Electric for the February electricity bill. Write check number 8952 for $237.50 to Fort Worth Water Utilities for the February water bill.

EOM	Prepare the following end-of-month adjusting entries.
	Refer to the Jan. 31 entry for depreciation expense and record the February depreciation entry. Turn this entry into a recurring entry that posts through November 30, 2009.
	Accrue five days of wages and make it a reversing entry. Post the liability to Wages Payable. Calculate the accrual using the gross pay for all employees for the month of February divided by four weeks. Reverse this entry on Mar. 1.

	Write and print check number 8953 to Cash for $154.50 to replenish petty cash fund. Debit the following expense accounts.
	
	    Office Supplies $ 27.50
	    Meals and Entertainment $127.00

	Expense one month of Prepaid expenses to insurance expense, $300.00.
	Prepare the following bank reconciliations and print the detail reconciliation report.
	Regular Checking Account statement balance using the statement that follows.
	Payroll Checking Account statement balance is $296.17. All items have cleared.
	Print the following reports for February.
	General Ledger Trial Balance report. Review for accuracy.
	Aged Receivables and Aged Payables detail reports as of February 28 and Inventory Valuation Detail report for month of February. Reconcile these reports to the appropriate account balances on the Trial Balance report.
	Payroll Liability report dated Jan. 1 to Feb. 28. Reconcile report totals to the appropriate payroll liability and expense accounts on the trial balance.
	Open Purchase Orders report.

	Print the following February financial statements.
	    Profit & Loss Standard
	    Balance Sheet Standard
	    Statement of Cash Flows

Backup the company data file to a backup file named **OlsenProj2**.

Olsen Office Furniture
Bank Statement February 28, 2009

Beginning Balance from January Statement				$	89,258.36
February Deposits					
	Feb 2, 2009		8,774.88		
	Feb 2, 2009		30,575.25		
	Feb 4, 2009		5,403.50		
	Feb 4, 2009		34,595.00		
	Feb 5, 2009		4,825.57		
	Feb 16, 2009		2,549.85		
	Feb 16, 2009		5,950.00		
	Feb 25, 2009		2,999.80		
	Feb 25, 2009		9,523.00		
Total Deposits for February					105,196.85
February Checks Cleared					
	Jan 28, 2009	8936	2,166.64		
	Feb 2, 2009	8938	1,875.00		
	Feb 2, 2009	8939	147.58		
	Feb 2, 2009	8940	800.00		
	Feb 2, 2009	8941	575.00		
	Feb 2, 2009	8942	5,500.00		
	Feb 9, 2009	8943	2,186.42		
	Feb 13, 2009	8944	859.87		
	Feb 23, 2008	8945	2,166.64		
	Feb 23, 2008	8946	1,125.00		
	Feb 23, 2008	8947	2,600.00		
	Feb 23, 2008	8948	5,500.00		
	Feb 23, 2008	8949	1,910.00		
Total Cleared Checks for February					27,412.15
Less Bank Transfers					
	Feb 9, 2009		8,500.00		
	Feb 23, 2009		8,500.00		
Total February Transfers					17,000.00
February Service Charges					75.00
Ending Bank Balance February 28, 2009				$	149,968.06

CHAPTER 12   CREATE A NEW COMPANY

LEARNING OBJECTIVES

In this chapter you create accounting records for a merchandising business named Electronics Supply. To perform this task, you will:

1. Create a new data file for the company using QBP's wizard.
2. Setup the chart of accounts and enter beginning balances.
3. Set preferences for the new company data file.
4. Create customer accounts and enter beginning balances.
5. Create vendor accounts and enter beginning balances.
6. Create inventory items and enter beginning balances.
7. Setup payroll and enter employee information.
8. Customize forms used by the company.
9. Complete a practice set at the end of the chapter where you post transactions and print financial statements for the new company.

NEW COMPANY DATA FILE WIZARD

Launch QBP and select *File>>New Company* on the main menu. In the window illustrated in Figure 12:1 click **Skip Interview**.

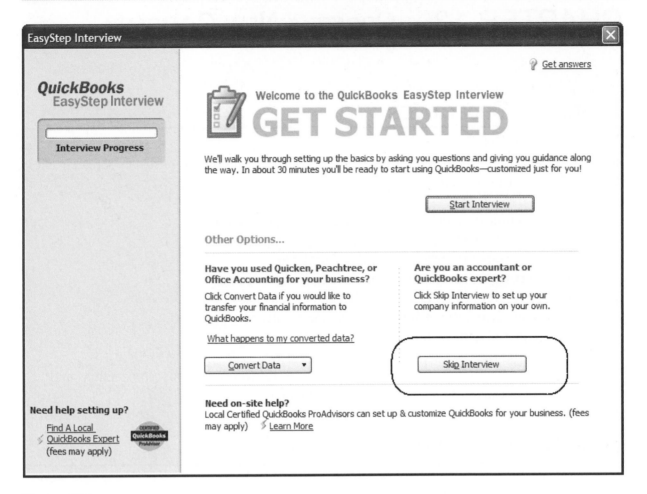

Figure 12:1

Now enter the company information as illustrated in Figure 12:2. **Add your initials to the end of the Company name and Legal name.**

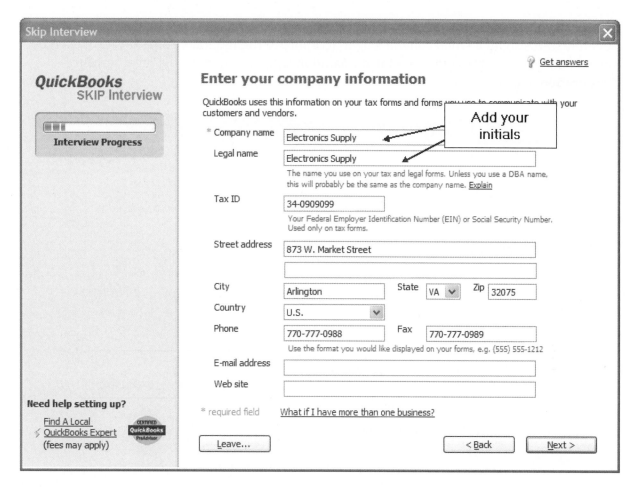

Figure 12:2

Click **Next** to reach the screen (Figure 12:3) where you select the business's legal status. QBP sets this status so it can map general ledger accounts to the federal income tax form used by the company, thus integrating with tax preparation software. Choose the legal status of **Corporation** and click **Next**.

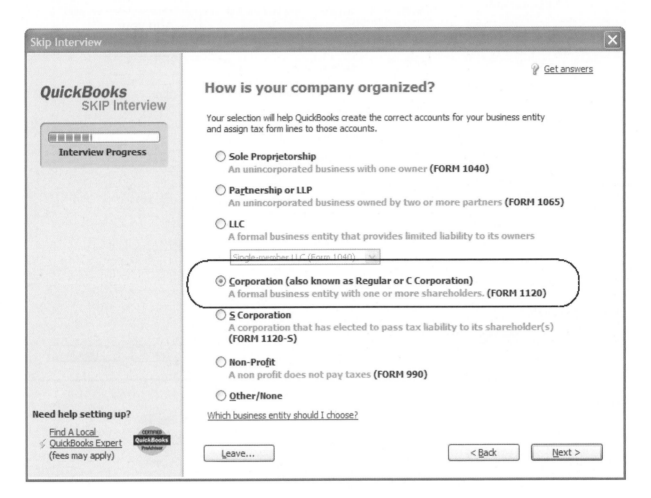

Figure 12:3

You are at the screen (not shown) for choosing the company's beginning month in its fiscal year. Keep January as the selected month and click **Next**.

In Figure 12:4 QBP offers to create a basic chart of accounts for the new company based on an industry type. Highlighting one of the industry choices will display a proposed chart of accounts to the right. We will be creating our own chart of accounts so select **Other/None** and click **Next**.

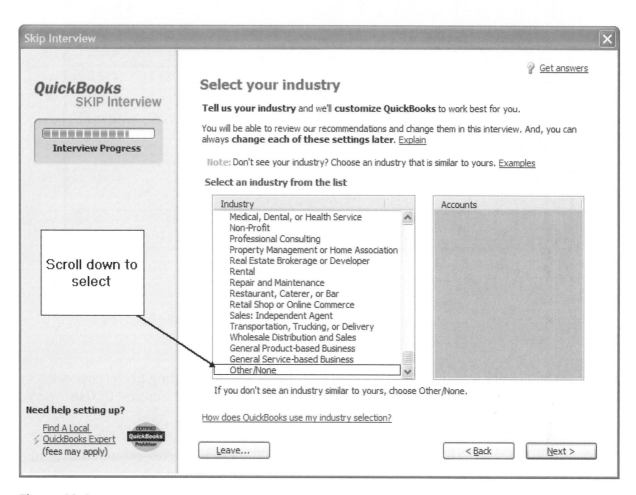

Figure 12:4

Click **Next** and QBP prompts for a file name (not illustrated). Keep the name of **Electronics Supply.QBW** and click **Save**.

Click **Next** and QBP prompts to create an online account. Click **X** to close this window.

The Home page now opens and we are ready to create the chart of accounts. Press **Ctrl + A** on the keyboard to find that QBP has created the basic accounts illustrated in Figure 12:5.

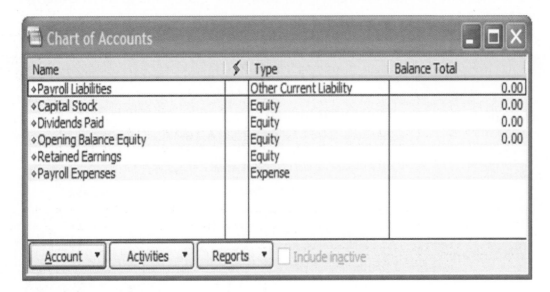

Figure 12:5

We will now customize these accounts and add remaining accounts. We begin by setting the company preference that turns on account numbers.

Select *Edit>>Preferences* on the main menu and choose the **Accounting** preference area. (See Figure 12:6.) Select the **Company Preferences** tab and mark the option to **Use account numbers**.

Set the closing date to 12/31/2008. Click **OK** and turn off future messages before clicking **No**.

Click **OK** to save the changes and you now see account numbers for existing accounts.

Preferences

| | My Preferences | **Company Preferences** | | OK |

- Accounting
- Bills
- Checking
- Desktop View
- Finance Charge
- General
- Integrated Applications
- Items & Inventory
- Jobs & Estimates
- Multiple Currencies
- Payroll & Employees
- Reminders
- Reports & Graphs
- Sales & Customers
- Sales Tax
- Send Forms
- Service Connection
- Spelling
- Tax: 1099
- Time & Expenses

Accounts
☑ Use account numbers   ☑ Require accounts
☐ Show lowest subaccount only

☐ Use class tracking
☐ Prompt to assign classes
☑ Automatically assign general journal entry number
☑ Warn when posting a transaction to Retained Earnings

Date Warnings
☐ Warn if transactions are [90] day(s) in the past
☐ Warn if transactions are [30] day(s) in the future

Closing Date
Date through which books are closed: (not set)

[Set Date/Password]

OK
Cancel
Help
Default

Also See:

General

Payroll and
Employees

Click to set date

Set Closing Date and Password

To keep your financial data secure, QuickBooks recommends assigning all other users their own username and password, in Company > Set Up Users.

Date
QuickBooks will display a warning, or require a password, when saving a transaction dated on or before the closing date. More details...

Closing Date   [12/31/2008] 📅

Password
Quickbooks strongly recommends setting a password to protect transactions dated on or before the closing date.

Closing Date Password   [   ]

Confirm Password   [   ]

To see changes made on or before the closing date, view the Report in Reports > Accountant & Taxes.

[OK]   [Cancel]

Figure 12:6

CHART OF ACCOUNTS SETUP

You are now ready to finish creating the chart of accounts. The account list should be open from the previous topic so begin by editing existing accounts.

Highlight account the **Capital Stock** account and click the **Account** button to select **Edit Account**. *(Note: You can also use shortcut key **Ctrl +E** after highlighting an account.)*

Change the **Number** to **3910** (Figure 12:7).

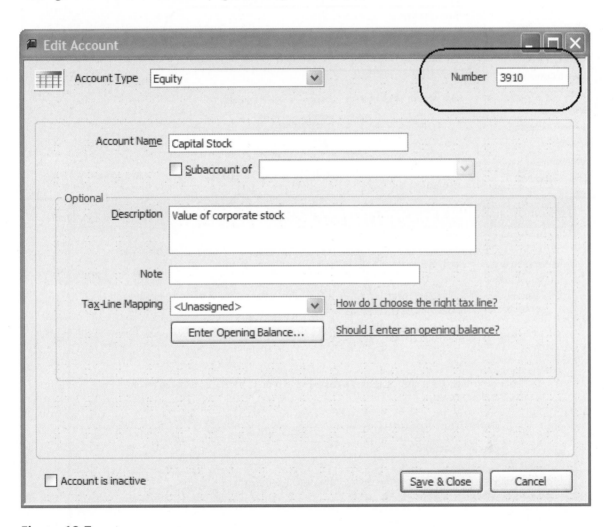

Figure 12:7

Click **Enter Opening Balance** and enter the balance and date shown in Figure 12:8. Click **OK** to return to the Edit Account window. Click **Save & Close** and **Yes** to confirm entering a beginning balance for 12/31/2008.

Figure 12:8

Change the remaining accounts by referring to Figure 12:9. *(Note: These accounts do not have a beginning balance.)*

Electronics Supply			
Chart of Accounts			
Current Account No.	Current Account Name	New Account No.	New Account Name
24000	Payroll Liabilities	2330	Federal Payroll Taxes Payable
30000	Opening Balance Equity	3000	Opening Balance Equity
32000	Retained Earnings	3930	Retained Earnings
30200	Dividends Paid	3940	Dividends Paid
66000	Payroll Expenses	6000	Wages Expense

Figure 12:9

Figure 12:13 and Figure 12:14 list remaining accounts to complete the chart of accounts along with beginning balances. We next illustrate creating the first account.

Click **Account** and select **New** or use shortcut key **Ctrl+N**. Select **Bank** as the **Account Type** before clicking **Continue**. (See Figure 12:10.)

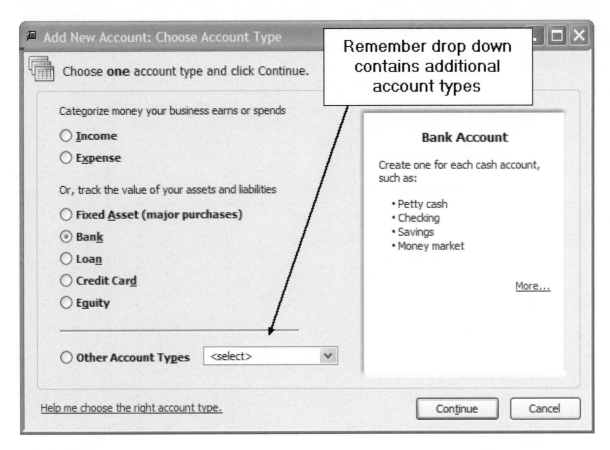

Figure 12:10

Type in the **Number** and **Account Name** illustrated in Figure 12:11.

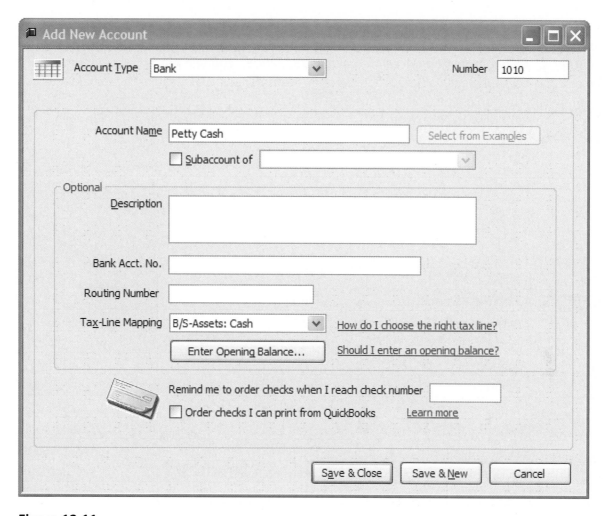

Figure 12:11

Click **Enter Opening Balance** and enter the amount and date shown in Figure 12:12. Click **OK** to return to the Add New Account window.

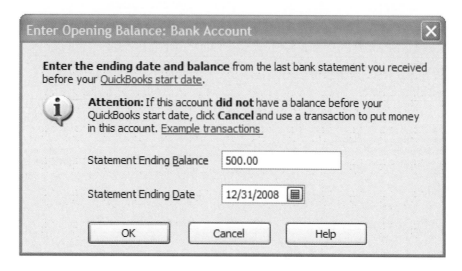

Figure 12:12

Click **Save & New** and **Yes** to confirm entering a beginning balance for 12/31/2008.

Continue adding accounts and beginning balances by referring to Figure 12:13 and
Figure 12:14. *You must use a minus sign when entering beginning balances listed in red
parenthesis. All beginning balances are as of 12/31/2008.* You will not enter beginning
balances on Accounts Receivable, Inventory, and Accounts Payable because these balances
are entered in the topics that follow. Account types are selected from the dropdown list on
field and shortcut key **Alt+N** saves the current account and clears the window for entering the
next account.

Electronics Supply

Chart of Accounts

Account ID	Description	Type	Beginning Balance
1010	Petty Cash	Bank	$500.00
1020	Checking Account	Bank	$162,000.00
1030	Payroll Checking Account	Bank	$5,000.00
1100	Accounts Receivable	Accounts Receivable	$0.00
1150	Allowance for Doubtful Accounts	Other Current Asset	($3,000.00)
1200	Inventory	Other Current Asset	$0.00
1400	Prepaid Expenses	Other Current Asset	$900.00
1500	Furniture and Fixtures	Fixed Asset	$30,000.00
1501	Accum Depr - Furn and Fixt	Fixed Asset	($4,286.00)
1510	Equipment	Fixed Asset	$27,000.00
1511	Accum Depr - Equipment	Fixed Asset	($5,400.00)
1520	Vehicles	Fixed Asset	$35,000.00
1521	Accum Depr - Vehicles	Fixed Asset	($11,667.00)
2000	Accounts Payable	Accounts Payable	$0.00
2340	FUTA Payable	Other Current Liability	$0.00
2350	State Payroll Taxes Payable	Other Current Liability	$0.00
2360	SUTA Payable	Other Current Liability	$0.00
2370	Health Insurance Payable	Other Current Liability	$0.00
2380	Income Taxes Payable	Other Current Liability	$0.00
3920	Paid In Capital	Equity	$150,000.00

Figure 12:13

Electronics Supply

Chart of Accounts Continued

Account ID	Description	Type	Beginning Balance
4000	Sales Income	Income	$0.00
4500	Sales Discounts	Income	$0.00
4600	Sales Returns and Allowances	Income	$0.00
5000	Cost of Goods Sold	Cost of Goods Sold	$0.00
5100	Freight Expense	Cost of Goods Sold	$0.00
5500	Purchase Discounts	Cost of Goods Sold	$0.00
5600	Purchase Returns and Allowances	Cost of Goods Sold	$0.00
5900	Inventory Adjustments	Cost of Goods Sold	$0.00
6100	Payroll Tax Expense	Expense	$0.00
6110	Employee Benefit Expense	Expense	$0.00
6200	Rent Expense	Expense	$0.00
6210	Maintenance and Repairs Expense	Expense	$0.00
6220	Utilities Expense	Expense	$0.00
6300	Office Supplies Expense	Expense	$0.00
6310	Telephone Expense	Expense	$0.00
6320	Advertising Expense	Expense	$0.00
6330	Postage Expense	Expense	$0.00
6400	Travel Expense	Expense	$0.00
6410	Meals and Entertainment Expense	Expense	$0.00
6500	Bank Fees	Expense	$0.00
6600	Insurance Expense	Expense	$0.00
6800	Depreciation Expense	Expense	$0.00
6810	Bad Debt Expense	Expense	$0.00
8000	Interest Income	Other Income	$0.00
8100	Other Income	Other Income	$0.00
8500	Interest Expense	Other Expense	$0.00
8600	Gain or Loss - Sale of Assets	Other Expense	$0.00
9500	Income Tax Expense	Other Expense	$0.00
9999	Suspense Account	Other Expense	$0.00

Figure 12:14

Print an Account Listing when finished to verify your entries. Select *Reports>>Accountant and Taxes>>Account Listing* on the main menu.

Click **Modify Report** and remove the **Description**, **Accnt. #**, and **Tax Line** columns. Click **OK** to refresh the report and compare your results to Figure 12:15.

Electronics Supply
Account Listing

Account	Type	Balance Total
1010 · Petty Cash	Bank	500.00
1020 · Checking Account	Bank	162,000.00
1030 · Payroll Checking Account	Bank	5,000.00
1100 · Accounts Receivable	Accounts Receivable	0.00
1150 · Allowance for Doubtful Accounts	Other Current Asset	-3,000.00
1200 · Inventory	Other Current Asset	0.00
1400 · Prepaid Expenses	Other Current Asset	900.00
1500 · Furnitures and Fixtures	Fixed Asset	30,000.00
1501 · Accum Depr - Furn and Fixt	Fixed Asset	-4,286.00
1510 · Equipment	Fixed Asset	27,000.00
1511 · Accum Depr - Equipment	Fixed Asset	-5,400.00
1520 · Vehicles	Fixed Asset	35,000.00
1521 · Accum Depr - Vehicles	Fixed Asset	-11,667.00
2000 · Accounts Payable	Accounts Payable	0.00
2330 · Federal Payroll Taxes Payable	Other Current Liability	0.00
2340 · FUTA Payable	Other Current Liability	0.00
2350 · State Payroll Taxes Payable	Other Current Liability	0.00
2360 · SUTA Payable	Other Current Liability	0.00
2370 · Health Insurance Payable	Other Current Liability	0.00
2380 · Income Taxes Payable	Other Current Liability	0.00
3000 · Opening Balance Equity	Equity	85,047.00
3910 · Capital Stock	Equity	1,000.00
3920 · Paid In Capital	Equity	150,000.00
3930 · Retained Earnings	Equity	
3940 · Dividends Paid	Equity	0.00
4000 · Sales Income	Income	
4500 · Sales Discounts	Income	
4600 · Sales Returns and Allowances	Income	
5000 · Cost of Goods Sold	Cost of Goods Sold	
5100 · Freight Expense	Cost of Goods Sold	
5500 · Purchase Discounts	Cost of Goods Sold	
5600 · Purchase Returns and Allowances	Cost of Goods Sold	
5900 · Inventory Adjustments	Cost of Goods Sold	
6000 · Wages Expense	Expense	
6100 · Payroll Tax Expense	Expense	
6110 · Employee Benefit Expense	Expense	
6200 · Rent Expense	Expense	
6210 · Maintenance and Repairs Expense	Expense	
6220 · Utilities Expense	Expense	
6300 · Office Supplies Expense	Expense	
6310 · Telephone Expense	Expense	
6320 · Advertising Expense	Expense	
6330 · Postage Expense	Expense	
6400 · Travel Expense	Expense	
6410 · Meals and Entertainment Expense	Expense	
6500 · Bank Fees	Expense	
6600 · Insurance Expense	Expense	
6800 · Depreciation Expense	Expense	
6810 · Bad Debt Expense	Expense	
8000 · Interest Income	Other Income	
8100 · Other Income	Other Income	
8500 · Interest Expense	Other Expense	
8600 · Gain or Loss - Sale of Assets	Other Expense	
9500 · Income Tax Expense	Other Expense	
9999 · Suspense Account	Other Expense	

Figure 12:15

If you find a mistake naming an account then double click it on the report to reopen, make changes, and resave. If you find a mistake on a beginning balance then click **Change Opening Balance** after reopening the account and follow the next steps to correct.

1. The account register will open as illustrated in Figure 12:16. Follow the instructions on the illustration.

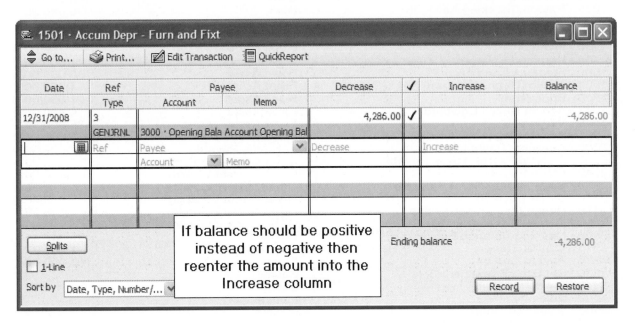

Figure 12:16

2. Click **Record** to store the change and **X** to close the register.

3. Click **Save & Close** on the account.

4. **Refresh** the Account Listing to see the change.

Close the Account Listing report and the Chart of Accounts list. In the next topic you set up company preferences.

COMPANY PREFERENCES SETUP

Select **Edit>>Preferences** on the main menu and follow the next series of illustrations to configure preferences for the new company. Select the **Preference** category and tab illustrated in the following figures and click **Yes** each time you change the category.

Bills

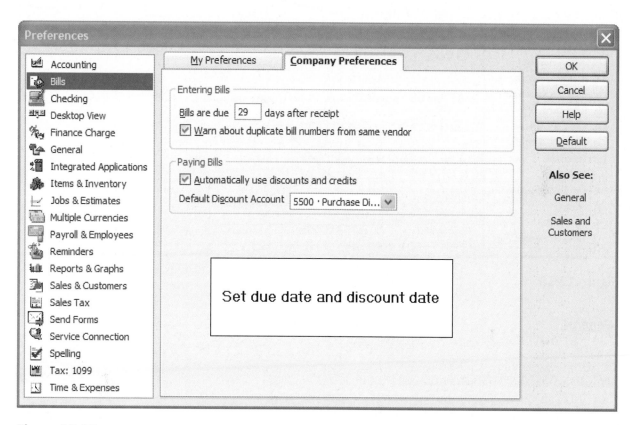

Figure 12:17

Checking

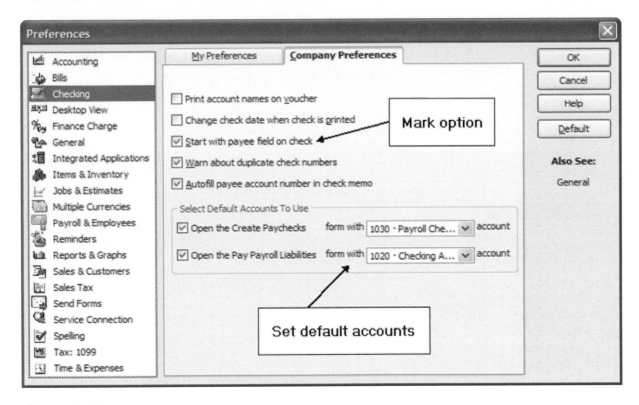

Figure 12:18

General

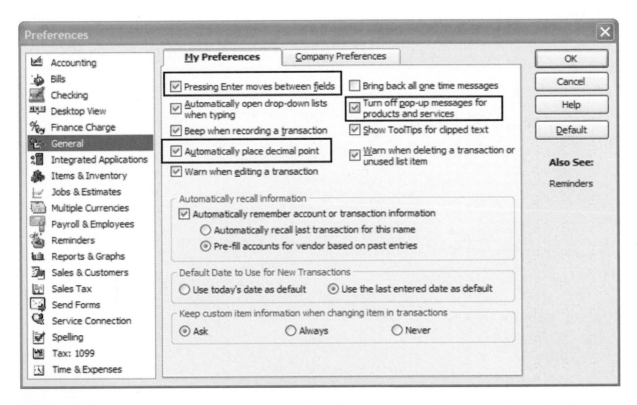

Figure 12:19

Items & Inventory

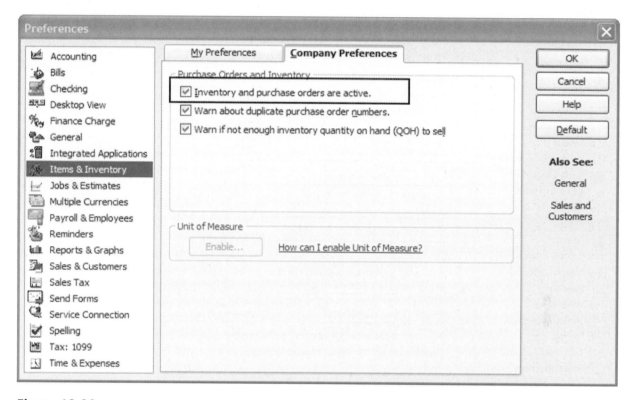

Figure 12:20

Jobs & Estimates

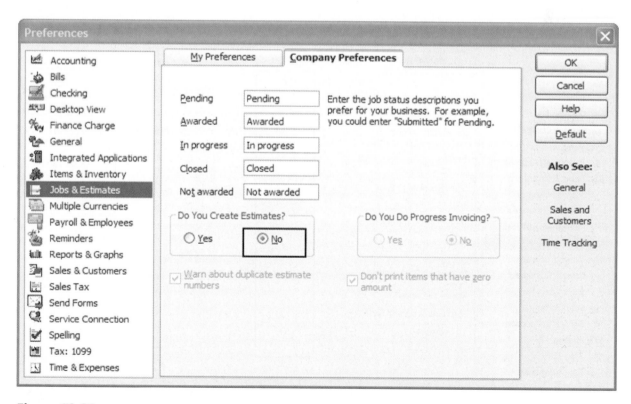

Figure 12:21

Payroll & Employees

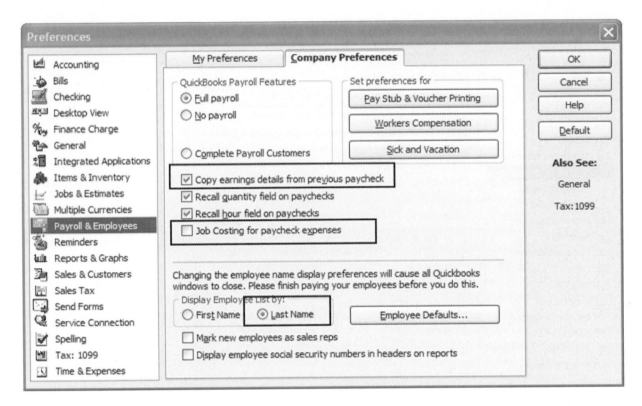

Figure 12:22

Reminders

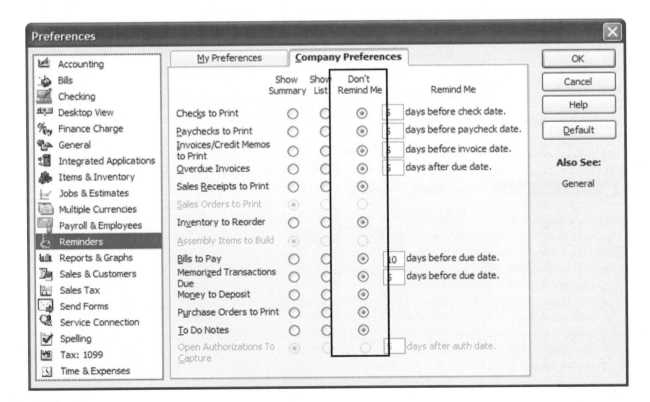

Figure 12:23

Reports & Graphs

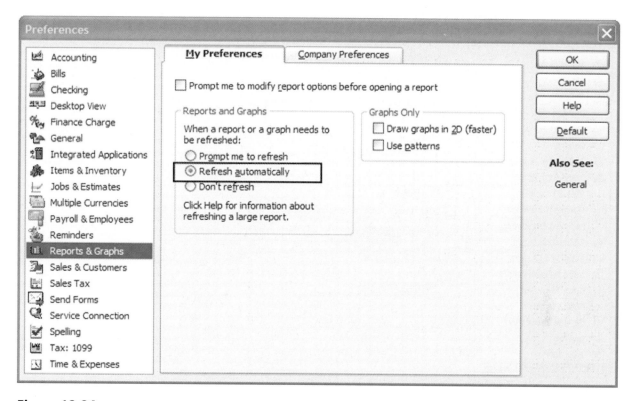

Figure 12:24

Sales & Customers

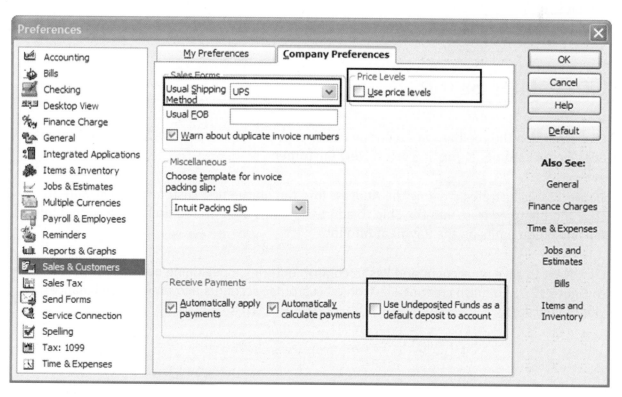

Figure 12:25

Time & Expenses

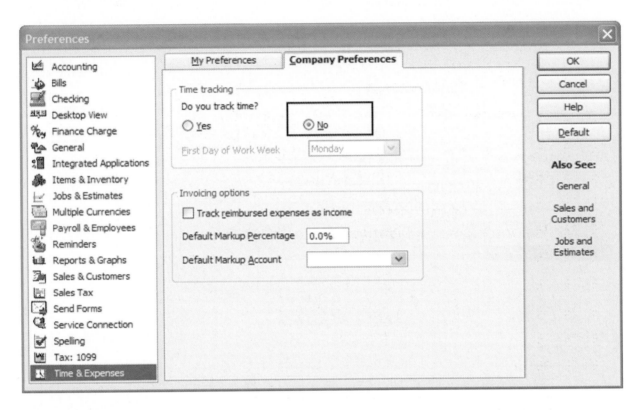

Figure 12:26

You have completed setup of company preferences so click **OK**. You will next create customer accounts and enter beginning balances.

CUSTOMER SETUP

Click **Home** on the toolbar to reopen the Home page and then open the **Customer Center**. Click **New Customer & Job** and select **New Customer**.

Figure 12:27 illustrates creating the **Address Info** tab on the first customer. Make sure to copy the **Bill to** address into the **Ship to** address. Terms are entered on the **Additional Info** tab and credit limits on the **Payment Info** tab.

Click **Next** to save an account and **Yes** to confirm entering a beginning balance for 2008. Refer to Figure 12:28 to finish creating Electronics' customer accounts and enter open balances where indicated.

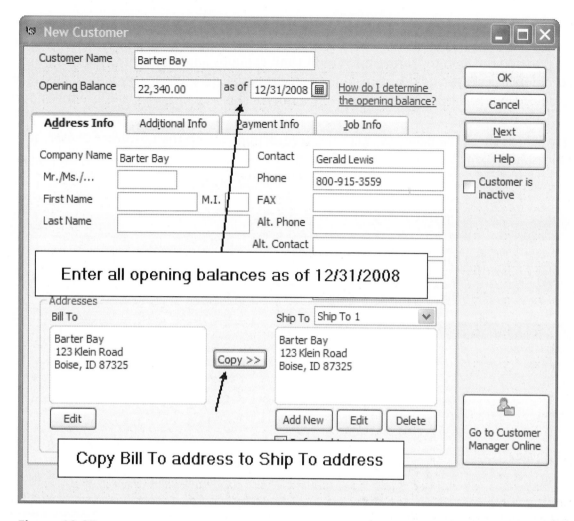

Figure 12:27

Electronics Supply

Customer List

Customer	Contact	Telephone	Address	City	State	Zip	Terms	Credit Limit	Beginning Balance
Barter Bay	Gerald Lewis	800-915-3559	123 Klein Road	Boise	ID	87325	Net 30	30,000.00	22,340.00
Better Buy	Jeremy Michael	800-924-4766	825 W. Exchange St	Chicago	IL	60609	2% 10 Net 30	50,000.00	27,000.00
Discount Electronics	Jamie Foxtrot	800-940-9594	33 Rodeo Drive	Berstow	CA	65841	Net 30	30,000.00	9,670.00
Electronic Town	Clarice Tompson	800-945-1080	3454 Broadway Ave	Aliquippa	PA	42251	Net 30	30,000.00	23,500.00
GG Hregg Stores	Trevor Logan	800-958-1442	454 Sanford St	Lansing	MI	60543	Net 30	30,000.00	9,600.00
Television World	Tina Filmore	800-997-3373	25 Saturday Ave	New York	NY	36544	Net 30	30,000.00	0.00

Figure 12:28

When finished, click **OK** and then print the Customer Contact List to verify your entries. Select ***Reports>>Customers & Receivables>>Customer Contact List*** on the main menu. Modify the report to add the **Ship to**, **Terms**, and **Credit Limit** columns and remove the **Balance Total** and **Fax** columns, click **OK** and compare your results back to Figure 12:28. If you find a mistake at this point, double click the account to reopen, make changes, and resave. Close the report.

You will next check the balances. Click the **Transactions** tab on the **Customer Center**, select **Invoices**, and change the **Date** filter to **All** (Figure 12:29). If you find a mistake, double click the transaction to reopen it, make changes, and resave.

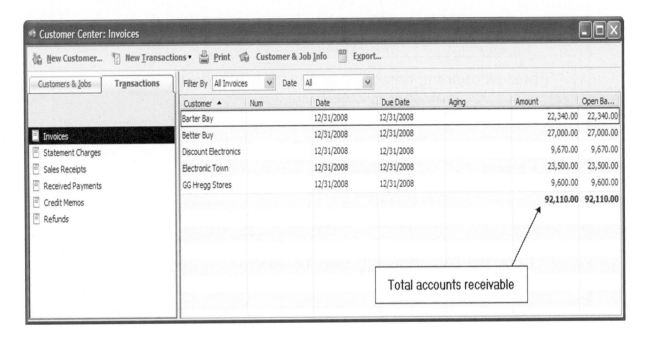

Figure 12:29

Close the Customer Center. You will next create vendor accounts.

VENDOR SETUP

Open the **Vendor Center** and click **New Vendor**. Figure 12:30 illustrates creating the first vendor account and opening balance. Refer to Figure 12:31 to create vendors and opening balances. Terms are added on the **Additional Info** tab. *(Note: The Net 5 payment terms can be added "on the fly" from the vendor account.)* General ledger accounts are selected on the **Account Prefill** tab.

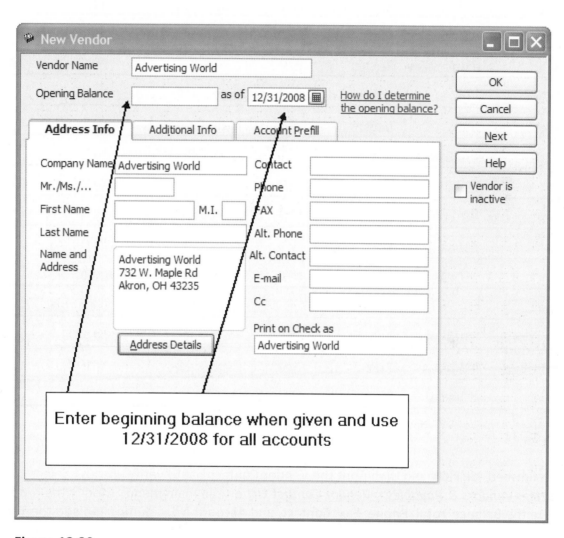

Figure 12:30

| Electronics Supply Vendor List | | | | | | | |
Vendor	Address	City	State	Zip	Account Prefill	Terms	Beginning Balance
Advertising World	732 W. Maple Rd	Akron	OH	43235	6320 Advertising Expense	Net 30	0.00
Bank Amerex	2332 Arlington Dr	Arlington	VA	23532	2330 Federal Payroll Taxes Payable	Net 5	0.00
Canyon Cam	8754 Anthony Lane	Harrisburg	PA	15237		2% 10 Net 30	7,740.00
Cooleys Repair	8 Ripley Ave	Blacksburg	VA	43253	6210 Maintenance & Repairs Expense	Net 30	0.00
CSB Telephone	2 Rich St	Arlington	VA	45325	6310 Telephone Expense	Net 15	0.00
Federal Xpert	903 Mulberry Ave	Montpelier	NH	17325	6330 Postage and Freight Expense	Net 15	0.00
Javix Cam	898 Main St	Albany	NY	09325		Net 30	7,760.00
Mutual Health Insurance	7542 Golf Way	Concord	NH	45789	2370 Health Insurance Payable	Net 15	0.00
Neer Pio	896 Angel Rd	Salem	OR	23456		Net 30	41,400.00
Office Rex	105 Curl Ave	Arlington	VA	44333	6300 Office Supplies Expense	Net 30	0.00
Petty Cash					6300 Office Supplies Expense	Due on receipt	0.00
SumSang Corporation	78123 Mulberry Ave	Santa Anita	CA	09827		Net 30	0.00
Travelor's Insurance	7895 Cat Drive	Salem	OR	78453	1400 Prepaid Expenses	Net 15	0.00
Virginia Electric	41 Cala Road	Arlington	VA	42353	6220 Utilities Expense	Net 15	0.00

Figure 12:31

When finished, click **OK** and then print the Vendor Contact List to verify entries. Select *Reports>>Vendors & Payables>>Vendor Contact List* on the main menu. Modify the report to remove the **Balance Total**, **Phone**, **Fax**, **Contact**, and **Account No.** columns and add the **Terms** column. *(Note: There is no option for listing the Account Prefill.)*

Click **OK** and then compare your results to Figure 12:31. If you find a mistake, double click to open the account, make changes, and resave.

Close the report. Now click the **Transactions** tab on the **Vendor Center** and select **Bills**. Change the **Date** filter to **All** and compare your results to Figure 12:32. If you find a mistake, double click to open the transaction, make changes, and resave.

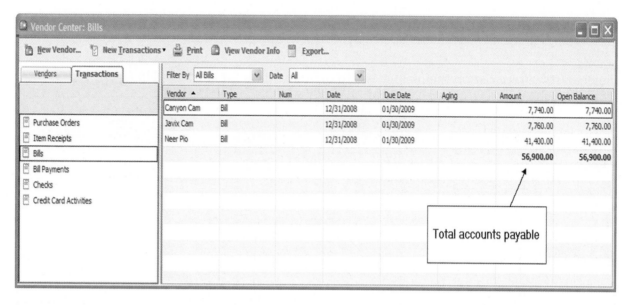

Figure 12:32

Close the Vendor Center. You will next create inventory items.

INVENTORY SETUP

Select *Lists>>Item List* on the main menu to open the Item list illustrated in Figure 12:33.

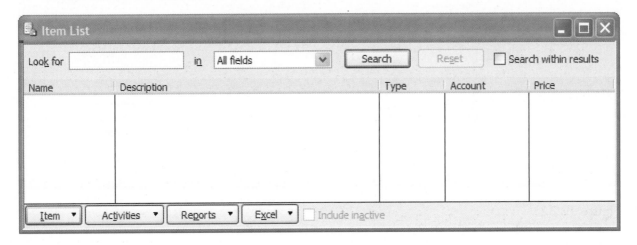

Figure 12:33

Click **Item** and select **New** or use the **Ctrl+N** shortcut key. Select **Inventory Part** as the **Type** and refer to Figure 12:34.

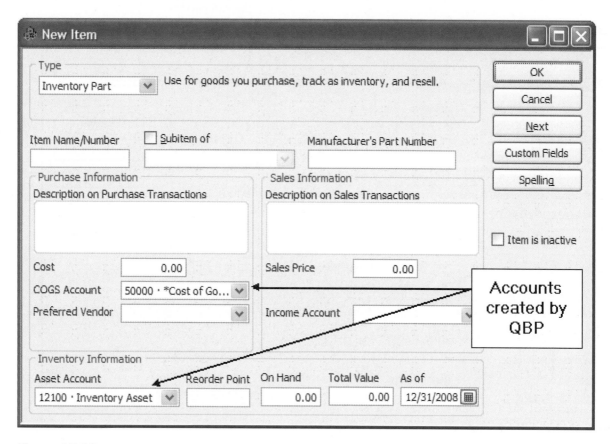

Figure 12:34

QBP has overridden your chart of accounts to create its own cost of goods sold and inventory accounts (i.e., 50000 *Cost of Goods Sold and 12100 Inventory Asset). We will delete these accounts in a subsequent topic. Instead, you will use the 5000 Cost of Goods Sold and 1200 Inventory accounts created earlier.

Add the first item by referring to Figure 12:35. Click **Next** and continue entering the items listed in Figure 12:36. All items are of the **Inventory Part** type and use the **COGS Account**, **Income Account**, **Asset Account**, and **As of date** illustrated in Figure 12:35.

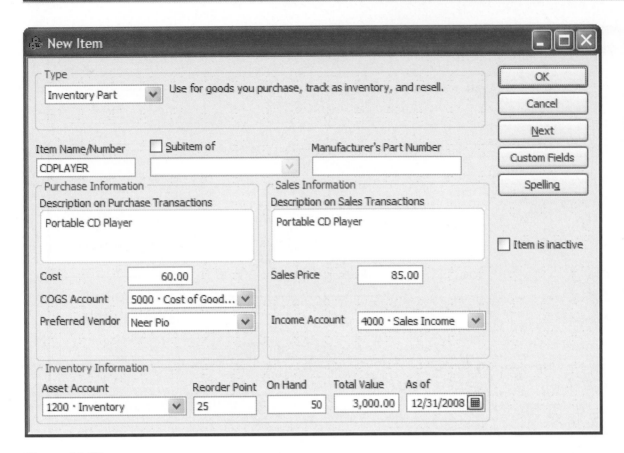

Figure 12:35

Electronics Supply							
Item List							
Item Name / Number	Description on Purchase and Sales Transactions	Cost	Preferred Vendor	Sales Price	Reorder Point	On Hand	Total Value
CDPLAYER	Portable CD Player	60.00	Neer Pio	85.00	25	50	3,000.00
DIGCAM	Digital Camera	191.00	Canyon Cam	285.00	25	50	9,550.00
DIGCORD	Digital Camcorder	394.00	Javix Cam	588.00	20	60	23,640.00
DVDPLAY	DVD Player	131.00	SumSang Corporation	195.00	25	50	6,550.00
DVRREC	DVR Recorder	67.00	SumSang Corporation	95.00	30	80	5,360.00
ENTSYS	Dolby Surround System	837.00	Neer Pio	1,350.00	15	25	20,925.00
HDTV	HD Television	1,620.00	SumSang Corporation	2,700.00	15	20	32,400.00
HOMSTER	Home Stereo	600.00	Neer Pio	895.00	25	30	18,000.00
LCDTV	LCD Television	2,700.00	SumSang Corporation	4,500.00	15	20	54,000.00
PRINTER	Color Printer	175.00	SumSang Corporation	250.00	20	90	15,750.00

Figure 12:36

When finished, click **OK** and then return to the **Item List**. Click **Item** and select **Customize Columns**. Now add, remove, and rearrange columns to match Figure 12:37.

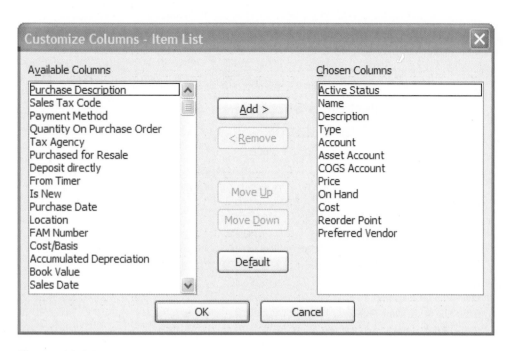

Figure 12:37

Click **OK** and compare your results with the next illustration.

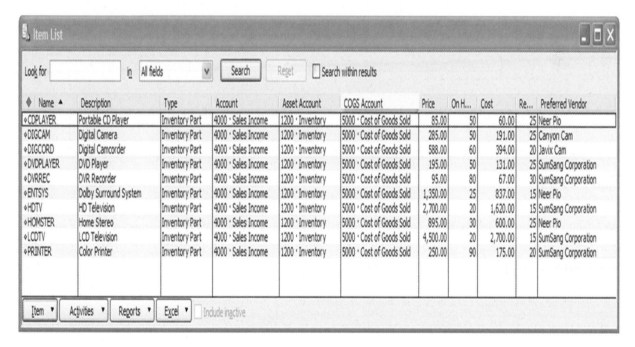

Figure 12:38

Close the **Item List** and open the **Trial Balance** report for 12/31/2008. Compare your balances to those illustrated in Figure 12:39.

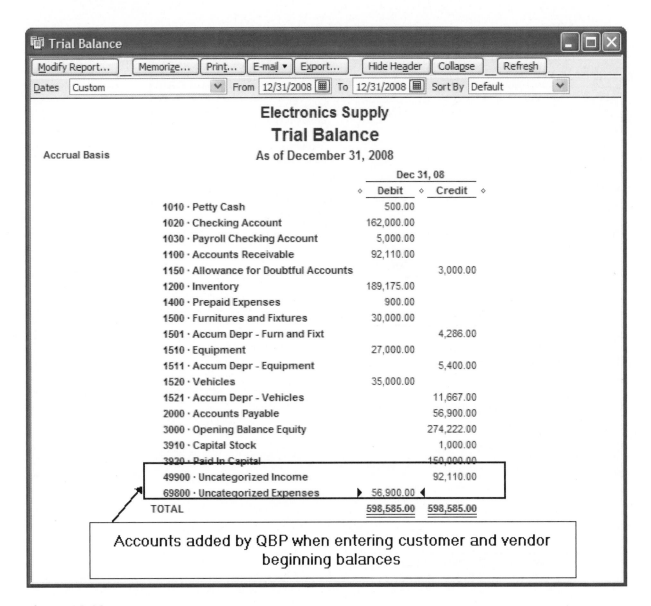

Figure 12:39

We will now make an entry to reclassify certain balances to retained earnings. Open a new journal entry and record the following entry. (See Figure 12:40.) *(Note: Turn off future messages on assigning numbers and click OK.)*

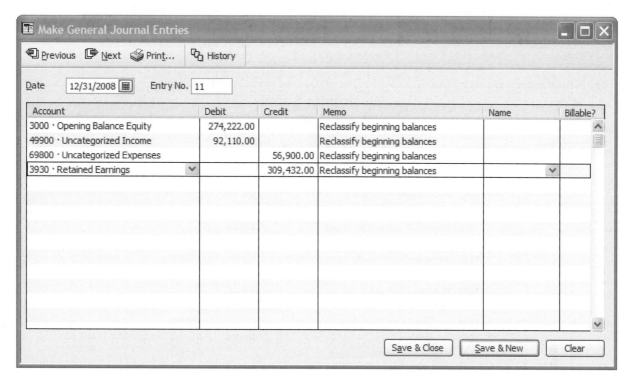

Figure 12:40

Click **Save & Close** and then **OK** to post the entry to Retained Earnings.

Return to the Trial Balance and compare yours to the one illustrated in Figure 12:41.

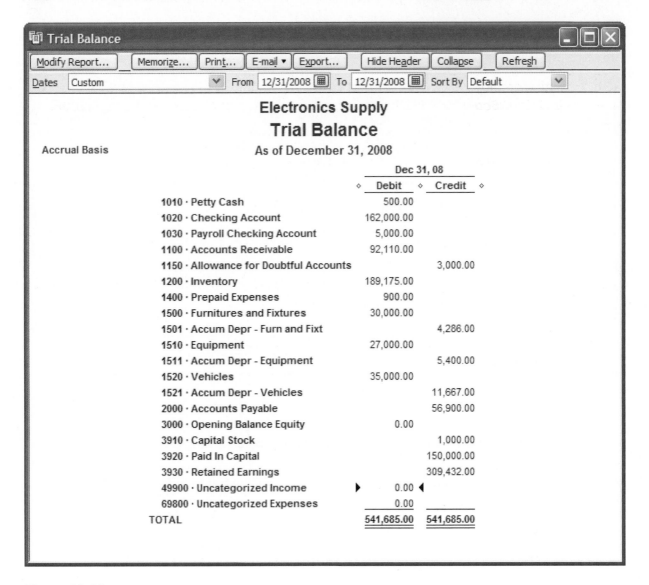

Figure 12:41

Reopen the **Account List**. Right click the following accounts and select **Make Account Inactive**.

> 12100 Inventory Asset
> 3000 Opening Balance Equity
> 49900 Uncategorized Income
> 50000 *Cost of Goods Sold
> 69800 Uncategorized Expenses

Close the Chart of Accounts and Trial Balance. You are now ready to begin setting up payroll and creating employees.

PAYROLL AND EMPLOYEE SETUP

Before creating employees, you need to set up the data file to manually calculate paychecks.
Select *Help>>QuickBooks Help* on the main menu. Refer to Figure 12:43 as we explain the
steps.

1. On the **Search** tab, type in "manual payroll" and press enter.

2. Click the first topic to process payroll manually without a subscription.

3. Scroll down the topic and click the "manual payroll calculations" link.

4. In the topic that opens, click the **Set my company file to use manual calculations** link
   to activate manual payroll. Click **OK** to confirm.

The Employees section of the Home page will now display the icons shown in Figure 12:42.
Close the QuickBooks Help window.

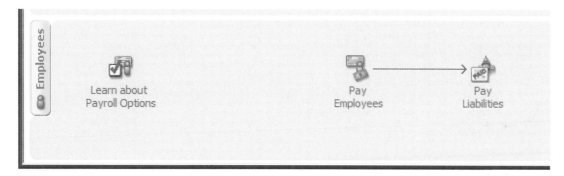

Figure 12:42

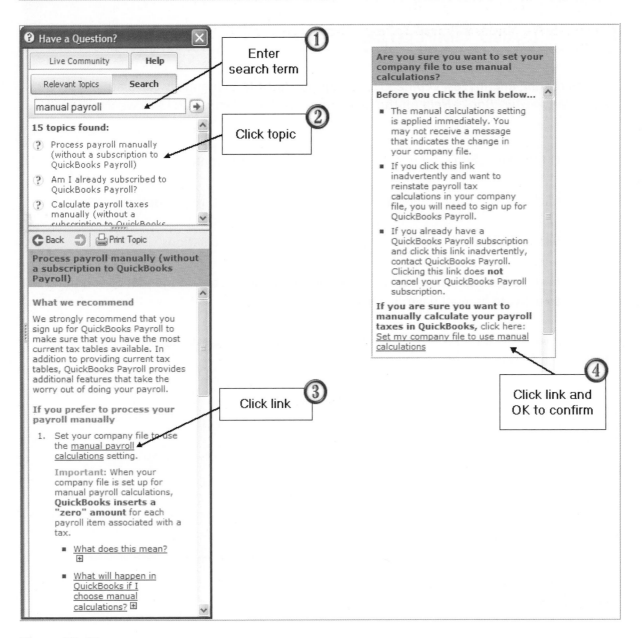

Figure 12:43

Now select *Employees>>Payroll Setup* on the main menu to begin the setup interview. (See Figure 12:44.)

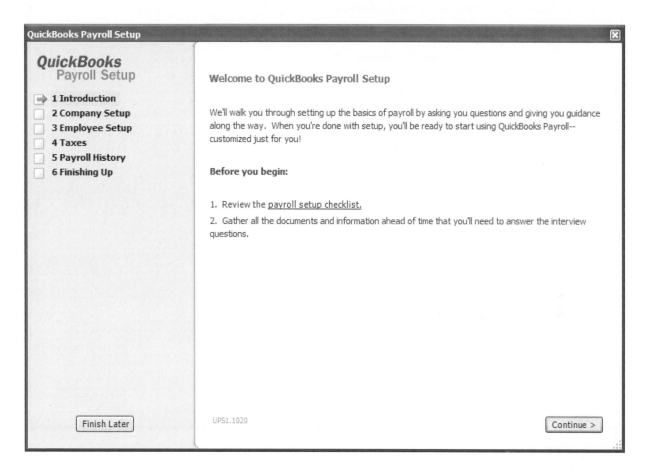

Figure 12:44

Click **Continue** and **Continue** on the next screen. Mark the options illustrated in Figure 12:45 and click **Finish**.

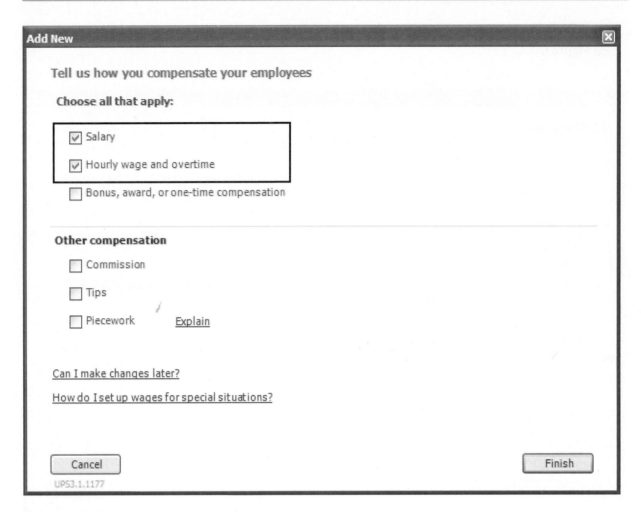

Figure 12:45

When compensation items appear, highlight **Double-time Hourly** and click **Delete** then **Yes** to confirm. You now have the items illustrated in Figure 12:46.

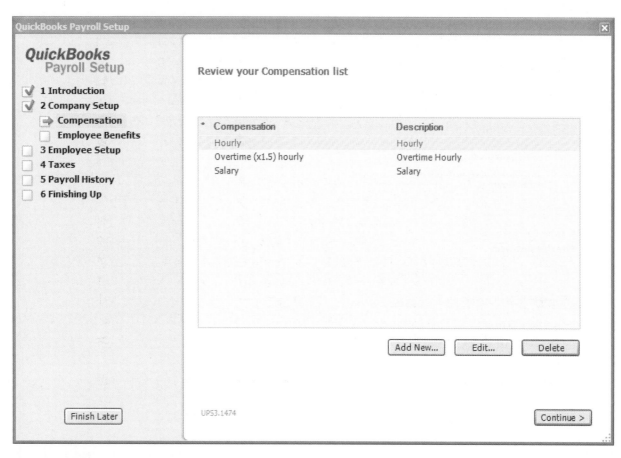

Figure 12:46

Click **Continue** and **Continue** again. Click **Health insurance** (Figure 12:47) and click **Next**.

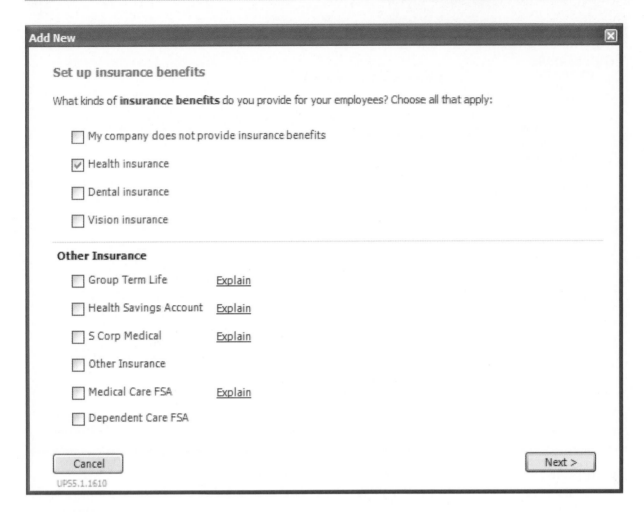

Figure 12:47

On the next screen (not illustrated) keep the option provided so that the company pays for all insurance costs and click **Next**. Fill out the payment schedule as illustrated in Figure 12:48.

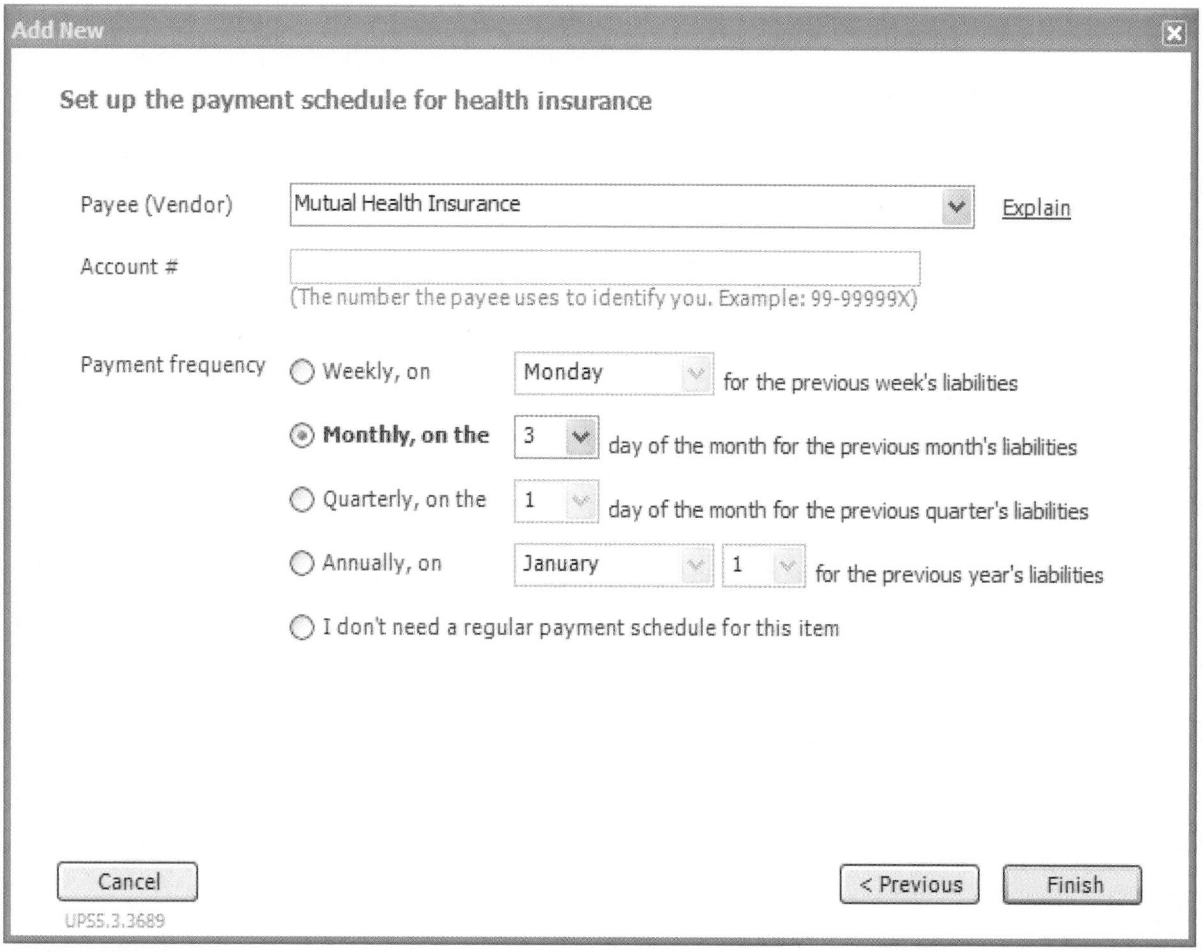

Add New   [x]

Set up the payment schedule for health insurance

Payee (Vendor) | Mutual Health Insurance   ∨ | Explain

Account # | _____ |
                   (The number the payee uses to identify you. Example: 99-99999X)

Payment frequency   ○ Weekly, on | Monday   ∨ | for the previous week's liabilities

                    ⦿ **Monthly, on the** | 3 ∨ | day of the month for the previous month's liabilities

                    ○ Quarterly, on the | 1 ∨ | day of the month for the previous quarter's liabilities

                    ○ Annually, on | January   ∨ | | 1 ∨ | for the previous year's liabilities

                    ○ I don't need a regular payment schedule for this item

[Cancel]   [< Previous]   [Finish]
UP55.3.3689

Figure 12:48

Click **Finish** and then **Continue**. Click **Finish** on the retirement benefits screen and click **Continue**.

Click **Finish** without setting up paid time off options and click **Continue**. Click **Finish** on setting up additions and deductions and click **Continue**.

You will now create employee accounts. Click **Continue**. The next series of illustrations helps you set up the first employee.

Employee Ashton Fleming   [x]

Enter employee's name and address

Legal name

First name   Ashton   M.I. [   ]

* Last name   Fleming

Print on check as   Ashton Fleming

Employee status   Active   [v]   Explain

Contact information

* Home Address   2533 Storer Ave

                    [   ]

* City   Arlington

* State   VA - Virginia   [v]

* Zip Code   43201

* required field

[Cancel]   [Next >]

UPS10.1.1496

Figure 12:49

Employee Ashton Fleming   [x]

Enter Ashton Fleming's hiring information

Employee type   Regular   [v]   Explain

Other hiring information

* Social Security #   111-22-7300

* Hire date (mm/dd/yyyy)   1/1/2008

Release date   [   ]
                       Last day of employment

Birth date   [   ]

Gender   [   ] [v]

* required field

[Cancel]   [< Previous] [Next >]

UPS10.2.1395

Figure 12:50

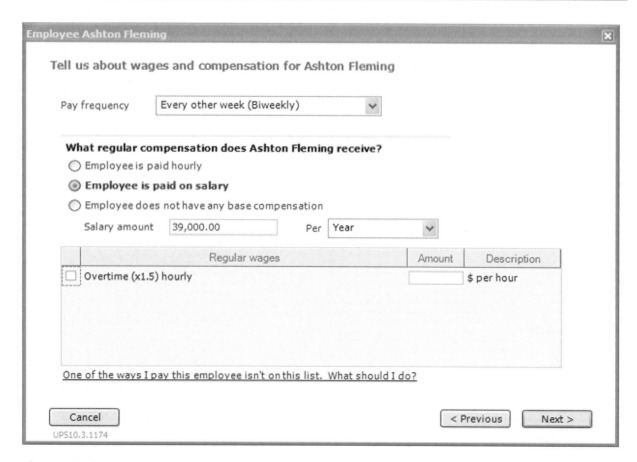

Figure 12:51

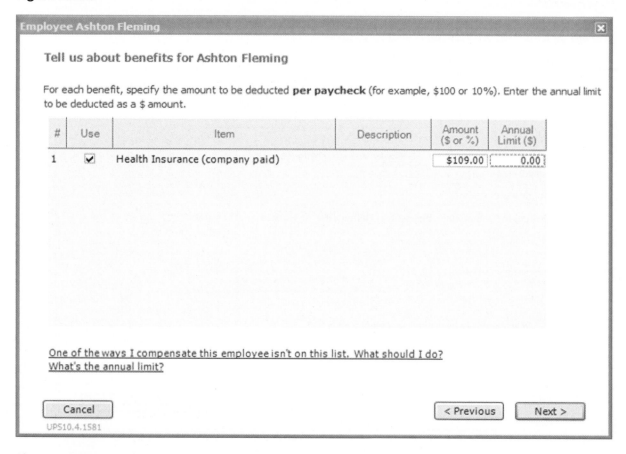

Figure 12:52

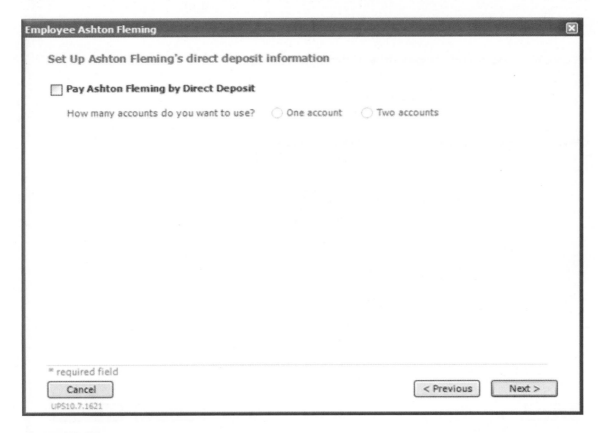

Figure 12:53

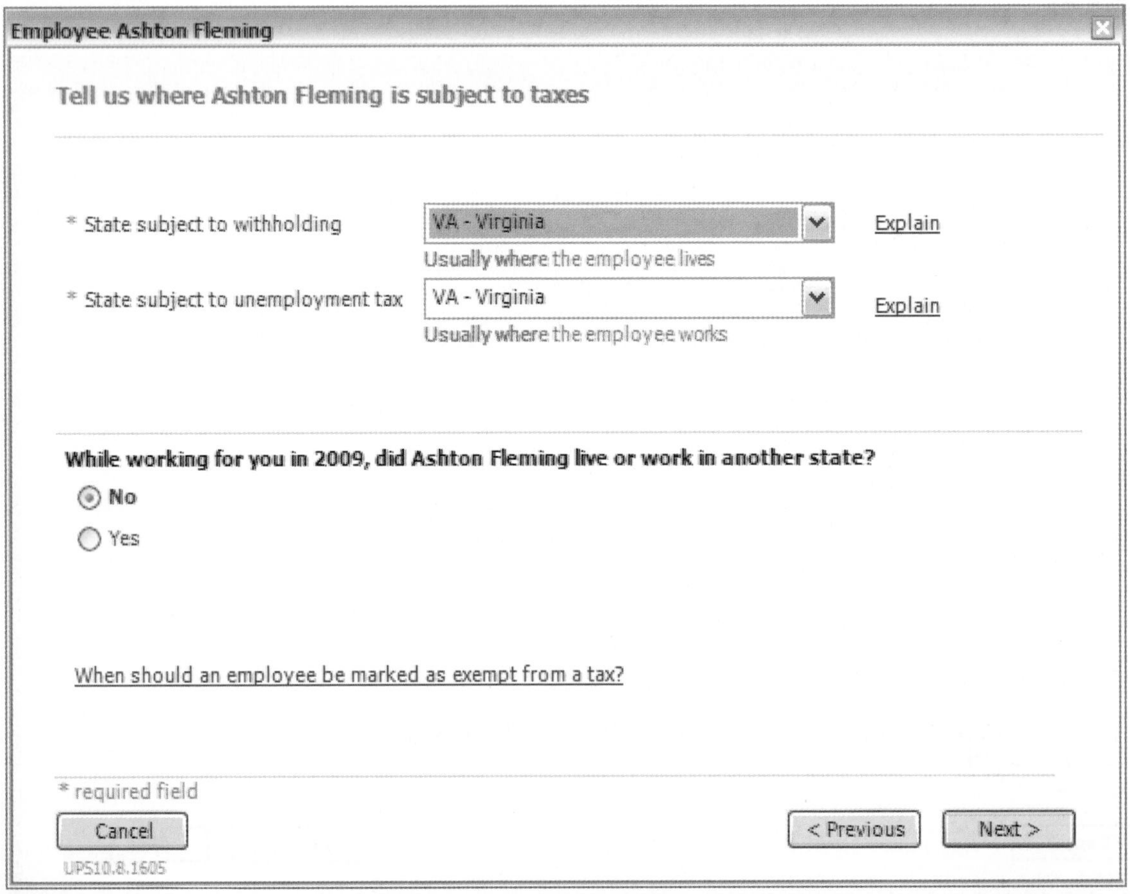

Figure 12:54

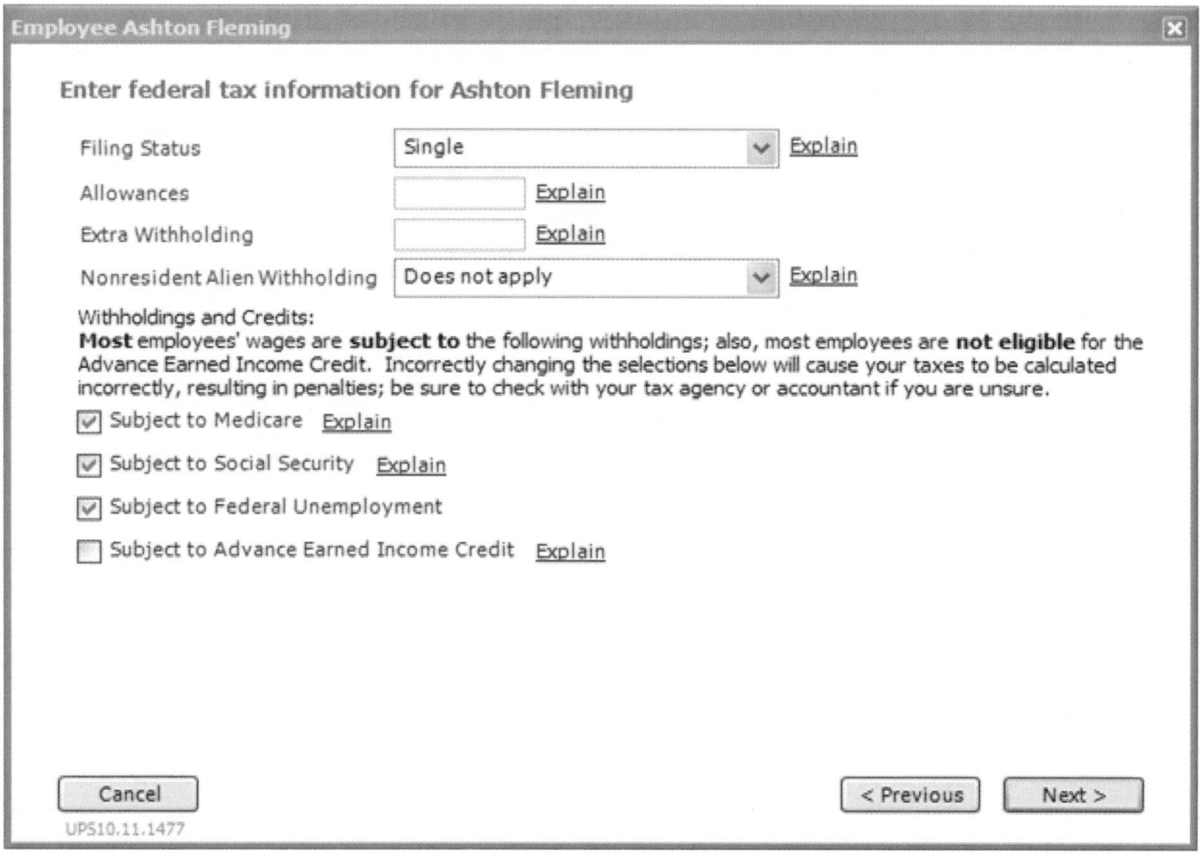

Enter federal tax information for Ashton Fleming

Filing Status	Single ▼	Explain
Allowances		Explain
Extra Withholding		Explain
Nonresident Alien Withholding	Does not apply ▼	Explain

Withholdings and Credits:
Most employees' wages are **subject to** the following withholdings; also, most employees are **not eligible** for the Advance Earned Income Credit. Incorrectly changing the selections below will cause your taxes to be calculated incorrectly, resulting in penalties; be sure to check with your tax agency or accountant if you are unsure.

☑ Subject to Medicare Explain

☑ Subject to Social Security   Explain

☑ Subject to Federal Unemployment

☐ Subject to Advance Earned Income Credit   Explain

Cancel

< Previous   Next >

UPS10.11.1477

Figure 12:55

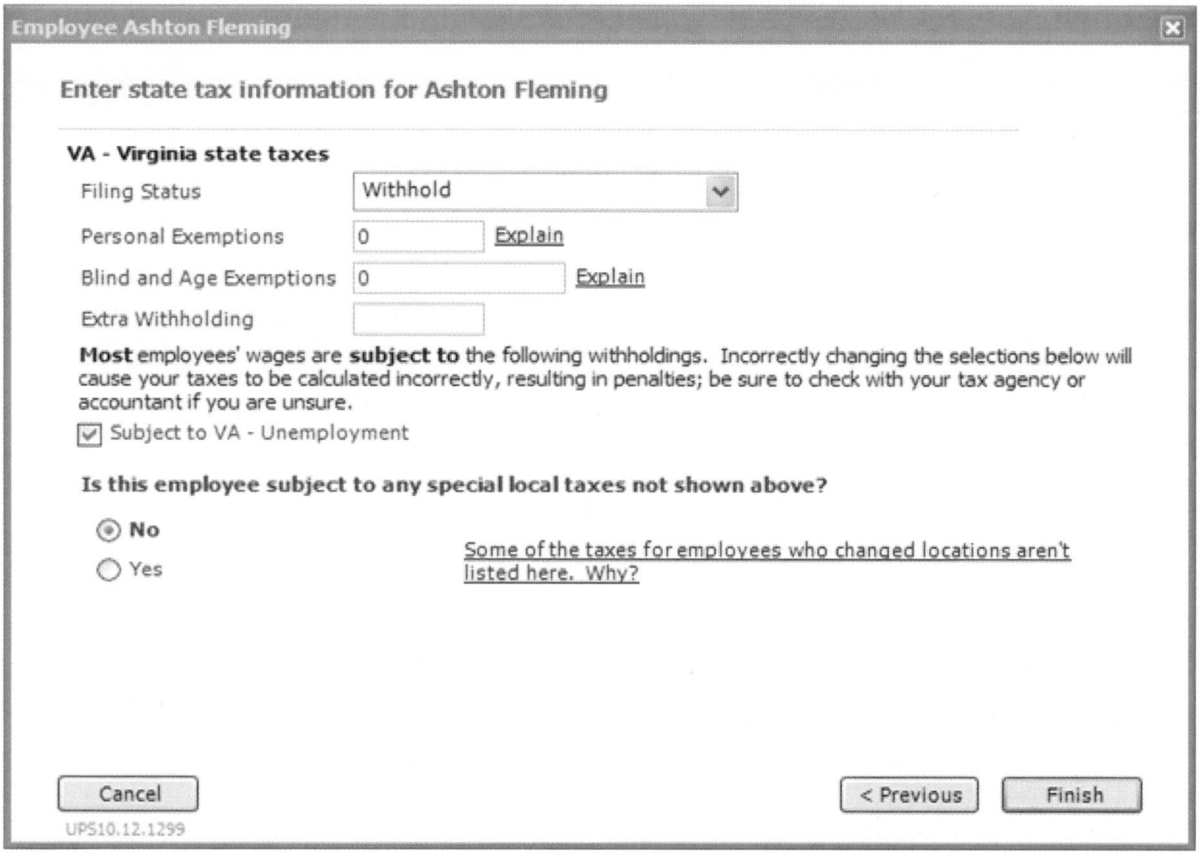

Enter state tax information for Ashton Fleming

VA - Virginia state taxes

Filing Status	Withhold ▼	
Personal Exemptions	0	Explain
Blind and Age Exemptions	0	Explain
Extra Withholding		

Most employees' wages are **subject to** the following withholdings. Incorrectly changing the selections below will cause your taxes to be calculated incorrectly, resulting in penalties; be sure to check with your tax agency or accountant if you are unsure.

☑ Subject to VA - Unemployment

Is this employee subject to any special local taxes not shown above?

⦿ **No**

◯ Yes   Some of the taxes for employees who changed locations aren't listed here. Why?

Cancel

< Previous   Finish

UPS10.12.1299

Figure 12:56

Click **Finish** and then click **Add New** to enter the three remaining employees listed in Figure 12:57. All employees have zero allowances for state tax purposes.

Electronics Supply
Employee Information

Employee	Address	City	State	Zip	Telephone	SS No	Hire Date
Ashton Fleming	2533 Storer Ave	Arlington	VA	43201	770-554-3253	111-22-7300	1/1/08
Susan Gonzales	18 Birdlane Dr	Blacksburg	VA	43231	770-555-1144	011-08-3253	1/1/08
Lebron Johns	873 Star Ave	Arlington	VA	43232	770-555-8923	110-09-0098	1/1/08
April Levine	998 Maplewood Dr	Gunther	VA	43235	770-783-8323	011-10-0939	1/1/08

Employee	Frequency	Annual Salary	Hourly Regular	Hourly Overtime	Health Insurance	Federal Filing Status	Federal Allowances
Ashton Fleming	Biweekly	39,000.00			109.00	Single	0
Susan Gonzales	Biweekly	67,600.00			109.00	Married	2
Lebron Johns	Biweekly		12.50	18.75	109.00	Single	1
April Levine	Biweekly		18.00	27.00	109.00	Married	0

Figure 12:57

Click **Continue** and **Continue** again to arrive at federal payroll tax items (Figure 12:58).

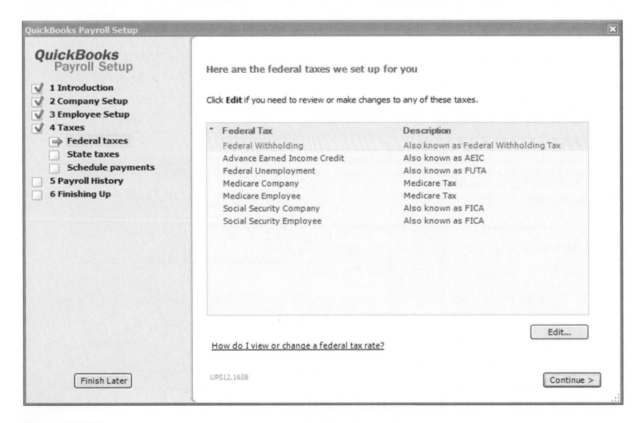

Figure 12:58

Click **Continue** and enter the information on Figure 12:59 for Virginia unemployment tax.

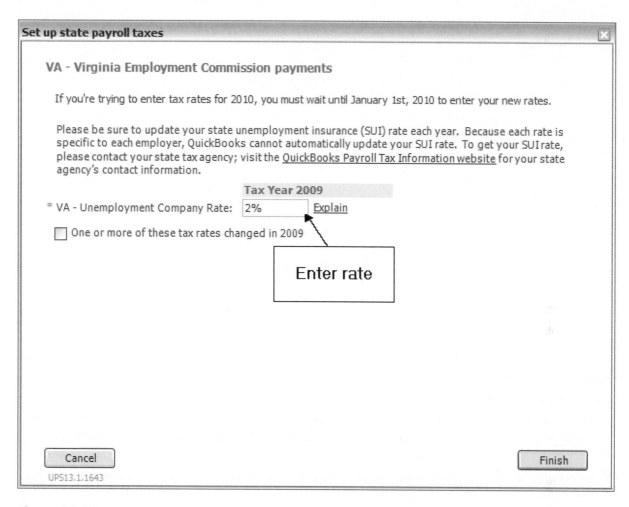

Figure 12:59

Click **Finish** and the screen displays state payroll tax items (Figure 12:60).

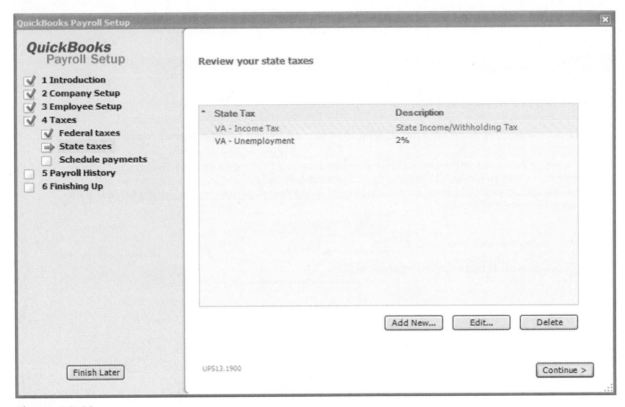

Figure 12:60

Click **Continue**. In the next series of illustrations, you schedule payroll tax due dates and choose a vendor account for paying the tax. Figure 12:61 sets the vendor account to Bank Amerex because the company pays federal tax liabilities through the local bank. Keep clicking **Next** until you complete this task.

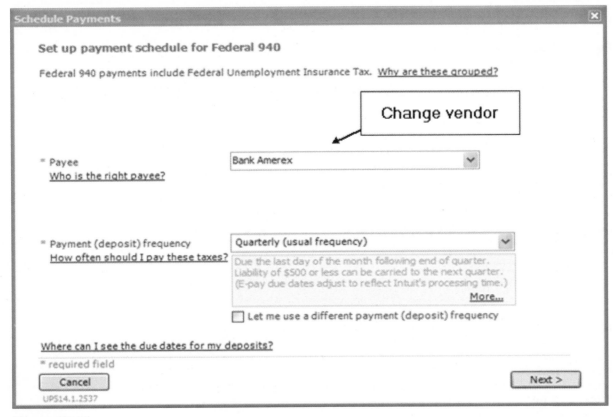

Figure 12:61

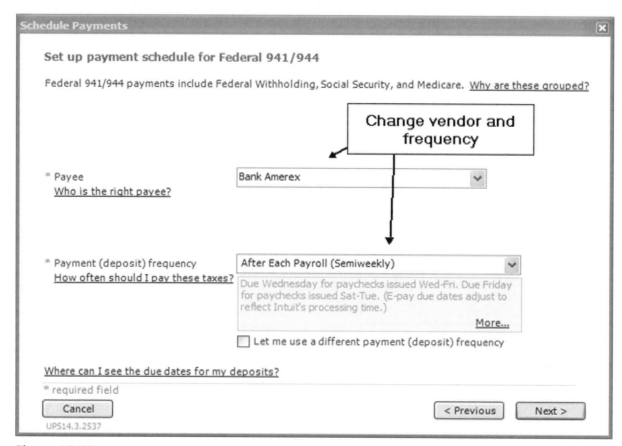

Figure 12:62

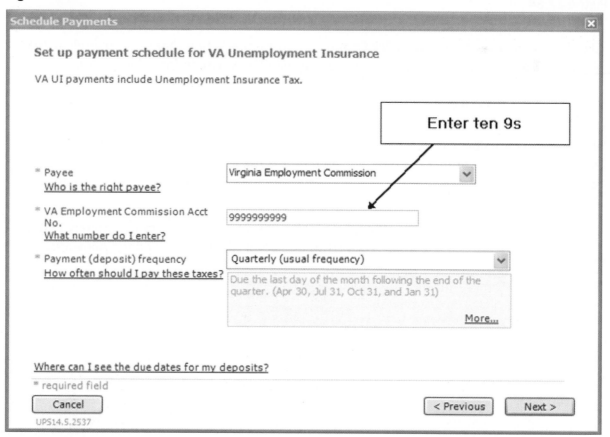

Figure 12:63

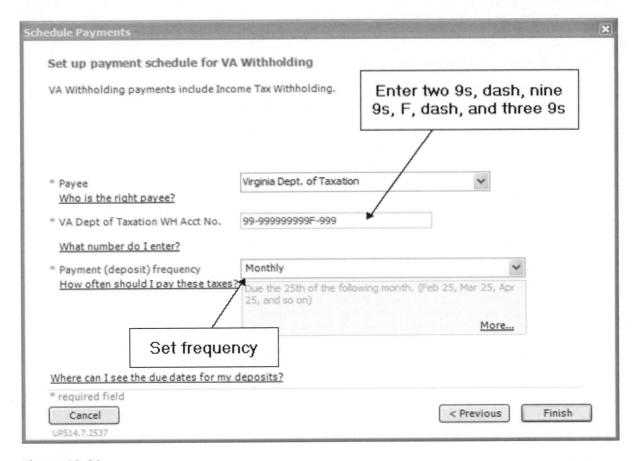

Figure 12:64

Click **Finish** and then **Continue**. Click **Continue**. Choose the option that starts payroll in **2009** and mark **No** if asked whether paychecks have already been issued (not illustrated).

Click **Go to the Payroll Center**.

Now print the Employee Contact List to verify your entries. Select *Reports>>Employees & Payroll>>Employee Contact List* on the main menu. Click **Modify Report** and make the following column changes.

Add:	Hire Date, Salary, Pay Period, Earnings 1/Rate, Earnings 2/Rate, Adjust1/Amt/Limit, Federal Filing Status, Federal Allowances
Remove:	Gender

The report is illustrated in Figure 12:65 for you to compare results. If you find a mistake, double click the employee to reopen, make changes, and resave.

Electronics Supply
Employee Contact List

Employee	SS No.	Phone	Address	Hire Date	Salary	Pay Period	Earnings 1/Rate
Fleming, Ashton	111-22-7300	770-554-3253	2533 Storer Ave Arlington, VA 43201	1/1/2008	39,000.00	Biweekly	Salary 39,000.00
Gonzalez, Susan	011-08-3253	770-555-1144	18 Birdlane Dr Blacksburg, VA 43231	1/1/2008	67,600.00	Biweekly	Salary 67,600.00
Johns, Lebron	110-09-0098	770-555-8923	873 Star Ave Arlington, VA 43232	1/1/2008	0.00	Biweekly	Hourly 12.50
Levine, April	044-10-0939	770-783-8323	998 Maplewood Dr Gunther, VA 43235	1/1/2008	0.00	Biweekly	Hourly 18.00

Earnings 2/Rate	Adjust 1/Amt/Limit	Federal Filing Status	Federal Allowances
	Health Insurance (company paid) 109.00 0.00	Single	0
	Health Insurance (company paid) 109.00 0.00	Married	2
Hourly overtime (x1.5) 18.75	Health Insurance (company paid) 109.00 0.00	Single	1
Hourly overtime (x1.5) 27.00	Health Insurance (company paid) 109.00 0.00	Married	0

Figure 12:65

Close the report and open the Payroll Item List by selecting *Lists>>Payroll Item List* on the main menu. Click **No** to using QBP's payroll service.

Click **Payroll Item** to select **Customize Columns** and then add the **Expense Account** and **Liability Account** columns to appear after the **Annual Limit column**. Also remove the **Account ID** column. Click **OK**. We will now customize posting accounts for a few of these items.

Double click the **Health Insurance** item and click **Next**. Change the **Liability** account and **Expense** account to the accounts shown in Figure 12:66.

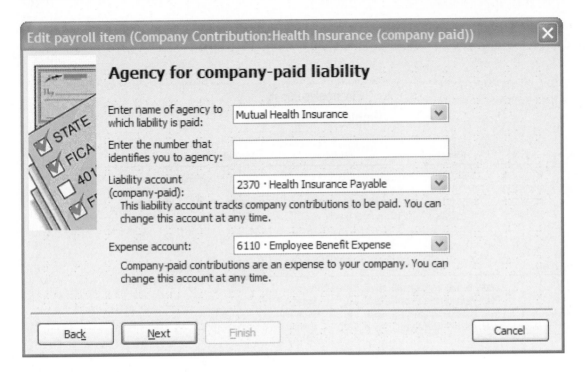

Figure 12:66

Click **Next** until you reach the screen containing Finish and then click **Finish**.

Close the list and the Employee Center. Reopen the Home page and return to the Vendor Center. You need to adjust vendor accounts created by QBP when adding payroll tax items.

First, delete the **United States Treasury** account by highlighting it and clicking *Edit>>Delete Vendor* on the main menu. Click **OK** to confirm.

Next, open the following vendor accounts to enter the vendor information provided.

> Virginia Dept. of Taxation
> > PO Box 8721, Arlington, VA 32513
> > Terms: Net 5
> > Account Prefill: 2350 State Payroll Taxes Payable

> Virginia Employment Commission
> > PO Box 8181, Arlington, VA 32513
> > Terms: Net 5
> > Account Prefill: 2360 SUTA Payable

Close the Vendor Center.

CUSTOMIZING FORM TEMPLATES

Customizing the forms used by a company is the last step to finalizing a new data file. Select *Lists>>Templates* on the main menu to access QBP's form templates (Figure 12:67).

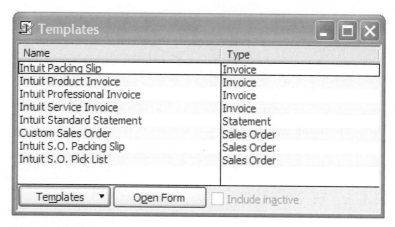

Figure 12:67

We will customize the product invoice first. Double click the **Intuit Product Invoice** and click the **Print Preview** button. Click **Zoom In** to enlarge the view and the form appears as illustrated in Figure 12:68.

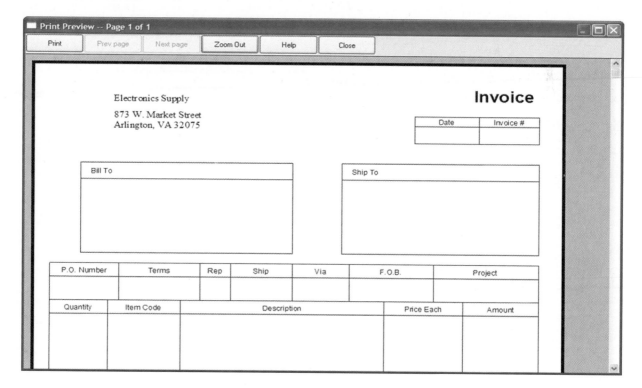

Figure 12:68

We want to add the company's phone and fax numbers and remove the **Project** field from the form. Click **Close** and then click **Manage Templates**.

Highlight **Intuit Product Invoice**, click **Copy**, and change the name to **Electronic Invoice** (Figure 12:69). Click **OK**.

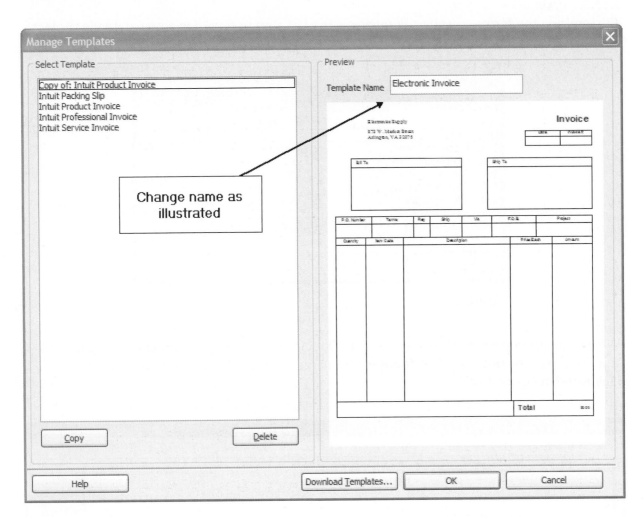

Figure 12:69

Click the **Phone Number** field (Figure 12:70), causing QBP to prompt to use the **Layout Designer**. Select the option to turn off future messages and click **OK**. Also click the **Fax Number** field.

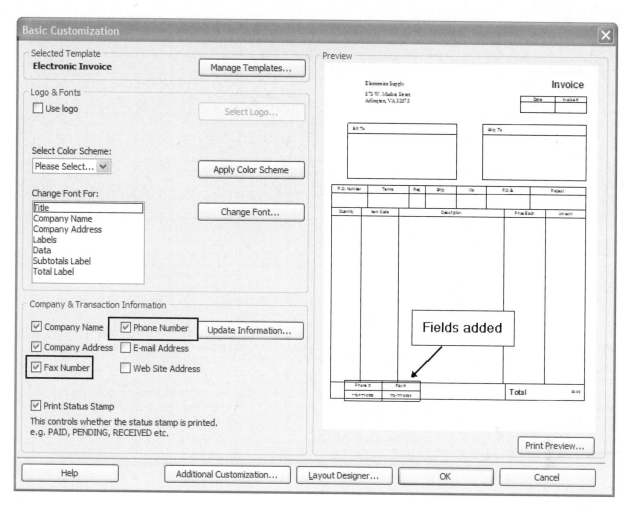

Figure 12:70

The new fields were added to the bottom of the form so you will move them to the top. Before that, click **Additional Customization** to remove the **Project** field. With the **Header** tab selected, turn off the **Project/Job** field. (See Figure 12:71.)

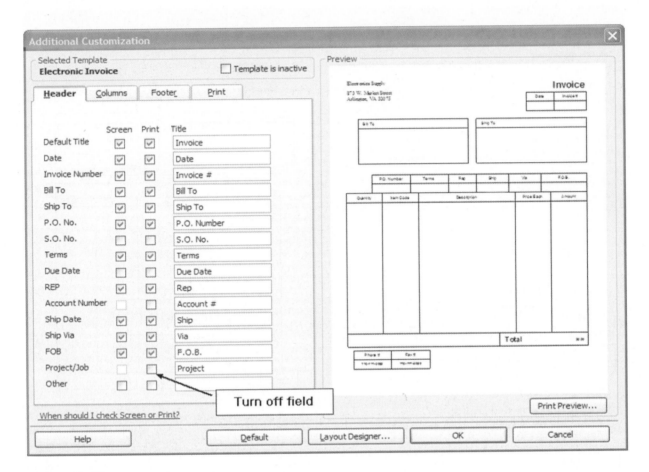

Figure 12:71

The **Header** tab sets the fields and titles that print at the top of the form. The **Columns** tab (not shown) sets the fields and titles that appear in the body of the form. The **Footer** tab sets information for the bottom of the form. Finally, the **Print** tab sets printing attributes.

Click **Print Preview** and scroll to the bottom of the form. Notice that the phone fields you added are at the bottom of the form. (See Figure 12:72.) We will reposition them next.

Figure 12:72

Click **Close** to exit the preview pane and click **Layout Designer** so you can reposition these fields.

Scroll to the bottom of the form and locate the phone fields. Each field is comprised of a field title and the field value. You can move all four fields simultaneously using the next instructions.

Click the **Phone #** title first and then hold down the Shift key as you click the three remaining fields. When finished, the four fields are grouped together. (See Figure 12:73.)

Figure 12:73

Using your mouse, drag the fields to reposition them at the top of the form (Figure 12:74). *(Note: The arrows on your keyboard will move the fields.)*

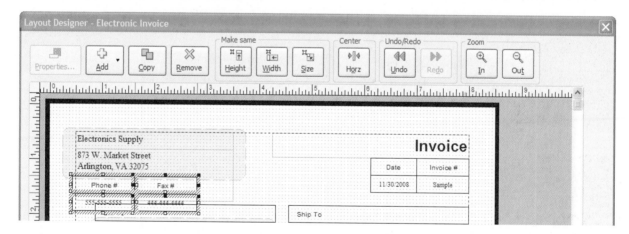

Figure 12:74

Click on the body of the form to ungroup the fields. Now resize and reposition each field individually so each appears as shown in the next illustration.

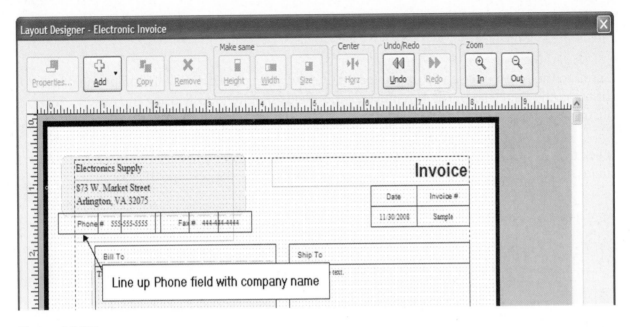

Figure 12:75

Click the **Phone #** field and select 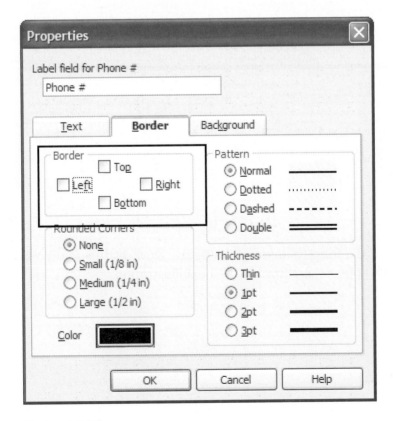. Select the **Border** tab to turn off the field borders (Figure 12:76). Click **OK** and do the same for remaining fields.

Figure 12:76

Click **OK** to save the changes and then click **Print Preview** to view the redesigned form. (See Figure 12:77.)

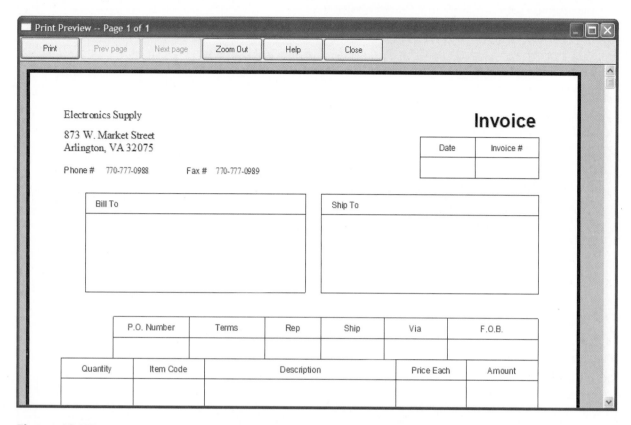

Figure 12:77

Click **Close** and then **OK** on the designer screen. Click **OK** on the customizing screen. The Electronic Invoice template now appears at the top of the template list.

You also need to redesign the PO form. The template does not appear on the list so click **Vendors>>Create Purchase Orders** on the main menu to open a purchase order and then click **X** to close the order.

Return to the list and open the **Custom Purchase Order** form. Click **Additional Customization** and select the **Columns** tab. Change the **Title** of "Rate" to "Unit Price" as illustrated in Figure 12:78.

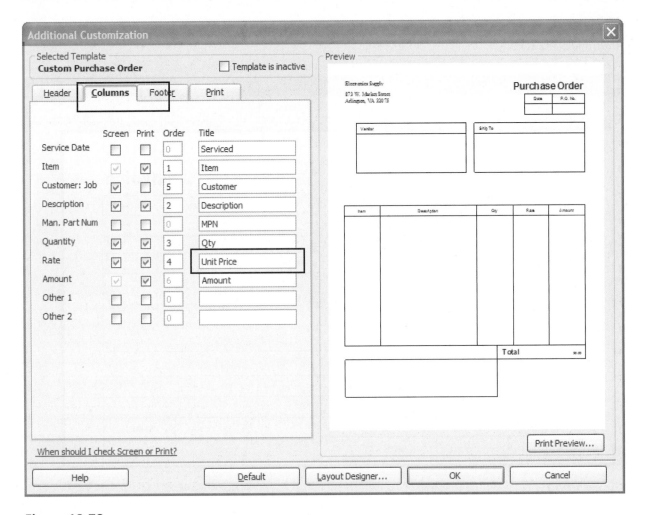

Figure 12:78

Click **OK** and **OK** again. Click **X** to close the Templates list.

You have finished creating the new company file. ***Create a backup of it using the backup filename of "Electronics Supply New Company".***

SUMMARY

Congratulations! You have created a new company. You first established the company data file and then created the chart of accounts and entered opening balances. You then set the company's preference options. From there you created customers, vendors, and inventory items, making sure to verify opening balances after creating. Finally, you established the company's payroll options, created employees, and customized forms. You are now ready to complete the following Practice Set where you record Electronics' accounting transactions for January.

PRACTICE SET

1. Enter the following January 2009 accounting transactions for Electronics Supply. Click OK whenever QBP warns that a transaction exceeds a customer's credit limit because the owner has approved these transactions. Print transactions only when instructed. Reports are printed in Steps 2 and 3.

Jan. 2	Sales Invoice 2000 for $11,400 to Barter Bay for 40 items of DIGCAM, unit sales price $285. ***Change the template to Electronics Invoice.*** Print the invoice.
	Check number 783 from Discount Electronics for $9,670 paying opening balance in full. *(Note: If asked to accept credit cards, mark No and turn off future messages.)* Change the Deposit field to 1020 Checking Account.
	PO 101 for $41,850 to Neer Pio for 50 items of ENTSYS, unit price $837. PO 102 for $48,600 to SumSang Corporation for 30 items of HDTV, unit price $1,620. Print both POs.
	Vendor Invoice 1235 for $3,000 from Travelor's Insurance; $1,200 for 6 months of prepaid auto insurance and $1,800 for 6 months of prepaid business insurance.
Jan. 5	Check number 132 from GG Hregg Stores for $9,600 that pays the opening balance in full.
	Sales Invoice 2001 for $90,000 to Television World for 20 items of LCDTV, unit sales price $4,500.
	PO 103 for $108,000 to SumSang Corporation for 40 items of LCDTV, unit price $2,700.
	Vendor Invoice 3729 for $48,600 for all items on SumSang Corporation PO 102.
Jan. 6	Vendor Invoice 3733 for $108,000 for all items on SumSang Corporation PO 103.
	Sales Invoice 2002 for $38,500 to Better Buy for 50 items of DVRREC, unit sales price $95, and 25 units of ENTSYS, unit sales price $1,350.
	Check number 0888 from Electronic Town for $23,500 that pays the opening balance in full.
	Check number 632 from Better Buy for $27,000 that pays the opening balance in full.

Jan. 7	Vendor Receipt RCT3253 from Neer Pio for all items on PO 101. Make sure to mark Waiting on Bill.
	Check number 772 from Barter Bay for $22,340 that pays the opening balance in full.
Jan. 8	Vendor Invoice 7333 for $41,850 from Neer Pio for Receipt RCT3253. *(Remember to change transaction date and document number.)* Vendor Invoice 45 for $350 from Advertising World for January advertising expense.
	Credit Memo CM2000 for $1,425 to Barter Bay for returning 5 items of DIGCAM on Invoice 2000. Apply to the invoice.

Jan. 12	Create the following payroll checks for the biweekly pay period ended January 11. Print checks from Payroll Checking Account on starting check number 1236.

Electronics Supply
Pay Period 12/29/2008 thru 1/11/2009

Check No.	Employee	Filing Status	Allow	Pay Type	Pay Rate	Regular Hrs	OT Hrs	Gross Pay	Federal Income Tax	Soc. Sec. (FICA) Tax	Medicare Tax	VA State Tax	Net Pay
1236	Fleming, Ashton	Single	0	Salary	1,500.00			1,500.00	217.00	93.00	21.75	60.00	1,108.25
1237	Gonzalez, Susan	Married	2	Salary	2,600.00			2,600.00	275.00	161.20	37.70	104.00	2,022.10
1238	Johns, Lebron	Single	1	Hourly	12.50	80.00		1,000.00	101.00	62.00	14.50	40.00	782.50
1239	Levine, April	Married	0	Hourly	18.00	80.00		1,440.00	141.00	89.28	20.88	57.60	1,131.24
	Totals					160.00	0.00	6,540.00	734.00	405.48	94.83	261.60	5,044.09
	Tax Basis								Circular E	6.20%	1.45%	4.00%	
	G/L Accounts								6000	2330	2330	2350	1030

Electronics Supply
Employer Costs for Period 12/29/2008 thru 1/11/2009

Employee	ER Soc. Sec. (FICA)	ER Medicare	ER FUTA	ER SUTA	Health Insurance
Fleming, Ashton	93.00	21.75	12.00	30.00	109.00
Gonzalez, Susan	161.20	37.70	20.80	52.00	109.00
Johns, Lebron	62.00	14.50	8.00	20.00	109.00
Levine, April	89.28	20.88	11.52	28.80	109.00
Totals	405.48	94.83	52.32	130.80	436.00
Tax Basis	6.20%	1.45%	0.8%	2.0%	
G/L Accounts	2330 / 6100	2330 / 6100	2340 / 6100	2360 / 6100	2370 / 6110

Check your totals before printing.

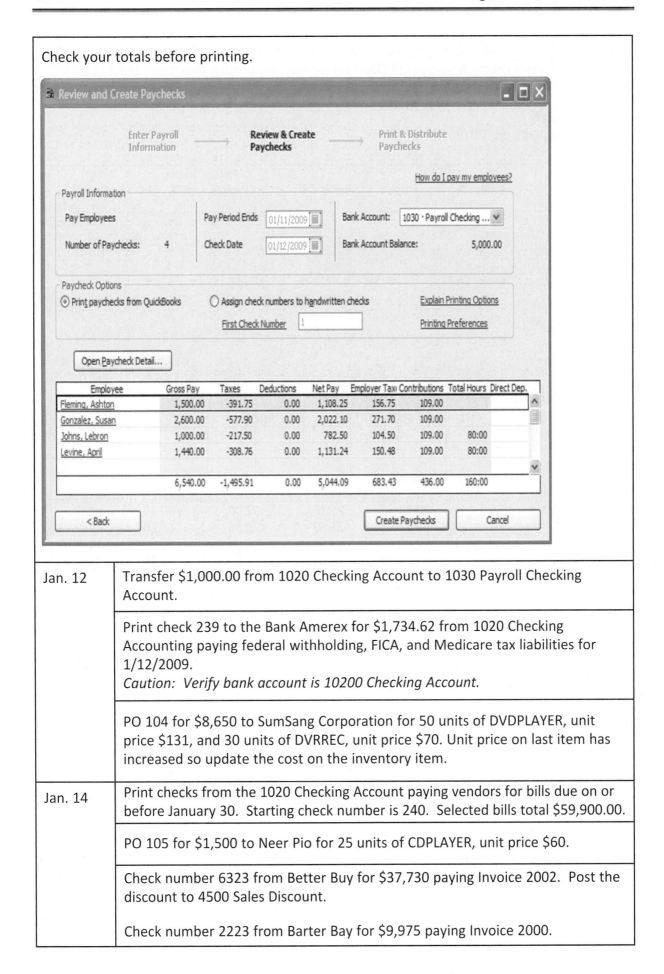

Jan. 12	Transfer $1,000.00 from 1020 Checking Account to 1030 Payroll Checking Account.
	Print check 239 to the Bank Amerex for $1,734.62 from 1020 Checking Accounting paying federal withholding, FICA, and Medicare tax liabilities for 1/12/2009. *Caution: Verify bank account is 10200 Checking Account.*
	PO 104 for $8,650 to SumSang Corporation for 50 units of DVDPLAYER, unit price $131, and 30 units of DVRREC, unit price $70. Unit price on last item has increased so update the cost on the inventory item.
Jan. 14	Print checks from the 1020 Checking Account paying vendors for bills due on or before January 30. Starting check number is 240. Selected bills total $59,900.00.
	PO 105 for $1,500 to Neer Pio for 25 units of CDPLAYER, unit price $60.
	Check number 6323 from Better Buy for $37,730 paying Invoice 2002. Post the discount to 4500 Sales Discount.
	Check number 2223 from Barter Bay for $9,975 paying Invoice 2000.

Jan. 16	Sales Invoice 2003 for $112,500 to GG Hregg Stores for 25 units of LCDTV, unit sales price $4,500.
	Vendor Receipt RCT332 for all items on Neer Pio PO 105.
	Vendor Invoice 88935 for $8,650 for all items on SumSang Corporation PO 104.
	Check number 7325 from Television World for $90,000 paying Invoice 2001.
Jan. 20	PO 106 for $9,550 to Javix Cam for 50 units of DIGCAM, unit price $191.

	Post the following vendor bills dated January 20.
	    CSB Telephone for January telephone, $230
	    Virginia Electric for January electric, $370
	    Cooleys Repair, Invoice 7722 for $275 for furnace repair expense
	    Office Rex, Invoice 4234 for $673 for office supplies expense

Jan. 21	PO 107 for $24,000 to Neer Pio for 40 units of HOMSTER, unit price $600.
	Sales Invoice 2004 for $53,850 to Electronic Town for 30 of HOMSTER, unit sales price $895 and 10 units of HDTV, unit sales price $2,700.
	Vendor Receipt RCT55533 for all items on Javix Cam PO 106.
	Vendor Invoice 7395 for $1,500 from Neer Pio for Receipt RCT332.
Jan. 23	Sales Invoice 2005 for $33,270 to Discount Electronics for 40 units of DIGCORD, unit sales price $588, and 50 units of DVDPLAYER, unit sales price $195.
	Sales Invoice 2006 for $20,000 to Barter Bay for 80 units of PRINTER, unit sales price $250.
	Sales Invoice 2007 for $14,310 to Better Buy for 30 units of CDPLAYER, unit sales price $85, and 20 units of DIGCORD, unit sales price of $588.
	PO 108 for $15,760 to Canyon Cam for 40 units of DIGCORD, unit price $394.

Jan. 26	Create the following payroll checks for the biweekly pay period ended January 25. Print checks from Payroll Checking Account on starting check number 1240.

Electronics Supply
Pay Period 1/12/2009 thru 1/25/2009

Check No.	Employee	Filing Status	Allow	Pay Type	Pay Rate	Regular Hrs	OT Hrs	Gross Pay	Federal Income Tax	Soc. Sec. (FICA) Tax	Medicare Tax	VA State Tax	Net Pay
1240	Fleming, Ashton	Single	0	Salary	1,500.00			1,500.00	217.00	93.00	21.75	60.00	1,108.25
1241	Gonzalez, Susan	Married	2	Salary	2,600.00			2,600.00	275.00	161.20	37.70	104.00	2,022.10
1242	Johns, Lebron	Single	1	Hourly	12.50	80.00	2.00	1,037.50	104.00	64.33	15.04	41.50	812.63
1243	Levine, April	Married	0	Hourly	18.00	80.00		1,440.00	141.00	89.28	20.88	57.60	1,131.24
	Totals					160.00	2.00	6,577.50	737.00	407.81	95.37	263.10	5,074.22
	Tax Basis								Circular E	6.20%	1.45%	4.00%	
	G/L Accounts							6000	2330	2330	2330	2350	1030

Electronics Supply
Employer Costs for Period 1/12/2009 thru 1/25/2009

Employee	ER Soc. Sec. (FICA)	ER Medicare	ER FUTA	ER SUTA	Health Insurance
Fleming, Ashton	93.00	21.75	12.00	30.00	109.00
Gonzalez, Susan	161.20	37.70	20.80	52.00	109.00
Johns, Lebron	64.33	15.04	8.30	20.75	109.00
Levine, April	89.28	20.88	11.52	28.80	109.00
Totals	407.81	95.37	52.62	131.55	436.00
Tax Basis	6.20%	1.45%	0.8%	2.0%	
G/L Accounts	2330 / 6100	2330 / 6100	2340 / 6100	2360 / 6100	2370 / 6110

Check your totals.

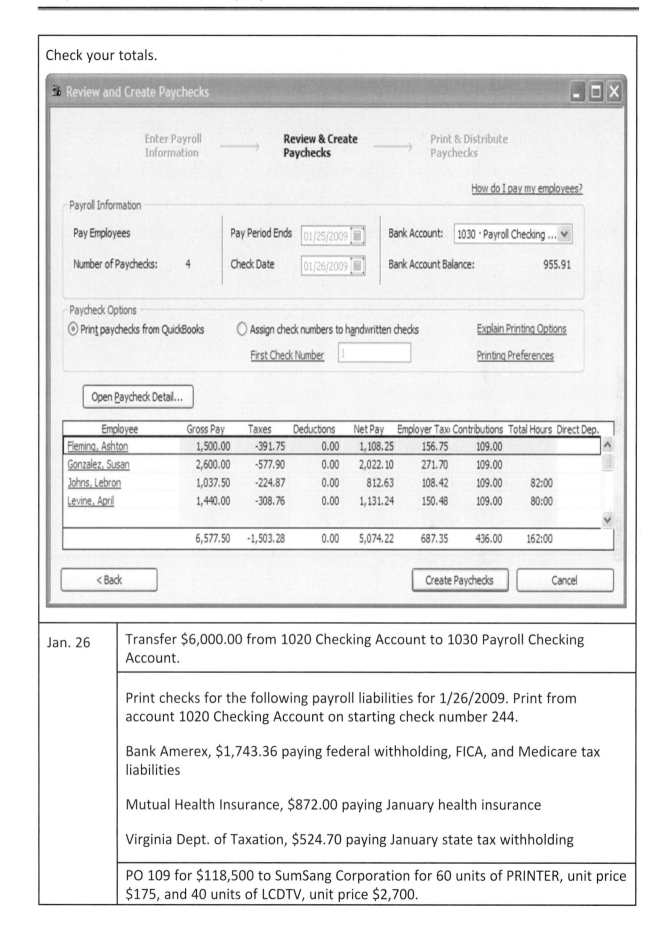

Jan. 26	Transfer $6,000.00 from 1020 Checking Account to 1030 Payroll Checking Account.
	Print checks for the following payroll liabilities for 1/26/2009. Print from account 1020 Checking Account on starting check number 244. Bank Amerex, $1,743.36 paying federal withholding, FICA, and Medicare tax liabilities Mutual Health Insurance, $872.00 paying January health insurance Virginia Dept. of Taxation, $524.70 paying January state tax withholding
	PO 109 for $118,500 to SumSang Corporation for 60 units of PRINTER, unit price $175, and 40 units of LCDTV, unit price $2,700.

Jan. 28	Vendor Invoice 89323 for $18,000 for only 30 units of HOMSTER on Neer Pio PO 107.
	Vendor Invoice 2232 for $15,760 for all items on Canyon Cam PO 108.
	Print checks out of 1020 Checking Account paying vendor bills due before or carrying a discount that expires before February 13. Set the discount account to 5500 Purchase Discounts. Starting check number is 247. Selected bills total $214,844.80.
Jan. 29	Vendor Invoice for $1,000 from Rental Experts for February rent on storage warehouse. Create the vendor account "on the fly" using the following information.
	Rental Experts, 872 Alum St, Arlington, VA 36544, Terms Net 5, account 6200 Rent Expense
	Vendor Invoice 66323 for $500 from Federal Xpert for freight expense. *(Note: Check the account that defaulted to the Expenses tab.)*
	Write check number 253 for $450 from 1020 Checking Account to Petty Cash, expensed as follows: Travel $210 Meals and Entertainment $240

EOM	Record January depreciation of $1,779. Accum Depr - Equipment $450 Accum Depr - Furn and Fixt $357 Accum Depr - Vehicle $972
	Accrue $4,125 for 5 days of payroll. Create account 2100 Accrued Wages on the fly. Reverse the entry as of February 1.
	Record expired prepaid insurance. Auto insurance $200 Business insurance $300

2. Reconcile January 31 bank statements. Print the detail reconciliation report for each account.

The Payroll Checking Account ending statement balance is $1,854.69. All January checks and deposits have cleared and bank service charges are $27.00.

The Checking Account statement is on the next page.

Electronics Supply, Inc.
Bank Statement Date: January 31, 2009

Beginning Balance from December Statement				$ 162,000.00
January Deposits				
	Jan 2, 2009		9,670.00	
	Jan 5, 2009		9,600.00	
	Jan 6, 2009		23,500.00	
	Jan 6, 2009		27,000.00	
	Jan 7, 2009		22,340.00	
	Jan 14, 2009		37,730.00	
	Jan 14, 2009		9,975.00	
	Jan 16, 2009		90,000.00	
Total Deposits for January				229,815.00
January Checks Cleared				
	Jan 12, 2009	239	1,734.62	
	Jan 12, 2009	240	7,740.00	
	Jan 12, 2009	241	7,760.00	
	Jan 12, 2009	242	41,400.00	
	Jan 12, 2009	243	3,000.00	
	Jan 24, 2009	244	1,743.36	
Total Cleared Checks for January				63,377.98
Less Bank Transfers				
	Jan 12, 2009		1,000.00	
	Jan 26, 2009		6,000.00	
Total January Transfers				7,000.00
January Service Charges				102.00
Ending Bank Balance January 31, 2009				$ 321,335.02

3. Print the following reports.
   a. Trial Balance as of January 31, 2009
   b. Sales by Customer Detail for the month of January
   c. Deposit Detail for month of January
   d. A/R Aging Detail as of January 31
   e. Purchases by Vendor Detail for month of January
   f. Open Purchase Orders for month of January. Modify the Filters tab and change Received to Either
   g. Missing Checks for Checking Account
   h. Missing Checks for Payroll Checking Account
   i. A/P Aging Detail as of January 31
   j. Inventory Valuation Detail for month of January
   k. Employee Earnings Summary for month of January
   l. Payroll Liability Balances for month of January
   m. Standard Profit and Loss for month of January
   n. Standard Balance Sheet as of January 31
   o. Cash Flow Statement for month of January

4. ***Back up the Electronics Supply data file to a backup file named "Electronics Supply Chpt 12".***

APPENDIX A   INSTALLING QUICKBOOKS PRO 2009

You begin by verifying that your computer meets the following minimum system requirements for a single-user installation.

Hardware/Software	Requirements
Computer processor	2 GHz Intel Pentium 4 or equivalent (2.4GHz recommended)
Memory	At least 256MB of RAM (512MB recommended)
Hard disk	1 GB of available disk space to install plus additional space for data files
Internet functionality	Broadband service or dial-up with at least 56 Kbps modem and Internet Explorer 6.0
Operating system	Windows XP with Service Pack 2 or later or Vista
Display	High color (16 bit) SVGA supporting 800x600 resolution with small fonts, optimized for 1024x768
CD ROM	4x CD-ROM drive
Optional Items	
Microsoft Office Outlook with Business Contacts	190 MB of additional hard disk space required
Integration functionality	Microsoft Word, Excel, and Outlook versions 2000, 2002, 2003, or 2007

To locate your computer's processor, RAM information, and operating system version, right click the **My Computer** icon on your desktop and select the **Properties** menu (Figure: A:1).

Figure: A:1

Click to select the **General** tab (Figure: A:2) listing your computer's system information. *(Note: The window view is based on the computer operating system; therefore, your view may vary from the illustration.)* After reviewing, click **OK** to close the System Properties window.

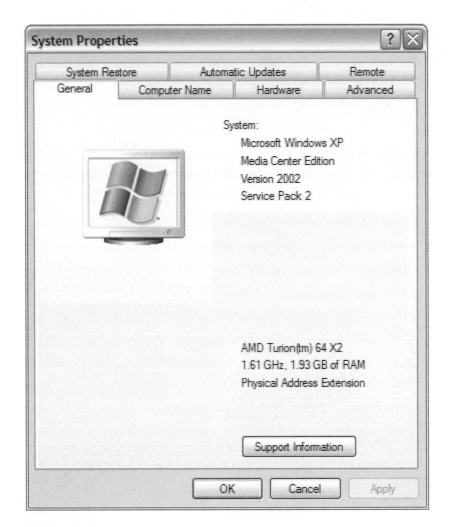

Figure: A:2

To review your computer's available hard disk space, double click the **My Computer** icon and locate the drive labeled **C** (Figure: A:3). *Note: Your window may list folder contents differently than illustrated. You can click the icon noted to change the view.*

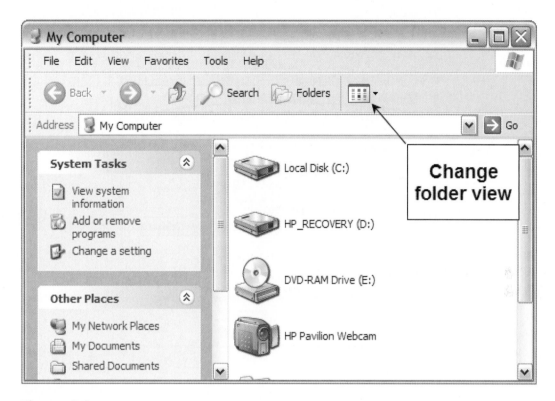

Figure: A:3

Right click the drive labeled **C** and select **Properties** to view the free space on your drive (Figure: A:4). When finished, close the Local Disk Properties and the My Computer windows by clicking **X**.

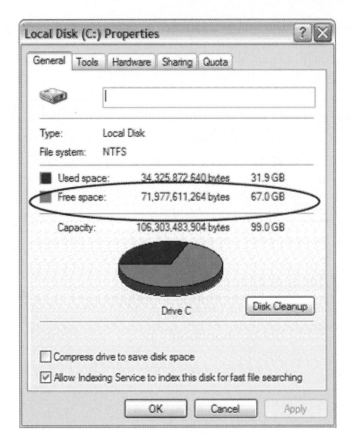

Figure: A:4

After confirming that your computer meets minimum system requirements, close all programs currently running and insert the **QuickBooks Pro 2009** software CD into your computer's CD drive.

*Note: If the CD does not automatically run, click the **Start** menu and select **Run**. In the Run dialog box, click the **Browse** button. Click the dropdown list on the **Look in** box to select your CD drive and then click the file labeled **SETUP**.*

When the window in Figure: A:5 opens, click to select **No** and then click **Next**.

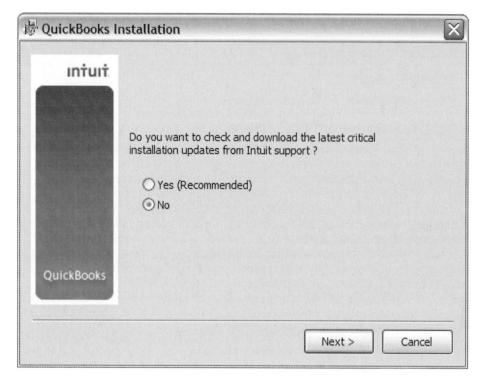

Figure: A:5

Click **Next**, if you receive a screen to install required components. Confirm that all open programs are closed and click **Next**. (See Figure: A:6.)

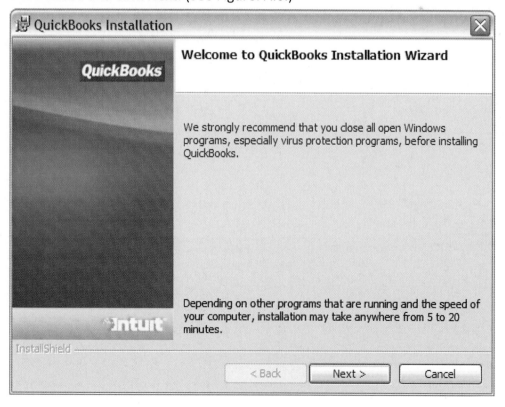

Figure: A:6

The next screen (Figure: A:7) displays QuickBooks' license agreement. Read the agreement, click **I accept** and then click **Next**.

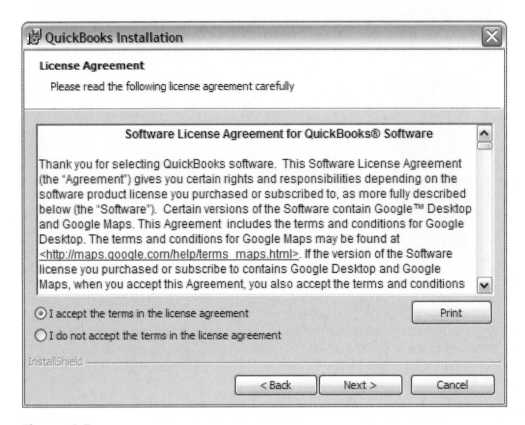

Figure: A:7

Choose to install one user and click **Next**. (See Figure: A:8.)

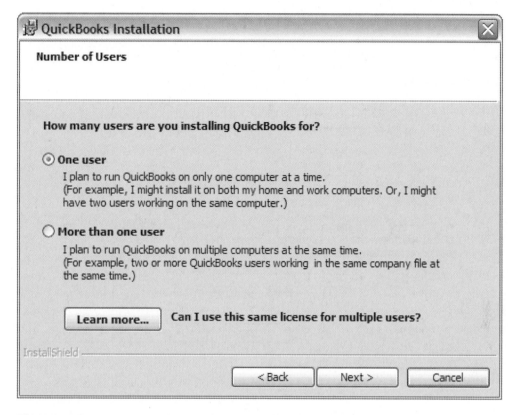

Figure: A:8

On the screen illustrated in Figure: A:9, enter the **License Number** and **Product Number** located on your software case and click **Next**.

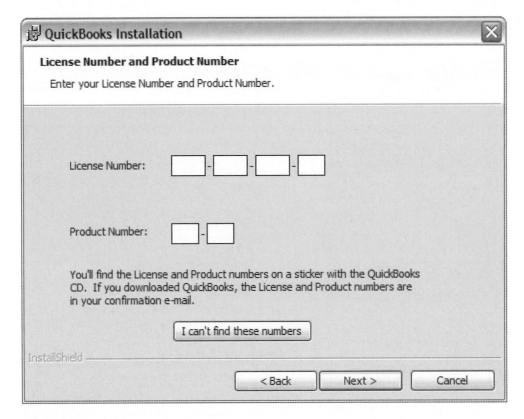

Figure: A:9

On screen that follows (Figure: A:10), keep the installation path provided and unmark **Add other services and support shortcuts to your desktop**. Click **Next**.

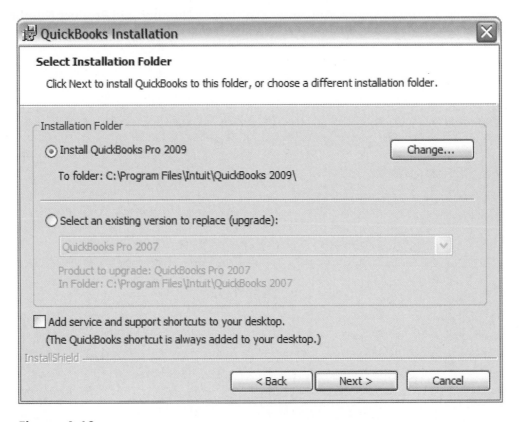

Figure: A:10

Click **Next** again and then click **No** to installing Google Desktop and click **Next**. (See Figure: A:11.)

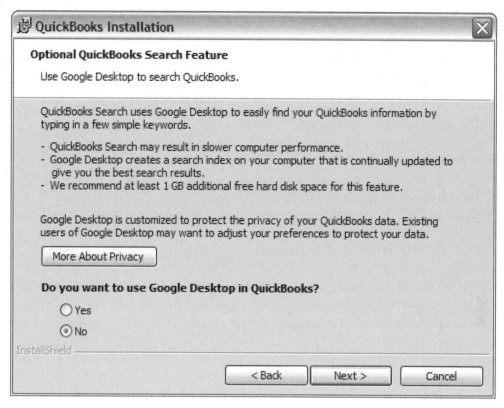

Figure: A:11

Click **Install** when you receive the confirmation screen in Figure: A:12.

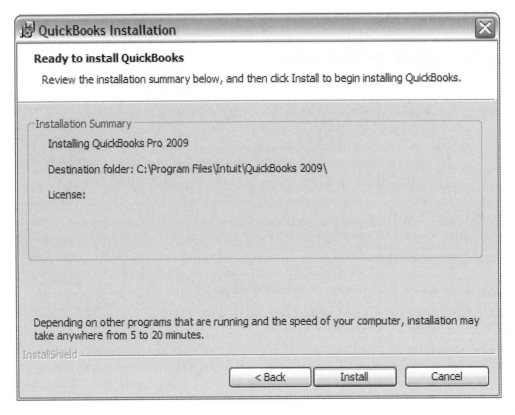

Figure: A:12

The installation process will take approximately 10 to 15 minutes. When you receive the screen in Figure: A:13, click **Finish**.

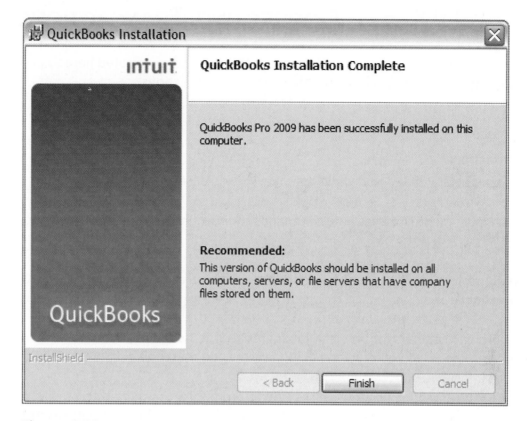

Figure: A:13

Remove the software CD from the drive and store it in a safe place. Return to Chapter 1 to load the sample company data files into QuickBooks.

APPENDIX B   CORRECTING TRANSACTIONS

The information in this topic appears throughout the text and is repeated here to provide a central location for locating instructions on correcting transactions.

New Transactions

You can change data in any field while entering a new transaction.

Edit on the main menu accesses data commands for inserting and deleting transaction lines or copying and pasting text.

The **Clear** button on the transaction window clears data on a new transaction without saving the transaction.

When invoicing customers for time and job materials, the **Add Time/Costs** button will reopen the selection window so you can add additional time and materials.

Clicking **X** on a transaction window causes QBP to prompt for instructions on saving or discarding the transaction. Selecting **No** exits the transaction without saving; **Yes** exits and saves the transaction; **Cancel** returns you to the window to continue working on the transaction.

Posted Transactions

Although the software will let you change and delete a saved transaction, you must be careful when altering posted transactions that have interacted with other transactions, such as changing a customer invoice that has been paid. The transaction categories below guide you on correcting posted transactions.

❖   Sales Invoices

You can modify, delete, or void a posted sales invoice *as long as you have not posted a customer payment against the invoice*. The first step is locating the posted invoice. This is done by opening the Customer Center and locating the invoice on the customer account. You then double click to reopen.

After reopening you can modify, delete, or void the invoice. When modifying you repost the transaction by clicking **Save & Close**. Invoices are deleted by selecting *Edit>>Delete Invoice* on the main menu. You void an invoice by selecting *Edit>>Void Invoice* on the main menu and then clicking **Save & Close**.

When the posted invoice involves employee time or job materials, deleting or voiding the invoice will not reinstate hours or materials. This means that you cannot reuse previously invoiced employee timesheets or vendor bills to reinvoice the customer.

Before deleting or voiding an invoice of this nature, print the invoice to use as a reference for reinvoicing the customer.

After posting a customer payment against an invoice you should not alter the invoice without first deleting or voiding the customer payment. (Caution: Read the instructions that follow before deleting a customer payment.)

❖ Customer Payments
You can modify or delete a posted customer payment by opening the payment on the customer account. You can use Edit on the main menu to delete the payment.

Modifying or deleting a transaction appearing on a reconciled bank account will alter the reconciliation report. QBP will warn you prior to making such changes. To track changes made to a reconciled bank account, print the ***Reports>>Banking>> Reconciliation Discrepancy*** report.

❖ Purchase Orders
Purchase orders do not post so these transactions do not interact with other vendor transactions ***until after you apply a vendor bill or receipt to the PO***. You can modify or delete a PO after locating the transaction on a vendor account. Use the Vendor Center to locate the transaction. You then double click to reopen the transaction.

POs are deleted by selecting ***Edit>>Delete Purchase Order*** on the main menu.

After receiving all items on a PO, the PO's status changes to **Closed PO** and you cannot make change to the transaction without first deleting the vendor transaction used to receive the items. *(Caution: Read the topic that follows before deleting a posted vendor bill or receipt.)* After deleting the vendor transaction, the PO status will be reinstated to open and you can make changes or delete the PO. If you receive all items for only some items on the PO then only those items are closed to editing.

❖ Vendor Bills and Receipts
Vendor receipts can be changed, deleted, and voided. Vendor bills can also be changed, deleted, and voided ***as long as you have not paid the bill***. Locate the vendor bill or receipt on the vendor account using the Vendor Center and then double click to reopen. To delete or void, select the appropriate command on the Edit menu.

After paying a vendor bill, you should not change, delete, or void it without first deleting or voiding the vendor payment. (Caution: Read the topic that follows before deleting a vendor payment.) After deleting or voiding a payment, the bill will be reinstated so you can repay the vendor.

❖ Vendor Payments
You can change, delete, or void a vendor's check by using the Vendor Center to locate the transaction on the vendor account. Double click to reopen the transaction and then

select the appropriate command from the Edit menu. In the real world, checks that have been printed are not changed because altering data does not affect the printed check. After voiding, you can reselect the vendor bill to print a new check.

If you select the wrong vendor bills to pay but have not printed the checks then you can delete the unprinted checks by opening them under the Bill Payments section of the Vendor center. You can then return to selecting bills to pay.

Modifying, voiding or deleting a check on a reconciled bank account will alter the reconciliation report. QBP will warn you prior to making such changes. To track changes to a reconciled bank account, print the **Reports>>Banking>>Reconciliation Discrepancy** report.

❖ Employee Time and Paychecks
You can correct employee timesheets *as long as you have not paid employees for the time*. After paying the employee for recorded time, you must void the paycheck to release the time. Timesheets are changed by clicking the Enter Time icon to reopen the Weekly Timesheet window and then scrolling to the week containing the error.

If you find an error prior to printing paychecks and are still in the Confirmation and Next Steps window, click Close to exit the window and then reopen the window. Select the same pay ending date and then click Find Existing Paychecks. QPB will open the Edit/Void Paychecks window for you to double click an employee check to open it for changes. After entering changes, click Save & Close. You are then returned to the Edit/Void Paychecks window. Reopen any listed paycheck and then click the dropdown menu for Print to select Print Batch for printing the paychecks.

If you find an error after printing paychecks, void the check by selecting **Employees>>Edit/Void Paychecks** on the main menu. Enter the check date, highlight the check with errors, and click Void. To reissue the paycheck, click Pay Employees and complete the window by entering the pay period end date and check date. If you voided a paycheck for an hourly paid employee, then reenter pay period hours. (Note: QBP will not repay previously paid timesheet hours.) Click the employee's name to reopen paycheck data. Reenter the data and then complete the steps that print the paycheck.

❖ General Journal Entries
You can change, delete, or void general journal entries by reopening the entry, Entries are voided or deleted by selecting the appropriate command from the Edit menu.

APPENDIX C BACKING UP AND RESTORING DATA FILES

For your convenience, the instructions for backing up and restoring company data files from Chapter 1 are repeated below. You will also find the instructions for creating and restoring a portable backup file. Portable backup files are used if you need to reduce a backup file size to fit on a removable storage device but these files store only financial data, not related data such as customized templates.

All instructions assume that you are either backing up or restoring the Practice Baxter Garden Supply data file.

Regular Backup and Restore Procedures

❖ *Backup Step 1*

Select *File>>Save Copy or Backup* on the main menu or click the **Backup** icon on the **Icon Bar** to open the window illustrated in Figure: C:1. Choose the option shown and click **Next**.

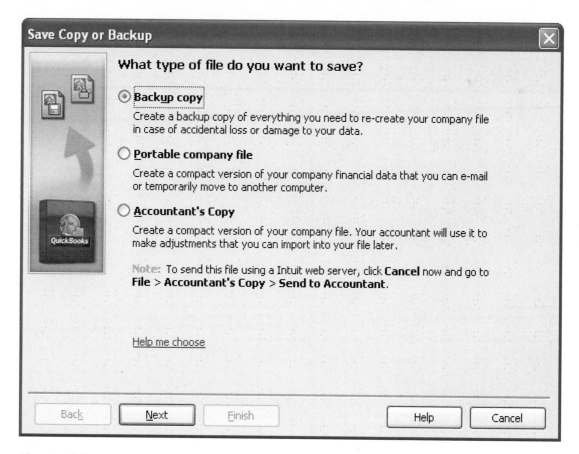

Figure: C:1

❖ *__Backup Step 2__*

On the screen illustrated in Figure: C:2, select **Local backup**.

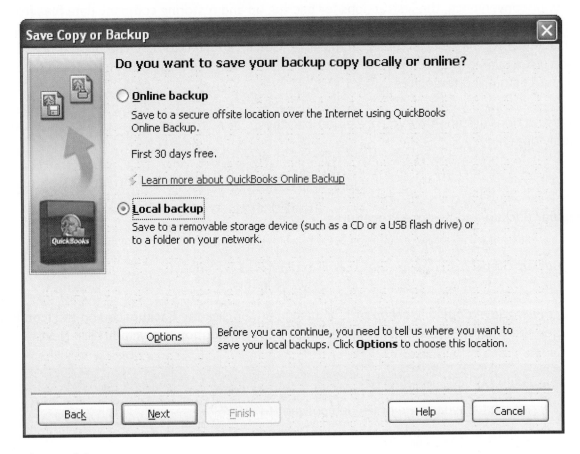

Figure: C:2

❖ **_Backup Step 3_**

Click **Options** to set options for creating the backup (Figure: C:3).

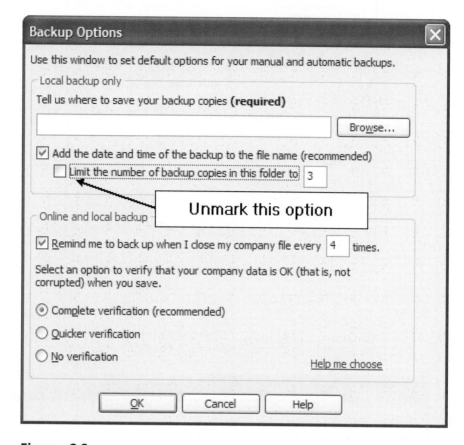

Figure: C:3

Click **Browse** to choose a path for storing the backup file. To make it easy to locate the file in the future, highlight **My Documents** and click **OK**. (See Figure: C:4.)

Note: You can also select the drive labeled CD-RW Drive. You can also select a USB drive, which is normally labeled "E." However, when storing backups to these devices you may need to use the instructions in Appendix C and create a portable backup to reduce the backup file size.

Figure: C:4

The window in Figure: C:5 now opens, showing the exact location for storing the backup file.

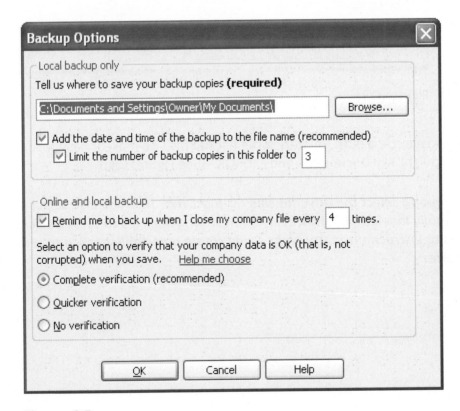

Figure: C:5

Click **OK** and you are prompted to change the location (Figure: C:6). Click **Use this location**.

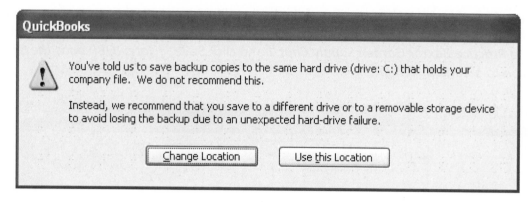

Figure: C:6

❖ _**Backup Step 4**_

Click **Next**, select **Save it now** (Figure: C:7), and click **Next**.

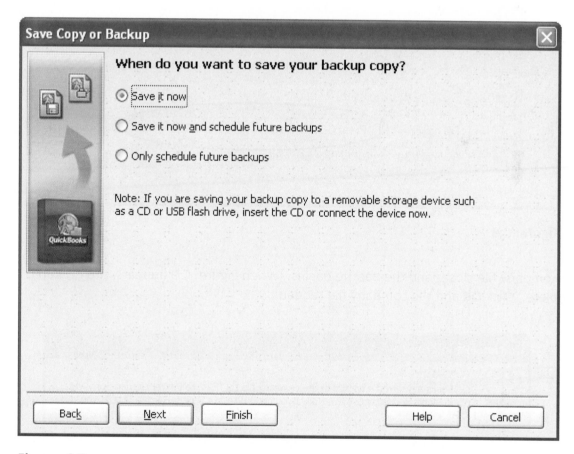

Figure: C:7

❖ *Backup Step 5*

We suggest replacing the date portion of the backup file name with the chapter name you are currently working on. Therefore, in the window illustrated in Figure: C:8, change the **File name** to *Practice Baxter Garden Supply Chpt 1* and click **Save**. *(Note: QBP adds the QBB extension to a backup file name.)*

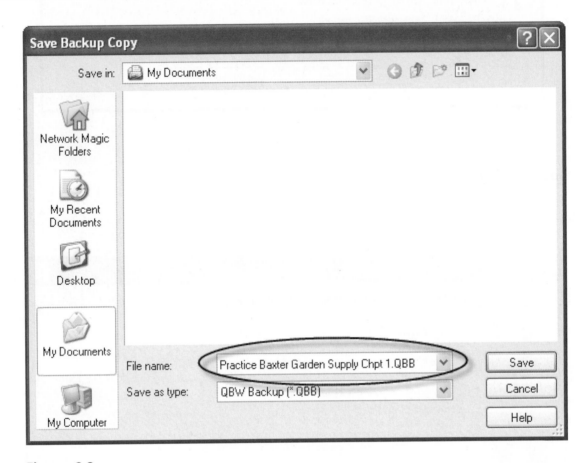

Figure: C:8

The company file closes and the backup begins. When Figure: C:9 appears, the backup is complete. Click **OK** and the company file reopens.

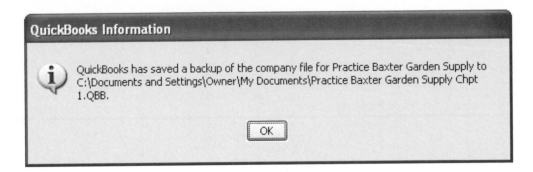

Figure: C:9

❖ *Restore Step 1*

Note: You cannot restore previous work unless you have created a backup file; however, you can always return to using the original data files downloaded from the textbook's Website.

Note: Restoring a backup file overwrites all existing data. Therefore, you should backup existing data using a unique filename before restoring a backup file.

Open the company to be restored by selecting *File>>Open or Restore Company* on the main menu. *(Note: You can actually open any company file.)* Choose the option illustrated in Figure: C:10 and click **Next**.

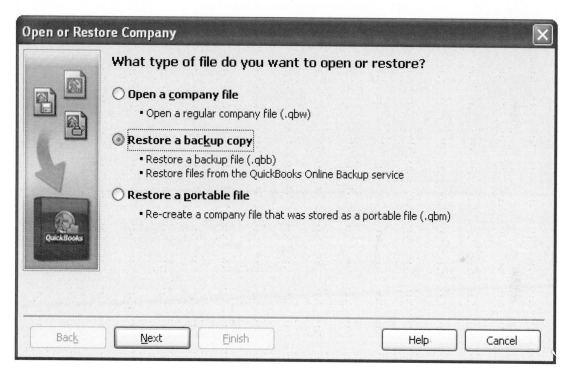

Figure: C:10

❖ *Restore Step 2*

Select **Local backup** and click **Next** (Figure: C:11).

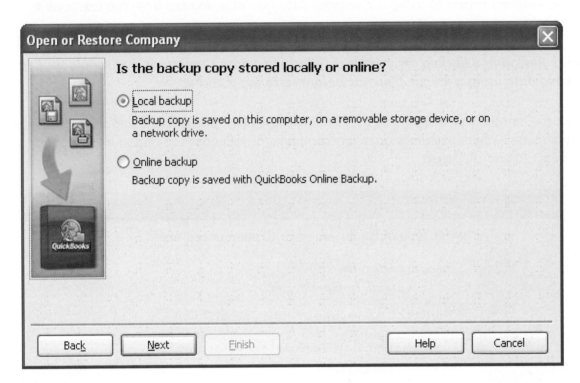

Figure: C:11

❖ *Restore Step 3*

Highlight the backup file name and click **Open** (Figure: C:12).

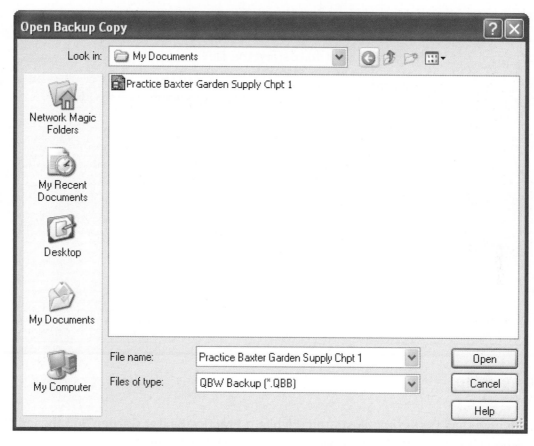

Figure: C:12

❖ *Restore Step 4*

On the window illustrated in Figure: C:13 click **Next**.

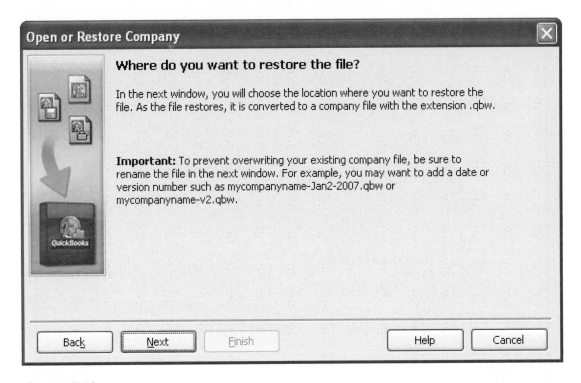

Figure: C:13

In the window that opens (not illustrated) highlight **Practice Baxter Garden Supply** and click **Save**. When QBP warns that the file already exists, click **Yes** to replace it.

The company closes and opens a confirmation screen to delete existing data by restoring data from the backup file (Figure: C:14). Type "YES" in all caps and click **OK**.

Figure: C:14

Click **OK** when QBP prompts and the company reopens.

Creating Portable Backup Files and Restoring These Files

If you're using a USB or CD drive, you may need to create a portable backup file of your company. Portable backup files are small enough to fit on a removable storage device because they store only financial data, not related files like templates. The following provides the steps for creating and restoring a portable backup file.

Be aware that portable backups do not fully protect company data so you should still create regular backup files.

❖ *Portable Backup Step 1*

Select *File>>Save Copy or Backup* on the main menu or click the **Backup** icon on the toolbar to open the window in Figure: C:15. Select the option shown and click **Next**.

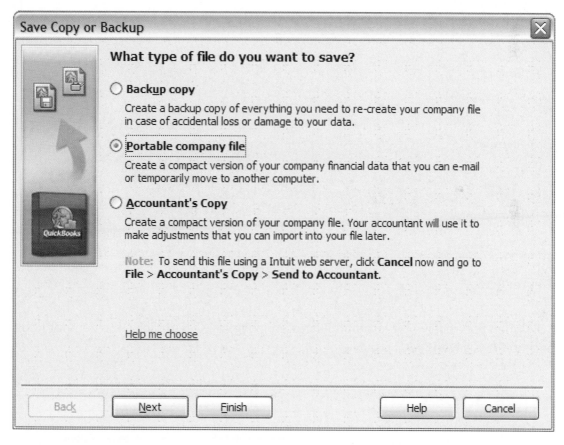

Figure: C:15

❖ **_Portable Backup Step 2_**

Set the path for storing the backup file by using the **Save in** dropdown list, enter a name for the backup file, and click **Save** (Figure: C:16). *Note that QBP assigns QBM as the file extension for a portable backup file.*

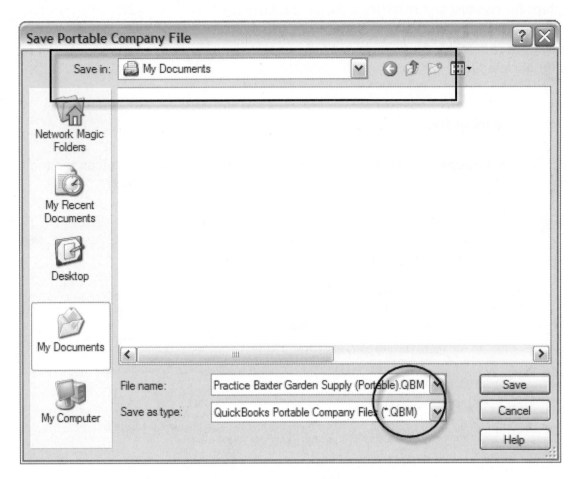

Figure: C:16

Click **OK** when you receive the prompt illustrated in Figure: C:17. Click **OK** when notified that the backup file is saved.

Figure: C:17

❖ *Restore Portable Backup Step 1*

Open Practice Baxter Garden Supply and select *File>>Open or Restore Company* on the main menu. Select the option illustrated in Figure: C:18 and click **Next**.

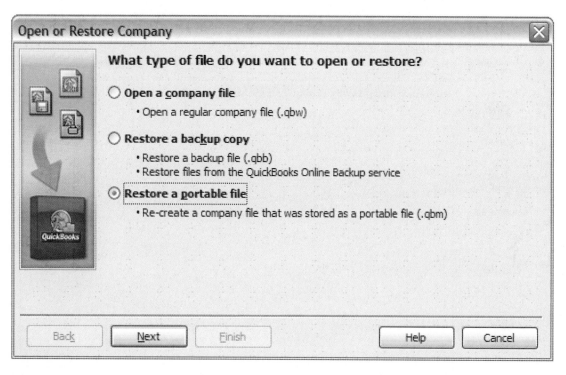

Figure: C:18

❖ *Restore Portable Backup Step 2*

In the window illustrated in Figure: C:19, highlight the backup file and click **Open**. *(Note: The file name must have a QBM extension.)*

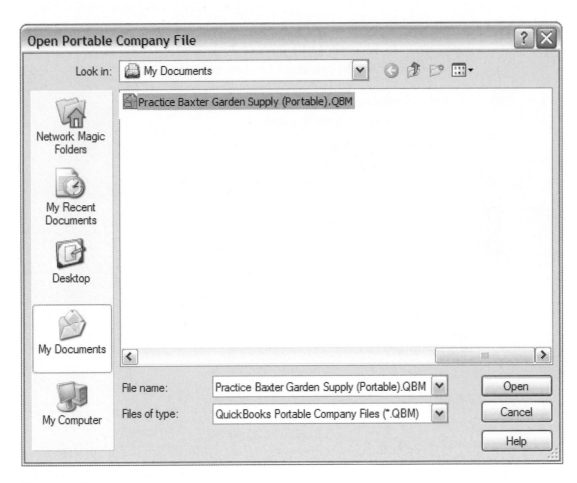

Figure: C:19

❖ *__Restore Portable Backup Step 3__*

In the window illustrated in Figure: C:20, click **Next**.

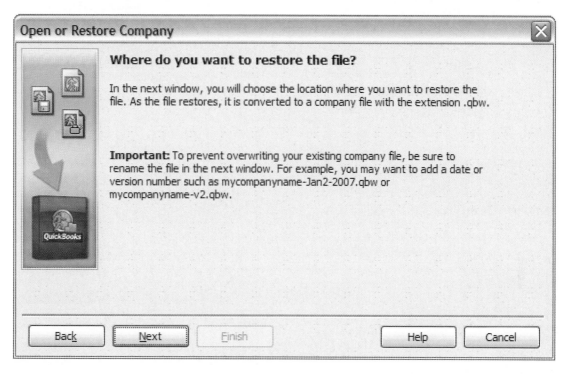

Figure: C:20

❖ *__Restore Portable Backup Step 4__*

In the window that opens (Figure: C:21), use the **Save in** dropdown list to set the path of
C:\Documents and Settings\All Users\Shared Documents\Intuit\QuickBooks\Company Files.

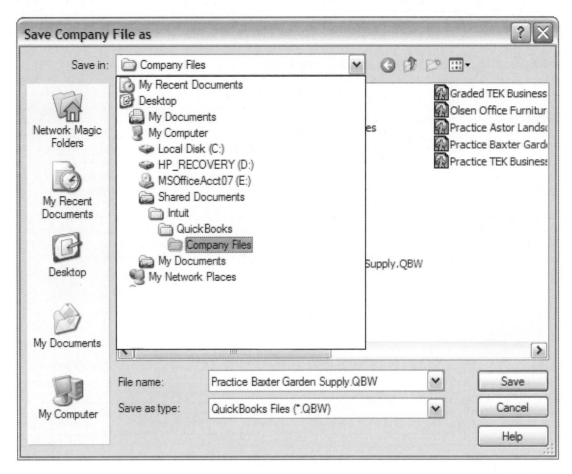

Figure: C:21

Highlight **Practice Baxter Garden Supply.QBW** and click **Save**. When QBP warns that the file already exists, click **Yes** to replace it.

The company closes and QBP opens the window in Figure: C:22. Type **YES** in all caps and then click **OK**.

Figure: C:22

Moving Data Between Home and School

You can use the regular backup and restore procedures or the portable backup and restore procedures to move your data files between home and school by following the next steps.

1. On the current machine, open each company to be moved and follow the steps for creating a regular backup or portable backup file. Remember to set the path for saving the file to your USB or CD drive.

2. On the second machine, follow the steps for restoring a regular backup file or a portable backup file. Open the file from your USB or CD drive and restore it to the second machine, making sure to select the correct the company name that you are restoring.

APPENDIX D   IRS CIRCULAR E TAX TABLES

The IRS tax tables used in the text begin on the next page. These tables are from the IRS's Circular E publication for 2008 because the 2009 tables were not available at the time of publishing the text.

SINGLE Persons—BIWEEKLY Payroll Period
(For Wages Paid in 2008)

If the wages are—		And the number of withholding allowances claimed is—										
At least	But less than	0	1	2	3	4	5	6	7	8	9	10
		The amount of income tax to be withheld is—										
$0	$105	$0	$0	$0	$0	$0	$0	$0	$0	$0	$0	$0
105	110	1	0	0	0	0	0	0	0	0	0	0
110	115	1	0	0	0	0	0	0	0	0	0	0
115	120	2	0	0	0	0	0	0	0	0	0	0
120	125	2	0	0	0	0	0	0	0	0	0	0
125	130	3	0	0	0	0	0	0	0	0	0	0
130	135	3	0	0	0	0	0	0	0	0	0	0
135	140	4	0	0	0	0	0	0	0	0	0	0
140	145	4	0	0	0	0	0	0	0	0	0	0
145	150	5	0	0	0	0	0	0	0	0	0	0
150	155	5	0	0	0	0	0	0	0	0	0	0
155	160	6	0	0	0	0	0	0	0	0	0	0
160	165	6	0	0	0	0	0	0	0	0	0	0
165	170	7	0	0	0	0	0	0	0	0	0	0
170	175	7	0	0	0	0	0	0	0	0	0	0
175	180	8	0	0	0	0	0	0	0	0	0	0
180	185	8	0	0	0	0	0	0	0	0	0	0
185	190	9	0	0	0	0	0	0	0	0	0	0
190	195	9	0	0	0	0	0	0	0	0	0	0
195	200	10	0	0	0	0	0	0	0	0	0	0
200	205	10	0	0	0	0	0	0	0	0	0	0
205	210	11	0	0	0	0	0	0	0	0	0	0
210	215	11	0	0	0	0	0	0	0	0	0	0
215	220	12	0	0	0	0	0	0	0	0	0	0
220	225	12	0	0	0	0	0	0	0	0	0	0
225	230	13	0	0	0	0	0	0	0	0	0	0
230	235	13	0	0	0	0	0	0	0	0	0	0
235	240	14	0	0	0	0	0	0	0	0	0	0
240	245	14	1	0	0	0	0	0	0	0	0	0
245	250	15	1	0	0	0	0	0	0	0	0	0
250	260	15	2	0	0	0	0	0	0	0	0	0
260	270	16	3	0	0	0	0	0	0	0	0	0
270	280	17	4	0	0	0	0	0	0	0	0	0
280	290	18	5	0	0	0	0	0	0	0	0	0
290	300	19	6	0	0	0	0	0	0	0	0	0
300	310	20	7	0	0	0	0	0	0	0	0	0
310	320	21	8	0	0	0	0	0	0	0	0	0
320	330	22	9	0	0	0	0	0	0	0	0	0
330	340	23	10	0	0	0	0	0	0	0	0	0
340	350	24	11	0	0	0	0	0	0	0	0	0
350	360	25	12	0	0	0	0	0	0	0	0	0
360	370	26	13	0	0	0	0	0	0	0	0	0
370	380	27	14	0	0	0	0	0	0	0	0	0
380	390	28	15	1	0	0	0	0	0	0	0	0
390	400	29	16	2	0	0	0	0	0	0	0	0
400	410	31	17	3	0	0	0	0	0	0	0	0
410	420	32	18	4	0	0	0	0	0	0	0	0
420	430	34	19	5	0	0	0	0	0	0	0	0
430	440	35	20	6	0	0	0	0	0	0	0	0
440	450	37	21	7	0	0	0	0	0	0	0	0
450	460	38	22	8	0	0	0	0	0	0	0	0
460	470	40	23	9	0	0	0	0	0	0	0	0
470	480	41	24	10	0	0	0	0	0	0	0	0
480	490	43	25	11	0	0	0	0	0	0	0	0
490	500	44	26	12	0	0	0	0	0	0	0	0
500	520	47	27	14	0	0	0	0	0	0	0	0
520	540	50	29	16	2	0	0	0	0	0	0	0
540	560	53	32	18	4	0	0	0	0	0	0	0
560	580	56	35	20	6	0	0	0	0	0	0	0
580	600	59	38	22	8	0	0	0	0	0	0	0
600	620	62	41	24	10	0	0	0	0	0	0	0
620	640	65	44	26	12	0	0	0	0	0	0	0
640	660	68	47	28	14	1	0	0	0	0	0	0
660	680	71	50	30	16	3	0	0	0	0	0	0
680	700	74	53	33	18	5	0	0	0	0	0	0
700	720	77	56	36	20	7	0	0	0	0	0	0
720	740	80	59	39	22	9	0	0	0	0	0	0
740	760	83	62	42	24	11	0	0	0	0	0	0
760	780	86	65	45	26	13	0	0	0	0	0	0
780	800	89	68	48	28	15	2	0	0	0	0	0

SINGLE Persons—BIWEEKLY Payroll Period
(For Wages Paid in 2008)

At least	But less than	0	1	2	3	4	5	6	7	8	9	10
$800	$820	$92	$71	$51	$31	$17	$4	$0	$0	$0	$0	$0
820	840	95	74	54	34	19	6	0	0	0	0	0
840	860	98	77	57	37	21	8	0	0	0	0	0
860	880	101	80	60	40	23	10	0	0	0	0	0
880	900	104	83	63	43	25	12	0	0	0	0	0
900	920	107	86	66	46	27	14	0	0	0	0	0
920	940	110	89	69	49	29	16	2	0	0	0	0
940	960	113	92	72	52	32	18	4	0	0	0	0
960	980	116	95	75	55	35	20	6	0	0	0	0
980	1,000	119	98	78	58	38	22	8	0	0	0	0
1,000	1,020	122	101	81	61	41	24	10	0	0	0	0
1,020	1,040	125	104	84	64	44	26	12	0	0	0	0
1,040	1,060	128	107	87	67	47	28	14	1	0	0	0
1,060	1,080	131	110	90	70	50	30	16	3	0	0	0
1,080	1,100	134	113	93	73	53	33	18	5	0	0	0
1,100	1,120	137	116	96	76	56	36	20	7	0	0	0
1,120	1,140	140	119	99	79	59	39	22	9	0	0	0
1,140	1,160	143	122	102	82	62	42	24	11	0	0	0
1,160	1,180	146	125	105	85	65	45	26	13	0	0	0
1,180	1,200	149	128	108	88	68	48	28	15	1	0	0
1,200	1,220	152	131	111	91	71	51	30	17	3	0	0
1,220	1,240	155	134	114	94	74	54	33	19	5	0	0
1,240	1,260	158	137	117	97	77	57	36	21	7	0	0
1,260	1,280	161	140	120	100	80	60	39	23	9	0	0
1,280	1,300	164	143	123	103	83	63	42	25	11	0	0
1,300	1,320	167	146	126	106	86	66	45	27	13	0	0
1,320	1,340	172	149	129	109	89	69	48	29	15	2	0
1,340	1,360	177	152	132	112	92	72	51	31	17	4	0
1,360	1,380	182	155	135	115	95	75	54	34	19	6	0
1,380	1,400	187	158	138	118	98	78	57	37	21	8	0
1,400	1,420	192	161	141	121	101	81	60	40	23	10	0
1,420	1,440	197	164	144	124	104	84	63	43	25	12	0
1,440	1,460	202	168	147	127	107	87	66	46	27	14	0
1,460	1,480	207	173	150	130	110	90	69	49	29	16	2
1,480	1,500	212	178	153	133	113	93	72	52	32	18	4
1,500	1,520	217	183	156	136	116	96	75	55	35	20	6
1,520	1,540	222	188	159	139	119	99	78	58	38	22	8
1,540	1,560	227	193	162	142	122	102	81	61	41	24	10
1,560	1,580	232	198	165	145	125	105	84	64	44	26	12
1,580	1,600	237	203	170	148	128	108	87	67	47	28	14
1,600	1,620	242	208	175	151	131	111	90	70	50	30	16
1,620	1,640	247	213	180	154	134	114	93	73	53	33	18
1,640	1,660	252	218	185	157	137	117	96	76	56	36	20
1,660	1,680	257	223	190	160	140	120	99	79	59	39	22
1,680	1,700	262	228	195	163	143	123	102	82	62	42	24
1,700	1,720	267	233	200	166	146	126	105	85	65	45	26
1,720	1,740	272	238	205	171	149	129	108	88	68	48	28
1,740	1,760	277	243	210	176	152	132	111	91	71	51	31
1,760	1,780	282	248	215	181	155	135	114	94	74	54	34
1,780	1,800	287	253	220	186	158	138	117	97	77	57	37
1,800	1,820	292	258	225	191	161	141	120	100	80	60	40
1,820	1,840	297	263	230	196	164	144	123	103	83	63	43
1,840	1,860	302	268	235	201	167	147	126	106	86	66	46
1,860	1,880	307	273	240	206	172	150	129	109	89	69	49
1,880	1,900	312	278	245	211	177	153	132	112	92	72	52
1,900	1,920	317	283	250	216	182	156	135	115	95	75	55
1,920	1,940	322	288	255	221	187	159	138	118	98	78	58
1,940	1,960	327	293	260	226	192	162	141	121	101	81	61
1,960	1,980	332	298	265	231	197	165	144	124	104	84	64
1,980	2,000	337	303	270	236	202	169	147	127	107	87	67
2,000	2,020	342	308	275	241	207	174	150	130	110	90	70
2,020	2,040	347	313	280	246	212	179	153	133	113	93	73
2,040	2,060	352	318	285	251	217	184	156	136	116	96	76
2,060	2,080	357	323	290	256	222	189	159	139	119	99	79
2,080	2,100	362	328	295	261	227	194	162	142	122	102	82

$2,100 and over   Use Table 2(a) for a **SINGLE person** on page 38. Also see the instructions on page 36.

MARRIED Persons—BIWEEKLY Payroll Period
(For Wages Paid in 2008)

If the wages are—		And the number of withholding allowances claimed is—										
At least	But less than	0	1	2	3	4	5	6	7	8	9	10
		The amount of income tax to be withheld is—										
$0	$250	$0	$0	$0	$0	$0	$0	$0	$0	$0	$0	$0
250	260	0	0	0	0	0	0	0	0	0	0	0
260	270	0	0	0	0	0	0	0	0	0	0	0
270	280	0	0	0	0	0	0	0	0	0	0	0
280	290	0	0	0	0	0	0	0	0	0	0	0
290	300	0	0	0	0	0	0	0	0	0	0	0
300	310	0	0	0	0	0	0	0	0	0	0	0
310	320	1	0	0	0	0	0	0	0	0	0	0
320	330	2	0	0	0	0	0	0	0	0	0	0
330	340	3	0	0	0	0	0	0	0	0	0	0
340	350	4	0	0	0	0	0	0	0	0	0	0
350	360	5	0	0	0	0	0	0	0	0	0	0
360	370	6	0	0	0	0	0	0	0	0	0	0
370	380	7	0	0	0	0	0	0	0	0	0	0
380	390	8	0	0	0	0	0	0	0	0	0	0
390	400	9	0	0	0	0	0	0	0	0	0	0
400	410	10	0	0	0	0	0	0	0	0	0	0
410	420	11	0	0	0	0	0	0	0	0	0	0
420	430	12	0	0	0	0	0	0	0	0	0	0
430	440	13	0	0	0	0	0	0	0	0	0	0
440	450	14	0	0	0	0	0	0	0	0	0	0
450	460	15	1	0	0	0	0	0	0	0	0	0
460	470	16	2	0	0	0	0	0	0	0	0	0
470	480	17	3	0	0	0	0	0	0	0	0	0
480	490	18	4	0	0	0	0	0	0	0	0	0
490	500	19	5	0	0	0	0	0	0	0	0	0
500	520	20	7	0	0	0	0	0	0	0	0	0
520	540	22	9	0	0	0	0	0	0	0	0	0
540	560	24	11	0	0	0	0	0	0	0	0	0
560	580	26	13	0	0	0	0	0	0	0	0	0
580	600	28	15	1	0	0	0	0	0	0	0	0
600	620	30	17	3	0	0	0	0	0	0	0	0
620	640	32	19	5	0	0	0	0	0	0	0	0
640	660	34	21	7	0	0	0	0	0	0	0	0
660	680	36	23	9	0	0	0	0	0	0	0	0
680	700	38	25	11	0	0	0	0	0	0	0	0
700	720	40	27	13	0	0	0	0	0	0	0	0
720	740	42	29	15	2	0	0	0	0	0	0	0
740	760	44	31	17	4	0	0	0	0	0	0	0
760	780	46	33	19	6	0	0	0	0	0	0	0
780	800	48	35	21	8	0	0	0	0	0	0	0
800	820	50	37	23	10	0	0	0	0	0	0	0
820	840	52	39	25	12	0	0	0	0	0	0	0
840	860	54	41	27	14	0	0	0	0	0	0	0
860	880	56	43	29	16	2	0	0	0	0	0	0
880	900	58	45	31	18	4	0	0	0	0	0	0
900	920	60	47	33	20	6	0	0	0	0	0	0
920	940	63	49	35	22	8	0	0	0	0	0	0
940	960	66	51	37	24	10	0	0	0	0	0	0
960	980	69	53	39	26	12	0	0	0	0	0	0
980	1,000	72	55	41	28	14	1	0	0	0	0	0
1,000	1,020	75	57	43	30	16	3	0	0	0	0	0
1,020	1,040	78	59	45	32	18	5	0	0	0	0	0
1,040	1,060	81	61	47	34	20	7	0	0	0	0	0
1,060	1,080	84	64	49	36	22	9	0	0	0	0	0
1,080	1,100	87	67	51	38	24	11	0	0	0	0	0
1,100	1,120	90	70	53	40	26	13	0	0	0	0	0
1,120	1,140	93	73	55	42	28	15	1	0	0	0	0
1,140	1,160	96	76	57	44	30	17	3	0	0	0	0
1,160	1,180	99	79	59	46	32	19	5	0	0	0	0
1,180	1,200	102	82	62	48	34	21	7	0	0	0	0
1,200	1,220	105	85	65	50	36	23	9	0	0	0	0
1,220	1,240	108	88	68	52	38	25	11	0	0	0	0
1,240	1,260	111	91	71	54	40	27	13	0	0	0	0
1,260	1,280	114	94	74	56	42	29	15	2	0	0	0
1,280	1,300	117	97	77	58	44	31	17	4	0	0	0
1,300	1,320	120	100	80	60	46	33	19	6	0	0	0
1,320	1,340	123	103	83	63	48	35	21	8	0	0	0
1,340	1,360	126	106	86	66	50	37	23	10	0	0	0
1,360	1,380	129	109	89	69	52	39	25	12	0	0	0

MARRIED Persons—BIWEEKLY Payroll Period
(For Wages Paid in 2008)

If the wages are—		And the number of withholding allowances claimed is—										
At least	But less than	0	1	2	3	4	5	6	7	8	9	10
		The amount of income tax to be withheld is—										
$1,380	$1,400	$132	$112	$92	$72	$54	$41	$27	$14	$1	$0	$0
1,400	1,420	135	115	95	75	56	43	29	16	3	0	0
1,420	1,440	138	118	98	78	58	45	31	18	5	0	0
1,440	1,460	141	121	101	81	61	47	33	20	7	0	0
1,460	1,480	144	124	104	84	64	49	35	22	9	0	0
1,480	1,500	147	127	107	87	67	51	37	24	11	0	0
1,500	1,520	150	130	110	90	70	53	39	26	13	0	0
1,520	1,540	153	133	113	93	73	55	41	28	15	1	0
1,540	1,560	156	136	116	96	76	57	43	30	17	3	0
1,560	1,580	159	139	119	99	79	59	45	32	19	5	0
1,580	1,600	162	142	122	102	82	61	47	34	21	7	0
1,600	1,620	165	145	125	105	85	64	49	36	23	9	0
1,620	1,640	168	148	128	108	88	67	51	38	25	11	0
1,640	1,660	171	151	131	111	91	70	53	40	27	13	0
1,660	1,680	174	154	134	114	94	73	55	42	29	15	2
1,680	1,700	177	157	137	117	97	76	57	44	31	17	4
1,700	1,720	180	160	140	120	100	79	59	46	33	19	6
1,720	1,740	183	163	143	123	103	82	62	48	35	21	8
1,740	1,760	186	166	146	126	106	85	65	50	37	23	10
1,760	1,780	189	169	149	129	109	88	68	52	39	25	12
1,780	1,800	192	172	152	132	112	91	71	54	41	27	14
1,800	1,820	195	175	155	135	115	94	74	56	43	29	16
1,820	1,840	198	178	158	138	118	97	77	58	45	31	18
1,840	1,860	201	181	161	141	121	100	80	60	47	33	20
1,860	1,880	204	184	164	144	124	103	83	63	49	35	22
1,880	1,900	207	187	167	147	127	106	86	66	51	37	24
1,900	1,920	210	190	170	150	130	109	89	69	53	39	26
1,920	1,940	213	193	173	153	133	112	92	72	55	41	28
1,940	1,960	216	196	176	156	136	115	95	75	57	43	30
1,960	1,980	219	199	179	159	139	118	98	78	59	45	32
1,980	2,000	222	202	182	162	142	121	101	81	61	47	34
2,000	2,020	225	205	185	165	145	124	104	84	64	49	36
2,020	2,040	228	208	188	168	148	127	107	87	67	51	38
2,040	2,060	231	211	191	171	151	130	110	90	70	53	40
2,060	2,080	234	214	194	174	154	133	113	93	73	55	42
2,080	2,100	237	217	197	177	157	136	116	96	76	57	44
2,100	2,120	240	220	200	180	160	139	119	99	79	59	46
2,120	2,140	243	223	203	183	163	142	122	102	82	62	48
2,140	2,160	246	226	206	186	166	145	125	105	85	65	50
2,160	2,180	249	229	209	189	169	148	128	108	88	68	52
2,180	2,200	252	232	212	192	172	151	131	111	91	71	54
2,200	2,220	255	235	215	195	175	154	134	114	94	74	56
2,220	2,240	258	238	218	198	178	157	137	117	97	77	58
2,240	2,260	261	241	221	201	181	160	140	120	100	80	60
2,260	2,280	264	244	224	204	184	163	143	123	103	83	63
2,280	2,300	267	247	227	207	187	166	146	126	106	86	66
2,300	2,320	270	250	230	210	190	169	149	129	109	89	69
2,320	2,340	273	253	233	213	193	172	152	132	112	92	72
2,340	2,360	276	256	236	216	196	175	155	135	115	95	75
2,360	2,380	279	259	239	219	199	178	158	138	118	98	78
2,380	2,400	282	262	242	222	202	181	161	141	121	101	81
2,400	2,420	285	265	245	225	205	184	164	144	124	104	84
2,420	2,440	288	268	248	228	208	187	167	147	127	107	87
2,440	2,460	291	271	251	231	211	190	170	150	130	110	90
2,460	2,480	294	274	254	234	214	193	173	153	133	113	93
2,480	2,500	297	277	257	237	217	196	176	156	136	116	96
2,500	2,520	300	280	260	240	220	199	179	159	139	119	99
2,520	2,540	303	283	263	243	223	202	182	162	142	122	102
2,540	2,560	306	286	266	246	226	205	185	165	145	125	105
2,560	2,580	309	289	269	249	229	208	188	168	148	128	108
2,580	2,600	312	292	272	252	232	211	191	171	151	131	111
2,600	2,620	315	295	275	255	235	214	194	174	154	134	114
2,620	2,640	318	298	278	258	238	217	197	177	157	137	117
2,640	2,660	321	301	281	261	241	220	200	180	160	140	120
2,660	2,680	324	304	284	264	244	223	203	183	163	143	123
2,680	2,700	327	307	287	267	247	226	206	186	166	146	126

$2,700 and over   Use Table 2(b) for a **MARRIED person** on page 38. Also see the instructions on page 36.

APPENDIX E   SOLUTIONS FOR YOU TRY EXERCISES

CHAPTER 1

No in-chapter exercises presented.

CHAPTER 2

The Chart of Accounts reports for sample companies are not illustrated.

CHAPTER 3

RECORD TEK'S JANUARY TRANSACTIONS

Journal report listing January transactions.

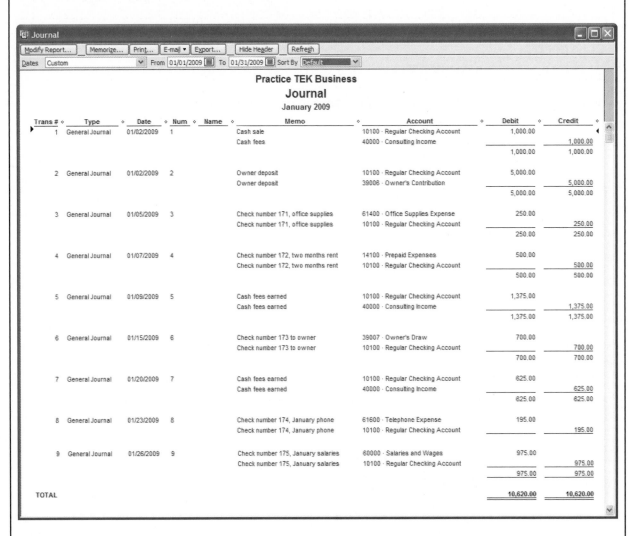

Figure: E:1

RECORD ADDITIONAL JOURNAL ENTRIES

Journal report filtered for dates specified.

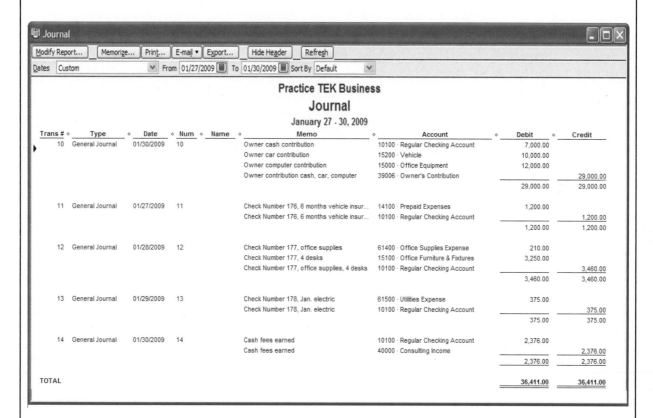

Figure: E:2

RECORD JANUARY ADJUSTING ENTRIES

Journal report for January 31, 2009.

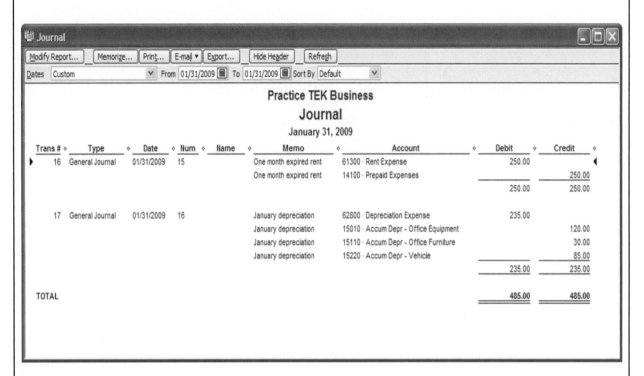

Figure: E:3

CHAPTER 4

 CREATE A NEW CUSTOMER ACCOUNT

Graphic Printing Services' Address Info tab.

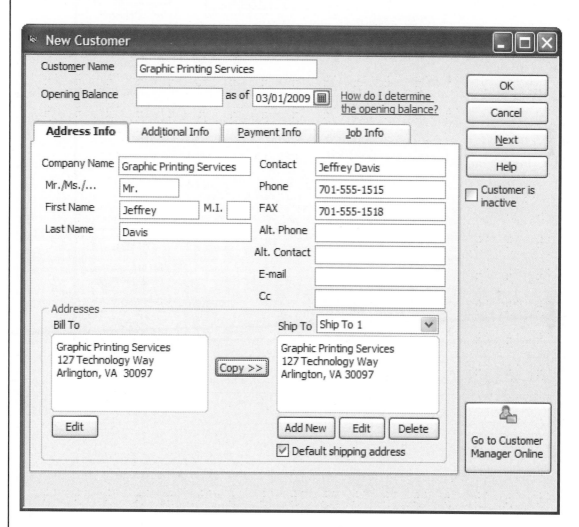

Figure: E:4

Graphic Printing Services' Additional Info tab.

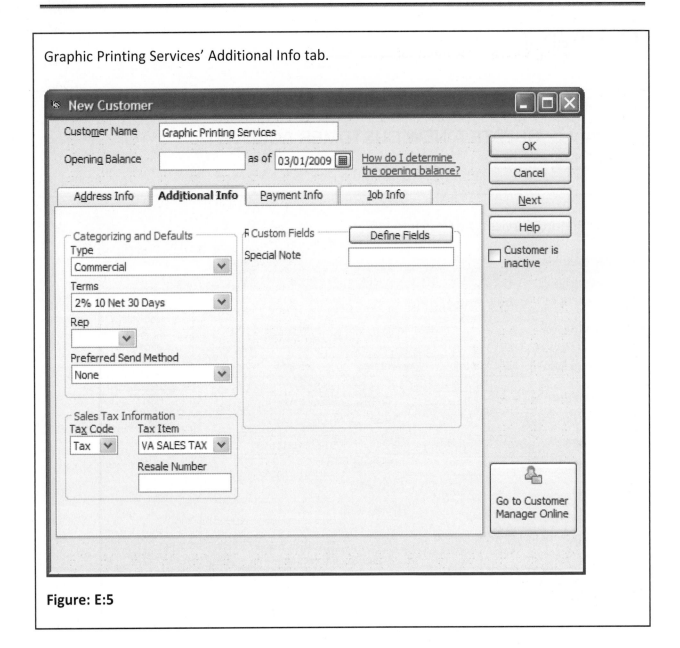

Figure: E:5

Graphic Printing Services' Payment Info tab.

Figure: E:6

Graphic Printing Services' Job Info tab.

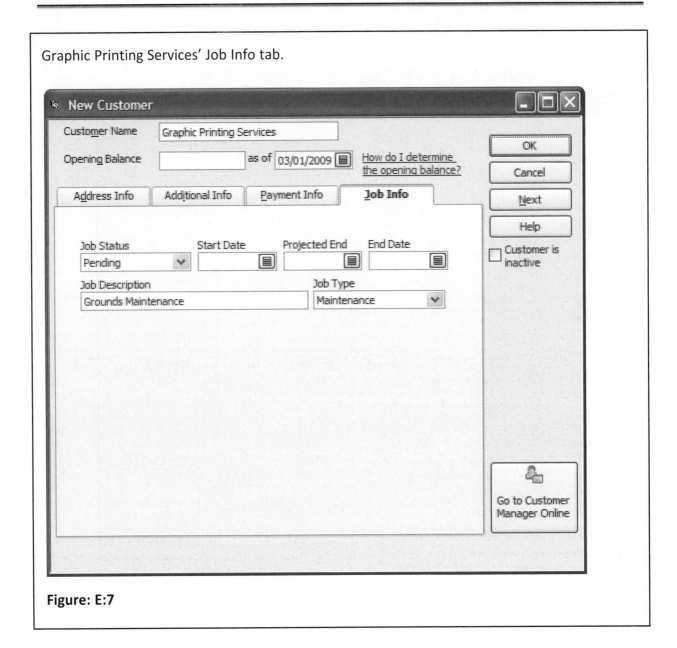

Figure: E:7

INVOICE A CUSTOMER FOR JOB COSTS

Time ticket selected for invoicing.

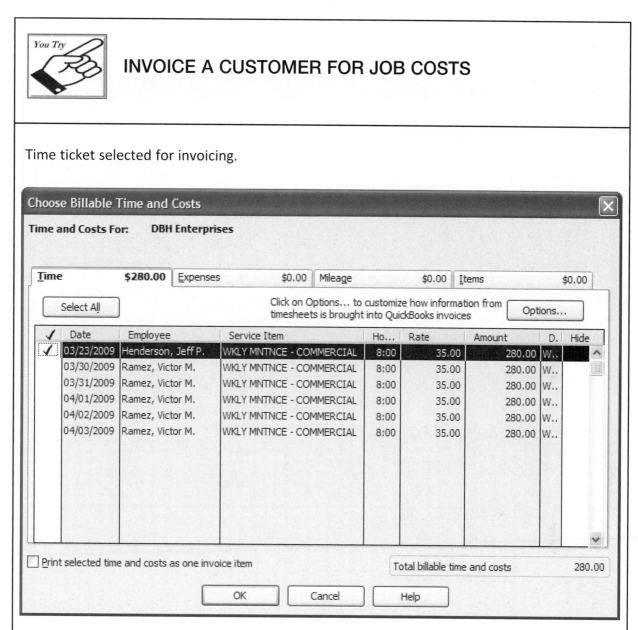

Figure: E:8

Invoice created.

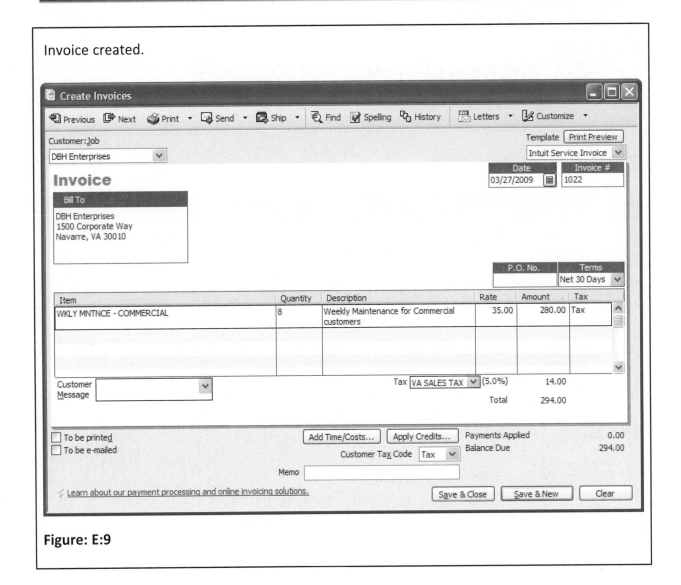

Figure: E:9

CREATE A JOB REPORT

Time by Job Summary report.

Practice Astor Landscaping
Time by Job Summary
March 2009

	Unbilled	Mar 09
Ashford Hill Apartments		
WKLY MNTNCE - COMMERCIAL	▶ 56:00	◀ 104:00
Total Ashford Hill Apartments	56:00	104:00
DBH Enterprises		
WKLY MNTNCE - COMMERCIAL	16:00	64:00
Total DBH Enterprises	16:00	64:00
Hutcheon, Brian		
INSTL HARD - RESIDENTIAL	0:00	68:00
INSTL LAND - RESIDENTIAL	0:00	72:00
Total Hutcheon, Brian	0:00	140:00
O'Hara Homes:Redesign Gardens		
INSTL HARD - COMMERCIAL	80:00	241:00
INSTL LAND - COMMERCIAL	32:00	54:00
Total O'Hara Homes:Redesign Gardens	112:00	295:00
Reynolds Court Subdivision		
WKLY MNTNCE - COMMERCIAL	40:00	110:00
Total Reynolds Court Subdivision	40:00	110:00
Silver Homes		
DESIGN - COMMERCIAL	0:00	12:00
INSTL HARD - COMMERCIAL	0:00	32:00
Total Silver Homes	0:00	44:00
Sugar Hill Tennis Club		
WKLY MNTNCE - COMMERCIAL	16:00	16:00
Total Sugar Hill Tennis Club	16:00	16:00
Sycamore Homes		
INSTL HARD - COMMERCIAL	0:00	80:00
Total Sycamore Homes	0:00	80:00
White and Associates		
INSTL HARD - COMMERCIAL	24:00	24:00
Total White and Associates	24:00	24:00
Zara Apartment Homes		
DESIGN - COMMERCIAL	0:00	27:00
Total Zara Apartment Homes	0:00	27:00
TOTAL	264:00	904:00

Figure: E:10

How to use: The Time by Job Summary report not only shows the amount of time spent in March working on customer jobs but it also shows the time that needs to be invoiced to customers.

RECORD CUSTOMER PAYMENTS

Ashford Hill Apartments' payment.

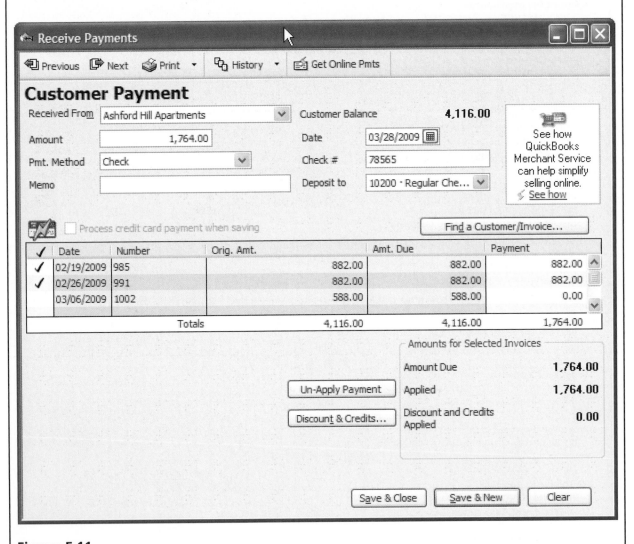

Figure: E:11

O'Hara Homes' payment.

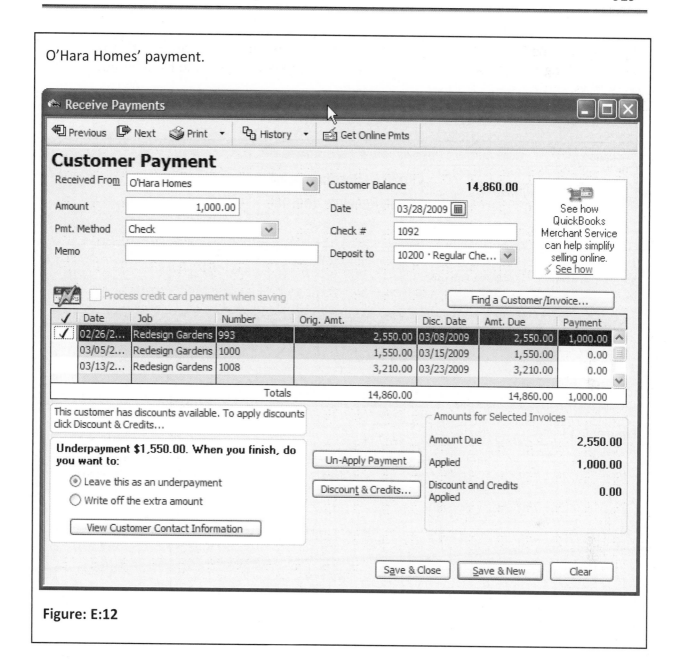

Figure: E:12

Cash Receipts Journal for March 28, 2009.

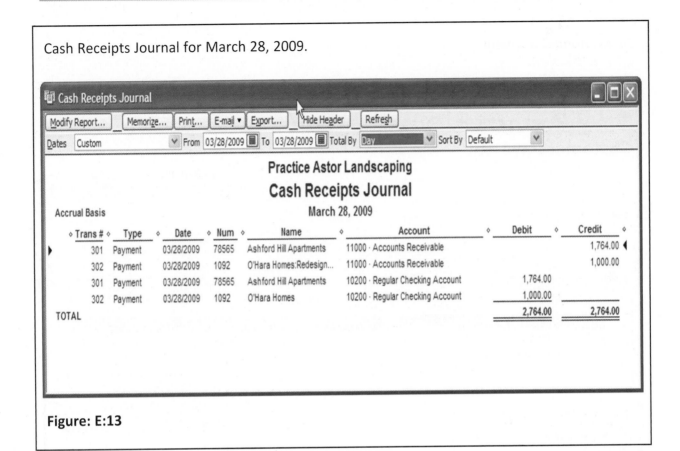

Figure: E:13

CHAPTER 5

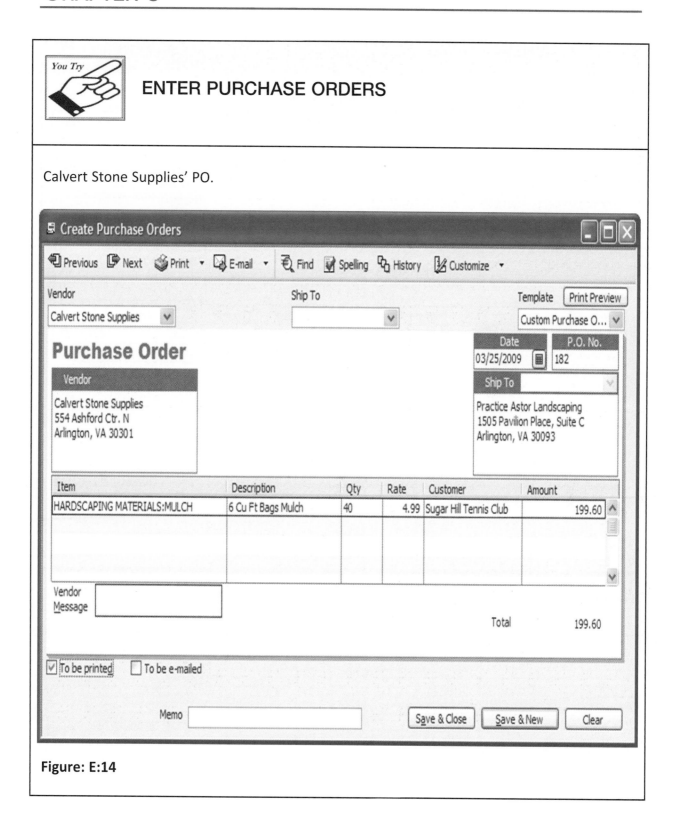

ENTER PURCHASE ORDERS

Calvert Stone Supplies' PO.

Figure: E:14

Southern Garden Wholesale's PO.

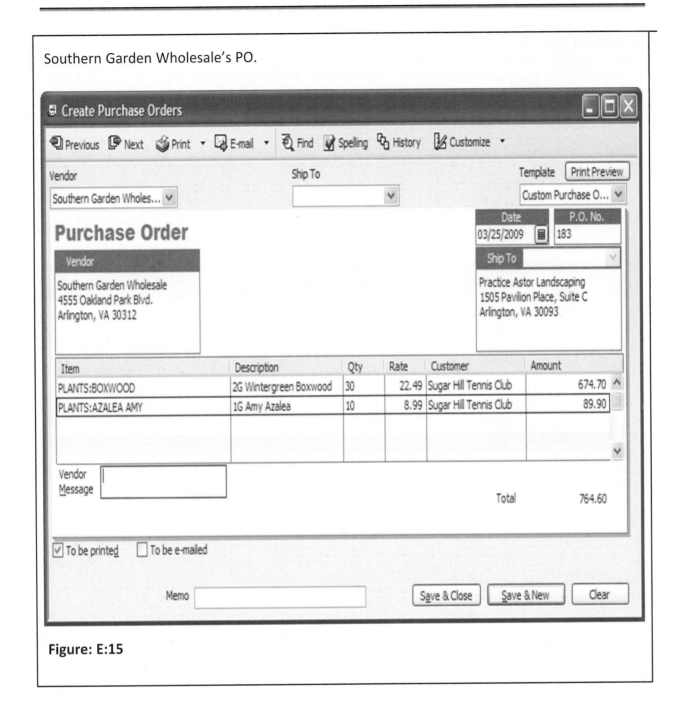

Figure: E:15

ENTER VENDOR RECEIPTS AND BILLS FOR PURCHASE ORDERS

Calvert Stone Supplies' vendor bill.

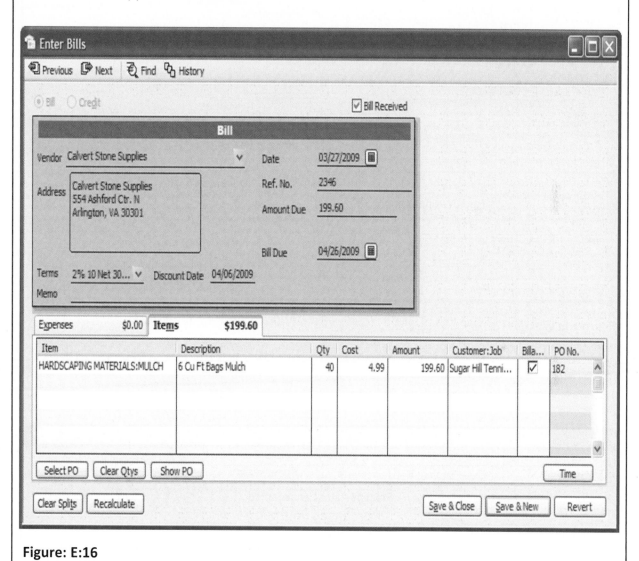

Figure: E:16

Southern Garden Wholesale's Receipt. *Note: Remove the quantity on the second line item.*

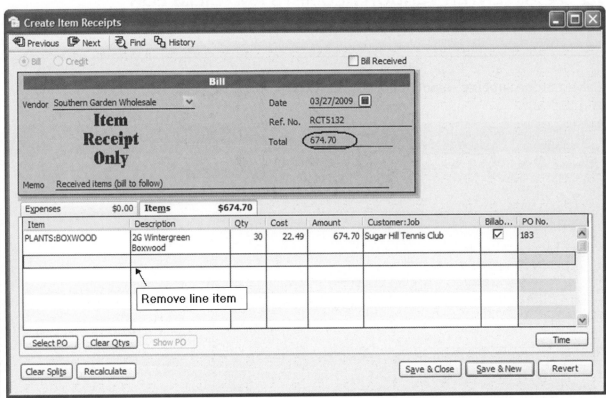

Figure: E:17

Purchases Journal.

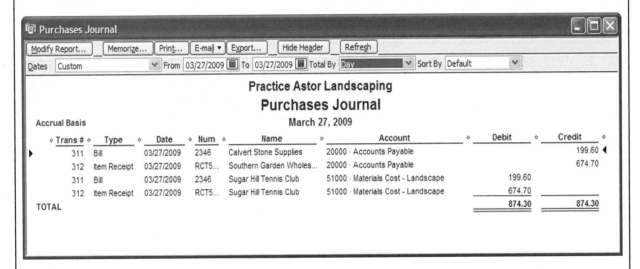

Figure: E:18

ENTER VENDOR BILL FOR VENDOR RECEIPT

Southern Garden Wholesale's bill. *Note: Click Show PO to reopen the PO and enter "1" as the Qty received.*

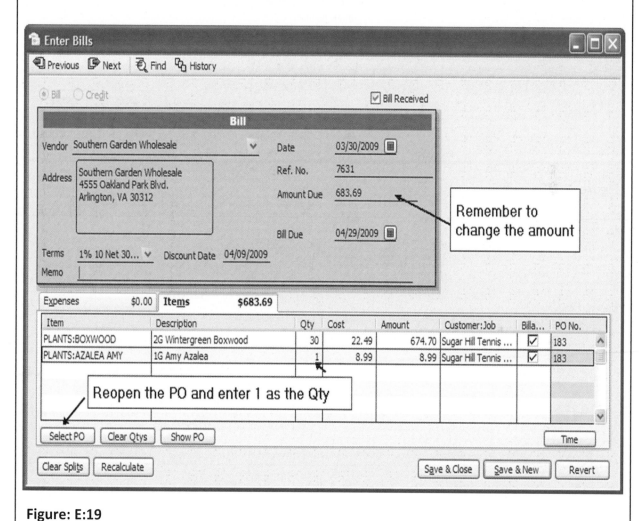

Figure: E:19

Purchases Journal.

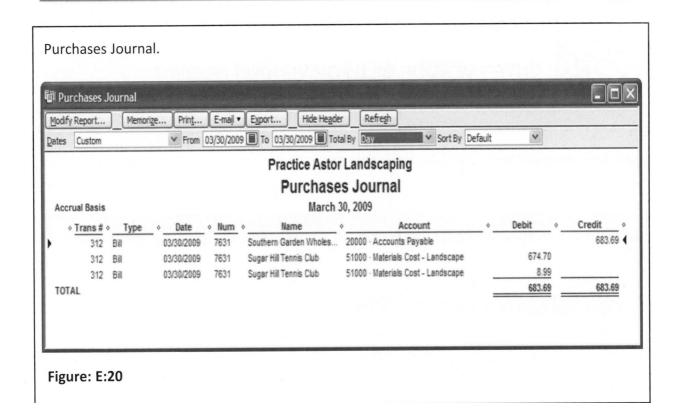

Figure: E:20

CREATE A NEW VENDOR ACCOUNT

Jackson Hyland Tax Service's Address Info information.

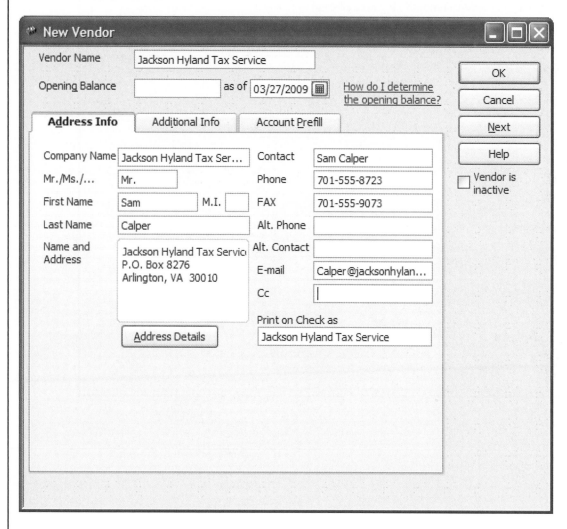

Figure: E:21

Jackson Hyland Tax Service's Additional information.

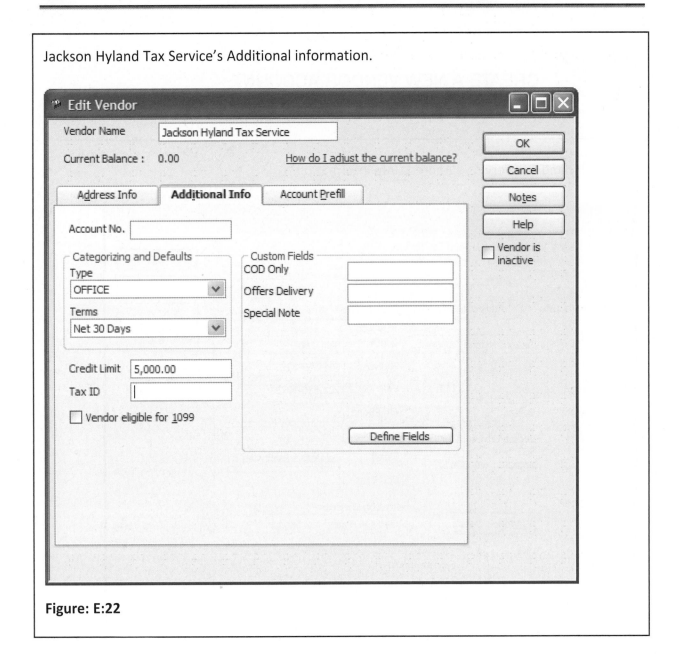

Figure: E:22

Jackson Hyland Tax Services' Account Prefill information.

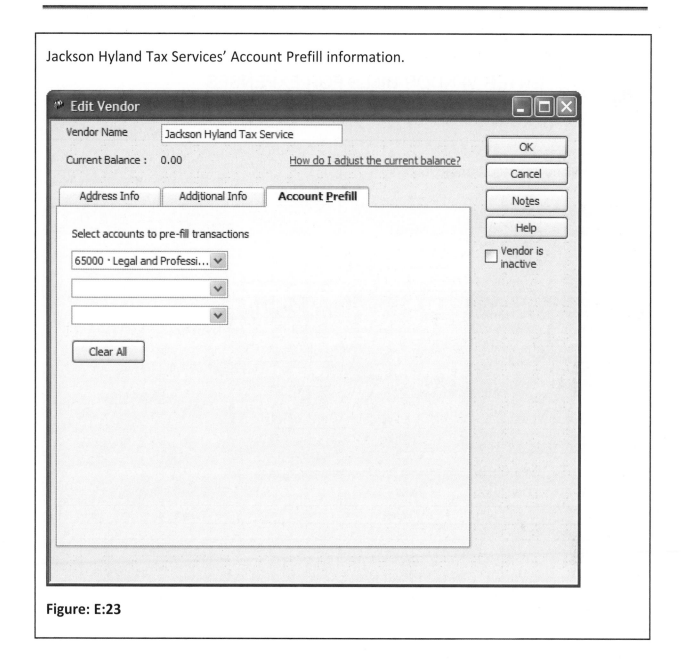

Figure: E:23

ENTER VENDOR BILLS FOR EXPENSES

Jackson Hyland's posted transaction.

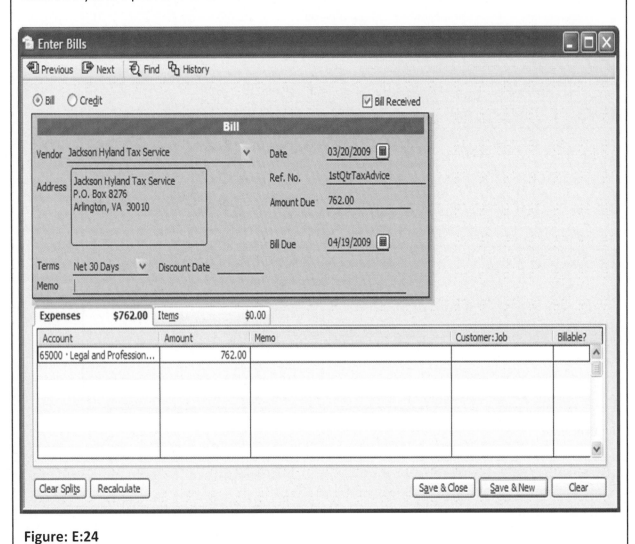

Figure: E:24

PAY VENDORS

Check Detail report for April 6, 2009.

Practice Astor Landscaping
Check Detail
April 6, 2009

Type	Num	Date	Name	Item	Account	Paid Amount	Original Amount
Bill Pmt -Check	442	04/06/2009	Anderson Whole...		10200 · Regular C...		-9.98
Bill	3807	03/12/2009	DBH Enterprises	HARDSC...	51000 · Materials C...	-9.98	9.98
TOTAL						-9.98	9.98
Bill Pmt -Check	443	04/06/2009	Calvert Stone Su...		10200 · Regular C...		-3,195.61
			Calvert Stone Sup...		20000 · Accounts ...	3.99	-3.99
Bill	901	03/17/2009	Silver Homes	HARDSC...	52000 · Materials C...	-661.66	1,032.00
			Silver Homes	HARDSC...	52000 · Materials C...	-2,218.22	3,459.80
			Silver Homes	HARDSC...	52000 · Materials C...	-120.12	187.35
Bill	2346	03/27/2009	Sugar Hill Tennis C...	HARDSC...	51000 · Materials C...	-199.60	199.60
TOTAL						-3,195.61	4,874.76
Bill Pmt -Check	444	04/06/2009	General Leasing...		10200 · Regular C...		-2,500.00
Bill	Marc...	03/03/2009			71000 · Rent Expe...	-2,500.00	2,500.00
TOTAL						-2,500.00	2,500.00
Bill Pmt -Check	445	04/06/2009	Jackson Adverti...		10200 · Regular C...		-175.00
Bill	Mont...	03/13/2009			64000 · Advertisin...	-175.00	175.00
TOTAL						-175.00	175.00
Bill Pmt -Check	446	04/06/2009	Neighbors Telep...		10200 · Regular C...		-262.43
Bill	MarT...	03/20/2009			71100 · Utilities Ex...	-262.43	262.43
TOTAL						-262.43	262.43
Bill Pmt -Check	447	04/06/2009	Southern Garde...		10200 · Regular C...		-676.85
			Southern Garden W...		20000 · Accounts ...	6.84	-6.84
Bill	7631	03/30/2009	Sugar Hill Tennis C...	PLANTS...	51000 · Materials C...	-674.70	674.70
			Sugar Hill Tennis C...	PLANTS...	51000 · Materials C...	-8.99	8.99
TOTAL						-676.85	676.85

Figure: E:25

CHAPTER 6

WORKING WITH TIMESHEETS

Roy Dillion's timesheet. Notice that hours on the first line have already been invoiced to the customer.

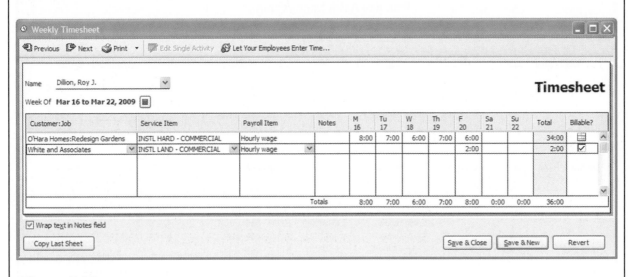

Figure: E:26

Jan Folse's timesheets for the biweekly pay period.

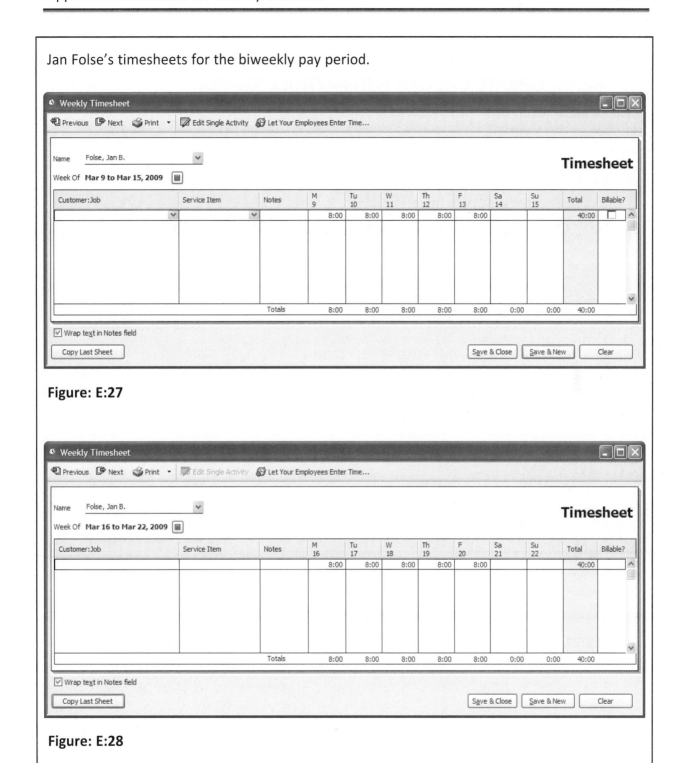

Figure: E:27

Figure: E:28

CREATE CHECKS FOR PAYROLL TAXES

Pay Liabilities window.

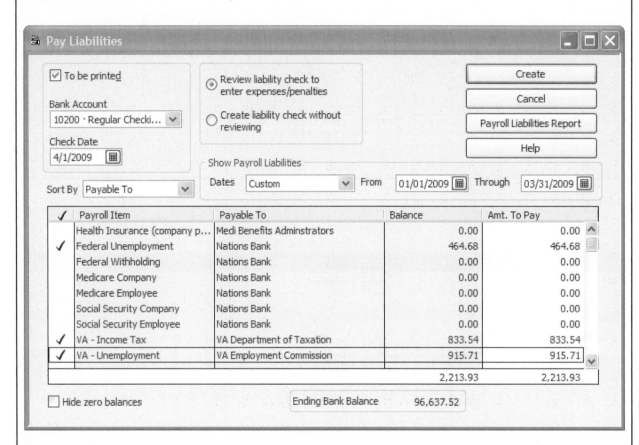

Figure: E:29

Check Detail report.

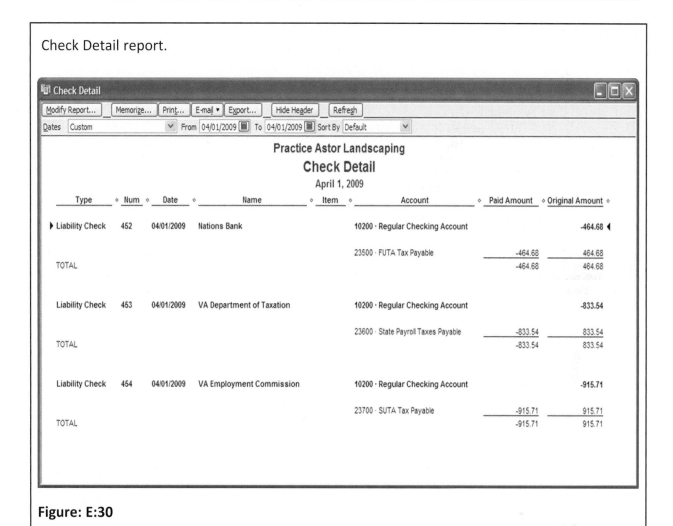

Figure: E:30

CHAPTER 7

FINISH RECORDING MARCH ADJUSTING ENTRIES

Petty Cash Check.

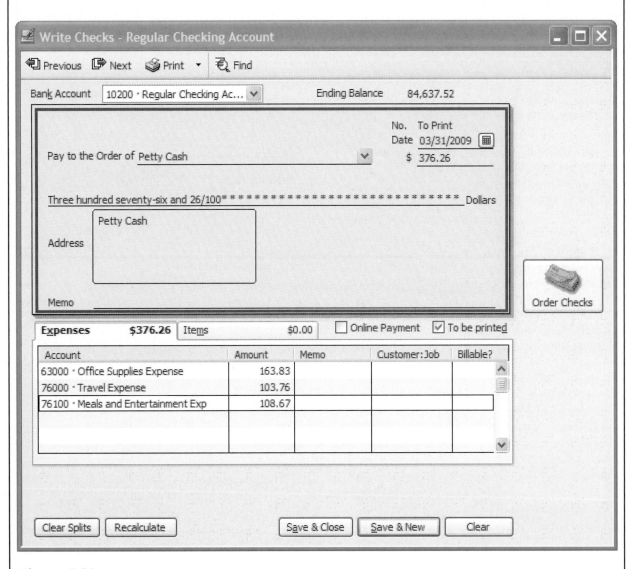

Figure: E:31

Accrued wages entry.

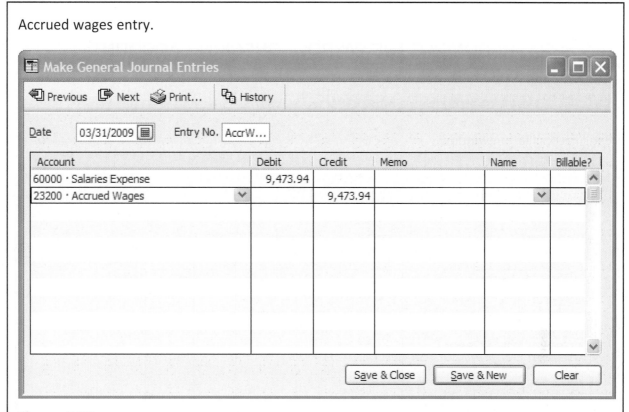

Figure: E:32

Note: In practice, you would also post a reversing entry dated 4/1/2009 to reverse this expense because the 7 days expensed in March will post again when paying wages for these days in April. In essence, the reversing entry reduces April expense for the 7 days expensed in March.

Here is an example of the reversing entry. Do not post this entry.

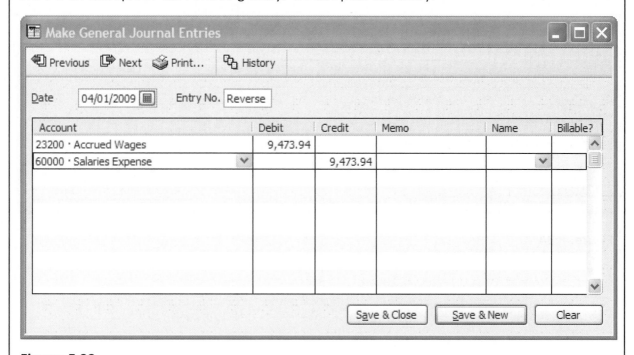

Figure: E:33

RECONCILE THE PAYROLL CHECKING ACCOUNT

Bank reconciliation window.

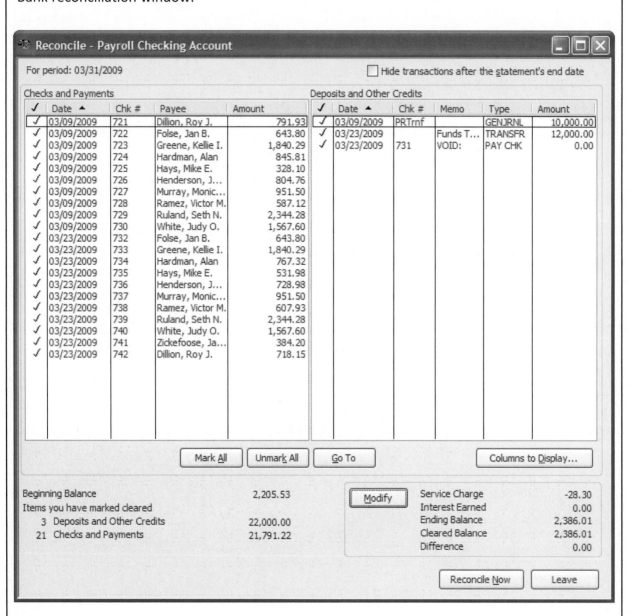

Figure: E:34

Reconciliation Detail report.

Reconciliation Detail

Modify Report... | Memorize... | Print... | E-mail ▼ | Export... | Hide Header | Refresh

Practice Astor Landscaping
Reconciliation Detail
10300 · Payroll Checking Account, Period Ending 03/31/2009

Type	Date	Num	Name	Clr	Amount	Balance
Beginning Balance						2,205.53
Cleared Transactions						
Checks and Payments - 22 items						
▶ Paycheck	03/09/2009	729	Ruland, Seth N.	✓	-2,344.28	-2,344.28 ◀
Paycheck	03/09/2009	723	Greene, Kellie I.	✓	-1,840.29	-4,184.57
Paycheck	03/09/2009	730	White, Judy O.	✓	-1,567.60	-5,752.17
Paycheck	03/09/2009	727	Murray, Monica D.	✓	-951.50	-6,703.67
Paycheck	03/09/2009	724	Hardman, Alan	✓	-845.81	-7,549.48
Paycheck	03/09/2009	726	Henderson, Jeff P.	✓	-804.76	-8,354.24
Paycheck	03/09/2009	721	Dillion, Roy J.	✓	-791.93	-9,146.17
Paycheck	03/09/2009	722	Folse, Jan B.	✓	-643.80	-9,789.97
Paycheck	03/09/2009	728	Ramez, Victor M.	✓	-587.12	-10,377.09
Paycheck	03/09/2009	725	Hays, Mike E.	✓	-328.10	-10,705.19
Paycheck	03/23/2009	739	Ruland, Seth N.	✓	-2,344.28	-13,049.47
Paycheck	03/23/2009	733	Greene, Kellie I.	✓	-1,840.29	-14,889.76
Paycheck	03/23/2009	740	White, Judy O.	✓	-1,567.60	-16,457.36
Paycheck	03/23/2009	737	Murray, Monica D.	✓	-951.50	-17,408.86
Paycheck	03/23/2009	734	Hardman, Alan	✓	-767.32	-18,176.18
Paycheck	03/23/2009	736	Henderson, Jeff P.	✓	-728.98	-18,905.16
Paycheck	03/23/2009	742	Dillion, Roy J.	✓	-718.15	-19,623.31
Paycheck	03/23/2009	732	Folse, Jan B.	✓	-643.80	-20,267.11
Paycheck	03/23/2009	738	Ramez, Victor M.	✓	-607.93	-20,875.04
Paycheck	03/23/2009	735	Hays, Mike E.	✓	-531.98	-21,407.02
Paycheck	03/23/2009	741	Zickefoose, Jack A	✓	-384.20	-21,791.22
Check	03/31/2009			✓	-28.30	-21,819.52
Total Checks and Payments					-21,819.52	-21,819.52
Deposits and Credits - 3 items						
General Journal	03/09/2009	PRTrnf		✓	10,000.00	10,000.00
Paycheck	03/23/2009	731	Dillion, Roy J.	✓	0.00	10,000.00
Transfer	03/23/2009			✓	12,000.00	22,000.00
Total Deposits and Credits					22,000.00	22,000.00
Total Cleared Transactions					180.48	180.48
Cleared Balance					180.48	2,386.01
Register Balance as of 03/31/2009					180.48	2,386.01
Ending Balance					180.48	2,386.01

Figure: E:35

CHAPTER 8

CREATE A NEW CUSTOMER ACCOUNT

Frost Garden Center's Address Info.

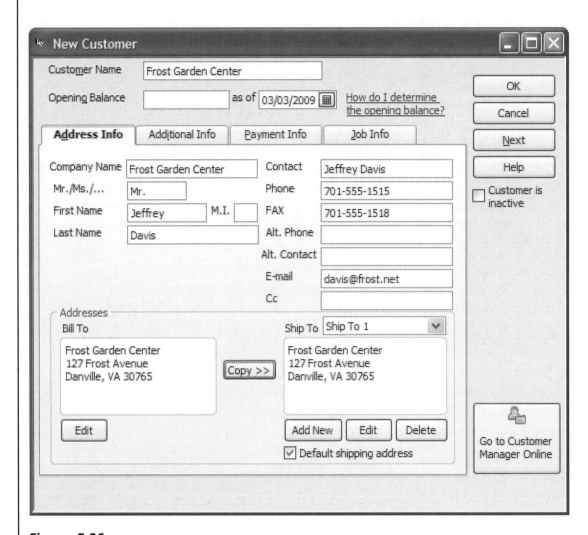

Figure: E:36

Frost Garden Center's Additional Info.

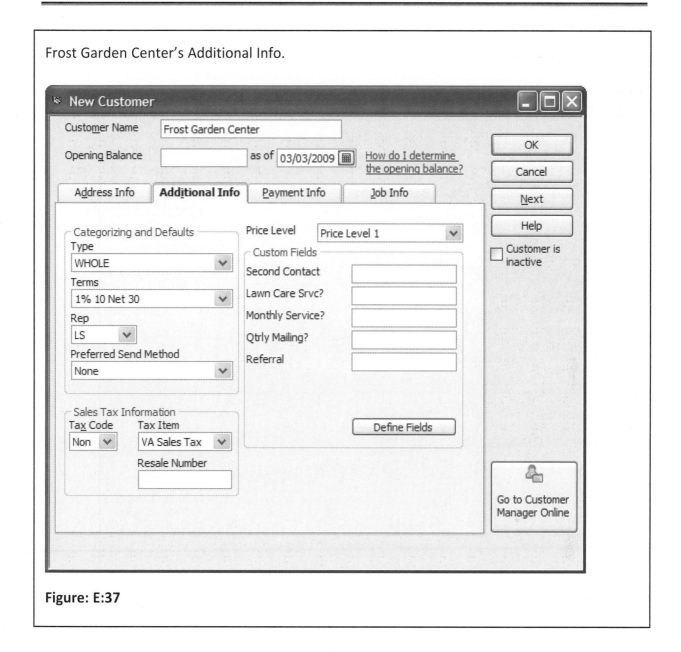

Figure: E:37

Frost Garden Center's Payment Info.

Figure: E:38

CREATE A NEW INVENTORY ITEM

New item and Item Listing report.

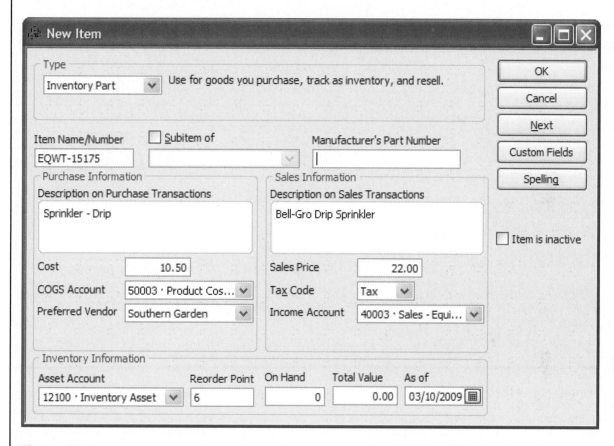

Figure: E:39

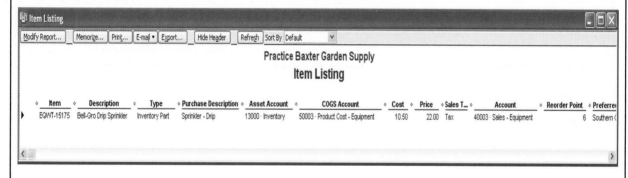

Figure: E:40

ENTER A STOREFRONT SALE OF MERCHANDISE

Freemond Country Club's sale.

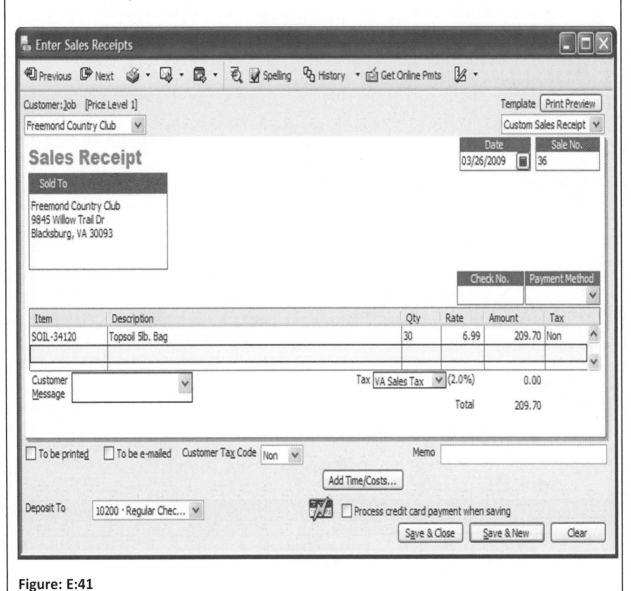

Figure: E:41

RECORD CUSTOMER PAYMENTS

Snyder Securities' payment. Note the option of applying an underpayment because the customer underpaid the invoice.

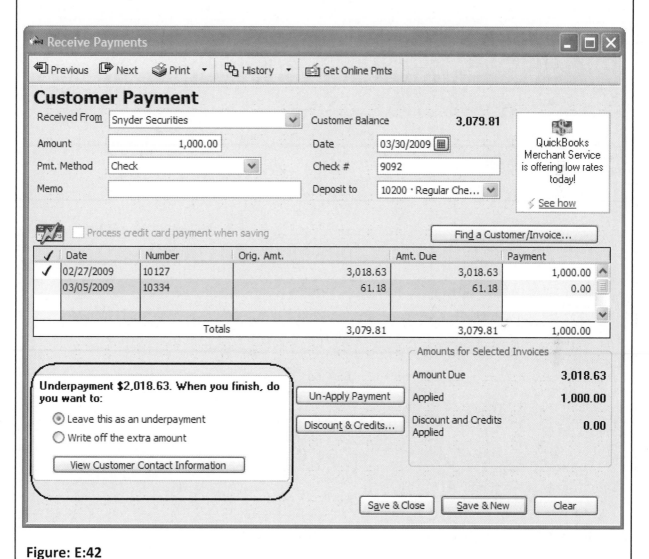

Figure: E:42

Cash Receipts Journal.

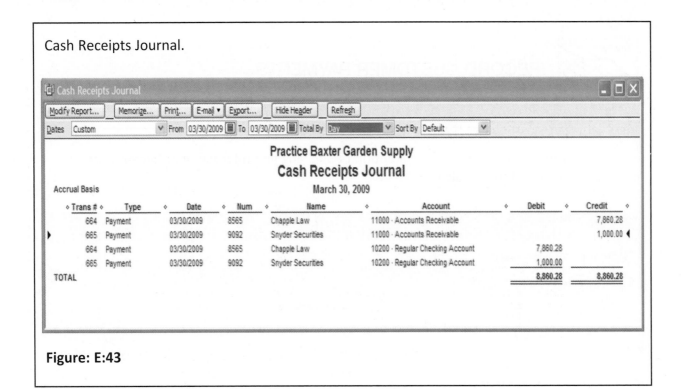

Figure: E:43

CHAPTER 9

ENTER PURCHASE ORDERS

DeJulia Wholesale Suppliers' PO.

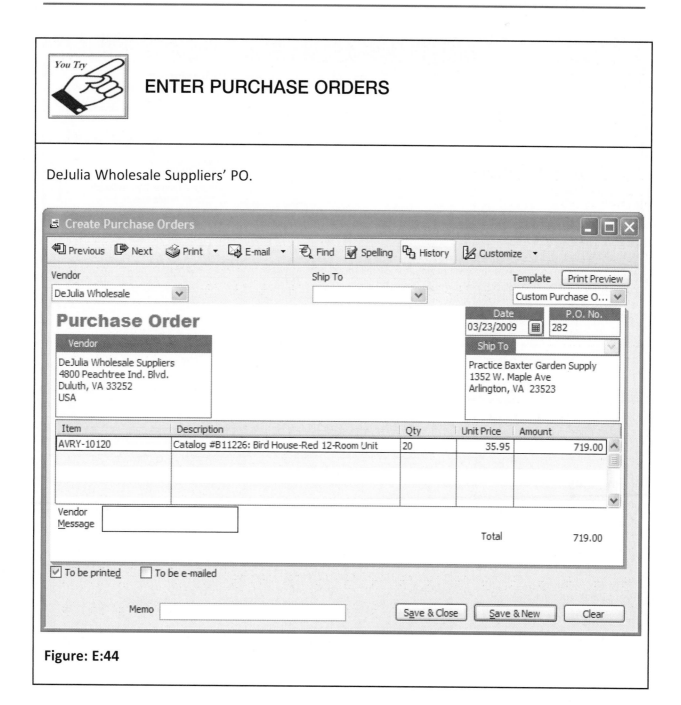

Figure: E:44

Abney and Son Contractors' PO.

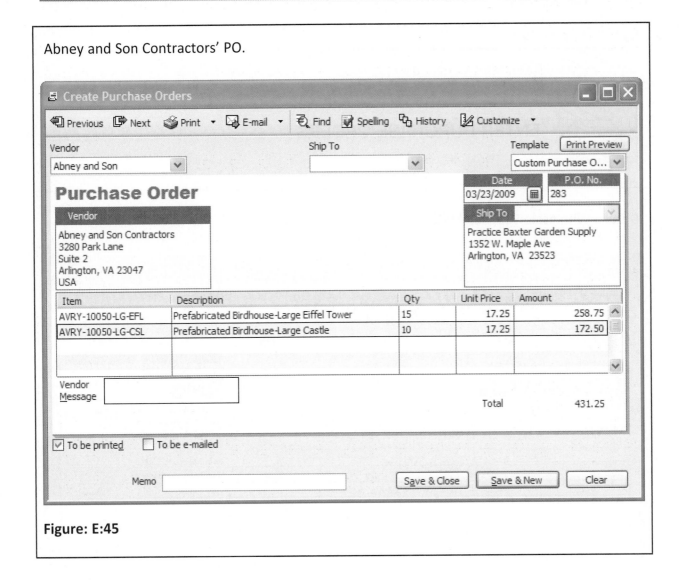

Figure: E:45

ENTER VENDOR RECEIPTS FOR A PO

DeJulia Wholesale Suppliers' receipt.

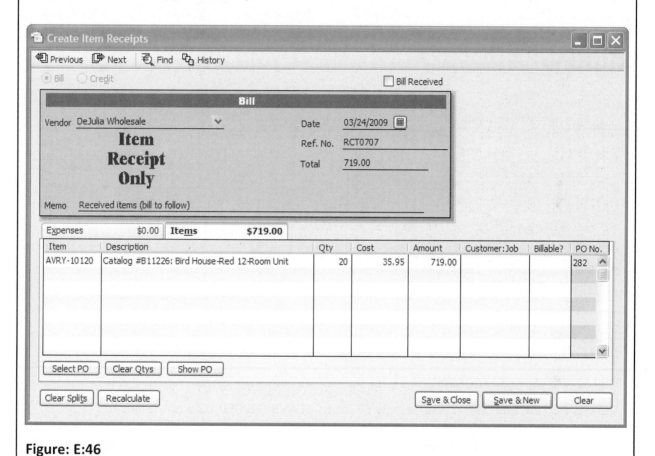

Figure: E:46

Abney and Son Contractors' receipt.

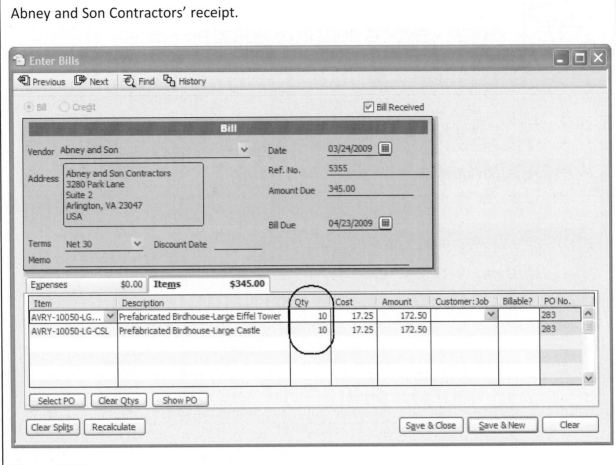

Figure: E:47

Abney's PO remains open because only 10 items of AVRY-10050-LG were received.

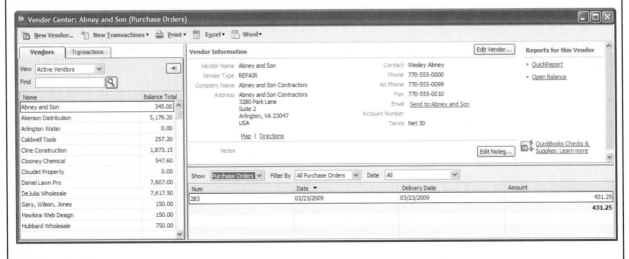

Figure: E:48

ENTER VENDOR BILL FOR VENDOR RECEIPT

DeJulia Wholesale Suppliers' invoice.

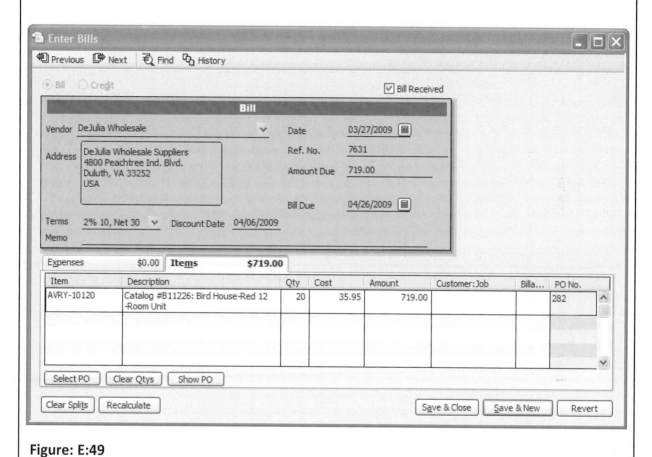

Figure: E:49

Purchases Journal for March 27. *(Note: Southern Garden's transaction already existed.)*

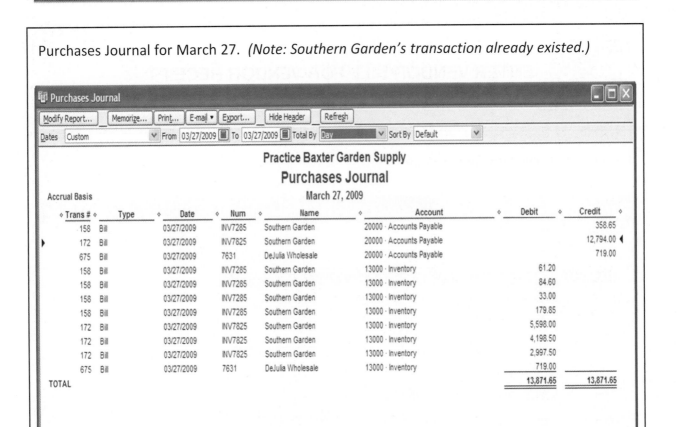

Figure: E:50

CREATE A NEW VENDOR ACCOUNT

Sullivan Buyer Supplies' Address Info.

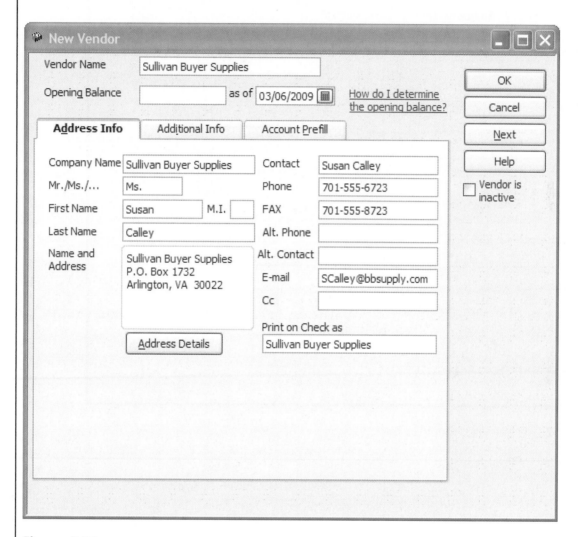

Figure: E:51

Sullivan Buyer Supplies' Additional Info.

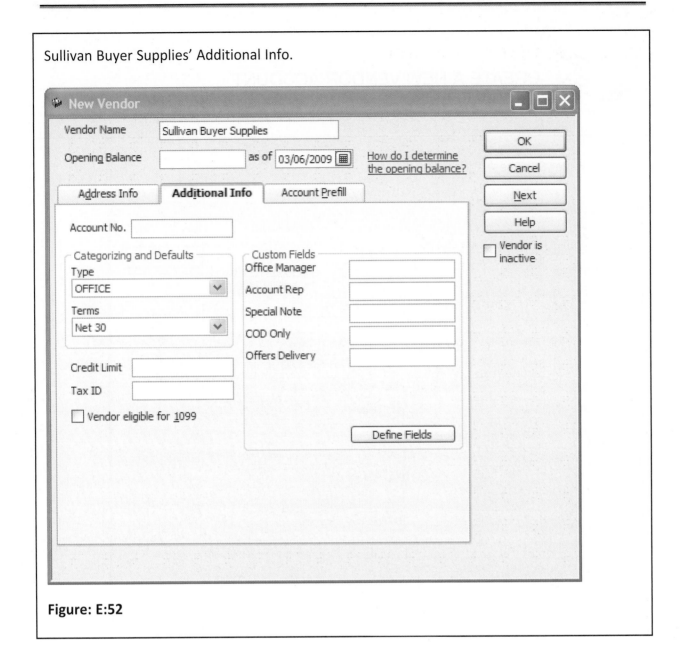

Figure: E:52

Sullivan Buyer Supplies' Account Prefill.

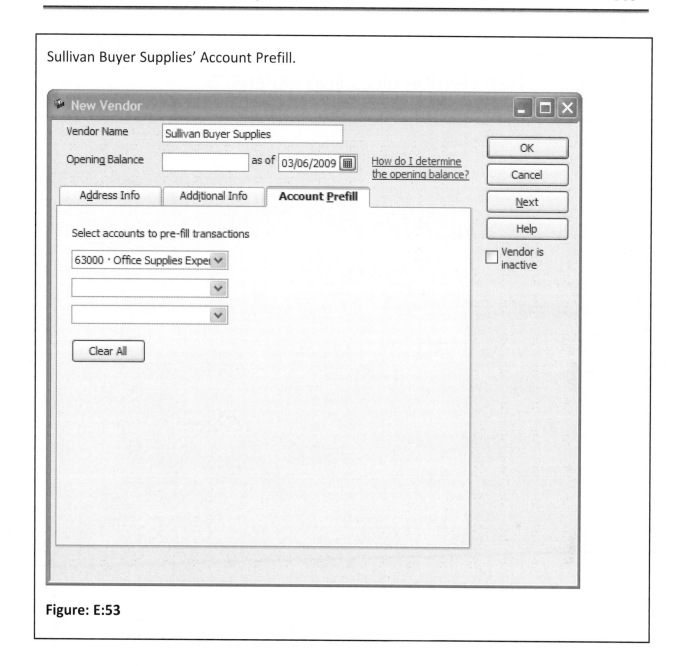

Figure: E:53

ENTER VENDOR BILLS FOR EXPENSES

Juan Motor Tools & Tires' transaction.

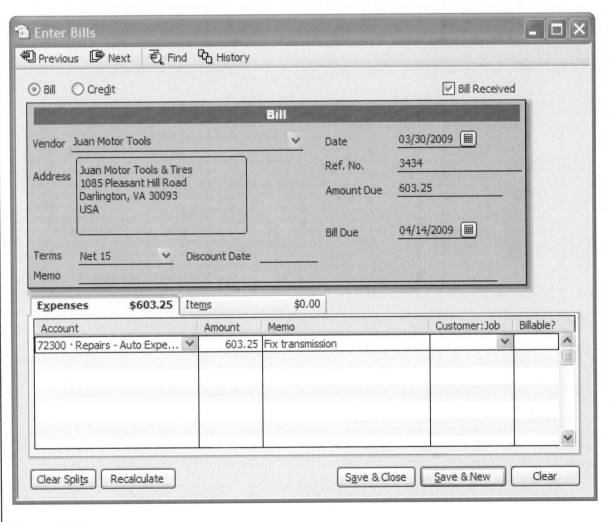

Figure: E:54

Neighbors Telephone Company's bill.

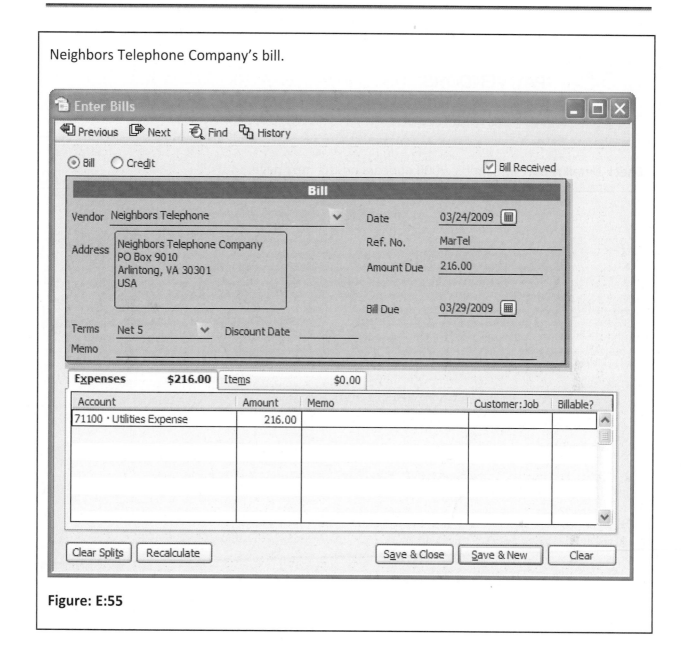

Figure: E:55

PAY VENDORS

Check Detail report for April 3, 2009 appears on the next page.

Practice Baxter Garden Supply
Check Detail
April 3, 2009

Type	Num	Date	Name	Item	Account	Paid Amount	Original Amount
Bill Pmt -Check	10254	04/03/2009	Akerson Distribution		10200 · Regular Checking Acco...		-5,000.00
Bill	4679	03/06/2009		AVRY-10100	13000 · Inventory	-2,050.70	2,124.20
				NURS-21900	13000 · Inventory	-796.46	825.00
				NURS-22000	13000 · Inventory	-1,385.35	1,435.00
				NURS-23010	13000 · Inventory	-767.49	795.00
TOTAL						-5,000.00	5,179.20
Bill Pmt -Check	10255	04/03/2009	Cline Construction		10200 · Regular Checking Acco...		-55.65
Bill	B1023	03/06/2009		TOOL-35220	13000 · Inventory	-23.85	23.85
				TOOL-35230	13000 · Inventory	-31.80	31.80
TOTAL						-55.65	55.65
Bill Pmt -Check	10256	04/03/2009	Clooney Chemical		10200 · Regular Checking Acco...		-297.60
Bill	1166...	03/12/2009		EQFF-13100	13000 · Inventory	-119.70	119.70
				EQFF-13140	13000 · Inventory	-79.50	79.50
				FERT-16130	13000 · Inventory	-56.40	56.40
				FERT-16170	13000 · Inventory	-42.00	42.00
TOTAL						-297.60	297.60
Bill Pmt -Check	10257	04/03/2009	Daniel Lawn Pro		10200 · Regular Checking Acco...		-75.00
Bill	45541	03/06/2009			71200 · Building Maintenance Expe...	-75.00	75.00
TOTAL						-75.00	75.00
Bill Pmt -Check	10258	04/03/2009	DeJulia Wholesale		10200 · Regular Checking Acco...		-4,144.85
			DeJulia Wholesale		20000 · Accounts Payable	75.65	-75.65
Bill	22113	03/10/2009		BOOK-11010	13000 · Inventory	-31.20	31.20
				BOOK-11030	13000 · Inventory	-62.40	62.40
				POTS-30210	13000 · Inventory	-28.20	28.20
				SEFL-31100	13000 · Inventory	-6.60	6.60
				SEFL-31140	13000 · Inventory	-6.60	6.60
				SEVG-33100	13000 · Inventory	-5.40	5.40
				AVRY-10140	13000 · Inventory	-90.00	90.00
				AVRY-10150	13000 · Inventory	-207.80	207.80
Bill	INV3...	03/26/2009		AVRY-10130	13000 · Inventory	-596.25	596.25
				BOOK-11000	13000 · Inventory	-956.00	956.00
				BOOK-11010	13000 · Inventory	-156.00	156.00
				BOOK-11020	13000 · Inventory	-119.50	119.50
				POTS-30200	13000 · Inventory	-797.50	797.50
				POTS-30210	13000 · Inventory	-58.75	58.75
				POTS-30410	13000 · Inventory	-98.75	98.75
				SEFL-31110	13000 · Inventory	-9.35	9.35
				SEFL-31150	13000 · Inventory	-6.60	6.60
				SEFL-31160	13000 · Inventory	-6.60	6.60
				SEFL-31170	13000 · Inventory	-6.60	6.60
				SEGR-32100	13000 · Inventory	-79.50	79.50
				SEHB-32100	13000 · Inventory	-5.40	5.40
				TOOL-35110	13000 · Inventory	-42.60	42.60
				TOOL-35120	13000 · Inventory	-28.20	28.20
				TOOL-35250	13000 · Inventory	-95.70	95.70
Bill	7631	03/27/2009		AVRY-10120	13000 · Inventory	-719.00	719.00
TOTAL						-4,144.85	4,144.85
Bill Pmt -Check	10259	04/03/2009	Juan Motor Tools		10200 · Regular Checking Acco...		-274.56
Bill	26171	03/03/2009			72300 · Repairs - Auto Expenses	-274.56	274.56
TOTAL						-274.56	274.56
Bill Pmt -Check	10260	04/03/2009	Southern Garden		10200 · Regular Checking Acco...		-1,829.00
Bill	8326...	03/06/2009		NURS-21800	13000 · Inventory	-127.50	127.50
Bill	IV3253	03/10/2009		NURS-21900	13000 · Inventory	-375.00	375.00
				EQWT-15100	13000 · Inventory	-599.50	599.50
Bill	IV23...	03/10/2009		NURS-21800	13000 · Inventory	-127.50	127.50
				EQWT-15100	13000 · Inventory	-599.50	599.50
TOTAL						-1,829.00	1,829.00
Bill Pmt -Check	10261	04/03/2009	Sulley Printing		10200 · Regular Checking Acco...		-17.10
Bill	B1024	03/10/2009		SEVG-33140	13000 · Inventory	-3.60	3.60
				SEVG-33160	13000 · Inventory	-6.75	6.75
				SEVG-33170	13000 · Inventory	-6.75	6.75
TOTAL						-17.10	17.10

Figure: E:56

CHAPTER 10

CREATE CHECKS FOR PAYROLL TAXES

Pay Liabilities window.

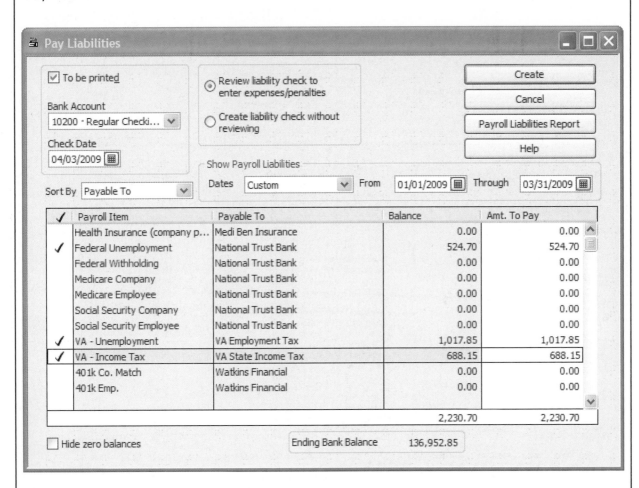

Figure: E:57

Check Detail report modified to filter for Transaction Type of Payroll Liability Check.

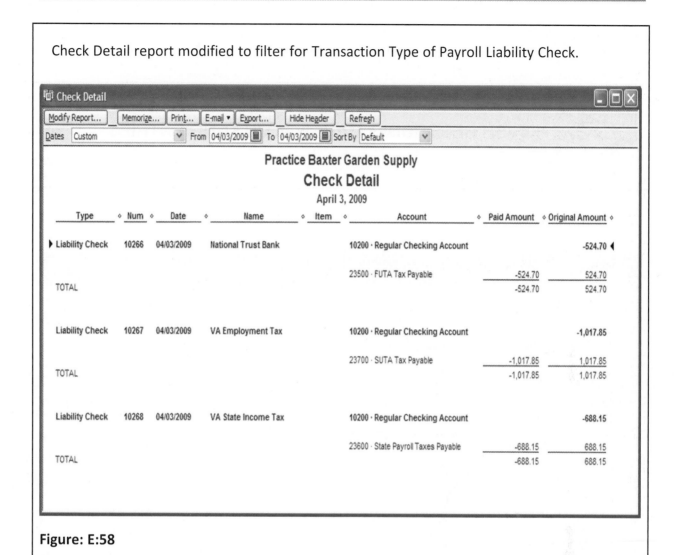

Figure: E:58

CHAPTER 11

 FINISH RECORDING MARCH ADJUSTING ENTRIES

Bank transfer entry.

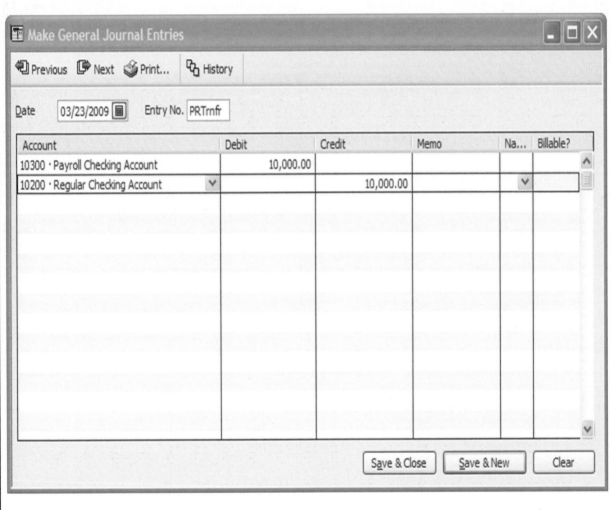

Figure: E:59

Expired prepaid expense entry.

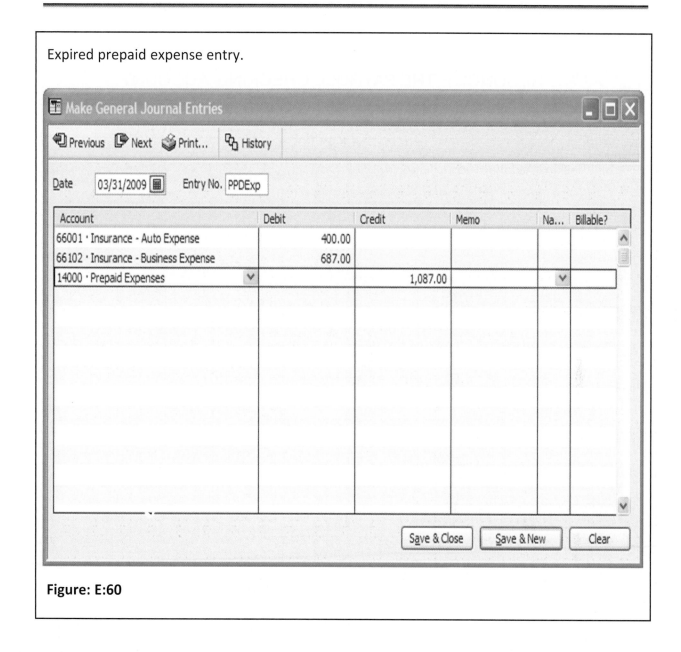

Figure: E:60

RECONCILE THE PAYROLL CHECKING ACCOUNT

Payroll Checking Account reconciliation window.

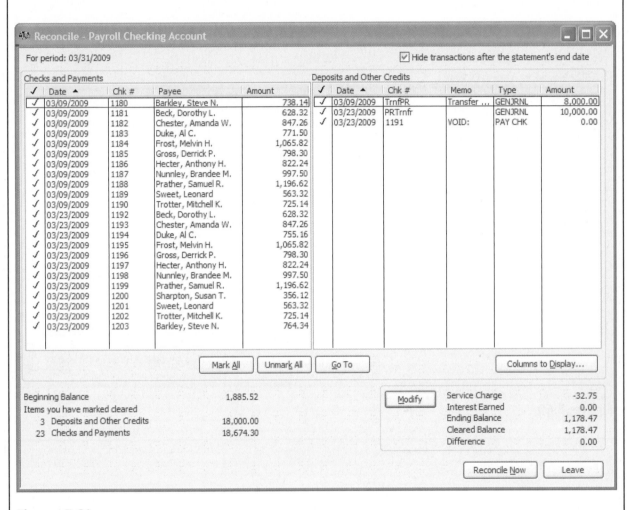

Figure: E:61

Payroll Checking Account bank reconciliation.

Practice Baxter Garden Supply
Reconciliation Detail
10300 · Payroll Checking Account, Period Ending 03/31/2009

Type	Date	Num	Name	Clr	Amount	Balance
Beginning Balance						1,885.52
Cleared Transactions						
Checks and Payments - 24 items						
Paycheck	03/09/2009	1188	Prather, Samuel R.	✓	-1,196.62	-1,196.62
Paycheck	03/09/2009	1184	Frost, Melvin H.	✓	-1,065.82	-2,262.44
Paycheck	03/09/2009	1187	Nunnley, Brandee M.	✓	-997.50	-3,259.94
Paycheck	03/09/2009	1182	Chester, Amanda W.	✓	-847.26	-4,107.20
Paycheck	03/09/2009	1186	Hecter, Anthony H.	✓	-822.24	-4,929.44
Paycheck	03/09/2009	1185	Gross, Derrick P.	✓	-798.30	-5,727.74
Paycheck	03/09/2009	1183	Duke, Al C.	✓	-771.50	-6,499.24
Paycheck	03/09/2009	1180	Barkley, Steve N.	✓	-738.14	-7,237.38
Paycheck	03/09/2009	1190	Trotter, Mitchell K.	✓	-725.14	-7,962.52
Paycheck	03/09/2009	1181	Beck, Dorothy L.	✓	-628.32	-8,590.84
Paycheck	03/09/2009	1189	Sweet, Leonard	✓	-563.32	-9,154.16
Paycheck	03/23/2009	1199	Prather, Samuel R.	✓	-1,196.62	-10,350.78
Paycheck	03/23/2009	1195	Frost, Melvin H.	✓	-1,065.82	-11,416.60
Paycheck	03/23/2009	1198	Nunnley, Brandee M.	✓	-997.50	-12,414.10
Paycheck	03/23/2009	1193	Chester, Amanda W.	✓	-847.26	-13,261.36
Paycheck	03/23/2009	1197	Hecter, Anthony H.	✓	-822.24	-14,083.60
Paycheck	03/23/2009	1196	Gross, Derrick P.	✓	-798.30	-14,881.90
Paycheck	03/23/2009	1203	Barkley, Steve N.	✓	-764.34	-15,646.24
Paycheck	03/23/2009	1194	Duke, Al C.	✓	-755.16	-16,401.40
Paycheck	03/23/2009	1202	Trotter, Mitchell K.	✓	-725.14	-17,126.54
Paycheck	03/23/2009	1192	Beck, Dorothy L.	✓	-628.32	-17,754.86
Paycheck	03/23/2009	1201	Sweet, Leonard	✓	-563.32	-18,318.18
Paycheck	03/23/2009	1200	Sharpton, Susan T.	✓	-356.12	-18,674.30
Check	03/31/2009			✓	-32.75	-18,707.05
Total Checks and Payments					-18,707.05	-18,707.05
Deposits and Credits - 3 items						
General Journal	03/09/2009	TrnfPR		✓	8,000.00	8,000.00
Paycheck	03/23/2009	1191	Barkley, Steve N.	✓	0.00	8,000.00
General Journal	03/23/2009	PRTr...		✓	10,000.00	18,000.00
Total Deposits and Credits					18,000.00	18,000.00
Total Cleared Transactions					-707.05	-707.05
Cleared Balance					-707.05	1,178.47
Register Balance as of 03/31/2009					-707.05	1,178.47
Ending Balance					-707.05	1,178.47

Figure: E:62

Index

A

Account Types. *See*, Chart of Accounts
Accounting Periods
    Open and close, 100, 128, 452, 786
    Preclosing checklist, 421, 755
Accounting software, 3
Accounts. *See*, Chart of Accounts, *See*, General Ledger
Accounts Payable Aging report, 271, 600, 602
Accounts Receivable Aging Report, 213, 544
Accrued Payroll, 756
Adjusting Entries, 122, 422, 756
    Manual system, 476
Application Software, 3
Audit Trail. *See* MAPS, *See* Behind the Keys

B

Backing Up Data Files. *See*, Data Files
Balance Sheet. *See*, Reports
Bank Reconciliations
    Prepare, 427, 760
    Reports, 433, 436, 770
Behind the Keys
    Tracing Cash Receipt entries, 201, 535
    Tracing General Journal entries, 114
    Tracing Paycheck entries, 366, 699
    Tracing Sales Invoice entries, 154, 491
    Tracing Vendor Bill entries, 248, 581
    Tracing Vendor Payment entries, 276, 606
    Tracing Vendor Receipt entries, 248, 581

C

Cash Disbursements Journal
    QuickBooks, 276, 606
Cash Flow Statement. *See* Reports
Cash Receipts
    Correcting, 209, 541
    Recording payments, 197, 531
    Recording storefront sales, 528
    Recording with a discount, 203, 536
Cash Receipts Journal
    QuickBooks, 201, 535
Centers
    About, 22
    Customer, 22, 141, 478
    Employee, 26, 323, 661
    Report, 77, 440, 522, 774
    Vendor, 25, 231, 563
Change Item Prices, 518
Chart of Accounts
    Account framework, 55
    Account types, 57, 59, 444, 778
    Adding accounts, 59
    Listing, 26
    Maintain accounts, 56
    Printing, 53
Circular E, 307, 642, 912
Company Preferences, 827
Correcting
    Cash Receipts, 209, 541, 893
    Employee Paychecks, 363, 695, 894
    General Journal Entries, 117, 894
    Payroll Tax Errors, 392, 726
    Purchase Orders, 240, 571, 893
    Reclassifying entries, 416, 748
    Sales Invoices, 158, 496, 892
    Vendor Bills and Receipts, 255, 584, 893
    Vendor Payments, 284, 613, 893
Create a Company. *See* New Company
Credit Memos
    Recording Customer, 210, 542
    Recording Vendor, 291, 620
Customer Receipts
    Correcting, 893
    Creating, 197, 531
    Creating with a discount, 203, 536
Customers
    Adding accounts on-the-fly, 148, 485
    Aging reports, 213, 544
    Job Account, 165
    Maintain accounts, 160, 499
    New company, 832
    Payment terms, 163, 501
    Reconciling activities, 213, 545
    Sales defaults, 163, 501
    Statements, 216, 548
    Transaction reports, 155, 493
    Write off invoice, 214, 546
Customizing
    Company Names, 28
    Form Templates, 863
    Reports. *See*, Reports

D

Data Files
    Backing up, 38, 895
    Backing up to a portable backup file, 905
    Customizing company name, 28
    Loading, 5
    Moving, 48
    Restoring, 44
    Restoring a portable backup file, 907
    Sample data file names, 4
Depreciation Expense, 424, 751
Drilldown Features, 66

E

Emailing Reports. *See*, Reports
Employees
    Allocating time to jobs, 374
    Earnings Summary report, 368, 701
    Enter compensation information, 328, 666
    Enter payroll tax information, 329, 667
    Filing status, 308, 643
    Maintain accounts, 325, 663
    New company, 845
    Paychecks. *See*, Paychecks
    Payroll tax computations, 308, 643
    Record timesheets, 339
    Tax withholdings, 304, 639
    Terminating, 338, 675
    Time reports, 344
    Voluntary deductions, 305, 640
Employer
    Additional compensation, 306, 641
    Payroll taxes, 306, 641
Exit QuickBooks, 48
Exporting Reports. *See*, Reports

F

Financial Statements. *See*, Reports
Finding Transactions, 73
Fiscal Year, 28
Form Templates
    Customizing, 863

G

General Journal
    Adjusting entries, 122
    Creating entries, 110, 119
    Manual system, 106
    QuickBooks, 114
General Journal Entries
    Adjusting, 422, 756
    Correcting, 117, 894
    Memorized, 424, 752
General Ledger
    Account framework, 55
    Account types, 57, 59, 444, 778
    Adding accounts, 59
    Analyzing transactions, 414, 746
    Maintain accounts, 56
    Printing Chart of Accounts, 53
    QuickBooks, 116
General Ledger Detail Report, 157, 254, 495, 583
General Ledger Report, 79, 414, 746

H

Hardware and operating software, 2
Help Files, 31

I

Icon Bar
    About, 15
    Customize, 19
Income Statement. *See*, Profit & Loss
Install QuickBooks Pro 2007, 881
Inventory Adjusting Entry, 476
Inventory Items
    About, 510
    Out-of-stock merchandise, 530
    Pricing, 515
    Reporting, 522
IRS Circular E, 912
Items
    Adjusting inventory, 525
    Changing prices, 518
    Inventory, 510
    Listing, 177
    New company, 838
    Non-inventory, 176
    Payroll, 311, 647
    Physical Inventory, 525
    Physical Inventory Worksheet report, 524
    Reporting, 522
    Service, 176

J

Jobs
    Allocating employee time, 374
    Assigning employee time, 340
    Assigning vendor bills, 237, 239, 245
    Employee time reports, 344
    Item Profitability report, 196
    Maintain accounts, 160, 499
    Profitability report, 192
    Status, 166
    Types, 166
    Unbilled Cost report, 195

K

Keyboard Shortcuts, 29

L

Lists
    Chart of Accounts, 26
    Non-inventory Items, 177
    Payroll Items, 311, 647
    Price Levels, 515
    Service Items, 177
    Task windows, 27

M

Manual Accounting. *See* MAPS
MAPS
    Customer activities, 137, 472

Employee activities, 303, 638
General Journal entries, 106
T-Accounts, 105
Vendor activities, 226, 558
Maximize button, 27
Memorized Transactions, 266, 595, 752
Memorizing Reports. *See*, Reports
Minimize button, 27
Moving Data Files, 48
Multi-tasking in QuickBooks, 26

N

New Company
  Create, 811
  Customers, 832
  Customize forms, 863
  Employees, 845
  Inventory items, 838
  Payroll setup, 845
  Preference setup, 827
  Vendors, 835
Non-inventory Items
  About, 176
  Listing, 177

P

Paychecks
  Correcting, 363, 695, 894
  Creating, 346, 676
  Printing, 348, 678
Payroll
  Circular E, 307, 642
  Correcting payroll tax errors, 392, 726
  Employee Earnings Summary, 368, 701
  Employee voluntary deductions, 304, 305, 639, 640
  Employee withholdings, 304, 639
  Employer additional compensation, 305, 306, 641
  Employer taxes, 305, 306, 641
  Items, 311, 647
  Listing items, 311, 647
  Payroll Liability Balances report, 376, 707
  Payroll Register, 307, 642
  Payroll Tax Forms, 385, 719
  Remitting taxes, 376, 707
Payroll Register
  Manual System, 307, 642
  QuickBooks, 368, 701
Payroll Setup, 845
Payroll Transaction Journal, 366, 699
Physical Inventory, 525
Preclosing checklist, 421, 755
Preference Options, 61
Prepaid Expense, 418, 751
Printing Transactions. *See Index for transaction type*
Profit & Loss. *See*, Reports
Purchase Discounts, 273

Purchase Orders
  Correcting, 240, 571, 893
  Creating, 236, 568
  Printing, 239, 570
  Reporting, 628
Purchases Journal
  QuickBooks, 248, 581
Purchasing Reports. *See*, Reports

Q

QuickBooks
  Centers. *See*, Centers
  Data integration, 130
  Desktop elements, 13
  Drilldown features, 66
  Email features, 159, 497
  Exiting software, 48
  Find feature, 73
  Help files, 31
  Home page, 16
  Icon Bar, 15
  Installing, 881
  Keyboard shortcuts, 29
  Launching, 4
  Lists. *See*, Lists
  Loading sample data files, 5
  Menu commands, 15
  Multi-tasking, 26
  Open and close company, 12
  Preferences, 61
  Reports. *See*, Reports
  System requirements, 881
  Title Bar, 15

R

Reports
  Accounts Payable Aging, 271, 294, 600, 602, 623
  Balance Sheet, 125, 444, 778
  Bank Reconciliation, 433, 436, 770
  Cash Disbursements Journal, 276, 606
  Cash Receipts Journal, 201, 535
  Center, 77, 440, 522, 774
  Chart of Accounts, 53
  Customer & Receivables, 213, 544
  Customer Statements, 216, 548
  Customer transactions, 155, 493
  Customize Statement of Cash Flows, 447, 781
  Customizing, 81
  Emailing, 89
  Employee Earnings Summary, 368, 701
  Employee time, 344
  Exporting, 89
  General Journal, 114
  General Ledger, 79, 116, 414, 746
  General Ledger Detail, 157, 254, 495, 583
  Inventory, 522

Inventory Stock Status, 629
Job Item Profitability, 196
Job Profitability, 192
Memorizing, 89, 252
Menu, 77
Payroll Liability Balances, 376, 707
Payroll Taxes, 385, 719
Payroll Transaction Journal, 366, 699
PDF version, 98
Physical Inventory Worksheet, 524
Profit & Loss, 89, 125, 441, 774
Purchase Orders, 628
Purchases Journal, 248, 581
Purchasing, 627
Sales Journal, 154, 491
Sales Tax Liability, 289, 618
Statement of Cash Flows, 125, 445, 779
Statement of Retained Earnings, 125
Transaction Journal, 71
Trial Balance, 66, 123, 438, 772
Unbilled Job Costs, 195
Vendor 1099, 297, 627
Vendor transactions, 253, 277, 582, 606
Vendors & Payables, 294, 623
Reversing Entries, 758

S

Sales Invoices
    Correcting, 158, 496, 892
    Creating, 147, 484
    Creating for out-of-stock merchandise, 530
    Creating Job Cost Invoices, 184
    Emailing, 159, 497
    Printing, 153
Sales Journal
    QuickBooks, 154, 491
Sales Receipts
    Recording with a discount, 203, 536
Sales Tax Liability Report, 289, 618
Service Items
    About, 176
    Listing, 177
Statement of Cash Flows. *See*, Reports
Suspense account, 419, 753
System requirements. *See*, QuickBooks

T

Tax Year, 28
Timesheets, 339
Title Bar, 15
Transaction Journal. *See*, Reports
Transaction List by Customer. *See*, Reports
Transactions. *See also*, Correcting
    Adjusting entries, 122, 422, 756
    Adjusting inventory, 525
    Bank Reconciliations, 427, 760
    Cash Receipts for storefront sales, 528
    Cash Receipts with a discount, 203, 536

Customer Credit Memos, 210, 542
Customer Receipts, 197, 531
Data entry tips, 109, 148, 485
Dates, 189, 496
General Journal entries, 110, 119
Memorized transactions, 424, 752
Memorizing, 266, 595
Paying employees, 346, 676
Paying Sales Tax, 287, 617
Printing. *See Index for transaction type*
Purchase Orders, 236, 568
Reclassify entries, 416, 748
Sales Invoice for out-of-stock merchandise, 530
Sales Invoices, 147, 484
Sales Invoices for Job Costs, 184
Sales Receipts, 203, 536
Suspense account, 419, 753
Timesheets, 339
Vendor Bills and Receipts, 243, 573
Vendor Bills for Expenses, 263, 592
Vendor Bills for Receipts, 256, 585
Vendor Credit Memos, 291, 620
Vendor Payments, 270, 600
Write Checks, 278, 607
Write off customer invoice, 214, 546
Trial Balance. *See*, Reports

V

Vendor Bills
    Correcting, 255, 584, 893
    Creating, 243, 263, 578, 592
    Memorizing, 266
    Payroll taxes, 376, 707
    Write checks, 278, 607
Vendor Payments
    Correcting, 284, 613, 893
    Purchase Discounts, 273
    Recording, 270, 600
    Sales Tax, 287, 617
Vendor Receipts
    Correcting, 255, 584, 893
    Creating, 245, 574
Vendors
    Adding accounts on-the-fly, 278, 607
    Aging reports, 294, 623
    Maintain accounts, 259, 587
    New company, 835
    Purchasing defaults, 260, 589
    Reconciling activities, 295, 624
    Terms, 260, 589
    Transaction reports, 253, 277, 582, 606

W

Windows
    Listing task windows, 27
    Minimizing and maximizing, 27
Write Checks
    Creating, 278, 607

Y

You Try

Create a Job Report, 197
Create a New Customer Account, 175, 509
Create a New Inventory Item, 528
Create a New Vendor Account, 263, 592
Create Checks for Payroll Taxes, 385, 719
Enter a Storefront Sale of Merchandise, 530
Enter Purchase Orders, 242, 573
Enter Vendor Bill for Vendor Receipt, 258, 587
Enter Vendor Bills for Expenses, 266, 595
Enter Vendor Receipts and Bills for Purchase Orders, 256, 585

Finish Recording March Adjusting Entries, 426, 760
Invoice a Customer For Job Costs, 190
Pay Vendors, 287, 616
Printing The Chart of Accounts For Other Sample Companies, 55
Reconcile The Payroll Checking Account, 437, 771
Record Additional Journal Entries, 122
Record Adjusting Entries, 123
Record Customer Payments, 209, 541
Record TEK's January Transactions, 119
Working With Timesheets, 343

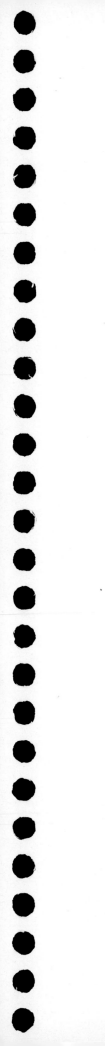

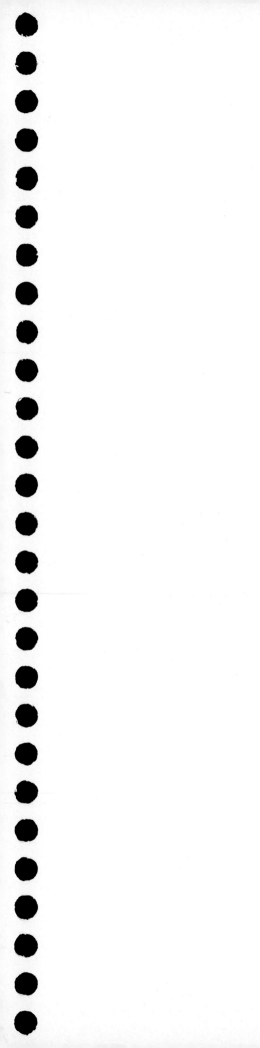